ISRAEL

THE

EMBATTLED

ALLY

With a new Preface and Postscript by the Author

NADAV SAFRAN

THE BELKNAP PRESS OF HARVARD UNIVERSITY PRESS

Cambridge, Massachusetts, and London, England

To Gaby

In memoriam

Preface, 1981

American-Israeli relations and their underlying dynamics, I wrote in the original Preface to this volume, have been characterized by change and evolution. If that was true of the first three decades of Israel's existence, it proved to be much more so of the three and a half years since those words were written. It can indeed be said that since the latter part of 1977, the change and evolution were so far-reaching as to attain revolutionary rather than incremental dimensions. Hence the need for a substantial addition to this volume.

The principal fundamental change that took place was, of course, the signing in March 1979, under American aegis, of the Egyptian-Israeli Peace Treaty, the first ever between the Jewish state and any Arab nation. Matching that event in importance and an indispensable prelude to it was President Sadat's historic visit to Jerusalem sixteen months earlier. If until November 1977 American-Israeli relations could conveniently be described in terms of stages demarcated by Arab-Israeli wars, since that date they could only be considered in terms of the transition from war to peace. That is what the additional chapter in the present volume attempts to do.

The Egyptian-Israeli peace embodies the potential for momentous diplomatic-strategic realignments in a region which has come to assume vital importance for the Western industrialized countries. Although that potential is still too far away and uncertain to warrant discussion at present, some of its outlines may deserve mention here. Clearly, the Egyptian-Israeli peace broke the historical dichotomy of Arabs versus Israel and opened up the possibility of combinations including Israel and some Arab states in opposition to groupings of other Arab states. This, in turn, opened up for the United States the possibility of viable formal or informal regional defense arrangements long sought by it but hitherto frustrated by the overriding intrusion of the Arab-Israeli conflict. For the time being, such possibilities are limited to Israel, Egypt, and perhaps small but strategically located Oman;

but intelligent diplomacy might be able to avail itself of existing leverages to enlarge the scope of the possible combinations so as to include Saudi Arabia, Jordan, and other countries relevant to securing Western access to Middle East oil. Finally, the Egyptian-Israeli peace has created a new arena for American-Israeli relations in addition to the one that centered on the two countries' relations to the Middle East arena as a whole and on their traditional one-to-one relationship. The triangle comprising the United States, Israel, and Egypt has alrady begun to function in several ways, including at least one instance where Egypt and Israel lined up in opposition to the United States over the issue of the best avenue for furthering the peace process.

On a more immediate level, the Egyptian-Israeli peace has reduced considerably, though it has by no means eliminated, the chances of a large-scale Arab-Israeli war in the foreseeable future. It is easy to conceive scenarios in which an Arab coalition excluding Egypt deems itself sufficiently strong to challenge Israel to some kind of war; however, such scenarios must presuppose a preparation period of many years, among other more or less difficult conditions. In the meantime, the danger of an American-Soviet confrontation over the Arab-Israeli conflict would be reduced, as would the chances of another Arab oil embargo, nondeliberate or deliberate. The diminished war prospects provide a breathing spell in which the Western dependence on Middle East oil could be eased.

Notable developments in Israel's internal affairs during that period included the complete fizzling out of the Democratic Movement for Change and the evaporation of the possibilities of a new alignment of political forces that had been briefly raised by that party's meteoric rise. The decline was the result of internal splits and defections, the resulting rump party's lack of any programmatic coherence and organizational underpinnings, and the political ineptitude manifested by its once star-leader, former General and Professor Yigael Yadin. An additional reason was that the rump party hitched its fortunes completely to Begin's own, which reached a zenith after the conclusion of the Camp David Accords in September 1978 and then tumbled down a precipitous slope as a result of disastrous mismanagement of the economy. The Labor Party was the residual beneficiary of these developments, and the latest opinion polls show it gaining an absolute majority in any imminent election. Were that to happen in fact, it would be an almost revolutionary development in Israel's politics.

The economic troubles underlying the political changes are reflected in an inflation that seems to have run amuck. From a rate of about 35 percent in the year the Begin government was installed, in 1977, inflation jumped to an annual average of over 50 percent in 1978, close to 80 percent in 1979, and more than 130 percent in 1980, the highest rate in the world. It is easy to misunderstand the significance of these figures. In many another society, such a pace of inflation would soon destroy democracy and disintegrate the social order, but in Israel, such results have been prevented by the fact that almost everybody is organized in some interest group and almost everything is indexed to everything. Nevertheless, the effects that did take place have been serious enough: indices have not always assured automatic compliance, and their application to specific instances has been the cause of constant disputes and bitter struggles. The net result has been that Israeli society has been running a treadmill, with all groups exerting themselves ever harder to stay in the same place.

N. S.

Cambridge, Massachusetts
January 1981

PREFACE

About the United States and Israel one might say that seldom in the history of international relations has such a world power been involved so intensely for so long with such a small power. What significance this phenomenon may have is a question for the philosophers of history to ponder. How it came to pass and the relevance of what happened to the further unfolding of American-Israeli relations is the subject of this study.

In order to assay properly that extraordinary relationship, I have attempted first to depict a comprehensive portrait of Israel before going on to analyze the historical development of the relations between the two. The keynote of both sections of this book is change and evolution, their dynamics and their implication. For nothing is more inimical to an adequate understanding of either Israel or American-Israeli relations than a static conception of them, which all too many Americans have been prone to entertain, perhaps because of their intense involvement with the subject on an almost daily basis.

An inkling of the scope, depth, and rapidity of the transformation that took place may be gained by looking at what has happened since 1963, when I wrote a similar, much smaller book—*The United States and Israel*—on the subjects discussed here. General wars tend to constitute watersheds in the international and internal histories of most nations; Israel fought two such wars in the intervening years—in 1967 and 1973—in addition to a grueling "war of attrition" in 1969–1970. One consequence of these wars has been that the nature of the United States' relationship with Israel has evolved from a connection of qualified friendship to a bond of alliance between friends. Thus, whereas in 1956–1957, for instance, the United States applied relentless pressure on Israel to force it to surrender the fruits of its victory in the Sinai War, in 1967 it stood firmly behind Israel to help it retain the gains achieved in the Six Day War until the Arab states were prepared to negotiate a settlement that satisfied the Israeli and American basic interests. On the same principle, the United States intervened in the 1973 Yom Kippur War with a massive airlift of arms to help Israel frustrate the attempt of the Arab states to settle the conflict on their terms by resorting to force. In the process, American and Israeli relations with the Soviet Union, Europe, the Arab countries, and the Third World were significantly reshaped again and again.

One crucial result of these events was that the United States emerged after the 1973 war in the role of peacebroker between Israel and the Arabs. In pursuing that role, the United States was able to bring about a series of partial agreements between the belligerents, but in the process of promoting these accords the United States assumed such extensive commitments and obligations toward Israel that they amounted to a formal alliance in all but name. In the meantime, American practical support for Israel was increasing by leaps and bounds. During the entire fourteen years covered by my earlier volume, for example, American aid to Israel amounted to about $800 million; the average *annual* aid in the past four or five years has been more than twice that total amount, and in the crucial year of 1973 it amounted to three times as much.

Indicators of internal changes in Israel during that period are no less dramatic. Annual defense outlays, for example, multiplied twelvefold in constant dollars between 1961 and 1975. As a percentage of Gross National Product they increased fourfold. The GNP itself grew threefold in real terms in those years, involving corresponding changes in the structure and sophistication of the economy. The population grew by about 60 percent, and its composition and character underwent even greater change. The very physical environment changed drastically, as Israel assumed control of conquered territories six times its original size, and as rapid economic development left its not-always-pretty imprint on its pre-1967 territory. Naturally, these transformations could not but profoundly affect the temper and workings of the Israeli polity and politics; and although the change there remained for some time concealed from all but the most penetrating eyes, in May 1977 it exploded in an electoral upheaval that overthrew a half-century of labor dominance and installed a new regime led by the Likkud. Only with regard to one issue discussed in my previous volume can it be said that the change has been less impressive than the continuity, and that is the problem of religion and the state. But that fact itself is so remarkable that it begged for elaboration, if only by way of providing a new case-study illustration.

This book seeks to reach the broad public as well as specialists, and this aim has guided my treatment of even highly technical material, including economic and military affairs. I have avoided referring to the massive and often confusing sources underlying the facts cited, or expounding fully the complex deliberations behind all the judgments stated. To the professional student of international politics and history I offer two partial compensations for those omissions: I have dwelt in greater detail in the text itself on the lesser-known events of recent years, and I have provided in the Bibliography references to available sources that are extensive in direct proportion to the degree to which a subject matter is unfamiliar. I should point out, however, that the available data, especially for the diplomacy of recent years, are scarcely of the kind that permits definitive historical conclusions. Therefore, in trying to make sense of the material that could be assembled, I have had to rely a great deal on my intuition, trained and enlivened, I hope, by a quarter-century of systematic study and teaching of the Middle East, traveling in its various parts, and discussing its problems with Israeli as well as Arab and American leaders, officials, and people in all walks of life. This book should therefore be viewed as a preliminary attempt at an overall understanding of Israel and Israeli-American relations—what Max Weber called *Verstehen*—a necessary prelude to the pursuit of definitive particular studies as the comprehensive data needed for such endeavors become available.

Cambridge, Massachusetts   N.S.

ACKNOWLEDGMENTS

This book owes more than can be specifically acknowledged to generations of students who have worked with me on the multitude of subjects treated in it. Particular thanks are, however, due to David Pollock and Mark Heller, two bright young scholars who have been my assistants in recent years.

My old friend Professor Sanford Lakoff of the University of California at San Diego read most of the manuscript at an early stage and contributed a great deal by his criticism and even more by his silence.

The Middle East Committee of the Social Science Research Council awarded me a sabbatical grant for the academic year 1972–73 which enabled me to make a good start on my project, and the Center for Middle Eastern Studies and the Center for International Affairs, Harvard University, provided supplementary summer grants and overhead support which enabled me to see it through to completion. Barbara Henson and Sharon Cronan of the Middle East Center favored my endeavor with attention beyond the call of duty.

I am grateful to the Bobbs-Merrill Company, Inc., for permission to use some material from Chapters VI and VII of my book *From War to War,* copyright © by Western Publishing Company, Inc. The citation on pages 545–547 has been reprinted by permission from *Foreign Policy,* vol. 22 (Spring 1976), copyright © 1976 by National Affairs, Inc., for which thanks are herein given.

I am grateful to my wife, Anita, and my children, Nina, Abby, and Lizzie, for putting up more or less stoically with the book's encroachment on time and attention to which they felt they had prior claim.

CONTENTS

Book One / The Evolution of Israel

Part One / The Origins of Modern Israel

Introduction 4

1 The Jewish Connection with Palestine 7
   The Ancient Hebrew Civilization 7
   The Diaspora and the Idea of Return 10

2 Zionism: The Dynamics of Its Internal
   Success 14
   *Zionism, the Yearning for Return, and the
      Jewish Problem 14*
   *Zionism, World Jewry, and the Building of the
      National Home 20*

3 The Balfour Declaration and the Mandate 24
   The Balfour Declaration 24
   *The Application of the Mandate: Internal
      Development 26*
   *The Application of the Mandate: External
      Political Aspects 28*

4 The United Nations, the United States, and the Birth
   of Israel 32
   *America's Palestine Relations Prior to the
      United Nations Resolution 33*
   *The United States and the Emergence of
      Israel 37*
   *Appraisal of America's Position in
      1947–1948 39*

5 The War of Independence and the Birth of Israel 43
   The Civil War's Course 44
   The Regular War's Course 48
   Consequences of the War 60

Part Two / The Physicial, Human, Economic, and Constitutional Environment

6 The Country   67
   Political Geography   *67*
   Physical and Economic Geography   *70*
   Land Tenure System   *80*

7 The People   83
   The Formation and Transformation of Israel's
      People until 1967   *84*
   —ꜛ *The Wars of 1967 and 1973 and the People*
      of Israel   *94*
   The Wars and the Future Composition of
      the Population   *99*
   The Stratification of Israel's People Today   *104*

8 The Economy: Development,
   Characteristics, Problems   107
   Growth of the Economy   *108*
   Role of Government in the Economy   *111*
   Pattern of Production   *114*
   Foreign Trade   *118*
   Problems and Prospects   *120*
   —ꜛ *Impact of the 1973 War*   *124*

9 The Constitutional Order   126
   Foundations of the Democratic System   *126*
   Basic Framework of Government   *128*

Part Three / The Pattern of Internal Politics

Introduction   138

10 The Inherited Party System and Its
   Characteristics   140
   Multiplicity of Parties   *140*
   Ideological Orientation and Intensity   *148*
   Extension of Party Activity   *152*
   Centralization of Party Authority   *154*
   Effect of Party Character on the Political System   *156*

11 Pressures and Adaptations, 1948–1967   161
   Effect of the State   *161*

    Effect of Immigration 162
    Effect of Threats to National Security 165

12 New Pressures and Readjustments, 1967–1977   172
    Impact of the 1967 Crisis and War 172
    Impact of the 1973 War 179
    *Preliminary Effect of the Changes on the Political
       System 188*
    The Upheaval of May 1977 191

13 Religion and the State   200
    Origins of the Religion-State Problem 200
    Pattern of Religion-State Relations 202
    Dynamics of the Religion-State Problem 206
    *An Illustration: The Case of the
       Mamzerim, 1965–1972 213*

Part Four / National Defense: Threats, Responses, Implications

    Introduction   222

14 National Security, 1949–1967: Challenge
and Response   224
    The Arab Challenge 224
    The Israeli Response 227

15 The Test of 1967: The Six Day War   240

16 National Security, 1967–1973: New
Challenges, New Responses   257
    Israel's Military Posture after the 1967 War 258
    The War of Attrition and Israel's Reactions 261
    *The Challenge of the Fedayeen and Israel's
       Response 266*
    *The Contest of Threat and Deterrence,
       1970–1973 271*

17 Trial by Ordeal: The 1973 Yom Kippur War   278
    The Prelude to the War 279
    The Course of the War 288
    *The Aftermath: The War and Israel's
       Future Security 312*

18 The Defense Effort and the Israeli Polity   317

Book Two / Israel and America in International Politics

Introduction   332

19   Striving for Security in the Absence of Peace,
1949–1956   334
> The First Phase, 1949–1953:
> Propositions and Dispositions   335
> The Second Phase, 1953–1956:
> Deterioration and War   347

20   A Decade of Consolidation and Hope,
1957–1967   359
> The Powers' Struggle, 1957–1958   360
> The Shaping of a Stalemate, 1959–1964   365
> Israel's Improved Position after Sinai   368
> Further Consolidation of Israel's International
> Position after Sinai   375

21   The 1967 Eruption   381
> The Remote Background   382
> The Immediate Causes of the War   387

22   New Options, Alignments, and Tribulations,
1967–1970   414
> Basic Considerations Affecting the Parties   415
> The Shaping of Positions and Alignments,
> 1967–1969   425
> The Diplomacy of the War of Attrition,
> 1969–1970   431

23   The Prevailing of the Israeli-American
Partnership, 1970–1973   448
> The Erosion of the Rogers Policies   449
> The Merging of American and Israeli
> Conceptions   464

24   The Cataclysm of October 1973   476
> The Diplomacy of War   477
> Israel's Position in the Wake of the War   495

25 Readaptations and Step-by-Step Diplomacy,
    October 1973–May 1974   506
    *Cease-Fire Problems; Israeli-American
       Strains 507*
    *Preparations for Negotiations; Improved
       Israeli-American Climate 513*
    Peace Rendezvous at Geneva 520
—ʒ *Israeli-Egyptian Disengagement; American
       Engagement 521*
    *Israeli-Syrian Disengagement; Greater
       American Engagement 528*

26 Faltering Steps, Reassessment, Realignment, Pause,
    June 1974–May 1977   535
    Disagreement on Jordan 536
    Falling Out of Step on Egypt 539
    Reassessment and Realignment 548
    Diplomatic Pause and Prospective Trials 560

27 American-Israeli Relations: An Overview   571
    America's Special Connection with Israel 571
    The Stages of American-Israeli Relations 577
    The Next Stage in American-Israeli Relations 594

Postscript   599

Bibliography   624
Index   637

War of Independance: 1947
Six Day War: 1967
Yom Kippur War: 1973
Invasion of the Sinai: 1956
War of Attrition: 1969

MAPS

UN Partition Boundaries and Initial Arab Invasion,
  May 15–June 11, 1948   51
The 1949 Armistice Demarcation Lines   61
Israel and Occupied Areas, 1977   68
The Six Day War: Egyptian Front   244
The Six Day War: Jordanian Front   249
The Six Day War: Battle of Jerusalem   251
The Six Day War: Syrian Front   254
The Yom Kippur War: Egyptian Front   290
The Yom Kippur War: Syrian Front   295
First Israeli-Egyptian Sinai Agreement, January 18, 1974   526
Israeli-Syrian Golan Agreement, May 31, 1974   533
Second Israeli-Egyptian Sinai Agreement, September 4, 1975   555

BOOK ONE

THE EVOLUTION OF ISRAEL

PART ONE

THE ORIGINS
OF MODERN ISRAEL

INTRODUCTION

In an immediate sense, Israel is first and foremost the creation of Zionism. This movement is closely linked to the wave of nationalism that has swept the world since the American and French Revolutions, and has given rise to over one hundred independent nations in the last quarter century alone. Zionism cannot, indeed, be understood apart from its origin in the political, social, and intellectual currents that washed Europe in the nineteenth century and were the common source of many nationalist movements. Its success cannot be imagined apart from the two world wars of the twentieth century which broke up empires, revolutionized international power relations, and made possible the triumph of many movements of national liberation. However, so different were the circumstances of the Jewish people from those of other peoples aspiring to sovereign national status, so different was the connection of the Jews to the territory they sought to make their national home from that of other peoples to their national territories, and so peculiar, therefore, were the tasks that confronted the Jewish nationalists and the conditions under which they had to work, that any attempt to understand Zionism by looking at it as just another nationalist movement is bound to obscure the subject rather than clarify it, and is certain to become a handicap in any effort to grasp the forces that shape Israel.

Zionism endeavored to obtain national sovereignty for a people scattered over much of the world in a land it had not effectively occupied for nearly two thousand years. The only link among the dispersed groups of the people had been religious, and between the people and the country the connection had been essentially spiritual. Yet Zionism, while capitalizing on these links, was not a religious movement in the commonly accepted sense of the term. It did not arise out of a religious impulse, nor did it seek to meet some religious need. In fact, Zionism emerged when the hold of religion on Jews was weaker than in any previous period of their history, and when Jews themselves were endeavoring for the first time to blur religious elements that stressed their separateness so as to be able to merge more easily among the Gentiles. The Zionist program did not seek to reverse this trend but sought rather to provide another way—in its view the only feasible one—to make the Jews in all respects like others.

The specific doctrine and ultimate program of Zionism were never accepted by more than a small minority of Jews in the world or in any particular country, and were in fact actively and vigorously opposed by many powerful Jewish groups in many communities. Nevertheless, the Zionist movement was able to mobilize the support of most Jews nearly everywhere for one aspect or another of its many endeavors in Palestine, which the supporting groups viewed as ends in themselves but which the Zionists viewed as elements of their nation-building goal. At a critical moment in Jewish history, after the Nazi slaughter of most of Europe's Jews, the Zionists were able by this process to mobilize the backing of nearly all of world Jewry for the creation of a Jewish state as the only means to rescue the survivors and relieve the oppressed. But the Zionist doctrine remained even then the faith of a minority.

While Zionism provided the leadership and drive and mobilized the resources for the overall Jewish endeavor in Palestine, the entire undertaking would have been impossible had not Britain sponsored the Zionist movement at the end of the First World War and given it the opportunity to establish a secure base in the country through the Balfour Declaration and the Mandate. A quarter century later, when Britain felt impelled to trade its support of Zionism for Arab goodwill, the embryonic Jewish national community that had emerged in the meantime in Palestine was already strong enough to defy its initial sponsor. With aid from the Zionist movement and the benefit of favorable circumstances, it was able to gain friends and supporters elsewhere who helped to bring about the termination of Britain's rule in Palestine and the establishment of Israel. One of these friends was the United States. American pressure on Britain immediately after the end of the Second World War to allow large-scale immigration was crucial in compelling that country to bring the whole Palestine question before the United Nations in 1947, and American support was decisive in winning the decision of this organization in November of that year in favor of partitioning Palestine between a Jewish and an Arab state.

The United Nations resolution was forcibly resisted by the Palestinian Arabs with outside assistance, and in the civil war that ensued between them and the Jews of Palestine, the Zionist dream of achieving statehood teetered for a while between fulfillment and frustration. Eventually, the Jews of Palestine, also with outside assistance, prevailed and proclaimed their independent state on May 15, 1948. However, the new state was immediately confronted with an invasion by the regular forces of the neighboring Arab countries, and this time the Zionist dream teetered between consummation and complete destruction. Against all apparent odds, the Jewish state triumphed, demonstrating in the process the extraordinary dedication of the Zionist settlers and the thoroughness with which they had built the makings of a nation. Moreover, in the course of the war the Jewish state captured more territory than had been allocated to it by the partition resolution, and the Arab states were compelled to concede to it control over these territories in formal armistice agreements.

For their victory in the civil war and the war with their neighbors, the Jews of Palestine paid very heavily in blood. For the Arabs, the cost of defeat was misery and the loss of homeland and home for hundreds of thousands of Palestinians, and humiliation and turmoil for the governments and states involved. For all sides, the events from the end of 1947 to the beginning of 1949 left a residue of bitterness and suspicion that conditioned their subsequent actions in ways that prolonged the conflict among them to the present day, while taking it through several crucial convolutions.

In the nearly three decades that have elapsed since the proclamation of the state of Israel, much has been written about the origins of that state by friends and foes. Because Israel was born in the midst of war, many, including extreme Israeli nationalists and most Arabs, have seen the origins of the Jewish state in the successful use of fire and sword, disregarding the conditions that made possible the success of Jewish arms. Others have looked upon the United Nations resolution to partition Palestine as the critical moment; and, because of President Truman's support of Zionist positions in the events leading up to that decision, have assigned to the United States a crucial role in the creation of Israel. Not a few Jews and many Arabs go back to 1917, and praise or condemn the Balfour Declaration as the root from which Israel grew, while some Zionist historians consider the Jewish state to have been historically "inevitable" from the moment Jewish national consciousness became crystallized in the Zionist movement a century or so ago. Finally, some Jews and Gentiles go back several thousand years and view the real source of Israel in God's covenant with Abraham granting the Land of Canaan to his descendants for all time.

All these conceptions express some truth but none the whole of it. Each of the factors mentioned did indeed make a necessary contribution to the creation of Israel, but none of them would have been sufficient, or even conceivable, without the others. This will become clear upon closer consideration of the origins of modern Israel.

1

The Jewish Connection
with Palestine

The Ancient Hebrew Civilization

The origins of the Jewish connection with Palestine go back to remote times in which history is merged with legend, myth, and religious tradition. The Bible tells the story of God's command to Abraham to go forth from his native land of Ur, in present-day Iraq, to what became known as Palestine, which country He promised to grant to his descendants forever, though not before they had passed a period of four hundred years as persecuted strangers in an alien land. In accordance with the divine forecast, Abraham's grandson Jacob, or Israel, was compelled by famine to go to Egypt with his entire family, in the circumstances described in the moving story of Joseph and his brothers, and settle there in the Land of Goshen. From seventy souls in all, the Children of Israel multiplied so rapidly that in the course of time they aroused the anxiety of Egypt's rulers, who took drastic measures to check their growth and keep them under control. At the proper time, God appointed Moses His prophet and entrusted him with leading the Children of Israel out of Egypt and back into the land He had promised Abraham. After many trials, during which God continually supported Moses with signs and miracles, and after forty years of wandering in the desert, during which the multitude of the Children of Israel were forged into a "nation" sworn to the exclusive worship of God and endowed with His laws, Moses at last brought his people to the gates of the Promised Land. God called Moses when his mission was fulfilled, and Joshua led the Israelites into their homeland.

With regard to most points of this story, history is able to tell us little that is certain. We do know that during the second millennium before Christ there were periodic incursions of Semitic tribes from the Syrian desert into the lands lying on the coast of the Mediterranean; that one tribe, or group of tribes, who claimed descent from Abraham of Ur and were known as Hebrews, or Israelites, had migrated into the territory of Palestine; and that by 1100 B.C.

the Israelites were in firm possession of most of the hill country. They were already distinguished by their religion from the Phoenicians and Philistines of the coast and from the nomads who dwelt on the eastern side of the Jordan.

For the next twelve hundred years the Children of Israel were settled in Palestine. They were never the sole occupants of the land, nor were they always its "sovereign" masters. But they were definitely rooted in it, and it was there that they developed the great spiritual heritage which they have contributed to mankind.

During the twelfth and eleventh centuries B.C., the Israelites lived as separate tribes that were often in conflict with each other and with their neighbors. This phase of their history is broadly sketched in the Book of Judges. But under the pressure of foreign enemies, particularly the Philistines, the tribes were driven to establish a monarchy which, after a halting beginning under Saul, became consolidated and reached the height of its power under King David (1010–970 B.C.) and King Solomon (970–930 B.C.). David decisively defeated the Philistines and other enemies, and Solomon extended the influence of the realm he had inherited from his father over nearly the entire area lying between the two rival powers of Assyria and Egypt. The glory of Solomon's reign was crowned by the construction of the Temple in Jerusalem, which gradually became the focal point of the religious and national life of the Israelites.

After King Solomon's death, the ten tribes inhabiting the northern half of the country seceded and formed their own kingdom, which became known as Israel. The Philistines reasserted their independence in their coastal city-states, as did other subject nations. What remained of Solomon's realm became known as the kingdom of Judah and continued to have its center in Jerusalem and its Temple. The two kingdoms, as well as the city-states of the coast, managed to preserve their independence for nearly two hundred years, despite their small size and relative weakness, until 721–715 B.C. At that time the Assyrian giant conquered the kingdom of Israel, destroyed its capital, and deported the able and the wealthy among the population to distant lands. Judah escaped this fate by submitting to Assyrian suzerainty. But several generations later, in 585 B.C., Nebuchadnezzar of the new Babylonian empire, which had dispossessed Assyria, conquered the Judeans, destroyed their Temple, and deported many of them to Babylon. This ended the era known in Jewish tradition as the period of the First Temple. Politically, the record of that period was rather unimpressive after the reigns of David and Solomon. Spiritually and culturally, however, it witnessed in its latter half the soaring of the human spirit, the deepening of the moral consciousness, and the flowering of the great rhythmic prose evident in the legacy of the prophets Amos, Hosea, Isaiah, and Jeremiah.

The captivity of Judah in Babylon did not last long. In 538 B.C. Cyrus the Great, the founder of the Persian Empire, occupied Babylon and in the next year gave permission to the Judean exiles to return to their country. Nearly 40,000 of them, a small part of the total Jewry of Babylon, availed themselves of the opportunity and returned to their homeland to rebuild the Temple and to reconstitute their national life as a small vassal state. Little was known until recently about the life of the "men of Judah," or Jews, for the next three of four hundred years, apart from the fact that they were under the suzerainty of the Persians and afterward of the Ptolemaic Greeks. But recent research, much of it done in Jerusalem, indicates that it was in this period that the cultural identity of the Jews was fixed and secured. It was then that the Torah (Pentateuch) took its final form and became the focus of Jewish life, and it was then that the books of Job, Ruth, Ecclesiastes, Proverbs, the Song of Songs, and some of the finest psalms were written.

A new phase began with the conquest of Palestine by the Seleucid rulers of Syria in 198 B.C. Hellenism had made deep inroads among the Jews, but when the Seleucids tried to hasten the assimilation process by banning adherence to rules of the Torah, a revolt broke out that succeeded in recovering the independence of Judea. The revolt had been led by the priestly Hasmonean family, who then established a dynasty of priest-kings. Under some of its more able members Judea expanded in all directions, so that by 150 B.C. it had reached something resembling the limits of the kingdom of David and Solomon. Less than one hundred years later, however, Judea succumbed once more to the power of another great empire when, in 63 B.C., Pompey captured Jerusalem. Palestine was not to become an independent realm for the next two thousand years, until the state of Israel was established in A.D. 1948.

During the century after their conquest the Romans ruled Judea indirectly and did not, on the whole, disturb the community life of the Jews. At times, they allowed native rulers like Herod to assume the title and many of the prerogatives of a king. But the heavy burden of taxation, internal feuds, and above all the growth of a fierce national spirit that fed on a fanatical attachment to religion led to continual strife and tension, which culminated in a general revolt in A.D. 64. It took Rome seven years of bitter fighting to subdue the Jews. The Temple, which was the seat of the last resistance, was burned to the ground by Titus and his soldiers. But the Jews were not yet completely crushed; they revolted again in 115 and in 132. This last revolt, led by Shim'on Bar Kochba, was so nearly successful that Rome determined to make its repetition impossible. In 135 Jerusalem was destroyed and its site was plowed up. Countless Jews were slaughtered and countless others were carried off to slavery. For two more centuries the pacified Jews of Palestine were able to maintain a communal life under the leadership of a patriarchate sanctioned by Rome, during which time the great work of elaborating the Torah into the legal-moral compendia known as the Mishna was completed. But subsequent centuries saw the dwindling of Jewish life in Palestine until only a few thousand and impoverished Jews remained in their ancient homeland. Long before this point had been reached, Jewish history had ceased to be the history of Palestine and began to be what it still is in large measure today: the history of Jewish communities dispersed over much of the world.

The Diaspora and the Idea of Return

The long, fascinating, and often tragic history of the Jewish communities outside of Palestine is beyond the scope of this work. However, its bare outlines are important for setting the Jewish connection with Palestine in its historical context.

The history of the Jewish Diaspora, or dispersion, began long before the disastrous end of the Bar Kochba uprising in A.D. 135. Many, if not most, of the Jews who had been exiled to Babylon in 585 B.C. did not return in 538 B.C. or thereafter. Their descendants, their numbers swollen by waves of immigration, grew in the course of time into a very large community that kept in close touch with Palestine and developed a creative cultural-religious life centered on the Torah. When Palestine declined as the center of Jewish culture (around the third century of our era), that function passed to the Babylonian Jewish community and remained with it through the Arab conquest in the seventh century and the golden age of Arab-Muslim civilization in the next three centuries. During this long period, the academies established by Babylonian Jewry collected and produced the immense corpus of commentaries and elaboration upon the Mishna known as the Talmud, worked out the principles of Jewish jurisprudence, assembled the homilies and legends known as the Midrash, and elaborated the first Siddur, or prayer book. This body of material has served ever since as the core of traditional Jewish learning everywhere and has provided Jews in the Diaspora with a common heritage of doctrine, law, and lore that contributed enormously to preserving the unity of the Jewish people until the dawn of modern times. Even today, over one hundred *Yeshivot* (religious colleges) in Israel and many others all over the world devote themselves mainly to the preservation and enrichment of the heritage bequeathed by Babylonian Jewry.

A Jewish community had been established in Alexandria, Egypt, almost since the founding of the city by Alexander the Great. Over time the community had grown to such an extent that it dared, in A.D. 115, to revolt against Roman power and was able to secure the relaxation of an old Roman law against mutilation of the body, which had been used before the uprising to ban circumcision. But jealous as it was of its faith, that community nevertheless participated fully in the Hellenistic culture and shared in the glory of Alexandria when it was the center of Hellenistic civilization. The Septuagint (the Greek translation of the Old Testament) and the work of the great Jewish philosopher Philo testify to the community's effort to reach an accommodation with Greek culture and thought which, incidentally, influenced in turn the philosophy of the Church Fathers. In later Roman times, the Jewish community in Alexandria declined in importance and numbers, just as did Palestine's Jewry with which it had kept in close contact, but the Jews of Alexandria flourished again under the generally tolerant Arab-Muslim rule. Once more the Jews of Egypt adopted the language, way of living, and culture of the surrounding society, while retaining their separateness in matters pertaining to their faith. Some of them attained positions of power and honor in the government, in finance, in science, and in learning.

In the wake of the Arab conquest Jews migrated from the Near East, from Egypt, and from North Africa to Spain and reinforced Jewish groups who had migrated to that country in earlier times. There they became full-fledged partners with the Arabs in the brilliant civilization that developed under a succession of magnificent princes. All walks of life, rural and urban, were open to the Jews, and many of them attained the highest positions in the economic, social, cultural, and political life of the various Arab states. While the Spanish Jews, like those in Egypt, assimilated by adopting Arabic names, the Arabic language, and Arab ways, they managed at the same time to produce a bright revival of Hebrew culture, including a rich religious and secular literature. The record of the period between the tenth and twelfth centuries, studded with names like Hasdai ibn Shaprut, Shmuel Hannagid, Shlomo ibn Gabirol, ibn Janah, Bahya ibn Pakuda, Yitzhak al Fasi, Moshe ibn Ezra, Yehuda Halevi, Abraham ibn Ezra, and Moshe ibn Maimon, or Maimonides, constitutes a glorious chapter in Jewish history. Unfortunately this period came to a premature end with the Almohade persecution of the Jews of Spain and North Africa, exceptional in its ferocity in the record of Muslim treatment of Jews, which compelled Maimonides, among many if his coreligionists, to seek refuge on the more hospitable shores of Egypt.

In the Western world, the Jews fared nowhere nearly so well as in the lands that came under the dominion of Islam. In Europe the Jews were compelled until the seventeenth and eighteenth centuries to live an isolated community life, assimilating little of the culture and ways of the peoples among whom they lived. From Rome and other cities of Italy, where large Jewish communities had existed by the first century A.D., Jews had penetrated into the European provinces of the Roman empire and, after its collapse, into Germany and England. When Christianity became dominant in these areas, the Jews were subjected to various restrictions and prohibitions which marked them off as distinct and inferior people because of their presumed denial of the central belief of Christianity.

The Gulf established by discriminatory ecclesiastical decrees was widened over time by the effect of social factors. The Jew could not find a place on the land or in the artisan guilds. Consequently, he became a middleman, merchant, or peddler; and since usury was forbidden to Christians, he also became the moneylender. Concentrated in the towns where they were confined to special quarters known as ghettos, foreigners and foreign-looking, keeping to themselves, occupied in unpopular albeit useful professions, clinging stubbornly to their faith, and viewed as bearing collectively and for all time the guilt of the crucifixion, the Jews became intensely disliked by the populace.

The feelings of hostility toward the Jews broke out into action from time to time. During the period of the Crusades, it became as much an act of piety to kill the Jews in Europe as to kill the Saracens in the Holy Land. Later, waves of persecution, increasingly brutal, spread over Western Europe. In England, France, and parts of Germany, Jews were despoiled, tortured, some massacred, and the rest finally expelled. For a time, there was less brutality in the parts of Spain reconquered by Christians. But in the second half of the fifteenth century the Inquisition took up its task of hunting and burning heretics, and in 1492 all Jews who refused to be converted were expelled.

The refugees from Western Europe went to the eastern frontiers of the expanding continent, to Lithuania, Poland, and Hungary. This migration continued through the centuries until half the Jews in the world were congregated in that area. At first the Polish Kings protected them, but the respite was short-lived. In the middle of the seventeenth century came the Tartar invasion and later, Russian rule. A sort of territorial ghetto, the "pale of settlement," was established from the Baltic north of Warsaw to the Black Sea near Odessa to keep the Jews from penetrating Holy Russia.

Most of the refugees from Spain went to the Mediterranean provinces of the Ottoman empire, to North Africa, Egypt, the Balkans, Asia Minor, and to Constantinople itself. A few trickled into Italy and southern France, where they were followed in subsequent generations by Marrano Jews—Jews who had remained in Spain by bowing to the Inquisition in outward form but not in conviction—who also infiltrated Holland, Germany, and England and paved the way for the return to all these countries of undisguised, professing Jews. The Spanish refugees who went to the Muslim lands merged with the Jewish communities already existing there and enjoyed relative freedom from the worst forms of persecution. But just as these Jews had shared in the glory of the Muslim countries in the previous centuries, so in the centuries that followed they shared in the decay and stagnation that engulfed them at the very time when the Western Christian peoples were forging ahead toward a new world.

By the time of the American and French Revolutions, Jews had lived in dispersion for one and a half to two and a half millennia without losing their identity and their essential unity. Certain minor differences in ritualistic detail and much larger sociological and even racial differences had crept in among various communities or groups of communities over the centuries, giving rise to three major divisions: the Ashkenazim—literally, Germans, but actually those who had lived under Christianity outside of Spain before the expulsion of the Jews from that country; the Sefaradim—literally, Spaniards, but actually the Spanish outcasts and all the communities of the Mediterranean basin with which they intermingled; and the Orientals—the various communities which existed uninterruptedly in the Middle East from before the destruction of the Second Temple, notably the Yemenites and the Iraqis. But the differences among these divisions were outweighed by the enormous body of religious law, ritual, customs, lore, and knowledge that they shared, and above all by the common conception of the history and destiny of the Jew, centering on the ideas of Galuth and Geullah, which they all held.

Galuth, meaning Exile, defined the condition of the Jews in their own eyes, and Geullah, Delivery from the exile and Return to the ancestral homeland, defined their expected destiny. Among various Jewish communities at various times these two concepts were overlaid with metaphysical meaning, but never until the nineteenth century was the idea of actual return to Palestine missing in any interpretation. Assertions of the conviction of Jews that their current status was that of an exiled people and expressions of their faith in delivery and return are to be found in countless rituals, from the daily prayers through the ceremonials attending birth, marriage, and death. But the belief in these concepts drew its strength from its roots in the traditional Jewish view of the world. This view, which saturates much of the Old Testament, conceives of the universe as governed by a divine design operating continuously, the chief motif of which is God's relation to His Chosen People. Empires rise and fall, nature pursues or modifies its prescribed course, and the earth proffers or withholds its bounty in order to serve an identifiable purpose in the cosmic moral drama that had its historical beginning in God's covenant with Abraham. It followed that such events as the destruction of the Temple and the scattering of the Jews, the most momentous since the Exodus, could not be accidental or definitive, but served a certain purpose and had to have a sequel. That purpose was viewed as the chastising of the Jews in Exile, and the sequel was viewed as redemption and Return to the land God gave to Abraham. The fact that both the Christian and Muslim societies among which the Jews served their sentence of exile conceded the special relation of the Jewish people with God in the past and confirmed the cosmic moral significance of its dispersion—even as they differed in assessing its present status and the sequel to its dispersion—further confirmed the Jew in his conviction. For the belief in the Delivery and Return yet to come became one of the most important criteria continuously separating and demarcating him from the peoples among whom he lived.

2

Zionism: The Dynamics of Its Internal Success

Zionism has been viewed by some as a nationalist movement representing the ripening of the religiously inspired yearning for Zion and by others as an essentially secular movement of national liberation triggered by the difficulties and problems encountered by Europe's Jews in the course of the nineteenth century. Both views have their adherents among Zionists themselves and can find support in the facts of Zionist history. Indeed it is possible to point out that the actual initiators of the Zionist movement, Pinsker and Herzl, were prompted to issue their call for a Jewish state by purely practical assessments of the conditions of the Jews in Europe and did not even consider Palestine as the only conceivable site for that state. But a critical look at the evolution of the Zionist movement as a whole in the context of a broad historical perspective would show that it could not have succeeded if it really were only one or the other. Its strength lay precisely in the fact that it combined the traditional yearning for Return with consideration of the practical needs of the Jews into a new synthesis, in which the needs activated the traditional yearning even as they stripped it of its strictly religious content; while the yearning for Return endowed the practically inspired suggestion of a Jewish state with emotional power even as it directed it toward Palestine specifically.

Zionism, the Yearning for Return, and the Jewish Problem

The Return to the ancestral homeland has been viewed throughout most of Jewish history as something to be accomplished through miraculous divine intervention in the context of a cosmic upheaval and as the prelude to an era of universal peace and justice. This conception did not, however, preclude certain minority opinions which envisaged the Return as coming about through the divine will operating in what would appear as normal historical processes, nor did it prevent self-appointed Messiahs from arising now and then to lead the people back to their homeland and gaining considerable numbers of followers on the basis of flimsy credentials. The traditional conception did not, in any case, rule against anybody going to live in the Holy Land without awaiting the Messiah; on the contrary, Jewish tradition extolled such an act as a good deed, almost a religious obligation, and cultivated a fervent unconditional affection for the ancestral home in and of itself. Throughout history there never lacked individuals and groups who uprooted themselves from their environment and went to live in Palestine out of piety and yearning for Zion.

In the early part of the nineteenth century, the stimulus of general European nationalism began to awaken the traditional yearning for Return and give it a nationalist turn. Sefaradi and Ashkenazi religious leaders in various parts of Europe, such as Rabbi Judah Bibas (d. 1852) of Corfu, Rabbi Judah Alcalay (1798–1878) of Semlin, Serbia, Rabbi Zvi Hirsch Kalisher (1794–1874) of Posen, in Prussian-occupied Poland, and Rabbi Joseph Natonek (1813–1892) of Nagysurány, Hungary, basing themselves on the minority opinions, urged their fellow Jews to take action to effect their Return to their homeland in the same way that other nationalists strove to redeem themselves. In the tracts they wrote and the sermons they preached they presented arguments and advocated measures which foreshadowed those subsequently adopted by the Zionist movement. But these appeals went almost unnoticed and made no significant impact until they were rediscovered and used by some groups in the Zionist movement several decades later, when necessity endowed them with a sense of urgency.

The idea of Return was a tenet of faith not only for the Jews, but also for some influential groups among the Christian, particularly Protestant, powers in modern times. And for them too the idea was not only eschatological. During the nineteenth century, sympathy for nationalist causes in general and unsettled conditions in the Near East and Palestine encouraged the notion among some enthusiasts of the Jewish Return that the time for the fulfillment of the Biblical prophecy had come. These enthusiasts, while they were personally moved by religious sentiment, advanced all sorts of political arguments to win the support of their governments for their schemes. Some argued, for instance, that a Jewish settlement in Palestine would prove a reliable support for the tottering Ottoman regime, when support of that regime seemed to be in the national interest. Others argued that the Jews in Palestine would be the most trustworthy successors to the Ottomans and the guardians of the eastern approaches to Suez in alliance with the power that would sponsor their settlement. Schemes of this sort engaged at times the attention and imagination of very serious statesmen like Palmerston; but, again, nothing enduring came of them until the Zionist movement appeared and was able to capitalize on them and on the sentiment underlying them.

The Zionist movement did not, in fact, produce any new idea when it advocated the establishment of a National Home for the Jewish people in Palestine, nor did it invent any new argument in approaching the various powers for support. If it nevertheless succeeded where its antecedents among both Jews and Gentiles had failed, it was because it wedded the idea of Return to the Jewish Problem as it appeared in the nineteenth century and thus responded to an urgent practical need with an emotionally rich formula.

In its modern version, the Jewish Problem is the product of the Enlightenment and the issue of identity raised by the emancipation of the Jews in many European countries in the wake of the French Revolution. As a matter of historical record, the United States was the first country in the world to grant to the Jews full civil and political rights and the freedom to engage in any occupation. However, the American example had no repercussions in Europe except insofar as the American Revolution generally influenced the French Revolution in its libertarian and egalitarian thrust.

Prior to the French Revolution, we have seen, the Jews of Europe, comprising the majority of world Jewry, had led their own life in the ghettos or villages of the "pale of settlement" in almost complete seclusion from gentile society except for business contacts. The confinement had been imposed on them together with other restrictions as a mark of the curse lying on them for rejecting the true faith, but they had rationalized their status and the frequent outbursts of active persecution in the concept of Galuth as a penance to be followed by Geullah; in the meantime, they had developed a complete, poor and inbred, but spiritually satisfying way of life. The French Revolution upset this doctrinal and social order which had stood for centuries by offering to the Jews freedom and equality with the non-Jewish citizens, provided they ceased to look upon themselves as a separate nationality and assimilated into the national culture while retaining only their separate cult and faith.

After an initial period of hesitation and fear, the French Jews welcomed their new freedom and endeavored to live up to the terms under which it had been proffered. France became a model for the other European countries, and the emancipation of the Jews went hand in hand with the spread of the Enlightenment and the advance of the liberal creeds of the French Revolution, so that by the 1860s most European states had liberated their Jews. The emancipated Jews plunged into the new modernizing world opened for them and proceeded to make the necessary doctrinal adaptations to accomodate their new identity and life style. In particular, they reinterpreted the concepts of Galuth and Geullah in various terms—mythical, allegorical, metaphysical, universalistic—so as to free them effectively from any separatist nationalist connotation. Many of them also supported additional doctrinal and ritualistic reforms in their religion, designed to suit it to modern thought as well as to discard anything that might impose excessive barriers between themselves and their fellow citizens. But the Jewish Problem was not to be solved so easily.

Although most European countries emancipated their Jews in the course of the nineteenth century, Tsarist Russia, containing most of Europe's Jews, and Rumania, containing the next largest number, did not do so. During the reign of Alexander II (1855–1881), it looked for a while as though Russia's Jewry, too, was on its way to liberation as curbs on Jews were eased and as many of them acquired modern education and mixed with Russian society. But the assassination of the Tsar in 1881 precipitated a general reaction that had begun a few years before and ushered in a period of repression and pogroms against the Jews such as had not been seen since the height of the Middle Ages. Many Jews reacted in the tradition of their ancestors by taking to the road and seeking more hospitable lands, thus starting the most massive wave of migration in Jewish history. But among the millions who remained, the masses were caught in a mixture of despair and messianic anticipation while members of the enlightened minority urged various courses and solutions. Some still believed in emancipation as the desirable solution, but, convinced that it could not be achieved under the existing regime, advocated participation in the efforts of the many Russian revolutionary groups to overthrow it entirely. Others lost all hope of emancipation from above and doubted its efficacy even if attained. One of these was a physician from Odessa by the name of Leo Pinsker (1821–1891), who published a pamphlet in 1882 entitled *Auto-emancipation: A Warning of A Russian Jew to His Brethren* that marked the beginning of Russian Zionism. Pinsker argued in his pamphlet that anti-Semitism was an inescapable passion provoked in Gentiles by the character of the Jewish people as an abnormal nation, a "ghost nation." Emancipation was no remedy to this predicament, which could be cured only by the Jews' taking their fate into their own hands and seeking to establish a state of their own which would convert them into a "normal" and equal nation among nations.

The significance of *Auto-emancipation* was not in first stirring nationalist feelings toward Palestine among the Jews of Russia and Rumania. For one thing, Pinsker did not specifically insist on Palestine as the site of the envisaged state, but mentioned it as only one possibility alongside any place in America. For another thing, nationalist stirrings and writings, focusing on Palestine, were widespread before he wrote and were leading, under the impact of the pogroms, to the first nationalistically oriented emigration to Palestine. Rather, Pinsker's contribution lay precisely in the fact that he provided the more or less inchoate religious and nationalist yearnings for Zion with a rationale based on an analysis of "the Jewish condition," and that he attacked in the process the assimilationist solution as an illusion. The attack was all the more credible because it came from a man who had been for many years the head of the Odessa branch of a society devoted to the dissemination of secular culture and the promotion of assimilation among the Jews.

Pinsker's pamphlet served to rally many of the small groups of proto-Zionists that had sprung up spontaneously in Eastern Europe, who constituted, together with disappointed assimilationists, a loose organization called Chovevei Tzion (Lovers of Zion). The movement held the first of a series of congresses in 1884 under the leadership of Pinsker, who was persuaded in the meantime that Zion was the only appropriate site for his scheme.

The Jewish Problem in the nineteenth century was not confined to Russia and Rumania. Even in Central and Western Europe, the emancipation which had been achieved formally did not proceed smoothly in practice. In the first place, emancipation had been much more an act prescribed by rational consistency in an age that valued reason than an expression of a spontaneous feeling of brotherhood, equality, and justice. The ideas of the Enlightenment were hostile to medieval corporatism; the status of the Jews was part of that system; therefore it had to go. Liberalism, with its conception of society as a conglomeration of free and equal individuals united by a compact, was particularly impelled by its own logic to eliminate the abnormal status of the Jews as an inferior group within but not of society. Emancipation on the basis of rational philosophical considerations alone could lead to political equality and economic freedom, but it could not and did not lead to actual social acceptance. In matters that were outside the province of the law, the Jews were still often treated as inferior. Second, in the latter half of the nineteenth century the rational philosophical theories of the Enlightenment and liberalism themselves came under heavy attack from political and social philosophies resting on evolutionism, historicism, romanticism, and race theories which viewed society as an entity that had been formed by many centuries of common history, as a living organism, or as a compact of blood rather than a deliberate artificial creation. Such schemes allowed no room in the national society for the Jews, who were a distinct group and had lived their own life in seclusion until recently, and some of them explicitly regarded the Jews as harmful to the nation or necessarily disloyal to it. Finally, because liberalism was closely associated with the emancipation of the Jews, its political opponents endeavored to arouse suspicion and dislike of the Jews on every conceivable ground with the purpose of using these feelings as a means of embarrassing or overthrowing the liberals.

The pressures generated by these hostile trends caused many Jews to discard more and more of their specifically Jewish baggage in an effort to merge more easily into the surrounding environment. Not a few crossed over and were formally baptized, like Heinrich Heine and the parents of Benjamin Disraeli and Karl Marx. Most tried to convince themselves that the progress of civilization and evidence of their own loyalty and attachment to their respective nations would finally eliminate the remaining prejudices against them. But a few gave up hope in the effectiveness of assimilation and suspected that anti-Semitism was ineradicable. One of these few was Theodor Herzl, who became the father of political Zionism, the founder of the World Zionist Organization, and the prophet of the Jewish state.

Herzl was born in Budapest in 1860 to a well-to-do, assimilated family and was brought up in the tradition of German-Jewish enlightenment of the time. After attending a Jewish elementary school and public high school in his native city, he moved to Vienna with his family in 1878 where he studied law at the university. He completed his studies six years later, but shortly thereafter he abandoned the legal profession to devote himself to literature, where he achieved a measure of fame as a writer of short stories, feuilletons, and plays. From 1891 to 1895 he served as the correspondent of the liberal Viennese daily *Neue Freie Presse* in Paris, where his life took a sharp turn as a result of the unfolding of the Dreyfus affair in the winter of 1894–95.

Herzl first encountered the Jewish Problem as a student in the University of Vienna. In 1882 he had read Karl Eugen Dühring's anti-Semitic book, *The Jewish Problem as a Question of Race, Morals, and Culture.* A year later he resigned from a student fraternity in protest against its anti-Semitic attitude. However, the problem did not weigh heavily on him in the next decade or so while he was making his career in Vienna, judging by his diaries and his writings which consisted of society and drawing room comedies without any specific Jewish reference. It was only after he arrived in Paris that the problem began to preoccupy him again, not because Paris before the outbreak of the Dreyfus affair was more anti-Semitic than Vienna, but because of a repeatedly confirmed tendency of Jews to be more sensitive to ostensibly anti-Semitic manifestations in other societies than in their own. Thus in 1892 he wrote for the *Neue Freie Presse* an article entitled "French Anti-Semites," which inaugurated his active concern with the problem. A year later he argued that the Jewish Problem was a social question that could be solved only by having the younger generations baptized en masse in an organized effort, or by having them all join the socialist movement. Two years later, in 1894, he wrote a play entitled *The New Ghetto* in which he depicted emancipation as having merely cast the Jews into a new spiritual and moral ghetto from which there seemed to be no possible escape.

In the latter part of that year Herzl attended as a journalist the trial of Captain Dreyfus. The climax of that episode in the ceremony at the Ecole militaire (January, 1895), in which Dreyfus was stripped of his rank and given a dishonorable discharge amid mob cries of "Death to the Jews," finally convinced him that assimilation was not realizable and that the only solution to the Jewish problem was a mass exodus of the Jews to a state of their own.

Herzl worked out a memorandum embodying his ideas and began to lobby for it among Jewish philanthropists like the Rothschilds and Baron Maurice de Hirsch, famous personalities, rabbis, and community leaders. It was only then that he became aware of the existence of Russian Zionism and Pinsker's similar conclusions reached thirteen years before on the basis of an assessment of the condition of the Jews in Russia. Most of the Chovevei Tzion societies generally supported him, but most of the "establishment" Jews of

Western Europe opposed him on grounds of principle as well as practicality. When Baron Edmond de Rothschild, who had been supporting for some time the first Russian Zionist settlers in Palestine, objected to Herzl's scheme on the grounds of the impossibility of organizing the Jewish masses, Herzl decided to go to the public to disprove this contention. After reworking his memorandum into an essay entitled *The Jewish State,* published in 1896, he initiated a meeting of what came to be known as the First Zionist Congress in Basle, Switzerland, in August 1897. The congress, which was attended by representatives of Jewish groups from seventeen countries including the United States, adopted Herzl's aim and established the World Zionist Organization to advance it. At the end of the congress Herzl confided to his diary: "In Basle I founded the Jewish State. If I were to say this aloud I would meet with general laughter; but in another five years, and certainly in another fifty years, everyone will be convinced of this. The state is created mainly upon the people's will for a state." He was wrong by a year.

In *The Jewish State* Herzl had expressed preference for Palestine as the site of the Jewish state because of its historical association with the Jews, but, like Pinsker, he was also willing to consider a suitable place anywhere else. The First Zionist Congress, however, opted unanimously for Palestine. A few years later, the choice of Palestine was put to the test when the British government offered Herzl a territory in East Africa for Jewish settlement. Herzl and many of the Western Zionists were inclined to accept, but among Zionists from Eastern Europe there was bitter opposition to any alternative to Zion, which threatened to pull the movement apart. Eventually the Seventh Zionist Congress, which met in 1905 soon after Herzl's death, rejected the East Africa proposal and rededicated itself to Palestine. Those who still favored any territory, about forty delegates led by Israel Zangwill, seceded from the movement and formed the Jewish Territorial Organization. The history of that organization is perhaps an indication of what might have happened to the Zionist movement as a whole had it not tapped the deeply rooted popular attachment to Palestine to sustain its endeavor to find a practical solution to the immediate Jewish problem. Despite its sponsorship by many outstanding Jews and its very able leadership, the Jewish Territorial Organization failed to advance its cause beyond the stage of exploration of possibilities in Surinam, Libya, Iraq, Angola, Canada, Honduras, Australia, Mexico, Argentina, and even Siberia. In the process, it became converted into a philanthropic group which did some useful work in several countries before sinking into insignificance within a decade of its creation.

Zionism, World Jewry, and the Building of the National Home

Zionism as a doctrine that rejected outright the possibility of the Jews' being able to live as citizens of various countries on equal terms with non-Jews, and asserted that Jews everywhere constituted a single nation for which it sought to secure a National Home in Palestine was never more than the faith of a relatively small minority of Jews. In 1899, two years after its founding, the World Zionist Organization had a registered membership of 114,000, even though membership in practical terms involved no more than payment of a small biennial poll tax. Fourteen years later, on the eve of the First World War, the number had increased to 130,000, after periods of considerable decline from the original number. In 1921, after the Balfour Declaration had been issued and the Zionists had proved that they were not merely a group of dreamers but an internationally recognized force worthy of the sponsorship of mighty Britain and the other great powers, the membership of the organization attained 778,000. Even if we assume that all these figures understate the strength of the movement, since Zionism was formally outlawed in both Tsarist and Soviet Russia, the adherents of the movement still represented a minority of the world Jewish population, which counted at that time 14 million.

Not only was Zionism the faith of a minority, but it was actively opposed nearly everywhere by powerful Jewish forces. In Russia and Eastern Europe it was opposed vehemently by the Bund, the General Jewish Workers' Organization in Russia and Poland, which was founded in the same year as the Zionist organization. The Bundists argued that the Zionists were diverting Jewish energies to a hopeless dream to the detriment of their own more realistic efforts to improve the lot of the Jews where they were. They sought instead to marshal Jewish effort on behalf of a Russian revolution while safeguarding what they conceived to be the interests of the Jewish working class. When revolution did come, the Bundists, characterized by Lenin using Plekhanov's words as "Zionists afraid of seasickness," were liquidated in the Soviet Union, but their anti-Zionist role was taken over by the fanatic *Yevsektzia,* the network of Jewish sections in the Communist party. The Bund continued to operate in Poland which contained within its boundaries nearly 3 million Jews, and on the eve of World War II it constituted probably the most important Jewish party in that country.

In Western Europe and the United States, the Zionist movement was opposed by most of the religious establishments and the Jewish organizations. The Orthodox rabbinates objected to Zionism for tampering with the messianic idea, and the ultra-Orthodox set up in due course a world organization which had as one of its main purposes combating Zionism. Reform rabbinical groups attacked Zionism for giving Jewishness generally and the messianic idea specifically a "parochial" nationalist meaning instead of the universalist sense they were wont to attach to them. Leaders of communal organizations and powerful and famous individuals were indignant at the Zionist suggestion that Jews everywhere constituted one nation and were unassimilable—a claim that tended to cast doubt on their loyalty to their respective countries and to strengthen the hands of the anti-Semites who asserted just that. So conscious were the Zionists of the Jewish opposition and so hemmed in by it that, until the rise of Hitler, their bête noire was not any persecutor of the Jews, nor was it, as in the case of other nationalist movements, a foreign occupying power, but other Jews—the non-Zionists and the anti-Zionists. If Zionism succeeded nevertheless in representing itself to the world as the spokesman of the national aspirations of the Jewish people and achieving its goal of a Jewish state, it was because of two crucial considerations: the comprehensiveness of its program and the tragic history of the Jewish people culminating in the disaster of Hitler's program of extermination.

As a nationalist movement, Zionism was confronted with the peculiar task of having not only to win sovereignty for a nonsovereign nation, but also of having virtually to create that nation before winning sovereignty for it. For even according to the Zionists, the Jews constituted only a disembodied abnormal nation that had to be normalized and given more substance before it could be called a nation in the full sense of the term. Zionism, therefore, had to gather the people in Palestine from the various countries, settle them on the land, teach them new skills and induce them to change their occupations, give them jobs, create towns and villages, build factories, hospitals, and schools, revive a defunct national language, start a new national culture, history, and mystique, and do a hundred other things which most nationalist movements elsewhere could take for granted. Many of these tasks taken separately appealed to non-Zionist Jews everywhere on philanthropic, religious, cultural, scientific, and humanitarian grounds, and they gave their unstinting support to achieve them. The Bund, for instance, though violently anti-Zionist, strove vigorously to preserve and promote Jewish culture; non-Zionist organizations of German Jews helped build a technological institute in Palestine; French Jews founded agricultural schools and farms; British Jews supported agricultural research stations; American Jews supported the Hebrew University. Ultra-Orthodox Jews set up religious schools, settlements, and urban quarters to combat Zionist secularism. All of these enterprises, while they were set up by their supporters without ulterior political motives, did in fact contribute greatly to the creation of that organic national strength in Palestine which in due course made the Zionist political claims all the more powerful.

An even more important factor in the success of the Zionist movement in becoming the most powerful and most widely recognized voice of the collective will of the Jewish people was the renewal of active and brutal persecution of Jews in many countries in the last quarter of the nineteenth and in the present century. Jews everywhere were unanimous in viewing it imperative to lend help to their persecuted brethren. Such help took many forms, including relief aid and intercession directly and through intermediaries with the offending authorities. But when the trouble was serious, there was no other recourse for the persecuted than flight, and flight became more and more difficult after the 1920s. As one country after another passed exclusion acts or adopted restrictive measures that blocked the way to massive Jewish immigration, Palestine became one of the few places of refuge and the only country which Jews could enter, in Churchill's words, "by right, not on sufferance." Increasingly, therefore, Jewish opinion in the world, regardless of political inclination, supported the struggle of the Zionists to keep the gates of Palestine wide open. When, after the massacre of European Jewry, the issue of providing a place of refuge for the survivors became inextricably involved with the issue of ultimate sovereignty in Palestine, virtually the whole of world Jewry, with its center by then in the United States, threw its weight on the side of the Zionists and pressed for a Jewish state. Thus it came about that, in the matter of building the foundations of a nation in Palestine as well as in the matter of winning sovereignty for it in most of the Palestinian territory, the Zionists were able to enlist the sympathy and support of most of world Jewry, though for motives other than their own and not on the basis of their complete interpretation of the position and destiny of the Jews in the world. These differences of motive and approach are at the root of the confused wrangles that still periodically agitate relations between and among the leaders of Israel, the Zionist movement, and spokesmen for Jewish organizations outside Israel.

3

The Balfour Declaration
and the Mandate

The triumph of Zionism as expressed in the establishment of Israel was not only the outcome of the convergence of the wills and forces of the Jewish people just described. The support of powerful individuals, groups, and governments for various aspects of the Zionist cause was also crucial on several occasions, even as it is essential today for the survival and development of Israel. One of the most important of these occasions was the issuing of the Balfour Declaration by the British government on November 2, 1917. It was this declaration that laid the foundation for the development of the Jewish community in Palestine from 56,000 divided and squabbling people scattered in two dozen settlements and a few mixed Arab-Jewish towns at the end of World War I into the disciplined and prospering embryonic nation of 700,000 that was able to withstand the combined assault of all the surrounding Arab states in 1948.

The Balfour Declaration

The declaration consisted of a single long sentence in the form of a letter dated November 2, 1917, addressed by Foreign Secretary Arthur Balfour to Lord Rothschild as representative of the Zionists. It read: "His Majesty's Government view with favor the establishment in Palestine of a national home for the Jewish people, and will use their best endeavours to facilitate the achievement of this object, it being clearly understood that nothing shall be done which may prejudice the civil and religious rights of existing non-Jewish communities in Palestine, or the rights and political status enjoyed by Jews in any other country."

The reasons that had prompted the British government to issue the Balfour Declaration are of interest because they reflect the grounds for the appeal of Zionism to a great gentile power like Britain and reveal the origins of the subsequent trouble in British-Zionist relations. They also incidentally provide an object lesson in the complexity of motives, the inconsistency of arguments, and the poverty of information that often go into the making of fateful decisions, even those as thoroughly studied as this one was. A definitive study by Leonard Stein distinguishes between immediate and long-term grounds for the issuing of the declaration. One of the immediate reasons was to help keep Russia in the war. Russia was then in the throes of revolution in which Jews played a prominent part, and the British Cabinet hoped that the declaration might provide an incentive to the Russian Jews to exert their influence against their country's pulling out of the fighting. This expectation was little less than fantastic in view of the rabid anti-Zionism of the Russian Jewish revolutionaries, which could have been missed only as a result of either incredible ignorance or a conviction that at bottom all Jews are or ought to be Zionists, even though the Cabinet had an example of active opposition to Zionism on the part of prominent British Jews within its very ranks. A second immediate reason was a desire to counter the apathy of a considerable section of American Jewry toward the war because of hostility to Jew-baiting Tsarist Russia, which, it was feared, might contribute to dampening the American war effort. This argument not only exaggerated the extent of Jewish influence in the United States at that time, but also rested on a premise that was no longer valid because by the time the declaration was issued, tsarism had been overthrown. A third immediate reason was the expectation of reaping some propaganda benefits in all the countries where Jews lived, and a fourth was the desire to forestall an expected German declaration in favor of the Jews. Once more, the reasons could be assumed to have practical significance only on the assumption that Jews were powerful and that their behavior would be significantly affected by British support for Zionism.

Beneath these immediate tactical considerations lay a variety of deeper sentiments and motives in favor of the object of the declaration that conditioned the climate in which the immediate reasons were discussed. These sentiments were reflected at one time or another in the course of the long process of interviews, discussions, and negotiations that preceded the moment of decision. Among these, there was an intuitive sympathy with Zionist aspirations, nurtured by the Bible, on the part of many British statesmen, which expressed itself as soon as Turkey entered the war and its partition became a major war object of the Allies. There was also the impression made on the British government by men like Chaim Weizmann and Sir Herbert Samuel that Zionism was a powerful force among Jewry and that Jewish goodwill was an intangible asset worth acquiring. There was the response of some imaginative British minds to the suggestion that a large-scale Jewish settlement in Palestine might have a stabilizing influence in an area where important British interests were at stake, and might contribute to the regeneration of the Middle East as a whole. There was the hope that a chance given to Zionism might serve as an antidote to the subversive movements in which

Jews, in rebellion against their lot, were finding an outlet for their frustrated energies. There were the romantic dreams of men like Mark Sykes to help a great but corrupted people regenerate itself through the renewal of its life in the cradle of its civilization, coupled with the desire to use the sponsorship of Zionist aspirations as a means to help nullify French claims to parts of Palestine and bring the whole country under British auspices. Finally, there was the more comprehensive view expressed by Balfour a few weeks after the declaration that "the Jews ought to have their rightful place in the world: a great nation without a home is not right." In short, the declaration was issued out of broad humanitarian considerations, for supposed immediate tactical political advantages, and for perceived long-range strategic interests—an irresistible combination to any imaginative Anglo-Saxon statesman.

The declaration was approved by the chief Allied powers, including the United States, and its principles were incorporated into the terms of the Mandate approved by the League of Nations by which Britain was to govern Palestine. The instrument of the Mandate recognized "the historical connection of the Jewish people with Palestine and . . . the grounds for reconstituting their national home in that country." The Mandatory power was directed to encourage immigration and close settlement of Jews on the land; and, as a sign of the Jewish cultural renaissance, Hebrew as well as Arabic and English was to be an official language. The instrument prescribed the establishment of a Jewish Agency representing the Jewish people to advise and cooperate with the British administration in economic, social, and other matters that might affect the establishment of the Jewish National Home, and assist and take part in the development of the country.

The Application of the Mandate: Internal Development

The story of the application of the Mandate as far as the Jews are concerned appears as a history of increasing frustration, despair, turmoil, and strife in the external political sphere, and of steady growth, prosperity, and achievement in the internal economic, social, cultural, and political fields. In retrospect, it seems oddly enough, that the frustrations as well as the achievements operated in favor of the creation of the state of Israel. For had the external political situation been less intolerable to the Jews by the end of the Second World War, they might not have risen against the prevailing order for a few more years at least, and this might very well have made all the difference in terms of obtaining international support for partition and the establishment of a Jewish state. In any case, the overall development of the Mandate was such that by the time its initial spirit and purpose had been completely whittled away, the Jewish settlement had grown in every respect to the point where it could take its fate into its own hands and forge ahead to create and sustain the state of Israel.

In terms of internal development, the history of the Yishuv (the Jewish community in Palestine) during the Mandatory period is marked by three phases. The first, which lasted from the confirmation of the Mandate in 1922 until the end of 1932, was characterized by a rather slow evolution. The basic institutions of Jewish Palestine were established or consolidated during that period—the instruments of communal self-government, the Jewish Agency, the labor movement, the main forms of settlement, the political parties, the Hebrew education system, the university, a national press, and so on; but the flow of immigration was disappointingly, almost fatally, slow. In his appearance before the Peace Conference in 1919, Chaim Weizmann had estimated the expected level of immigration to the envisaged National Home at between 70,000 and 80,000 a year. Louis D. Brandeis had had notions of transferring a million Eastern European Jews to Palestine in a few years. In contrast, the number of immigrants in the period under consideration averaged slightly more than 10,000 a year, and in 1927–1928 the number of Jews who emigrated from Palestine actually exceeded that of Jews who immigrated to it. It is true that the closing of the exit gates before Russia's Jews was partly responsible for the disparity between the expectations of the Zionist chiefs and the reality; but there can be no doubt that these men had grossly overestimated the eagerness of the Jews to avail themselves of the opportunity offered to them to build a homeland without the constant prodding of persecution, and economic necessity. Thus, despite the important qualitative development of the Yishuv during that decade, its slow quantitative growth carried with it the danger that the Jewish National Home in Palestine might shrivel to something not unlike the interesting but ultimately unimportant Jewish agricultural settlement in Argentina sponsored by Baron de Hirsch. That this did not happen was largely due to Hitler's coming to power in Germany.

The persecution of the Jews by the Nazis induced or compelled tens of thousands to leave Germany, then Austria, then Czechoslovakia and all of Central Europe, with nowhere to go but Palestine. Such were the skills and qualifications of these people, or such was the capital they were able to take out, that very large numbers of them passed the tests of the Mandatory government devised to restrict immigration in accordance with the economic absorptive capacity of the country. And as those who entered invested their money in various enterprises and built houses and facilities, they created further absorptive capacity for more Jews from everywhere. Thus it came about that in the course of the six years from 1934 to 1939, more than twice as many immigrants came to the country as had entered it in the previous twelve years. By the outbreak of World War II, the Yishuv had not only grown to a substantial community of more than half a million, but its overall potentialities had greatly expanded by the injection of new capital and vast numbers of excellently trained professionals, technicians, entrepreneurs, and highly educated people generally.

The third phase in the growth of the Yishuv dates from 1940 until the foundation of the state. Because of the war and political restrictions, the number of immigrants who came in during this period was relatively small, averaging about 15,000 a year; nevertheless this phase was of great importance to the formation of the Yishuv in all other respects. It was a period in which the economic and technical capacities of the Yishuv were fully utilized as the dwindling of imports to the entire Middle East and the Allied war effort stimulated the growth of new Jewish industry, the reorganization of agriculture, and the expansion of the entire economy through vast new expenditures. It was a period in which the Yishuv was able to acquire valuable military experience through the 30,000 men it contributed to the British forces, and to accumulate a substantial arsenal of clandestine weapons from the vast stocks that circulated in the area. Above all, it was a period when the Yishuv, screened against its own will from any vast inflow of new immigrants, totally engaged in the war and, fired by the shame, agony, and hatred caused by the savage destruction of millions of fellow Jews, was able to merge all the previous waves of immigration into a national community as cohesive and determined as any the world has seen. It was the insufficient appreciation of this moral-psychological factor, the outcome of the strains of the war and its aftermath, that completely confounded the estimates of the Yishuv's real strength made in Cairo and Damascus as well as in London and Washington.

The Application of the Mandate: External Political Aspects

In the political sphere, the story of the Mandate is the history of the continual narrowing of its original intent and purpose as these came increasingly into conflict with the interests of Britain in the Middle East as a whole. Already at the beginning of the Mandate, the immediate tactical political calculations that stood behind the issuing of the Balfour Declaration had become irrelevant. The broad humanitarian impulse that had moved statesmen in London to adopt a decision of principle in favor of the Jews was naturally less effective when it came to the question of influencing the decisions and actions of officials in London and Jerusalem concerned with the routine application of the Mandate in the face of mounting practical difficulties. Finally, the long-range strategic considerations began to turn more and more decisively against the Zionist case as Arab opposition to the Jewish National Home deepened and broadened and as the world headed toward an international crisis in which the goodwill of the Arab mass of the Middle East seemed to weigh more and more heavily in the eyes of the British government.

Even before the Mandate had been confirmed, the Palestinian Arabs manifested their resistance to the policy it embodied in serious riots in 1920 and 1921. The following year, the British government issued an interpretation of the Mandate designed to assuage Arab fears and to check any extravagant expectations on the part of the Jews. The interpretation, known as the Churchill White Paper, excluded the area of Transjordan from the purview of the Jewish National Home. It also explained that the development of that home did not mean the imposition of Jewish nationality upon all the inhabitants of Palestine, but the full development of the existing Jewish community to become a center in which the Jewish people could take pride. Having constricted the territorial scope of the Jewish National Home and given it this cultural twist, the White Paper then went on to insist that the Jewish community in Palestine was there "as of right, not on sufferance."

For seven years comparative peace reigned in Palestine. Then, in 1929, Arab religious and national feeling, excited by a conflict involving the Wailing Wall (a remnant of the Second Temple), which stands in an area sacred to both Arabs and Jews, burst out in a series of murderous attacks on the Jewish population. A number of British commissions visited Palestine to inquire into the causes of the trouble and recommend remedies. Their reports suggested the imposition of qualifications and restrictions on Jewish immigration and, in general, stressed those provisions of the Mandate safeguarding the rights of the non-Jewish inhabitants to an extent as great or greater than those designed to secure the establishment of a Jewish National Home.

Once again there was a seven-year period of peace followed by another outburst of Arab violence and another spate of commissions of inquiry which submitted recommendations designed to appease the Arabs. This time, however, the issues were more significant, the commissions were of a higher caliber, the recommendations were more basic, and the stakes were consequently much higher.

The grounds for the Arab outburst had been the sudden increase in the rate of Jewish immigration following Hitler's rise to power. Although this immigration gave a fillip to the economic life of the country from which everybody benefited, the Arabs became fearful of the prospect, now real for the first time, that the Jews might soon become a majority in the country. As a sop to their apprehensions, the Palestine government suggested in 1936 the formation of a legislative council in which Arabs could outnumber Jews and government-appointed members. But the scheme was severely criticized in the British Parliament and withdrawn; whereupon the Arabs initiated acts of violence which soon assumed the character of an open, all-out revolt against British authority.

A Royal Commission, sent in 1937 to inquire and make recommendations, did not content itself with suggesting new restrictions, but reached the drastic conclusion that the Mandate itself was altogether "unworkable." Instead of the Mandate, the commission suggested partitioning Palestine into an Arab and a Jewish state and a British zone. The Arabs rejected the scheme outright, the Jews accepted the principle of partition, and the British government sent another commission to work out the details of partition which concluded that partition was impracticable. To break the deadlock, British Prime Minister Neville Chamberlain summoned a conference of Arabs and Jews in London. In recognition of the character which the Palestine question had begun to assume by that time, and as an indication of the context in which the British government now viewed it, not only the Jewish Agency and the Palestinian Arabs were invited to attend, but also the representatives of all the neighboring Arab countries.

The conference assembled in London at the beginning of 1939 in the shadow of a new climax in the international crisis. Hitler had just violated the Munich Agreement by annexing the rest of Czechoslovakia and even Chamberlain realized by then that war could no longer be avoided. In this context, the foremost concern of the British government was to win Arab goodwill, or at least to check the spread of pro-Axis sympathies, in order to secure Arabian oil and protect the Middle East link of its imperial communications. Consequently, when the conference, as had been expected, got nowhere, the British government issued a unilateral statement of policy (the White Paper henceforth) which proposed to give up the Mandate in favor of an independent, predominantly Arab Palestine that would be established in ten years if a constitution protecting Jewish rights could be secured. In the interim period, Jewish immigration was to be fixed at a maximum of 75,000 in the entire first five-year period, after which it would depend on Arab consent. The Jews would be allowed to acquire land from the Arabs only in a very small portion of the country. In short, the Jewish National Home was to be frozen at the level it had attained by then, and Palestine was to remain predominantly Arab.

Throughout the years of the Mandate, the majority of the Zionist movement, under the moderate leadership of Chaim Weizmann, had perforce reconciled itself to the successive British restrictions on its aims as long as the residual policy still allowed the growth of the National Home at a reasonable rate. The general feeling was that the political future of Palestine would ultimately be determined more by the established realities of relative strength and number than by any legal or political formula. The promulgation of the White Paper policy, by foreclosing further growth of the Jewish proportional strength, disrupted this approach and threw the whole movement into agitation. Dissident rightist groups resorted to systematic terror against the British as soon as the Nazi threat to the area receded. The majority of the movement formally adopted a program that, for the first time since the Balfour Declaration, spoke no longer of a Jewish National Home but redefined its aim as the establishment of a Jewish state. A substantial minority on the left opposed the new program as impractical or premature and urged the establishment of a binational Jewish-Arab state with freedom of immigration. Despite all the ringing proclamations and programs, however, it is almost certain that all sections of opinion would have been content with the abolition of the White Paper and the restoration of the status quo ante with large-scale immigration.

For a moment right after the war, the chances of achieving just that seemed propitious. The Yishuv had made an important contribution to the war effort, the world was horrified at learning the fantastic extent of the horrors perpetrated by the Nazis against the Jews, and the Labor party had come to power in Britain soon after its conference had adopted far-reaching pro-Zionist resolutions. But it soon became apparent that, under the aegis of Foreign Secretary Ernest Bevin, Britain's Palestine policy was more than ever wedded to the aim of winning Arab support for a new Middle East order based on an Anglo-Arab alliance. Pressure from President Truman on the British government to admit to Palestine immediately 100,000 survivors of the Nazi extermination camps brought about the appointment of an Anglo-American commission to inquire into the whole much-inquired-into Palestine question. The commission reported favorably on the admission of 100,000 people but also made some political recommendations which included the need to dismantle and disarm all illegal forces. President Truman and the Zionists hailed the conclusion concerning immigration and pressed for immediate application, while the British government made it contingent upon the disarming of illegal armies and upon American financial and military support in the enforcement of the entire scheme. There was another committee, another plan, another conference, and a long series of embittered exchanges among British, Jews, Arabs, and Americans, but it was obvious that the issue was getting nowhere. In the meantine, tension in Palestine built rapidly to a climax. The dissident groups extended their acts of terror. The Haganah (the underground army under the authority of the Yishuv leadership) engaged in sabotage and brought in numerous unauthorized immigrant ships; and the British responded with hangings, martial law, curfew, arrest of Yishuv leaders, and deportation of illegal immigrants to camps in Cyprus and even back to Germany. When the last device—an Arab-Jewish-British conference—collapsed, the harassed British government finally decided on April 2, 1947, to place the whole Palestine issue squarely in the hands of a special assembly of the United Nations.

4

The United Nations, The United States, and the Birth of Israel

The Palestine problem was brought before a special session of the General Assembly of the United Nations on April 28, 1947, and seven months later the regular session of the world body adopted the well-known resolution to partition Palestine into an Arab and a Jewish state. Although all the practical arrangements made by the United Nations for the application of its resolution were nullified by British obstruction and Arab resistance, and although the Jews of Palestine had to fight a costly war for their state, the resolution was nevertheless crucial for the emergence of Israel. It was crucial because it liquidated the Mandate and defined the legal framework within which the Yishuv could conduct its struggle and establish its state while placing its enemies in the position of aggressors. It was crucial because it made it possible for the Yishuv to obtain material help from abroad and diplomatic support from the Soviet Union, the United States, and the United Nations at critical moments in the war. It was crucial, above all, because it provided the Yishuv with a definite goal and a program around which it could rally its forces. Only five years before the United Nations resolution, the adoption by the Zionist movement of a program redefining its immediate aim as the setting up of a Jewish state instead of simply assuring the further development of the National Home had encountered great difficulties and in the end left a substantial minority in opposition. Only one year before the United Nations resolution, the energies of the movement had been concentrated on promoting acceptance of the recommendations of the Anglo-American Commission, although these explicitly ruled out a Jewish state. It was only after the majority of the United Nations' own inquiry commission (UNSCOP) recommended partition and a Jewish and an Arab state that the stragglers, not to be less "Zionist" than the commission, and the extremists, not to miss the opportunity of getting what could be obtained, rallied to the center, and that the entire Yishuv, from the extreme left of the Communists to the extreme right of the Irgun, could fight for a common program.

The United States was intimately involved in the adoption of the partition resolution as well as in the chain of events that had brought the Palestine question before the United Nations. In the very intense struggle that developed between supporters and opponents of partition, the United States not only stood on the side of partition, but in the crucial moments before the decision, threw its full weight into the effort to mobilize the votes that were still needed. Without this effort, it is very doubtful that the partition resolution would have obtained the statutory two-thirds majority of the General Assembly.

In many quarters in the United States, including some departments of the government, the role played by America in the Palestine controversy under the leadership of President Truman has been severely criticized as unwise and unfair in terms of the Palestine issue itself and as damaging to the interests of the United States. Actually, as we shall see, the United States' stand in favor of partition can be justified on any and all of these grounds at least as adequately as the alternatives implied by the critics. The real trouble was that that stand, as well as all the positions advocated or adopted in connection with the Palestine question, had not been carefully thought through by anybody in any terms. Various groups exerted pressure on the President to favor or oppose specific measures, but nobody presented him with any suggestion for a feasible, comprehensive, consistent policy on Palestine. The result was vacillation and inconsistencies, which did more harm to the issue and more damage to American prestige and interest than did the substance of the final position taken.

America's Palestine Relations Prior to the United Nations Resolution

The absence of a definite, comprehensive American policy on Palestine when its fate was being decided stemmed partly from the fact that although the United States had had connections with Palestine and the Middle East going back at least a century, it had few interests there until just a few years before the problem came up in the United Nations. Until Woodrow Wilson's brief sally into world politics during and after the first World War, United States concern with the area had been almost purely a function of the academic, missionary, and philanthropic interests of some of its citizens in that part of the world. The activities of the American government in connection with these interests were uncontroversial and worked directly or indirectly for the benefit of Arabs and Jews equally. On the Arab side, the government afforded protection to the educational work of American missionaries which helped spark a cultural revival that marked the birth of Arab nationalism. On the Jewish side, American consuls provided protection to large numbers of Jerusalem Jews under the capitulations system, and American representatives in

Constantinople wrestled with discriminatory laws against Jews because they affected the few hundred American Jews then residing in Palestine. In the course of the war, American naval vessels helped evacuate Palestinian Jews expelled by the Turks from Jaffa to Alexandria, and were commissioned to transport food, gasoline, medicines, money, and other relief to the Jews of the Holy Land, who were cut off from their sources of aid in the rest of the world by the British blockade and abandoned to their fate by the Turks. These activities either derived from the concern of the American government that American citizens should not be discriminated against or placed under unjust laws, or they were undertaken out of humanitarian considerations in response to appeals of American Jews on behalf of their distressed brethren.

For a brief period after the end of World War I, the nature of America's involvement in Palestine and the Middle East changed abruptly. Although it had not declared war against Turkey, the United States became concerned with the political future of the area as part of the general peace settlement. The United States government still had no special interest of its own to advance; but its influence was vigorously sought by opposing forces which then began to crystallize and were destined henceforth to become a permanent factor in the Palestine question in its American context. As early as October 1917, President Wilson, under the influence of his Zionist friend and adviser Louis D. Brandeis, had conveyed to the British government his support for one of the last drafts of the Balfour Declaration, unknowingly helping its advocates in Britain to overcome the last obstacles in their way. But the President had given that support in an offhand way and did not act in the Peace Conference as though he had already committed himself on the Palestine question. To the dismay of Brandeis and his associates, the President and some of his aides from the State Department entertained suggestions about the future of Palestine and Syria which took no account whatever of the Balfour Declaration or were opposed to it. Such suggestions had been made by, among others, groups of missionaries who feared that their work would be undone by the Jews, and who unfolded instead the vision of a united Arab world under American tutelage. They were reinforced by the opposition to the declaration of anti-Zionist Jews who were fearful of the charge of dual allegiance and by the opposition of some American business interests— notably Standard Oil—which had acquired concessions from the Turks in the Negev and feared the Zionists. In the end, President Wilson reaffirmed his support of the Balfour Declaration in strong and unequivocal terms; but his initial casual involvement, his subjection to opposing pressures, his vacillation and final commitment, were a remarkable preview of what was to happen on a grand scale with President Truman thirty years later.

With the failure of Wilson's internationalism and the return to isolationism, the United States government lost any interest it may have had in the political fate of the Middle East and Palestine, and its concern with the area reverted once more to being subsidiary to the private interests of American citizens there. By then, however, these interests were no longer confined to the sphere of religion, humanitarianism, and philanthropy but had come to include economic and political interests of increasing importance.

As early as 1920 American oil concerns had appealed to their government to secure for them equal opportunity in the Middle Eastern countries under the control of the French and the British. The American government responded to this appeal and obtained for a group of American companies a 23.75 percent share in the Iraq Petroleum Company. Thereafter, the United States government strove to obtain from the powers controlling the Middle Eastern countries commitments to an Open Door policy that would not discriminate against private American business. In this connection, the United States concluded the Anglo-American Treaty of 1924 which regulated relations between the two countries in connection with the Palestine Mandate and secured the protection of business and missionary interests of Americans in Palestine. Incidentally, the preamble to this treaty included a reference to the Balfour Declaration, inserted at the insistence of the British negotiators, which was to be interpreted later by various parties as giving the United States the right to have a say in any changes in the Mandate.

As for the political interest of American citizens in the Middle East, this had already manifested itself in the pressure on President Wilson by American Zionists, headed by men like Brandeis, Felix Frankfurter (later justices of the Supreme Court), Judge Julian Mack and Rabbi Stephen Wise, to support the Balfour Declaration and the granting of the Palestine Mandate to Britain. Having attained its object, the political activity of the American Zionists subsided for most of the interwar period. But in the 1930s, as persecution of Jews in Hitler's Reich mounted and as the British put increasing restrictions on Jewish immigration to Palestine, the American Zionists bestirred themselves once more in an effort to induce their government to press the British to alter their policy. At that juncture the Zionists did not obtain much satisfaction from the President or the State Department, but Congress was another matter. The legislature of the United States, partly because it was not directly responsible for America's foreign policy and could therefore afford to look at the matter in abstract humanitarian terms, and partly because its members were more sensitive to the electoral implications of their position, had by then an already established tradition of sympathy with Zionist aspirations and wishes. In 1922, for example, Congress had adopted a joint resolution in support of the Balfour Declaration; and the sponsor of the resolution in the Senate was none other than Senator Henry Cabot Lodge, the spearhead of American isolationism in the postwar years. Now, in 1939, a majority of the House Foreign Affairs Committee and twenty-eight senators publicly protested against the restriction of immigration to Palestine at that critical moment for the Jews. They called the defense of Jewish interests in Palestine "a moral obligation of the United States" and declared that the White Paper was a violation of the Anglo-American Treaty of 1924.

During the Second World War the private interests of American citizens in the Middle East became much more intense and, in addition, the American government itself developed new interests of its own in the area. In 1933 American companies had obtained from the ruler of Saudi Arabia extensive oil concessions which reached the stage of large-scale production by 1940. Toward the end of the war, the excessive drain on America's own oil reserves caused the government itself to show interest in the Middle East oil. In 1944, for instance, Secretary of the Interior Harold Ickes sought to give the government a stake in Arabian oil by suggesting to the companies concerned that it should finance the building of a pipeline from the Arabian oil fields to the Mediterranean. The oil companies balked at the proposal, but official concern with ensuring the flow of oil from the Middle East continued in government quarters, especially after the oil companies themselves undertook to build the pipeline and to expand their operations at a cost of hundreds of millions of dollars.

The outbreak of war and the initial disasters suffered by the Allies made it difficult for the Zionists to draw much attention to the problem of Palestine and the Jews. But as the tide of the war began to turn and victory loomed upon the horizon, and as news of the Nazi projects for exterminating the Jews reached the United States, the American Zionists, supported by the entire Jewish population and by large sections of the non-Jewish public, exerted a persistent and desperate pressure on the government to persuade the British to open the gates of Palestine and commit themselves to the support of a Jewish commonwealth. Congress responded with a series of resolutions and declarations in the period 1943–1945 in favor of unrestricted immigration and a Jewish state in Palestine. President Roosevelt gave a number of clear pledges during the election campaign of 1944 of his intention to help bring about the realization of a Jewish commonwealth in Palestine, which he counterbalanced with ambiguous pledges to King ibn Saud that he would take no action which might prove hostile to the Arab people without full consultation with both Arabs and Jews. The War Department expressed concern lest the declarations made by Congress and the President should endanger the war effort of the Allies, while the State Department held to the line that Palestine was Britain's responsibility, except insofar as the American government was interested in the general problem of the tragedy of European Jewry and was eager to help. This last qualification was quite important: it was to prove the opening wedge of the American government's involvement in the Palestine question right after the war, which began with President Truman's appeal to Prime Minister Clement Attlee to admit 100,000 survivors of the Nazi camps to Palestine.

While the private interests of its citizens were drawing it into greater involvement in Middle Eastern matters, the American government was also acquiring its own interest in the area. During the war, the United States became directly interested in the Middle East as a theater of operations, as a strategic base, and as a supply route to Russia. At the end of the war, it looked for a time as though the United States might pull out of the area entirely and leave it under the responsibility of Britain. But the civil war in Greece and Soviet pressure on Turkey and Iran compelled the American government to become more and more engaged, first politically on the side of Britain, and then both politically and militarily as the chief actor. The turning point came in the spring of 1947 when, after Britain notified the United States of its intention to divest itself of responsibility for Greece and Turkey, the United States proclaimed what came to be known as the Truman Doctrine. The doctrine committed the United States specifically to guarantee the security of Greece and Turkey and declared the intention of the American government to contain Communist aggression everywhere. Thus, both by implication and as the hinterland of the American defense perimeter established along the above-mentioned countries, the Middle East now came directly into the orbit of American global strategy.

The United States and the Emergence of Israel

When the Palestine question came up for decision before the United Nations in the fall of 1947, the implications of the various involvements of the United States in the Middle East had not yet been fully worked out. There was a general sense that it was important to have the goodwill of the governments of the Arab landmass right behind the American defense perimeter. There was a belief that an effort should be made to ensure the undisturbed development and flow of Arabian oil. And there was a generally accepted notion that something ought to be done to relieve the survivors of the Nazi slaughter and thus assuage the agitation of Palestine's Jews, alleviate the pressure of their American brethren, and meet a demand endorsed by public opinion generally. But all these considerations had not been assessed together in the context of the realities and possibilities of the Palestine situation in an effort to formulate an appropriate policy. What happened, instead, was that different individuals and sections in the government and among the public seized upon one aspect or another of the question in disregard of others and endeavored to press it upon President Truman while impeaching the arguments and even the motives of others. The President was left to steer his own course by hunch or impulse amid conflicting views and opposing pressures; and his instinct guided him now one way, now another.

In the fall of 1947, the President decided, apparently without much difficulty, to support partition, against the judgment of people in the State Department. He, like everyone else, had been impressed by the fact that a majority of a United Nations commission, composed of representatives of countries with no direct interest in Palestine which had just investigated the problem, had recommended this solution. (These countries were Australia, Canada, Czechoslovakia, Guatemala, India, Iran, the Netherlands, Peru, Sweden, Uruguay, and Yugoslavia.) The solution also seemed to accord well with the humanitarian impulse that had induced him in the course of the two previous years to press for the admission to Palestine of a large number of survivors of Nazi concentration camps. Moreover, the proposed partition plan had been accepted with barely hidden enthusiasm by the Jewish masses of America whose votes seemed particularly important in that election year, when Truman was the underdog in the contest against Governor Thomas Dewey of New York.

But the partition plan did not work out according to the schedule prepared for it by the United Nations. The British refused to cooperate with the world organization in easing the transition to the new order and even seemed to be doing their best to make it difficult. At the same time, the Arabs of Palestine rose up in arms in December 1947 with the encouragement and support of the neighboring Arab states, and the country was plunged into a vicious civil war in which the Jews seemed to be getting the worst of it. The United Nations considered organizing an international constabulary to enforce partition, but a force of the size thought to be needed was impossible to raise without Russian participation, to which the United States was opposed. The President was under mounting pressure to send American troops to do the job, but he was disinclined to commit the country further and, moreover, his military advisers informed him that the United States did not have the necessary forces available in any case. In these circumstances, the President accepted the advice of the State Department, and the American representative to the United Nations declared in March 1948 that the partition plan was impracticable and submitted instead a proposal for a United Nations trusteeship over Palestine.

This reversal of policy brought frantic protests and appeals from American Zionists and other Jews, congressmen and other politicians, and prominent and plain American citizens. It also encouraged the Arabs to believe that whatever the political decisions were, it was the military facts that counted. But while the United Nations became entangled in fruitless discussions about trusteeship and how *it* could be enforced, the Jews of Palestine, having received a shipment of Russian arms and enjoying greater freedom of action as the British forces kept withdrawing from the country, launched an offensive that reversed the course of the civil war and brought most of the territory allocated to them by the partition plan under their effective control. On May 14, 1948, notwithstanding State Department advice to the contrary, they proclaimed their state, calling it Israel. A few hours later, as army columns from the neighboring Arab states poured into Palestine in an attempt to establish a new set of military facts, the American chief delegate to the United Nations had to interrupt a speech in favor of trusteeship to announce that the American government, that is, the President, had just awarded de facto recognition to the new state of Israel. The trusteeship proposal was, of course, buried.

President Truman's recognition of Israel, undertaken without even notifying all the men who were in charge of executing America's foreign policy, was not the last act in the unseemly spectacle of United States inconsistency. Once again, the secretary of state himself was to support a modification of the partition resolution, known as the Bernadotte Plan, in the forum of the United Nations, only to see the President repudiate it publicly at home; and more than once the President was to go over the heads of his State Department, as he did in choosing and instructing the first ambassador to Israel. All this seesawing and confusion, besides causing great damage to the prestige of the United States and encouraging the belligerents to believe and act as though military facts were the only important considerations, has left as residue the notion that the United States' support of Israel and the partition plan had been forced upon a well-meaning but weak President by sinister pressure groups regardless of the damaging effect on America's interest. To what extent is such a notion justified?

Appraisal of America's Position in 1947–1948

That the President of the United States was subjected to unusually strong and sharp pressures in connection with the Palestine problem which helped to confuse his judgment is beyond doubt. As the published records of the period indicate, however, these pressures came from the opponents as well as from the supporters of partition. As to the question whether America's support of the partition plan was unwise, unjust, and contrary to the national interest, an appraisal of the situation in 1947, taking into account the background of the Palestine problem and the basic aims of the United States at that time—to maintain peace and gain Arab goodwill, to protect the oil interests, and to help the escapees of Hitler's massacres—would seem to indicate that partition was, if not the best, at least the only available solution worthy of support.

It should be recalled that by the fall of 1947, two basic facts in regard to the Palestine problem were clear to all. One was that the Mandate could not go on and had to be terminated. This was a conclusion which had been reached by the British, the Arabs, and the Jews and was included among the unanimous recommendations of the United Nations inquiry committee. The second fact was that Arabs and Jews were determined to fight: the former to prevent large-scale Jewish immigration, the latter to achieve just that. These two facts must be taken as premises in any attempt to assess the most desirable and practical policy for the United States at the time.

Before the United Nations and the world, three competing solutions to the Palestine problem were presented. Two of these were suggested by the United Nations inquiry committee which, given its composition, could not be said to have had any interest in the question other than providing a fair and viable solution under the circumstances. The majority of the committee recommended partition into two sovereign, independent Arab and Jewish states and an international zone linked by an economic union, and allotted to the proposed Jewish state nearly 55 percent of the territory of Palestine in order to give it some living space for future immigration. The minority recommended a single federal government for all of Palestine with two constituent states, Arab and Jewish, endowed with a considerable degree of autonomy. Immigration, together with defense and foreign affairs, was to be entrusted to the federal government whose legislature was to be bicameral, with equal Arab and Jewish representation in one house and proportional representation in the other. All legislation was to require a majority of both houses. Deadlocks were to be resolved by an arbitral committee in which the decisive voice would belong to an outsider. The third solution was suggested by the Arabs themselves. It called for an independent, unitary, sovereign state in Palestine in which the Jews would enjoy guarantees of their status as a minority and would be awarded a large measure of municipal and cultural autonomy. Immigration, like all other matters, would depend on the decision of the legislature which would, of course, be predominantly Arab.

Now, the Arab solution was the one that least endangered the oil inter-ests, and support for it would have gained for the United States the goodwill of the Arabs at least in the short run. But from the point of view of the United States it had at least three major disadvantages. First, it precluded in practice any substantial Jewish immigration for which the United States had been pressing Britain. After all, an important factor in exacerbating the Palestine crisis right after the war had been the plea made by President Truman to the British government to admit a large number of survivors of the Nazi massacres into that country in the belief that such tragic necessity could hardly be resisted. Even the Morrison-Grady plan of 1946, worked out by the State Department and the British but rejected by the President, had envisaged an immigration of 100,000 immediately and held out the promise of more thereafter. It is true that the embarrassment of appearing inconsistent did not prevent the United States government from changing its mind several times later on; but at least in those cases it could plead *force majeure* whereas, in this instance, supporting the Arab plan would have required it to accept and even urge something much less than what it had previously rejected as inadequate at a time when the United Nations committee was recommending more. Second, it was extremely doubtful that the Arab solution, even with American support, would have gained the required two-thirds majority vote of the General Assembly. considering its extreme remoteness from even the minority report of the United Nations committee. Third, the application of such a solution would have required measures to suppress the Jews of Palestine even more drastic than those adopted by the British to no avail in the previous two years. It would have needed something like an international force or a great power sealing the country while the armed forces of the Arab states crushed the Jewish settlers—and this right after the Nazi massacre of Europe's Jews.

I have deliberately dwelt at some length on the Arab solution because it was the only one that seemed to offer the prospect of satisfying the "real," tangible, and immediate interests of the United States, and it is therefore important to stress how unfeasible it was. The other two proposals, that of the majority and that of the minority of the United Nations committee, were labeled "absurd" by the Arabs and were vehemently rejected. Consequently, United States support for either seemed to entail a risk of alienating the needed Arab goodwill and endangering the oil interests. It is of course true that in the perspective of later events it became clear that the Arabs would have preferred the minority plan; but in this same persepctive the Arabs have expressed their acceptance of partition too. As things stood in 1947, support for the minority plan would have entailed almost the same risk for United States interests without satisfying the Jewish aspirations and having the Jewish support that the majority plan enjoyed. Furthermore, supposing the minority plan were capable with the United States' active support, of mustering, the needed vote—which is not at all certain—its realization and viability depended so much on continual Arab-Jewish cooperation that once the two partners of the envisaged state opposed it, they in fact doomed it. Realization of the plan in the face of such opposition would have required the indefinite presence of a third power, which almost surely was not to be found and which in any case would gain the hostility of both sides very quickly. The problem of Palestine would have remained to plague the United Nations, and in all likelihood one of the federated states would have seceded sooner or later and reopened the entire issue.

In the light of the circumstances of 1947, there seems to be no doubt that the partition plan offered the best hope for a solution to the Palestine problem. It had the support of the Jews, which greatly simplified the problem of application. Violence and difficulties might have been expected from the Arab side, but if handled wisely and with determination, the extent of the violence might have been limited, and, after a transition period, there would have been two independent states capable of taking care of themselves. From the point of view of the United States, there was undoubtedly some risk of losing standing among the Arabs and endangering the oil interests of its citizens in which the government too was interested; but these were in less danger from the quick surgical operation of partition than from the festering open wound of a federal state or some similar scheme. Finally, the partition plan did offer some prospect of closing the painful episode of Jewish martyrdom which weighed heavily on the conscience of the Western world. If subsequent circumstances disproved the calculations that might have been made in 1947, it was in great degree because the calculations were *not* made and therefore the support given to partition was uncertain, hesitant, and incomplete. Who knows whether the Arab armies would have intervened had the United States as well as the Soviet Union provided arms to the Jewish militia in March and April of 1948 instead of knuckling under to Arab violence and repudiating the partition plan? The Jewish state might have been erected then within the boundaries provided for it by the United Nations, and a Palestinian Arab state might have emerged at its side. Further, the bulk of the refugee problem would not have existed, much bloodshed and misery would have been avoided, the entire heritage of the tragedy of Palestine might have been less bitter, and a salutary precedent might have been set for Arabs and Jews, as well as for other nations, in those crucial formative years of the international body that the United Nations' will cannot be flouted with impunity.

5

The War of Independence and the Birth of Israel

Whatever might have been the course of events had the United States acted differently in 1947–1948, the fact was that Israel had to confirm its right to come into existence through the ordeal of war. Indeed, it had to do this twice in succession, once in a civil war with the Palestinian Arabs aided by the neighboring states, and immediately after that in a war with the neighboring states themselves.

Israelis have called these contests the War of Independence, which is a slight misnomer. At stake was not only the issue of subjection to alien rule or self-rule but also the question of the survival or destruction of the entire Zionist endeavor and of everything that it had achieved up to that moment, and perhaps even the physical survival of the Jews of Palestine as individuals. With hindsight, this characterization may appear to be overly dramatic. It might be thought that, whatever the stakes were in theory, Israel was in little danger of losing, as is evidenced by the fact that it won, and went on to withstand successfully more than a quarter century of Arab confrontation and to win a whole series of wars. But such retrospective wisdom does not accord with the record of the events, which clearly shows that Israel's victory was by no means a foregone conclusion. At several points events might have led to a completely different outcome.

The War of Independence began on December 1, 1947, immediately after the United Nations General Assembly passed the partition resolution, when Palestinian Arab irregulars opened fire on a Jewish bus, and the Arab Higher Committee (the umbrella organization of the Palestinian political groupings) declared a general strike in preparation for an all-out struggle. The fighting spread rapidly to the entire country and raged uninterruptedly for the next five and a half months. On May 15, 1948, as the leadership of the triumphant Yishuv proclaimed the establishment of the state of Israel, the regular forces of Egypt, Transjordan, Syria, Lebanon, and Iraq crossed the boundaries of Palestine and turned the waning civil war between the Jews and

Arabs of Palestine into an international war between the newly born state of Israel and its neighbors.

That war lasted formally for nearly eight months, until Egypt agreed on January 7, 1949, to enter into armistice negotiations. However, actual hostilities were repeatedly interrupted by truces and cease-fires, so that large-scale fighting took place during only about one-quarter of that period, in four intervals. The general aims of the Arab and Jewish sides were the same in both phases of the war, before and after May 15, 1948. However, the nature of the struggle and the conditions under which it took place were entirely different.

The Civil War's Course

Although the civil war was fought by both sides with relatively small, loosely organized, and more or less haphazardly armed forces, it was no less critical or costly than the regular war that followed, and was in many respects more cruel. For until the Jewish and Arab areas became segregated from each other, people from each side going about their daily business were exposed to sudden violence and death. Even after the segregation was completed, the disintegration of public order exposed those remaining within their respective sectors to hardships and shortages, and those who ventured outside them, to ambush. Before the opponents worked out coherent strategies, fighting consisted mainly of terror and counterterror; and even after the two sides concentrated on clearly perceived military objectives, neither would forgo an opportunity to wreak elemental violence on the other. As the party satisfied by the political verdict of the United Nations, the Jews initially tried to minimize the scope of violence by restricting themselves to relatively static defense; but as their casualties mounted and it became apparent that Arab resistance was general, they too turned to all-out war.

On the eve of the civil war the Jewish forces consisted of the Haganah—the underground militia controlled by the authorities of the Yishuv—and two small dissident organizations: the *Irgun Zvai Leumi,* better known abroad as simply the Irgun, and *Lochamei Herut Yisrael,* known also as Lechi or as the Stern Gang. The Haganah comprised some 47,000 men and women, only half the strength which it was generally credited to have had since the end of World War II. Of these, only 15,000 were incorporated in "field formations." The rest were a local home guard consisting of those who knew how to handle a light weapon and were assigned to night guard duty and to village or neighborhood defense in emergencies. In the field formations, 4,000 troops were mobilized, with the remainder in reserve. Weapons were available for only about one-third of the total force, and consisted of rifles, submachine guns, light and medium machine guns, hand grenades, and explosives. The heaviest weapons in the Haganah arsenals were some 800 two- and three-inch mortars.

Since the end of World War II the Haganah had had a secret network of missions in Europe and America attempting to acquire war surplus weapons and arms-making machinery to be smuggled into Palestine. Following the United Nations partition resolution and the outbreak of fighting, the network was expanded, the missions were better provided with funds, and their activities were accelerated so that within the next year or so they were able to acquire enough weapons to equip an army of 90,000, not only with small arms, but also with some two dozen warplanes, scores of ships, tanks, and armored vehicles, and hundreds of artillery pieces. However, because of the naval blockade maintained by the British until May 15, 1948, only about 10 percent of that equipment could be smuggled into the country during the last stages of the Mandate—just enough to equip all the 15,000 troops of the field formations.

On the eve of the war, the Irgun comprised some 5,000 members in all its formations, including a teenagers' Youth Guard. However, not more than 10 percent of these were in full-time service at any given period and only a small percentage of the remainder were actually mobilized and equipped after the outbreak of fighting. Lechi had 1,000 members, also with a small core of people in full-time service and a somewhat larger reserve component for which arms were available. The two organizations had their own command and control structures and had developed in defiance of recognized authorities in the Yishuv controlling the Haganah. After the war broke out, they made a series of agreements with these authorities (and then with the government of Israel) for coordination of action and cooperation with the Haganah; but after severe crises resulting from their independent actions, they were outlawed by the government and forcibly incorporated into the armed forces of Israel.

The Arab forces in the civil war had three components: (1) irregular bands gathered around local or regional leaders; (2) the Arab Liberation Army, composed of volunteers from Palestine and the neighboring Arab countries, organized, financed, and equipped by the Military Committee of the Arab League, and trained and marshaled in Syria before being sent into Palestine; and (3) masses of villagers and townspeople haphazardly armed and barely organized for local defense into a "national guard," which would rally around an irregular band, or a unit of the Liberation Army for a particular action and disperse after it. Some of the irregulars had received sustained military training; the rest, as well as the armed villagers, knew how to handle small weapons and were instinctively skillful in fieldcraft, but were inclined to operate as groups of individuals rather than as organized formations.

The Liberation Army was established from the outset along regular lines and was intended to constitute eight battalions of 1,000 men each. In January 1948, about 1,500 crossed into Palestine, and by March of that year their numbers had reached 4,000. At that time, the irregulars numbered about

9,000, of which 3,000 operated in the north of the country in cooperation with the Liberation Army; 5,000 operated in the center along the Tel Aviv–Jerusalem axis and its vicinity, under leaders from the well-known Husseini clan; and the rest (including several hundred Muslim Brethren volunteers from Egypt) operated in the south.

Command and control of all Arab forces was ostensibly vested in the Military Committee of the Arab League (headed by Iraqi General Ismail Safwat Pasha), to which the Arab states contributed arms and financing. Actually the committee had little control even over the Liberation Army it had created, and could provide military guidance only to the extent that its directives were accepted by the military leaders or as a consequence of its bargaining power, which derived from the arms and monies at its command. The Jews had a very distinct advantage over the Arabs in this respect since the bulk of their forces were under the effective control of the Haganah General Staff, which fell in turn under the authority of a single political leader in charge of defense, David Ben Gurion—a man of monumental willpower who applied himself single-mindedly to marshaling all the resources needed for victory. Nevertheless, the Arab forces were eminently successful in the first stage of the civil war, owing to the different strategies prescribed for the two parties by their respective aims and by the circumstances in which the war was fought.

The principal aim of the Jews was to gain effective control over the territory allotted to them by the United Nations partition plan. The Arabs' chief aim was to frustrate the aim of the Jews, and thus force a different resolution, one more favorable to themselves. Within the territory allotted to the Jewish state, the areas of actual Jewish settlement were dispersed among large chunks of Arab-inhabited areas, except for the coastal plain between Tel Aviv and Haifa and the Valley of Jezreel. However, even in areas of heavy Jewish concentration, Arab settlements often occupied intruding positions from which Jewish communications could be harassed. Furthermore, several of the largest cities, including Jerusalem, Haifa, Tiberias, and Safed had mixed populations living in mixed or crisscrossing neighborhoods; and even the entirely Jewish city of Tel Aviv was situated cheek by jowl with the wholly Arab city of Jaffa and shared with it the same outside lines of communication.

For the Jews to achieve their aim under these circumstances, they needed to capture and hold positions occupied by the Arabs along main arteries linking Jewish settlements, and to subdue the Arab enclaves within the thickly inhabited Jewish areas. Such operations required much larger and better-equipped forces than the Jews had at the outset. Moreover, they were certain to be opposed by the British, who were determined to prevent any drastic change in the status quo as long as they formally retained the Mandate over Palestine, and as long as they had enough military force left in the country to do so. In contrast, for the Arabs to achieve their aim it was enough to disrupt

Jewish lines of communication and cut off outlying areas of Jewish settlement from localities and positions they already occupied, and to defend these against seizure by the Jews long enough to permit British intervention. This strategy was inoffensive to the British authorities and perfectly suited to the character, size, and organization of the Arab forces.

Thus, after the initial random killings had given way to a recognizable pattern of fighting, the Arabs gained the upper hand. The several attempts they made to overrun outlying Jewish settlements were repelled; but they managed by the beginning of March to cut off from the coastal plain the entire Negev, most of Galilee, and the Jerusalem region and to isolate from one another many of the settlements within each of these regions. Efforts made by the Jews to break this isolation were often frustrated as their armed convoys fell easy prey to Arab ambushes that inflicted heavy casualties in men and equipment. In four months of fighting, the Arabs killed 900 Jews and wounded three or four times that many (more than five times the relative losses suffered by Israel in the entire Six Day War in 1967, which engaged fifteen times more soldiers and infinitely more firepower). More importantly, the Arabs came within reach of their principal political objective when the United States formally proposed that the United Nations put aside the partition resolution as unrealizable and establish instead a trusteeship over Palestine.

The threat of a political disaster made it imperative for the Jews to try to reverse the fortunes of war, and circumstances were propicious for such an attempt. The evacuation of British forces had proceeded so far as to reduce the chance of a serious intervention on their part, the first substantial shipment of Czech arms had been safely brought home, and the mobilization of Jewish forces had reached the 20,000 level. The Jewish High Command decided to launch a series of large-scale operations aimed at *seizing and holding* Arab-controlled areas in the territory assigned to the Jewish state and related strategic areas, and opening up lines of communication between Jewish settlements. It happened that just then, the Liberation Army too decided to launch an ambitious operation. On April 4 it began an attack on Mishmar Haemek which might have led to cutting off the Haifa region and the Valley of Jezreel from the coastal plain. The Jews repelled this attack, and then proceeded with their own offensive which proved to be eminently successful. The road to Jerusalem was broken open after bitter fighting over its mountain passages, and the 100,000 beleaguered Jewish inhabitants of the Jerusalem region received large quantities of supplies that were to prove vital because the road was soon to be blocked again more tightly than ever by regular Arab forces. All the Arab towns and villages and the mixed cities within the territory designated for the Jewish state were overrun in rapid succession, including the vital port city of Haifa, which fell to the Jews on April 22, 1948. A few days later, the Irgun launched an offensive on the all-Arab city of Jaffa, which according to the partition plan was meant to be included in the Arab state. But after the Irgun broke through part of the city in heavy fighting, British forces intervened, blocked the assault, and stabilized the front line. Following the British evacuation of the region the assault was resumed, and the city surrendered on May 13, 1948. Similarly, the all-Arab city of Acre north of Haifa (also intended to be part of the Arab state) was besieged by Jewish forces and capitulated on May 17. In Jerusalem, Jewish troops seized all the buildings and facilities evacuated by the withdrawing British, completed the capture of nearly all quarters of the new city, and isolated the mostly Arab-inhabited old city. As a result of these operations, the organized resistance of the Palestinian Arabs collapsed entirely, their leadership structure disintegrated, and hundreds of thousands of them fled to areas beyond Jewish control.

Thus, by the time the British Mandate came to an end on May 14, 1948, the Jews had largely managed to achieve their strategic aim. In some respects they exceeded it, as in their capture of Jaffa and Acre; in others they fell short of it, as in their failure to establish secure access to the Jerusalem region and the scattered Jewish settlements in the Negev. But even as they capped their military successes by proclaiming the birth of their state, the armies of the neighboring Arab states were marching in.

The Regular War's Course

The war that began on May 15, 1948, was peculiar in several respects. In the first place, it was not, like other wars, a free trial of force in which the contestants could accomplish whatever their relative military power permitted. Rather, it was a series of rounds of combat, each interrupted by a cease-fire or truce imposed by the big powers working through the United Nations Security Council, and intended to permit a diplomatic settlement of the conflict. Since the diplomatic efforts reflected in large measure the situation on the battlefield, first one contestant then the other sought by resuming the fighting to achieve a better bargaining position before the next cease-fire. While military campaigns became a continuation of policy and policy a continuation of military campaigns, military power was prevented from taking a free course to the extent of permitting one side to dominate completely.

Second, the war was fought among contestants who had not previously known one another in a context of peace. With the possible exception of the Transjordanians, the leaders, soldiers, politicians, writers, and journalists of the Arab countries (not to speak of the common people) had had no contact with the Jewish community in Palestine and had only a faint idea of its composition, organization, aspirations, achievements, weaknesses, and strengths. The Arab governments had been drawn into the diplomatic arena of the Jewish-Arab conflict in Palestine only a short time before, and until only a few weeks before the war had not expected to become directly involved in a military capacity. The same ignorance of the other side held true in the case of the Yishuv, but to a somewhat lesser extent. Even a man like Ben Gurion, who was unique among his colleagues in the Zionist leadership in foreseeing as early as 1945 an armed clash with the Arab states and in getting preparations for it under way even then, knew so little about the Arab countries as to confuse the secretary general of the Arab League with the Prime Minister of Egypt all during the period he was involved in war with that country.

The nearly total mutual ignorance of the two sides (compounded rather than mitigated by information they hastily gathered about each other on the eve of the war) gave the fighting a haphazard character, at least in its early and critical stages, and led first one side then the other to score successes or suffer setbacks that bore little relation to the overall balance of forces. It was as though two armed groups found themselves fighting from room to room in one large building while the whole building was immersed in darkness. The decisions of the fighters—whether and when to attack and with what force, and whether to fight back or flee—were determined more by impressions of the situation and by the inner motivation of the fighters than by the realities, to which they were blind.

Third, the war was fought on the Arab side by a group of five armies, only two of which (the Transjordanian and the Iraqi) worked more or less in tandem, while the others operated without any coordination either at the military or the political level. Of course, as von Clausewitz pointed out long ago, all war coalitions are precarious (especially when they fail to achieve promptly the common aim that has brought them together), because of the diverse particular aims, interests, and calculations marring their unity. However, in the case at hand the mutual mistrust among the principal partners was so deep that the Egyptian and the Transjordanian forces, for example, did not even pretend to coordinate their actions, and indeed they guided their respective operations as much by the desire to frustrate each other's suspected intentions as by the requisites of defeating the enemy. Initially, the Israelis were not aware of this situation and therefore acted as if they faced a clever common plan. But once they got wind of what was happening, they were able to concentrate most of their strength on one enemy at a time and were thus able to deal with it while the others remained idle or were in no position to help.

Finally, during the course of the war the balance of forces changed considerably over what it had been at the outset. Particularly striking was the fact that Israel, with a population of 700,000, won the race for mobilization and armament against the Arab states, which collectively had a population forty times larger. Israel ended up with an army that was superior to the Arab armies not only qualitatively but quantitatively as well. The ghost of Voltaire might feel smug satisfaction that in this instance, too, God gave victory to the side with "the biggest battalions." But he would have to use intellectual leger-demain to explain how the side with the much smaller population was able to marshal the larger army.

Initially, the total strength of the invading Arab armies was about 24,000 troops, including 10,000 in the Egyptian army, 4,500 in the Arab Legion of Transjordan, 3,000 Syrians, 3,000 Iraqis, and 3,000 Lebanese and Arab Liberation Army troops. Israel had at that time over 30,000 troops, three-quarters of which were organized in combat formations. The Arab forces had an enormous advantage in firepower and organization since they were established armies, usually equipped with warplanes, armor, artillery, and other heavy weapons, whereas the Israeli forces were an improvised, ragtag army whose heaviest equipment remained one hundred 3-inch mortars and four just-acquired, antiquated, 65-milimeter guns. The Arab armies were fresh, while the best of Israel's forces had been exhausted and bled by six months of civil war.

The Arab forces had the initiative, were able to seize many undefended jumping-off points in areas already under Arab control, and could select the targets on which to concentrate superior forces. On the other hand, the Israelis enjoyed the advantage of interior lines of communication, and their fortified settlements provided them with many very useful bases of operations and with some substantial obstacles along various routes of enemy advance.

Again, Arab armies did not have a common plan of operation, except for the Transjordanian and Iraqi forces. They simply started from different directions and headed toward the heart of the Jewish area—the Lebanese from the north, the Syrians from the northeast, the Iraqis and Trans-jordanians from the east, and the Egyptians from the south. The Israeli High Command, however, saw the initial Arab moves as parts of a clever plan de-signed to draw Israeli forces to the north and the south in order to permit the Transjordanian and Iraqi forces (taking off from the Arab-controlled hills of Samaria and Judea) to strike in the most vulnerable sectors: in the narrow waist of Israel at the coastal plain, where the country could be cut in two by a ten-mile dash from the Arab lines to the Mediterranean, and in the Tel Aviv–Jerusalem corridor to consolidate the isolation of Jerusalem and its environs. Consequently, the Israeli command decided to concentrate its maximum ef-fort in the central sectors, and to let the relatively thinly deployed forces in the north and south fend for themselves. The results might have been disastrous had the Arab armies attacking in the north and south known the situation fac-ing them and pressed their offensive harder.

In the north, the Syrian army opened its attack on the evening of May 16 with an artillery barrage on the Israeli border settlements of Ein Gev, east of the Sea of Galilee, and Massada and Shaar Hagolan south of it. On the 17th, a column of infantry supported by armor attacked Samakh, a small Arab town at the southern tip of the Sea of Galilee held by the Israelis and situated at a

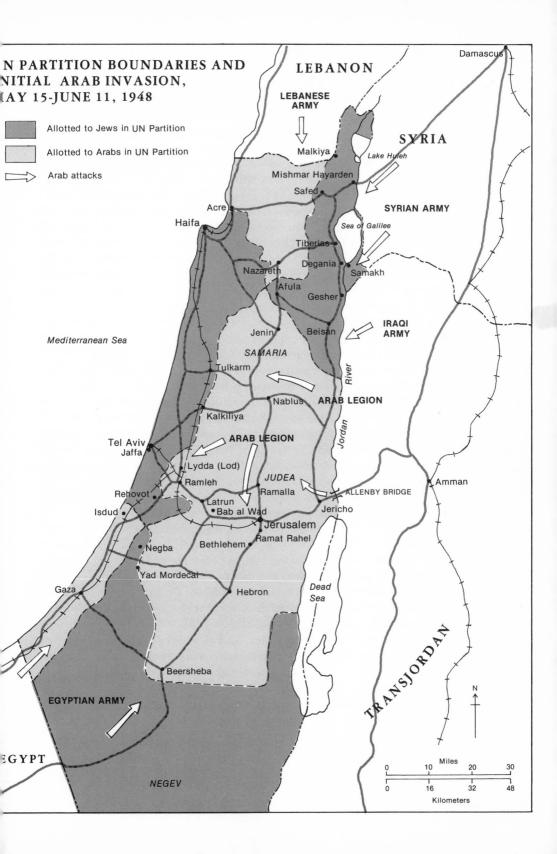

UN PARTITION BOUNDARIES AND
INITIAL ARAB INVASION,
MAY 15-JUNE 11, 1948

Allotted to Jews in UN Partition

Allotted to Arabs in UN Partition

Arab attacks

LEBANON

Damascus

SYRIA

LEBANESE
ARMY

Malkiya

Lake Huleh

Mishmar Hayarden

Safed

SYRIAN ARMY

Acre

Haifa

Sea of Galilee

Tiberias

Degania

Nazareth

Samakh

Afula

Gesher

Jenin

Beisan

IRAQI
ARMY

Mediterranean Sea

SAMARIA

Tulkarm

Nablus

ARAB LEGION

Kalkiliya

Jordan River

Tel Aviv
Jaffa

ARAB LEGION

Lydda (Lod)

Ramleh

JUDEA

Ramalla

Amman

Rehovot

Latrun

Bab al Wad

ALLENBY BRIDGE

Isdud

Jericho

Jerusalem

Negba

Bethlehem

Ramat Rahel

Yad Mordecai

Dead
Sea

Gaza

Hebron

TRANSJORDAN

Beersheba

N

EGYPT

EGYPTIAN ARMY

NEGEV

Miles
0   10   20   30

0   16   32   48
Kilometers

junction of roads leading west, north, and south into Israeli territory. At the same time, other columns attacked Massada and Shaar Hagolan a short distance south and east of Samakh. The Syrians captured Samakh but the Israelis continued to hold a police fortress that controlled the exit from the town. The attacks on Massada and Shaar Hagolan also were repulsed. On the next day, however, the Samakh police fortress fell to the Syrians after all its forty-two defenders were killed, and after a relief attempt by an Israeli force had been thrown back with heavy losses. These successes of the Syrians, attributable mainly to their possession of artillery and armor against which the Israelis did not yet know how to cope with their light weapons, created a sudden panic in the Jewish camp. That night, Massada and Shaar Hagolan were abandoned by their settlers, who took refuge in settlements further west and southwest, next on the line of the Syrian advance. Materially, these latter settlements were no better prepared to face artillery and tanks than the positions that had already fallen, and their loss would have been a very heavy psychological as well as military blow since they included the oldest kibbutz, Degania Alef, and its offspring, Degania Bet, which symbolized and led the entire collective settlement movement.

The Israeli High Command was pressed by the settlers to send reinforcements, but in view of the situation on the other fronts, all it could spare was an unemployed commando officer with the rank of major called Moshe Dayan, whom it rushed northward to take over command of the area's defense, together with a handful of fighters he picked up along the way and two of the four 65-milimeter guns which were "lent" to that front for forty-eight hours. Dayan got there in time to position his "artillery" and introduce a minimum of order before the Syrian attack on the two Deganias began. On May 20 after an artillery bombardment two columns of Syrian infantry advanced on the two settlements behind widely deployed light tanks and armored cars. In Degania Alef, the two leading tanks broke through the barbed wire into the settlement, but were put out of action by "Molotov cocktails." The remainder of the armor hesitated, and the infantry hugged the ground. At this moment, Dayan ordered the two artillery pieces to open fire. After suffering two direct hits, the Syrians hurriedly withdrew. That night, Dayan sent a small unit to raid Samakh, only to discover that the Syrians had withdrawn from the town as well as from Massada and Shaar Hagolan, which were promptly reoccupied. Obviously, panic had visited the Syrians in their turn, once they realized that the enemy could offer stiff resistance even to armor and, above all, once they discovered that the Israelis, too, had artillery.

For the next twenty days, the Syrians caused little trouble from behind the international frontier line to which they had withdrawn. Then, on June 10, one day before the first truce was to come into effect, they launched a carefully prepared surprise attack some twenty-five miles to the north, seized intact the Bridge of Jacob's Daughters spanning the Jordan, established a two-mile wide bridgehead, and defended it against Israeli counterattacks for the remainder of the war.

In the northernmost "finger" of upper Galilee, the Israelis had sought to anticipate a Lebanese invasion by sending, on May 13, an elite battalion to seize the border village of Malkieh and the adjoining police fortress of Nebi Yusha which controlled the invasion route. Upon reaching its objectives after a long night march, the battalion was met by the Lebanese expeditionary force, which had arrived before it, and was thrown back with heavy losses. Five days later, the Israeli battalion returned and succeeded in capturing Malkieh, but early in June the Lebanese recaptured the position from the occupation unit that had replaced the elite battalion. By that time, however, the initial thrust of the Arab invasion had been blunted, and Arab Liberation Army units that descended from Malkieh to Arab-inhabited central Galilee were unable to pose a serious strategic threat.

Some ten miles south of the initial Syrian penetration but not coordinated with it, the Iraqi expeditionary force attacked. Its immediate target was the Israeli settlement of Gesher and neighboring positions that controlled the route across the Jordan River to Beit Shaan and the Valley of Jezreel. On May 17 the Iraqis crossed the river without resistance and began to probe Israeli positions. Three days later, they launched a general multi-pronged attack preceded by heavy artillery bombardment. The greatly outnumbered defenders held their ground everywhere for four days, after which the Iraqis withdrew beyond the river, recrossed it farther south into Arab-inhabited Samaria, and deployed there to relieve the Transjordanian forces who had preceded them into the area. The Iraqis arrived in Jenin, at the northern end of Samaria, just in time to block an Israeli attack designed to divert Arab forces from any offensive projects along Israel's narrow waist.

The Arab Legion of Transjordan began its operations well before the end of the Mandate. On May 11, 1948, it mounted an assault against the Etzion bloc, a group of four Jewish settlements halfway between Hebron and Jerusalem that had been isolated by Arab irregulars for several months. A week before, the Legion had shelled the complex heavily to prevent harassment of Legion convoys which, under the control of the British, were shuttling between the British military depots along the Suez Canal and Legion bases in Transjordan, carrying ammunition and supplies in preparation for the war. On May 11 these Transjordanian units, which still operated in Palestine under the authority of the British Mandate, launched an all-out attack to capture the settlements. After two days of fighting, Legion armor broke through at the village of Kfar Etzion and subdued its decimated and exhausted defenders. While the prisoners were being rounded up and Palestinians from the neighboring villages were looting the settlement, shooting was renewed, in the wake of which all the surviving Jewish defenders, most of them already disarmed, were killed. The next day, May 14, the other three villages of the bloc surrendered and their inhabitants and defenders were taken prisoners.

After withstanding five months of siege and repelling several massive Arab attacks in the course of the civil war, the quick collapse of the Etzion bloc had a shattering effect on the morale of Jewish Jerusalem, whose population had been under siege on and off for several months. To the defenders of the city, who were thinly deployed along a large perimeter, the armor, artillery, drill and British command of the Legion appeared nearly irresistible. Had the Legion been able to follow up on its victory over the Etzion bloc with a prompt assault on the city, it might well have forced capitulation, and would then have been in a position to move most of its troops down to the coastal plain for a final blow against the Jewish heartland. Fortunately for Jerusalem and Israel, the Legion was not prepared to act so boldly, and when, five or six days later, it appeared on the outskirts of Jerusalem, the defenders had recovered their morale and were better prepared materially than they would have been in the absence of delay.

On May 15 the main forces of the Arab Legion crossed the Jordan River unopposed over the Damia and Allenby bridges into Arab-controlled areas, and proceeded to deploy themselves in various positions in Arab Samaria. On May 19 the first group of an eventual force of 700 legionnaires, comprising infantry supported by armored cars and artillery, began to attack the Jewish-held part of Jerusalem with an assault on the important quarter of Sheikh Jarrah, in the north. This quarter cut off the old city of Jerusalem from Arab Ramalla and linked the Jewish-held new city with Mount Scopus, the site of the Hebrew University and the Hadassah medical complex. The Jewish defenders were easily overcome and the Legion captured the quarter, cutting off Mount Scopus and completing the isolation of the Jewish quarter of the old city and its 2,500 inhabitants, mostly elderly people with a few young defenders. The Jews made several desperate attempts to break through the wall of the old city in various places in order to link up with the Jewish quarter; all efforts failed except one, which established contact long enough to permit the introduction of modest reinforcements. This, however, only prolonged the agony of the besieged until May 28, when they surrendered to the Legion.

In the meantime, the Legion forces that captured Sheikh Jarrah tried to continue their advance through the next, Jewish-inhabited, quarters of the new city. Here, to their surprise, they encountered the first serious Jewish resistance. The defenders had learned how to ambush the Legion's armor with Molotov cocktails and antitank rifles in the thickly built-up area; and each time the Legion captured a row of houses after using its artillery point-blank, the Jews counterattacked, often at night, and reoccupied the positions. The fighting went on in this way for five whole days. On one occasion, fighting went on for two days and nights in the gardens and the building of the vast Notre Dame convent. By the time it was over, the Jews remained in possession after having suffered and inflicted very heavy casualties. With no reserves and little capacity to absorb losses, the Legion finally gave up all efforts to storm the city and set about trying to subdue it by siege and bombardment.

While one critical battle with the Legion was going on in the northern quarters, another began in the south of the city, against Egyptian forces that had arrived there unopposed along the Ismailia-Auja-Beersheba-Hebron road. On May 21 the Egyptians began an attack on Ramat Rahel, a collective settlement commanding the approaches to the southern quarters of the city. After several hours of point-blank artillery bombardment, the Egyptians stormed and captured the settlement; but before they were able to entrench themselves, a Jewish reinforcement unit counterattacked and reoccupied the position. This unit was rushed north immediately thereafter, leaving the settlement in the hands of second-line troops who were unable to hold on when the Arabs attacked again the next day. Once more, Jewish reinforcements were rushed back and fought their way up the settlement hill again to win the position, lose it, and finally win it again, and thus stem the threat to the city from the south.

While resistance inside Jerusalem prevented its immediate fall, it was clear that sooner or later the city was doomed unless the mountain road linking it to the coastal plain (the road had been closed during most of the civil war, twice reopened and twice closed again) were once more reopened to let in supplies, reinforcements, and ammunition. Consequently, even before the fighting within the city had subsided, the Israeli High Command, spurred on by Ben Gurion, made desperate efforts to break through to the besieged city. The key positions blocking the way were in the Latrun area and had been held by units of the Arab Legion since May 18, although the Israelis did not know this until they mounted their first attack. Against these positions the High Command threw on May 25 a brigade formed a mere seventy-two hours before, composed in large measure of immigrants taken almost straight off the ship. The inexperience of the force, the improvised command, hasty planning, and poor intelligence told in the results, which were utter failure and near disintegration of the attacking unit.

The Israelis took a few days to regroup, bring in an experienced battalion for reinforcement, and work out a new plan. They then returned to the assault. This time the armored unit of the force broke through and reached the police fortress that was the hub of the enemy positions; but the infantry that was supposed to back it up failed to follow, and an attack from the rear went awry, with the result that the second attempt, too, collapsed, bringing to some 600 the number of casualties suffered in the two efforts.

The Israelis made a third attempt against the Latrun area on June 9, this time from both the Jerusalem and the coastal sides, but fared no better than before, except perhaps in suffering fewer casualities. However, between the second and third attacks, the Israelis discovered a path leading through the mountains and skirting the Arab positions and decided to turn it into a road for vehicular traffic. They set to work on it twenty-four hours a day, often under Legion artillery fire from Latrun, and completed it by the time the third attack failed. When a truce came into effect two days later, the Israelis used that road to supply Jerusalem freely, and independently of limited supply arrangements agreed upon as part of the cease-fire.

In the south, Egyptian forces invaded Palestine along two routes. The main body took the coastal road stretching from Kantara on the Suez Canal through el Arish, Rafah, Gaza, and on to Tel Aviv, while a substantial but more lightly equipped force took the road leading from Auja on the Egyptian-Palestinian border through Beersheba and Hebron to Jerusalem. Moving through uninhabited or Arab-inhabited area, the latter force advanced rapidly and reached the outskirts of Jerusalem by May 21 when, as we have seen, it attacked Ramat Rahel.

The main Egyptian force, too, began by advancing rapidly but was soon compelled to proceed more cautiously. While the bulk of the force advanced through Gaza, several units were assigned the task of eradicating three small settlements in the vicinity of the main road—Kfar Darom, Nirim, and Beerot Yitshak. This turned out to be more difficult than expected, for all three outposts successfully repelled the attackers and inflicted substantial casualties, compelling the Egyptian command to content itself with investing the stubborn villages to prevent interference with Egyptian traffic. Farther north, the main Egyptian column had done the same to the settlement of Yad Mordecai in its advance to the Arab town of Majdal, expecting it to fall of its own accord. But after the experience with Kfar Darom and Nirim, the Egyptians decided to eliminate that settlement before proceeding farther. On May 19 they began their attack with heavy artillery bombardment followed by an advance of infantry supported by armor. The assaulting force approached the perimeter of the settlement, actually penetrating it before being thrown back. The next day the Egyptians repeated their attempts four times, and four times they were repelled. Over the next two days they continued to shell the settlement and on the 23rd they assaulted it again and succeeded in seizing some of its positions. That night the survivors managed to evacuate the settlement and slip away to safety through Egyptian lines with the help of a small commando rescue unit. The defense of Yad Mordecai had cost the Egyptians 300 casualties and five precious days during which the Israelis were able to set up a defense line of sorts farther to the north.

The Egyptians were delayed another two days on their way to the north by kibbutz Nitzanim, which they were able to bomb into submission. By the 29th they had reached the Arab village of Isdud, some twenty miles south of Tel Aviv, where the area of thick Jewish settlement began. Barring their way was the Israeli Givati brigade, composed of some 4,500 lightly armed men deployed in over seventeen positions to cover all possible routes of enemy advance. Since the Egyptian contingent that had taken the coastal road consisted of two regular brigades supported by armor and ample artillery, and since it had the advantages of initiative and concentration of force, the odds seemed to be all on its side. However, the Egyptian command did not know exactly what it faced, and it had acquired a healthy respect for the enemy. When an Israeli force supported by the first fighter planes (four Messerschmitts that had just arrived from Czechoslovakia) launched the first counterattack, the Egyptians decided to stop the march and dig in. Over the next few days, the Israelis continued a series of unsuccessful attacks on Egyptian positions, while the Egyptians failed in a resolute attack on kibbutz Negba, intended to open up an alternative advance route. This kind of fighting for an opening through enemy lines continued until the cease-fire began on June 11. The Egyptians had by then cut off the Negev from Israel, but their advance on Tel Aviv had been decisively stopped.

On all fronts the Israelis had, through a mixture of tenacity, boldness, improvisation, and luck, managed to withstand the initial critical moments of the Arab assault, absorb the first setbacks, and block the thrust of the Arab invasion—before the four-week truce ordered by the United Nations Security Council. The Arab states had definitely failed to stifle the Jewish state; but the Israelis desperately needed the respite afforded by the truce. Their hastily mobilized army was in a deplorable state of disorganization, with many of the units lacking the most elementary items of equipment. Their best formations had been fighting continuously for many months and had suffered very heavy attrition of personnel through casualties and exhaustion. For example, of the three elite Palmach brigades one had suffered 837 casualties and was left with only 200 worn-out fighters, another had 550 casualties, and the third had suffered similar losses while its men had fought in the Negev for seven months without leave. Jewish Jerusalem had been saved and the Arab vise around it loosened, but the city was hungry, bleeding, and shell-shocked. It had been in a state of near-siege for six months, had been hit by 10,000 artillery projectiles in the course of three weeks, and had suffered over 4,000 casualties, most of them military. The Egyptian drive on Tel Aviv had been stopped, but the entire Negev was cut off by a linkup across a lateral road south of Isdud between Egyptian forces that had advanced along the coastal and interior roads. The Arab war machine had also worn itself out and was badly in need of overhaul if it were not to collapse entirely.

During the truce both Israelis and Arabs refitted themselves for fighting, but the Israelis made much better use of the respite because they needed it more. For example, the Arabs increased their forces by one-third to some 35,000, while the Israelis doubled theirs to over 60,000. And while the Arab forces, who were mainly regular troops to begin with, hardly improved qualitatively, the Israeli forces, composed for the most part of hastily mobilized recruits with minimal training in regular warfare who had ample room for improvement through training, used the truce period to correct deficiencies.

During the lull, the mediator appointed by the United Nations, Count Folke Bernadotte, proposed to the belligerents a prolongation of the truce. The Israelis agreed at once because they saw in the end of the fighting a confirmation of the existence of their state and an opportunity to try to put it in order. The Arab side was initially agreeable, but when it became apparent that Bernadotte intended to propose to the parties and the United Nations a settlement based on awarding the Negev and Jerusalem to Transjordan and western Galilee to Israel, the Egyptian government balked. It insisted on the resumption of fighting in pursuit of the originally proclaimed Arab aim of liberating all of Palestine, and forced its reluctant allies to follow suit. The fact that the original Arab aim was no longer attainable was obscured for Egypt by its repugnance at the idea of having gone to war merely to secure for Transjordan the portions of Palestine that were wrested from the Jews.

Hostilities resumed on July 9 and lasted for ten days, after which a "final" cease-fire came into effect. This time the Israelis had seized the initiative in most sectors, while concentrating their main effort against the Arab Legion in the approaches to Jerusalem. This decision was based partly on the respect which the Israeli High Command accorded the Legion as the most effective Arab fighting force, and partly on a desire to redeem failures suffered by Israeli forces at Latrun. But above all it was intended to alter in a fundamental way the military realities in that sector that had obviously served as a basis for Bernadotte's recommendation to give Jerusalem to Transjordan. Accordingly, the Israelis launched a two-stage offensive designed to eliminate Legion forces along the Tel Aviv–Jerusalem corridor, and then to turn back Legion forces in Jerusalem itself by wheeling around Latrun and cutting the Jerusalem-Ramalla road. The first stage was accomplished quickly and cheaply as the towns of Ramleh and Lydda (Lod), the Lydda international airport, and the surrounding areas were seized, and the corridor to Jerusalem was widened in several places. In the second stage, however, the Israelis stumbled once more against the Latrun position, which though assaulted by large forces converging from all directions, repelled the attackers while inflicting heavy casualties. In view of the relation of forces between defenders and attackers, Latrun would most probably have succumbed to subsequent assaults, were it not that a cease-fire took effect once again. The Legion command must have realized this, for henceforth Transjordan's King decided to sit out the war even while his allies were being taken apart by the Israelis, as long as the Israelis would leave him alone. And they did leave him alone once they had secured their position in Jerusalem.

In the southern sector, the Israelis sought essentially to contain the Egyptians while trying to improve local positions. Except for a major Egyptian assault on Negba, which was once again repelled, the fighting took the form of seasaw battles for positions in the vicinity of the junction of the coastal and lateral roads—possession of which could either keep the Negev cut off or open it for the Israelis, but only at the cost of splitting the Egyptian forces into two. In the end the Egyptians retained the main positions while the Israelis captured a few secondary ones that gave them a claim of access to the Negev after the cease-fire came into effect.

In the north, the Israelis launched a major assault on the Syrian bridge-head at Mishmar Hayarden but failed to dislodge the enemy. They also lost some ground to Iraqi attacks in the Jenin sector. On the other hand, they launched a very successful offensive against the Arab Liberation Army, which netted them the city of Nazareth and most of central Galilee.

The second cease-fire was supposed to have been final and to permit set-tlement of the conflict by diplomatic means. However, on October 14 a third round of fighting began, this time between the Israelis and the Egyptians only, except for some secondary action against the Liberation Army in central Gal-ilee. The grounds for resuming the hostilities were basically the desire of the Israelis to alter the military situation in the Negev in order to undermine Ber-nadotte's recommendation to give that area to Transjordan—just as their operations against the Arab Legion had undermined his initial recommen-dation to give Jerusalem to Transjordan. (His final report recommended in-stead the internationalization of the Holy City.) However, the Egyptians were foolish enough to give the Israelis the opportunity they sought to renew the fighting by forcibly barring them from supplying their settlements in the Negev, in clear violation of the terms of the cease-fire.

This time the Israelis had all the advantages on their side, including nu-merical superiority, surprise, concentration of force, and freedom to select the most convenient areas for attack along a lengthy and relatively thin Egyp-tian front. In a sharp campaign lasting nine days, they were able to smash their way to the south, cut the Egyptian front into pieces, trap one-fourth of the Egyptian forces in a pocket, neutralize another fourth, and drive the rest back to an untenable arc stretching from Gaza to Asluj, some twenty miles south of Beersheba. In the north, the Israelis routed the remnants of the Lib-eration Army in a sixty-hour campaign, in which they cleared all of central Galilee and moved beyond the international borders of Palestine to occupy some Lebanese villages.

The last round of fighting occurred at the turn of the year 1948–49 and lasted for about two weeks. On November 16, 1948, the Security Council had ordered the parties to the conflict to conclude armistice agreements. When the Egyptians refused, the Israelis launched an offensive intended either to secure their acquiescence or to complete the destruction of their army in Palestine. As in the previous offensive, the Egyptians obligingly gave the Israelis legal cover for breaking the truce by overreacting to provocations.

And again, the other Arab armies sat still while the Israelis concentrated their superior forces against the Egyptian front. The Israelis easily broke up the Egyptian line at Auja and drove into the territory of Egypt proper in a wide flanking movement aiming at el Arish. The entire Egyptian army was thus reduced to one tight pocket left over from the past round of fighting, and another almost completely enclosed pocket extending from Gaza to el Arish, which the Israelis were pounding. With nowhere to retreat, the Egyptians did some of their best fighting of the entire war, but were saved from a heroic doom only by a virtual British ultimatum to the Israelis to pull out of Sinai, followed by the timely agreement of the Egyptian government to conclude an armistice.

The fighting stopped on January 7, 1949, and by February 24 the Egyptians had signed a separate armistice agreement with Israel—leaving their allies to face the potential wrath of Israel alone. But Israel's government had had enough of fighting and wanted to get on with the conclusion of peace and minding the business of the new state; and so, after toying with the idea of a campaign to expel the Arab Legion and take over all of Palestine, it contented itself with concluding an advantageous armistice with Transjordan in April 1949. Lebanon had signed a month before, and Syria followed in July. Israel's War of Independence thus came to a victorious end.

Consequences of the War

The War of Independence not only assured the birth and immediate survival of Israel but also produced a host of effects that left a deep imprint on the future of the Jewish state. The most obvious of these effects was the far-reaching modification of the original United Nations partition plan. The Arab state envisaged by that plan failed to emerge, and the territory allocated to it was divided by the armistice agreements between Israel, Transjordan, and Egypt. Israel got the largest share, some 2,500 square miles, which it formally annexed to the 5,600 square miles alloted to it by the partition plan. Transjordan acquired 2,200 square miles, which it formally annexed as well, transforming itself into the state of Jordan. Egypt retained control of the Gaza Strip, some 135 square miles, which it held in the status of Egyptian-administered territory. As for Syria and Lebanon, the international frontiers of Palestine became the armistice lines between them and Israel. Jerusalem, intended by the partition plan to be under an international regime, was divided between Israel and Jordan. Several small demilitarized zones were created on the borders between Israel and Egypt, Jordan, and Syria. The specific boundaries that defined Israel's territory were relatively very long and were highly vulnerable strategically, but they were infinitely better than the partition boundaries. The former at least left Israel with a modicum of territorial continuity, whereas the latter envisaged three blocks of Jewish territory inter-

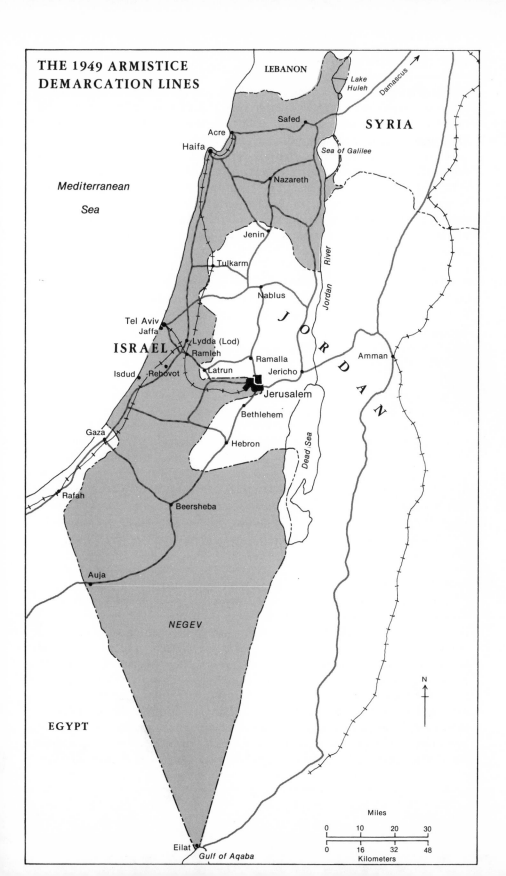

THE 1949 ARMISTICE
DEMARCATION LINES

LEBANON

Lake
Huleh

Damascus

SYRIA

Safed

Acre

Haifa

Sea of Galilee

Mediterranean

Sea

Nazareth

Jenin

Tulkarm

Nablus

Tel Aviv
Jaffa

ISRAEL

Lydda (Lod)

Ramleh

Isdud   Rehovot

Latrun

Ramalla

Jericho

Amman

JORDAN

Jerusalem

Bethlehem

Gaza

Hebron

Dead Sea

Rafah

Beersheba

Jordan River

Auja

NEGEV

N

EGYPT

Miles

0   10   20   30

0   16   32   48

Kilometers

Eilat

Gulf of Aqaba

sected by three blocks of Arab territory, with the links among the Jewish and the Arab areas respectively consisting, literally, of dots on the map.

The war also involved a major reshuffling of population. Some 700,000 Palestinian Arabs who lived in the area that came under Israeli control were displaced in the course of the fighting before and after May 15, 1948, and ended up as refugees in Jordan (60 percent), the Gaza Strip (20 percent), and Syria and Lebanon (20 percent). This development gave Israel a much more homogeneous population than that envisaged by the partition plan, which contemplated an Arab population nearly as large as the initial Jewish population within the boundaries assigned to the Jewish state. In the boundaries that Israel actually achieved through the armistice agreements, there would have been an Arab majority had the Arab population remained in place. On the other hand, the displaced Arabs also created a refugee problem that has remained to haunt Israel's existence and its relations with the Arab countries ever since, besides involving untold misery for large numbers of human beings.

A vast controversy has since raged over the question of whether the refugees left the territory under Jewish control of their own accord or were compelled to leave by threat or force. At the risk of sounding banal, it can be safely asserted that the truth in this instance lies in the middle ground between the two positions, almost exactly. That is to say, as long as the fate of the partition plan and of the Jewish state appeared uncertain to both sides, the Arabs left of their own accord in the face of persistent Jewish pleas to stay. Once that issue ceased to be in doubt, the Arabs wanted to remain in the areas that fell under Israeli control, but most of them were forcibly driven out by the Jews, who sought thereby to secure the advantage of a more homogeneous population. The numbers involved in each phase were almost equal. An entry in Ben Gurion's diary dated June 5, 1948, published in his book *Israel; A Personal History,* reveals that on that day a plan was brought to his attention "to deal with the situation created by the de facto transfer of populations that has taken place" (p. 122). That date may be taken roughly as the dividing line between the two phases; and at that time, according to the diary, the number of Arabs that had left was 335,000—a figure that is confirmed by independent calculation.

In addition to these consequences, the war had a profound psychological impact on the people of Israel. It is a tragic fact of life that war, the most brutal manifestation of intergroup antagonism, often serves to promote the most comprehensive intragroup solidarity; the War of Independence accomplished that for Israel's people. The people of Israel had not lacked in shared ideals and aspirations, but the experience of the war indelibly stamped a sense of unity and common destiny on the psychic fiber of all those who partook of it; and by the time it had reached its last stages, virtually every corner of the country had experienced it. From beginning to end, the war entailed some

30,000 casualties—more than Israel has suffered in all the wars and violent incidents since. Since the population amounted to about 700,000, this meant that there were not many in the country who had not had several relatives or friends killed or maimed. The culmination of this ordeal in triumph not only confirmed those who went through it in their sense of nationhood, but also provided the succeeding generations of native and immigrant Israelis with ample material for mythology, legend, and history with which to nourish theirs.

A particularly significant effect of the War of Independence on the collective spirit of the Jews of Israel, and for that matter on the spirit of Jews everywhere, had to do with the fact that that war was fought and won only a short time after the massacre of Europe's Jews at the hands of the Nazis. Much as they agonized over the calamity, empathized with its victims, and endeavored to stress every manifestation of resistance they had put up, many Jews had never been able to suppress completely a nagging, painful whisper within themselves that "they"—the condemned—should have fought back more, should have sold their lives more dearly, should have clawed their murderers; that "they" should not have allowed themselves to be led like sheep to the slaughter. The Jews of Palestine, who felt themselves the bearers of the Jewish national consciousness, the vanguard of Jewish national self-regeneration, were particularly sensitive to this agonizing remorse. Consequently, their desperate and ultimately victorious fight against what seemed to be crushing odds entailed for them not only their own survival and the survival of their work, but a kind of partial catharsis, a redemption of Jewish history, which made it possible for them to face the future with a somewhat easier heart and much greater confidence.

Finally, the fact that it took a grueling war to accomplish the Zionist goal of Jewish national sovereignty had another, not unrelated, effect. The Zionist movement had stressed from the outset that it sought to accomplish its purposes by peaceful means and in accordance with "Public Law," to use the expression of the Basel Program. Perhaps at the beginning the movement had no choice, considering that it had no firm footing in the land that was the object of its aspiration; but after the Mandate came into effect and a Jewish national community began to take shape in Palestine, that was no longer the case. A minority of the movement, led by Vladimir Jabotinsky, began to stress military means and, after seceding from the Zionist Organization, gave birth eventually to the Irgun, which expressed its conviction in the refrain of its favorite song: "By blood and fire Judah fell, by blood and fire Judah shall arise." However, the mainstream of the movement, dominated by self-styled "Practical Zionists" and "Labor Zionists," persisted in maintaining that the conquest of Palestine was to be accomplished by work and toil and confirmed by Public Law. To the fiery slogan of the dissenters (whom they dubbed "dissidents"), they consciously opposed the prosaic motto: "Yet another acre, yet another cow." To be sure, the dominant leadership did not neglect the military side altogether and did sponsor the creation of the Haganah organization. However, as its name (Defense Organization) implied, it was conceived essentially as an instrument for the protection of Jewish life and the fruits of Jewish labor on a local basis, in case the authorities responsible for the maintenance of law and order should falter. Later, during World War II and after, the functions of the Haganah were expanded to include participation in the Allied war effort against Nazism, the smuggling of immigrants in defiance of the British authorities, and occasional acts of sabotage against British military installations in Palestine. These activities, in turn, created in the world at large an impression that the Yishuv was endowed with a substantial military capacity, which swayed the relevant international opinion toward the notion that the Zionist aspirations could not be suppressed and had to be at least partly met. However, with the notable exception of Ben Gurion and one or two others, the mainstream Zionist leaders at no point imagined that the Yishuv would have to use military means, much less to fight an all-out war to establish its right to sovereign nationhood.

That things actually came to that, despite the accumulation of many acres and cows and despite the fact that the right of the Jews to a state in Palestine had been proclaimed by "Public Law" in the form of the United Nations resolution, initiated a basic transformation in the thinking of most Israelis. The leadership could not own abruptly that the convictions it had voiced all along proved to be faulty, and so for a while it went on to argue that labor and toil were essential for securing the right, and that both were essential for succeeding in the ordeal of war. However, before long, the leadership joined the bulk of the rank and file in the conviction that right without might was useless, which, since right was taken for granted, meant emphasis on might—that tough, stiff-necked, go-it-alone propensity that has become characteristic of Israeli attitudes in matters relating to their existence and security as they see them.

PART TWO

THE PHYSICAL, HUMAN, ECONOMIC, AND CONSTITUTIONAL ENVIRONMENT

6
The Country

Political Geography

The state of Israel as it emerged from the War of Independence included almost four-fifths of Palestine. Since the Six Day War of June 5–11, 1967, Israel has also occupied the remainder of Palestine, including the territory known as the West Bank, which it took over from Jordan, and the Gaza Strip, which it took over from Egypt. In addition, Israel has occupied the Egyptian Sinai Peninsula and the Syrian Golan Heights. When speaking of Israel throughout the remainder of this study, I shall have in mind the country in its pre-1967 borders. The areas conquered in the 1967 war will be referred to collectively as "the occupied areas" and individually by their particular appelations. Israel as here defined and the occupied areas together will be referred to as "Israeli-controlled areas."

The name Palestine goes back to Roman times. However, it did not designate a distinct political entity until recent times, when it emerged as one of the successor states to the Ottoman Empire that was dismembered in the wake of the First World War. It was constituted out of the southern halves of the former Ottoman provinces of Beirut and Damascus and the entire district of Jerusalem. No sooner was that entity established than it underwent its first division. In 1921 Britain, then in the process of acquiring the Mandate from the League of Nations over that territory, divided it into two administrative segments separated by the Jordan River. The eastern segment was ruled by an Arab Prince advised by British officers, while the western portion was directly administered by the British. Although both segments formally constituted the Mandate of Palestine, the eastern territory grew into the independent kingdom of Transjordan (later Jordan) and only the western part retained the name of Palestine. The fact that Palestine had been for many centuries almost indistinguishable from the Syrian provinces has been a factor in the involvement of Arabs outside Palestine in the country's destiny; while the fact that the original Mandate of Palestine included the territory that became Jordan has been a factor underlying irredentist claims among some Israelis.

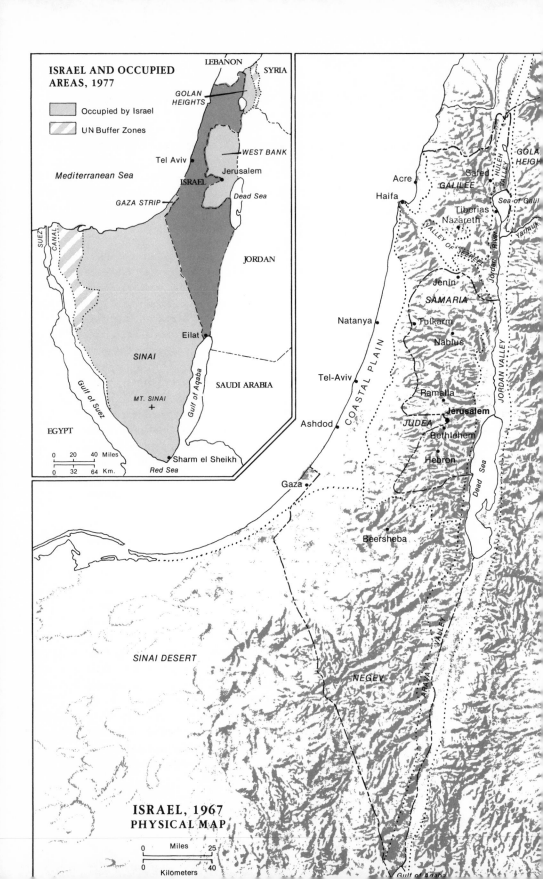

ISRAEL AND OCCUPIED AREAS, 1977

Occupied by Israel

UN Buffer Zones

LEBANON

SYRIA

GOLAN HEIGHTS

WEST BANK

Tel Aviv

Jerusalem

Mediterranean Sea

ISRAEL

Dead Sea

GAZA STRIP

JORDAN

SUEZ CANAL

Eilat

SINAI

SAUDI ARABIA

Gulf of Suez

MT. SINAI

Gulf of Aqaba

EGYPT

0 20 40 Miles

0 32 64 Km.

Sharm el Sheikh

Red Sea

LEBANON

SYRIA

GOLAN HEIGHTS

Acre

Safed

Galilee

HULEH VALLEY

GOLAN HEIGHTS

Haifa

Tiberias

Sea of Galil

Nazareth

VALLEY OF JEZREEL

Jordan River

Yarmuk

Jenin

SAMARIA

Natanya

Tulkarm

Nablus

Tel-Aviv

COASTAL PLAIN

Ramalla

JORDAN VALLEY

Jerusalem

Ashdod

JUDEA

Bethlehem

Hebron

Dead Sea

Gaza

Beersheba

SINAI DESERT

ARAVA VALLEY

NEGEV

ISRAEL, 1967
PHYSICAL MAP

0 Miles 25

0 Kilometers 40

Gulf of Aqaba

Israel is situated on the eastern shore of the Mediterranean at a meeting point of three continents. The successive invasions of that part of the world by Assyrians, Babylonians, Persians, Greeks, Egyptians, Syrians, Romans, Arabs, Mongols, Turks, and British testify to its importance as a bridge or a buffer between the Nile and the Euphrates, between Africa and Eurasia. That area also connects the Mediterranean and the Atlantic to the west with the Red Sea at the Gulf of Aqaba and the Indian Ocean to the east. Israel, occupying the only land route between Egypt and the countries of the Fertile Crescent, has so far served as a buffer rather than as a bridge between the Arab countries to its south and southwest, and those to its north, east, and northeast. Although this fact is outwardly lamented by all the Arab states and has been a crucial factor in their unrelenting hostility to Israel, it has actually benefited several Arab regimes by posing an obstacle to Cairo's drive for hegemony over the Arab nations. Israel's position linking the Mediterranean and the Red Sea began to be exploited on a limited basis for oil passage and transit trade after 1957. Between 1967 and 1975, when the Suez Canal was closed and Israel controlled the entire Sinai Peninsula, the exploitation of that position acquired a substantial international significance. A new 42-inch oil pipeline with a potential throughput capacity of 60 million tons annually was laid between Eilat and Ashdod, in addition to the 16-inch Eilat-Haifa pipeline that existed before; and the possibility of large-scale transit of containerized bulk cargo was also actively explored. In addition, the rapid emergence of the Soviet Union as a naval power in the Mediterranean and the Indian Ocean gave to the areas of Israel and Sinai controlling passage between the two seas a greatly enhanced strategic importance.

Israel's shape is awkward and vulnerable. On the map it looks like an irregular triangle standing on its apex, connected by a long, narrow, irregular rectangle to a small, irregular square. The clumsy frontiers, the result of the freezing of the battle lines of the 1948 war, look as though they had been drawn to achieve the maximum length and unmanageability. Thus, for a territory of 8,000 square miles, Israel has 613 miles of land frontier in addition to 158 miles of seafront. At the tip of the triangle, the country is only 8 miles wide; at the triangle's base, where it achieves its maximum width, it spreads only 69 miles from border to border; through the long rectangle, the width varies between 9.5 miles to 16 miles; and in the north, the square is never wider than 41 miles. Before 1967, a traveler was thus never far from the frontiers wherever he went; and in a place like Jerusalem he met them while walking down the street since the city itself was divided between Israel and Jordan. The oddity of the boundaries, and the fact that they connect Israel with four Arab countries—Lebanon, Syria, Jordan, and Egypt—had much to do with the frequent border incidents that characterized Israel's history and with the obsessive preoccupation of Israel's leaders with the problem of national security. The 1967 cease-fire lines altered the situation greatly.

Although they brought under Israeli control 26,500 additional square miles—more than three times its original 8,000—they shortened its land demarcation lines by nearly 25 percent to 471 miles. The shoreline under Israeli control increased by nearly two and a half times to 564 miles. These changes entailed a radical reversal of relative geostrategic advantage between Israel and its enemies, which was only slightly modified by the Israeli withdrawals in accordance with agreements concluded in the wake of the 1973 war.

Physical and Economic Geography

Although Israel is only the size of Massachusetts, it encompasses a great deal of geographic variety, including some features to which the superlative, in world-geographic terms, is applicable. Taking Palestine as a whole, four basic geographic features may be discerned: (1) At the center of the country there is a range of hills stretching from Lebanon down to the heart of the Negev; (2) west of that range there is a coastal plain of varying width; (3) east of the hills there is the Jordan depression; and, finally, (4) to the south of all these there is the Negev desert. Variations in these basic features produce at least six geographic regions which are worth brief separate examination.

(1) In the extreme north, the mountains of Lebanon continue without a break, though at lower altitudes, to form the hills of Galilee, whose highest peak is just under 4,000 feet. Abundant seasonal rainfall has eroded the hillsides and formed small fertile valleys which can be farmed without irrigation. The countryside is dotted with a considerable number of Jewish settlements but with even more Arab villages and townlets, this being the area where most of the Arab population of Israel is concentrated. Here is located the town of Nazareth and many other places mentioned in the New Testament as associated with the life of Jesus; and here too is the town of Safed, the old seat of Jewish mysticism. Today Nazareth is a town of 35,000, mostly Arabs engaged in commerce, light industry, and services connected with the numerous religious establishments in the area. On hills overlooking Nazareth, a new all-Jewish industrial town, Natserat Illit, with a population of about 18,000, has been built. Safed, with a population of 15,000, is essentially a resort town with some light industry. The country is famous for its olives and tobacco.

(2) The hills of Galilee fall away abruptly on three sides. On the east they end at what is the beginning of a nearly 300-mile-long narrow rift with a maximum width of 14 miles in which the Jordan River flows. The Jordan rises partly inside Israel, partly just inside the frontiers of Syria and Lebanon, and, after flowing for 60 miles in Israel, continues for another 97 in West Bank territory. This provided additional grounds for contention between Israel and the Arab states, especially in 1964–1965 when Israel diverted some of the river's waters as part of a national irrigation scheme, and the Arab states

threatened to turn away the waters at the sources located in their countries. During the Six Day War, Israel made certain to bring the river's source in Syria under its control in addition to establishing itself along the entire length of the river.

A few miles from its source, the river used to flow into Lake Huleh, a marshy expanse of shallow water that had been a breeding ground for malaria until drained by Israel and converted into 10,000 acres of agricultural land. Further down its course, the Jordan flows into the biblical Sea of Galilee, later called Lake Tiberias, which covers an area of 122 square miles, all included in Israel, and constitutes the most important water reservoir of the country. For a dozen miles south of the Sea of Galilee the Jordan Valley is blessed with conditions that favor a very rich and variegated agriculture, including rice, cotton, groundnuts, corn, and tropical fruits. From there on, the river flows through barren country dotted by a dozen or so Israeli military-agricultural settlements established after 1967, until it reaches the lush Jericho oasis near the Dead Sea. The latter is a saltwater lake 40 miles long and 10 miles wide, the southern half of which is under Israeli sovereignty for most of its width. The shore of the Dead Sea lies 1,300 feet below sea level and is the lowest spot on earth. Its waters are fabulously rich in salts and minerals which are exploited on a large scale by Israel.

(3) To the west, the hills of Galilee fall away to a coastal plain which stretches from a point south of the Lebanese border all the way through the Gaza strip. From its starting point to Haifa, the plain assumes the shape of a crescent forming the Acre-Haifa Bay with the mountain reaching down to the sea at the crescent's tips. Not far from the Lebanese border is the town of Nahariya with 25,000 inhabitants, having grown fifteenfold since the establishment of Israel. Farther south is the ancient town of Acre, the Hellenistic Ptolemais of St. Paul, the principal harbor and stronghold of the Crusaders, today a mixed Arab-Jewish town of some 35,000 people. Still farther south is the city of Haifa, climbing up the slopes of Mount Carmel, including a modern harbor which constitutes Israel's main gateway to the world. At the end of the Mandate, Haifa had a population of 120,000, of whom two-thirds were Jews and the rest Arabs. During the fighting that preceded the 1948 war, the Arab population fled and has since been replaced by more than three times as many Jews, bringing the total population to about 230,000. The area from Nahariya to Haifa is a major industrial center going back to Mandatory days. Clustered together are foundries, flour mills, textile mills, shipyards, power stations, large oil refineries, cement works, railway repair shops, automotive plants, and an entire steel complex, the "steel town." Through the northern outskirts of Haifa runs the small perennial river of Kishon, once marshy but now cleared and its mouth enlarged to take in large ships.

Going south from Haifa, the coastal strip opens into the fertile Plain of Sharon which broadens into a wide but increasingly sandy expanse some twenty miles south of Tel Aviv until it eventually becomes loose sand dunes and merges into the Sinai Desert. The coastal plain is the heart of Israel. It is the center of Israel's citriculture which provides the country with one of its most important exports. It is the site of most of the country's industry. There two-thirds of Israel's population and most of its cities and towns are concentrated. About halfway between Haifa and the Gaza Strip border rises the city of Tel Aviv, the economic center of Israel and its largest urban concentration. Started in 1909 as a garden suburb of neighboring Arab Jaffa, Tel Aviv has since grown into a city of more than 400,000 which has swallowed its mother town. Together with the townships of Bat Yam, Holon, Ramat Gan, Petach Tikva, Herzliya, and others that merge with it physically, the Tel Aviv area forms an urban conglomeration of about a million people, which, for various reasons, suffers much more than its due share of traffic congestion, air pollution, neighborhood deterioration, and other urban blights. A twelve-mile-long perennial river, the Yarkon, cuts across "greater Tel Aviv"; half this stream's waters are carried away by pipeline to the south for some seventy miles. Midway between Tel Aviv and the Gaza Strip lies the ancient Philistine city of Ashdod, where an economically and strategically vital second deep-water harbor was built and a city of about 50,000 developed in the course of the last decade. To the east of it is the Lachish region, one of Israel's show pieces of land reclamation and planned settlement.

(4) To the south, the hills of Galilee look down upon Emek Yizreel—the Valley of Jezreel—or, as the Israelis call it, *the* Emek. This is a valley descending southeastward from the Mediterranean to reach the Jordan Valley. At its western end by the Acre-Haifa Bay, the vale is fifteen to twenty miles wide, but it narrows inland to only a mile or two before opening up once again where it joins the Jordan Valley. For millennia the Emek has been a corridor of major importance linking the Mediterranean coast and Egypt with the interior of southwest Asia and has served as a passageway for ethnic, cultural, and military invasions. In the centuries prior to World War I, this lowland of very fertile soil, adequate rainfall, and abundant water springs had become converted by a chain reaction of nomad raids, desertion of the settled population, and neglect into a largely uncultivated malarial area. In the 1920s, the Jews bought up most of the valley, drained the swamps by relatively primitive methods that cost the lives and health of many, and transformed it in the course of time into a vast granary and garden. Looking down from one of the many surrounding hills at the Emek with its dozens of neat settlements tucked in the midst of woods, the geometric designs of its meticulously cultivated, multicolored fields and its resplendent fish ponds, one beholds the spirit of the Jewish endeavor in Palestine at its inspiring best.

(5) South of the Emek, the central mountain chain resumes its course in the form of an upland plateau 3,000 feet high extending for nearly one hundred miles to a point south of Hebron where the hills come down to meet

the Negev. This region was the heartland of the ancient kingdoms of Judah and Israel, with Jerusalem and Shomron as their respective capitals; the coastal plain was settled for the most part by non-Jews. In modern times the situation has been reversed, with this area remaining almost exclusively Arab while the Jews concentrated on the coast and in the plains. Consequently, in the 1948 war the plateau was taken over by the Transjordanian army except for the new city of Jerusalem and a corridor from it running east and west, fifteen miles long and ten to fifteen miles wide, which pierces through the Judean hills to connect the city with the coastal plain. In the 1967 war Israel expelled the Arab Legion from this area as well as from the Jordan rift to the east of it, which, together, constitute the West Bank.

In the north the plateau soil has been eroded into valleys, many of which are fertile; in the south rainfall is reduced, streams are less frequent, and the hills are more bare. The region as a whole was fairly thickly inhabited even before it received several hundred thousand Arab refugees from the 1948 war; nevertheless, it produced enough agricultural surplus for export to the East Bank and to neighboring Arab countries. A chain of towns runs along the spine of the plateau, including Nablus, the biblical Shekhem, with a population of 50,000 Arabs, and Ramalla, with 25,000 inhabitants, in the northern part; and in the southern part Bethlehem, the site of Christ's birth, with a population of about 35,000, and Hebron, the burial place of Abraham, Isaac, and Jacob according to the Bible and the first capital of King David, with a population of some 40,000. For many centuries Hebron had a small community of pious Jews who cherished living in that holy city. During the riots of 1929, the community suffered a brutal pogrom at the hands of the Arab populace which caused it to flee the town. Some three decades later, after the 1967 war, religious Jews returned to Hebron in defiance of the government of Israel to establish a new urban settlement bearing the town's biblical name of Kiryat Arbaa, which comprises some 2,000 souls by now.

In the center of the central plateau there is, of course, Jerusalem. The 1948 war had left the city divided into two rigidly isolated parts. The old walled city together with the northeastern suburbs became part of Jordan, while the new city became the capital of Israel. Until 1967, Jewish Jerusalem was a curious city: it was the center of government and the seat of many of the country's most important cultural and religious institutions—the Hebrew University, the National Museum, the Chief Rabbinate, tens of religious colleges, and so on; but it was a city that led nowhere. The world literally ended at some mined ravine or ugly cement wall accross a street for all but a few privileged diplomats and for pilgrims who could cross over to and from the Arab part of the city on stated occasions. This is why Jerusalem remained economically unimportant despite all the government's efforts to stimulate its development. In 1967 the Israelis conquered the old city in the fiercest and most costly battle of the Six Day War, and "unified" it with the new city. Since then, united Jerusalem has become a different city—a communication center, a road junction, a diverse, open, bustling, sprawling city. The multitude of holy places for Christians, Muslims, and Jews on either side of the former dividing line—now freely accessible to all—attract masses of tourists from within the country as well as from abroad, including Arabs from beyond the Jordan. Buildings are rising like mushrooms everywhere, and plans are afoot to develop a center for science-based industries. The growth of the population gives a partial reflection of all this: from 170,000 Jews and 60,000 Arabs in June 1967, it grew to a total of some 340,000 eight years later.

(6) At the southern end of the central plateau lies the Negev. This area, comprising more than half the territory of Israel, is shaped and acts like a wedge driven into the surrounding Arab expanses. Geographically, it is divided in two by a north-south range of hills which is a continuation of the central plateau, and in an east-west direction it is crossed by an imaginary line running somewhat south of Beersheba that delineates the progress of the Israeli agricultural settlement frontier. The northern part of the Negev was populous until late Byzantine times, but in the centuries that followed it turned into a desert after the nomads drove off the cultivators. Since the establishment of Israel, water has been brought to the area from the north and this, together with science, hard work, and a lot of money, has managed to bring the countryside to life once again. The center and symbol of this area as of the entire Negev is Beersheba, a sleepy market townlet of 2,000 people in 1948, now grown into a bustling, booming town of 95,000 well endowed with industry, hospitals, a university, an Institute for Arid Zone Research, and all the urban amenities. The southern part of the Negev is mostly an extension of the Sinai Desert. Agricultural settlements are sparse and experimental, but several urban centers based on mining and industry have been developed. One of these is Dimona, a lively town of about 25,000 people twenty miles southeast of Beersheba which serves as residence for scientists and technicians from the nearby nuclear reactor, workers and employees of the multimillion dollar potash and chemical works at Sodom, on the Dead Sea, and also has its own textile industry. Another is the beautiful town of Arad, established in 1961 on a hill 2,000 feet above sea level in the vicinity of newly discovered natural gas fields. A less successful center is Mitzpeh Ramon, halfway between Beersheba and Eilat, planned to be based on the exploitation of nearby stone and ceramic clay quarries. The Timna copper mines, reputedly exploited in the days of Solomon three thousand years ago, are a few miles before Eilat itself, lying at the southernmost tip of the Negev touching the Gulf of Aqaba. The function of this growing town of 16,000 as a gateway to the East makes it a vital spot in the country. Eilat has an operating harbor which serves as a base for a regular freight line to Africa and the Far East, and is the starting point of a 16-inch oil pipeline leading to the refineries in Haifa and a 42-inch pipeline leading to Ashdod, built since 1967.

The Occupied Territories

The geography of the West Bank and the Gaza Strip has been discussed together with Israel's since all three areas constitute a single geographic continuum. The Sinai Peninsula, on the other hand, is quite different and separate, as are the Golan Heights to a lesser extent.

The Golan Heights are part of a larger geographic unit that was known in antiquity as Bashan and in modern times as Hauran. That unit is a trough cutting through wide expanses of lava which erupted from ancient volcanos in connection with the formation of the Jordan rift. Along the trough runs the ancient King's Highway, the medieval Pilgrims' Route, and the modern road from Damascus to Dar'a and Amman. The Hidjaz railway too passed there before Lawrence and his bands chopped it up. The Golan Heights rise gently to the west of this trough but descend steeply toward the Huleh Valley and the Sea of Galilee in scarps with elevations of about 2,000 feet. They also slope from the north, where they abut the majestic Mount Hermon and reach a height of 3,000 feet, to the south and east, where they come down to about 1,000 feet above sea level. That geographic area has a north-to-south length of about forty miles and a width of about ten miles. Israel occupies most of it.

The Golan Heights are mostly strewn with basaltic boulders, but a few areas are covered with fertile soil formed of volcanic dust. In these areas there was before 1967 a considerable number of villages inhabited by Circassian Muslim refugees from the Caucasus, who were settled there by the Turkish authorities in the nineteenth century. The town of Kuneitra, lying on an important road junction, was the most important urban center. In the course of the Six Day War, the entire population of the Golan Heights—some 150,000—fled in the wake of the retreating Syrian army, except for 5,000 Druzes (members of a heretical Muslim sect) who lived in the villages on the slopes of Mount Hermon. Between 1967 and 1973, the Israelis established sixteen settlements in the area, which were evacuated in the course of the 1973 war and repopulated after the Syrian forces were repulsed.

The Sinai Peninsula is a land bridge between Asia and Africa with a surface area of 23,000 square miles. It consists of two different regions, the triangular peninsula and the continental bridge. Neither part receives sufficient rain for agriculture, and the southern portion is extremely arid.

The peninsular part is bounded by the Gulf of Suez on the west and the Gulf of Aqaba on the east. Its core is a granitic massif which reaches its peak in Jebel Musa (Moses' Mountain, 7,496 feet), thought by some to be the biblical Mount Sinai. At the foot of the mountain there is one of the earliest Christian monasteries, called after St. Catherine, and near it there is the oasis of Firan, the only one in the region. The massif is bounded on the north by a succession of plateaus over 5,300 feet high which slope toward the center of Sinai. All these mountainous parts form a maze of cliffs and scarps dissected by canyons and deep valleys. They are completely roadless, impassable, and uninhabited except for the monks of the monastery and the few inhabitants of the Firan oasis.

The mountains reach the east coast of the peninsula along its total length leaving no coastal plain and barely room for a coastal road in some parts. Only near the southern extremity does the coast widen to form the cove of Sharm el Sheikh, opposite the island of Tiran. From here the Egyptians blockaded the entrance to the Gulf of Aqaba leading to Eilat before 1956, and (after Israel had secured passage by force in the 1956 war) again in May 1967, leading to the Six Day War. Since the capture of Sharm el Sheikh Israel has built a road linking it to Eilat and developed a powerful military base in its vicinity. Continued control of this area has been the principal bone of contention between Israel and Egypt at least since February 1971, when the latter agreed in principle to conclude a peace agreement with Israel. The west coast consists of a wider plain which carries the road from Suez to Sharm el Sheikh. Here lies the small town of el Tur, which was an important medieval port and has served since the nineteenth century as a quarantine station for Muslim pilgrims returning from Mecca. Farther north there are the important oil fields of Abu Rodeis, which supplied half of Egypt's needs before 1967. Israel exploited and developed these fields to supply half its needs, until returning them to Egypt by viture of the second Sinai Agreement, concluded in September 1975.

The continental bridge part is mainly a low plateau bounded by the Mediterranean on the north and the foot of the Tih Plateau on the south. The low northern margin is covered by a belt of sand dunes which attains the width of thirty miles in some places. The center is crossed by two rows of folded limestone ridges which form a direct continuation of the mountains of the Negev. Along the gaps between the ridges and along the coast run historic routes that linked Asia and Africa throughout the centuries and formed the main lines of advance during the wars of the twentieth century. The coast is separated from the Mediterranean by the Lagoon of Bardawil, which runs from Port Said to the vicinity of el Arish and prevents any use of the coast for harbors.

The Sinai Peninsula is thought to contain important mineral resources. However, except for oil and manganese, these have not been adequately explored, let alone exploited. The population of the entire peninsula in 1967 amounted to about 50,000, half of them in el Arish and its vicinity, a few thousand in settlements along the east bank of the Suez Canal, in the oil fields, and the manganese mines, and the remainder Bedouin nomads. Because Sinai is essentially a vast desert, its political demarcation lines were left vague during the centuries when it was part of the Ottoman Empire. Early in the twentieth century these lines were the subject of a dispute between the Ottoman government and the British, acting on behalf of the Egyptian government, which was terminated in 1906 in an agreement that set the boundary along a line from Rafah to the Gulf of Aqaba, the same line that became the boundary between Egypt and the Palestine Mandate and the armistice line between Egypt and Israel except at the Gaza Strip. It is interesting to point out that in the course of the dispute the Egyptian nationalists supported the claims of the Ottoman government against their own, which would have set the boundary at a line running south just east of el Arish.

The Transportation Network

Israel inherited from Mandatory days a good network of roads which was then and still is today the most important means for the transportation of passengers and freight. In the years of its independent existence, the new state has expanded that network very considerably to meet the requirements of defense, the immense growth of the population and its very substantial redistribution, and the needs of economic development and of bringing new areas into use. In terms of coverage, Israel's highway system is quite good today, comprising some 2,800 miles of metaled road that reaches almost every corner of the land actually inhabited or planned for development. In terms of quality, however, it leaves much to be desired, especially in the thickly inhabited coastal plain and the corridor linking it to Jerusalem. In recent years an effort has been made to widen and improve the quality of existing arteries, but this has failed to keep pace with the almost incredible increase in the number of vehicles—this has doubled every six years on the average over the last twenty-four years. The congestion of the roads coupled with suicidal driving habits has placed Israel among the countries with the highest traffic accident rate in the world. In addition to the roads, practically all of the railway system of Mandatory days remains in the area belonging to Israel; but that system was not very extensive and its chief importance as an international link in the Paris-Cairo system is nullified by the hostility between Israel and its neighbors. The principal railway line, laid by the British army in 1918, runs from Sinai northward to Haifa and the Lebanese frontier along "the way of the sea." An important extension links this line to Beersheba and Dimona, and from there the line might be extended to Eilat. Another line, built by the French in Ottoman days, goes from Jaffa to Jerusalem through Lod. The tracks of this line constituted the agreed boundary between Israel and Jordan at several points in the Tel Aviv–Jerusalem corridor until 1967. Finally, a third line—a branch of the Hidjaz railway—runs through the Valley of Jezreel to Damascus. Under Israel, the railway has been moderately extended, relaid in several places, and reequipped with modern rolling stock and diesel engines to allow faster traffic. The total length of track currently in operation is about 470 miles.

Israel's connections with the outside world were exclusively by sea and air until 1967, when a relatively modest route across the Jordan River bridges began to develop. To insure its international link in emergencies, Israel developed a substantial, variegated, modern merchant fleet of about 120 ships with a deadweight of about 3.5 million tons. Part of that fleet normally operates exclusively between foreign ports; the rest touch at the ports of Haifa, built under the Mandate, and Ashdod and Eilat, built since the establishment of the state. Israel also developed a large, highly successful airline which has carried more than 75 percent of the nearly 2 million passengers that flew into or out of the country every year in recent years. Israel's only international airport, at Lod, has never caught up with the pace of growth of the air traffic despite its continuous expansion.

Climate

Israel has a typical Mediterranean climate modified considerably by varying altitude. There is a cycle of hot, dry summers when the temperature reaches ninety to a hundred degrees Fahrenheit, and short, mild, rainy winters. But while Jerusalem and Judea may have several inches of snow in winter and Galilee several feet, the lowlands rarely see any, and Tiberias, by the lake of that name, and the Negev never do. The valleys, especially the Emek and adjacent parts of the upper Jordan, which lie below sea level, can become extremely hot (over a hundred degrees) and humid. Rainfall, too, fluctuates a great deal from one part of Israel to another. Galilee receives an average of forty-two inches annually and parts of it even more; Jerusalem gets about twenty-six inches, the Gaza plain rarely gets more than ten inches, while Eilat gets less than one.

Natural Resources

Israel is relatively poor in natural resources, but the little there is has been or is being intensively exploited. Of its known mineral resources, the most important are potash, bromine, magnesium, salt, and other minerals which can be drawn from the unlimited reserves of the Dead Sea. Actual production was about a million tons of potash in 1973, representing a sixfold increase since 1960. Mining of phosphates began at Oron in the Negev in 1951, and important new deposits have been discovered since. Today's production amounts to close to 800,000 tons of ore annually with 31 percent content. At Timna, near Eilat, geological surveys found proven deposits of 50 million tons of low-grade cooper ore (1.43 percent content). A mill was completed in 1958 to process these ores and reached an annual level of production of 11,000 tons of copper ten years later, but then declined and was closed down in 1975. Oil was discovered in the south in small quantities in 1955; production reached a high point of 200,000 tons of crude per year in 1965, meeting about 8 percent of the country's oil consumption at the time. Since then it has declined to less than one-third as much. In 1959, 1961, and 1962, gas fields were discovered in the Dead Sea area, two of which have an estimated annual capacity of 20 million cubic feet of gas, equivalent to 200,000 tons of crude oil. Other mineral deposits currently exploited on a significant scale include gypsum, ball clay, marble, and glass sand. Israel has no known usable deposits of iron or coal and has no important source of hydroelectric power. It relies for energy on electricity generated from steam produced mostly by imported fuel.

Agricultural Land

Land for agriculture is the most important natural resource of Israel, and the use made of it is still the greatest feat of its people despite growing diversification of the economy and industrialization. Men and women of diverse nationalities and backgrounds have disagreed violently about the ultimate rights and wrongs of the Jewish-Arab conflict over Palestine; but there are few who fail to be impressed by the great work of reconstruction and conservation that the Jews have accomplished in the land. For the country that they "invaded" or to which they "returned" had long ago ceased to flow with milk and honey: it was a country whose valleys were largely malarial swamps, whose pastures had been grazed down to the ground and turned into dustbowls, whose hills had been denuded of forests and washed off to bedrock, whose terraces were mostly in ruin, and whose hundreds of ancient prosperous villages had become mounds of dirt or heaps of weather-beaten stones. To this land the Jews brought organization, skill, capital, science, and, above all, infinite devotion—the early settlers had literally developed a cult of the soil, nature, and work. They drained its swamps, checked spreading sand dunes, planted tens of millions of trees, improved seeds and farming methods, and made the land yield a farm produce that supplies nowadays all but the meat and grain needs of the population on a Western European level and leaves large quantities for export.

Potentially usable agricultural land is plentiful in Israel, but water resources are relatively scarce. Surveys of land-use potential carried out by the Israeli government estimate that of the state's total area of 20.7 million dunams (a dunam equals approximately one-quarter acre), more than 4 million dunams are potentially available for dry farming, and more than 5.5 million dunams are potentially available for farming under irrigation. Of the potential dry farming area, nearly two-thirds is actually cultivated; while of the area available for farming under irrigation, less than one-third is actually worked. To realize even that degree of irrigated agriculture in addition to meeting industrial and personal needs, Israel has had to tap nearly the totality of its water resources at the cost of enormous investments.

Israel's water resources include the Jordan River and its tributaries (37 percent of total yield), groundwater formations in the north of the country

(38.5 percent), the Yarkon River (14 percent), intermittent storm runoff in dry creeks (5.5 percent), and reclaimed wastewater from major cities (5 percent). Together, these sources yield an annual average of 1,400 million cubic meters. Virtually all these waters are fed into a fully interconnected water supply system, the backbone of which is formed by the National Water Carrier. This is a $300 million project completed in 1964 that essentially draws water from the Sea of Galilee, lifts it up more than 1,100 feet, joins to it waters from other sources in the north and the coastal plain, and pumps it all ninety miles southward through a system of open concrete canals, reservoirs, 108-inch prestressed concrete pipeline, and branches of smaller diameter that end up in the northern Negev. As of now, utilization of these resources is approaching 100 percent. Water for further growth is being sought at present through efforts to devise more effective methods of using existing waters, experiments in modifying natural factors limiting water supply, such as cloud seeding and improvement in soil and vegetative cover to increase water conservation, and desalination of brackish water, a field in which Israel has been for some time one of the pioneering countries of the world.

Land Tenure System

Israel's mineral resources are the property of the state and the most important known ones are exploited by companies owned wholly or partly by the state. This is fairly common practice in many parts of the world. But what is unusual is that the land itself, especially agricultural land, is overwhelmingly the property of the state—not merely in the nominal sense in which land in many Latin American countries, for instance, is said to belong to the state, but in a very real sense that effectively determines its use.

Of the total area of Israel, 92 percent belongs to the National Land Authority, which was set up in 1959 to administer all the lands formerly under the authority of the Jewish National Fund and the state; only the remaining 8 percent is privately owned, half by Jews and half by Arabs. If account is taken only of the farmed and built-up area, then the proportion of privately owned land increases to 20 percent; but this means that virtually all the land reserves of the country are in the hands of the National Land Authority.

The idea of public ownership of the national land goes back more than seventy years to the establishment of the Jewish National Fund by the World Zionist Congress to purchase Palestine land piecemeal for settlement. The principle prescribed for the disposal of lands acquired by the fund was the biblical injunction that "the land shall not be sold in perpetuity." This principle was not, however, adopted for the reason given in the rest of the injunction, namely that the land and its fullness belongs to God, but because it was thought to be suitable for the practical purposes of the Zionist Organization.

These purposes were essentially two: to ensure that colonists settled on land acquired through public funds used the land for making a living, not for speculation, and to prevent as far as possible the reversion of land acquired by Jews to non-Jewish ownership. Consequently, the fund gave out land in 49-year leases, which would be invalidated if the lessee failed to work his land for no sufficient reason or if he worked it with the help of hired labor. With the establishment of the state of Israel and its assumption of control over most of the land of the country as the custodian of refugee property and heir to the Mandatory government, the practical purposes that had moved the National Fund either became irrelevant or could be achieved by other means; but by that time social considerations reinforced the already established tradition and led to the retention of the fund's basic principles.

There are other conditions for leasing national land that also had their origins in practical grounds but were later reinforced by considerations of social policy. In the days when the Jews constituted a minority of the population in Palestine, living in a hostile environment, it was largely impractical to lease out fund lands to individual private farmsteads, if only for security reasons. The practice therefore developed of awarding land leases mainly to small groups, organized in some form of cooperative or collective association. Since the establishment of the state, security conditions have changed considerably, at least in regard to many parts of the country; nevertheless, the practice of leasing land only to groups has continued with few exceptions, because cooperation and association have come to be viewed as desirable for social, economic, and ideological reasons. Thus, though there is no rule prohibiting it, a potential private farmer cannot in practice set himself up on leased national land; he has to join with other aspiring farmers and form a cooperative settlement, which must undertake to employ no hired hands. The alternative for him is to lease or buy the land he needs from the very limited private sector at costs that are likely to affect severely the competitiveness of his products.

Within the frame of the formal and informal conditions of land rental mentioned above, publicly owned agricultural land is almost free for Jews. The rents charged for such land average about 0.5 percent of the gross value of the agricultural product, and even this trivial rent is not exacted regularly. In contrast, a private Arab farmer, for instance, usually has to pay his landlord about one-third of his crop or its equivalent in money as rent.

The reasons for this extraordinary policy go back, once again, to the nature of the Zionist endeavor in Palestine. The Zionist movement wanted to create a class of Jewish land settlers out of people who had had almost no agricultural tradition for centuries. It would have been difficult enough for inexperienced, often frail, urbanized young Jews to transform themselves into farmers in the best of circumstances. In the period before the establishment of the state this difficulty was compounded by the fact that the new farmers had to settle on land that had been neglected for ages, in areas often infested with malaria and almost always surrounded by hostile neighbors. The elimination of rent made the task somewhat easier economically and constituted a sort of subsidy given to the products of Jewish farmers to enable them to compete with those of the Arabs, who were accustomed to a very low standard of living. By the time the state came into being the material conditions had eased a great deal, but the people who came to the country in the massive waves of immigration were far less ready than earlier settlers to accept any hardships. The rent-free land system was therefore retained as an inducement to attract people to agriculture.

In addition to these reasons, the free rent system served another purpose. The leaders of the Yishuv and the state of Israel wanted not only to create a class of agricultural settlers, but also to locate some settlements in areas that were important from a political or strategic point of view, although they may not have been the best in agricultural terms. The elimination of rent made it easier for the authorities to direct aspiring settlers to the desired areas. Of course, other factors had a bearing on the settlers' choice, such as access to water and proximity to markets; but here too the authorities set up various compensatory schemes such as equalizing the cost of water all over the country.

Economists and free-enterprise–minded Americans may find many features of this system objectionable. For Israel, however, deficiencies in the details notwithstanding, the system as a whole has so far proved of enormous benefit. Thanks to it, Israel is, for instance, free from the agrarian problems that beset many developing societies and have been at the root of many social upheavals elsewhere. It has no masses of land-hungry peasants confronting a few big landowners; no oligarchy deriving its power from the ownership of land; no vast ecclesiastical estates; no class of absentee landowners interested only in collecting rents and leaving the work entirely to tenant farmers who have neither the means nor the incentive to care for the soil. And it has experienced a soaring of land values as a result of speculation only in urban areas, where private ownership has prevailed. How viable the system will prove to be cannot, of course, be foretold; but the increasing resort to hired labor, which the authorities pretend to ignore, should serve as an illustration of how it might gradually become subverted altogether over the years.

7

The People

Israel, we have already observed, is unique among the multitude of new states in that not only its sovereignty but also its people are new. The people is new in the elementary sense that the great bulk of it did not live in the territory over which it eventually achieved sovereignty until relatively recent times; it was constituted by immigrants and their offspring who came to Palestine from the four corners of the world, absorbed the small native Jewish community, and wittingly or unwittingly displaced most of the native Arab population. A hundred years ago there were only 25,000 Jews in all of Palestine living amid some 500,000 native Arabs. Twenty-eight years ago, when the state of Israel was born, there were 650,000 Jews in addition to a residue of 150,000 Arabs who remained in the territory of the Jewish state. Nowadays, there are nearly 2.9 million Jews and 520,000 Arabs, excluding the population of the territories occupied since 1967 except for East Jerusalem (the old city). The formation of Israel's people in the simple demographic sense is still far from stabilized and may yet undergo far-reaching changes in the coming decade as a result of the final settlement of the status of the occupied territories and their Arab population, and of the opening of the gates of immigration to Jews from the Soviet Union.

Israel's people is also new in the more elusive sense of national identity and character. As was previously indicated, the prestatehood immigrations had congealed by the eve of independence into a highly integrated national community with a very distinct character. However, the influx of immigrants in massive numbers and of largely different types in the poststatehood period loosened many of the bonds of the prestatehood community and precipitated a process of change in the character of the people that is still going on at present. As with the demographic aspect, here too the Six Day War may yet prove to be a watershed.

I shall try to elucidate this difficult subject by analyzing the process by which Israel's people was formed and transformed both demographically and qualitatively in the time until 1967. I shall follow with an examination of the impact of the Six Day War and the 1973 war, and will conclude with an effort to evaluate the prospects of growth of Israel's population in the next ten years and their implications for the general character of its people.

The Formation and Transformation of Israel's People until 1967

Israel's people was formed by a succession of immigration waves over a period of ninety years. The waves are known in Zionist historiography as aliyot, plural of the Hebrew term aliyah, denoting ascent or immigration to the Holy Land. Each aliyah had its own characteristics, made a particular impact on the existing population, and brought its special contribution to the development of Israel's people as a whole. A broad distinction may, however, be drawn between the aliyot that preceded and those that followed statehood. Generally speaking, the prestatehood aliyot were more distinctly defined than the poststatehood ones which, except for the first, were more like a continuous stream than a succession of waves. Moreover the poststatehood immigration was much more diverse and came at a much higher average rate than the prestatehood one. Finally, whereas the later prestatehood aliyot "stuck" readily to the core national community constituted by the earlier ones and merely enriched and enlarged that core, the poststatehood aliyot not only did not stick so well but they precipitated a reaction in the core itself which, together with other related factors, weakened the cohesiveness of the community and gave rise to a serious problem of national integration.

The Prestatehood Aliyot

The First Aliyah began in 1882 and continued until 1903. It brought to Palestine 25,000 Jews, mainly from Tsarist Russia, whose arrival doubled the Jewish population of the country. Nearly half of the previous inhabitants were Sefaradi and Oriental Jews who were thoroughly Turkified or Arabicized except for religion, and the rest were Ashkenazi Jews, mainly old people who had trickled into the country over the years for pious reasons. The initial inhabitants were concentrated in the holy cities of Jerusalem, Hebron, Safed, and Tiberias where they led a thoroughly apolitical, traditional existence and were primarily concerned with religious observance and study. They eked out a living from crafts and petty trade or subsisted on donations made by Jewish communities all over the world. In the 1870s, the first winds of change came to ruffle the settled life of the community. Eliezer Ben Yehuda, a young man obsessed with the idea of reviving the Hebrew language and putting it to daily use, appeared in Jerusalem and began to preach and practice his gospel. In 1878, a group of Hungarian Jews set out from Jerusalem to found an agricultural colony eight miles from Jaffa which they called Petach Tikva (an opening for hope). A few years before, the Alliance Israélite universelle, a French Jewish philanthropic-cultural organization, founded an agricultural school near Jaffa, Mikve Yisrael (the gathering place of Israel). But when the new immigrants arrived, Ben Yehuda was encountering fanatical resistance from the older inhabitants who held that the use of Hebrew for secular purposes was sacrilegious. The Petach Tikva settlement had failed, and the graduates of Mikve Yisrael had nowhere to practice their skills outside the school's own farm.

The newcomers differed from the older inhabitants in almost every respect. Many of them were young and had been exposed to modern education and ideas. They had come to Palestine in the wake of the Russian pogroms of 1881 with the express intent of paving the way for a restoration of Jewish national existence in Palestine. Some of them adopted as their slogan the verse from Isaiah 2:5, "O house of Jacob, come ye and let us go," from the Hebrew initials of which they derived their name of Biluim; but they were not themselves religious. They all meant to pursue their aims by leaving behind them in Europe the customary Jewish occupations and engaging in manual work and tilling the soil. Some of them refounded Petach Tikva while others set out to establish the new colonies of Rishon le-Tzion, Nes Tzionah, Rosh Pinna, Zichron Yaacov—all in areas which were by the standards of those days far removed from the relative security and the "amenities" of the existing towns. The people of the First Aliyah were thus the initiators of Jewish colonization in Palestine fifteen years before the World Zionist Organization had been conceived.

The first settlers did not have an easy time in their adopted country. Their own inexperience, malaria, the long-untended soil, the suspicious Turkish officials, the predatory Arab neighbors, and the sullen hostility of Jews of the old settlement conspired to make their life miserable. The whole experiment would probably have collapsed had not Baron Edmond de Rothschild of Paris come to their assistance after Chovevei Tzion had interceded with him. The baron bought land and built houses for the settlers, advanced money, tools, and stock, subsidized or bought their products, and sent instructors from France to organize them and teach them farm management. But the settlers had to pay for all that by giving up many of their brave ideals and settling down to a comfortable life as docile farmers relying primarily on cheap Arab labor and depending on the munificence of the baron and the goodwill of the bureaucratically minded supervisors he sent. For, although we know now that the baron privately entertained his own visions of Jewish national redemption, he acted outwardly at that stage as though his motives were purely philanthropic, and he was opposed to the assertion of any nationalist, not to mention radical social aspirations on the part of the settlers that might create difficulties with the Turkish authorities and nullify the prospect of Palestine's serving as a place of refuge for persecuted Jews. At any rate, had Jewish colonization continued along the same pattern, the history of Palestine and the fate of hundreds of thousands of Jews and Arabs might have been quite different. Instead of a nation, or at least the makings of one, there would have grown in Palestine a class of Jewish *colons,* who might have led a comfortable existence for a shorter or longer period only to be swept away eventually by the tide of awakening indigenous nationalism. That this did not happen was largely owing to the character and drive of the men of the Second Aliyah.

The Second Aliyah, too, came overwhelmingly from Russia and brought to the country nearly 40,000 Jewish immigrants in the decade between 1904 and 1914. This wave of immigration was prompted by the renewal of large-scale pogroms in Russia in 1903, but the newcomers were moved by much more than the desire and need to escape terror and oppression. The pogroms, renewed tsarist repression, and the dislocation of Jewish life caused by the beginning of the industrial revolution in Russia had set in motion the most massive Jewish migration in history, which carried westward over two and a half million Jews in the years between 1882 and 1914. But the majority of these Jews went to the United States and most of the remainder went to other non-European countries. Only 3 percent went to Palestine, and more than half of these arrived after 1904 and constituted the Second Aliyah. These were people who chose Palestine because, like their predecessors, they aspired to build a National Home there; but they were much more conscious of themselves as part of a nationalist and socialist movement on the rise. They were affiliated with the World Zionist Organization and many were also members of labor and socialist movements, founded almost simultaneously with the Zionist movement, which aspired to transform the Jews as individuals and as a people by revolutionizing their thought, their life, and their occupations, and above all by rooting them in the soil of their ancient homeland. They were for the most part sons and daughters of middle-class families who sought deliberately to become farmers and workers in order to establish the base for a new, "normal," healthier occupational pyramid for the Jewish people while striving to ensure that the new society should be free of injustice and exploitation.

The men and women of the Second Aliyah and those of the next set their stamp indelibly on the development of Jewish Palestine. They endowed the country with its most typical institutions and spirit and decisively shaped its orientation for two generations. To the extent that Israel has had any "aristocracy," it has been definitely composed of members of the Second and Third Aliyot. Until recently, they were to be found in all the leading positions of the country. Thus, for example, two of Israel's first three Presidents have been men of these aliyot as well as its first three Knesset speakers. Of the first five Prime Ministers, two have been men of these aliyot, one the offspring of

Second Aliyah parents, and a fourth, Golda Meir, is a Third Aliyah woman by chronology and by adoption.

The immigrants of the Second Aliyah immediately launched a struggle against the comfortably settled people of the first for the replacement of Arab by Jewish labor on their farms. The struggle was long and bitter because Arab labor was cheaper and better than the inexperienced newly arrived youth, and because the latter considered that on its issue hinged not only their immediate livelihood but the future of their dreams of turning the country into a self-supporting Jewish homeland resting on a Jewish society built from the bottom up. Their eventual victory in this struggle was crucial for the entire Jewish endeavor in Palestine.

People of the Second Aliyah developed unions of rural and urban workers, cooperative enterprises, and mutual aid societies which became the foundation of the Histadrut—the impressive General Federation of Jewish Workers—of which more later. They gave a powerful impetus to the Return to the Soil movement and endowed it with an ideology that made a cult of manual labor, some of which persists today. They founded the kibbutz (collective settlement) movement which gave Palestine-Israel a unique institution and an instrument that rendered inestimable service to the Zionist endeavor and to the survival of Israel before becoming an exceptionally adaptable entrepreneurial unit. They gave a decisive stimulus to the revival of the Hebrew language and ensured its triumph as the national tongue over several rivals.

The Third Aliyah began in 1918 and brought 25,000 Jews, mainly from Russia, in the course of the next five years, after which the exit of Jews from that country was barred. Essentially, this was in most respects a continuation of the Second Aliyah, which had come to an abrupt end with the outbreak of the First World War, except that the new immigrants now came into a country ruled by a new master, Britain, which had committed itself to promoting the Zionist endeavor. The people of the Third Aliyah were predominantly pioneers belonging to the Zionist-socialist movements and shared the ideologies and aspirations of the people of the second. They confirmed the patterns already set by their predecessors and brought some of the enterprises begun by them to full fruition. Thus the kibbutz was transformed from an uncertain experiment to a growing movement and the Histadrut from a project to a reality. In addition, the two aliyot established an autonomous Jewish school system from kindergarten to university where Hebrew was the language of instruction, and laid the foundations for self-governing institutions encompassing all the Jews of Palestine. The Third Aliyah also set up the moshav (a smallholders' cooperative village), which became another major form of agricultural settlement in Palestine and Israel.

The Fourth Aliyah, lasting from 1923 to 1926, brought in 60,000 people, mostly from Poland. This wave was already substantially different from the second and the third. It was composed for the most part of middle-class people who intended to continue their occupation in their new country. They tended to cluster in Tel Aviv, founded fifteen years previously, in Haifa, and in Jerusalem. The aliyah in which they came had in fact been triggered by a series of measures taken by the Polish government that had hurt Jewish business in particular, and it came to an abrupt end when an economic crisis in Poland and the devaluation of the zloty caused an economic crisis in Palestine itself. The relatively large size of that aliyah was attributed at the time to the tightening of the immigration laws in the United States, which deflected remnants of the great East European Jewish migration to Palestine.

As the depression in Palestine gradually faded, immigration resumed at a slowly increasing pace. In 1932, it suddenly spurted to 12,000 and heralded the beginning of the Fifth Aliyah, the biggest wave of immigration in all the period preceding the establishment of Israel. From 1932 until 1939, nearly 225,000 Jews came into Palestine. About one-third came from Eastern Europe and constituted in fact a continuation of the previous flow which had been interrupted between 1927 and 1930. But another third came from Germany and Central Europe as a result of the Nazis' rise to power and brought a new element into the Yishuv. There were very many doctors, lawyers, engineers, journalists, technicians, men with experience in administration, finance, and business organization, scholars, and scientists, some with an international reputation, in addition to a large number of people with substantial capital. The Fifth Aliyah thus gave a powerful impetus to the development of industry, commerce, science, culture, and many other aspects of the Yishuv's life. It also gave the Yishuv a decidedly European character and composition. The old Sefaradi-Oriental core, though reinforced continually by a thin stream of immigration and by a high rate of reproduction, was reduced by 1939 to a mere fifth of the total Jewish population.

Although the Fourth and Fifth Aliyot were impelled by necessity, the immigrants, once in Palestine, became quickly integrated into the Yishuv and strengthened its national drive. For one thing, these aliyot, though predominantly middle-class, still contained many *chalutzim* (pioneers) who had been brought up in their countries of origin on the ideals of the men and women of the Second and Third Aliyot and came to Palestine ready to join them in doing the most difficult work. Moreover, many others among the new immigrants, though not ready to become workers, live in a kibbutz, and drain marshes, were convinced Zionists and fitted quickly into the ethos of the Yishuv. Even those who had not been Zionists abroad were at least familiar with the Jewish national movement and, once in Palestine, considered themselves part of it. Thus, by the time World War II broke out, the very young Yishuv was no formless conglomeration of immigrants and refugees but a well-organized, politically conscious national community, which was able, through voluntary recruitment alone, to contribute 30,000 soldiers to serve with the British forces. The tragedy of Europe's Jewry, news of which became known early in the war, only tightened the community more and permitted it to absorb another 120,000 immigrants by 1948 without any strain.

The Poststatehood Aliyot and the Communal Problem

The establishment of the state brought about a revolution in the size and composition of the aliyot. In the first three and a half years after the proclamation of independence, there was a tidal wave of immigration that brought in 684,000 Jews, more than the entire previously existing Jewish population. From the beginning of 1952 until the first half of 1954, there was a lull owing to economic difficulties, the adoption by the authorities of a temporary policy of selective support for immigration, and the imposition of restriction on Jewish emigration in some East European countries. Fewer than 40,000 immigrants came in during that period, and in 1953 there was a net excess of emigration from Israel over immigration to it. Beginning with 1955 a substantial flow began pouring in again bringing between 20,000 and 70,000 immigrants each year for the next ten years. In 1964 there was once more a sudden dwindling of the flow which persisted for more than three years before picking up again after the Six Day War. Altogether, over 700,000 immigrants came in during the twenty years since the initial massive wave, slightly more than half of them in the first ten years. During the entire period from 1948 to 1973, some 260,000 Jews emigrated from Israel as against the more than one and a half million that immigrated to the country.

The poststatehood immigrants came from more than fifty countries. However, until 1967, 90 percent of them came from six European countries (Rumania, Poland, Bulgaria, Hungary, Czechoslovakia, Yugoslavia), four Asian countries (Iraq, Yemen, Turkey, Iran), and the five North African countries (Morocco, Algeria, Tunisia, Libya, Egypt). Western Europe contributed some 4 percent, and the Soviet Union, the United States, and other American countries contributed 1 percent each.

The sheer size of the poststatehood immigrations would probably have made it impossible for the established community to absorb them in the same way it did the prestatehood aliyot, by a mixture of adaptation of existing institutions and socialization of the newcomers. The fact that these immigrations included masses of Oriental Jews from Africa and Asia, who differed sharply in relevant historical background, culture, education, motivation, and even physical appearance from the European Jews—those already settled in the country as well as new arrivals—definitely ruled out such a prospect and gave rise to a situation in which the existing community was subjected to a very strong disintegrative pressure. Perhaps vis-à-vis the outside world national unity remained unimpaired, but internally, national integration became as much an aim as a reality.

The immigrants from Africa and Asia as well as those from Europe differ considerably according to particular country of origin; but the two groups of communities constitute two recognizable sectors differing from one another in several ways. The most obvious difference relates to the general conditions of the society of origin. European societies varied a great deal from one another, but they were all relatively advanced by comparison with the Oriental societies, which included some that were in the process of emerging into modern life and some that were still pacing the treadmill of tradition.

The immigrants reflected these differences upon their arrival and were conditioned by them as they made their way in Israel. Thus, for example, the Oriental families are much larger than the European. As late as 1967, one out of every six Oriental families had seven or more members, whereas only one in a hundred European families was of that size. More than one in three Oriental families included six or more members, while among the Europeans only one in twenty-five families was of that size. Oriental parents who had completed their families in the country of origin had had more children than parents who had most of theirs in Israel; however, because of the better sanitary conditions of Israel, nearly all the children born in Israel survive whereas a very high proportion of the children born in the original country died young. At the time of immigration, 56 percent of the Oriental females over fourteen were illiterate; as of 1967, 44 percent of the Oriental female population of the same age group was still so. The rates for Oriental males are considerably lower: 26 percent illiterates among the immigrants and 18 percent among the 1967 Oriental male population; but this still contrasted sharply with the 95–99 percent literacy rate for Europeans, males and females, immigrants and overall population.

Poor education and large families have meant relatively low income. The average per capita income in an Oriental family was about 48 percent of the average for a member of a European family in 1960. This represented a rise from lower levels in previous years, but it declined to a low of 44 percent in 1968 during a recession from which the Orientals suffered more than the Europeans. By 1973 the rate was back to 48 percent, but the record suggests that the recovery was due mainly to the restoration of full employment, and thus points out the greater relative vulnerability, as well as relative poverty, of the Orientals.

Poor education, large families, and low income have meant inadequate education for the children and the perpetuation of the cycle. For although kindergarten and primary schools are free and compulsory in Israel, secondary education, which is still the critical dividing line in the correlation between education and income, social outlook, and family size, is neither and is in fact rather expensive. For many years Oriental children constituted 60 percent of the entrants to kindergartens but only 5 percent of the graduates of secondary schools and 2 percent of recipients of university degrees. The Ministry of Education and other public bodies made considerable special efforts to improve the situation and in 1971–72, 50 percent of Oriental children of secondary school age attended secondary school as against 80 percent of European children. However, much larger proportions of the Oriental children were enrolled in vocational postprimary schools and were unable to complete their studies. The difference is also seen in the figures for enrollment in universities. Among people in the 20–29 age group, the proportion of Europeans enrolled was thirteen times higher than that of Orientals in 1964–65. Eight years later, the gap was considerably reduced, but the Europeans still retained a fivefold advantage.

The gap between Orientals and Europeans is, of course, reflected in a very low representation of the former in positions that are usually correlated with a high level education and seniority, such as the senior civil service, the higher ranks of the officer corps, the professional and managerial positions, and so on. But it is also reflected no less strongly in political power positions that depend more on political organization than on formal qualifications. Orientals have held only one or two Cabinet posts out of 16–20 and not more than 16 out of 120 Knesset seats since 1949. In local government, where the dimensions of political organization are more manageable, the Orientals have been able to score substantial gains over the years. In 1950 only 13 percent of the municipal and local councilmen and less than 1 percent of the mayors and council chairmen were Orientals; by 1973 the percentages were 44 percent and 30 percent respectively. Significantly, however, the Orientals continued to be grossly underrepresented in the very large municipalities, such as Tel Aviv and Haifa.

A particularly significant manifestation of the gap between the two communities is seen in a much greater frequency among the Orientals of slum-dwelling and crowded housing, and in much higher rates of criminality, juvenile delinquency, and other kinds of antisocial behavior. Because these differences are the most visible on a day-to-day basis, they are perhaps particularly serious in their consequences. They tend to provide underpinnings for prejudice insofar as this needs any; and they "justify" an "empathy gap" that has its deeper roots in the very different historical experience of the Jewish Problem that the two groups of communities had had before coming to Israel.

The Europeans had experienced the Jewish Problem in several immediate and practical ways. Various segments of them had sensed it as an intellectual conflict between modern thought and norms and the traditional Jewish faith and practice, or as an internal conflict between the desire to become equal partners in the surrounding society and culture and the fear of losing their Jewish identity, or as an external contradiction between the will to assimilate and their rejection by non-Jewish society, before they finally experienced it as active persecution culminating in extermination camps. The Orientals, on the other hand, had faced the Jewish Problem mainly as a religious-metaphysical question for which the ideas of Galuth and Geullah provided a satisfactory answer. They had suffered none of the crises of their European brethren, and had lived within a surrounding society that was itself organized for the most part on a regional and communal basis. Even where the host society's traditional structure had begun to crumble under the impact of nationalism and modernization, the bulk of the Jews had not yet been called upon to make the kind of drastic adjustments to that society that gave rise to the sort of dilemmas European Jews faced.

This different historical experience of the Jewish Problem translated into a different conception of Israel. The Orientals revere the country as the Holy Land; they understand their own immigration as the traditional "Ingathering of the Exiles"; and they are good patriots; but they do not see the Jewish state as a means of solving individual or collective problems of identity or religious-intellectual conflicts. For them, the act of coming to Israel is the realization of their yearning for Zion and the completion of their aspiration as members of the Jewish collectivity, and their primary commitment from the moment of their arrival was therefore to their families and themselves except for the obligation of national defense. The dreams of the founders of Zionism and the builders of the Yishuv envisaging the Jewish state as a means or an opportunity for creating a model socialist society or a perfect liberal democracy, for allowing the "Jewish ethical genius" to flourish and be a light to humanity, or for raising a New Jew free from all the horrible and mean characteristics he allegedly acquired in the Diaspora—these and many other ideas which had their roots in the conditions and predicaments of the Jews in various countries of Europe and had become the moving forces of their endeavor in Palestine-Israel, are beyond the ken of most Oriental Jews. So are most of the seemingly homegrown ideas articulated by the native Israeli offspring of European parents, since these are very largely reactions against the attitudes and visions of the parents. A good illustration of this point is provided by a book by Amos Elon entitled *The Israelis: Founders and Sons*, which achieved a substantial circulation in the United States. Elon, himself a native Israeli of European parentage, tried to depict the mind of present-day Israelis in terms of the dialectic between generations, and he did so with a display of learning, insight, and sensitivity that deservedly earned him high praise from critics in Israel and abroad. However, the Oriental Jews, fully one-half of the Israelis, occupied no place whatsoever in his analysis. The omission may be partly explained by the fact that the Oriental Jews were not significantly present among "the founders"; but their exclusion from the discussion of the intellectual makings and emotive promptings of "the sons" clearly reflects the psychic gap between Orientals and Europeans, intuitively perceived by the author and obviously affecting his own group.

American readers may be tempted at this point to make analogies between Israel's communal problem and the race or color problem in the United States. Such analogies would be more instructive in the contrasts than in the similarities they would underscore. For, notwithstanding the varieties of historical experience, the Jews of East and West have had a very strong sense of unity and solidarity founded on a common religion going back over thousands of years, which is not true of the ethnic groups, let alone the races, that went into the making of the American people. Moreover, that sense of unity and solidarity has been a central premise of the movement of Jewish national revival and is an undisputed principle of the state and the society that it created. More importantly, the empathy gap and even the expressions of antipathy between Orientals and Europeans, to which the divergences discussed above have given rise, have focused almost without exception on ethno-cultural motifs, which are acquired and malleable in principle, rather than on race or color, which are ostensibly inherited and fixed for generations. An Oriental Jew who "makes it," for example, can ipso facto become a fully accepted, even a "noble" Israeli; a black in America, no matter what his achievement, would have much greater difficulty becoming fully accepted. This is why intermarriage between members of different communities in Israel has been getting increasingly frequent. The endogamy index in Israel in 1972 was 0.65, where an index of 1 means marrying strictly within one's community in the narrow sense. This is still very high, of course, but it is much lower than among races in the United States and it is considerably lower than the endogamy index of 0.80 that obtained in Israel in 1960.

Many writers have referred to the communal problem in Israel in terms of Disraeli's metaphor of two nations. That might be a more appropriate image than one derived from relations between races in the United States, but it is somewhat overdramatic and tends to convey a static picture which does violence to the changing reality. It will have been noticed that some of the very indices used above to illustrate the gap between Orientals and Europeans have been changing. Moreover, there is in Israel a very substantial common ground on which the two groups of communities stand despite their divergences: for example, the language of Israel. A visitor to the country in the early 1950s may have seen Hebrew written on all signs and official forms, but he would have heard a Babel of tongues, among which Hebrew would have been distinguished more by the assertiveness of its speakers than by its spread. Ten or fifteen years later, Hebrew was so universally spoken and used that a visitor coming to the country for the first time then may not even have realized that three out of every four adults he saw had had a different mother tongue, and that most of them had learned and adopted Hebrew in the years since 1948. Considering that the last time that language was the daily tongue of the Jewish people was thousands of years before, its complete and rapid triumph bespeaks a truly extraordinary degree of national will in which all Israelis shared. The difference in intonation that does exist between Orientals and Europeans is of small significance in this context and anyway tends to disappear in a generation without need for any Drs. Higgins.

Another manifestation of national unity is the consensus encountered among Israelis of all origins regarding certain basic issues of Israeli existence. The hypothetical visitor of the 1960s would have noticed, for example, that Israelis took a passionate interest in even minute affairs of their country and were prone to argue violently about them all; however, on a number of subjects, he would have encountered an unbelievable, almost complete, and most assertive unanimity of views. Such unanimity covered the rights and wrongs of the Palestine conflict and the ins and outs of Israel's dispute with its neighbors, a belief in the universal unity of the Jewish people and in a notion of mutual obligation between Jews everywhere and Israel, the imperative of immigration and the sanctity of the open gate principle, identification with the achievements of the collectivity and a sense that the collectivity has an almost unlimited responsibility for the welfare of its members, and the primacy of national defense and support for all sacrifices required in that connection. Such an agreement on fundamentals, and such strong national will as manifested in the successful revival of an almost forgotten language are not common among nations of the world. They suggest that Jewish history and the circumstances of the Jewish state made the people of Israel of the mid-1960s at one and the same time a more pointed and less integrated nation than most established, older nations.

The Wars of 1967 and 1973 and the People of Israel

The 1967 war affected the character, size and composition, and future prospects of the people of Israel in many obvious ways. The 1973 war operated sometimes to reinforce the effects of the 1967 war and sometimes to check them; in all instances, however, the impact was of great significance.

The 1967 Six Day War was a crucial, fateful experience in which all Israelis partook equally, which provided a powerful and enduring sense that they all constituted one nation and shared in one common enterprise and destiny beyond their communal differences. The 1973 Yom Kippur War gave further expression and reinforcement to that sense and contributed to its prevailing over the differences in outlook going back to diverse historical-psychological experiences.

The Six Day War also triggered a new wave of immigration, which was even more notable for its composition than for its size. For the first time in the history of the people of Israel, that wave comprised large numbers and percentages of Jews from the Soviet Union and the United States. The Yom Kippur War checked that development or slowed it down six years after it had begun. Whether it did so "for good" or only temporarily remains to be seen.

Finally, the Six Day War brought under Israeli control nearly a million Palestinian Arabs in the West Bank and Gaza, apart from the nearly half million Israeli Arabs in the prewar boundaries. The future of these Arabs became an issue along with that of the territories where they live; and whatever that future, it was bound to have a greater or lesser effect on the future character and composition of Israel's people. However, even apart from any resolution of the territorial issue, the Arabs of the occupied territories have already affected both the social-occupational patterns of Israel's Jews and the political orientation of Israel's Arabs. The 1973 war and its immediate aftermath mitigated or intensified these problems but did not substantively alter them.

The Wars and the Communal Problem

The Six Day War and the crisis that preceded it gave the most dramatic demonstration of the capacity of Israel's people to act as one nation despite all communal divergences. The Arab states and their Soviet ally had counted on these differences to weaken Israel's resolve and undermine the effectiveness of its military reserve system, which depended entirely on willing cooperation. Israel's government did show a certain weakness of resolve during the crisis; but this had nothing to do with any divisions among the people, which proved to be more united and more eager to act than its leaders and indeed in large measure forced their hand and compelled them to close ranks. Moreover, the people responded to the mobilization orders 100 percent and occasionally even more, and its unity of purpose and solidarity endowed the military units with the momentum that drove them to victory.

The 1967 war not only tested the capacity of Israel's people to act as one nation but provided also a critical shared experience that greatly enhanced the feeling of its various segments that they belonged to one community. Hitherto, Oriental and European Jews had felt themselves equal partners in the mythical Israel, the object of their common millennial yearnings; but in the Israel of here and now, the European Jews had acquired most of the rights and privileges and felt entitled to them by virtue of their labors in building the country, creating a state, and defending it. The Oriental Jew who complained about getting a smaller share of the desired things in Israel was taunted, in reply, with the question where *he* was when the European or his kinsmen were draining the swamps, building villages and towns, and fending off the enemy with their lives. Now, after a fateful war in which the Oriental Jews, who constituted the majority of the armed forces, performed their duty impeccably, even the European Jew had to concede that his Oriental brethren had earned an equal right of property in the actual Israel that was reborn by overcoming the threat of destruction. One could thus witness, sometime in 1972, a European mother who was visibly tempted to make some mean remarks about Orientals in connection with a "racket" that some children were making near her home, check her own indignation by reminding herself that the youngsters' parents had defended her home, and one of them had lost his life while doing so.

Besides providing a crucial common present experience to counter-balance the divergent past experiences, the 1967 war also contributed in a very practical way to the narrowing of the gap between Orientals and Europeans. The war and its aftermath abruptly terminated an economic recession coupled with widespread unemployment that had been going on for two or three years, and triggered a boom and a shortage of labor that went on unabated for six years. The Orientals, who had been the chief victims of the recession, became the disproportionate beneficiaries of its reversal; and while their relative share of per capita income perhaps just went back to the level it had attained before the recession, the trend upward stimulated a feeling of buoyancy and hopefullness which was reflected in high rates of consumption on the basis of anticipated income. Thus, for example, the relative percentage of Orientals owning durable goods, which are usually purchased on credit, increased dramatically, as did the percentage who improved their housing conditions through purchase of more spacious dwellings. At the same time, the government accelerated some of the special efforts it had been making on behalf of the Orientals in such crucial fields as education, a "headstart" program for promising Oriental young men within the framework of the armed forces, and so on.

Observing the revolution wrought by the Six Day War in the psychological standing of the Orientals and the substantial narrowing in the material gap between them and the Europeans, many students of Israeli society rashly concluded that the communal problem was on its way to a solution if not actually solved. Those students failed to realize that if the part the Orientals played in the war made them feel better, it also increased their expectations from the Israel of here and now, and their impatience with delays in the realization of these expectations. The consumption on future account was a benign expression of that inclination; but it was followed in 1972 by a not-so-benign manifestation in the form of the activity of the "Black Panthers" of Israel, an organization that threatened to use the methods of its American namesake to advance the cause of Oriental Jews. Three years later, the Black Panthers seem to have been an ephemeral phenomenon, but the mood of impatience in the face of slow progress in the realization of more intensely felt rights underlying the emergence of that organization clearly is not. In fact, it may well have been reinforced by the experience of the 1973 October War.

The Yom Kippur War provided Israel's people with an additional experience of national unity and common fate that was even more profound than that of the Six Day War because the peril was greater and the sacrifices and efforts to ward it off much more onerous. Although the 1973 war gave rise to bitter quarrels and divisions which openly assailed even the ranks of the armed forces for the first time since the War of Independence, these clashes cut across communal lines and, in a sense, demonstrated all the more the extent to which Israel's people as a whole had come to be swayed and rippled by the same winds in regard to fundamental issues. On the other hand, the Yom Kippur War was also followed by a period of severe economic strain which inevitably tends to victimize the weaker and poorer Oriental Jews more than their European brethren. The combination of a more intense awareness on the part of the Orientals of rights due them, and a decrease in the capacity of Israeli society to satisfy those rights resulting from the October War is obvious. Miraculously, it has not so far manifested itself in exacerbated acts of discontent by the Orientals, conceivably because of the sense of national emergency which has persisted since the Yom Kippur War.

The Wars and Soviet and American Immigration

The Six Day War and its aftermath released a new flow of immigration that brought in about 250,000 newcomers in the years 1968–1973. But the most important feature of this flow is that it brought in large numbers of Soviet and American Jews—about one-half and one-eighth of the total respectively— for the first time since the birth of Israel and even before. The October 1973 War was followed by a dwindling of the general flow for which the decline of Soviet and American immigration was largely responsible—in 1974, as in 1964 and 1954, there was more emigration than immigration. A question of crucial importance for the future size, composition, and character of Israel's people is whether the 1968–1973 phenomenon represented a new trend, which was temporarily interrupted by the October War and its aftermath, or whether the phenomenon was instead the result of a special conjuncture of factors that came to an end in 1974. The answer to that question was not clear at the time of writing.

With regard to the immigration of Soviet Jews, little that is certain is known as to why so many of them manifested a strong desire to emigrate to Israel after the 1967 war, and even less is known as to why the Soviet authorities allowed large numbers of them to go, when Zionism had been banned for half a century and when the Soviet Union had been pursuing for over a decade an inimical policy toward Israel that culminated in the breaking off of diplomatic relations. This much, however, seems clear from the record: first, that an immigration of 130,000 Soviet Jews out of some 2.5 million over a six-year period cannot be considered a marginal phenomenon, especially in view of the great difficulties placed by the Soviet authorities in the way of the prospective emigrants. Second, that although the Soviet authorities have done much to discourage emigration of Soviet Jews—harassment, intimidation, deprivation of jobs, "exit tax," circulating horror stories about the experience of immigrants in Israel, jailing "activists," and so on—they have refrained from adopting more draconian measures for fear of reviving Stalinism at home and jeopardizing the country's relations abroad. Third, that while the degree of pressure applied by the Soviet authorities proved of little avail in deterring Soviet Jews from going to Israel when Israel was booming in 1968–1973, that pressure was effective in reducing the level of emigration as Israel entered into a difficult period in the wake of the 1973 war. In short, it seems that the impulse to emigrate is by now strongly active among Soviet Jews, and that the extent to which it will lead to action in the future will depend on the balance between the attraction of Israel and the sanctions imposed by the Soviet authorities. Soviet Jews seem to be prepared to run the gauntlet of sanctions if they can look forward to reasonable prospects in Israel at the end of their ordeal. Otherwise, they either bide their time or go elsewhere, as nearly half who left the Soviet Union have done in the last two years.

As far as the immigration of American Jews is concerned, the difficulty in evaluating its significance is no less considerable. The coming of 35,000 American Jews to Israel in six years when only one-third that number had settled there in the previous twenty years would seem to suggest that immigration to Israel can no longer be viewed as idiosyncratic behavior of some individual Americans. On the other hand, can an immigration of less than 0.5 percent of the total number of American Jews be viewed as indicative of a trend among those Jews, especially when the possibility of returning to the United States remains open to them and has been used extensively by American immigrants in the past? Limited inquiries have shown that the post-1967 immigrants from the United States came for a variety of reasons: the sharpening of the sense of Jewish consciousness and solidarity as a result of the crisis and war of 1967; a feeling that the quality of life in America was deteriorating and the desire to bring up children in a more purposeful social environment; the recession that visited the United States in those years, and the boom in Israel, coupled with the opening up of opportunities for highly trained and experienced people in sophisticated industries, business, the universities, and research institutes. None of these reasons is decisive in indicating future immigration prospects. Enhanced feelings of solidarity may cool off or may find outlets in forms of behavior other than immigration; thoughts about the quality of life in America may readily change, especially after a realistic experience of the quality of life in Israel; recession can give way to boom and boom to recession; and even if the boom in Israel were to go on indefinitely, it could make room for only so many people a year from a very highly educated community and a much more advanced economy. The decline of immigration after 1973 suggests that this was precisely the case.

Should American Jewry nevertheless become a source of large-scale immigration to Israel, and/or if the immigration of Soviet Jews should resume its momentum, the effect on the people of Israel could be very far-reaching indeed. Obviously, it would mean a very rapid proportional growth in size, considering that these two sources contain three times more Jews than Israel. Obviously, too, the intercommunal problem would be greatly affected by the influx of large numbers of Russians and Americans, although it is not at all clear in what ways—there would certainly be a swing toward the West and away from the East in the general character of the people, but the newcomers could affect the material and psychological gap between Orientals and Europeans for better or for worse or both ways at once. Less obviously or not obviously at all, a massive immigration of Soviet and/or American Jews, if it should begin to materialize in the next few years, could have a significant effect on Israel's decision as to how many *Arabs* presently under its control it could afford to incorporate and therefore how much territory it should seek to retain.

The Wars and the Future Composition of the Population

The Six Day War brought under Israeli control the West Bank and the Gaza Strip and triggered a profound dispute among Israelis about the future of these territories. In principle, nearly all Israelis consider them to be part of the historical homeland and feel entitled to them; however, they have been deeply divided on the practical advisability and feasibility of annexing them as a whole or in parts. Some of these grounds have been external-political— whether Israel could "get away" with annexation without having to pay an excessive cost; others, however, have centered on the consequences for the composition and character of Israel's people of absorbing all or part of the 690,000 Arabs of the West Bank and the 370,000 Arabs of the Gaza Strip.

By about the beginning of 1972, Israelis were generally agreed that it was probably within their country's power to annex the entire West Bank and the Gaza Strip if it wanted; but they were deeply divided as to the desirability of doing so. The debate involved many issues, but one of the most crucial of these was the so-called "demographic problem." Considering that Israel had already an Arab minority of 460,000 whose natural growth rate was a phenomenal forty per thousand (compared with sixteen per thousand for Jews), how many more Arabs could Israel absorb without losing its Jewish character and/or some of its other prized characteristics, such as democracy and a "healthy" social structure?

As of 1971, the Arab minority amounted to somewhat less than 15 percent of the total population of Israel in the pre-1967 boundaries plus East Jerusalem. Were Israel to annex the Gaza Strip, the percentage of Arabs would rise to 24 percent. Were it to annex the West Bank in addition to the Gaza Strip, the Arabs would attain 35 percent of the population. Because of the vast differences in the natural rate of growth of Jews and Arabs, the proportion of the latter would constantly rise, so that by 1990, the Arabs would come to nearly 50 percent of the total population if Israel annexed the West Bank and the Gaza Strip. The addition of Jewish immigration to natural growth would offset this development to some extent depending on its size.

Table 1. Population projections (in thousands) under alternative boundaries and immigration levels.

| | 1971 population | | | | Projected 1990 population based on annual net Jewish immigration | | | | | | | | | | | |
| | | | | | 25,000 | | | | 40,000 | | | | 70,000 | | | |
Boundaries	Total	Jews	Non-Jews	% Non-Jews	Total	Jews	Non-Jews	% Non-Jews	Total	Jews	Non-Jews	% Non-Jews	Total	Jews	Non-Jews	% Non-Jews
1967 borders plus East Jerusalem	3,095	2,637	458	15	4,809	3,870	940	20	5,131	4,191	940	18	5,796	4,856	940	16
Above plus Gaza Strip	3,465	2,637	838	24	5,569	3,870	1,699	30	5,890	4,191	1,699	29	6,555	4,856	1,699	26
All above plus West Bank	4,155	2,637	1,518	37	6,984	3,870	3,114	45	7,305	4,191	3,114	43	7,970	4,856	3,114	39

At a rate of 25,000 a year, which is the average net rate (subtracting emigration) for the previous ten years, the percentages of Arabs by 1990 would be 20 percent without further annexation, 30 percent if the Gaza Strip were annexed, and 45 percent if the West Bank too were added. Were immigration to come at the rate of 70,000 a year, which is the highest figure for any single year since the massive wave of 1948–1951, the Arab proportions would decline to 16, 26, and 39 percent respectively. At a rate of 40,000 a year, which is roughly the average for the 1951–1971 period, the proportions would come to 18, 29, and 43 percent. These calculations, together with the relevant absolute numbers, are summarized in Table 1.

Virtually all Israelis, except for a few whose dissent is notable mainly because of its rarity, wanted to retain the Jewish character of their state. Most of them also agreed that that character would be greatly jeopardized long before 1990 by the annexation of the West Bank and the Gaza Strip *if* the above-stated assumptions about Arab natural growth and Jewish immigration were to prove true. However, they disagreed violently as to whether these assumptions needed be so. Many did consider them essentially valid and therefore ruled out any substantial annexation and thought instead of alternative schemes (such as the Allon Plan or a Palestine Entity) that would assure for Israel the security it desires without saddling it with additional large numbers of Arabs. Others, however, rejected these calculations completely and insisted on the "unification" of all of Eretz Yisrael (Palestine). Once Israel unequivocally annexed the Gaza Strip and the West Bank, these others argued, many Arabs would prefer to emigrate to other lands rather than live in the Jewish state, while the birthrate of those who would remain would decline sharply as they became more modernized. At the same time, a determined public effort could boost the natural rate of growth of the Jewish population and stimulate immigration in much larger numbers than assumed. Adherents of this view pointed to the large increase in the number of immigrants from the United States and the Western countries after 1967 to support their position, and emphasized above all the prospects of massive immigration from the Soviet Union, which began to materialize contrary to all previous expectations.

In addition to these considerations, the debate also had a qualitative dimension. Opponents of general annexation argued that, regardless of the percentage the Arabs would represent, one or two million of them living concentrated in predominantly Arab areas and having all the makings of a nation could not be prevented for long from seeking to assert their right to self-determination, perhaps with the help of their brethren from across the borders, and would thus plunge Israel sooner or later into civil strife and war. Had not the Jews themselves acted this way when they were a minority in Palestine? If that should come to pass, Israel would not be in a position to "disgorge" the Arabs it would have failed to digest and assent to a new partition without suffering enormous damage itself, since the Arabs would have become integrated into the economy and the country would have come to depend on them. Even apart from such far-reaching though not improbable convulsions, the great likelihood that the Arabs would come to occupy predominantly the more menial sectors of the economy would turn them into "hewers of wood and drawers of water" to the Jewish masters who would concentrate in the "higher" occupations, and thus undo much of what the Zionist-socialist revolution had done by way of creating a "normal" Jewish occupational pyramid.

To these arguments the proponents of annexation answered that the Palestinian Arabs have never been a nation; that if they were indeed to become one, they would not be content with what the opponents of annexation had to offer them anyway, and Israel would thus have to face them down in any case. As for the impact of the Arabs on the Israeli economy and society, that too would have to be faced regardless of formal boundary lines and definitions of citizenship, since Israel had already established free movement of people and goods throughout the occupied territories and even beyond them, and would certainly want to maintain that condition under any kind of peace settlement. The Six Day War, these Israelis concluded, had for better or for worse terminated once and for all the insulation of the Jewish economy and society from their immediate Arab environment, which the Arab states had imposed on Israel since 1948, and which the Yishuv had deliberately pursued in the preceding half century.

Until the 1973 war, the government of Israel was as divided on these issues as the Israeli public at large and therefore adhered to a decision, going back to 1968, not even to try to decide what Israel should seek as long as no substantial number of its members felt that real options they desired were within reach or were being foreclosed. Since no significant number of ministers felt so with sufficient conviction to be willing to force the Cabinet to make a decision and incur division, the government of Israel in effect presided over the continuation of the uncertainty. Shortly after the 1973 war, the decline of immigration to Israel, on the one hand, and the considerable international recognition given to "Palestinian rights", on the other hand, appeared for a while to foreclose the annexationist position. However, the emergence of the Palestine Liberation Organization as the sole spokesman for the Palestinians, and its insistence on a single Palestine, but under *Arab* control gave the Israeli annexationist position a new lease on life. In any case, it provided new grounds for the Israeli government to continue to adhere to its decision to refrain from decision.

The Six Day War also reopened the question of the Arab population of Israel itself, which numbered some 440,000 people at the end of 1971. From the time of Israel's creation it was clear that that population was destined to remain a minority that neither meant on its part nor was meant by Israel to assimilate eventually into the majority. On the one hand, Israel's Zionist vocation and the particular way in which religion and nationalism combined in the Zionist ethos necessarily gave the Jewish state a certain exclusivist tendency that barred the Arabs from full membership. On the other hand, the fact that the Arabs of Israel had been part of an Arab majority in Palestine that was dispossessed and scattered by war and defeat and that they were linked religiously, linguistically, and culturally to the peoples of the hostile Arab states surrounding Israel inevitably entailed a certain measure of resentment of the Jews as perpetrators of their downfall and an inner identification with their enemies. However, despite these barriers, the necessity of living together, the demoralized state of the Arabs in defeat, and the flight of their traditional leadership, on the one hand, and the severity of the sanctions against resistance, the activity of strong libertarian forces among the Jews that strove for improvement of the lot of the Arabs, and the work of economic forces, on the other hand, combined to produce in the course of time a "pragmatic adaptation." Acts of virtual dispossession of Arabs from their land on ostensible grounds of security became less and less frequent, military rule over thickly Arab-inhabited areas was gradually relaxed and then abolished, the Arabs learned to use the franchise that was granted to them from the outset more and more effectively to secure advantages to their community, and the general prosperity and shortage of manpower drew ever larger numbers of Arabs into the orbit of relative affluence. By the early 1960s, the Arabs of Israel still suffered the agonies of identity and alienation, but in their day-to-day life they made up a generally free, prosperous, healthy, educated community. The Jewish majority still looked upon the Arab minority as a potential fifth column, but it had learned to repress that suspicion and refrain from acting upon it in its day-to-day dealings with the Arabs. There was a potentially disturbing factor in the situation in that the modernized, educated younger Arabs were beginning to feel restless and to look across the borders for broader mental horizons, but the traditionally minded older generation was relatively content with the situation, and its weight still prevailed in the community.

The Six Day War went a long way toward undoing that adaptation. One might have supposed that the very rapid and seemingly definitive victory of Israel should have only confirmed the existing situation by eliminating any hopes that it might be changed by some outside force; but things worked out differently in reality. As a result of the war, contact was restored between the Israeli Arabs and their brethren in the occupied territories, who in turn were allowed to maintain close contacts with the broader Arab world by the Open Bridges policy adopted by Israel. The Arabs of the occupied areas were not only more numerous, but this time, unlike 1948, defeat did not destroy their organization and leadership. These instead remained intact and rapidly overshadowed the incipient leadership of the Israeli Arabs and came to speak in the name of all the Palestinian Arabs. Moreover, to the extent that the Israeli Arabs were distinguished at the outset from their brethren in the occupied areas by higher standards of living, the distinction was subsequently blurred by the accelerating economic boom in which the latter were allowed to share through the policy of free movement of people and goods. Finally, not a few of the restless among Israel's Arabs were drawn into the Palestinian guerrilla and resistance movements, thus stirring the dormant suspicions among Israelis that "their" Arabs were no different from the others. Thus, while the Arabs of Israel gained a large measure of relief from the psychological malaise of isolation and alienation as a result of the war, the price of this relief has been a reopening of the question of their relationship to Israel, and the linking of their future with the future of Arab-Israeli relations in general and the future of the Arabs of the occupied areas in particular. The 1973 war only enhanced those tendencies as Israel appeared to be militarily vulnerable, and as the Palestine Liberation Organization came to acquire a dominant position as spokesman for all Palestinians.

The Stratification of Israel's People Today

When Israel started its career as a sovereign state, it had probably the most egalitarian community in the world, the nearest approximation to a "classless society." Since then, mass immigration, especially its Oriental component, together with rapid economic development has loosened up the egalitarian social structure just as it has diluted the ideological compactness and relative homogeneity of the initial settlers. When Israel was established, its economy was young and small and had not given the opportunity for any significant number of people to accumulate large amounts of capital; since then, very rapid economic development and inflation have given rise to a large class of successful entrepreneurs and nouveaux riches. At the beginning of the state, Israel had had for a decade and a half an excessive supply of highly educated and professional people so that the difference between the salaries of these people and the wages of the manual workers was very small; since then, the needs of the economy and the low proportion of highly educated people among the massive Oriental immigration have reversed the situation and have brought about a much greater differentiation of salaries and wages. When Israel began, the traditional difference in standard of living, social characteristics, and outlook that exists everywhere between town and country people was practically nonexistent, because farm incomes were high and the farmers were themselves city people who had taken to tilling the soil out of "idealism"; since then farm incomes have declined in relation to urban incomes, and masses of unprepared, uneducated Orientals burdened with large families have been diverted to agriculture, creating a new class of farmers with limited income and limited horizons. In the early days, the pioneering, cooperative, and socialist-egalitarian tradition of the Second and Third Aliyot was still the dominant ethos; since independence, reliance on the sovereign state, economic development, and a massive immigration of people devoid of pioneering and Zionist background have all but washed away that tradition.

Today the distribution of income in Israel shows a very considerable measure of inequality. A recent study indicates that the lowest tenth of the urban Jewish families received only 2.2 percent of the total income, while the highest tenth received as much as 27.5 percent. The poorer half of the families received less than one-quarter of the total income while the richer half received more than three-quarters. One-half of the urban families, in other words, had an average income three times higher than that of the other half, while the top 10 percent of families received more than 12 times the income of the lowest 10 percent. Between these two extremes, income rises or falls gradually. Reliable comparable figures for the period around 1948 are not available, but all existing indications point to a very substantial increase in inequality. A remarkable thing is that this spreading of the income structure took place even though the natural resources of the country, including most of the land, are publicly owned and despite the fact that the government and the Histadrut own and operate almost half the country's industry and control very large portions of every other aspect of its economy.

Despite these differences, however, Israel still remains among the most egalitarian countries in the Free World—as egalitarian as Sweden, for example. Moreover, as in Sweden, the inequality is considerably mitigated by a progressive taxation that falls heavily on the rich, and by extensive state welfare services that benefit the poor. In addition, the figures cited represent somewhat less inequality than the figures for a decade before, which suggests that the trend toward greater disparities may have decelerated if it has not been altogether checked. On the other hand, it should be noted that wealth is now displayed more conspicuously than ever, and that it has come to prevail increasingly over other criteria in bestowing status. Even distinguished military service, which used to grant uncontested standing in itself, is now often rewarded with positions and perquisites associated with affluent living if not wealth, be it in the form of a company directorship or a concession on a gas station. Above all, one must never lose sight of the communal problem, which has relegated whole sections of the population to an inferior status and tends to perpetuate their position there.

Occupationally, nearly 7.5 percent of Israel's working population is engaged in agriculture, 34 percent in industry and construction, 25 percent in public services, 7 percent in transportation and communications, and 26 percent in commerce, banking, and personal services. This structure is still heavily weighted on the side of traditional Jewish occupations, but there can be no doubt that the founders of the Yishuv and the leaders of Israel have accomplished the Zionist dream of creating a "normal" structure for Jewish society in its homeland resting on a broad new base of farmers and workers. That this real revolution has been achieved without compulsion or violence and largely through self-sacrifice makes the accomplishment all the more impressive.

Israel's population is heavily urban. In 1973, 86 percent of the total population lived in about 104 cities and towns and 14 percent lived in about 800 rural settlements. Among Jews, the urbanization is even heavier, reaching over 90 percent, in contrast with the Arabs, 59 percent of whom live in urban settlements. Today, as in 1948, most of the Jewish population is concentrated in the three districts, out of the country's six, which are composed of Tel Aviv, Haifa, Jerusalem, and their respective surroundings. But thanks to a deliberate and very expensive effort on the part of the government, a substantial redistribution has taken place in the last twenty-five years. Thus the Tel Aviv district, which accounted for 43 percent of the Jewish population in 1948, now accounts for only 33 percent; while the South district, including the Negev, which comprised only 1 percent of the Jewish population in 1948, now accounts for 12 percent of a population that has grown more than four-fold. The Haifa and Jerusalem districts, too, have had their share reduced, while that of the Central district, including the hilly corridor between Tel Aviv and Jerusalem, has correspondingly increased from 15 to 20 percent. The North district, including Galilee, increased its share from 8 to 10 percent, but much of this is accounted for by the natural growth of the Arab population which is heavily concentrated in that district.

8

The Economy: Development, Characteristics, Problems

Five years after Israel had been established, a prominent economist entirely without bias in favor of Israel astounded a distinguished American academic audience by suggesting that that country might be able to "make a go" of its economy in a decade or two and that, fundamentally, its economic position was perhaps more manageable than that of its neighboring countries. The astonishment reflected the belief current at the time among all but the most confirmed of Zionists that a complete economic collapse of Israel was imminent. And, indeed, Israel presented a sad picture then. Here was a country, small, half of it wilderness, devoid of any significant natural resources with one or two exceptions. It was surrounded by hostile neighbors who made no secret of their intention to wipe it off the map, and in the meantime compelled it to divert much of its scarce resources to maintain a defense establishment disproportionate to its size and means, while inflicting on it heavy losses through an economic boycott. Since its foundation, the state had welcomed all Jewish immigrants, and now its countryside was strewn with primitive canvas and tin hut camps in which hundreds of thousands of them wilted in misery and frustration, living on doled-out food and clamoring for relief work. For some time, the government had financed much of its work by "creating" money and trying to suppress the inflationary consequences through a comprehensive price-control and rationing system; but the system had just broken down completely, and rampant inflation was wreaking havoc on prices, wages, and currency. Everything was short, the black market was rife, and the population was utterly demoralized. In 1952–1953 emigration from the young nation actually exceeded immigration.

Two decades later, in 1973, only the wildest of wishful thinking could possibly expect Israel to break down under economic strain. Going about the country, one was struck by signs of vitality and affluence everywhere. Hundreds of new villages and factories dotted the countryside; new towns had grown like a mirage in desert landscapes; scores of thousands of buildings rising at any one time made the entire country look like one single con-struction site. No trace remained of the depressing immigrant camps, and the tens of thousands of new arrivals in each of the previous few years from the Soviet Union and the West were almost immediately housed in comfortable, fresh, monotonous developments of a quality and size that many veterans deemed luxurious. Despite the addition of some 370,000 people to the labor force in the previous five years—an increase of more than 20 percent—and the employment of some 70,000 Arabs from the occupied areas, there were more jobs available than people to fill them. Inflation was still a problem for the economy as a whole, but shortages were a mere memory, evoked most often in conversations about the waste accompanying the present abundance and conspicuous consumption. Refrigerators and gas stoves, once an index of rare wealth, were to be found in virtually every home in Israel. One in five Israelis left the country in 1973, but only a handful of these were emigrants; the rest simply went for business, study, or pleasure. Almost one Israeli fam-ily in four owned a private car, until ten years before a privilege of one family in fifteen; and the rapid spread of ownership had brought about the whole "automobile culture," with its suburban dwelling, accelerated living, outing and dining out, as well as its traffic congestion, parking and pollution problems, and its road accidents.

Underlying this transformation, there was undoubtedly a record of solid economic achievement; but it was still as erroneous to think then that Israel was on the high road of self-sustaining economic growth as it was to think twenty years before that it was heading for collapse. The country still con-fronted some serious economic problems whose solution was not even in sight. It will be the task of the next pages to analyze briefly Israel's economic development in the first quarter century of its existence and to point out the chief problems still facing it today. While doing this, there will be occasional digression from the main subject to dwell in some detail upon related topics that seem relevant to Israel's position today or appear to be of social or politi-cal interest in their own right.

Growth of the Economy

At about the time Israel celebrated the second anniversary of its birth, its economy, measured by per capita product, stood close to the level of develop-ing countries like Argentina and Colombia or of poor European countries like Ireland and Italy, but was considerably below that of Western European countries and only a quarter that of the United States. Since then, it has grown at a very rapid rate and, with a per capita product of about $2,700 in 1973, has come to rank eighteenth among all the countries of the world, immedi-ately behind Japan, Britain, Finland and New Zealand, at about 40 percent the level of the United States. The total amount of goods and services produced (gross national product, or GNP) multiplied eightfold during that period, increasing at an average annual rate of close to 10 percent. This magnitude sustained over such a long period represents the highest rate of development in the world, higher even than Japan's 9.6 percent. It is more than three times the equivalent American rate and five times the equivalent British rate during much the same period.

During the twenty-three-year period mentioned, Israel's labor force multiplied threefold, creating some presumption that total product would rise significantly. But even when this factor is taken into account and economic growth is examined on a per capita basis, this still comes out to an impressive average rate of 5 percent a year. Though no longer the highest in the world, this rate would be warmly welcomed by any nation seeking economic development. It represents two to three times the per capita rate of growth of the United States and Britain.

The magnitude of Israel's achievement becomes all the more apparent if we recall that it took place against a background of very limited natural resources, hardly any sources of energy, a relatively poor initial economy, and several serious handicaps. The new immigrants, especially the 750,000 who came during the first three years of statehood, included a very high proportion of children, and most of them possessed no skills other than those of artisans and small traders. Many of them needed more or less extensive aid before they could start to take care of themselves and the majority had to spend a long period getting settled, learning the Hebrew language, or acquiring a trade before they could become productive. Among immigrants from Muslim countries, tradition and very large families confined women to their homes. All these factors reduced the participation of the immigrants in the labor force to a small fraction of their number and contributed to making the proportion of the working population and the proportion of those directly engaged in the production of goods in Israel among the lowest in the world.

In addition to these physical and human hindrances, Israel has labored under several handicaps owing to the hostility of the neighboring countries. The Arab economic boycott, begun in 1950, denied Israel the advantages of regional economies, scared away potential investors with businesses in Arab countries when they were most needed, and cost the country $40–50 million annually in higher shipping costs, oil prices and insurances rates when it could least afford them. Much more important, the Arab military threat forced Israel to devote a consistently higher share of its GNP to defense than any country outside the Soviet bloc, and to divert some of the best minds and energies at its disposal into military service. Besides the direct costs, considerations of national security have frequently been the motive behind many costly, uneconomical endeavors which might not have been undertaken otherwise or might have been differently conceived. In view of all this, the question becomes all the more urgent: how did Israel do it?

From a technical economic point of view, the answer appears simple: Israel has achieved that high rate of development per capita thanks to a very heavy investment program financed from outside sources. Indeed, throughout the period between 1950 and 1973, Israel has invested on the average the equivalent of over 25 percent of its GNP every year in capital stock. This proportion has rarely been exceeded outside the Soviet bloc during those years. Put differently, Israel has invested more net dollars for every person living there, every year, than any country other than the United States. The money for this investment came overwhelmingly from loans, grants, contributions, and investments from sources outside Israel, including notably United States government grants-in-aid and loans, proceeds from the sale of bonds, German government reparation payments to the Israeli government and restitution payments to Israeli citizens, donations by world Jewry, direct foreign investments, transfers by immigrants, and miscellaneous other sources. In the course of Israel's first twenty-five years of existence, the total amount thus transferred reached the astronomical figure of more than $18 billion, more than half of it received in the last quarter of that period or since the Six Day War. The net contribution of domestic savings to the process of capital formation for that period as a whole has been relatively negligible.

There can be no dispute, of course, that the vast flow of money from abroad was an indispensable condition for the success achieved by Israel's economy. Nor can there be much doubt that this very heavy reliance on foreign aid, and especially the failure of domestic savings, confronts Israel with severe problems, as we shall presently see. But in relation to economic achievement, at least two points should be mentioned that qualify the simple explanation just given.

The first is that the growth of GNP achieved by Israel was not entirely due to heavy capitalization. Calculations of various serious and critical analysts suggest that one-third to one-half of the increase in per capita output was due to greater productivity. This degree of improvement in "efficiency" is roughly equal to that attained by many other advanced countries. But since Israel has an unusually large service sector, which is not susceptible to rapid advances in productivity, its overall per capita advance in productivity signifies an unusual degree of improvement in industry and agriculture.

The second point is that the vast inflow of capital from abroad, though a necessary condition, is not a sufficient one for achieving the economic advance generally attributed to it. Such an inflow involves many complex adaptations and adjustments that cannot be taken for granted, and have not, in fact, been achieved by other countries, with the consequence that large amounts of foreign aid or windfall oil revenues have been ineffectively used. It involves, among other things, the setting up of a reasonably efficient overall economic administration, the assimilation of new techniques over a wide range of industries and the adaptation of human skills to them, making many internal adjustments in the structures of consumption, production, and distribution, and rearranging the network of external relationships.

Both the increase in productivity and the making of adjustments must be largely credited to the Israeli human factor, and indeed a look at the human resources with which Israel started shows it to have been exceptionally well endowed. To the extent that formal education can be used as a criterion, Israel's population in 1948 seems to have been the most highly educated in the world. According to comparative data assembled from United Nations sources, Israel had that year a higher proportion of people who had completed their university education than the United States, and twice the proportion of the next highest country. A similar picture emerges with regard to the proportion of people having completed secondary education, where Israel ran ahead of the United States, particularly with respect to people past middle age. This large volume of very high quality "human capital" provided a valuable foundation for subsequent development, especially since much of it was underutilized before the state was established. The massive immigration of Oriental Jews in the late 1940s and the 1950s temporarily lowered the quality considerably but still left it among the highest in the world. More recently, the level has been rising again owing to the large-scale immigration from the Soviet Union, the United States, and other Western countries after 1967 and to an explosive expansion of the number of Israelis pursuing higher education in the country and abroad.

To summarize, then, in the course of its first quarter century of existence, Israel was able to increase its GNP to eight times the original size and to raise its per capita product more than three times. It has realized this outstanding growth while absorbing into its economy three times as many people as the state had at the beginning, while maintaining a large and ever more expensive defense establishment, and while dramatically raising the standard of living of the population. It was able to accomplish all this without infringing upon its democratic institutions and procedures and without invoking any extraordinary powers, that is, powers not practiced by free governments elsewhere. This remarkable record was attained thanks to a combination of extremely generous assistance from the Jewish people in the world and friendly powers, and exceptionally high human resources. In other respects, however, Israel has not done nearly so well and has suffered a number of failures. Before looking into these, I shall turn for a moment to some features of Israel's economy.

Role of Government in the Economy

One of the most important features of Israel's economy is the central role played in it by the government, understood as including local government and the Jewish Agency, the arm of the World Zionist Organization, and other Jewish organizations entrusted with various aspects of assistance to immigrants and land reclamation. Of course, in the era of Keynesian economics and the welfare state, large-scale governmental intervention in the economy has become a common feature even in self-proclaimed free enterprise societies; however, the magnitude and scope of the economic activities of the government of Israel are unusually extensive by comparison with any society outside the Soviet bloc. Throughout the 1950s and most of the 1960s, for example, the budgetary expenditures of Israel's government amounted on the average to more than one-third of GNP, and they have risen after the Six Day War to a highpoint of over 50 percent in 1971. Moreover, the government has used some of these resources to engage directly in the production of goods and services.

From the outset, the government of Israel has owned and operated directly certain enterprises, such as railways, the post, telegraph, telephone, and broadcasting services, which are publicly owned in many other countries, and has carried out typical public works such as road construction, irrigation and drainage schemes, afforestation, conservation, and so on. These undertakings are financially integrated into the national budget. In addition, the government has itself established nearly two hundred public corporations not integrated into the budget, of which it owns more than 50 percent of the shares. Among these are enterprises engaged in the production of oil and petrochemicals, electricity, potash, bromine, phosphates, fertilizers, copper, ceramic materials, and so on, in addition to plants producing defense wares. Altogether, the government and its various undertakings generate about one-quarter of GNP. Adding the somewhat smaller share of the Histadrut to it, this would leave private enterprise as the source of a little more than half the national product.

Large as it is, the direct share of the government in GNP is only part of its total contribution to it. Throughout Israel's existence, the government's share of total capital investment in the country has been probably higher than in any non-Communist country. In the early 1950s, the government was responsible for financing nearly two-thirds of total investment. In the 1960s this proportion declined to about 43 percent, but rose again after the Six Day War. The areas in which government-financed investment is concentrated have varied over the years: in agriculture and irrigation, the government has financed over 80 percent of the investment from the outset; but in mining, quarrying, and power, government financing declined from 50–90 percent of investment in the 1950s to 10–40 percent in the 1960s; in manufacturing the government's share declined from 32–43 percent in the 1950s to 6–39 percent in the 1960s; in public transportation the government's share fluctuated throughout between 40 and 70 percent; in trade and services between 34 and 57 percent; and in home building between 32 and 48 percent.

The government investments have been made in the form of loans to Histadrut and private enterprises as well as in the form of acquisition of assets, with increasing emphasis being placed on the former in the course of time. This approach has had the effect of reducing the government's role in direct production below what it might have been. On the other hand, since the government insisted as a rule on the participation of additional funds from private sources as a condition for granting investment loans, this approach has given it an even greater influence on capital formation throughout the country than its share in investment might indicate.

In addition to its direct and indirect investments, the government has exerted a very large influence on the economy through other means. It has used the fiscal and monetary controls employed by governments everywhere to guide the general course of the economy, only more so, since taxation together with compulsory loans accounted for about 40 percent of GNP in recent years. It has supplemented these with a vast array of direct controls, subsidies, tax concessions, differential export incentives, and bank loans at low interest rates designed to achieve specific purposes such as promoting exports or tourism, encouraging agriculture, keeping down the price level of essential commodities, and others. It has used its political relationship with the Histadrut leadership, in addition to statutory provisions, to influence the wage structure and level, and it has affected the entire economy through its immigration policy, its land-use policy, and its defense policy. All these factors together make governmental activity the real axis of the economy and endow it with the means of affecting the everyday life and well-being of the citizens to a degree unusual in other free countries.

The extraordinary involvement of the government in the economy has only little to do with the domination of all the governments of Israel since its establishment by the mildly socialist Israel Labor Party and its antecedents. Had nonsocialist parties been in control all that time, they might have been more lenient on certain controls, they might have used a different order of priority in making allocations, and they might have decided to stimulate private enterprise sooner than the government actually did. But essentially, they would have altered very little the fact of the government's predominant role and position in the economy because this has rested mainly on three factors: the Zionist conception of the state; the poverty of the country's resources; and the particular defense requirements of Israel.

The Zionist view, which considers the state as an instrument for solving the Jewish Problem, implies, among other things, that the state should open its gates to unrestricted immigration of Jews who want to come. This principle was expressed in Israel's Declaration of Independence and was embodied in a fundamental law of the country by unanimous agreement. In the economic sphere, this view meant that all governments, regardless of political orientation, were bound to intervene in the economy on a large scale in order to increase its capacity to absorb new immigrants and to channel them and fit them for productive work. The experience of Western governments in the 1930s, to whom intervention in the economy was more repugnant on principle than to any Israeli party, points out that the absorption of masses of unemployed into the economy necessitated extensive public measures even when the question was not one of creating new capacity, as it has been in Israel, but of making full use of existing resources.

But even without a continual massive immigration, any government of Israel was bound to assume a leading role in the economy for many years in order to insure its growth at a satisfactory rate. This is because Israel's natural resources are poor and the financial means of the Yishuv were modest; and these two factors, together with the Arab boycott, ruled out private investment, local as well as foreign, as immediate sources for significant financing of economic development. The only other resources available to Israel were foreign public and nonprofit funds, and most of these could be tapped only by the government. With the bulk of investment money coming from these sources into its hands, it was inevitable that the government should play the central role in the economy.

Finally, Israel faced from the outset a very serious military threat to its existence and integrity from enemies that exceeded it many times in size and numbers and potential power. Israel could hope to resist this threat successfully only by a thorough, continual, centrally directed planning and development of its own defense potential. This has meant not only a high level of military spending, but the orientation of the whole economy in accordance with the strategic and tactical requirements of the country as well as economic considerations. Such a task required a high degree of intervention in and direction of the economy, and these would have been undertaken by any government of Israel.

Pattern of Production

One of the striking features of Israel's economy is the exaggerated size of its service sector. Commerce and banking, transportation and communications, and personal and government services occupy over 57 percent of Israel's labor force and account for approximately the same percentage of its GNP. These proportions are very high compared with those of other countries at a similar or higher level of development such as Germany and France, or even those of Switzerland, the land of banking and tourism par excellence. Moreover, they have changed relatively little in the years since Israel's birth despite the great changes in the size and composition of the population and the enormous growth of the national product during that quarter century. Calculations for 1947, for example, indicate that 53 percent of the Jewish labor force of Palestine was employed in roughly the same service sector.

The fact that the percentage of the labor force employed in the service sector remained approximately the same while the economy grew more than three times on a per capita basis and eight times in absolute terms indicates, of course, a very considerable adjustment of the occupational structure, since normally the service sector grows bigger as the economy grows richer. In other words, the Israeli economy as a whole caught up in a large measure with an initially highly exaggerated concentration in services. However, the remaining disparity between Israel and other countries on the same economic level as well as the previously greater inflation of services still requires explanation.

One of the reasons advanced by economists to explain this phenomenon is the strong demand for public services and public administration because of the size and composition of immigration. This argument seems to fit well with the fact that the size of the service sector remained more or less constant while the economy grew richer, since at the same time immigration declined and the initial immigrants became increasingly self-supporting. It does not, however, fit so well with the fact that the service sector was equally high in 1947, when immigration was low and the economy was relatively poor. Another explanation points to the enormous relative excess of imports over exports, which consisted mainly of commodities, and maintains that this excess necessitated a compensatory shift of the domestic resources toward the service sector. This argument applies to the prestatehood period as well as to the period since Israel's birth, but internal evidence—such as the "normal" size of the transportation and communication areas within the service sector—gives it only a limited validity. The unusually large defense establishment that Israel has had to maintain has been offered as another reason, but this too can only have limited validity since most of Israel's armed forces consist of trained reserves and only a moderate number is at any time under arms. Other explanations include the small size of the settlements and productive units, making for duplication of service functions, and simple inflation of the civil service. These factors are true in themselves, but are even more important as symptoms of a general tendency among the people of Israel that underlies all the suggested explanations. Despite the great and partly successful efforts of the Zionist movement as a whole to induce new arrivals in Palestine-Israel to change their traditional commerce and service occupations, former habit and predilection have continued to reassert themselves whenever the opportunity presents itself.

Of the 43 percent of the working population engaged in the goods-producing sector, one-fifth more or less is engaged at any time in construction. This, again, is an exceptionally high rate, but it is understandable in view of the pressing need for housing to meet the large immigration and rising standards of living, and for plants and roads to meet the demands of an expanding economy. As a matter of fact, construction is one of the fields that has suffered recurrent shortages of workers, particularly skilled ones, and this has sometimes led to the suspension of licenses for building projects deemed "unessential." One consequence of the manpower pressure has been that construction made considerable improvements in technique and productivity at least in the years before 1967, and that it has since drawn upon Arab workers from the occupied territories in very large numbers. These two reasons account for the fact that in 1973, for example, construction contributed 12.9 percent of GNP while employing only 8.8 percent of *Israel's* labor force.

Agriculture employed 7.5 percent of the labor force in 1973 and accounted for 6.5 percent of the national product. These percentages represent respectively somewhat less and somewhat more than half the percentages of twelve years before, which in turn were the same as those of 1951. Yet now, as twelve years ago, agriculture supplied virtually all the food needs of the country on a very high level with respect to quantity, quality, and variety except for cereals, fodder, and fats, and produced, in addition, a surplus for export that is equivalent in value to the food imports, thus directly and indirectly providing or paying for the entire diet of the country. This impressive achievement was attained without even increasing the cultivated acreage, which remained at slightly over one million acres throughout the last decade, and with only a 20 percent increase in the irrigated acreage, to about 450,000 acres in 1973. Simple increase in productivity enabled less than half the proportion of the population engaged in agriculture twelve years ago to meet the needs of the present population at the same or higher levels, while using much less land per capita—one-third instead of one-half acre.

Responsible for this accomplishment is a combination of factors that makes Israeli agriculture one of the most original as well as one of the most efficient in the world. Besides careful planning, intense capitalization, high-order research, and effective supply and marketing organization, which are common to advanced farming everywhere, Israeli agriculture benefits from some unique advantages. The land is publicly owned and inalienable, but the users can have it in perpetual lease for a nominal rent, which gives them every incentive to improve it and encourages rapid capital accumulation. Because of the very high priority assigned to agriculture by Zionist ideology, the public authorities have not only provided the land virtually rent-free, but have invested heavily in its improvement through national, regional, and local schemes of irrigation, drainage, road construction, afforestation, and so on, and have put at the disposal of farmers vast amounts of credit at favorable rates and many other facilities. The same feature of Zionist ideology also initially channeled into agriculture from other occupations and backgrounds some of the best human elements, reversing the farm-to-city trend that takes place everywhere else. Finally and most importantly, the great bulk of Israeli farmers are organized in collective and cooperative farming villages functioning through elected managing committees, which are federated on the regional and national levels and maintain their own cooperative enterprises and facilities for marketing, supply, credit, technical assistance, market research, legislative lobbying, and so on. Even private farmers, mainly citrus and vine growers, are tightly associated in joint-interest organizations that also run cooperative enterprises. This setup facilitates effective planning, permits economies of scale, encourages a high level of capitalization, allows for a quick translation of research findings into advanced technology on the farms, and generally maximizes the possibilities of adaptation to changing needs and opportunities. This is how new crops, such as beets, cotton, and groundnuts were introduced, out-of-season fruits, vegetables, and flowers for export were developed, old crops were improved, and general productivity increased at an annual average rate of 5 percent or more, attaining in several areas world-record or near record yields. The extraordinary degree of adaptability of the organized farmers of Israel is perhaps best reflected in the entry of kibbutzim into the field of industry in a big way, thus setting up another unique Israeli institution: the "agrindustrial" collective village.

Industry and mining employed 28 percent of Israel's working population in 1972 and generated the same proportion of the national product. These figures are nearly 25 percent higher than those of twenty years before and only slightly higher than those of ten years before; however, in view of the very great increase in population in the intervals between these dates, the proportions indicate a great absolute growth. Thus, industrial production has grown more than fivefold since 1958, threefold since 1962, and somewhat more than twofold since 1967. More importantly, the relative composition of the products and their "exportability" has changed considerably, especially since 1967. For example, electrical and electronic equipment, which ranked tenth among industrial products in terms of value of output in 1966, advanced to fifth place in 1973 with an output valued at $374 million; basic metal and metal products advanced from fourth place to second behind food and beverages and ahead of textiles, with a 1973 output valued at $656 million. As for the improvement in "exportability," this is indicated by a more than eightfold increase in the value of industrial exports since 1960, and a threefold increase since 1968.

The development of Israel's industry was helped by various measures of protection, including a high tariff wall. Since 1962 a process of gradual exposure to international competition has been in effect, and has resulted so far in tariff reductions of nearly 50 percent. This has provided an important stimulus for the transformation of the industry, which was further spurred by the launching in 1968 of a vast and ambitious program to make Israel self-sufficient in the production of defense hardware within a relatively short period of time. As a result of this program, military-industrial production exceeded $500 million in 1973, a fivefold increase over the 1966 level. The hardware manufactured locally includes highly sophisticated weapons such as the Gabriel sea-to-sea guided missile, said to be superior to any such missile in service anywhere, the Kfir supersonic fighter-bomber, said to be superior to the French Mirage, and a medium-range surface-to-surface guided missile.

Israel's industrial exports amounted to $1.2 billion in 1973. Polished diamonds, which have a relatively low added value, accounted for some 44 percent of these; nevertheless the magnitude of the remainder, together with the net value added of diamonds export, should put to rest the skepticism that prevailed until recently about the prospects of Israel's industry. True, most of that industry runs on imported equipment, is powered by imported fuel, and uses mainly imported raw materials. It is also true that the internal market is limited, labor costs are fairly high, and the units of production are small—of the 6,000 industrial units employing five workers or more, only 6 percent employ more than one hundred workers and 2 percent, or 128-odd units, employ 300 workers or more and average 600. However, the success achieved so far points out the foundations for a prosperous and expanding industry. It shows that despite all the handicaps mentioned, Israel can reach out for the world market and have a comparative advantage by making maximum use of its endowment in human resources, stressing products that involve skilled labor, distinctive techniques, and high level of organization.

Foreign Trade

Israel is a very active participant in foreign trade with a total trade movement of $7.8 billion in 1973. Even allowing for $1.3 billion in defense imports, Israel exhibits an extremely high level of per capita participation, typical of economically advanced countries like Switzerland and Norway or Britain and Japan, who compensate for their limited markets or natural resources with intensive economic activity on the international level. However, unlike these countries, Israel's role in the international market is much more that of a buyer than a seller: it imports almost twice as much as it exports, and pays for the surplus from funds it receives in loans and assistance from abroad.

Israel's exports of goods and services have increased more than fifty times in the period since 1949 and more than seven times since 1960, amounting in 1973 to $2.6 billion. Of that total, services and goods accounted for roughly half each. A little less than 40 percent of the value credited to services is accounted for by transport of passengers and goods, chiefly the earnings of Israel's merchant fleet and international airline. Both have been undergoing constant expansion and renovation designed to keep them in the forefront among competitors in quality of equipment. The merchant fleet included in 1973 108 ships with a deadweight tonnage of nearly 3.9 million tons, compared with 50 ships and 290,000 tons in 1960. The bulk of the increase in tonnage is accounted for by tanker capacity, which increased fiftyfold, from 41,000 tons in 1960 to 2.4 million in 1973, and is connected with the expanded oil-carrying activity of Israel since the building of the 42-inch Eilat-Ashdod oil pipeline after the Six Day War. Israel had fifty-two new ships scheduled for delivery by the end of 1974, which would increase the capacity of its merchant fleet by an additional one million tons and further reduce the average age of its vessels, already among the lowest in the world.

Israel's international airline, El Al, operated in 1973 a fleet of fifteen jet aircraft, which carried over 800,000 passengers and 35,000 tons of freight and mail.

Second to transportation, tourism contributed about 20 percent to the earnings from services. In 1973 some 700,000 tourists visited the country and spent $230 million, a tenfold and twentyfold increase respectively over 1961. With a 75 percent value added, tourism has become the number one net exporter as well as the most rapidly growing branch of Israel's economy.

Of the nearly $1.4 billion of commodities exported in 1973, nearly seven-eights were industrial and the remainder agricultural. These proportions reverse the percentages of the two sectors that obtained twenty-three years ago and testify to Israel's firmly acquired vocation as an industrial country. It is also important to notice the trend toward increasing diversification in both sectors. In agriculture, citrus fruits continue to provide two-thirds of the exports ($172 million in 1973), but a large variety of products, such as winter fruits and vegetables, flowers, groundnuts, cotton lint, and poultry produce have been added to the list and account for the remaining third. In the industrial export sector, now as ten years ago, polished diamonds account for about 40 percent of the total value, placing Israel in second place in the field in the world after Belgium and in first place in the export of medium-sized stones. The remaining 60 percent of industrial exports include a substantial variety of goods, some of which have only recently broken into the export field. The most important of these products, listed in descending order (and rounded numbers) after diamonds ($560 million), are textiles and clothing ($150 million), processed food ($105 million), chemicals ($80 million), metal products ($60 million), electric and electronic equipment ($29 million), rubber and plastic products ($29 million), transportation equipment ($29 million), machinery ($20 million), paper and printed material ($17 million), and wood products ($16 million). The entire export picture reflects Israel's economic posture as a country in an advanced stage of transition toward a modernized economy, producing a substantial variety of merchandise and capable of shifting emphasis according to circumstances and market conditions.

A similar effort to achieve greater maneuverability through diversification is detected in the search for markets, but with only limited success. Israel has diligently built up a clientele of more than seventy countries, most of them in Asia, Africa, and Latin America, and has increased its exports to them from 8.1 percent of total exports in 1956 to 16 in 1961 and 24 percent in 1973. However, the great bulk of its aggregate sales to those areas—nearly 70 percent—went to only four Asian countries: Japan, Hong Kong, Iran, and Singapore. All of Africa accounted for only another 12 percent (or 5 percent of total exports) and all of Latin America for another 6 percent (1.7 percent of total exports). In contrast, the United States and Canada alone accounted for 20 percent of Israel's total exports in 1973, and the nine European Common Market countries (including Britain, Denmark, and Ireland) for 39 percent. Other West European countries bought 12 percent, while the East European countries of the COMECON bought only 1.3 percent, most of it accounted for by Rumania. The overall pattern clearly shows that Israel, like other economically advanced countries, trades mostly with other advanced countries, contrary to the hackneyed notions that dominated political-economic thinking in the heyday of imperialism and colonialism about the need of industrialized countries to exploit the markets of the nonindustrialized.

Israel's imports of goods and services have increased tenfold in the last twenty-two years, slightly less than fourfold in the last decade, and amounted to $4.2 billion in 1973. Of the total imports, until 1966, goods amounted for an annual average of about 61 percent, services for 30 percent, and defense imports 9 percent. Since 1967 the share of defense imports increased to an average of 26 percent and that of goods to 55 percent. In absolute amounts, defense imports came to $1.2 billion in 1973.

The structure of Israel's commodities imports reflects the already familiar pattern of the economy's production and growth. The bulk of the bill— over 63 percent in recent years—covers raw materials and fuel and lubricants for industry, agriculture, and construction. An additional 30 percent consists of the costs of investment goods, and the remainder of consumer goods. The single most important source of Israel's imports is the United States, which in recent years accounted for 33 to 45 percent of total imports of goods and services, far exceeding $1 billion a year in the last few years. The European Common Market, in its 1973 membership, supplied 47 percent of Israel's goods in recent years, with Britain and West Germany accounting together for over half the amount.

Problems and Prospects

Despite the impressive record of economic development in its first twenty-five years, Israel still confronted even before the 1973 war a number of very difficult problems that seriously threatened its future welfare and growth. Among these problems are to be found the kindred troubles of inflation, excessive consumption and low saving, rising labor costs, and distortions in the allocation of resources. But overshadowing all the troubles and lending them a particular relevance is the issue of Israel's excessive dependence on outside assistance as reflected in an import surplus of enormous magnitude.

Israel's use of the vast inflow of outside capital to realize a very high rate of growth of aggregate and per capita GNP was an outstanding achievement, but its failure to use this growth to reduce significantly its dependence on foreign assistance was a signal shortcoming. The record of this failure is quite clear despite all innocent and deliberate attempts to befog it. Although GNP grew by some 800 percent between 1950 and 1973, the proportion of the import surplus in relation to it at current prices remained virtually the same at the end of the period as at its beginning. No significant portion of the expanded national product went into new net investment, the whole GNP being just about equal to total consumption plus depreciation. In other words, all the increase in production went for consumption, and the increased need for investment resources was supplied by an enlarged import surplus financed from the outside.

The failure of Israel to provide at least part of the sinews of growth domestically is connected to a multitude of interrelated reasons. Proximately, it has to do with a very high level of consumption on the part of the public sector because of the desire of the government to provide at one and the same time for the large defense needs of the country, stimulate and absorb immigration on a large scale, and maximize social justice and public welfare; and on the part of the private sector, it has to do with the coupling of the natural desire for better living conditions with inflation and monetary instability, the ability of the workers to have their way in wages, and the habit of employers to pass on the costs to the consumers without fearing foreign competition. Ultimately, the failure is the result of two general factors: the security position of the country and its Zionist vocation, on the one hand, and the nature of its government as a coalition dominated by workers' parties, on the other hand. The first commits the country to rapid economic growth; the latter prevents the government from taking the tough measures needed to provide domestically more of the resources for growth and to check the disturbances attending rapid development, as long as other alternatives, however temporary, are available.

Because of this situation, Israel has sought to meet the problem of economic dependence almost exclusively by using the expanded economy to increase exports at a faster rate than imports, and thus bring the two to the point of equality. In theory, this approach is feasible, and, as a matter of fact, it is much more humane than the painful methods of indigenous capital accumulation through enforced greater savings. The question is whether it can be done in practice, and at what alternative costs. More specifically, the question is: (1) whether exports can actually be expanded continually at a significantly faster rate than imports to close the gap between the two within a reasonable period of time; (2) whether the outside capital resources needed to finance the gap while it lasts can be found—keeping in mind that the size of the gap is bound to increase for some time in absolute terms even while it decreases in proportional terms; and (3) what political costs, if any, are incurred in the course of mobilizing these resources. A look at Israel's past record puts these questions in bold relief.

Between 1949 and 1965, Israel's exports grew almost continually much faster than imports. Over the 1955–1965 decade in particular, exports grew at almost twice the rate of imports—17.1 percent as against 9.4 percent. At the end of that period, exports paid for 60 percent of imports, but because of the initial great disparity in the size of the two, the absolute size of the import surplus still grew from some $280 million in 1955 to $520 million in 1965. Nevertheless, had the process continued at more or less the same pace, the size of the absolute gap would have soon reached a maximum point, after which it would have started to move rapidly toward the zero point where exports equaled imports. What happened instead was that the process was suddenly reversed as imports shot up faster than exports, increasing considerably the proportional as well as the absolute gap. Whereas exports had reached 66 percent of imports in 1966, they fell back to 65 percent in 1967, 62 percent in 1968, and 52 percent in 1970 before picking up again to 57 percent in 1971. In the meantime, the size of the absolute gap had risen from about $450 million to over $1.2 billion. Israel's march toward economic independence was thus set back by nearly a decade, at the same time that the burden of financing the gap each year increased enormously and was virtually certain to increase even more.

The reasons for the abrupt reversal of the trend after 1967 were a resumption of full employment and rapid growth after two or three years of recession, the resumption of large-scale immigration after a similar period of slowdown, and above all the tremendous expansion of defense expenditure. Between 1966–67—the last full year of "peace"—and 1971–72, defense allocations increased fivefold in absolute terms and two and a half times as a percentage of GNP, while defense imports rose from $116 million in 1966 to over $800 million in 1972. A recognition that the reasons for the reversal were all "good" only underscores the difficulty of the problem by indicating that little could be done about them and that they were not very likely to "go away" soon. Defense spending in particular was expected in 1972 to amount to some 40 billion Israeli pounds in the following six years, 50 percent more than in the previous six, according to the forecast of Israel's civil and military leaders. This means that it was expected to remain at the 1972 relative level taking into account the growth of GNP, even under the best military and political assumptions, presumably because the spending was connected with long-term planning and programming of the country's security needs. It was thus clear before the 1973 war that it was going to be very difficult to resume the trend of increasing exports at a faster rate than imports, and extremely difficult to sustain it over anything like the period in which it had been sustained in the past. In any case, Israel was bound to face the problem of finding the resources to finance a deficit of an ever larger absolute size.

In discussing this last problem with responsible Israelis before the 1973 war one often came up against a disconcerting measure of insouciance. One was reminded that throughout the 1950s and most of the 1960s, nearly every book or essay that dealt with the Israeli economy ended up with a forecast that the flow of outside capital on which Israel depended was in danger of dwindling or drying up, and concluded with dire warnings about its economic fate if it did not take immediate measures to become more self-providing in investment resources. Yet, throughout the years of its existence, Israel managed somehow to raise the amounts it needed to finance the rising import surplus, and in many years it even raised more than was needed and put the surplus in the reserves. Thus, in the years between 1967 and 1971 alone, Israel raised almost as much capital as in all the previous eighteen years of its existence to meet the growing balance of payments gap. The German government, which provided an average of $125 million a year before 1967, provided an average of $210 million after. The United States government, which supplied $50 million a year on the average before 1967, contributed an average of $450 million a year since. World Jewry, the third major source, made available $200 million a year before 1967 and $700 million a year since then. In the face of such almost incredible facts, warnings about the availability of capital in the future sounded to Israelis like one more familiar false cry of wolf.

Yet, even the very impressive record just cited bore some ominous portents. Before 1967, for example, 90 percent of the contribution of the German government consisted of outright grants (in the form of reparations and restitutions) and 10 percent was in the form of loans; since then the percentage of loans has increased to 20 percent of the total amount. Before 1967, 40 percent of the American government's aid was in the form of grants and 60 percent loans; since then 90 percent of it has been in loans and only 10 percent in grants. The contribution of world Jewry comprised the same percentages of loans and grants before and after 1967—30 and 70 percent respectively; but in 1971 and 1972 there was a tendency for the share of loans to increase. Altogether, where loans were below 40 percent of unilateral transfers as recently as in 1968 ($178 million as against $435 million), in 1971 they attained double that proportion ($641 million as against $798 million).

The mounting share of loans in the financing of Israel's import surplus meant a mounting foreign debt, the servicing of which mortgaged an ever larger part of Israel's exports. This in turn made the resumption of the pre-1967 process of closing the gap between imports and exports much more difficult to contemplate. Already before the 1973 war the foreign debt needed $400 million to service, according to the budget proposal for 1973–74. That was the equivalent of 20 percent of the value of the expected exports for that year. Thus, Israel faced the prospect of having to work ever harder for a long time in order to advance relatively little toward independence, while having to find ever larger amounts of foreign capital to do so.

Even if it were to succeed in raising the amounts needed, could it do so without jeopardizing its political freedom; without restricting too much its policy options in the international arena? Israel was investing enormous amounts of money and effort in building up military industries in order to expand such options and gain an added measure of capacity to resist pressures. Yet its increasing dependence on loans was very likely to frustrate that aim of its labors. Israelis perhaps thought that financial dependence on other powers was less serious than dependence on them for weapons; they were not perhaps sufficiently aware that in the Anglo-Saxon tradition, the power of the purse has always been the instrument that held the power of the sword in check.

Impact of the 1973 War

The 1973 October War demonstrated the high degree of strength and resilience achieved by the Israeli economy. Helped by an upsurge of voluntary effort by the population, the economy was able to make the transition to a wartime footing in a matter of days, remain mobilized for several months, and then go back to peacetime norms without suffering undue damage and with a minimum of snags and friction. Despite the mobilization of up to one-quarter of the country's manpower and a large part of its transportation facilities, essential supplies and services were maintained and, on the whole, export orders were met. And despite the injection of huge amounts of money into the economy, runaway inflation has been averted (at least so far) by the application of fiscal and monetary brakes, voluntary and compulsory loans, and by a marked restraint on the part of the public in purchases of goods and services.

However, the war also underscored and exacerbated the economy's major weakness. The gap in current account increased from $1.1 billion in 1972 to $2.7 billion in 1973 and $3.4 billion in 1974, while the percentage of imports covered by exports dropped from 60 in 1972 to 50 in the next two years. Most of the increase in the deficit—fully 58 percent—was due to a higher increase in the price of Israel's imports than in that of its exports in connection with global inflation; but, of course, the effect was so large only because the gap between export and import was wide to begin with and had become even wider. Another 29 percent of the increase in the deficit was due to larger direct defense imports. The remainder—nearly half a billion dollars—was due to a fall in the rate of growth of exports from 12 percent before the war to 8 percent in 1973 and 1974, and an increase in nondefense imports by an average of 12 percent in the latter two years.

The deficit in the 1973 current balance was more than offset by capital imports of $3.2 billion, making possible a $500-million transfer to foreign currency reserves. Unilateral transfers—mainly grants from the United States ($788 million), contributions from world Jewry ($742 million), and personal transfers ($650 million)—accounted for 82 percent of capital transfers, or nearly the totality of the deficit in current account. However, in 1974, capital imports fell short of the $3.4-billion deficit by a full billion, which was financed from short-term sources—short-term loans and drawing on currency reserves. Moreover, the share of unilateral transfers in capital imports dropped to 50 percent, with the United States' contribution dropping slightly (to $625 million), personal transfers remaining nearly the same ($676 million) and contributions from the world Jewry dropping by almost half from their wartime high (to $383 million). The result was a large addition to the foreign debt, which amounted to $6.25 billion in 1974 and required to service it $872 million, or one-quarter of that year's exports. For 1975, the burden of debt servicing was expected to be much higher—over $1.3 billion—because of the increase in short-term borrowing in 1974.

These developments have undoubtedly foreclosed the prospect of economic independence and placed Israel in a position of strong dependence on the United States for quite some time to come. The challenge confronting Israel in the remainder of the 1970s is to undertake drastic reforms— reallocate resources toward production for export, restrict domestic consumption, restrain inflation, limit import growth, and so on—not so much in order to eliminate that dependence as to keep it within the limits of practical feasibility. Otherwise Israel would have to plead continuously for ever larger amounts of American aid; and even if these several billion dollars a year were to be forthcoming, they would constrain more and more Israel's already limited freedom of political maneuver.

9

The Constitutional Order

Foundations of the Democratic System

Israel is a parliamentary democratic republic; that is the character of its regime in fact, not by virtue of any self-definition in a constitution. For one of the unique features of that state is that it does not have a constitution at all in the proper sense of the term. Certain laws enacted by the Knesset (Israel's parliament) are tagged "Basic Laws" and are intended in due course to form the basis of an integral written constitution; but not all laws dealing with matters normally included in constitutions are so designated, and even those that are have, with few exceptions, no extraordinary legal standing. They do not require any special majority for their passage or amendment as articles of a constitution normally do, and do not therefore constitute any particular limitation on the usual powers of the legislature. Thus, in theory at least, the legislature can alter the nature of the regime altogether and change completely the structure of government by the same process it follows in enacting the simplest of laws.

The existence of a working democracy in Israel despite the absence of a constitution may provide a refreshing contrast to the habit of so many states, new and not so new, of adopting high-sounding democratic constitutions that have little relation to actual practice. Nevertheless, the American observer, accustomed to a fairly rigid constitution and a delicate system of checks and balances which he regards as necessary for the protection of democracy and liberty, is apt to find the Israeli arrangement somewhat dangerous. It seems to grant too much power to a simple majority of the legislature, which, in the circumstances of modern politics, often means the few leaders of the party or parties commanding that majority and exposes the entire regime to the passions of a fleeting popular will. True, Britain does not have a constitution or any limitation on the power of Parliament, and its democracy does not seem to be the worse for it. But then, could a young nation-state such as Israel be expected to have the equivalents of the long parliamentary tradition, the political experience, and the kind of public opinion which have acted as informal restraints on the power of the majority and as buttresses of liberty in Britain?

Israel does have some unwritten checks and balances that have enabled it to do without a constitution so far. These consist of a balance of political forces in the country and a tradition of voluntary cooperation and egalitarianism going back to Yishuv days. With respect to the first of these factors, the discussion of political parties will show that their character and their relative numerical strength have been such that no one of them could achieve exclusive control of the legislature, and no combination of them could agree on any comprehensive program that might subvert the existing order. As a matter of fact, the absence of a constitution is largely due to the failure of any combination of parties to produce an appropriate majority in favor of any integral constitution to replace the existing ad hoc arrangements. But this balance of forces may not endure for any length of time, and there are signs that it is indeed altering under the impact of the rapid changes in the country's economy, the composition of its population, its leadership and its culture, and of issues raised by the 1967 and 1973 wars.

As for the democratic tradition of the Yishuv, this rested primarily on two basic facts. One was that Jewish society in Palestine had been newly founded by idealistic pioneers imbued with a utopian socialist spirit and rested overwhelmingly on self-supporting labor. No important social barriers or vested interests arose, therefore, which needed to be overthrown or suppressed. The large labor movement that developed did not grow in antithesis to capital but had the conditions for its existence within itself: it created the work that made the workers. All this has altered a great deal in the last two dozen years. Israeli society may still be driven to some extent by the momentum of the Yishuv tradition, but that momentum has slowed down considerably under the impact of rapid economic expansion and massive immigration, especially of Oriental Jews. The other fact at the root of the democratic tradition of the Yishuv was that the community as a whole had no means of compulsion at its command and needed the cooperation of all its members for its immediate nation-building endeavor and its ultimate struggle to win sovereign statehood. Consent and cooperation were therefore its only means not only on the all-community level of organization, but also on the level of each undertaking connected with nation-building, such as a village, a town, a school system, or self-defense. This situation naturally altered with the establishment of the sovereign state of Israel with its power to compel. Although the tasks of national defense, the reclamation of the wilderness, and the absorption of huge immigration call for a spirit of dedication and participation beyond anything that can be achieved by laws, and although they have in fact acted to mitigate the spirit of extreme partisanship in Israel, nevertheless the urge to obtain the consent of the minority and to elicit popular cooperation has diminished greatly and the temptation to rely on mechanical majorities and compulsion has increased accordingly. Altogether, then, it seems that if Israel's leaders had some good grounds for not being overly concerned with the adoption of a constitution immediately after the establishment of the state, they may be guilty of shortsightedness if they allow too long a time to pass without adopting one.

Basic Framework of Government

The institutional framework of Israel's government was largely established by the Provisional Government which ruled the country in the first nine months of its independent existence. That government consisted of a Provisional Council of thirty-eight members, which acted as a legislature, and a Cabinet of thirteen members which acted as an executive. Oddly enough, the Provisional Government exercised a tremendous influence on the form of government in Israel although it had no legal authority, strictly speaking; it was a self-appointed body composed of leaders of the Zionist movement residing in Israel and active in the Jewish Agency, leaders of the community institutions of the Yishuv, and delegates of parties and groups not represented in those two organizations. The respect and support it commanded, which have not been surpassed by any elected assembly or Cabinet since, were due to its success in organizing the urgent services of the state out of the chaos left over by the Mandate and leading the nation to victory in the war that accompanied its birth.

The Provisional Government set the pattern for the present form of Israel's government by organizing itself on a parliamentary basis, whereby the Cabinet derived its power from the Council, exercised it with its approval and under its scrutiny, and remained in power for as long as it retained the Council's confidence. By its Elections Ordinance of November 1948, the Council established also the method of representation in the legislature of Israel, fixed that body's size, and determined the mode of its election. Finally, the Provisional Government provided for the continuation of the laws of the Mandate with some exceptions (notably the restriction of immigration and land purchase by Jews) and of the judicial system of the British administration, adding to it a Supreme Court.

All these crucial acts and many others of slightly lesser importance were adopted by the Provisional Government with a minimum of discussion and hardly any dissent. This was due partly to the enthusiastic mood and the sense of national emergency that gripped all Israelis in those fateful days, and to the fact that the acts made no radical innovation in the spirit and forms familiar to Israelis from the institutions of the Yishuv, the Jewish Agency, and the Zionist Organization. Above all, however, this was due to the realization that these were after all only temporary measures, subject to confirmation or revision by a constituent assembly that would draft a constitution. But what actually happened afterward was that the various combinations of parties were unable either to agree on any constitution that would modify the status quo established by the Provisional Government or to make that status quo itself final by embodying it in a constitution. The result was a compromise decision to leave things as they were but to work out the elements of a future constitution on a piecemeal basis over a period of years. The record of the debates suggests that the discussants had in mind a period of ten to twenty years at the most; in fact, in the twenty-seven years that have elapsed since, only four Basic Laws have been enacted pertaining to the Knesset (1958), national lands (1960), the state President (1964), and the government (1968).

The Knesset

As things stand today, the Knesset is the supreme authority of the land. This is a single chamber of 120 members elected by universal suffrage of adults eighteen years of age and older on the basis of proportional representation of party lists. A Cabinet, now formally called "government," is considered legally constituted only after it faces the Knesset and obtains its confidence. A vote of no confidence at any time must entail the immediate resignation of the government. The Knesset also elects the President of the republic and can impeach and dismiss him.

The Knesset is the sole legislative authority; although the Prime Minister, the competent minister, and the President must sign bills before they become law, none of them has veto power, and the signatures of all three denote merely a compulsory formality. The Knesset fixes the budget of the government by a new law each year and checks on its application through a state comptroller appointed by it. It exercises continual control over the executive and the administration by means of a question period at the beginning of its meetings, the right to ask for a plenary discussion of any subject whatsoever (the "motion for the agenda"), the right of the Knesset committees to inquire into the subjects under their jurisdiction and call for witnesses and records, and, again, through the state comptroller who reports not only on accounts but also on the efficiency of government offices and government-supported enterprises in the country.

Unlike the practice in Britain, which has served as a model for Israel in many respects, no authority in the land—neither the Prime Minister nor the President—can dissolve the Knesset and call for new elections, nor does even the resignation of the government necessarily mean the termination of the Knesset. Only the Knesset can dissolve itself and fix the date of the new elections. This anxiety to preserve the independence of the Knesset in principle was allowed to prevail even at the risk of possibly serious crisis in the event that the government having resigned and efforts to form a new one having failed, the Knesset nonetheless does not muster a majority in favor of dissolution. The government, which is bound to remain in office until the formation of its successor, would then continue to act as long as that situation persisted without being responsible in fact or in law to the Knesset. Until 1958, when a Basic Law was passed fixing the regular term of all Knessets to four years unless any decides to dissolve itself, each Knesset fixed its own duration and could, presumably, prolong it indefinitely. That law also set a fixed time and place for the automatic convening of a new Knesset and established for the first time different majority requirements for certain laws and functions. Thus the electoral system based on "universal, nationwide, direct, equal, secret and proportional" elections can be changed only by an absolute majority of Knesset membership (sixty-one votes). A similar majority was set for the election of a President on the first and second ballots and a three-fourths majority for dismissing him. A minimum vote of eighty was made necessary to amend the Basic Law of the Knesset by means of emergency regulations. Normally, the Knesset needs no quorum to transact its business.

Formally, then, the Knesset has even more powers than the British Parliament, of which it was said that it could do everything except turn a man into a woman and vice versa. But, as in the case of the British Parliament and unlike that of the American Congress, the exercise of the tremendous powers of the Knesset is, in practice, overwhelmingly under the control of the government, which commands a Knesset majority through strict party discipline and which has by law a decisive say in fixing the Knesset's agenda.

The Government

Israel, like Britain, has a much less definite separation of powers among its three branches, especially between the legislative and the executive, than the United States. The executive (the government), as has been said, is under the authority of the Knesset. After elections, the President charges the head of one of the parties with the task of forming a government from Knesset members as well as from outsiders; but the government is not considered legally installed until it confronts the Knesset and receives an explicit vote of confidence. There is no fixed number of ministries or ministers, and these have generally varied to suit the needs of the country as well as the political considerations attending the formation of a government.

The government has very broad capacities in law and even broader ones in fact. In practice, the government leads the Knesset in most essential functions more than it is led by it, and has charge, in addition, of the executive functions which are all its own. It not only determines internal and foreign policies and executes the laws, but possesses the initiative in legislation almost exclusively. Unlike the practice in Congress, it is virtually impossible for a Knesset member to initiate a law, although he is legally entitled to do so, unless the government is willing to surrender the priority it has for its own business and to allow its supporters in the Knesset to back the private member's bill. The government collectively, and each minister in his own sphere singly, are empowered to issue the regulations necessary for the execution of legislation, and these regulations have the force of law subject to the tacit consent of the Knesset and the interpretation of the courts. In foreign affairs, the government can itself enter into international agreements that commit the country without reference to the Knesset, although the latter can discuss all acts of the government and vote it out of office any time. The Transition Law of 1949 requires Knesset ratification of treaties with foreign states, but the government has tended to put a strict construction on the term so as to exclude from Knesset prerogative a wide variety of "agreements."

Powerful as the government is in Israel, it is less powerful than the British Cabinet in theory as well as in practice. It lacks the right of dissolving the Knesset, and its freedom of action has been limited by the fact that the division of political forces in the country has made possible so far only coalition governments, which lack internal cohesiveness and unity. The Israeli Prime Minister does not have the power of his British equivalent to nominate or ask for the resignation of any or all of his ministers. The parties in his coalition appoint their own ministers whom the Prime Minister can dismiss only if the parties violate the principle of collective responsibility by voting against the government, or if he himself resigns and thus brings down the entire government. All in all, the pattern of legislative-executive relations that has emerged in Israel seems to strike a compromise between the continental European tradition favoring an omnipotent assembly and the British system of an extremely powerful Cabinet.

The President

The President of Israel presides but does not rule. He has only formal and ceremonial functions except for two prerogatives: that of granting pardon and that of designating a person to form a government. The latter right is usually circumscribed since the President has to choose a candidate who can muster the support of the majority of the Knesset and this, in the circumstances of Israel so far, has meant, with one exception without consequence, the leader of the largest Knesset faction. It is conceivable, however, that under certain circumstances this right may become of practical importance. Should the leadership of the largest party not be settled on one person, for instance, or should two Knesset factions emerge that would both be capable of marshaling a coalition, the President would have a real choice in determining the Prime Minister.

The President is elected by the Knesset for a term of five years and for a maximum of two consecutive terms. On the first and second ballots he needs to obtain a majority of the total Knesset vote, or sixty-one; thereafter a majority of the votes cast is sufficient. He can be impeached by a vote of three-quarters of all the members of the Knesset Committee and can be dismissed by three-quarters of the entire Knesset itself on the grounds of behaving in a manner not in keeping with his position. The Knesset can also depose him on the grounds of incapacitating ill health. A Basic Law passed in 1964 established that a candidate to the presidency must be an Israeli citizen residing in Israel. Prior to that the pertinent laws required no qualification whatsoever, which pointed out the extent to which the Israeli legislators viewed that office as honorific. The extremely weak position of the President provides an assurance against conflicts between him and the other branches of the government. On the other hand, it has also deprived the Israeli political system of a potential stabilizing influence which could have been very useful in view of the highly fragmented nature of political opinion in the country.

The Judiciary and the Legal System

Israel has an eclectic judicial and legal system in which British influence is nevertheless predominant. There are two networks of courts in the country, one general and one special. Not all the courts operate on the basis of legislated laws. The Ecclesiastical Courts and the Arbitration Courts, though sanctioned by the state, operate on the respective bases of the religious law of the state's residents and of equity and tradition. The special courts deal with matters that fall under municipal, military, and administrative laws and regulations; the general courts supervise the special courts and deal with all the matters not covered by them. They are organized in a three-tier hierarchy culminating in a Supreme Court of nine members, which acts as the highest court of appeal and as High Court of Justice to hear charges of arbitrary and illegal action by public authorities. In 1948 and 1949, when a constitution was being considered, it was suggested that the Supreme Court should have the power of judicial review, but the proposal found no favor. Nevertheless, in 1969 a precedent was set that may have opened the way for judicial review of legislation. In that year the Court ruled that certain provisions of a law for the public financing, limitation, and control of election expenses violated the "equality" provision of the 1958 Basic Law on the Knesset, and the Knesset accordingly amended the law in question. The Supreme Court, together with other courts, exercised quite vigorously from the outset the power to void regulations as unauthorized by the law on which they rest, or as unnecessary for its proper execution.

All judges are nominated by an Appointment Committee which consists of the minister of justice, two members of the Knesset elected by secret ballot, three justices of the Supreme Court, two ministers, and two elected representatives of the Israel Bar Association. The nominations are forwarded to the President who makes the appointments, subject to Knesset confirmation. This procedure is one of the most important innovations in the emerging constitution of Israel. Together with other, more conventional, measures it is intended to secure the independence of the judiciary, which has in fact availed itself fully of its position. Judges hold office during good behavior and are required to retire with pension at the age of seventy (seventy-five for judges of the Religious Courts). Their salaries are fixed by the Finance Committee of the Knesset and are at present set on a level that gives the chief justice of the Supreme Court a salary equivalent to that of the Prime Minister.

The laws applied in Israel derive from several sources. Upon the establishment of the state, the Provisional Government adopted the entire body of law that ruled in Mandatory Palestine, with the exception of a few laws that restricted Jewish immigration and land purchase and laws that were contradicted by ordinances issued by it. The establishment of the Knesset brought an addition of new laws and modification of old ones, but did not change the situation with any large-scale new codification. The laws inherited from the Mandate themselves derived from three sources. One was the Ottoman laws that prevailed in Palestine on November 1, 1914, the day Turkey joined in the war against the Allies, to the extent that they were not subsequently changed or cancelled by the Mandatory government. These laws were themselves a composite body that included survivals of Muslim religious law, important elements of French law, laws enacted by the Ottoman legislator, and the religious law of the non-Muslim communities. A second source of Palestinian law consisted of laws and ordinances issued by the Mandatory government and the Palestinian local authorities. Finally, a third source consisted of the common law and laws of equity of Britain, which were used to fill the gaps in the previous two sources to the extent that they were deemed suitable to the local conditions. Among the legal elements from the British tradition inherited by Israel were the prerogative writs of habeas corpus, mandamus and certiorari, and the order *nisi* which, in the hands of the Supreme Court sitting as a High Court of Justice, have been used very effectively to protect citizens against arbitrary or illegal behavior by public authorities and to instill respect for the rule of law.

These, then, are in brief the basic institutions and procedures of the government of Israel. They fall far short of a constitution not only in the sense, already mentioned, that they rest for the most part on acts which have the standing of simple laws and which can be abrogated or modified by a relatively easy process, but also in the sense that they leave many gaps that need to be filled. There is, for example, no period fixed by law or usage within which elections must take place after a Knesset dissolves itself, but each Knesset fixes anew the date of the election of its successor. The relations between the state and the various religions are still technically governed by Mandatory and Ottoman laws whose foundations were completely altered by the establishment of the state of Israel. There is no Bill of Rights, and the protection of the citizens' liberties rests mostly on the assumption that everything is permissible which is not specifically prohibited by the regular law or by the emergency regulations which have been kept from Mandatory days. As may be gathered from all these examples, some of the gaps have remained because the practical need to fill them has not yet been felt. But others exist because the circumstances of party politics have conspired to leave them unfilled, and still others because they relate to highly divisive subjects such as religion, or such delicate issues as the balance between civil liberties and the needs of national security.

An issue worthy of special mention at this juncture is that of the emergency powers exercised by the government. Among the laws that Israel inherited from the Mandate were the Defence (Emergency) Regulations, 1945, promulgated by the British High Commissioner under the authority of the Palestine (Defence) Order-in-Council, 1937. These regulations gave the High Commissioner—and the administrative and military authorities of Israel as his successors—very far-reaching powers to restrict the liberty of the individual, his freedom of movement, expression, assembly, and his property rights by administrative action, without resort to the courts and to the processes and conditions attaching to any comparable restrictions under normal legal procedures. In May 1951 the First Knesset, in a resolution carried almost unanimously, ruled that these regulations were incompatible with a democratic state and instructed the Constitution, Law and Judicial Committee to submit a bill to the Knesset within a fortnight for the annulment of these regulations and their replacement by a permanent State Security Law. However, for reasons that are not clear, this instruction has not to date been implemented and the regulations have therefore remained in force. They provided the legal basis for military rule in some Arab-inhabited border areas of Israel until that rule was abolished in 1964, and they provide the basis for most of the security measures enforced by the Israeli authorities since the Six Day War. The manner of application of the regulations has come under frequent scrutiny in the press and periodical scrutiny by the High Court of Justice; nevertheless, the failure to give the regulations themselves a thorough scrutiny by the legislative authority and the retention of an emergency act promulgated thirty years ago by a nonrepresentative government under vastly different circumstances is a severe blemish in Israel's democratic and libertarian record, especially since, as the First Knesset suggested, Israel's security concerns could have been taken care of by more appropriate legislation.

As the state of Israel enters into the twenty-eighth year of its existence, the absence of a constitution symbolizes both its basic internal strength and weakness. There is evidence of basic strength in the fact that the democratic regime of the country has rested for twenty-seven years not on formal constitutional definitions and arrangements but on a practical modus vivendi worked out by the political forces active in it. But insofar as these forces have been unable to extend that modus vivendi to fill remaining gaps and to transform it into a normative pattern enshrined in a constitution, there is evidence of a combination of rigidity and tension in the system that may undermine it by barring it from making the necessary adjustments. These deficiencies will be encountered again and again in the specific topics discussed in the next chapters. To overcome them is a serious internal challenge confronting Israel.

PART THREE

THE
PATTERN
OF INTERNAL
POLITICS

INTRODUCTION

If the constitutional order of Israel is poorly delineated in comparison with the United States, its party system is probably more powerfully articulated than any in the Free World. In the United States, parties were "invented" to make the constitution work; in Israel, what there is of a constitution was "invented" by parties and constricted by the nature of the party system and the way it worked. Parties in Israel not only antedated the constitution but were prior to the state itself and were the principal instruments that created the one as well as the other. At the outset of statehood, the parties not only represented the people, but were themselves in a very real sense the people organized under various political banners.

Over the years of its sovereign existence, Israel developed an elaborate administrative apparatus, an extensive civil service, a powerful military establishment, strong pressure groups, and a substantial independent press which have played important roles in its political life. It has also been exposed to tidal currents and stormy events originating at home and abroad. However, so powerful and pervasive has been the influence of parties that none of these developments can be fully understood without significant reference to their interaction with the party system, its characteristics and dynamics.

Because of the extraordinarily powerful articulation of the party system at the time Israel was born, the subsequent political life of the country may be seen as centering largely on the interaction between the thrust of the initial party system and the counterpressures for change generated by the realities of Israel's experience as a sovereign state. That interaction set in motion a process of adaptation that slowly altered the character of the party system, although it left its form and external appearance largely intact. The process went through two distinct stages, separated by the crisis and war of 1967.

In the course of the two decades preceding the war, a multitude of events and social currents slowly eroded the differences among the parties, reduced the heat of interparty struggles, and generated an ever wider consensus on basic issues among the parties. This trend reflected itself in attempts at fusion between various pairs or groups of parties and in a greater ability among all of them to cooperate within the framework of government coalitions or as government and opposition. The 1967 crisis and war brought this process to a climax and at the same time gave rise to new basic issues that divided the public across existing party lines and created a new political environment. Rather than realign themselves on the basis of the new issues, the existing parties and alliances sought to avert the uncertainties of division by deciding to avoid decision, thus preserving unity of ranks to the detriment of unity of aims.

This adjustment may have been politically expedient but was inherently unstable since it depended on the ability of Israel's government to resist outside pressures to make decisions it sought to avoid. Although the adjustment lasted for some six years, it eventually collapsed under the impact of the October 1973 war, which threw the political system into a deep crisis of adaptation from which it has not yet emerged.

Despite the difficulties presently gripping Israel's party system, the record of its past performance gives reasonable grounds for hope that it will eventually find a satisfactory way to deal with them. It is, at any rate, possible to visualize several plausible solutions to the problems the system now confronts that would put it in a better position to carry on its functions in the future. That much cannot, however, be said about another issue of Israeli political life related to party politics but transcending them: the problem of the relationship between religion and the state. Opinion on this vital question remains almost as sharply divided now as it was when the state came into being, and the pragmatic compromise that was adopted at that time has only served as a constant irritant to the partisans of theocracy and of complete secularization. The explosive potential of the problem has been contained so far by the external threat to national existence, but the persisting tension has obstructed social cohesion and disrupted political stability, and gives grounds for fears about the future of Israel's internal peace if and when external peace is achieved.

10

The Inherited Party System and Its Characteristics

The political parties of Israel had their origins in the complex and feverish life of the World Zionist Organization and in the self-governing organization of the Yishuv in the Mandatory period. For decades before the establishment of the state, groups that called themselves parties or movements competed vigorously with one another for control of these two organizations and for influence within and upon them. By the time Israel declared its independence, these parties had been so completely formed that they simply changed the target of their operations and otherwise continued to operate without the least disturbance. The party system with which Israel thus began its internal political life had four major characteristics: an extraordinary multiplicity of parties, a very strong ideological orientation and extremely intense party politics, an extension of party activities to all spheres of life, and a very high degree of centralization of party authority. These traits tended to reinforce one another, giving the system as a whole a very strong "conservative" inclination.

Multiplicity of Parties

In the elections to the First Knesset of Israel that took place in January 1949, twenty-four parties and organizations competed with separate lists and sixteen managed to elect one or more candidates to the 120 seats. Of the successful lists, ten represented "major" long-established parties, and two represented Arab parties affiliated with Jewish ones. Table 2 shows the principal parties and the percentage of the total votes each of them drew in that election. The reasons for this multitude of parties are the same ones underlying any multiparty system: the multiaxial division of opinion, or the crystallization of organized opinion around a number of issues that cut across each other, and a system of proportional representation.

Table 2. Results of elections to the First Knesset, 1949.

Party	% of votes[a]	Seats
Mapai	35.7	46
Torah Front		
Mizrachi	12.2	16
Hapoel Hammizrachi		
Agudat Yisrael		
Poalei Agudat Yisrael		
Herut	11.5	14
Mapam		
Achdut Haavoda	14.7	19
Hashomer Hatzair		
Poalei Tzion Smol		
General Zionists	5.2	7
Progressives	4.1	5
Communists	3.5	4
Minorities lists	3.0	2
Other lists	10.1	7
Total	100	120

[a] Eligible voters: 506,567.
  Valid votes: 434,684.
  Valid votes as a percentage of eligible voters: 85.8%.

Opinion in Israel was divided in 1949 over five major issues all inherited from prestatehood experience and minimally modified by the fact of the state's establishment. First, there was the issue of basic socioeconomic doctrine. It differentiated five leftist parties—the Palestine Communist party, Mapam, Mapai, Hapoel Hammizrachi, and Poalei Agudat Yisrael—from five rightist parties—the Progressive party, the General Zionist party, the Herut Movement, the Mizrachi party, and Agudat Yisrael. Within each group of parties, too, there were important differences of doctrine and practice on socioeconomic issues, such as those separating Mapam with its dogmatic Marxism from Mapai with its fluid pragmatic socialism, and Herut's inclination to national managerialism from the Progressives' faith in free enterprise. But among at least some of the parties—the Communists and Mapam; Mapai and Hapoel Hammizrachi and Poalei Agudat Yisrael; Herut or the Progressive party and any and all of the other rightist parties—socioeconomic differences were minimal or absent and would not have justified separate parties, were it not that other issues cut across their similar socioeconomic views and differentiated them on those other grounds. One of these is the religious question, which constituted the second main axis of opinion.

The issue of the place of religion in the state separated Hapoel Hammizrachi and Poalei Agudat Yisrael from the other left-wing parties, and the Mizrachi and Agudat Yisrael from others of the right. All these four parties sought to establish in Israel a state based upon the Jewish religious law; but the Mizrachi and its labor offspring, Hapoel Hammizrachi, had for many decades taken part fully in the Zionist enterprise, while Agudat Yisrael and its workers' offspring, Poalei Agudat Yisrael, had opposed the Zionist endeavor as an encroachment upon the idea of redemption through miraculous divine intervention, and their members had come to Palestine for purely religious or practical considerations. The establishment of the state led them to make the major adjustment of accepting it as a fact and working to influence its policy from within its institutions, a step which a few of their numbers have refused to take to the present day.

The religious parties as a group confronted in the other parties varying attitudes toward the religious question. All the other parties were opposed to a theocratic state, although all but the Communists recognized the national cultural value of the Bible and certain elements of Jewish tradition. On matters specifically relating to religion, attitudes differed *within* the other parties on a range extending from considerate tolerance to mild anticlericalism, except for Mapam and the Communists who were militant atheist secularizers.

Another issue that served to justify the division within both the Right and the Left was connected with the definition of the national and territorial claims of Zionism. Until the Soviet Union announced its support of partition and the establishment of a Jewish state, the Communist party of Palestine had opposed altogether the Zionist endeavor and aspiration to statehood. This opposition had defined that party's main difference from Hashomer Hatzair, one of the two components of Mapam, which considered itself Zionist but otherwise shared with the Communists their orthodox Marxist doctrine and attachment to the Soviet Union. Hashomer Hatzair, in its turn, had differentiated itself from the other left-wing parties by advocating a binational Jewish-Arab state instead of an exclusively Jewish state in Palestine.

On the other side of the socioeconomic divide, Herut's antecedents, the Revisionist party and its underground military offshoot, the Irgun, had differentiated themselves from the General Zionists with whom they shared very similar socioeconomic tenets, and from the other parties in general by their claim to the whole of Palestine west and east of the Jordan and by their readiness to fight for their goal alone, outside the framework of the Zionist institutions. The latter disposition had confronted the Yishuv with the threat of civil war and had led Ben Gurion, the Prime Minister in the Provisional government, to order the shooting and sinking of an Irgun-mustered armship, the *Altalena,* a few weeks after the state came into being.

The establishment of the state and the imposition of its authority impelled the Communists, Hashomer Hatzair (united with Achdut Haavoda in Mapam), and Herut to adapt themselves to these facts, but their past attitudes found new forms of expression that continued to distinguish them. The Communists, for example, while accepting the fact of Israel's existence, continued to reject the Zionist doctrine underlying it, which viewed Israel not just as a Jewish state but as the state of the Jews, and to oppose all its theoretical and practical implications. Mapam, while giving up the idea of a binational state, considered itself the guardian of the rights of the Arab minority and pressed for the easing of restrictions imposed on it on grounds of security. Herut, while limiting open talk about *Israel irredenta* and submitting its armed forces to the authority of the state after the *Altalena* showdown, pressed for greater militancy in the country's relations with its neighbors and continued to favor "direct action" to promote its aims and oppose the government, such as street demonstrations.

Foreign policy orientation reinforced the division on the previous issue and gave it an added justification. The Soviet Union's active support of Israel appeared to Hashomer Hatzair finally to vindicate its own long-nurtured faith that the socialist Motherland would some day recognize the merits of Zionist socialism and thus remove the one reservation that Hashomer Hatzair had in its otherwise complete identification with the Soviet Union and boundless devotion to it. Consequently, even while the fighting for the establishment of Israel was still going on, Hashomer Hatzair impelled Mapam to advocate fervently a completely pro-Soviet foreign policy orientation and to look askance at any sign of American or bourgeois-Zionist influence in Israel. At the other end of the spectrum, Herut and the General Zionists were profoundly anti-Soviet and favored a policy of open alignment with the West. Between the two groups stood Mapai, whose nondoctrinaire socialism committed it to neither East nor West. Mapai began with a tentative "positive neutralist" orientation (it called it "nonidentification"), adopted on pragmatic grounds and open to change on pragmatic grounds.

Relations with the Arab countries were not seen in 1949 as a major issue since everyone expected the armistice agreements just concluded or in process of negotiation to lead to peace. But implicit in some parties' perception of the recent war with the Palestinians and the Arab states was an attitude that was soon to engender divisions over policy orientation on this question too. Mapam viewed the armed opposition of the Arabs as having been instigated by the class of effendis and pashas for their own benefit to the detriment of the toiling masses, whose interests lay in peace and cooperation with the Jewish working class. Therefore, when the Arab governments refused to conclude peace agreements with Israel, Mapam professed not to be surprised and looked forward to the coming to power of revolutionary regimes in the Arab countries as the condition for the resolution of the Arab-Israeli conflict. Herut, on the opposite extreme, tended to view the war as well as the decades of strife that preceded it as some kind of Darwinian struggle for survival between two ethnic groups, which could only end in the complete triumph of one and the submission of the other. Consequently, strength and toughness were in its view the only assurance that the Jewish side would definitely win in the end. Between these two extremes, Mapai typically occupied a middle ground. It had a vague perception that the Arab masses stood to benefit from cooperation with the Jews and would not have been hostile to Zionism were it not for the incitement of their leaders who feared the example set by the progressive Yishuv and Israel. Consequently, it shared, albeit with a lesser degree of conviction, Mapam's hopes that social change in the Arab countries would work for better Arab-Jewish understanding. At the same time, it had an intimation that something more elemental, like a clash of cultures or national aspirations, might be involved and that therefore only strength and diplomacy would convince the Arabs to accept and make room for the Jews by their side.

A fifth issue creating political divisions had to do with the "communal problem." The Arabs formed in 1949 several small parties to make Arab grievances and demands heard. Long before, Sefaradi, Yemenite, and Central European Jews had set up separate political groups to advance their interests in the face of the ruling Ashkenazi and Eastern European Jews. Neither in 1949 nor later did separate "ethnically" based political organizations succeed in becoming important political forces on the national level. But the communal problem itself was soon to become a serious issue of social integration and to present a repressed threat of a new political division.

The proliferation of parties in Israel, and, before its establishment in the Zionist Organization and the Yishuv, has been strongly encouraged by the system of proportional representation adopted by all three. In the election system current in the United States and Britain, the candidates for office, be it the presidency, a governorship, or a seat in Congress or Parliament, compete with one another in a given constituency and the candidate who receives a plurality is elected while his rivals get nothing. A defeated candidate for the presidency may obtain many votes in the country and a candidate for a governorship may obtain many votes in his state, but all these votes entitle him to nothing because he did not make up the required plurality. Similarly, a party may run scores of candidates for Congress or Parliament in scores of constituencies and thus obtain a very large vote over the country as a whole, but unless it can get pluralities in specific constituencies, all its votes are wasted. Since elections involve a lot of effort and expenditure, a party under this system is not likely to run a candidate unless he has good chances of winning. Moreover, in elections to Congress or Parliament, unless a party is able to get a sufficient number of members elected so as to give it some leverage in these assemblies, it will tend to drop out of the race altogether or to pool its forces with some large party. This system of single-member constituencies and plurality elections thus discourages political fragmentation and encourages concentration.

In the system of proportional representation, on the other hand, everything conspires to produce the opposite result, especially when the system is applied consistently and without any modification as it is in Israel. There, the entire country is considered a single constituency to which all the Knesset seats are assigned, and these are divided after the elections among the various parties in proportion to the number of votes each of them drew. Thus a party may draw only a few votes in each locality—in the American system they would be completely wasted—but these may add up over the country as a whole to give it a few mandates. This in itself is an incentive for many parties to enter the elections independently, but the effect of the system goes further. Because many parties enter the elections and manage to gain some seats, the final result is that no single party is able to gain a majority in the Knesset and only coalition governments can be formed. This gives even a very small party a chance to place one or more of its members in the government and thus makes its whole effort worthwhile and worth continuing. There is no incentive for small parties to merge since this would not give them any significant advantage and there is, on the contrary, every inducement for a discontented minority within an existing party to split off and form a party of its own. Accordingly, the entire system discourages political concentration and encourages fragmentation. It encourages political groups to lay stress on the issues and features that divide them rather than on the interests they may have in common.

Having seen how the multiaxial division of opinion and proportional representation conspire to produce a multiplicity of parties, the next question is why these two factors became established in Israel or in the political organizations that preceded the establishment of the state—the World Zionist Organization and the Yishuv self-government.

In general, where a society is already divided into a number of fixed positions that cut across each other when it comes to setting up a representative system, and where that society does not want or is unable to repress one or more of these positions, there is no escape from setting up a system of proportional representation, which perpetuates and multiplies that initial division. Certain modifications of the system of proportional representation may reduce to some extent the number of divisions, but a basic remedy can be achieved only by mutual accommodations and voluntary mergers among the parties which may then be consolidated by a reform of the system of representation. On the other hand, where opinion is divided into only two crystallized positions or two sets of related positions at the time a representative system is to be set up, the community is free to choose any system of representation, and the system it chooses will have a decisive influence on the number of parties that may emerge over the course of time. If it adopts a system of single-member constituencies and plurality elections, the dual division is likely to become perpetuated. New issues may arise all the time, but the tendency will be for them to fall within the existing dual framework. They may upset the balance of forces between the two parties, change their character and their names, but they will not alter the dual pattern. Occasionally, a crucial issue may temporarily give rise to a third party, but the system of representation is likely in the long run to restore the dual division, either by the existing parties' "plundering" the successful ideas of the new party or by the new party's pushing aside one of the existing parties and becoming itself the second major party. But if the society initially divided into two set positions adopts the system of proportional representation, the next issue that arises or the next conflict within one of the existing parties is almost sure to produce another party, and yet another; once this happens, it is difficult to change altogether the method of representation without recourse to repression. The critical questions, then, affecting the number of parties are: how was crystallized opinion divided at the time the system of representation was set up? And, if opinion was not yet crystallized or if it was crystallized in a dual division, what sort of system of representation was adopted?

When Herzl established the World Zionist Organization to speak and act on behalf of the national political aspirations of the Jews, its adherents embraced a vast diversity of views. Coming from all over the world, from all sorts of environments, and from all levels in the social structure, they brought with them a wide variety of ideal political-social images derived from their different environments. And although at the time the organization was founded and for a few years thereafter these attitudes and images had not yet assumed the form of organized parties, the nature of the organization and the circumstances in which it operated precluded the setting up of a system of constituency and plurality elections, but rather prescribed the establishment of a method that quickly developed into proportional representation with all its inevitable consequences.

The Zionist Organization was called by its founder "the Jewish State on the way," and its institutions were often thought of in terms analogous to state institutions. These descriptions and comparisons, although they proved to be prophetic in a general historical sense, are less useful when one seeks to understand the political nature and dynamics of the organization and its institutions. Except for some formal analogies, these had nothing in common with the objects with which they were compared. In fact, the Zionist Organization differed substantially even from other nationalist movements—many of which, incidentally, may also be called "states on the way"—because the people on whose behalf the organization claimed to speak were dispersed all over the world and constituted an insignificant minority in the territory that was the object of its aspirations. Because the Zionist Organization, unlike a government, was not involved in ruling a given territory, a territorial constituency representation was pointless. And even if constituency representation were desirable on some other ground, it was highly impractical because the organization did not operate within defined territorial limits. In any case, a plurality vote was wholly undesirable because it involved an element of compulsion and, above all, because it was bound to leave unrepresented a substantial number, if not most, of the members—an absurd situation for an organization whose sole authority was the moral one of claiming to represent all sorts of Jews and which therefore, needed every additional member almost as much as he needed it. Nothing seemed more natural, therefore, than for the organization to adopt the system it did, which simply allocated to every so many members the right to send a delegate to the Congress, the supreme representative institution of the movement.

As the Zionist movement progressed in its endeavors and became a force of importance among the Jews and in the international political arena, the diverse backgrounds of its members combined with the method of representation adopted by its organized institutions to produce a large number of factions and parties. Some differentiated themselves on grounds of tactics to be followed by the movement, others on the grounds of personality, others still on the grounds of the religious, social, and economic character of the state to be. Some drew their inspiration from the liberal democracies of Western Europe, others from Wilhelmian German authoritarian capitalism, and still others from Eastern European idealist utopianism or revolutionary socialism. The varied orientations, coming together for a brief meeting in a biennial World Zionist Congress, could not be stamped out by a single overriding direction without crippling the whole organization, even if such direction had majority support. The Zionist movement, as a voluntary organization, was too weak to impose unqualified majority rule since the losers in an important showdown might depart and form separate Zionist bodies, fragmenting Zionism into feeble cliques. Thus, because of the vital need to preserve the formal unity of the World Zionist Organization, the rights of the minor parties were always respected; they were granted representation in the Executive and the Council, which ran affairs between World Congresses, and their members were appointed to posts in the Zionist bureaucracy.

In time, the Zionist parties developed their own organizations and agencies in the countries of heaviest Jewish concentration, and when their members emigrated to Palestine, they brought with them the party baggage and flag. In the 1920s the newly arrived Zionists set up a constitutional framework for the entire Jewish community in Palestine and sought recognition for it from the Mandatory administration together with the right to levy rates from the community's members. Both recognition and right were granted, but on condition of ensuring a proportional representation to ethnic groups in the community and of reserving to every individual the right to contract out of the community altogether. Thus, the same voluntary method and the same imperative to include as many members as possible and preserve external unity that prevailed in the World Zionist Organization acted in the self-governing institutions of the Yishuv to ensure the adoption of proportional representation and to protect the life of the smallest independent faction. In the case of the Yishuv, the drive toward individual party life was even accentuated because each of the units had the opportunity to implement its ideological utopia, whether in the form of a collective kibbutz, free-enterprise exploitation of orange groves, the setting up of cooperatives, or the establishment of religious colleges.

When the state was declared in 1948, the parties had been already too well established to allow for even the thought of change. Each had developed its own ideology, its own institutions, its own rhetoric, its own oligarchy, and its own vested interests, and most of them had been accustomed to living, working, and fighting with one another. When the Provisional government of Israel issued its ordinance calling for elections to the first sovereign Knesset, it prescribed proportional representation as the natural method of election.

Ideological Orientation and Intensity

In a climate suffused with the pragmatism of American and British politics, the term *ideology* carries connotations of dogmatism, lack of realism, and fanaticism in the same way that the term *propaganda* carries overtones of deception. When American and British parties and politicians talk about abstract ideas they speak of *principles,* never *ideologies,* and when they seek to spread their views they resort to *publicity,* never to *propaganda,* or—God forbid—to *indoctrination.* In the climate of Israel's politics, on the other hand, *pragmatism* was until not long ago a term of opprobrium connoting opportunism and shortsightedness when it did not denote the moral monstrosity of justifying the means by the end. A party that did not profess an elaborate ideology and did not engage actively in indoctrination was nothing but a group of opportunists who were only thirsty for power and self-aggrandizement. Every party in Israel had therefore at least one organ devoted wholly or in part to the discussion of "fundamental questions"; it had its specialists in ideology, its itinerant speakers, its school for "activists," its seminars and study days, its cultural committees and its clubs. Old-timers and keepers of the "party conscience" bemoaned the decline of ideological fervor as the years passed in the same terms and tones that the prophets of old used to decry Israel's neglect of God's Word. And, like their more famous models, they foresaw doom and desolation unless Israel "repented" and returned to living according to ideological inspiration.

The reasons for this addiction to ideology go back to the environment and historical circumstances in which the Zionist endeavor unfolded. Because Zionism was a movement that emerged among a widely scattered people who were everywhere a minority and because it lacked any means of coercion and had no substantial foothold in the territory to which it laid claim until long after it began, it could only rely on persuasion and moral pressure to achieve its aim, at least until it could establish a position permitting it to use other means. It needed to persuade the persecuted Jews that its program was the only solution to their suffering, the emancipated and assimilated that it offered them the only guarantee of their security and dignity, and the traditionalists that its scheme was in the best spirit of Judaism. It had to make some world powers believe that it was in their best interest to support it, and convince all and sundry that its project was realizable. To accomplish all this and to answer the objections of Jews and Gentiles, it had to develop a whole sociology of the nature and causes of anti-Semitism, produce a reinterpretation of the history and eschatology of Judaism, and make continual reassessments of world power realities as they might affect or be affected by Zionism and Palestine. All of these quickly built up into a general storehouse of ideology on which all parties in the movement drew and to which they made their specific additions, each according to its inclination.

Under the leadership of Theodor Herzl, the Zionist movement acted for a while as an international lobby aimed at obtaining a charter for the Jewish National Home prior to organizing a general exodus of Jews from Europe. But once this grand scheme failed, the movement directed its effort toward slow, piecemeal colonization work in Palestine based on the labors of small numbers of pioneers. Since conditions in the country were very difficult and life there involved great hardships and sacrifice, candidates to do the work could be recruited only through prior intensive indoctrination or ideological self-intoxication. As the Zionist endeavor progressed and succeeded, the original pioneers became the founders and leaders of most of the country's institutions and parties and left on them the imprint of their predilection for ideology.

But probably the most fundamental reason for the addiction of Israeli parties to ideology lies in the circumstances under which they originated and grew in Eastern Europe at the turn of the century. At that time Judaism there was confronting a most severe crisis as a result of the impact of the Enlightenment and the deterioration of the conditions of Jewish existence. Large numbers of Jews in Tsarist Russia and Poland who had managed to acquire a modern education during the short period of relative liberalism in the 1860s and 1870s became convinced, like many Christians around them in similar circumstances, that their religion was obsolete, superstitious, false, opposed to progress, or harmful. The initial reaction of many of them was to substitute for their faith a fervent belief in one of the many current liberal, populist, or socialist philosophies, and to join groups of Russians of similar persuasion in seeking to reform or transform Russian society in accordance with their favorite philosophy. However, the reaction that set in after 1881, and particularly the outbreak of pogroms that were often tacitly condoned by Russian "progressive" and revolutionary groups, made many of these Jews realize that their Jewishness set them apart and would make it impossible for them to live their philosophy even in a transformed Russian environment. They were thus alienated from their own still orthodox brethren as well as from the Gentiles. Other educated Jews, who had sought to redefine Jewish identity on the grounds of an enlightened secular Jewish culture that they tried to create themselves, found the ultimate aim of their endeavor menaced by the uncertain conditions and prospects of their people. Both groups saw in Zionism a timely resolution of their problem, allowing them to discard traditional Judaism for their preferred alternative while remaining Jews. Thus grew the multitude of hyphenated Zionist groups with ideologies that were not merely political doctrines but religion surrogates.

Because Zionist commitment filled the role of religion for a generation of people who had lost their inherited faith, Zionist politics assumed a total, passionate, explosive character that was carried over into Israeli politics. People fought each other with a bitterness and a relentlessness reminiscent of religious controversy out of a similar belief that salvation was at stake. The knowledge that they all must preserve at least the semblance of unity vis-à-vis both the enemies and potential supporters of Zionism on the outside set some limits upon the ultimate practical conclusions to which the parties might push their warfare, but these restraints served to heighten all the more the intensity and drama of the struggle within the vague boundaries of the permissible. Every group strove to maintain its ideological purity and viewed compromise as tainted with sin; even minor tactical differences were sufficient grounds for the definition of a new faction and for endless haggling amid flamboyant oratory.

Illustrations of the passion with which Israeli parties carried their politics are embarrassingly abundant. A left-wing faction seceded from Mapai in 1946 and two years later united with the extreme left-wing movement of Hashomer Hatzair to constitute Mapam, which became the chief rival of Mapai for the vote of the workers. The struggle between these two socialist parties became so intense that in many kibbutzim secessionists from Mapai and loyalists felt they could no longer live together. Whichever group was in the majority expelled the minority, and in some cases sections of one and the same kibbutz had to be segregated by barbed wire. Lifelong friendships were broken, children who had been raised together in children's communities were separated, families were sundered. All this over such issues as whether or not Mapai had sold out to the capitalists and whether or not Mapam had sold out to the Russians. Ironically, a short time after the climax of this controversy, Mapam itself was split three ways over the implications of the beginnings of de-Stalinization.

The sinking of the *Altalena* in 1948, which brought to a climax verging on civil war the long struggle between the organized institutions of the Yishuv and the Irgun, may be defended on the grounds of reason of state, and Ben Gurion's order to shoot may even be seen as an act of courageous statesmanship; but to gloat over the deed, to designate the weapon of the tragedy a "Holy Gun," and to treat the defeated opponent as nonexistent and its leaders as "nonpersons" for nearly twenty years afterward, as Ben Gurion did, was nothing but display of fanatical zeal.

Still another example may be seen in the notorious Lavon affair. The complete record of this issue is still not clear and not all of it is relevant to the present discussion; however, it is clear even now that the whole problem could have been resolved at several junctures were it not for the passion and the intransigence with which the protagonists preferred to pursue their struggle. What was basically a dispute between a minister and his subordinates, all members of Mapai, over the responsibility for giving orders to execute an ill-conceived and worse-fated sabotage operation in Egypt was turned in the end into a free-for-all that lasted over a year in 1960–1961, paralyzed normal government and political life, and splintered and nearly sundered Mapai. As if that were not enough, four years later Ben Gurion suddenly decided to reopen the affair after brooding on it for a year in his retirement retreat; this time what began as a request on the part of the veteran leader from his handpicked successor to establish a judicial committee to review the problem ended up as a convulsive struggle between Ben Gurion and Levi Eshkol within and outside Mapai in which the issue became nothing less than the soul of Israel and its integrity. When the dust of the battle finally settled, the fate of Israel's soul remained unknown, but Mapai's integrity was definitely disrupted as Ben Gurion and his followers, outvoted by their opponents, seceded from the party and formed one of their own.

Crises such as these tell much about the temper of traditional Israeli politics, but the uninitiated observer from more sedate political climates can easily read too much into them. One has to realize that Israeli politics are *normally* keyed to a very high pitch in order to assess the real importance of outbreaks of this sort. It is a normal thing to denounce the tactics of one's opponents not as opportunistic or base, but as sins and crimes. It is normal for a religious spokesman arguing against a bill to safeguard property acquired by a wife before marriage to denounce it as an instrument that is bound to lead to the utter destruction of family life in Israel. It is not considered unusual when an observation by the foreign minister that his interest in the punishment of Nazi murderers pales before his awe in the face of the holocaust brings upon his head charges that he is insensitive to the crimes committed against his people. Hyperbole, passion, cataclysmic oratory, and occasional outbreaks of fanatical zeal are the stuff of everyday politics in the tradition inherited by Israel.

Extension of Party Activity

If the manifold division of opinion was stimulated and enlivened by a strong addiction to ideology, it was given a powerful institutional buttress by the wide extension of party activity. In the United States, parties are organized primarily for the purpose of capturing power during electoral contests. In the interim, they may issue partisan political bulletins and serve as social clubs on the local level. During the heyday of bossism, the ward politicians also engaged in some social and charitable activities, but these were clearly subordinate to the function of vote-getting. In the system inherited by Israel, elections were a mere episode in the life of the party; most of its energies, staff, and financial resources were engaged day by day in widespread activities nowhere else associated with parties. Parties helped build agricultural settlements, industries, and urban housing projects; they founded schools, clinics, and ran medical insurance programs; they had their own publishing houses, issued newspapers and periodicals, established cultural centers and synagogues, maintained sports clubs, and sponsored youth movements. Until sometime after the declaration of independence, some of them even supported their own military and paramilitary organizations. To carry on all these activities the parties employed relatively large permanent staffs, and to finance them they founded their own banks and credit institutions and ran their own fund collections in the country and abroad.

The most remarkable manifestation of this tendency is the Histadrut—the General Federation of Workers. Founded in 1920 by two socialist parties whose total membership did not exceed a few thousand in order to stimulate and undertake the kind of activities described, this organization grew in the course of the next generation to the point where its affiliated enterprises accounted in the 1950s for nearly one-fourth of gross national product of Israel and employed the same proportion of the labor force, its trade unions affiliated 90 percent of the workers by hand and by brain, and its health insurance service embraced two-thirds of the total population. So powerful did this Workers Society become that some of its leaders claimed for it parity with or even priority over the state. The success of the Histadrut, controlled since the early 1930s by Mapai, led other parties to develop similar institutions in competition. The religious Hapoel Hammizrachi, for example, founded the Histadrut Hapoel Hammizrachi, and the Revisionists—the ancestors of Herut—founded the Histadrut Ovdim Leummiyim (the Histadrut of Nationalist Workers). These organizations never approached the Histadrut in wealth and power, but they became strong enough to prevent members of their founding parties from being absorbed by the Histadrut and contributed in any case to reinforcing the pattern of ramification of party activities beyond the immediate, strictly political sphere. Other parties that did not or could not aspire to imitate the Histadrut in the comprehensiveness of its operations, concentrated their extraelectoral activity in selected fields. Thus the Mizrachi concentrated on building a network of religiously oriented schools, the Agudat Yisrael on founding and supporting *Yeshivot* (Talmudic and theological colleges), and the General Zionists on general secular schools, sports, and boy scout organizations. All parties without exception published their own daily newspaper in Hebrew and, in most cases, put out other periodicals in several languages, and all of them had at least one bank or financing institution of their own and several cooperative economic enterprises or other types of economic association.

The reasons for this characteristic of the parties inherited by Israel go back to the fact that Israel was a new society as well as a new state. The society that gained its independence in 1948 did not exist at all only a generation or two before; it was created by the deliberate action of men and women who had lived elsewhere. These people came to Palestine and banded together into small groups to build a new society on the basis of definite ideas that each group had as to what that society should be like. As the total endeavor progressed and central institutions endowed with funds made available by Zionists and Jews everywhere were established, these small groups became political parties competing for influence over these institutions. Newcomers who did not already belong to a party abroad were immediately absorbed into one or another, so that at the time of the establishment of the state most of the population was politically affiliated. One can therefore say that whereas everywhere else societies gave birth to political parties and determined their character, in Israel it was the parties that gave birth to society and shaped its character.

The assumption of extrapolitical activities by the Israeli parties, together with their addiction to ideology, had the effect of making party affiliation into a way of life and of strengthening party loyalties to an extent unimaginable in America or in the West in general outside the hard core of devotees of Communist parties. The establishment of the state and its assumption of primary responsibility in fields that had been previously in the hands of partisan organizations, together with the mass immigration of Jews who had had no previous contact with Zionist politics have done much, as we shall presently see, to weaken or check the spread of this phenomenon. Nevertheless, the inertia and habit of the voters and the organizational adaptations of parties had combined to limit the floating vote in Israel to very small proportions until 1973. Prior to the elections of that year, which were exceptionally affected by the Yom Kippur War, seven national elections in the course of twenty years yielded only very small changes in the relative strength of the parties, taking into account the many fissions and fusions that took place, despite a fourfold increase in the electorate. This can be seen in table 3 on page 158.

Centralization of Party Authority

Americans are used to the idea that each of the national parties is a confederation of scores of sectional and local parties which comes to life once every four years to nominate and try to elect a president. For the rest of the time, and for purposes of other electoral contests, the local party is virtually independent of any central national organization. Hence it is not surprising to Americans that sectional or local leaders in state or local positions or in Congress are able for years and years to defy the national party leadership as long as they keep their fences mended back home.

In the system inherited by Israel, such independence from the party center in any position at any level was almost unheard of. The system did not allow even the slight degree of local and individual independence that is to be found in British parties, which have presented to American students of government models of centralization and discipline to be admired or denounced. In Britain, at least, the constituency parties have the main say in selecting their candidate for Parliament and, despite the proverbial docility of members of Parliament in general, this system has consistently produced a sufficient number of strong or troublesome individuals to compel the party leadership in Parliament not to take the support of its rank and file for granted.

In Israel, the electoral system barely recognizes even the theoretical possibility of an independent candidate. If someone wants to run for the Knesset on his own he has to constitute himself first into a party, present a "list" of himself approved by 750 signatures, and poll at least 1 percent of the total national vote before his list can be considered in figuring the outcome. In the Knesset, under the prevailing rule of proportional distribution of time, he will have exactly five minutes to speak on bills and major debates; and under the rule regarding representation in committees, he is not likely to receive any assignment at all. He can avail himself of the somewhat looser procedures guiding debate on a motion for the agenda and question period in order to play the role of a gadfly; otherwise he will be virtually useless unless he allies himself with some faction, in which case he ceases to be independent.

Israel's electoral system provides one key mechanism for maintaining central authority of the party leadership. The voters do not choose candidates but party lists; they have no right to change the order of candidates on the lists or to write any in. The lists are compiled and the ranking is done in all parties by their respective central bodies, and since the distribution of strength of the various Israeli parties has shown itself to be relatively stable, ranking on the list is tantamount to election or defeat except for a few borderline cases. Because the Knesset member owes his election so entirely to the central party authority—he was not personally elected, he has no constituency of his own to back him, the campaign was financed by the party, and his name was placed where it was by the party—his allegiance and obedience to that authority cannot be less than total if he cares to be reelected.

The import of the remarks about the subjection of the Knesset member to the party leadership must be qualified by the observation—itself of importance in understanding the power structure within the Israeli parties—that for the most part the Knesset members are themselves of that leadership. Because the number of parties is so large and the total membership of the Knesset is so small—only 120—each party can return only relatively few members. Mapai, the largest party never returned as many as 50 Knesset members by itself, while the single second largest party never returned more than 20. Such a small number of seats for each party does not even suffice to take care of all the members of the central committees that approve the lists of candidates, and in some cases the number of Knesset seats won is not even enough to provide for all the members of the respective party executives that draw such lists. Consequently the chances for candidates below the very top of the party hierarchy are exceedingly slim, and the names of old party stalwarts have in fact filled the rosters of the Knesset again and again. As a result, the Knesset has not served as a training ground for future leaders as the British Parliament and the American Congress have done, but has tended to be almost exclusively the club for the ruling elites of the various parties.

The extreme centralization of party authority has tended to perpetuate the multiplicity of parties by placing control of party affairs in the hands of small oligarchies that had a vested interest in the separate existence of their parties, or that personalized the differences and animosities between them Perhaps in the prestatehood and early poststatehood period the personalization of differences was more relevant than the vested interest because at that time the leadership of the parties tended to be more or less ideologically in tune with the rank and file, since both were effectively motivated by a strong, clearly discernible "General Will." Since then, the decline of ideology disrupted the mental unison between leaders and led, and the democratic-centralist procedures of the parties became a thin veil covering the domination of party bosses controlling powerful party machines built according to the classical patterns. These power groups naturally viewed party strategy from the perspective of their particular interests, and even when alignments and mergers between parties were effected, the groups tended to continue to defend their existence within the new setup as separate power factions.

In 1957 Ben Gurion tried to reform the system in his own party so as to give greater say to the branches in the selection of leadership in order to make room at the top for new, younger men. Thanks to his exceptional standing in the country, he was able to push through a considerable measure of formal decentralization of the selection processes in Mapai, which were promptly emulated by other parties. However, it seems that the main effect of the reforms was to impel the central power groups to extend their activities and holds to the branches rather than the other way around. At any rate, the reforms failed to produce the effect sought by Ben Gurion, and the few younger men that have risen up in Mapai, or in other parties, have attained their positions by co-optation rather than by being projected from the ranks below.

Effect of Party Character on the Political System

The multiplicity of parties and the wide variety of their ideological coloring offered the Israeli voter an unusual choice of programs and orientations. To that extent the multiparty system may seem more "democratic" than the two-party system which often gives the American voter, for example, few alternatives. It should be recalled, however, that having chosen the party that best expressed his wishes, the Israeli voter never had the chance of seeing that program realized in full, because under the existing system of proportional representation and firm party allegiance, no single party could obtain the necessary majority to put through its program. All governments had to be coalition governments based on compromise, which diluted considerably the programs of the parties included. Of course, compromise as such is a basic characteristic of democracy everywhere and takes place also within the two-party system; however, in a two-party system it takes place mainly *before* the election, and the voter can therefore often know in advance what sort of compromise he is voting for, whereas in Israel the voter could rarely be sure of the ultimate compromise since this depended on the nature of the coalition formed *after* the election.

The difference in timing of the inevitable compromise had further implications of great importance for Israeli political life. When a compromise has to be formulated after the elections, it is bound to be more difficult to achieve, is likely to be less enduring, and is sure to be more repugnant to the average voter from a moral viewpoint than when it is reached quietly before the elections. For elections everywhere, and especially in Israel, stress the differences rather than the common elements among the various parties, involve bitter attacks against the opposition, impel the parties to "rededicate" themselves to their original "pure and unsullied" principles, and in general arouse to a high pitch the spirit of partisanship and belligerence. To compromise at all after the bitterness of an election is likely to cast doubt on the sincerity of the leaders involved; to compromise easily, without giving ample evidence of a deep reluctance to do so and without standing unflinchingly on at least some points of "principle," is bound to be viewed by the recently aroused party faithful as plain cynicism. Hence, the formation of a government in Israel after elections has generally been a long, painful, wearing process involving a dangerous demoralization of the public and a considerable danger to the stability of democracy in the country. Parties had to agree over the prospective government's program in detail and the distribution of portfolios within it; in the process of bargaining the two topics invariably merged into one. A demand by a religious party to include in the program the enactment of a Sabbath or pork import law, for example, might be traded for a ministry or a department; and a demand for an "economic ministry" by Achdut Haavoda might be traded for a less important one plus a commitment not to sell arms to Germany in the lifetime of the envisaged government. Ministries were dismembered and their departments were shuffled around to allow greater maneuverability for the negotiators, and absurd combinations of titles and positions were made. The social security administration, for example, might be annexed to the Ministry of Labor or it might be shifted to the Ministry of Development; Tourism might be placed in the Prime Minister's Office, be shifted to Commerce and Industry, or be made into a separate ministry; one minister might hold three portfolios while other ministers might hold none; a ministry like Defense might duplicate the functions of several other ministries, while several separate ministries might be set up for Posts, for Information, for Police, for Religions, and for Tourism. All this was done in the glare of publicity while the public was left waiting for months and the Knesset was paralyzed, and all the while each party stressed the horrors of it all even as it threw the responsibility on the other parties. The irony of this situation was that after the long agonies of birth, the governments that finally ensued had for the most part a relatively short and contentious existence that ended in a storm long before the formally appointed term, and necessitated the resumption of the irritating process. The average life of a government extended to less than half its term and that of a Knesset to less than two-thirds.

The Israeli governments' character of precariously constructed coalitions led to a lack of central direction in the administration of the country and a great deal of unevenness in its development. Ministries tended to become the preserves of the various parties who ran them each according to its own conception of the national interest and the party's advantage. Projects sponsored by the various ministries tended to receive a higher or lower priority in budgetary allocations depending as much on the political coloration of the minister in charge as on their own intrinsic merit. Mapai's important ministries might recruit their staff more or less in accordance with the advanced civil service regulations of the country, while lesser ministries and ministries of other parties might be turned into agencies to subsidize the "higher" pursuits of party members.

A fourth and probably the most crucial effect of the system was the domination of all governmental coalitions by Mapai. This was partly due to the fact that, with the average one-third of the Knesset seats it was able to gain continually, it was by far the strongest party. But more than that, it was the result of the particular position that Mapai occupied at the center of the Israeli

Table 3. Results of elections to the Knesset, 1949–1973 (in seats won).[a]

Parties[b]	1973	1969	1965	1961	1959	1955	1951	1949
National Religious Party[c]	10	12	11	12	12	11	10	16
Agudat Yisrael	5	4	4	6	6	6	5	
Poalei Agudat Yisrael		2	2					
Total religious bloc	15	18	17	18	18	17	15	16
Herut		26	26	17	17	15	8	14
General Zionists				17[a]	8	13	20	7
Free Center	39[e]	2						
State list		4						
Total right bloc	39	32	26	30[f]	25	28	28	21
Progressives	4	4	5	—[g]	6	5	4	5
Citizens Rights (Aloni)	3			—[g]				
Total center bloc	7	4	5	4[g]	6	5	4	5

Rafi	—	—	—	—	—	10	—	—
Mapai	46	45	40	47	42	45	57[h]	51[h]
Achdut Haavoda			10	7	8			
Mapam	19	15	9	9	9	8		
Total labor bloc[i]	65	60	59	63	59	63	57	51
Moked (Israel Communists)						1	1	1
Rakah (Communists)	4	5	6	3	5	3	3	4
Total far left bloc	4	5	6	3	5	4	4	5
Minorities lists	2	5	5	5	4	4	4	3
Other lists	7	3	0	0	0	1	2	0

[a] Total Knesset seats: 120.
[b] Subtotals are groupings developed in this study.
[c] Includes Mizrachi and Hapoel Hammizrachi.
[d] Including Progressives.
[e] Likkud.
[f] Excluding an estimated 4 Progressives.
[g] Progressives included with General Zionists.
[h] Maarakh.
[i] Rafi, Mapai, and Achdut Haavoda formed Israel Labor Party in 1968.

political spectrum. Mapai could draw partners for a coalition from its immediate right and immediate left and from one and all of the religious parties; whereas its opponents could not muster a majority unless they all coalesced, and this they were never able to do because they were too far-flung to the right and to the left. The uninterrupted predominance of Mapai mitigated in large measure the instability of government and to a lesser extent the disjoined character of the country's administration by making possible a continuity of leadership personnel in some key areas that exceeded even that of the more stable two-party democracies. From 1948 to 1977, for example, Israel has had only five different Prime Ministers compared with six Presidents for the United States and eight Prime Ministers for Britain. It has had five or fewer different ministers for each of the Ministries of Defense, the Treasury, and Foreign Affairs, whereas the United States and Britain have had as many or more different men occupying the equivalent posts as they have had Presidents and Prime Ministers.

The dispersal of Mapai's opponents which ensured the dominant position of Mapai had the concomitant effect of ensuring the absence of a constructive and responsible opposition. As often as not the formation of a government by Mapai and its allies left an opposition that had very little in common beyond general hostility to the government. Its criticism did not therefore present any coherent pattern implying an alternative program; and since the opposition as a whole was never "in danger" of having some day to assume responsibility for making good on its suggestions, it could afford to take the most extreme positions suggested by the dictates of ideology or demagoguery. The Israeli voters thus found themselves over and again in a situation in which the majority had had quite enough of the rule of a Mapai grown fat and complacent, but had no hope of seeing any alternative materialize. The blame was of course largely theirs since they could not agree in sufficient strength on the alternative to Mapai; but this made the situation nonetheless troublesome for Israeli democracy.

Another peculiarity produced by the system inherited by Israel was the unusually strong influence of the religious parties in comparison with their real electoral strength. In principle, Mapai always favored the formation of broad coalitions because this made any one of its partners in the government dispensable and therefore more tractable. In practice, however, Mapai had to rely a great deal on the religious parties because these confined their demands until recent years to an area to which Mapai was on the whole indifferent, while the other parties insisted on concessions in the field of foreign and internal economic and social policies which were central to its interest. For Mapai, this arrangement had obvious advantages, but for the country at large it meant the imposition on the majority of the population of far-reaching restrictions based on religion owing to the balance-of-power position of minority religious parties.

11
Pressures and Adaptations, 1948–1967

Although the party system with which Israel started its career had a powerful inherent inertia, three sets of forces operated in the first two decades of sovereignty to counter that initial thrust and to force the parties into a process of readjustment. These were the fact of the creation of the state and the activities assumed by its authorities; massive immigration, the forced pace of economic development it entailed, and the consequences of both; and the imperatives of Israel's security needs in the context of changing international circumstances. Together these forces slowly but deeply modified almost every feature of the political system just as they did almost every other aspect of Israeli life.

Effect of the State

We have already seen that the very fact of the proclamation of the state of Israel effectively settled an issue that had previously been a source of grave contention between Hashomer Hatzair (with its idea of a binational state) and the two Agudah parties (with their opposition to a Zionist state) on the one hand, and other parties to which each was otherwise close. This, however, was only one example of the way in which the establishment of the state gradually reduced differences among parties by eliminating some hypothetical options that had served to justify division of opinion and by converting others into practical policy options subject to the test of experience. Ideological addiction and the habit of abstract thinking could and did delay this process of adjustment to reality, but they could not prevent it altogether.

The establishment of the state not only narrowed the scope of differences by discarding irrelevant hypothetical options but also provided a positive common focus of loyalty and emotional attachment that overarched particularistic loyalties to parties. So strong had these loyalties been that party members were at first inclined to subsume loyalty to the state to loyalty to party and to assume that what was good for their particular party was good for the state; but with the passage of time, the weight of the state, the richness of its symbols, and the influx of hundreds of thousands of immigrants whose loyalty was exclusively focused on it brought it to a position of primacy over parties.

The weight of the state made itself felt through its assumption of many functions that had been previously performed by political parties. Thus, education became national, as did social security, the labor exchanges, unemployment insurance, housing, frontier settlement, and recently, care for the immigrants, previously channeled through the Jewish Agency as well as the parties. These services and many other activities of the state have checked and rolled back the ramification of party activity and concomitantly contributed to loosening party allegiances.

Effect of Immigration

Immigration contributed to the change in a variety of ways. During the first four years of statehood, nearly 700,000 immigrants poured into the country more than doubling its Jewish population, and a comparable number followed in the next fifteen years. The absorption of these masses into the existing system could not but alter in fundamentally in the course of time. To begin with, half the new immigrants came from Muslim countries and brought no doctrinaire political tradition and little political experience of any sort in their meager baggage; most of the other half came from Communist Eastern Europe where they had known ideology mostly as a cover for repression and therefore tended to suspect and shy away from it. Since all these immigrants acquired the right to vote the moment they landed in the country, the political parties were compelled to appeal to them in terms that were relevant to them, such as national sentiment, the personality of the leaders, and bread-and-butter issues. This process gradually replaced the parties' near-religious ideological fervor with a practical, pragmatic bent that blurred the differences among them. Illustrative of the change is the answer that Yosef Almogi, campaign manager for Mapai in an election in the 1950s, gave to criticism that his down-to-earth appeal and methods alienated the intellectuals and the ideologically sensitive people from the party: "How many of them are there?" he asked rhetorically, "about one *ma'barah* worth?" (A *ma'barah* is an immigrant transit camp, of which there were many at the time).

Immigration also affected the party system through its effect on the economy. The massive influx of mostly destitute people confronted Israel with the immense task of sorting out the new arrivals, housing and caring for them, and above all providing them with productive jobs. Two critical questions had to be faced: where to get the necessary capital, and how to provide the organization and enterprise to put it into use. At first the various parties answered these questions each according to its abstract ideology. Mapai, which was responsible for the government, initially thought the answers were to be found in the miraculous powers of socialist planning. It sought to raise capital by printing money with one hand and imposing a strict regulation on demand with the other, and it relied for organization and enterprise on the cadres of the existing collective and cooperative sector and on a burgeoning new state bureaucratic apparatus. This approach worked for a while but then collapsed entirely as controls broke down, inflation mounted rapidly, and hundreds of thousands of immigrants piled up in miserable reception camps month after month in costly idleness because of the shortage of jobs and housing. By 1952 Mapai came to see salvation only through massive import of capital from any available source and through the utilization and encouragement of any enterprise that could work and make work. This recognition had much to do with Mapai's willingness to sign the reparations agreement with West Germany, which became possible just then, and to push it through in the face of fierce and widespread emotional opposition. It also underlay Mapai's agreement to enter into a coalition with the "capitalist" General Zionist party.

The participation of the General Zionists in the government signaled an adjustment on their part too, since Mapai's new pragmatic emphasis still involved the investment of much of the public resources through the "labor sector" of the economy and still gave the state a crucial role in channeling the activities of the "private sector." Other parties, however, took longer to free themselves from the hold of ideological dogmas. Herut, for example, violently opposed the reparations agreement with Germany on purely nationalist grounds in complete disregard of any other considerations, although it ceased to object to its application once it was ratified. Mapam not only opposed the agreement but also objected to the entire economic policy of Mapai and continued for some years to advocate its own ideologically inspired plan, which envisaged capital formation mainly through a domestic effort, by organizing the masses of immigrants into collective agricultural and industrial enterprises and "socializing" large private capital resources. The tenuousness of this approach was evident in the fact that even Mapam's own already existing kibbutzim had trouble recruiting enough personnel to allow them to expand production through the cultivation of newly acquired state lands. Like the kibbutzim (and the moshavim) of other movements, its own had to resort to hired labor, in effect turning the strongholds of Israeli socialism into collective capitalist enterprises.

Massive immigration and the character of the immigrants eroded not only the doctrinal boundaries of the parties but also many of the practices and institutions they had succeeded in establishing on the basis of doctrine. The example of hired labor in kibbutzim and moshavim was only one instance out of many; another crucial instance was the gradual erosion of the egalitarian wage structure established by the Histadrut from Yishuv days under the impact of the increasing demands of a growing economy for highly trained personnel and the relative abundance of unskilled labor among the new immigrants. Still other examples included the breakdown of the monopoly of cooperative marketing agencies owing to the resistance of new immigrant farmers, and the practical loss of control by Histadrut central bodies over their burgeoning industrial enterprises. The general effect of these changes was to loosen up all the parties, undermine their self-assurance and intolerance, and slowly transform interparty struggles to appear less as fights among tight sects and more as wrangles within one church, where doctrine still mattered but the claims of the world were also acknowledged and accommodated.

Immigration also helped ease the consequences of the division over the question of the relationship between religion and state even though it did little to advance a solution to the problem. As we shall see in the chapter devoted to the subject, the intricacy of the issues involved, the seeming impossibility of finding a viable middle ground between the opposed views, and the grave implications of any attempt to reach a decision by the simple application of majority rule led all the parties, except Mapam and the Communists, to agree to contain the religion-state problem by maintaining the status quo that prevailed at the time of independence and to postpone its final resolution to the indefinite future. However, this agreement did not prevent the outbreak of frequent clashes concerning its meaning and applications, which threatened to subvert it and lead to widespread civil strife. The masses of immigrants from Muslim countries helped to stem that danger and impose a measure of moderation on the opponents because their different historical experience had led them to hold much more nuanced views on the question of religion and state.

Mass immigration thus contributed greatly to the blurring of previous divisions of opinion or to the mitigation of their expression. True, the very high component of Oriental Jews in that immigration also gave rise to a new issue in the shape of the communal problem; however, this division did not give rise to any new, enduring, ethnically based parties. Rather, it manifested itself in ways that cut across the existing parties, and in this manner, by inflicting on them all a common problem, contributed to the growing similarity of concerns and views among them.

Initially, when the Oriental Jews began to arrive en masse to Israel, they were too destitute, too inexperienced politically, and too ignorant of the country's conditions to be able to organize themselves effectively into independent parties. The few attempts that were made to run ethnic lists proved unsuccessful. The existing parties, commanding strong organizations and extensive patronage, therefore had little difficulty in recruiting the new arrivals into their respective ranks. Curiously enough, for reasons that remain unclear to the present day, the Orientals were not only absorbed into existing parties but distributed themselves among them in such proportions that they did not significantly alter their relative strength. This at first led the leadership of the parties, and the government too, not to give to the ethnic question all the attention it deserved, and to expect the Oriental Jews to be further assimilated into the polity, economy, and society through the operation of such existing integrative mechanisms as social mobility, national education, membership in the Histadrut, and service in the armed forces. In the course of time, however, it became apparent that the partial integration of the Orientals in any sphere only made them more aware of the gap remaining and more impatient with it. Their resentment expressed itself in sporadic demonstrations, sit-ins, acts of defiance of authority, and even occasional outbreaks of violence and a few desertions from Tzahal (the Israeli Defense Force). It also found more enduring expression in increasingly successful attempts by Oriental Jews to promote ethnic candidates on the municipal and local council levels, both within the framework of existing parties and independently. The combination of external pressure and internal threats to the control of central party authorities compelled all the parties to compete in making special accommodations for the Orientals within their ranks, and spurred the government to make special efforts to hasten their more complete integration.

Effect of Threats to National Security

National security was the third and probably the most important countervailing force that helped to modify the initial characteristics of the Israeli party system and their consequences. The general concern with this problem not only prevented Israeli factionalism at its worst from tearing the whole political system asunder, but it also contributed more than any other factor to the development of a positive consensus among parties on some specific perceptions, policies, and procedures. After an initial period of indulging their divergent views, all the parties soon came to share in the perception of Israel as engaged in an inescapable confrontation with its neighbors. They all came to agree that building Israel's deterrent power was the main, if not the only, assurance against destruction and constituted a sine qua non for any prospect of peace. They therefore agreed, too, that the requirements of building Israel's military capacity should have first claim on the country's resources, and that security considerations should be the chief motive of its foreign policy. The armed forces of the state should be insulated from politics, and all disagreements on specific security issues should be resolved in camera in the appropriate constitutional bodies and not be fought out in public.

The agreement on these questions and their many ramifications was not at all easily achieved but required much adaptation by most political groups.

As was previously shown, the various parties differed greatly in their initial perceptions of the conflict with the Arabs and the desirable foreign policy orientation of Israel on the basis of ideological predisposition rather than experience. It took much time and a great deal of struggle before experience could assert itself over ideological predilection and force the various parties to meet on its ground.

The first perceptual adjustment made by all the parties was to renounce their expectation of a prompt liquidation of the conflict with the Arab countries through peace treaties, and to recognize that the Arab reticence on this score created a lasting security problem. All the parties also agreed that the security problem should be met by a combination of national armed power and international support capable of deterring potential Arab aggression. Neither of these adjustments was difficult to accomplish, since neither clashed with any party's ideological inclination. However, the difficulties began with views about the practical application of these realizations.

Mapam, which had felt its long attachment to the Soviet Union vindicated by that country's diplomatic and material support of the creation of Israel, naturally began by advocating a policy of cultivating Soviet friendship as a buttress for Israel's security while opposing cooperation with the United States. It denounced the government for accepting an American loan in 1949 and condemned it for welcoming the Tripartite Declaration of May 1950 by which the United States, Britain, and France made themselves the guarantors of the armistice between Israel and its neighbors and further proposed to enlist the countries of the area into some regional defense scheme. However, Mapam persisted in its advocacy of a pro-Soviet line even in the face of mounting Soviet hostility to Israel, the launching of a campaign against Zionism in the Soviet Union that degenerated into anti-Semitic agitation, the liquidation of Jewish cultural institutions, mass arrests, and the elimination of Jewish writers and artists. Not even the Prague Trials of December 1952, in which a Mapam leader figured as one of the accused, "confessed" to unspeakable crimes against the Soviet Union, and was convicted, and not even the notorious Moscow Doctors' Plot of January 1953 distracted Mapam from its line. On the contrary, it defended its position so passionately against the outraged attacks of members of Mapai that kibbutzim that included people of these two political persuasions had to split up. In March 1953, when Stalin died, Mapam went into official mourning and its organ bemoaned the loss of the "sun of all nations."

By a strange process well understood by specialists on Communist affairs, it was Soviet "liberalism" rather than harshness that began to erode Mapam's faith. Stalin's hard line could always be blamed on the "provocations" that the Mapai-dominated government of Israel perpetrated by selling out to American imperialism. But when, by mending Stalin's actions, repealing some of his sanctions, and restoring reasonable relations with Israel, his own successors implied that these provocations had not been after all so serious, Mapam's faithful became confused. One consequence was that Achdut Haavoda seceded from the party in 1954. Another was that the remainder of the party, torn by dissent, began to allow, even before the shattering revelations of Khrushchev in the Twentieth Party Congress, that Soviet policy and action could after all be less than impeccable. The ground was thus prepared for the about-face that came after the conclusion of the 1955 Soviet-Egyptian arms deal, when Mapam joined the government for the first time since 1949 in a coalition with Mapai and, incredibly, the religious parties. Several months later, when Ben Gurion prepared to attack Egypt in collusion with the British and French "imperialists," Mapam voted against the action in the Cabinet, but nevertheless remained in the government and abstained from opposing the attack in public. Subsequently, whether in the government or out, Mapam persisted in this peculiar method of balancing the dictates of its ideological conscience with the demands of Israel's security, which was more than enough to make it "coalitionable" with Mapai.

The rapprochement between Mapam and Mapai in the field of security and foreign policy involved considerable adaptation on the part of Mapai, too, although this was not nearly so painful. Mapai initially advocated a policy of positive neutrality through which it hoped to retain the favor that the United States and the Soviet Union had shown toward Israel at the outset, and to elicit from both powers maximum support for the goals of security, immigration, and economic development. However, because the United States was prepared to give Israel economic aid and the Soviet Union was not, and because the United States was better placed by its position in the Middle East to help Israel in its search for peace and security, Mapai's pursuit of its proclaimed policy inevitably inclined Israel more and more toward the United States. This inclination was particularly resented by the Soviet government, which at the time was intolerant of even genuine, balanced neutrality and which had internal reasons having to do with its own "Jewish Problem" for keeping some distance from Israel. As a result it turned violently against Israel, leaving Mapai with little choice but to give up neutrality and turn more completely toward the West.

After turning to the West, however, Mapai discovered that the West was not prepared to accept Israel fully. In 1954 NATO turned down a request for membership, and the United States declined a formal proposal for a mutual defense treaty that Israel had made in an effort to counterbalance the projected Western-Arab alliance that resulted eventually in the Baghdad Pact. Mapai's discovery turned into shock the following year when, after the Soviet Union concluded its massive arms deal with Egypt, the West refused to supply Israel with weapons to counter those acquired by Egypt for many critical months until France provided some secretly. It was then that Mapai, disabused of its illusions about the West, decided that Israel could rely for its security only on its own military strength, and on the influence of that strength on the interests and considerations of outsiders; and it was on this new ground that Mapam, disabused of *its* illusions about the Soviet Union, met Mapai.

The other parties with initial definite ideological inclinations about foreign affairs could rally to the new ground more easily than Mapam and Mapai. Achdut Haavoda had begun with less enthusiasm than Mapam (or Hashomer Hatzair) about the Soviet Union and was more inclined toward "activism" in defense. The General Zionists, pro-American before Mapai, were even more disappointed than Mapai by the rebuff of the West and drew identical conclusions from it. Herut, with its extreme nationalism and its predilection for toughness, felt quite comfortable in the new orientation and in the war to which it soon led. In the face of what it regarded as a general vindication of its outlook, Herut was even willing to act with a greater sense of responsibility—by respecting, for example, the reasons of the government in agreeing to withdraw from Sinai in 1957 to the extent of confining its opposition within parliamentary boundaries.

The 1955 Soviet-Egyptian arms deal and the ensuing security crisis and 1956 war rallied the various parties to another common ground with respect to their view of the dynamics of Israel's conflict with the Arab states. The critical factor here was the change of attitude of the new Egyptian regime on the Palestine question from one of apparent moderation to one that seemed bent on mobilizing Egypt's military resources and leading the Arab countries in an assault on Israel. Strangely enough, this change presented fewer problems of adjustment for Herut and Mapam than for the more pragmatically inclined Mapai. Herut, with its nationalistic, power-oriented perspective, had seen the new Egyptian regime from the outset as more dangerous because more effective than the corrupt monarchy and was not therefore surprised to see it act as it did. Mapam, with its classical Marxist approach, never viewed the military coup as the real revolution of the working classes it deemed necessary for a new approach to the conflict on the part of the Arabs. At most it might have been inclined to follow the Soviet lead and look upon the new regime as an anti-imperialist nationalist-bourgeois revolution that bore no hopeful implications for Israel. It was Mapai with its vague populistic perception of Arab hostility as fanned by antiprogressive forces that had had the most hopeful expectations from the new Egyptian regime and was most shocked by the intensified anti-Israeli turn it appeared to take. This initial hopefulness was reflected in the assumption of the prime ministership by Moshe Sharett, replacing the more militant Ben Gurion, and in the secret contacts he entertained with the Egyptian regime in an effort to promote a settlement. The disappointment was reflected in the return of Ben Gurion to the leadership of the government and the dropping of Sharett even from the post of foreign minister he had occupied before the shuffle. It is indicative of the consensus already developed on procedure for settling disagreements on matters of security that the grounds for the removal of Sharett from any role in the government and the extent of the breach that this action caused within Mapai were not disclosed at the time by anyone and became dimly apparent only ten years later.

The overall effect of these adjustments was to lower or abolish barriers between the various parties and to reduce the intensity and heat of party struggles, making possible widespread attempts at formal fusion among various pairs or groups of parties. Thus the four religious parties at one time combined in a formal political alignment called the National Religious Front, and the two veteran Zionist religious parties of the right and left, Mizrachi and Hapoel Hammizrachi, merged to constitute the National Religious Party (Mafdal). The centrist Progressive party united with the General Zionists to its right to form the Liberal party, and the latter in turn subsequently merged with right-wing Herut to make the Herut-Liberal Bloc (Gachal). Finally, Achdut Haavoda and Mapai reached an agreement to merge and began its application with the formation of an alignment popularly called the Maarakh (Alignment).

Even more indicative of the growing rapprochement of parties was their growing capacity to work together as reflected in their participation with Mapai in coalition governments on the basis of common programs. The religious parties were Mapai's first partners and have continued to work with it almost without interruption ever since. The bases of this partnership were, as noted above, an agreement to maintain the status quo in religious affairs and the political convenience of both sides. Next, the experience with economic development and immigrant absorption prepared the ground for the adhesion of the General Zionists to a coalition with Mapai together with the Progressives and the religious parties. The same experience and the weakening of differences in the sphere of security and foreign affairs subsequently made it possible for Achdut Haavoda, and finally for Mapam, to enter into a coalition agreement with Mapai that included the religious parties as well. With the participation of Mapam, all the parties outside of the Communists and Herut became in principle "coalitionable" on a routine basis, and even Herut was on its way to qualifying for partnership through its merger with the Liberal party which had qualified earlier.

But if the fusion and merger of separate parties and the eligibility of more of them for coalition partnership reflected the process of adaptation of the party system to the Israeli experience, a simultaneous series of opposite developments reflected the remaining strength of the original tendencies of that system. Thus the National Religious Front broke up after a brief experience and was never revived again; Achdut Haavoda seceded from Mapam after eight years of unhappy unity; a segment of the Liberal party, formerly the Progressive party, refused to go along with the merger with Herut and set itself up as the Independent Liberal party; and Mapai itself broke up from within in 1965 as Ben Gurion and a number of followers including Moshe Dayan and Shimon Peres seceded to form the Israel Workers' list (Rafi)

The last-mentioned split was particularly important because it struck the party that had been the mainstay of what political stability Israel had and could have had far-reaching consequences were it not that it was countered by an alignment between Mapai and Achdut Haavoda. Moreover, the split was the outcome of a crisis that had stirred up the worst features of Israel's political system. The crisis had developed over Ben Gurion's fierce insistence on reopening the Lavon affair, a complicated tangle that had been bitterly fought out once before in 1960–1961. The revived crisis pitted Ben Gurion, who had recently retired after thirty years of undisputed leadership of Mapai and the nation, against Prime Minister Eshkol, Ben Gurion's longtime collaborator and his handpicked choice as successor; and when Eshkol won at the party convention, Ben Gurion seceded. The electorate's rebuff of the national hero by giving his Rafi list only 20 percent of Mapai's vote in the general election, and the timely alignment between Mapai and Achdut Haavoda, which compensated for that loss almost exactly, not only saved the party and the political system but also gave a dramatic demonstration of the public's impatience with the stormy old-style politics. But that the crisis did occur at all showed how deeply entrenched this style of politics was and how difficult it was for it to die.

In summary, we can say that the Israeli political system underwent a gradual, not easily perceptible, but nonetheless profound substantive transformation in the course of the nineteen years of Israel's sovereign existence prior to the 1967 war. This transformation was a function of the interaction between the thrust of the party system inherited by Israel from the Yishuv and the World Zionist Organization and the exigencies of Israel's experience. The initial division of opinion on socioeconomic issues, the nature and scope of the state, and the question of security and foreign policy either disappeared or became much reduced, giving way to a broad practical consensus on these matters. The division on the religious question remained valid but was contained by a modus vivendi that postponed a showdown to the indefinite future. The communal problem, the fifth of the initial divisions, though alive and menacing, was politically diffuse because it did not produce a single strong party and because it elicited strong remedial measures that commanded the support of all existing parties.

The practical rapprochement among Israeli political groupings was enhanced by a simultaneous decline in ideological fervor generally, by a relative decline in the extrapolitical activities of parties, and by a loosening of their hold on enterprises that remained under their control. As a consequence of these developments, there was a tendency for parties to merge or align themselves into larger blocs, which went hand in hand with an expansion of the number of parties that could be coalesced in a government on the basis of common programs.

This process of adjustment had proceeded with great difficulty and was punctuated by many crises owing to the extremely powerful inertia of the initial system. That inertia and the psychological and material interest vested in it had not only prevented the process of adaptation from going further but had strong latent potentialities for setting it back. Thus the trend toward the fusion of parties was partly offset by a countertrend of fission, the healing of old antagonisms within an increasingly pragmatic atmosphere did not prevent the outbreak of the frenzied disputes surrounding the Lavon Affair in 1960–1961 and 1964–1965, and the gradual qualification of old pariah-parties for participation in the government did not prevent the emergence of a new pariah-party in the form of Rafi led by Ben Gurion. It was in this context that the May 1967 crisis and the war exploded, bringing in their aftermath momentous changes in the political dynamics of Israel.

12

New Pressures
and Readjustments,
1967–1977

Despite the difficulties and occasional setbacks that attended it, the gradual adaptation of the party system to Israel's experience in the course of the first nineteen years of sovereign existence was moving steadily in the direction of an improved and more efficient democracy. If carried further, the processes that were taking place could have led to the crystallization of organized opinion into something resembling a two-party system modified by the addition of one or two religious parties, which in turn would have made a reform of the electoral system both justifiable in theory and possible in practice. The result could then have been an enhanced political stability that at the same time reflected and respected the choice of the electorate; greater coordination and unity in the direction of government; more responsible opposition that had a prospect of realizing its program as an alternative government; closer contact between the voter and his representative, moderation of party centralization and discipline, vitalization of the Knesset; more frequent rise of leaders from below and better circulation of elites; and so on. Unfortunately, however, instead of moving gradually along these highly desirable lines, Israeli politics were thrust by crises and wars into precipitous developments that led the political system into swampy grounds from which it has not yet emerged. Not that the system ceased to be democratic or is in serious danger of ceasing to be so; however, it lost much of its coherence and its ability to face the country's problems. Ironically, the setback began in the guise of a major leap toward unity under the impact of the 1967 crisis and war, and proceeded in the guise of a further leap toward coherence and leadership renovation under the impact of the 1973 war.

Impact of the 1967 Crisis and War

The seeds of the evolution of the Israeli political system in the wake of the 1967 war were laid in the May–June crisis that preceded that war. A detailed analysis of that crisis is given in Chapter 21; for the purpose of the present discussion we need only point out a few highlights. The first is that by the last week of May 1967, nearly all Israelis perceived the situation that had developed as presenting a clear and imminent danger of destruction for their state, and perhaps for themselves as individuals. In the light of the complete and easy victory that followed, these fears may seem to have been highly unjustified; they were nevertheless experienced as very real at that time and left a lasting imprint on the subsequent behavior of Israelis.

The main focus of the crisis as far as the Israeli public was concerned was not so much the actions of Gamal Abdel Nasser or the position of Washington, Moscow, London, or Paris as it was the timid and fearful behavior of their government under Eshkol's leadership. Israelis had been nurtured for nearly twenty years on faith in Tzahal, and for ten years they, as well as the rest of the world, had taken it for granted that an Egyptian blockade of the Gulf of Aqaba would be an instantaneous casus belli. When, immediately after Nasser proclaimed a blockade, Eshkol made a speech on May 23, 1967, in which he did not spell out a clear warning of reprisal but instead called on "the world" to restore free navigation, Israelis began to wonder whether, in the terms of the time, there was "cover" for the credit they had been taught to give to Tzahal. Even those whose faith in Tzahal remained unshaken were distressed by the fear that its power to act was being dissipated by inept leadership. The anxieties and discontent reached their peak on May 29, 1967, after a mumbling speech by Eshkol in which he announced the government's decision to continue exploring the possibilities of resolving the crisis by diplomatic means, and resulted in the building up of enormous and eventually successful pressure on Eshkol to relinquish the defense portfolio to General Moshe Dayan.

The success of the pressure dramatically demonstrated the change that the crisis had wrought in the Israeli political system. The specific proposal for the appointment of Dayan originated outside the government coalition altogether, in consultations that brought together leaders of the two pariah parties of the time, Rafi and Herut, including sworn enemies like Ben Gurion and Menachem Begin who had never exchanged a greeting in their lives. It was endorsed by the National Religious Party, a partner in the ruling coalition, and was forcefully presented by this party's leader in the cabinet against strong opposition by Eshkol. Finally, as the popular dissatisfaction peaked, the proposal was endorsed by a majority of the leadership of Mapai, which voted for an opposition candidate against its own chief. Partly to disguise the humiliation of Eshkol, the appointment of Dayan was made part of a wider move to constitute a Government of National Unity embracing for the first time in Israel's history all parties except the Communists.

No sooner was this process of rapprochement among the parties finally consummated than they were all confronted with a situation that threatened to break up not only their collective alignment but their individual unity too. This situation was the product of two intertwined factors, both of them the result of Tzahal's victory: the emergence of crucial new issues in connection with Tzahal's conquests that divided opinion across party lines, and the development of a new but uncertain relation of political forces as a result of the retrospective allocation by public opinion of credit or blame to the various leaders. Mapai, as the strongest party of Israel and the mainstay of the political system, was naturally the primary focus of the new situation.

Tzahal's victory brought under Israel's control vast new territories about which it had no clear political plans. Judging by the clockwork precision with which the Israeli military operations unfolded, it is quite obvious that Israel's leadership had anticipated the kind of war that took place, including the capture of enemy territories, and had prepared for it meticulously. However, judging by what took place after the war, it is no less obvious that the question of the political use to be made of the territories after their capture had never been given serious consideration. Such a disparity between military and political planning is known to many societies, including the United States, and may be inherent in democracies. In the case of Israel, it may have been enhanced by an exclusive prewar obsession with the goal of peace and by the prevalence of a facile assumption, which has not disappeared entirely even today, that peace would automatically follow once the Arabs were shown conclusively that they could not defeat Israel in war.

It was within this frame of mind that Eshkol acted when he pledged to King Hussein that Israel would leave Jordan alone if it did not join the war, and when he solemnly announced shortly after the shooting began that Israel sought no annexation from the war but had lasting peace as its only aim. Two days later, however, Dayan contradicted Eshkol's announcement when he vowed before the Wailing Wall immediately after the capture of the old city of Jerusalem that Israelis had returned to their sacred city never to be parted from it again. Dayan's oath received immediate universal endorsement and proved to be the first of many statements by him and other leaders and personalities that revealed that Israelis were far from agreeing with Eshkol's definition of Israel's aims. Opinion in the country split increasingly over the future of the various occupied territories and parts of them; over what was to be retained by Israel and for what reasons; what was to be returned to whom and under what conditions; over the future status of the conquered populations and the present right of Israelis to settle in this or that part of the occupied lands; and so on. The divisions cut across existing party lines, although certain views tended to be strongly clustered in the extreme right and left parties.

Prime Minister Eshkol and his loyal party colleagues tried to regain control of the situation, but felt frustrated by Dayan's popularity and oppositionist tendency. Attempts were made to reduce the stature of the defense minister by deflecting the credit for victory onto Tzahal as a whole and its chief, General Yitzhak Rabin; by trying to build up Yigal Allon, a hero of the 1948 war, as a rival popular leader; and by leaking information to show that once the war began, Dayan restrained rather than spurred the troops and hesitated to send them down to the Suez Canal and up the Golan Heights. However, no device could undermine or outweigh the simple but crucial connection indelibly imprinted in the public's mind between the appointment of Dayan as defense minister and the end of the traumatic wait and crisis of indecision. If proof was needed of the failure of all efforts to dim Dayan's luster, it came in the form of a movement calling itself "Dayan for Prime Minister" which gathered enormous crossparty support within a very short time.

The problem of Dayan's popularity and defiance was particularly upsetting to the Mapai leadership because it was coupled with another political threat centered on Gachal. Since 1955 at least, the drift of Israel's orientation in matters of security and foreign policy had been toward greater toughness and reliance on the nation's armed forces, generally associated with Herut (Gachal's major component). However, the political gains that might have accrued to that party from the "vindication" of its approach had been restricted by the public's memory of its past defiance of the majority of the Yishuv, its identification with a seemingly unrealistic irredentism, and the political ostracism imposed on it by all the left-wing parties. Now that Gachal became at last respectable and responsible through its participation in the National Unity Government, and now that the conquest of all of Palestine this side of the Jordan plus other territories made its irredentism appear no longer so remote, two developments appeared possible: Gachal could, in an electoral contest, finally score major gains at Mapai's expense; and, whether it did or not, it could now become a partner with the party of Dayan and, together with the religious parties, they could all command a majority and dislodge Mapai from the leadership position it had occupied in Yishuv and Israel politics for nearly forty years. One need not be cynical to see why Mapai's leaders wanted to avoid that possibility almost at all costs; they honestly believed that it would be disastrous for the country as well as the party.

As the effort to check the "Dayan phenomenon" failed and the new political dangers became more apparent, the Prime Minister and his loyal Mapai collegues and Achdut Haavoda and Mapam allies responded in two ways. As an immediate reaction, they renounced any effort to advance in the government a coherent substantive policy regarding the future of the occupied territories and the multitude of related issues and contented themselves instead with promoting agreement on a limited formula insisting on peace and negotiations. A further agreement that the partners in the government should refrain from publicly advocating particular views on the major issues proved to be impossible to uphold, as ministers joined and abetted the proliferation and division of opinion in the country.

For the longer run, Mapai's leadership pursued a strategy of "if you can't lick them, join them." On one level, this took the form of promoting a union of all left-wing parties. Playing upon the dream of "unity of labor" long cherished by these parties and capitalizing on the fact that past differences among them on nearly all issues had vanished or diminished, Mapai was able, in January 1968, to bring about a merger of itself with Rafi and Achdut Haavoda to constitute the Israel Labor party, to which Mapam later allied itself to constitute a new, larger Maarakh. The diversity and opposition of views on the postwar issues among and within the component units was circumvented by an agreement to postpone the elaboration of any specific comprehensive policy, to keep all options open, and to meet unavoidable questions on a case by case basis. On another level, the strategy took the form of promoting an agreement with all the other parties to prolong the National Unity Government on the basis of a similar understanding. The government would simply insist on direct negotiations aimed at achieving peace and would strive to leave all options open as long as the enemy did not accept the proposed procedure and its aim. These measures succeeded completely in averting a political showdown, as was shown in the October 1969 general elections. At a time when opinion in the country was highly fragmented, these proved to be the least controversial of all Israel's elections. All the parties were anxious to continue the National Unity Government, the programs they presented to the public were general and similar, and the electorate returned all the lists in very nearly the same strengths, allowing for changes in labels.

Although Mapai's tour de force was prompted mainly by immediate tactical political considerations, it still had the potential of becoming an instrument of constructive adaptation to the postwar situation. Although their behavior and expression might not always suggest it, Israelis were in varying degrees aware that the options realistically open to their country depended in crucial measure on unpredictable economic, military, and international political developments. Mapai's action spared the country a political upheaval over differences that could turn out to be purely theoretical and provided a framework that gave the political system time to adjust gradually to the realities of the situation as these became apparent. The National Unity Government could provide a congenial forum for sober discussion of issues on the basis of shared information and thus, perhaps, allow the coalescence of views into a simpler division while blunting the edges of the remaining opposition. The united Labor party and the Maarakh could potentially achieve even more and succeed in crystallizing a substantive policy that would be acceptable to the party as a whole.

In fact, little of this came to pass and the unity frameworks tended to become ends in themselves that stymied rather than fostered the development of shared substantive policies. One reason for this was that the relevant external influences unfolded in ways that did not sufficiently encourage the sorting out and consolidation of views. The economic sphere provided no constraints at all on any views, as the country experienced a sustained boom which allowed it to bear without undue discomfort the financial burdens of occupation and stalemate and the rising cost of armament. In the military and diplomatic spheres there was a build up of pressures, especially after the spring of 1969, as Egypt launched a war of attrition and the United States, nervous about the explosion of all-out war, began to explore the parameters of a Middle East settlement, first together with the Soviet Union and then alone. However, because these pressures were not accompanied by proposals that even the most moderate Israelis could accept (and Nasser refused to contemplate peace, negotiations, or recognition), they only had the effect of driving all factions together into a joint stance of resistance. There was one exceptional episode in the summer of 1970 that actually proved the rule. At a moment of grave military danger owing to direct Soviet military intervention, the United States pressed Israel to accept what came to be known as the "Rogers Initiative" for a limited cease-fire and indirect peace negotiations. The government as a whole resisted at first, but then the majority gave in, resulting in the resignation of Gachal and the end of the National Unity Government, as well as in the consolidation of two clear positions. However, the evaporation of the pressures shortly thereafter caused a diversity of views to reassert itself within the ranks of the majority and thus a relapse into avoidance of decision until the fateful fall of 1973.

Another reason for the failure of formal unity to produce agreement on substantive policy, at least within the Labor party and the Maarakh, was related to the quality of the leadership of those bodies. Levi Eshkol may not have been up to the task of steering the party toward real unity; but in any case he died shortly after the consummation of the formal union and gave way to a leader who had all the strength and determination he lacked, but lacked a proper conception of the job, which he at least had. Golda Meir was elected by the party councils as a compromise candidate to end an incipient struggle for the succession between Dayan and Allon which threatened to tear asunder the newly united party. She proved to be acceptable to all because she was known to be strong and shrewd but, unlike the other contenders, uncommitted to any general policy line regarding the postwar issues. Moreover, because of her advanced age—she was seventy at the time of her election in February 1969 and had been called back from retirement—she was clearly seen as a "transient" leader who would see the party through the immediate crisis and then give way to someone else. By that time, perhaps, the country's situation might become clearer and its real options more apparent.

Meir's "transient" leadership lasted more than four years and would have gone on considerably longer had it not been terminated by the aftermath of the Yom Kippur War. Otherwise, however, she managed the government and the party during her period of stewardship exactly in accordance with the expectations of those who had unanimously elected her. She gave proof of enormous strength and determination in leading country and party in resistance to the mounting diplomatic and military pressures of 1969–1970, and she then showed great courage in leading them to accept the American initiative of the summer of 1970. However, as soon as the pressures abated, she not only refrained from committing herself to or advancing any policy line, but she continued to conceive of her role as being primarily one of holding the balance between the various views and personalities and preventing their clashes from tearing the party and government apart. Thus party unity, instead of gradually promoting substantive agreement, became a reason for the perpetuation of disagreements and factions.

A third reason for the failure of the formal union to produce a coherent, agreed policy was the existence within the Maarakh, and hence in the government, of a certain relation of forces between "moderates" and "hardliners" that worked against such a development. At any given time the moderates, however defined, had a preponderance of numbers, but the hardliners had the greater actual power because they held the implicit threat to secede and join Gachal. The moderates, on the other hand, had nowhere to go and feared that they would be worse off if the hardliners left and the Maarakh lost power as a result. Therefore they were compelled to refrain from using their numerical strength to force a decision on an overall policy, and they were forced to yield piecemeal to demands of the hardliners or to put up with faits accomplis they created, such as promoting settlements in the occupied territories, integrating the economy of the territories with Israel's, and so on.

The failure of the formal fusion and alignment of the labor parties to develop into substantive unity and coherence resulted, in effect, in institutionalizing disunity and incoherence at the levels of party and government. Central Labor party and Maarakh institutions of unity were maintained, but party and alignment affairs were actually managed by bargaining and maneuvers among faction leaders and bosses. At the governmental level, stability was preserved even after Gachal's resignation, but only at the price of rigidity of policy. Conflicts in the management of national affairs were minimized, but only by turning whole areas of national administration into virtual fiefs of party chieftains. Defense thus became the almost exclusive domain of Dayan, finance and the economy of Pinchas Sapir, and what was left over was parceled out to lesser lords and vassals. Meir, assisted by a handful of ministers and advisers who met informally in her home (thus known as "Golda's Kitchen Cabinet"), kept watch over the principal postwar issues, and particularly minded that they should not tear the precarious fabric of unity.

A good illustration of the way the system worked is provided by an episode that unfolded in the summer of 1973. Sometime before, the Defense

Ministry had drawn up ambitious plans to build a city and a port to be called Yamit in the Rafah approach, straddling the international border between Mandatory Palestine and Egypt. For years before, the ministry had been involved in setting up small military-agricultural settlements in border parts of the occupied territories, rebutting objections of the moderates as well as of friendly outside powers with the argument that these were merely defense outposts that could be removed if a peace settlement so required. However, the scope of the Yamit plans betrayed these rationalizations and revealed the intentions of the planners, and the dovish Finance Minister Sapir tried to block their realization by denying the necessary funding. This provoked Dayan to open the whole issue of the future of the occupied territories, and to agitate for a clear-cut decision regarding them in the party platform for the forthcoming elections, due in October 1973.

There followed a heated public debate between moderates and hardliners which spilled over onto many of the basic issues hitherto avoided and threatened to bring about the long-feared division. The matter was finally taken up by a committee of ministers from the various segments of the party, which eventually produced a "compromise" known as the "Galili Document," after Meir's closest adviser who drafted it. The document envisaged large-scale acquisition of land by the government and private bodies in the occupied areas, the creation of an "urban center" at Yamit, a new suburb near Jerusalem, and many agricultural settlements everywhere. It also called for stimulating industrial and general development in the territories and measures for the rehabilitation and resettlement of Arab refugees, and pointedly specified a sum of several hundred million dollars to be allotted to help carry out these projects. Many moderates were outraged by the document, seeing it as a charter for "creeping annexation," and were scandalized by Sapir's agreeing to it. But the chief boss of Mapai, the all-powerful lord of the economy, and the most prominent of moderates, faced with the danger of defection of Dayan and his followers and a consequent fall of the Labor party from power, preferred to give in to Dayan's demands as the lesser evil. In the party Secretariat, where the document came up for formal adoption, half the members abstained; but the majority of the other half approved it and it became part of the Labor party's platform for the October 1973 elections. That platform, however, was not destined to stand for long in the face of the sudden cataclysm that shook Israel.

Impact of the 1973 War

The 1973 Yom Kippur War shook the foundations of Israeli life and thrust the Israeli people into an emotional maelstrom. The political system was naturally affected and altered, but not so much as the violence of the war's impact or the initial agitation of the Israelis led one to expect.

The war and its aftermath forced the political parties to define more clearly their positions on the issues of territory and peace, which thus became the principal axis along which they differentiated themselves. The definition of positions was done in the context of a general election and this resulted in a considerable shift of strength that left the Maarakh dominant but altered the general balance of forces among the parties. Finally, the emotional upheaval caused by the war forced a substantial change in the leadership of the Labor party and thus of the government, as the remnants of the traditional political elite relinquished the top posts to men of the emerging sabra (native) elite.

At the time these changes happened they seemed to reflect or portend a major adaptation of the Israeli political system. However, in the perspective of only two years after the war they appeared to be more like temporary adjustments that left the system entrapped in new rigidities and its future wrapped in uncertainty.

Definition of Party Positions

When the war broke out, Israel was caught in the last stages of an electoral campaign in which twenty-one lists competed. Eleven of these were new and represented splinters from existing parties or tendencies that could find no room within the post-1967 party system. Of the remaining ten lists, the most important were, of course, the Labor party–Mapam Alignment and a new alignment called Likkud (unity), engineered by reserve General Ariel Sharon and constituted by the fusion of Gachal with two small parties and a new right-wing political group. Up to that time the campaign had centered mainly on socioeconomic issues. Although several new leftist formations attacked the Maarakh-dominated government for its policy with respect to the territories, the right-wing Likkud criticized the government mainly on the grounds of official corruption and failure to protect and advance the weaker classes of society. This reversal of traditional leftist and rightist concerns indicated the extent to which the drift of the Maarakh into a policy of creeping annexationism had stolen the thunder of the Likkud and forced it to try to fight the Maarakh on other grounds. It also reflected the extent of the absorption of the public with bread-and-butter issues, as it complacently assumed an indefinite continuation of the status quo secured by Israel's unchallengeable military deterrence and strong diplomatic position.

The war shattered these illusions and replaced them with a profound sense of bewilderment as to what had happened and deep anxiety about what lay ahead. These two questions and their ramifications and implications became the central issues in the election campaign, now prolonged to the end of December 1973. In the process of addressing themselves to them all, the parties were forced for the first time since the 1967 war to adopt clear-cut positions with respect to the questions of territories and peace.

In the renewed campaign, the Likkud started with the enormous advantage of being the only visible alternative to the ruling party, which bore the responsibility for the country's misfortunes. It also had a major asset in having as one of its top leaders General Sharon, who emerged from the war as the only hero among the country's top commanders. For quite some time after the war, opinion polls showed it to be neck and neck with the Maarakh. However, the Likkud dissipated much of its advantage by sticking to an uncompromising platform (annexing Judea and Samaria, ceding part of Sinai but only in exchange for full peace, resisting American pressure), and by concentrating the bulk of its efforts on belaboring the government for its blunders and failures. Even on the latter score, however, the Likkud, because it had itself shared in and largely influenced the general policy of the government, was forced to concentrate its attacks on the very narrow grounds of the government's failure to take the necessary precautions in the face of mounting evidence of an impending Arab attack. "Why weren't the reserves mobilized? Why weren't the tools [armor] brought forward?" That refrain of the Likkud's attack rubbed in the pain felt by the Israelis and stirred up their fury against those responsible for the failure, but it did not necessarily invite confidence in what the Likkud could do to help retrieve the situation. It appealed only to those whose sense of outrage over the past outweighed their concern about the future.

The leaders of the Maarakh, for their part, attempted to defuse the public's passion about past events, at least for the duration of the electoral campaign, by putting through the Cabinet a measure appointing a neutral commission headed by the President of the Supreme Court, Shimon Agranat, to investigate essentially the questions raised by the Likkud and their ramifications. This did not prevent public discussion of the issues while they were under consideration by the commission, but it at least allowed the leaders under attack to make a plausible plea for suspension of judgment until the commission reported. As for the public's anxiety about the future, the Maarakh leaders attempted at first to soothe it by pointing to the impending peace conference at Geneva in December and playing this up in general terms as an opportunity to realize Israel's long-cherished dream of peace and security. However, the necessity in which the government found itself, owing to American pressure and in order to make Geneva possible, to make immediate tactical concessions to the Egyptians in the battlefield stirred up feelings for and against the concessions within the Maarakh, and compelled the leadership to seek from the party a specific, clear-cut policy on the postwar issues and a mandate to pursue it.

A committee of fifteen members representing all factions and currents was appointed; it produced a fourteen-point program which it submitted to the party's Central Committee. The draft replaced the narrow and tough approach of the Galili Document with a broad and moderate if not dovish peace program. It described the scheduled Geneva Peace Conference as a "major event in the history of the Middle East" and looked to it to achieve a peace settlement ensuring "defensible borders based on territorial compromise and the preservation of the Jewish character of the state of Israel." No mention was made of any particular area as being indispensable, either in writing or as "oral doctrine," except for Jerusalem; and the reference to "the Jewish character of the state" clearly implied nonannexation of thickly-inhabited Arab territory. The draft rejected the idea of a separate Palestinian state in the West Bank, but for the first time recognized the need for a "Palestinian identity," which was to express itself in a "neighboring Jordanian-Palestinian state." Settlement would continue, but only in accordance with government decisions to be made from time to time, and "with priority for security considerations," rather than on a wholesale basis as in the Galili Document. The draft also envisaged the possibility of withdrawal from cease-fire lines in accordance with interim agreements that might be made "as temporary arrangements on the road to peace."

The draft program was presented to the Central Committee on December 5, 1973, and, after a full day's debate, was adopted by acclamation. Obviously, the program still left room for considerable differences of interpretation, but equally obviously it narrowed greatly the range of the differences by pulling the hardline views toward the moderate position. This in turn established a more distinct line of demarcation between the hardliners of the Maarakh and the Likkud, as evidenced by the posture adopted by the latter. The Likkud attacked the Maarakh's platform as a program "leading to surrender and endangering the nation's survival" and reiterated its opposition to any withdrawal from Judea and Samaria. It acknowledged the change in Israel's position in the wake of the war only to the extent of indicating willingness to compromise over Sinai in exchange for full peace. The Maarakh's program also differentiated it from the many leftist lists that advocated more decisive dovish programs, though that was not so important since no leftist group was strong enough to exert a potential attraction to Maarakh moderates.

Change in the Balance of Forces

The Maarakh's effort to direct attention to the future and depict itself as the party of peace and the Likkud as the party of war undercut the threat of its chief opponent on the right. A widespread conviction among Israelis that the Arabs had never been seriously interested in a settlement before the war helped spare it from the full effect of charges from the left that its immobilistic policy and creeping annexation had led to war. However, no amount of political maneuvering and no amount of good luck could have spared it from having to pay *some* price for the disasters that took place while it was in charge of the government, and pay it did.

The election returns showed a loss for the Maarakh of six Knesset seats out of its previous total of fifty-seven—a large shift in Israeli terms—and a gain of eight for the Likkud over its previous total of thirty-one—an even greater shift in absolute and percentage terms. Countering somewhat this shift to the right, the National Religious Party, which had run on a platform almost as hawkish as the Likkud's, lost one seat to come down to ten, and an entirely new dovish list called the Movement for Citizens' Rights, headed by Shulamit Aloni, won a surprise three mandates. The moderate Independent Liberals retained their previous four seats, and a new dovish list called Moked, made up of Jewish Communists and a splinter from Mapam, won one. The Torah Front, an alignment of Agudat Yisrael and Poalei Agudat Yisrael which ran on an apolitical religious platform, lost one of its previous six seats. The predominantly Arab Communist list, Rakah, gained one seat to bring its total to four, and the remaining three seats went to Arab minority lists affiliated with the Maarakh, for a loss of one. All in all, the election resulted in an almost exact balance of gains and losses for the out-and-out hawkish and dovish lists on either side of the Maarakh (see Table 3). Considering that the Maarakh itself had substantially altered its platform in a dovish direction after the war, the real outcome negates the initial impression of a shift of the electorate in a hawkish direction that one gets from the Likkud's gain of eight and the Maarakh's loss of six seats. However, the overall realignment of forces tended to qualify that real outcome.

The overall results left the Maarakh still the strongest single party and, on the basis of its platform, at the center of the dovish-hawkish spectrum that had come to be the main axis of Israeli politics. The Maarakh was thus in a position to combine with "harder" and "softer" parties to form a coalition, whereas the Likkud, its principal opponent, could only combine with the religious parties, a possibility that would still leave it short of a majority. However, the margin of maneuver of the Maarakh was narrowed a great deal, and the bargaining power of the religious parties increased correspondingly despite their loss of two seats, thus increasing the potential for instability of the entire system. For example, an additional gain of seven seats for the Likkud and the religious parties together, scored at the expense of *all* the other parties, would make a majority Likkud–religious parties coalition possible. A gain of only three seats would make the negation of a Likkud–religious parties minority government, or the survival of an alternative Maarakh-led minority government, dependent on the votes of the Arab minorities' and Communits lists. A gain of five seats would make the negation of one combination and the survival of the other dependent on the vote of the Arab Communists alone. The implications of these and similar scenarios for the content of Israeli national policy, the stability of government, and the integrity of parties can be readily imagined.

Because of the critical role of the religious parties, it became more important than ever for the Maarakh to do all it could to prevent the coalescence of the National Religious Party and the Torah Front and to avoid the gravitation of even the National Religious Party alone toward the Likkud. But what it could do was limited by the necessity to preserve the recently achieved concili- ation within its own ranks and by the need to keep the dovish and secularly in- clined Independent Liberal party content. The dilemmas and stresses and strains of the new alignment of forces were illustrated in the complicated process of government formation that took place in the wake of the elections.

As Golda Meir attempted to put together a coalition, the National Re- ligious Party insisted that the government's program should include a com- mitment not to give up any part of Judea and Samaria, and to enact legislation defining a Jew exclusively in terms of the *Halakha* (religious law). The first condition reflected the growing nationalist emphasis of the National Re- ligious Party, while the second reflected an effort of that party to draw the Agudah parties in a tacit alliance with it in order to enhance its own power and that of the religious bloc. Meir was prepared to meet the first condition to the extent of committing the government not to ratify any agreement in- volving surrender of West Bank territory without first submitting it to the test of general elections, but she could not meet the second condition without losing the support of the Independent Liberal Party and becoming totally dependent on the religious parties, which is precisely what the National Re- ligious Party wanted. Therefore, when the National Religious Party persisted in its demand, Meir proceeded to form, together with the Independent Liber- als, a minority government—for the first time in Israel's history. She left the door open for the National Religious Party to join later if it changed its mind by leaving available the portfolios of interior, welfare, and religious affairs that it traditionally held. In the meantime, she counted on the dispersal of the opposition to allow the coalition to run a government commanding only 58 votes (including the Arab minorities' seats) out of 120.

Meir resigned and the minority government fell almost as soon as it was confirmed by the Knesset for reasons of intra-Maarakh politics which we shall consider further on. Yitzhak Rabin, who was elected by the Labor party to succeed Meir, went over the same ground with the National Religious Party and ended up forming a coalition with the Independent Liberals and Aloni's Citizens' Rights Movement, which commanded a bare majority of sixty-one in Knesset. Although Rabin's government took office after the pat- tern of Israel's postwar policy had already been largely set by the conclusion, under the previous government, of two disengagement agreements with Egypt and Syria, the strong dovish character of the government (which com- prised Mapam as well as the Liberals and Aloni's movement) caused mount- ing restlessness in the ranks of the harder segments of the Labor party. More- over, harder and softer segments alike were anxious that the exclusion of the National Religious Party for long might cause it to acquire the habit of cooperating with the Likkud in opposition, which in turn could lead to a dangerous political alliance. Consequently, when the National Religious Party "repented" and indicated its willingness to join the government on the terms previously offered by Meir, Rabin and most of the Labor leaders welcomed it, although its return led to the withdrawal of Aloni's movement from the coalition. The Citizen's Rights Movement, unlike the National Religious Party, had nowhere to go where it could endanger the Maarakh.

Change of Leadership

The end of the war found Israel a seething sea of discontent which threw up wave after wave of demonstrations and protest movements demanding a revamping of the political system, more democracy, a greater degree of accountability of public officials, and, especially, the resignation of members of the government responsible for the blunders of omission or commission that had brought Israel to the verge of total disaster. The first wave broke out right after the end of the fighting but was somehow held in check by a widespread belief that the war might resume any time and by the timely appointment of the Agranat Commission to investigate some of the issues underlying the public restlessness. The fact that general elections were under way also helped, by causing some to feel the need to close ranks now and settle accounts later, and others to hope that the results would penalize the "guilty ones." As the elections were concluded and the process of coalition-formation that followed seemed to forecast the "same mixture as before," and as a disengagement agreement was concluded with Egypt that seemed to push further away the danger of renewed war, another massive wave of protest broke out, spearheaded by demobilized soldiers, which centered specifically on demanding Dayan's resignation. Dayan resisted, sought to elicit Likkud support by calling for the formation of a National Unity Government, but eventually broke down when bereaved parents spat on his car and declared that he would not take part in the next government which was forming.

In early March 1974 Meir submitted to the Central Committee of her party for approval a list of her next government, which included Rabin in the defense slot previously occupied by Dayan. During the deliberations, Meir was stung by criticism that the government did not include enough new faces and by insinuations about the way she ran matters in government and party and walked out of the meeting after submitting her resignation. Caught by surprise and fearing a destructive struggle for the succession, the party leadership sent delegation after delegation to plead with her to change her mind and save the party. After eliciting expressions of contrition from the critics and pledges of cooperation from all, Meir relented and agreed to resume her posts. For his part, Dayan, believing that Meir had finally tamed his critics in the party as well as hers, told her that he too was prepared to come back, and she willingly agreed. Publicly, Dayan justified his change of mind by citing the development of a security emergency in the north.

Meir had barely received the Knesset's endorsement of her new government, including Dayan, when the Agranat Commission published the long-awaited interim report of its investigation. The report was full of praise for Meir's handling of the crisis and the war. It also exonerated Dayan from any direct responsibility for the errors of judgment about the likelihood of war and for the failure to take adequate precautionary measures in the face of the enemy military buildup. On the other hand, the report came down harshly on the chief of staff, General David Elazar, for failures committed by his subordinates, and, although it considered his conduct of the war once it started to be beyond reproach, recommended his removal in the name of clarity of responsibility. The report raised the question of the parliamentary and ministerial responsibility of the minister of defense for shortcomings in the area under his jurisdiction, but it refrained from drawing any conclusion on this score on the grounds that the question was beyond its purview. General Elazar did not await any official action but immediately submitted his resignation, stating that the confidence of the armed forces in their chief of staff, essential for the proper fulfillment of his office, was now impaired. The public expected Dayan to do the same on similar grounds if not in acknowledgment of his parliamentary responsibility and in solidarity with his comrades in arms, and when he refused to do so the storm broke out. There then developed a movement to force Dayan out that was ironically reminiscent of the one that had forced him into the defense post in 1967. The popular unrest spread to Dayan's own associates and to the leadership of the Labor party, and led to mounting pressure on the Prime Minister to ask for the resignation of the defense minister. Meir would not do so out of collegial solidarity and because of her ceaseless concern for a possible breach in the party; but she brought about the demanded result by resigning from the prime ministership, thus bringing down the entire government, and from the party leadership, thus making room for the selection of a new candidate for the post of prime minister.

The aroused state of public opinion and Meir's identification with Dayan precluded a repetition of the scenario of the month before, when the party pleaded with her to come back. The state of public opinion also impressed the party chiefs with the need to break away from old names that were always mentioned in past talks of succession and to initiate some new procedure of selection. They decided to present to the Central Committee of more than six hundred members two fresh candidates and let it choose between them by secret ballot. One of the candidates was Yitzhak Rabin, promoted by Sapir because of his glorious record as chief of staff during the Six Day War and because he was untainted by any association, military or political, with the unfortunate Yom Kippur War. The other was Shimon Peres, whose candidacy was advanced as a sop to the Rafi wing of the party after the fall of Dayan, and whose association with the Yom Kippur War was limited by the relatively junior position he occupied in the Cabinet as minister of transport and communications. The result was a victory for Rabin, but only by a majority of 298 against 254 for Peres.

Rabin proceeded to form a government in which Peres, on the strength of his showing in the party election, was given the crucial portfolio of defense. Yigal Allon, who had been once again bypassed for the prime ministership, was compensated with the post of deputy premier and the foreign affairs desk. The Rabin-Peres-Allon triumvirate of sabras (Peres actually came to the country as a child) was reinforced by the reinstatement and addition of several ministers of a similar background, giving the entire government quite a new complexion. The new government waited for the old to terminate negotiations it had started with Syria before taking over, and the juxtaposition of the incoming team and the outgoing one, including Golda Meir, Moshe Dayan, Pinchas Sapir, and Abba Eban, underscored the extent of the change in leadership personnel that was taking place.

The accession of Rabin's government was viewed by many Israelis and outsiders as marking a turning point in the country's political history. In the lingering excitement caused by the success of public pressure in overthrowing Dayan and forcing the retirement of Meir, many were also disposed to see a triumph of the pressure for democracy in the fact that Rabin was chosen for the post of prime minister for the first time in an effective contest by secret ballot rather than in a prearranged selection by party oligarchs behind the scenes. Even the fact that the outcome was so close between the nominee of party boss Sapir from the Mapai faction and a former Rafi man and avid Dayan partisan was intepreted optimistically as signaling the disappearance of factional divisions within the party. A more sober view and a certain amount of perspective suggest that what actually took place was far less dramatic, and its implications, alas, much less hopeful.

The advent of Rabin and Peres to the top posts represented the culmination of a long process rather than a new start. Israel's political life had been dominated from the outset by an elite composed of people from the Second, Third, and Fourth Aliyot whose formative experience was in Zionist movement and Yishuv politics and whose orientation was heavily ideological; however, over the years of Israel's existence, that elite had co-opted into its ranks people of different background and experience, at first slowly and then, as its ranks were depleted by old age and death, more rapidly. This is how Dayan and Allon, Eban and Peres, Chaim Barlev, Aharon Yariv, Ezer Weizmann, Ariel Sharon, and many others made their way into the ranks of government or leadership of their respective parties. The co-optation of Rabin to the very top had, to be sure, a certain symbolic significance as a consummation of a process, but even that might have come about much earlier had not

Allon and Dayan, who are of the same general background as Rabin and Peres, managed to checkmate each other so often.

The contested election by secret ballot in the Central Committee *was* a rather novel experience, but the fact remained that at least Rabin's candidacy was totally the making of party boss Sapir and his fellow oligarchs. This qualifies considerably any idea of democratic processes being established in the party, but more importantly it spelled difficulties for Rabin later on. It should be remembered that in the Israeli system, the Prime Minister, unlike the President in the United States, continues to depend on party support after his election to office on a day-to-day basis, and can fall if he fails to get it. Rabin's lack of any significant record of service for the party meant that he could not count on such support by virtue of established credit and past associations, but had to earn it as he went along. Of course, Sapir could draw on his own credit to help him until he built his own, but this had its own inconveniences and, besides, Sapir happened to die not long after Rabin's accession.

The closeness of the vote between Rabin and Peres helped make Peres and his former Rafi colleagues feel that they were now finally accepted as full-fledged members of the Labor Party, entitled to aspire to any position. To this extent it may have laid to rest the ghost of that factional strife; however, even as it did so, it planted the seeds of a new factionalism based on personal rivalry and policy inclinations, fanned by the hostility of party regulars to outsider Rabin who was "parachuted" into the top position. That resentment probably accounts for the fact that so many members of the Central Committee availed themselves of the secrecy of the ballot to defy Sapir's wishes and vote for Peres. In the eyes of those who did so, Peres' record of many years of toil in the party field, misguided as it may have been, made him preferable to the newcomer Rabin who would painlessly reap what they had laboriously sown.

Preliminary Effect of the Changes on the Political System

Although a relatively short time has elapsed since the post-1973 changes took place, it might be useful before leaving this subject to consider briefly the collective impact of the changes on the system, to the extent that this can be ascertained.

The redefinition of party positions after October 1973 resulted in a much clearer demarcation among the parties than had existed in the interwar period on the issues that became the principal axis of division of opinion in the country. In principle, this made it possible for the electorate to express its preferences more meaningfully and to give a party or group of parties a more definite mandate to pursue certain broad policies. In practice, however, the way in which the electorate voted in the 1973 election tended to undercut those effects. The public collectively did opt for a dovish-to-moderate range of platforms extending through the Maarakh in preference to the annexationist platforms of the Likkud and the National Religious Party; however, the way it distributed its votes resulted in placing the National Religious Party, despite the slight loss it suffered, in a position to stymie the choice of the majority. One immediate reflection of this was the pledge Meir felt compelled to give to go to the country before completing any agreement involving withdrawal from the West Bank. That pledge was repeated by Prime Minister Rabin and led to his refusal to contemplate a limited agreement with Jordan when one was possible, with results that proved quite deleterious to Israel (see Chapter 26).

The inhibition imposed on the Maarakh leadership by the fear of alienating the National Religious Party was aggravated by the change that took place in the leadership. The accession of several new men to the key positions in the government helped end the postwar turmoil and held out the promise of inaugurating an era of greater vigor, coherence, initiative, and flexibility in managing the nation's affairs. However, after a short auspicious start, the very extensiveness of the change in leadership personnel and the way in which it had come about proved to be a source of renewed rigidity, friction, incoherence, and potential instability.

The root of the problem lay in the relations among the "triumvirate," especially between Prime Minister Rabin and Defense Minister Peres. In general, because defense always occupied a central role in the nation's policy and made enormous demands on its limited resources, relations between the occupant of the defense post on the one hand, and the remainder of the government, but especially the Prime Minister, on the other hand were always fraught with potential strain. Ben Gurion avoided that problem to a large extent by occupying both posts himself, though he clashed with Foreign Minister Sharett; Sharett as Prime Minister had a new, strongheaded defense minister and the result was the Lavon affair as well as the end of Sharett's political career; Eshkol reverted to the Ben Gurion pattern of holding both posts only to have Dayan imposed on him in the 1967 crisis and to suffer subsequently from the problem until his death; Meir "resolved" the problem by balancing off most of the Cabinet against Dayan and then giving Dayan a virtually free hand. The new government got caught in this same problem, but faced it in a particularly acute form for several reasons.

In the first place, unlike most of the Meir era, the breakdown of the Middle East stalemate confronted the government with the necessity to make frequent policy decisions, in which defense considerations were, naturally, centrally involved. Moreover, because of the course and consequences of the Yom Kippur War, defense made greater demands than ever on the nation's resources. These developments were apt under any circumstances to exacerbate the "normal" competition between the Defense Minister and the rest of the government for budgetary allocations and the usual contest between him and the Prime Minister and the foreign minister for influence on policy; but the particular background of the personalities who were actually involved made the problem even more difficult and practically barred any simple, visible solution to it. It so happened that the Prime Minister was a former victorious chief of staff and successful ambassador to Washington, and therefore considered himself to be much more knowledgeable about broad matters of defense and foreign policy than the defense minister. Foreign Minister and Deputy Prime Minister Allon, too, happened to be a former victorious general and a strategic thinker of note, who also claimed special competence in the field of security and foreign affairs. This ruled out any solution along the lines followed by Meir vis-à-vis Dayan of deferring to the defense minister. On the other hand, it was also out of the question that the defense minister should yield to his colleagues because, apart from the fact that he too had claims to considerable experience in defense matters (having served as deputy defense minister under Ben Gurion), he also commanded greater political support than either the Prime Minister or the deputy prime minister and foreign minister. In a long-run contest, he could see himself prevailing over them and succeeding to the prime ministership himself.

Prime Minister Rabin had received in the Central Committee's ballot 298 votes against Peres' 254. However, Rabin's strength was only "borrowed," while Peres' was his own. Moreover, Rabin lost much of the support that had been rallied for him by Sapir after the latter's death, partly because of the spontaneous erosion of that power bloc after the death of its boss and partly because of Rabin's lack of political skill, whereas Peres retained his and was able as an experienced politician to build upon it. Allon had only a limited political support of his own, as was shown in the fact that he had not even been nominated as a contestant for the prime ministership. Also, Peres, as heir to the leadership of the hardline wing of the Labor party after Dayan, could always count on the support of the National Religious Party's ministers who carried disproportionate weight in the government. Finally, he could, in the final account, confront the Maarakh itself with the threat of defection of the hardliners, which would throw it out of power.

Altogether, then, the changes wrought by the immediate aftermath of the Yom Kippur War unraveled the configuration of the political system that took shape in the wake of the Six Day War but did not produce one that seemed better adapted to dealing with the crucial issues confronting the country. It can be said, without much exaggeration, that if *unwillingness* to make decisions and incur the risk of divisions characterized the previous configuration, *inability* to make decisions because of a particular pattern of political division in the country, the government, and the dominant party was the hallmark of the new configuration. However, the very strains latent in the new configuration made it unlikely that it would endure unaltered. Conceivably, external pressures and events in the highly fluid regional and international arenas could impel the development of a pragmatic, piecemeal consensus on policy among the government and the majority of the country. Otherwise, the strains were apt to lead to fission in the Labor party or a breakdown of the government coalition, forcing new elections and perhaps a new distribution of forces. The process of negotiating the Second Sinai Agreement between March and September 1975 and the massive approval of the accord by the Knesset seemed to indicate evolution in the former direction. But that very success turned out to be the starting point of a backslide toward increasing strain on the postwar adjustment and its eventual breakdown.

The Upheaval of May 1977

The strains latent in the post–Yom Kippur War adjustment were instrumental in the failure to pursue a limited agreement with Jordan and the collapse of the March 1975 negotiations for an interim agreement with Egypt; but the American pressure during the period of "reassessment," coupled with the danger of renewed war, had compelled the various leaders, factions, and parties in the government to compose their differences enough to work out an agreed policy to meet the crisis of the moment. This pragmatic accommodation might have served as a basis for the development of a wider and deeper consensus. Instead, once the Sinai Agreement was concluded and ratified, the easing of the external pressures that ensued allowed the suppressed strains to manifest themselves more strongly than ever in the context of difficult internal problems, and led within a little more than a year, in December 1976, to the breakdown of the government coalition and the scheduling of new elections.

The elections, which were held five months later in May 1977, wrought a complete upheaval in the Israeli political landscape. The Labor party suffered a devastating loss of nineteen seats, which ended the half century dominance of Yishuv and Israeli politics by Mapai in its various incarnations. The Likkud gained four seats and was propelled into the position of the strongest party and the potential leader of a hawkish government coalition. An entirely new party, the Democratic Movement for Change (known as Dash, a shortened acronym of its name in Hebrew), which had entered the arena only six months before the elections, made a spectacular showing in Israeli terms by obtaining fifteen Knesset seats. The National Religious Party unexpectedly scored a gain of two seats and it and the Agudah parties were placed by the new configuration into a stronger position than ever as holders of the balance of power. There were several other less dramatic changes which may yet prove to be of crucial importance in some future contingencies.

These results—essentially a delayed consequence of the Yom Kippur War—clearly indicated the end of an era but drew much less clearly the contours of the new. True, the electorate this time gave a clear mandate to the Likkud and like-minded parties to govern Israel, but the mandate was slim and was spread over several parties with important secondary differences among themselves. Indeed, the Likkud itself is a front of several distinct competing factions and vivid personalities. This made the potential new coalition vulnerable to slight jolts which could topple it and bring about new alignments and perhaps a new distribution of forces. Such possibilities were all the more real because of the near-certainty that a Likkud-led government would clash severely with the United States, on which Israel has become strongly dependent economically, militarily, and diplomatically.

The unofficial results of the 1977 elections (only these are available at the time of writing) are shown in Table 4, together with figures for the 1973 elections to the Eighth Knesset for comparison. Before commenting further on them it might be useful to review the course of events that led to this outcome.

After the signing of the Second Sinai Agreement, Prime Minister Rabin, like the good former chief of staff that he was, worked out a general strategic conception to guide his direction of Israel's foreign policy and internal development, as well as his own political position in the years ahead. The strategy had two broad, related objectives. Rabin wanted to improve Israel's

Table 4. Unofficial results of the 1977 elections to the Knesset compared with the 1973 elections.

Party	Knesset seats 1977	Knesset seats 1973
Likkud	43	39
Maarakh	32	51
Democratic Movement for Change	15	—
National Religious Party	12	10
Democratic Front (Rakah and allies)	5	4
Agudat Yisrael	4	4
Shelli (Moked and allies)	2	1
Shlomtzion (Ariel Sharon's party)	2	—
Independent Liberals	1	4
Citizens Rights	1	3
Poalei Agudat Yisrael	1	1
Samuel Flatto Sharon (Independent)	1	—
United Arab list (Maarakh)	1	3
Total	120	120

bargaining position so that it could ultimately obtain a settlement that would meet its essential needs as he saw them, and he wanted to build up his own political standing in the country, the party, and the government so that when the time came he could gain approval for the settlement to which he would agree. To accomplish the first objective, Rabin sought to buy time during which the Israeli economy would be strengthened and the country's financial and military dependence on the United States would be reduced. He also believed that time would diminish the monetary power of the Arab countries through the commitment of their disposable funds, the increased dependence of their economies on the West, and protective devices worked out by the Western countries themselves. The realization of the second, personal political objective, Rabin expected, would follow partly from the demonstration of his success in strengthening the country economically and militarily, partly from a deliberate effort he intended to make to use the authority bestowed by his office to build for himself political strength. Rabin estimated that four or five years would be necessary to achieve his first set of goals, and that about halfway along he would have made sufficient progress to be able to win a strong mandate in the elections due at the end of 1977 that would then permit him to consummate these goals.

Rabin's conception was questionable on several grounds. For example, people with experience in international affairs, including his party colleague Abba Eban, strongly doubted that time would work in favor of Israel or that Israel would be able to buy it. Many professional economists were skeptical that Israel could remedy the ills of its economy and strengthen it while keeping up the level of defense spending necessary for its security and for reducing military dependence on the United States. Above all, it was highly dubious that the government Rabin headed had the coherence and authority to carry out the economic reform measures needed, or that in attempting to do so either it or he would gain politically. The course of events in 1976 and 1977 confirmed all these doubts and added unforeseen difficulties in the bargain.

Gaining time presented no great difficulty in the remainder of 1975 and 1976. For a short while after the conclusion of the Second Sinai Agreement the United States kept talking about the need to maintain the momentum for peace in the Middle East in order to sustain the patience of friendly Arab countries. In the course of 1976, however, the expanding civil war in Lebanon embroiled the Arab countries in conflict and absorbed their attention, while the United States became completely absorbed in the presidential elections. But by early 1977, with the American elections over and a new administration installed, and with the Arab states having resolved their differences over Lebanon, the United States began to apply gentle but ominous pressure on behalf of a settlement which raised serious doubts about the possibility of gaining much more time, if indeed it was still useful to do so. Very shortly after assuming office, President Jimmy Carter gave strong indication not only that he was determined to press right away with action to advance a settlement but also that he had fairly definite ideas as to what the settlement should look like. These ideas, as publicly voiced by the President during and after a visit by Rabin to Washington in March 1977, precipitated an anxious debate in Israel that was not calculated to help either Rabin or the Labor party in the election campaign in which they were already engaged.

Regarding the defense part of Rabin's conception, Israel did make important strides in developing its military industries and strengthening its armed forces in the course of 1976. Moreover, in connection with the Lebanese civil war, Israel seemed to strike the right policy, contributing to embroiling the Syrian forces with the PLO while compelling them both to keep a respectable distance from its northern border. The spectacular Entebbe rescue operation in July 1976 was another significant success of great symbolic importance which revived, at least momentarily, the Israelis' pride and confidence in Tzahal. However, these achievements did not in any way reduce Israel's financial and military dependence on the United States, nor did they involve any significant reduction of the internal defense burden. Furthermore, supporters of Peres sought to give him, as defense minister, all the credit for the achievements, and the attempts made by Rabin to claim his share and undercut his rival sometimes backfired and always exposed the rift between the two to the public, to the detriment of the Labor party as a whole. Finally, early in May 1977, in the last stage of the election campaign, the state comptroller published a highly critical report on the state of some Tzahal installations inspected by his officers which jolted the public and reminded it of the widespread shortcomings that contributed to the disasters of 1973. The attempt made by the defense minister and labor chief to downplay the criticism only brought back memories of the pre–Yom Kippur War complacency of the Labor government.

It was in the economic sphere, however, that Rabin's game plan suffered the worst setbacks and the Labor party the most discredit. The Yom Kippur War had triggered a rapid inflation that reached the rate of 50 percent in 1974 and 40 percent in 1975. Strengthening the economy required a drastic slowing down of that pace and redirection of resources toward export. The government tried to attack these problems by increasing taxes, reducing investment, cutting down public expenditures, seeking to restrain wage increases, and adopting a policy of "creeping devaluation" to defend Israel's competitive position in the world market. The drive to increase exports met with some success, but the effort to reduce inflation failed miserably and stirred up widespread unrest and waves of authorized and wildcat strikes that swept the entire country. Some substantial degree of inflation was inevitable as a result of the continuous 2 percent a month devaluation necessary to maintain Israel's position in the world market. Much of the failure, however, was due to weaknesses in the government and the Labor party. The defense minister, for example, opposed any meaningful reduction of the huge defense budget and was able to have his way. Lack of solidarity in the government ruled out firmness in the face of unauthorized strikes, and lack of harmony and coordination between Labor leaders in the government and the Histadrut either pitted the two against each other or undermined the latter's ability to control its unions, and the unions' to control the various work committees. The result was not only that the government failed to keep the lid on wages and prevent a wage-price spiral but also that its authority and credibility suffered heavily. And as in all such situations, the unorganized, the weak, and the poor were the ones who suffered most. Matters came to such a point that on one occasion in May 1976, slum dwellers in Tel Aviv took to the streets, threw up barricades, battled the police with firebombs and grenades, and were subdued only by tear gas.

As has happened often in the past, the public's discontent extended into the leadership councils of the party, only this time it led to no effective corrective measures. Already in February 1976, the secretary general of the Labor party, Meir Zarmi, resigned because Rabin and other representatives of the party in the government and the trade unions went their own divergent ways and ignored the party's decision-making and coordinating forums. Zarmi was induced to stay on after the leaders vowed to correct the situation and bring the party institutions into the picture, but the corrective actions undertaken or contemplated became themselves the grounds for dispute and maneuvering for position between the Rabin and Peres camps, especially as the time for the party's convention, scheduled for February 1977, approached. It was in connection with this struggle for influence in the party that Rabin and his political ally, Finance Minister Yehoshua Rabinowitz, took, in September 1976, the unfortunate step of nominating Asher Yadlin to the position of governor of the Bank of Israel, the equivalent of the American Federal Reserve Bank. Yadlin, an influential party stalwart who headed the Histadrut Sick Fund, was known to be inclined toward Peres, and Rabin and Rabinowitz wanted to lure him to their camp with the very prestigious and important bank job. Shortly after the nomination, however, an investigative reporter unearthed accusatory material which led to the investigation, arrest, and subsequent indictment of Yadlin on eight charges of bribery and fraud while managing the Sick Fund. The affair cast discredit on the entire Labor party, but it particularly damaged the already battered position of Rabin.

By the end of November 1976, Rabin's strategy was in tatters and his government had clearly reached the end of its tether. Earlier that month the government had increased basic food and public transit prices by 20 percent, and fuel, electricity, and water prices by 11 percent over the protests of the Histadrut, thus bringing on new waves of strikes and unrest. On November 16 the Executive Board of the Independent Liberal Party had voted to recommend to the party's Central Committee to leave the coalition, and some members of the National Religious Party spoke of doing likewise. In the previous days, the mass circulation daily *Maariv,* the prestigious *Haaretz,* and the usually pro-government *Jerusalem Post* had all called editorially for the resignation of the government and early elections. On November 23 Yigal Yadin, the highly respected former chief of staff, builder of the Israeli army, and prominent archeologist, announced the formation of a new party called the Democratic Movement for Change, dedicated to reforming the political system and the administration, which attracted immediate massive attention. By that time, the diplomatic truce had also approached its end as the American elections were finally concluded and the Arab leaders finally settled their differences, and it was generally agreed that the existing government was in no condition to deal effectively with the expected initiatives and pressures on behalf of a settlement. In these circumstances, Rabin needed only an appropriate excuse to end his government; this he found in an incident involving the National Religious Party.

On December 10, 1976, members of the government attended a welcoming ceremony for the first three F-15 jet fighters supplied by the United States. The ceremony was held shortly before the Sabbath, which meant that some ministers had to violate the holy day to drive home from the air base afterward. Four days later the Agudah parties filed a no-confidence motion against the government in the Knesset for desecrating the Sabbath which the government narrowly survived by a 55–48 vote. Nine of the ten members from the National Religious Party abstained, and this led Rabin on December 19 to oust the party from the coalition on the grounds of violating collective responsibility. The next day, Rabin himself resigned and called for the dissolution of the Knesset and new elections. By agreement of the parties, these were set for May 17, 1977.

As the Labor party began to prepare for its convention, Minister of Housing Avraham Ofer, a party leader with a reputation for integrity and dedication to principles, committed suicide in January 1977 after newspaper stories implicated him in scandal. Ofer left a note in which he protested his innocence and complained of being abandoned by his party colleagues in the face of his accusers. Six weeks later, Asher Yadlin plea-bargained guilty to four counts of bribery and tax evasion, and testified that he had engaged in illegal fund-raising for the party under the pressure of such leaders as Finance Minister Rabinowitz and Education Minister Aharon Yadlin, a cousin of his.

Preparations for elections have normally been strictly the business of the party oligarchies and machines, which usually set the list of candidates, formulated platforms, and presented both for routine approval to the parties' representative bodies. The 1973 elections exceptionally involved debates over platforms, and, in the Labor party, they were *followed* by arguments over ministerial appointments and eventually by the election of a new leadership by the Central Committee. Not so this time. Partly because of the example set by the Democratic Movement for Change, which decided to resort to direct primary elections and ranking of candidates, but mainly because of the rivalry between Rabin and Peres and the general disarray of the party, it was agreed from the outset to hold a regular primary contest for the leadership in a convention of 3,000 delegates, and to give the convention real authority in formulating a platform and deciding on rules for nominating and ranking candidates. This display of intraparty democracy was fine, but the electorate and the party members who had experienced for three years the consequences of the Rabin-Peres feud found little comfort in this when they saw the results of the balloting. Rabin won the formal contest against Peres, but only by the slim margin of 1,445 to 1,404, an even narrower margin than the one by which he had won in the Central Committee vote of 1974. Two days later, the convention adopted a platform which essentially reiterated that of 1973, except for indicating specifically willingness to return some territory to Jordan in a peace agreement. Dayan challenged the latter plank and lost, but only by a vote of 659 to 606.

The convention ended on an upbeat note, with the loser congratulating the winner and everyone calling for unity. Before long, however, supporters of Peres argued that their leader was entitled by virtue of the votes he had gained to the number two position in the future government and to half the Labor ministerial posts for his followers, while Rabin's camp spoke in terms of winner takes all. The argument over the spoils before they were even secured probably alienated many voters, but the manner in which it ended must have repelled many more. In March 1977 a *Haaretz* correspondent in Washington unearthed evidence that Rabin and his wife Leah had kept an active joint account in Washington since the days Rabin served as ambassador there, in violation of Israel's currency regulations. After making some lame excuses that did not withstand further probing, Rabin admitted guilt, resigned his leadership of the party, and took leave from his office as interim Prime Minister in early April. Peres succeeded him by unanimous vote of the Central Committee, but the party he now led was in even worse shape than it had been when it faced the electorate after the Yom Kippur earthquake.

If Labor projected the image of an unwieldy, divided, and corrupt party trying desperate improvisations to minimize the losses it expected to suffer, its principal traditional opponent, the Likkud, appeared to be an orderly, united, and principled organization but one that was so only because it was stuck in its ways and had a strictly limited relevance to the business of governing Israel. Its undisputed and venerated chief, Menachem Begin, had long outgrown his reputation as a ruthless demagogue and was by then highly respected even by his opponents as an honest, ascetic patriot and an able and dedicated leader. However, his complete dominance of the party and authoritarian bent allowed no other personality to emerge from his shadow and had made the organization inhospitable to people of charisma and strong character who tried to enter its top ranks laterally from the armed forces, business, or other political parties. At a time when all the other parties were rushing to "democratize" their procedures and make room for new blood on their lists, the Likkud followed its traditional way and produced a slate of candidates that reshuffled positions in accordance with the wishes of the leader and the oligarchy surrounding him. The party's platform was practically identical to that of 1973 in foreign policy, stressing the inalienability of Judea and Samaria (the West Bank), willingness to compromise on other territories in a peace settlement, maximizing Israel's deterrent power, mobilizing world Jewry, promoting mass immigration, and cultivating American friendship and backing. In internal affairs, the platform repeated, mutatis mutandis, the themes of the pre–Yom Kippur War platform except for the addition of a plank for compulsory arbitration of labor disputes in vital public services. It stressed the rooting out of corruption, eliminating as much as possible government interference in the economy, cutting down the budget drastically, rewarding initiative and enterprise, but also improving the lot of the poor through negative income tax, free secondary education, minimum wages, higher social benefits, and so on. Thus, although massive defections of the electorate from Labor appeared to be a foregone conclusion, the stodgy Likkud did not seem to be a likely major beneficiary—and would not in fact have been one but for the way in which the disgruntled voters distributed their vote.

The party that seemed to capture the attention of the country was the newly formed Democratic Movement for Change. Though launched only in November 1976, it quickly attracted important defectors from the top ranks of Labor as well as the Likkud and other groups and was expected to duplicate that feat on a large scale among the electorate. Its principal appeal was its emphasis on the need to reform the electoral system by a combination of constituency and proportional representation in order to bring the representative closer to the voter and improve the chances of producing majority parties. The fact that its top ranks comprised people from the entire hawk-dove spectrum was seen by many as a source of future factionalism, strife, and indecision of the kind that plagued the Labor party, but these apprehensions were in large measure countered by the present strong revulsion against Labor and were mitigated by the movement's adoption of thoroughly democratic procedures for leadership selection and decision-making. The movement's platform on foreign policy was almost identical to Labor's minus the explicit reference to returning part of the territories to Jordan. Its internal policy plank stressed, in addition to reform of the electoral system, reorganization of the administrative apparatus, purification of public life, encouragement of private initiative, and special care for the underprivileged Oriental Jews. The main weakness of the movement, besides the heterogeneity of foreign policy views among its leaders, was the homogeneity of their socioeconomic background, nearly all of them coming from the privileged and established classes. In addition, the movement had very little time to develop an effective organization before Rabin precipitated early elections, which was one reason why he did so.

The campaign was exceptionally dull by Israeli standards, despite the innovation of a televised debate between Peres and Begin. Until the very last moment, opinion polls predicted a substantial loss for Labor that would nevertheless leave it in the position of the dominant party. The only indication hinting at what actually took place was the very high proportion of respondents who reported undecided to the very end.

Several additional features on the results of the elections should be noted. First, although the Likkud became the strongest party, it did not quite inherit Labor's position as the dominant party, in the sense of being indispensable for the formation of a government. For in theory Labor could still combine with Dash and its own traditional partners—the National Religious Party, what survived of the Independent Liberal Party, and the affiliated Arab list—to constitute a majority and might well do so in practice in the future if a Likkud-led coalition should fail at some point. This opening up of the possibility of alternative governments led by either Likkud or Labor constituted a major change in the Israeli political structure, which was likely to be of considerable significance for the internal and external politics of the country.

Another important point is that the Democratic Movement for Change, besides being the principal beneficiary of the discontent with Labor, occupied the same position as that party at the center of the Israeli political spectrum. This could enable it to develop into a still greater and more influential force in the political system by drawing additional support from its immediate left and right. But this factor could also expose it to erosion toward the right and the left if it should fail to meet the main expectations of its supporters.

Other notable results were the near-destruction of the over forty-year-old Independent Liberal Party and the similar fate suffered by the Maarakh's minorities lists. The latter result left the Communist Democratic Front formed by Rakah as the almost exclusive representative of the Arabs of Israel.

Altogether, the 1977 elections amounted to a start, after a long detour, of the realignment of political forces in Israel that became necessary after the Six Day War and that Labor did much to prevent, to its own eventual detriment and perhaps to the country's. But while some definite features are already established, the realignment is not yet completed. This much is clear, however: if a Likkud-led government is formed, its encounter with the United States will have a crucial effect in determining the future course of the realignment.

13
Religion and the State

The question of the relationship between religion and the state is probably the most complex, the most vexing, and potentially the most explosive problem bequeathed to Israel by Jewish history and by the country's own more recent background. In a simplified form, the problem is that of a nation in the making, desperately needing to retain and consolidate its unity, confronting an irrepressible opposition between two segments of itself over an issue that both consider vital. One segment (consisting of about 15 percent) wishes in effect to turn the country into a theocratic state; the other, probably twice as large, wants to make it into a fully secular state. Between these two extremes, the center is divided in roughly inverse proportions between those favoring some link between religion and state while opposing others, and those leaning toward complete separation but prepared to tolerate at least temporarily some links. In the interest of national unity, which all desire, the opposing sides ostensibly agree to a modus vivendi based on the status quo that prevailed in the matter at the time the state was established. However, this arrangement is necessarily precarious and fraught with tension since the country has changed a great deal since 1948 and the status quo is complex, rigid, and vague. The result has been a state of continual friction, repeated crises, and frequent eruptions, which have been contained so far mainly because of extraneous considerations. But what would happen should these considerations weaken or disappear, or should some eruption get out of hand? One might well ask, paraphrasing the words Abraham Lincoln used in a situation bearing striking resemblances to Israel's problem, how long can a nation remain half-sacerdotal, half-secular?

Origins of the Religion-State Problem

Practically speaking, the problem of religion and state, in anything like the sense in which it has been known in the West, did not arise for the Jews until the establishment of Israel.

Diaspora Judaism recognized no central church with exclusive authority to determine and prescribe doctrine or ritual and no office empowered to enforce the legal compendia that were universally accepted as embodying orthodox doctrine and practice. Each community developed its own institutions, which usually comprised religious courts dealing, at the least, with all matters of personal status, educational institutions concerned with the transmission of religious knowledge, and various establishments necessary for the practice of the ritual. When the surrounding gentile society more or less separated church from state after bitter struggles, most Jewish communities needed to make only a few adjustments in the principles of their organization. The secular state may or may not have recognized the legal validity of acts performed by the communal institutions, but these could for the most part continue to dispense their services on a voluntary basis. True, the eagerness to bridge the gap between the institutions and practices of Jews and those of the surrounding society led in the case of some communities to a proliferation of styles and "denominations," but, typically, the conflict among them seldom went beyond the verbal level. It was only with the emergence of Israel that the question of the state's relation to what had been communal religious institutions arose with all the sharpness characteristic of church-state conflicts in Western societies.

The ideological conflict over the religion-state question goes back to the very origins of the Zionist movement. It assumed two forms, one of which, involving religious opposition to the very idea of a worldly Jewish state, was and is still peculiar to Judaism. Precisely because the Zionist idea of Return to the Promised Land is rooted in the religious concept of Geullah, not all religious Jews welcomed it. Opposition came from the ultra-Orthodox, who wished to await the divine Messiah to bring it about, and from some Reform Jews, who had deliberately reinterpreted the idea of Geullah in spiritual and universal terms in order to clear it of any Jewish separatist as well as any Jewish nationalist connotations. After the establishment of the state of Israel, the Reformist opposition dwindled to some marginal groups operating outside Israel, like the American Council for Judaism, or became converted into opposition to the exclusive dominance of Orthodox Judaism in the state of Israel. The ultra-Orthodox opposition, too, gave way after the emergence of Israel, but it persisted among various groups that live and operate in Israel such as the Neturei Karta (Guardians of the [Holy] City). Members of this group refuse on religious grounds to acknowledge the authority of the state, serve in its armed forces, or attend its schools; they often engage in violent acts such as stoning cars that pass near their neighborhoods on the Sabbath and burning down "sex boutiques"; and, when the authorities react against them, they complain to the United Nations and daub swastikas on official buildings in Israel and abroad. In terms of numbers, the Neturei Karta and other such groups are rather marginal; however, they exert a significant pull toward radicalism on the entire organized religious camp through their competition with Agudat Yisrael which formerly shared their opposition to the Jewish state.

The other, and more serious, form of ideological conflict over religion and state has its roots within the Zionist movement itself. From the beginning, the movement encompassed two conflicting visions with regard to the nature and character of the Jewish National Home it sought to promote. One group of Zionists considered the Jews a nation like all other nations, entitled to a home of its own in which it could work out its destiny in accordance with one or another of the political and social philosophies prevalent in the nineteenth century, all of which made a clear distinction between religion and state. Another group continued to view the Jews as constituting a "priestly people and a holy nation" and envisaged the Jewish National Home as a holy commonwealth in which the nation could once again live fully in accordance with its ancient sacred laws. Between these two groups there was an amorphous center that included many who hoped to establish some sort of continuity between selected elements of the ancient tradition and the modern social and political philosophies by restating those elements in a suitable secular form and incorporating them into the resurgent national life.

Adherents of all three positions came to Palestine and strove to influence the overall Zionist endeavor in accordance with their vision. The secularists far outnumbered the religious in the movement itself and, to an even greater degree, in Palestine. But the latter were helped at that stage by religious groups in the country who, while outside the Zionist fold, still sought to fight secularism and enhance religious life in the Holy Land. Above all, the religious were helped by the political and legal conditions that prevailed in the Palestine of the Mandate. Out of strivings of that period both the pattern of religion-state relations that obtains in Israel today and the protagonists in the continual struggle around it became crystallized.

Pattern of Religion-State Relations

The pattern of religion-state relations in present-day Israel includes the religious courts dealing with matters of personal status according to religious law, the institutions of the rabbinate supported by the state, the national and local Sabbath and dietary laws, the public education system which includes religious schools, the network of religious councils to provide for the religious needs of the population, and the Ministry of Religions which is involved in all the preceding in addition to its concern with the interests of the different religions and denominations in the Holy Land.

All these elements, with the exception of the ministry, were already established in Mandatory days, and they were established then as a result of the interplay of two factors that had little to do with the relative power of the religious groups. One factor was the need of the Yishuv to organize itself politically, and the other was the political and administrative circumstances in Mandatory Palestine as they affected this need. Soon after the First World War, the Jews of Palestine attempted to set up self-governing institutions to regulate their affairs and represent them before the Mandatory authorities. The authorities could not, however, grant recognition to such institutions without doing the same to some Arab self-government body. Since the Jews were not interested in promoting Arab political organization and did not, in any case, want to depend on what the Arabs did or failed to do, they availed themselves of an existing legal opening in order to achieve their aim. That opening was the *millet* system, continued by the British from Ottoman days, which allowed each *religious* community a high degree of autonomy in regulating its life in accordance with the requirements of its faith. The Jews built the self-government institutions they wanted as if they were appendages to the religious bodies they were entitled to set up, and so were able to obtain recognition from the Mandatory government for the whole system. The secularists among them had no choice but to swallow the religious courts, the rabbinate, and other institutions and practices desired by the religious in order to obtain the political institutions they wanted, and once the system was established it slipped unnoticed into the structure of the Jewish state when it was declared in the midst of war and administrative chaos.

As of today, Israel continues the *millet* system by allowing all religious communities to maintain their judicial institutions and follow their own laws in matters of personal status. For the Jews, however, this apparent continuity involves, in effect, important theoretical as well as practical changes in the position of the religious law and courts. Previously the religious courts were essentially communal institutions: their judges were appointed and paid by the communities. The Mandatory government lent its enforcement power to these courts, but it was the community itself that chose to submit to them in the first place. Certain groups could and did opt out of the community to establish their own institutions. Moreover, the jurisdiction of the Jewish religious courts was in practice rather limited because under mandatory law it was compulsory only for Jews who were Palestinian citizens. Foreigners and stateless Jews, who amounted to very large numbers, could either confer jurisdiction upon the religious courts voluntarily or turn to the secular district courts which applied to them the laws of their countries of origin on the matter. Not so in the state of Israel. The religious courts are an integral part of the state's judicial system supported by state funds and are imposed on all Jews residing in the state, regardless of formal citizenship.

The rabbinate is another institution inherited from the Mandate that has become directly integrated into the structure of the state. The Rabbinical Council, initially elected in 1921 by a gathering of Jewish community leaders and rabbis, was the first indigenous authority approved by the Mandatory government as part of the application of the Ottoman *millet* system. As subsequently confirmed and formalized, it consisted of two chief rabbis, one Ashkenazi (Western) and one Sefaradi (Oriental), and six associate rabbis, elected for a period of five years by a specially appointed Electoral Assembly of 42 rabbis and 28 laymen. In 1963, the Rabbinical Council was enlarged to 12 members and the Electoral Assembly to 125 members.

The Rabbinical Council has decisive control over the training and authorization of judges of the religious courts and of religious functionaries. The major source of its power and prestige, however, derives from its position as interpreter of the religious law, sitting on the apex of the religious judicial system. Although the rabbinate, in Israel as elsewhere, cannot *make* religious law but is bound by an elaborate code of law fixed by consensus, the multitude of new problems requiring answers that crop up in the first Jewish state in two thousand years give the Israeli rabbinate in practice a very extensive quasi-legislative authority. In addition, the rabbinate wields considerable power through its licensing of marriages and divorces and of *kashrut* (conformity with dietary law).

Laws and regulations relating to public religious observance were also inherited from the days of the Mandate. On the national level, such laws were naturally limited in Palestine because of its multicommunal character. But towns and cities inhabited entirely by one religious community had the power to make regulations concerning public religious observance, and most of the Jewish ones made extensive use of it. With the establishment of Israel, the flight of Arabs from previously mixed towns, and the emergence of many new urban settlements, religious regulations were extended to most of the country's towns. Besides, the central government itself introduced a number of new "blue laws" affecting the country as a whole. As a result, on the Sabbath and holy days, all government offices are closed, interurban public transportation is halted, and military business is restricted to a minimum. Ships arriving in Israel after sunset on the eve of such days cannot unload their passengers until the next day after sunset. National law requires all public institutions, including the army, to observe the Jewish dietary laws and prohibits the raising of pigs except in a limited area of the state inhabited mostly by Christians. Municipal regulations prohibit public transportation on Sabbath and holy days in most cities and towns, enforce the closing of places of public entertainment as well as stores and businesses except for a few restaurants, and restrict the production and sale of pork.

Israel inherited from the Mandatory days a tradition of a fragmented system of education. The Palestine government had failed to set up a national system of public education partly for lack of sufficient means to do so, and partly because the Jews preferred to set up their own schools and orient them as they wished. But the orientation the Jews chose was not uniform; various parties and local government bodies set up their own schools to ensure educa-

tion according to their own ideological inclinations. Four networks of
schools, known as "trends" thus emerged: a "general" network, maintained
by municipalities and adhering to a general Zionist orientation; a religious
network, founded and supported by the Mizrachi party and stressing its
Zionist-religious outlook; a labor network, supported by the Histadrut and
promoting a socialist-Zionist orientation; and an ultra-orthodox network,
founded and supported by Agudat Yisrael and emphasizing exclusively a religious outlook. Schools thus became an important arena for carrying on the
party struggle, especially the struggle for determining the character of the nation and its institutions with respect to the issue of religion and state. Promot-
ers of the various trends fought bitterly over enrollment of immigrant children and allocation of funds, especially after the establishment of the state
when the government passed a compulsory elementary education law that
recognized all four trends and provided for their complete support on the
basis of size of enrollment. In 1953, after several government crises, a law
was finally passed unifying all but the Agudat Yisrael network into a single
national system that specified certain schools as having a national-religious
orientation and allowed parents to choose between them and secular national
schools. Establishments of the Agudah network could receive financial support from the state if they complied with certain requirements of curriculum
and standard. This law did much to eliminate glaring disparities in the quality
and content of education and to reduce the spirit of partisanship within the
schools themselves. It did not, however, eliminate squabbles and friction over
the matter of secularism and religion since the religious parties gained control
over the national-religious schools and continued to view them as their particular preserve.

A new feature in the picture of religion-state relations has been added
since the establishment of the state with the creation of the Ministry of Religions, which was vested with the authority formerly held by the British High
Commissioner in connection with religious sects, jurisdiction of religious
courts, and registration of marriages and divorces. Initially, this special office
was established for primarily international political reasons. Israel wanted to
signify thereby its recognition of the importance of Palestine for the other
faiths and to indicate its readiness to accord continual and prompt attention
to the interests and claims of the faiths concerned. However, for various
reasons, including notably the fact that the ministry was placed at the outset
under the control of a minister from one of the religious parties, the initial
emphasis shifted soon to activities covering the whole range of the religious
establishment. The ministry became concerned with regulating the Rabbinical Councils and selecting some members of their Electoral Assemblies, su-
pervising the religious courts and providing for their budgets and administration, providing for the religious needs of the population through some two
hundred Religious Councils partly financed and appointed by it, assisting re-

ligious schools and colleges, and helping to apply laws concerning Sabbath observance and dietary regulations. As it now stands, the ministry has no parallel in any Western country; among Islamic states, however, similar institutions are frequently found. The services of the ministry are used extensively by Muslims as well as Jews, but less so by Christians, who prefer to look after themselves in order to retain greater autonomy.

Dynamics of the Religion-State Problem

It has been shown that Israeli institutions involving a very extensive intrusion of religion into public affairs originated in the particular circumstances of the Mandatory period; the next question is why these were continued, and even expanded, in the different circumstances of the Israeli state, and with what consequences?

The immediate reason for the continuation of the institutions and practices of Mandate days in the state of Israel has to do with historical accident. Unlike most of the new states, Israel was not born after an orderly period of transition and constitutional and administrative preparation. Israel came into being in the midst of war and chaos, and its first government, which was in any case provisional, had its hands full with the task of winning the war and ensuring physical survival. In these circumstances, the government did what was only natural and decreed the continuation of previously existing laws and regulations until a legally instituted constituent assembly took over. When such an assembly came into existence in 1949, it confronted in matters relating to religion a set of already established facts which it could change only by initiating a Kulturkampf—at a time when the country was surrounded by enemies, economically prostrate, and in the process of receiving hundreds of thousands of immigrants. The wise course seemed therefore to postpone thorough consideration of the question and in the meantime to give official sanction to the status quo. The record of the debates and of press comments at the time indicate a general lack of awareness that the sanctioning of the status quo itself involved a very considerable change in principle and in practice in the position of religion, as several of its manifestations in public life became compulsory emanations of the sovereign state rather than elements of voluntary communal organization.

Besides the desire to avoid an outright struggle over the issue of religion and state in a difficult period for the country, internal political considerations worked in favor of maintaining the status quo and even modifying it in favor of the religious parties. The political balance of forces in Israel has been such that no government could be formed without Mapai and none by Mapai alone. In its search for coalition partners, Mapai found the religious parties more convenient than any of the other parties, especially during the first years of the state's existence. Potential partners on the left and on the right insisted on far-reaching concessions in matters of economic, social, and foreign policy about which Mapai had very strong feelings as a condition for their participation in the government; whereas the religious parties were willing to let it have its way in all these questions provided it assured them that the status quo regarding the religious law and courts would be maintained, that Sabbath and dietary legislation would be firmly enforced, and granted them other seemingly minor concessions. Since the emergency situation in which Israel found itself at the time did not, in the judgment of Mapai's leaders, permit any drastic modification of the status quo in any case, the conditions of the religious parties seemed to them more acceptable than those which the other potential partners insisted upon. Only after many years and many incidents that pointed out the extent to which the seemingly innocuous confirmation of the status quo had in fact established a large measure of previously nonexistent religious compulsion did Ben Gurion, the architect of Mapai's alliance with the religious parties, express regrets about the price he had agreed to pay for it. By then, however, things had already gone too far to permit a reversal and other factors had come into the picture.

Ben Gurion's initial permissive position points up an element of ambivalence in the attitude and thinking of secularly inclined Israelis with respect to the Jewish religion and its relation to their state, which is essential to keep in mind if one is to have a proper understanding of this question. In Western democratic societies, the separation of church and state became a fundamental and unquestioned constitutional tenet only after centuries of conflict, civil strife, and religious wars in the course of which many other solutions were broached but proved inviable. The Jews as a collectivity have had no such experience of conflict to condition their attitude since they had had no state of their own for nearly two millennia prior to the creation of Israel. Of course, since the Emancipation European and American Jews have been involved in the issue of church and state in the societies in which they lived, where they generally took a very strong position in favor of the principle of separation of the two and its most strict application. However, this attitude derived from their experience of oppression at the hands of established alien churches and from their position as a religious minority in predominantly non-Jewish societies rather than from any "national" experience of their own. Evidence is found in the fact that Orthodox Jews upheld the principle no less fervently than Jews of all other doctrinal hues. When they came to build their own state in Palestine-Israel, the non-Orthodox Jews brought along from the West the ideal of a secular state, but in the new circumstances their commitment to the ideal was purely doctrinal and lacked any foundation in experience or necessity. Consequently, they did not view the separation of religion and state in the same categorical terms in which people of their conviction view it, or indeed they themselves had viewed it, in the West. They somehow entertained an element of doubt whether absolute separation would prove necessary in the case of a Jewish state and perhaps even a hope that it might not. As for the Orthodox Jews, they, of course, reversed their previous attitude upon coming to Palestine-Israel and became ardent advocates of having religion dominate public life.

The attitude of Israelis toward the question of religion and state is further affected by the absence of any fundamental opposition between religion and Jewish nationalism, and indeed the presence of a strong tie between the two. In the West, the modern nation-states could begin to emerge only at the expense of and in opposition to the idea of a Universal Christian Community. In the case of the Jews, however, there was no established "universal community of Jews" with a formal organization and vested interest in opposing the principle of nationality and vying against particular sovereignties. Insofar as the Jewish faith linked Jews everywhere in a community of belief and endowed them with a sense of solidarity, these rather supported the preservation and crystallization of a sense of Jewish national, or at least protonational consciousness. The most radical Israeli secularists recognize that it was Judaism as a religion that preserved the national identity of the Jews and prevented them from melting into the surrounding societies as so many other faiths, races, and ethnic groups had done. This is why most of them expressed vigorous concern about the Soviet drive against religion generally and the Jewish religion in particular. They recognized that the success or failure of that drive was likely to determine the question whether the Jews of Russia would some day find their place in Israel, or would be lost forever to Israel as well as to Judaism. Israelis sense that community of religion, be it formal, passive, and even merely negative, is the link between them and Jews in the rest of the world. For example, they have been repeatedly troubled by the question "who is a Jew?" in connection with incidents of registration of national identity, marriage and divorce, and eligibility to the privileges accorded to Jews by the Law of Return; and while the answers they gave to the question were sharply divided, they were all agreed, at least according to the evaluation of the Supreme Court, that one could not be a Jew by nationality while professing a religion other than Judaism—a position that, incidentally, could at times be more restrictive than the religious law itself. Because of these links between Judaism and nationality, many of the secularists in Israel are really people who have been thrown back to that position by their inability to regulate themselves the relations between religion and state, which is what they would have preferred, rather than people who would totally dissociate the two if they could.

The ambivalence arising from these considerations was reinforced by a substantial shift of opinion in the country since the time of independence away from secularism, though not exactly toward theocracy or even a broad construction of the status quo in favor of religion. Opinion studies, supported by direct observation and the changing composition of the population, suggest that while previously self-defined secularists constituted the great majority of the population, nowadays they account for not more than half of it, of whom only two-thirds are determined secularizers. The other half consists of one-third "theocrats" who would regulate public life according to religious law, and two-thirds people who favor only some links between religion and state, especially with respect to marriage and divorce laws, recognition of religious holy days, and general respect for tradition in the public education system and in other institutions. The principal reason for this change has been the massive influx of Oriental Jews, who had been conditioned by a totally different experience of the religion-state question in their countries of origin. Some observers are inclined to attribute the change to an ostensible "religious awakening" among Israelis connected with the general disillusionment with secular ideologies, the generational dialectic between founders and sons, the pressures of war, tension, and the conditions of modern life, and so on. However, while these factors have undoubtedly affected many people in the indicated sense, others, such as the general rise in the level of education and the troubled religion-state relations in Israel, have affected not a few people in an opposite way. Therefore, until the two tendencies are measured and analyzed simultaneously, the Oriental factor remains the most probable effective explanation.

Oriental Jews came from Muslim societies that took for granted some sort of link between religion and state. For reasons having to do with the particular character and history of Islam, these societies never experienced a church-state conflict in any form resembling its manifestations in the West. They either followed the *millet* system before the name, which rested the entire political organization of the society on a corporate-religious basis, or else, in more recent times, they combined residues of the *millet* system with the structure of a modern nation-state. Insofar as societies that did the latter faced a problem having to do with religion, the issue was not whether the state should be separated from religion but how to reform Islam so as to make it more applicable in a modern state and more suitable to the conditions of modern life generally. Moreover, the answers to the question broached by Muslim intellectual and political leaders very rarely suggested clear-cut solutions (as Kemal Ataturk did), but consisted mainly of more or less muddled improvisations coupled with a great deal of apologetic rhetoric extolling the inherent virtue of Islam and its suitability to all times and all circumstances. The Oriental Jews coming from these societies tended to view the relation between religion and state in Israel in similar terms. They either visualized the situation in Israel as a continuation of the *millet* system, with the difference that here Jews rather than Muslims constituted the dominant corporate group, or else they sensed a problem which they perceived and answered as a problem of modernism. That is to say, they tended to affirm a priori the eternal veracity of the Jewish religion and the applicability of its prescriptions to all conditions and aspects of life, while they were prepared in practice to tolerate all sorts of dissonant behavior and ad hoc accommodations. As for the question of relations between religion and state specifically, they favored a substantial formal role for religion in public life, on the understanding, however, that this would not be applied too strictly.

While all these factors have contributed to the establishment and prolongation of the status quo of religion-state relations, another set of factors, no less varied and effective, has worked to generate a constant and sometimes extreme tension around it which has made its existence contentious and its continuation precarious. In the first place, whatever the attitudes of people to the status quo in principle, the "politics of religion" have provided many grounds for widespread resentment of it. The cause of advancing religion in public life is actively promoted by several political parties; however, the dedication of these groups to their cause often tends to get confused with their dedication to their interests as parties. While this tendency is true of all political parties everywhere, and may even have a certain political-theoretical justification, it is also true that it is generally resented everywhere, and is particularly jarring in the case of religious parties that deal with an ostensibly holy cause and use a very elevated rhetoric. Also, leaders of the various religious parties have sometimes taken positions on important public issues that were indicated more by considerations of the rivalries within and between the parties than by the substance of the issues involved; and while this, again, is a common occurrence within and between all parties, in the case of the religious parties in Israel it has been particularly unsettling because it has often tended to stimulate extremism with regard to a highly charged subject on which opinion is sharply divided. Altogether, the exclusive dedication to a single cause makes the religious parties seem to much of the public more like organized pressure groups than political parties. Their tendency to bargain with issues of national interest for the sake of obtaining concessions in matters affecting religion sometimes appears as political blackmail in the eyes of even religiously inclined people who do not share their sense of priorities.

Second, the extension of the status quo that prevailed in Yishuv days to the statehood period ipso facto involved, as was shown above, important changes in the position of religion that were not noticed at the time. As the implications of these changes manifested themselves in the course of time, they inevitably gave rise to disputes and crises. For example, the rabbinate and the religious courts used their authority in the area of marriage and divorce to bar for many years a whole community of Jews from India, the *Bnei Yisrael,* from marrying other Jews, on the grounds that their Jewishness was in doubt. They revived laws that had fallen into disuse among Jews, if only for lack of means of enforcing them, and applied them to bar the marriage of whole categories of people—wives deserted by husbands whose whereabouts were unknown;

childless widows in case a brother-in-law is available anywhere but does not, as require by the Bible, renounce the obligation to marry his sister-in-law in a formal ceremony; a divorcee and a *kohen* (theoretically, a descendant of the priestly clan of Aharon, the brother of Moses, whose members are enjoined to marry only virgins, but practically, any man called Cohen or any of its many variations or any man known to have once borne such a name); and *mamzerim* (bastards). To the religious side, this kind of action may have seemed as nothing more than the application of the status quo, which recognized the jurisdiction of religious law and religious courts in the area of marriage and divorce; to the nonreligious, however, this appeared as creeping clericalism and heartless application of harsh, obsolete laws. In the absence of a constitutional document defining the status quo and of a recognized authority to interpret it, the disputes could only be fought out tumultuously and passionately in the public arena until the parties got weary or a behind-the-scenes compromise was worked out.

Third, the status quo of 1948 could not, objectively, cover all the contingencies and needs of a newly sovereign and rapidly changing society. I have already mentioned the example of public education, where a national system was an elementary imperative that was resisted by the religious parties as an infringement on the status quo but was pressed by other parties at the cost of more than one governmental crisis. Military or other national service for women is another example that also involved a governmental crisis and aroused feelings to the point where some zealots attempted to set fire to the Knesset for passing the pertinent legislation. Other examples in this category, less serious in their implications but the cause of no less public agitation, include disputes over broadcasts by the television service on the Sabbath, the observance of dietary laws in the kitchens of liners of a navigation company in which the government is partner, the licensing of import of nonkosher food, and so on.

Fourth, in the normal course of Israeli political life, small parties that did not deem themselves bound by the status quo agreement have taken advantage of favorable political conjunctures to introduce legislation that clearly infringed upon it. For example, the WIZO (Women's International Zionist Organization) faction in the Knesset availed itself of a temporary quarrel between Mapai and the religious parties to push through the Equal Rights for Women Law (1951). This legislation, which among other things protected property acquired by the wife before marriage, abolished polygamy, fixed a minimum age for the marriage of girls, and gave authority to secular authorities to break up marriages undertaken in violation of the law, undoubtedly trespassed deliberately on the sphere explicitly reserved for the jurisdiction of the religious law and courts. Nevertheless, the majority of the Knesset, temporarily freed by the quarrel from the calculations of coalition politics, enacted it to the consternation of the religious parties.

In the case just cited, the sponsors of the legislation clearly acted out of pure concern with the subject matter. In other instances the motives of the sponsors were to say the least mixed, and included the desire to embarrass Mapai, to torpedo its partnership with the religious parties, or to score points with the public. The effect in any case has been to help keep the issue of religion in the forefront and to exacerbate it.

For their part, the religious parties have not been remiss in using favorable situations to try to alter the status quo *their* way or to undo some of the effects of laws obnoxious to them. For example, after all the agitation about the national education system they managed to establish virtual control over the religiously oriented schools in the system through use of their political balance of power position. In 1958 the Knesset passed the Dayanim Law, which regulated among other things the appointment and tenure of religious judges in a manner that equated them with civil judges, except for one detail on which the religious parties insisted. While the civil judges must, on assuming office, take an oath of loyalty to the state and its laws, the religious judges are required to pledge loyalty to the state and "to the law according to which they must judge." In theory, therefore, the religious judges are not bound to follow in their work such state legislation touching the area of marriage and divorce as the 1951 Equal Rights for Women Law. In 1961 the religious parties took advantage of the weakened position of Mapai in the wake of the Lavon affair and its greater need for their support to extract from it a commitment to enact a national law banning the raising of pigs in most of the country and a pledge to consider a national law banning public transportation on the Sabbath, instead of the existing situation which left these matters to the municipal authorities.

Early in 1974, when the country was seething like a volcano and gripped by anxiety over the future in the wake of the unfortunate Yom Kippur War, the religious parties deemed it appropriate to raise the "who is a Jew" question and to try (vainly) to take advantage of the weakened position of the Labor Party to extract from it, as a condition for joining the next government, a commitment to have the definition of a Jew in law modified to conform strictly to *Halakha*.

Finally, in recent years the National Religious Party, under the influence of one of its factions dominated by new young leaders, has taken a very strong stand against returning any part of Judea and Samaria on ostensibly religious grounds. The Agudah parties and other religious personalities have strongly dissociated themselves from that stand and denied the relevance of religion to the issue, but the Ashkenazi rabbinate has upheld the party's view and both have supported a "direct action" group called Gush Emunim (Block of the Faithful) which has tried to force the hand of the government by establishing unauthorized settlements in the areas in question. Whether this development will in the long run help or check the extension of the sway of religion in the state is an open question, but there is no doubt that the injection of religious doctrine, not merely religious sentiment, into the question of the future of the occupied territories introduces an additional explosive factor in the religion-state situation.

Legislation extending the domain of religion and legislation restricting it, outcries against the sinister influence of religion in politics, and outbursts against the desecration of the holy, indignation at the revival of harsh archaic Judaic laws, and holy passion aroused by violation of God's law have maintained an atmosphere of persistent tension that has made precarious the life of any compromise and has pressed for a radical solution. If this pressure had been contained so far, it is only because of greater external pressure on the country as a whole. Whether this pressure will repress the conflict for another year, or ten or twenty years, is hard to tell. But that a showdown is due sooner or later seems certain.

An Illustration: The Case of the Mamzerim, 1965–1972

The relations between religion and state in Israel have given rise to a multitude of incidents that demonstrate the many facets and incredible ramifications of the problem. In addition to the incidents already alluded to in the course of this discussion, one could cite several times as many relating to areas not touched. There is, for example, the famous problem of "who is a Jew," which already caused one governmental crisis in 1958, has since manifested itself in several incarnations, and is still an issue on the agenda. There is the issue caused by the passionate opposition of some religious groups to the performing of autopsies, which subsided without resolution as suddenly as it flared up, but not before it led to violence and threats of violence against pathologists. Also unresolved and certain to raise trouble in the future are issues arising from the belated entry into action in Israel of Reform Judaism, which is anathema to the Orthodox. Conflict has already arisen as to what is proper and valid conversion to Judaism, and more is certain to arise in view of the large number of mixed marriages among immigrants from the Soviet Union. Besides these recurring problems there have been many "one-time" scandals over such diverse issues as the refusal of the religious authorities to allow burial in a consecrated cemetery to a baby because it was born out of wedlock, the opening of a mixed swimming pool in Jerusalem, the kidnapping of a child by his grandfather because the education chosen for him by his parents was not sufficiently religious, the holding of a flower show in Haifa on the Sabbath, the location of a playground, the operation of a subway, the opening of a new slaughterhouse, and the order of religious services at the Wailing Wall. Each of these issues, even the simplest, has usually involved several facets of the religion-state problem. However, no issue in Israel's twenty-seven years of existence has combined so many facets of it as the case of the mamzerim, and therefore no issue can better serve to illustrate the reality of the religion-state situation in the country.

In 1965 a brother and sister, Chanoch and Miriam Langer, and their respective fiancés routinely filed two marriage applications with the Marriage Registrar of the Tel Aviv rabbinate. To their amazement, the registrar rejected their applications on the grounds that the Langers were listed in his records as mamzerim (bastards) who, according to religious law going back to biblical times, are barred forever from "marrying into God's community." A mamzer (singular of mamzerim) is the offspring of a married woman from one other than her husband; and the definition ostensibly applied to the Langer brother and sister because their mother bore them during a second marriage which, though duly performed according to the religious law, was consummated before she had obtained a legal dissolution of her first marriage to a certain Mr. Borokowsky, a Catholic who had converted to Judaism. In law, therefore, she was still married to Borokowsky when she had the children by Langer.

The brother and sister appealed the registrar's decision to the Tel Aviv Rabbinical Court, but the court confirmed the decision. They appealed to the Supreme Rabbinical Court in Jerusalem, which decided to refer the case back to the Rabbinical District Court in Petach Tikva. That court confirmed the verdict of the Tel Aviv court. Once more the Langers appealed to the Supreme Rabbinical Court, and this time, as they had both served in the armed forces, they enlisted the assistance of Chief Chaplain, General Rabbi Shlomo Goren, who gathered and brought to the case new material that would impugn Borokowsky's conversion and thereby invalidate the mother's first marriage, validate the second, and legitimate the children. The Supreme Court referred the case back, once again, to the Petach Tikva Rabbinical District Court with instructions to look into the new material concerning Borokowsky's status. After so doing, the court decided that it could not itself legitimate the Langers, but added that, in view of Rabbi Goren's intercession, it thought there might be grounds for a reconsideration of the case by the Supreme Rabbinical Court. Finally, after receiving an additional appeal, the Supreme Court reviewed the case and decided definitely to turn it down. By then it was 1970, five years after the unfortunate brother and sister had begun their futile proceedings.

It should be pointed out here that despite the explicit injunction about mamzerim in the Bible, the subject has never been a major preoccupation of Jews since the destruction of the Second Temple. Certainly since the dawn of modern times, a situation such as the Langers found themselves in has been unheard of, either in Jewish communities throughout the world or in the Jewish community in Palestine before the emergence of Israel. A whole range of reasons account for that, including notably the lack of any central Jewish religious authority and the nonexclusive authority of the communal rabbinates.

The emergence of the case in Israel is therefore something novel, and it illustrates clearly the unforeseen consequences of the adoption by the sovereign state of Israel of the status quo in religious affairs that prevailed in the different circumstances of the Yishuv.

The Langers' case was not the only instance of the sudden revival or stricter application in Israel of archaic laws that had previously been forgotten or little used. Other instances include the cases of deserted wives, childless widows, and cohens and divorced women. The number of people involved in these cases amounted at the time of the Langers affair to several hundred. However, the mamzerim case is exceptional in that its victims were not only denied religious marriage but were stigmatized for life; moreover, their offspring too were likewise forever barred and stigmatized. In the other instances, the people involved could at least find relief from their problem by marrying in nearby Cyprus, for example; the same recourse would have allowed the Langers to marry but would not have erased their stigma and would have left their offspring saddled with the problem. The extreme harshness of the blow and its finality, coupled with the fact that the victims were attractive, young, loyal Israelis who had fought and risked their lives for their country in the Six Day War, even while the courts were tossing their case back and forth, served to dramatize to many Israelis the absurdity of some aspects of the status quo more than any of the many previous incidents.

As long as the case was still under judicial consideration, it stirred, as it moved from stage to stage, "only" the kind of polemics and furor among the public that scores of incidents relating to religion had caused over the years since Israel was born. However, after the final ruling of the Supreme Rabbinical Court, the case took a dramatic turn that brought into play all the complex forces involved in the religion-state problem in Israel.

Early in 1971, the Langers wrote a letter to Moshe Dayan, who, as defense minister, had a certain responsibility for them as members of the armed forces, in which they explained their plight and pleaded for help. Dayan was sufficiently moved to proceed immediately to familiarize himself with the technical aspects of the problem and within two weeks to raise the issue in the Cabinet. Probably on Rabbi Goren's coaching, he suggested that a new rabbinical court should be formed that would take account of new material collected by the Langers' attorney in order to legitimate them; if that should prove to be impossible, he argued that new legislation must be enacted that would permit all people who are barred from marriage according to religious law to marry according to civil law. The minister of religious affairs, a member of the National Religious Party, supported by Prime Minister Golda Meir, urged caution in order to avoid splitting the Jewish people, and advocated renewed efforts to find a solution to the problem according to religious law. This position having been accepted, the minister of religious affairs promptly assembled a conclave of men of law and religion to study the issue, and these decided to assign to Rabbi Goren, by now the chief rabbi of Tel Aviv, the task of preparing a religious-legal brief of the case to serve as a basis for its solution.

Rabbi Goren completed his assignment promptly and produced a legal opinion that invalidated Mrs. Langer's first marriage by impugning the conversion of her first husband, and consequently cleared her children. There remained, however, the problem of getting this opinion adopted by a proper religious court, and here new difficulties developed. The two chief rabbis announced that they were willing to have the Supreme Rabbinical Court reexamine the case in light of Rabbi Goren's findings; but the latter was convinced that the court, in its existing composition, was already deeply prejudiced, and that its members resented him personally. Goren urged instead the formation of a special court, headed by one or both of the chief rabbis, but neither agreed to this procedure. Whatever the substantive reasons of all concerned, it was clear that their position was also affected by the fact that elections to the posts of chief rabbi, in which both the incumbents and Rabbi Goren were certain to be candidates, were due in 1972. From the point of view of the incumbents, allowing Rabbi Goren to solve the Langers' case after all its previous perambulations would ensure his election, whereas luring him into a rebuff would seriously weaken him. As for Rabbi Goren, if he could not be assured a favorable resolution, then the promise he held of resolving it himself if elected chief rabbi could enlist for him the support of powerful political circles within and outside the National Religious Party, with considerable influence on the course of the elections. In the meantime, the case was stuck.

A new factor was injected into the situation when Gideon Hausner, the former attorney general who had prosecuted Adolph Eichmann and a member of the Knesset representing the Independent Liberal party prepared a private bill that would authorize civil marriage to all those who are denied marriage according to the religious law, and served notice that he would introduce it to the Knesset. Hausner's party declared that it would support the bill, but Prime Minister Meir, who feared the upheavals that would be caused by the introduction of civil marriage and who pinned her hopes of solving the problems to which the bill addressed itself on the election of Rabbi Goren, declared publicly that she opposed the bill and would view its introduction as a breach of the coalition in which the Independent Liberal party was partner. The Independent Liberals had only four Knesset seats and their passing to the opposition would have left the government still in command of a comfortable majority. However, it happened that at the same time the Central Committee of Mapam resolved, against the advice of the party's formerly venerated chiefs, to support the Hausner bill if introduced. This, assuming that the breach-of-coalition sanction applied to Mapam too, would have had very far reaching consequences. It would have broken up the Maarakh, the alignment between Mapam and the Labor party, which held out hopes of an eventual unity of the two parties and in the meantime allowed a certain balance of forces in the government and the Labor Party itself with respect to the fateful postwar issues. It would have eliminated the government's majority and necessitated new elections at a time when the question of succession and issues of basic policy were unsettled in the Labor party. Moreover, since the elections were bound to focus on the question of religion and state in Israel, they could have precipitated the long-feared Kulturkampf and wrought havoc in the existing party structure and alignments. Ominously, a debate on questions of religion and state was demanded by members of the Central Committee of the Labor party itself, and when it was held it revealed a deep divergence even within the committee. Veterans and the "young guard" of the party expressed a tough secularist stance, in opposition to the more accomodating and cautious approach of the people who represented the party in the government.

In the face of the magnitude of the impending crisis, the responsible politicians involved played for time while the minister of religious affairs hastened the preparations for the rabbinical elections and did his best to pack the Electoral Committee and Electoral Assembly with partisans of Rabbi Goren. In November 1972 the elections were finally held and Rabbi Goren won by a wide margin the seat of Ashkenazi chief rabbi. The seat of Sefaradi chief rabbi, however, was won by Rabbi Ovadia Yosef, the candidate of Goren's opponents and a man who had participated in the Supreme Rabbinical Court that had issued the final verdict in the case. As chief rabbi, Goren had the authority to set up by himself a special court to resolve the case, but for the sake of future working relations with his colleague and in order to protect himself against the anticipated reaction of the extremists, he sought first to associate Rabbi Yosef in the project of the special court. Yosef would only agree to sitting with Goren in the Supreme Rabbinical Court for a review of the case, an option that Goren had previously rejected.

In the meantime, Mrs. Langer's first husband, Borokowsky, who had been quiescent all the while, suddenly came to action, almost certainly at the instigation of Rabbi Goren's opponents. He presented a petition to the Petach Tikva Rabbinical District Court, the same court that had ruled against the Langer brother and sister twice before, to confirm his being Jewish, in view of current stories that his Jewishness was in doubt. A favorable response by the court, which was virtually certain, would have destroyed the foundation of Goren's case, locked the issue again, and released all the attending consequences. In the face of this unexpected threat, Rabbi Goren acted in a way that showed his previous rank of general not to have been entirely honorific. On the evening of November 19, 1972, he called a press conference at his home in which he announced that the Langer brother and sister had already been cleared by a Special Rabbinical Court of nine judges headed by himself that had assembled in secret earlier that day, and that they were married shortly thereafter in a secret double ceremony attended by family and friends and Defense Minister Dayan. Goren indicated that the composition of the court was to be kept secret for the moment, as were the grounds for its verdict, although the latter were presumed to be summed up in the previously known "Goren brief."

Rabbi Goren's action brought to a happy end, at last, the specific case of the long-suffering brother and sister and their patient fiancés. It also defused the threatening political crisis as the Independent Liberals decided to hold back the Hausner bill for the time being, Mapam announced that it considered itself absolved from its commitment to support it, and the responsible Labor party leadership indicated that it felt its confidence in the possibility of solving religious problems within the existing framework but under enlightened religious leadership vindicated. However, the action did not close the episode entirely and certainly promised no relief for Israel from tension and agitation over religion-state problems. Indeed the next round of stress and strain followed immediately. The secularists expected the chief rabbi to go on and solve the problem of other "unmarriageables" now that he settled the case of the alleged mamzerim, whereas the extreme Orthodox reacted with holy furor to what the chief rabbi had already done. Days after he announced his action, thousands of them gathered to perform a collective rending of clothes—the traditional ceremony performed at the death of a close relative, the desecration of the Torah, and excommunication. Heads of religious colleges and religious leaders issued learned denunciations of the chief rabbi, while some of them advocated seceding entirely from the formal community of Jews in Israel and setting up a separate community with its own courts and registers of "pure" Jews. Anonymous pamphlets and wall posters execrated and reviled the rabbi in the harshest, most hate-provoking terms in the traditional lexicon.

Between the expectations of the secularists backed by the threat of secular legislation, and the uproar of the extreme orthodox and its ever latent threat of violence for the sake of kiddush hashem (sanctification of the Holy Name), the new chief rabbi had to face a religious establishment composed in part of proven recalcitrant rabbis, supported by his own hostile colleague and secure in their tenure and their conviction, in part of terrorized rabbis who had made secrecy a condition for their participation in his special court, and in part of rabbis whose initial favorable disposition toward him was shaken by his use of the paratroopers' style in judicial proceedings and by the reaction that this approach evoked among relatively moderate and highly respected spiritual leaders in Israel and abroad. In these circumstances, for the chief rabbi to fulfill his role in a routine fashion in the years that followed required him to have in ample measure the learning of a sage, the courage of a soldier, the wisdom of the statesman, and much good fortune. For him to fulfill it so as to ameliorate the problem of religion-state relations in Israel required him to exceed these qualifications. It is a measure of the straits to which matters had come that very many people in Israel and not a few of its responsible leaders expected the Chief Rabbi (General) Shlomo Goren actually to bring relief to the religion-state problem.

PART FOUR

NATIONAL DEFENSE: THREATS, RESPONSES, IMPLICATIONS

INTRODUCTION

National defense and security have been the supreme concern of Israel throughout its existence. Before it saw the light of day as a sovereign state it had already to fight a civil war launched to abort it, and moments after its birth it had to fight another, regular, war launched by the neighboring Arab states with the aim of strangling it. Israel won both wars, but victory brought no peace—not then, not since. On the contrary, the unexpected success only stimulated its defeated enemies to try to husband better their superior military resources with a view to another round and another, and thus signaled the beginning of a confrontation that has still not ceased nearly three decades later.

The confrontation between Israel and its enemies assumed ever more diverse forms, escalated to ever higher levels, exploded in all-out war three times, and generated a "war of attrition" and continuous guerrilla and terrorist action and counteraction. In the process, the confrontation became embroiled in the ups and downs of pan-Arab politics and inter-Arab rivalries, and got entangled with the changing patterns of superpower competition and the fluctuations of relations within the world alliance systems. Although the military and the diplomatic aspects of the confrontation were thus inseparable in real life, it is important to focus on the military before going on to the diplomatic because of the very unique place that defense and security have occupied in Israel's life.

In the security problems that confronted Israel two stages may be clearly distinguished. Right after the War of Independence, the challenge Israel faced was to husband its limited resources and to use them in such a way as to deter any Arab coalition from going to war. In this, Israel succeeded brilliantly, especially in the 1957–1967 period. In the latter year, however, a series of accidents combined to deceive Egypt's Gamal Abdel Nasser about Israel's real strength in comparison with the forces at his command and drove him to precipitate war.

The fact that the kind of power it developed had not proved sufficient to deter its enemies impelled Israel to revise its basic strategy and seek to use the assets it had gained in the war to achieve security through forcing a favorable peace settlement. This switch to a strategy of "compellence" involved a much greater admixture of the political with the military than had the previous strategy of deterrence. It required definition of the desirable peace settlement and the deployment of means to induce the enemy to accede to it, in addition to denying to him the possibility of recovering his assets by military means. In dealing with the military aspects of the problem, which assumed the novel forms of a war of attrition, guerrilla action, and terrorism, Israel did very well, although perhaps not as brilliantly as in the previous stage. However, an uneven and generally mediocre handling of the political aspects of the strategy denied it the success it might have achieved and impelled the Arabs to gamble on a surprise general war rather than yield to open-ended demands. The impressive recovery of the military from the initial blunders of the 1973 Yom Kippur War prevented a complete failure of the compellence strategy. It remains to be seen, however, how long Israel can preserve what was salvaged, and, especially, how intelligent will be the handling of its political aspects.

The next few chapters will elaborate on the main themes of this introduction. One will be devoted to the security challenge and Israel's response to it in the stage of deterrence, and another will do the same in the stage of compellence. In addition, one chapter will describe the course of the 1967 war and another that of the 1973 war. Finally, because Israel's security concerns have involved total husbanding of its energy and resources for war for nearly three decades, one chapter will explore the implications of that effort for the Israeli polity and society. It will particularly address the questions whether and to what extent that effort has perverted or may yet pervert civil liberties and the democratic political system, and whether and to what extent Israel may have turned or may yet turn into a militaristic nation.

14
National Security, 1949–1967: Challenge and Response

The Arab Challenge

Even before the last armistice agreement terminating the 1948 war had been concluded, various efforts were under way, secret and open, direct and through the United Nations, to convert the armistice agreements into a final peace. However, by the summer of 1950 all these efforts had collapsed never to be resumed, and the war that was just concluded with Israel's victory, instead of deciding finally the long conflict over Palestine, became merely an episode in an open-ended conflict involving Israel and the surrounding Arab states.

This conflict went through several successive stages, each confronting Israel with a more severe security challenge than the preceding, until the showdown of the Six Day War. Thus, an initial implicit threat of *revanchisme* became an explicit threat of a "second round" supported by acts of hostility; a potential long-term threat became a real and present danger; and finally, the ostensibly limited aims that the enemy pursued at one stage became total in the next: the destruction of the Jewish state. Underlying the ever graver nature of the menace and lending it maximum credibility throughout was the enormous disparity in resources between Israel and its enemies and the extremely vulnerable geostrategic position it occupied.

Formally, the post-1948 peace negotiations between Israel and its neighbors failed because the parties could not reach an agreement on the question of the Palestinian refugees and the boundaries of the Jewish state. Actually, they failed because of a complex set of underlying reasons that prompted the Arab states collectively to reject the idea of peace with Israel. These reasons included the unlikelihood of Israel's renewing the war to compel them to come to terms, the paucity of material inducements for making peace and the counterbalancing of these by material disadvantages for most of the Arab countries, the mutual deterrence of the Arab governments against making separate peace and defense arrangements, the apprehension that peace would enhance the possibilities of Israel's diplomatic maneuvering among the Arab states and thus increase the danger of feared Israeli expansionism, the psychological reluctance of the Arab governments to admit final defeat and their fear of facing an outraged public opinion that had been encouraged in its expectations of easy victory, and finally the seduction exercised on some governments by the seemingly far superior potential of the Arabs, leading them to wish to keep the issue open until such time as a reversal in the balance of power would permit a radical reversal of the situation, the restoration of "justice," and the recovery of Arab honor.

Among these reasons for the refusal of the Arab governments collectively to make peace, only the last was of an offensive nature in that it involved not merely saying no to peace but looked forward to a time when the situation might be reversed. However, for reasons of internal and inter-Arab politics, the Arab governments felt impelled to stress that one reason above all others and present it as if it were the only one. Moreover, in their attempts to curry favor among their public or to score points against rivals, they suggested that revenge was not merely an open option for the distant future but an imminent project on which they were actively engaged. To underscore their point, they engaged individually and collectively in various acts of political, economic, and psychological warfare against Israel, punctuated by periodic acts of violence on a local scale.

Victorious states throughout history have tended to be wary of *revanchiste* urges on the part of their defeated enemies even when these had signified their acceptance of the war's outcome in peace treaties. Israel might therefore have felt a security challenge on this ground alone, even if its enemies had not refused to make peace and had not gone on instead to speak loudly of another round and to indulge in all sorts of hostile activities. Moreover, since the issue in the war that Israel won had been unlimited, centering on the very right of a Jewish state to exist in Palestine, the refusal of the Arabs to accept the war's verdict and their urge to reverse it appeared to Israel as a refusal to recognize its very right to survive as a nation and a desire to negate it in action. To be sure, for some time after the war the Arab states insisted officially that they only wanted Israel to return to the United Nations partition boundaries and to repatriate the Palestinian refugees, thus implying a willingness on their part to accept a Jewish state; however, even before they dropped that position in the mid-1950s in favor of one that frankly sought to eliminate that state, Israel felt that the realization of the Arabs' more limited demands would put them in a position to dismantle it at will anyway.

The gravity of the Arab threat was underscored by an enormous disparity in size and resources between Israel and its enemies. On the morrow of the armistice agreements Israel's Jewish population amounted to some 750,000 while that of the five Arab countries it had fought was 30 million. Egypt alone had twenty-five times more people than Israel. The national product of the five Arab countries was seven times greater than Israel's and Egypt's alone was four and a half times greater. Of course, Israel hoped that massive immigration and rapid economic development would gradually improve these proportions, but the initial gap was so wide that the residual gap seemed bound to remain enormous almost indefinitely.

Intensifying the challenge confronted by the Israelis was the political and physical geography of their country before 1967. Israel was surrounded on all sides but the western seashore by enemy countries. It had nearly 600 miles of frontier to defend, and its territory was so small and so shaped as to give little or no depth for defense. There was hardly a point of strategic importance in Israel that was removed from Arab positions by more than 30 miles, and in some instances Israel had no choice but to build important air bases within range of enemy artillery fire. Along the coastal plain, where most of Israel's population, economic life, and industry were concentrated, the country was only 9 to 15 miles wide; a slight enemy advance from any point in the Arab bulge westward could split the country at its waist and cut off the Haifa and Galilee regions from the Tel Aviv region and the Negev. Connections between Tel Aviv and Jerusalem depended on a corridor which narrowed down to 10 miles at some points; the capital itself was within range of light enemy weapons and was surrounded on three sides by enemy territory. Sea access to Eilat could be easily blocked by Egyptian batteries posted at the southern tip of the Sinai Peninsula, and the land reach to it could be cut by the convergence of enemy forces from Jordan and Egypt across the narrow, uninhabited triangle that constitutes its hinterland. In the far north, the jutting finger of eastern Galilee was exposed to enemy positions on three sides, and further down, Syrian batteries in the Golan Heights sat on top of Israeli settlements in the Huleh Valley and the area of Lake Tiberias. The only relief in this otherwise nightmarish situation was the fact that the most threatening geostrategic feature, the central Arab bulge, was occupied by Jordan, a relatively weak Arab state. This area offered a determined enemy so many possibilities for a quick, devastating thrust that its control by any other Arab army was seen by Israel as grounds for an immediate "preventive war." Indeed, the signing of an agreement establishing a unified command of the forces of Jordan, Syria, and Egypt in October 1956 and in May 1967 was one of the factors that made war inevitable in both instances.

To the challenge presented to Israel by the radical nature of the intentions of its enemies, their vastly superior resources, and its extremely vulnerable geostrategic position, history added its own dimension. At the end of the 1948 war Egypt, the most formidable of Israel's enemies, was hamstrung in its effort to realize its power potentialities by a most unmartial, corrupt, and inefficient regime, but in July 1952 a new regime of young officers took over that was untrammeled by internal obstacles and for whom the upbuilding of the armed forces was a paramount objective. From 1950 to 1955 Egypt and the other Arab countries could not make full use of their superior financial and manpower resources to prepare for another war because of limitations on the supply of arms to the entire area imposed by the traditional Western suppliers, but since 1955 Egypt and Syria were able to obtain at bargain prices from the Soviet Union all the arms they could buy in addition to all the instruction in their use they cared to get. In the early 1950s a large British army was encamped along the Suez Canal and constituted an effective separating wall between Egypt and Israel, which gave added credence to the expressed desire of the Western powers to preserve the military status quo; but after 1955 that wall was removed as a result of an Anglo-Egyptian agreement, and the Egyptian armed forces as a consequence were free to move eastward. They acquired the first-rate British facilities and stores of the canal base in the bargain. In short, prior to 1955 Egypt and the Arab states presented a formidable potential threat to Israel but the threat seemed to have an indefinite future due date; after 1955 the danger became real, clear, and present.

In addition to the need to confront the threat posed to its "basic" security by all the factors cited, Israel had to face the task of dealing with day-to-day or "current" security problems resulting from its exposed frontiers and Arab hostility. Immediately after the signing of the 1949 armistice agreements, Israel was plagued by repeated acts of infiltration of its borders and by sporadic armed disputes over the local application of the terms of the agreements. Newspaper readers throughout the world were constantly reminded of the Palestine conflict through such incidents and their frequent eruption into full-scale local battles, but probably few of them realized to what extent these incidents were an integral part of the brink-of-war situation in the area. Many border crossings, especially at the outset, were undoubtedly made by miserable refugees walking over to steal a few pieces of pipe, a sheep, or a sack of watermelons, but others were undertaken by organized Palestinians bent on provoking a fight between the Arab states and Israel while robbing and killing the hated Jew. Some border clashes were due to the bona fide conviction of an Arab government that Israel had infringed upon the armistice agreement in a demilitarized zone, but others were the outcome of deliberate action by one or another Arab government designed to pin down some of Israel's forces, harass and demoralize its people, score some political points at home or in the arena of inter-Arab politics, promote fifth-column work among the Arab minority, or carry out sabotage and intelligence activity. Israel confronted the task of developing the means to deal effectively with an agitated border or risk undermining the credibility of its existence and the sapping of its people's morale—its main asset in the contest with the Arabs.

The Israeli Response

The magnitude of the Arab challenge led Israel to make defense considerations the supreme concern in its international and internal endeavors. The international aspect of Israel's response will be discussed in detail further on.

228 | *The Evolution of Israel*

Suffice it here to mention that whatever Israel sought to achieve by diplomacy, it did not allow success or failure in the external endeavor to deflect it from exerting the maximum defense effort internally. Nor did it, in its strategic thinking, depend on the international factor to act in its favor, however much its diplomacy tried to foster that probability.

Internally, Israel's response took the form of adapting every relevant aspect of life to considerations of defense and strategy. The effort had a constant facet, related to the basic disparity in resources between Israel and its enemies and its inferior geostrategic position, and a variable one connected with the specific evolution of the Arab challenge and the changes in the size, armament, and capabilities of the enemy's armed forces relative to Israel's.

Defense and the Management of Civil Resources

Throughout its existence, Israel has had to devote very large portions of its national product to defense to compensate for the larger resources of its enemies and to keep its position in the arms race that developed between it and them, especially after the Soviets began to provide arms to Egypt and Syria. For the 1950–1966 period as a whole, Israel spent an average of 9 percent of its GNP each year on defense. This percentage was second only to that spent by the Soviet Union in that period and was similar to that of the United States, with its vast burden of international responsibilities and commitments. It was more than twice that of countries of Israel's economic class that carry a heavy defense burden, such as Sweden and New Zealand. Although Israel's GNP grew by an average of 10 percent a year during that period, the portion of GNP devoted to defense tended to rise rather than decline as a consequence of the acceleration of the arms race. Thus, spending on defense increased from about 6.5 percent of GNP in 1950 to 12.5 percent in 1966, while the absolute amounts involved increased nearly sixfold, from $80 million to $460 million a year.

Impressive—or depressing—as these figures are, they do not give a complete picture of the extent to which defense impinged on Israel's economic life. For, besides the direct defense activity reflected in these figures, Israel adapted many normal economic and social programs to defense considerations, sometimes at no extra cost, often at a very high price that does not appear on the defense bill. This tendency in itself may not be unusual in our times; what is unusual is the relative extent to which Israel pursued it. As a country that began to be built in relatively recent times in circumstances of ceaseless and violent hostility, Israel had the chance to build national defense into its very foundations. In the nineteen years between the War of Independence and the Six Day War alone, the authorities of Israel had the chance to direct or influence with an eye to the defense problem the use of fifteen times more land, three times more population, and perhaps twelve times more national wealth than existed at the birth of the state. Few other modern states have had such an opportunity, and none has made as much use of it as Israel.

The most important illustration of the incorporation of defense considerations into the foundations of the country is provided by Israel's agricultural substructure. From the early days of the Zionist endeavor in Palestine, the agricultural settlements, whatever their type, were viewed not only as economic enterprises or as a way of life for their members, but were also considered as outposts spearheading or consolidating the Zionist conquest of the country. Initially, the enemy was the lawless Bedouin, who had previously made settled life impossible for anyone irrespective of nationality, religion, or color. In the 1920s and the 1930s, it was the organized, politically-directed Arab bands bent on destroying the settlements and checking the progress of Zionism. At that time many of the settlements assumed the physical shape of early American frontier posts, with stockade and towers, and their semimilitary exploits became similarly part of the national mythology. During the War of Independence practically all the settlements became full-fledged military bastions, and many of them became formidable little hedgehogs with trench networks, prepared fire positions, rows of barbed wire, minefields, underground shelters, hospitals, and stores. The principal function of the settlements was to hold back enemy advance while the country mobilized its striking forces or while these forces concentrated on particular chosen targets, and with few exceptions they acquitted themselves of their task brilliantly as we have seen in the War of Independence.

After the 1948 war, the acquisition of vast land areas by the state, the inflow of one million immigrants, and the availability of billions of dollars for development work enabled Israel to establish hundreds of new villages and towns, planned more than ever before with a view to their role in the country's defense. Sites for the settlements were chosen by the authorities concerned in consultation with the General Staff. Their organization and the armament and training of their members were continually adjusted to cope with the advances achieved by the Arab armies and with the added security duties imposed on them, such as helping to check infiltration and guerrilla activity. Very often, the sites chosen for new settlements were not the best from an economic point of view, and their selection for military reasons involved a masked military expenditure in the form of greater and longer support for the villages from the settling authorities. In many cases, where defense requirements prescribed the setting up of settlements in certain areas but where conditions did not permit any livelihood to be derived from them for some time, special sections of the army known as Nachal (Pioneering-Fighting Youth) went on the land and took upon themselves the task of gradually improving it until it could be made to yield a livelihood for permanent settlers. The whole endeavor of colonization combining military and economic purposes was developed into a fine art which Israel imparted to friendly countries in Asia and Africa confronted with comparable problems.

Similar considerations affected the decisions concerning the country's urban and industrial development. For example, in planning the overall distribution of the masses of immigrants and the location of the thousands of new industrial establishments, economic reasoning alone would have prescribed encouraging people to go where there is water, and industry to go where there are people, power, markets, easy transport, and other facilities. Instead, Israel's planners endeavored to guide people and industry to areas chosen for their strategic value even though they might be barren, and to bring water, power, roads, and other facilities to them by means of enormously costly national schemes. Industries chosen for special solicitude were not only those that promised to make the quickest or greatest contribution to the economy and those that happily combined reasonable prospects of economic viability with potential defense use; they also included many that required prolonged assistance and much protection at great immediate cost before they could become solvent, because they were deemed militarily important. An aircraft industry, for example, was established in 1953 in Lod although Israel had no special qualifications for such an undertaking and had to pay a heavy learning and running-in cost before the enterprise began to pay its way, but the price was accepted in order to build a local reserve of technicians and repairmen for the air force, reduce the country's dependence on foreign suppliers of parts, and begin to produce warplanes locally. Hundreds of millions of dollars were poured through the years into acquiring more and more cargo ships at times when many of those available left Israeli ports half-empty or had to operate on charter between foreign ports. But the urge to keep Israel's only supply route open and the unwillingness to rely on foreign commercial shipping in emergencies overrode short-run economic considerations and impelled Israel to launch on a naval vocation regardless of cost. Much the same can be said about the Israeli shipyards, the large-scale integrated steel industry, the automotive industry, and about a very large number of smaller enterprises established in the 1950s and early 1960s.

Immigration provides another example of Israel's shaping basic policies of the state to defense purposes. The "ingathering of the exiles," or the return of the Jews to their homeland, has been, of course, of the essence of Zionism and of the state to which it gave birth. But while Israel's authorities might have chosen to at least regulate the rate of immigration in accordance with the need of distressed Jews and the country's economic capacity, they chose instead to throw the gates of the state wide open and to take measures to persuade the hesitant and the reluctant to come, in complete disregard of economic considerations. This policy involved enormous waste in the early years, as hundreds of thousands of people sat idly in reception camps eating the country's substance without producing anything, but the urge to increase the manpower pool for defense as quickly as possible prevailed over other considerations.

Further examples could be adduced almost indefinitely, from the incorporation into the National (social) Insurance system of a contributory scheme to cover the pay of reservists during their annual call-up periods to the inclusion of air raid shelters in all buildings, but the broad instances mentioned should suffice to indicate the extent to which defense thinking has pervaded Israel's life.

The Military Establishment

Israel's response to the challenge of Arab hostility came into sharpest focus, of course, in its military establishment proper, the principles guiding it, and its mode of operation. It is at this level that the country's security problems had to be specifically met and that its overall defense effort was ultimately tested.

Even when Israel expected the armistice agreements to lead to peace and when it was thought that providing against an implicit threat of *revanchisme* was the principal defense task, the enormous disparity in potential resources between Israel and its neighbors led its defense planners, headed by Chief of Staff Yigal Yadin (who has since become a world-famous archaeologist), to base the country's armed forces on a unique reserve system that has become the hallmark of Israel's military establishment. The essence of the system was to enroll every man and woman who could be of any use for military service into an accordion-like structure that allowed keeping the armed forces at reduced levels during peaceful intervals and expanding them in various measures to meet varying degrees of emergency up to total mobilization. This idea in itself is not novel, of course; what is novel is the thoroughness with which it was applied in Israel, the extraordinary rapidity with which the reserves could be mobilized, the high level of preparedness at which the reserves were constantly kept, and the extent to which reserves and regular forces were routinely integrated. For a brief period after Yadin's retirement there was a tendency among some of Israel's military chiefs who had been reared in the British military tradition to interpret Israel's system imitatively, which led to an effort to shape a polished regular army while paying scant attention to the reserves. It took a "revolution" from within, in which General Dayan was a leading spirit, to reverse that trend and give the Israeli armed forces the imprint of a nation at arms that they have borne ever since.

In the system as it crystallized, there is no regular army as such. Israel's armed forces consist of a relatively small professional cadre plus conscripts and reserves. The professional cadre includes a core of officers and NCOs of a size varying between 12,000 and 20,000 (during the period under discussion), who serve on the basis of renewable three-to-five-year contracts. They provide the leadership of the conscript and reserve formations, man their permanent framework, and "activate" them. Conscription applies to every male and female for periods of service that have varied from two to three years for men and from one to two years for women. Some exceptions are made for women on religious and family grounds, but none are made for men other than for physical or mental unfitness. Call-up age is eighteen, but immigrants arriving after that age are still conscripted and required to fulfill a period of service if they are subject to reserve liabilities. These liabilities are applicable after conscription up to the age of forty-nine for men and thirty-four for women and include up to thirty-one consecutive days a year plus one day per month. Officers are subject to an extra seven days a year of reserve services. Reservists are assigned to reserve units on a territorial basis whenever feasible; all reserve formations are activated in turn, either to train conscripts or to exercise their members on their annual call-up. Arabs of military service age are registered but only the Druzes (numbering some 37,000 in the country) are called up.

The size of the active forces at any given time varies with the size of the call-up for conscription and the security needs of the country. Around 1965, conscription brought in some 60,000; together with the permanent cadres this made for a standing military establishment of about 80,000. Total mobilization could multiply this almost fourfold, to an incredible 300,000 out of a total Jewish population of 2.6 million. Mobilization of various units in turn is frequently practiced and has been developed into a fine art. During the Sinai campaign of 1956, it was five days from the time the first reserve units were called up to the moment Israeli forces started their operations across the Israeli-Egyptian frontier; on that occasion considerably less than full mobilization capacity was ordered. In 1967 total mobilization *was* effected and brought to the colors close to 300,000 men and women, but on that occasion the authorities chose to proceed gradually over a two-week period.

The 1973 war put the system through its most severe test, as the first mobilization orders went out a few hours before the start of hostilities, and as strategic surprise was compounded by tactical surprise to create a critical situation at the fronts. There was a great deal of confusion, and many shortcomings grave and small became apparent, but all in all the system worked to meet the emergency. The first reserve reinforcements entered the battle in the Golan Heights after twenty-four hours, and enough units were mobilized in another twenty-four hours to permit Israel to launch counteroffensives on two fronts. The last units and pieces of equipment reached the fronts after four days.

The organization of the armed forces is designed to secure maximum flexibility, coordination, and economy of time and effort. The basic formation of Israel's army is the brigade, more or less equivalent to the American regiment, which has about 4,000 men. The strength and organization of a brigade's subunits are not rigid and have varied with the availability of weapons and vehicles. Brigades have their own reconnaissance and mortar companies and their own administrative, signal, engineering, medical, and antiaircraft units, each capable of expansion or contraction according to task. They do not have their own artillery, which is attached to them according to requirements and availability. Any number of brigades and subunits can be grouped into task forces of differing size and mix—conscript and reserve formations, armor, motorized infantry, paratroopers, and heliborne troops, artillery and auxiliary units.

All three branches of Israel's armed forces—army, navy, and air force—are controlled and guided by a single General Staff under a single chief who receives his orders from the minister of defense. The General Staff has the usual four departments—operations, manpower, supply, and intelligence—which service all three branches. In addition to the Central Command, there are three permanent territorial commands under it known as the North, Center, and South Commands. Initially established to meet the needs of the 1948 war, they were retained and developed so as to allow different parts of the country to go on fighting independently in case they are cut off and to provide added mobility and flexibility in any case. The commands are responsible for troops in their territory with respect to mobilization, training, and administration and are also in charge of directing military operations in their sectors and beyond the frontiers facing them. General Headquarters moves troops from one command to another; each command must therefore be ready on short notice to administer and feed large numbers of troops and to fuel and service their vehicles. This arrangement enables the permanent staff of each command to familiarize themselves thoroughly with the particular enemy and problems of their sector and to assimilate and deploy promptly large additions of forces, at the same time that it allows General Headquarters to move troops quickly from one front to another without too much concern about their supplies.

Israel's armed forces are reputed to have a very high ratio of combat-to-noncombat strength, though more so in the past than recently. It is estimated that before 1967 Israel's forces attained up to 50 percent "teeth" as compared with the twenty-to-eighty "teeth-to-tail ratio" of other large armies. This achievement was made possible to a large extent by the small size of the country, obviating the duplication of military installations (less true at present), and by a very heavy reliance on civilian facilities in cases of extraordinary activation (again less true now). All civilian vehicles, for example, were and are subject to call at any moment—infantry transport has consisted of buses and other commandeered civilian vehicles. Civilian hospitals were and are prepared at any moment to turn assigned sections into military hospitals, garages and garage men can be taken over as working units at a moment's notice, the Public Works Department, with its depots, garages, sheds, equipment, specialized vehicles, engineers, and other trained men are ready to be promptly utilized when needed, personnel of the sanitation, electricity, and water works are on call, and so on. All these arrangements make for vast economies and liberate the maximum number of soldiers for fighting duties, although they cannot be very efficient in a protracted war.

All other aspects of Israel's army reflect the integration of regular and reserve service and their equal orientation to combat. Discipline is strict but there is minimum attention to spit and polish. Completion of mission is stressed as the principal criterion for assessing action; all other considerations are viewed as subordinate. Training emphasizes speed and aggresiveness; initiative is vigorously cultivated. Assumption of responsibility by lower echelons is encouraged, and commanders are instructed to lead their men into battle even though this is bound to involve heavy casualties among officers, as was the case in the 1956, 1967, and 1973 wars. Relations between officers and ranks are easy and barrack regimentation is relatively casual; officers have for the most part to establish their ascendancy over their charges through competence rather than formal authority and distance. Promotion is exclusively through the ranks and is based solely on experience and attainment in the field. Senior officers are frequently rotated among different assignments and advanced studies to maximize their experience and knowledge. General-grade officers are retired to the reserves in their low or mid-forties in order to make room for fresh talent in the active service, and to inject still young vigor into the reserve command. In order to test the reserve units and keep them tempered for action, they are periodically called up and entrusted with military operations, even though these might have been performed entirely by standing army formations.

The air force and the navy are reared on the same principles as the army as far as cultivating an offensive spirit directed to the completion of the mission and maintaining close coordination with relevant civilian enterprises and installations, such as the commercial airlines, the aircraft industry, the merchant marine, the shipyards, the Ports Authority, and so on. They too have a professional core and a body of recruits and reserves, but in their case the ratio of the former to the latter has to be much higher than in the army because of their much greater need for men with technical competence. Nevertheless, the air force and the navy strive to train many more men than they need to operate the equipment available to them at any given time in order to make room for rapid expansion when and if more equipment is obtained.

A special feature of the Israeli armed forces is the Nachal—the above-mentioned army corps designed to combine fighting with the founding and manning of frontier settlements. Another unusual institution sponsored by the armed forces is the Gadna (Youth Battalions), a voluntary organization for boys and girls aged fourteen to seventeen for the purpose of promoting patriotism, physical fitness, and premilitary training. The Gadna maintains branches in the secondary schools and in the cities and towns and has its own camps and training sites. There are air and naval as well as army Gadna units

which help orient the youngsters toward the respective services in anticipation of reaching their induction age. While the purpose of the Gadna in
normal times is mainly social and educational, in emergencies Gadna
members can be useful in secondary military tasks.

Women serving in the armed forces is not an unusual feature in our time,
but it is unusual to submit them to compulsory service and to reserve duties in
peacetime as does Israel. Women constitute a high percentage of the standing
army of Israel at any given time—possibly up to one-third. At times this may
be more than needed, but women are kept on for national educational purposes. During the 1948 war, women often served in fighting units; now they
are mainly used as clerks, typists, drivers, signalers, computer operators, in
supply depots, clinics, and hospitals, for parachute packing, and in education
and social welfare tasks. By filling these and similar jobs, they allow the maximum number of men to be available in the "teeth" units. In an emergency
they can be used in static and civil defense tasks.

Strategy

Liddell Hart defined strategy as "the art of distributing and applying military
means to fulfil the ends of policy." For a war situation this definition seems as
good as any and better than most. However, for a situation of confrontation,
such as the one in which Israel has lived from the moment of its birth to the
present day, that definition needs to be modified to include the husbanding as
well as the distributing and applying of military means, and the sense of *military means* must be broadened to include such dual-purpose instruments as
settlements of the kind described. The definition as modified points to two related components of strategy: one organizational or structural and the other
dynamic, or pertaining more directly to application. Having already talked a
great deal about the former, I shall discuss here some central aspects of the
latter in conjunction with the former.

The policy ends that strategy was intended to serve in the case of Israel
until 1967 had the merit of being extremely clear and simple: to deter any
Arab attack against the integrity and sovereignty of Israel and repel it should
it occur. Its opponents, in contrast, had several policy aims which tended to
hamper maximum concentration of effort and to cause waste of resources.
Egypt under Nasser, for example, wanted its strategy to serve not only the
purpose of revising the status quo with Israel or subduing it, but also to secure
the regime and the home front against subversion, to advance the cause of
pan-Arabism and Arab unity to the extent that this can be done by military
means, and to defend the country against attacks by outside powers other
than Israel whose interests and policies clashed with Egypt's. Israel had no internal problems susceptible to being met by military means, no external aspirations of a nature that might bring it into armed conflict with third powers,

and no revisionist desires that impelled it to take the initiative to alter the status quo. Arab spokesmen may dispute the last statement and assert that Israel has ever been bent on expansion. However, when made not merely propagandistically such arguments are probably based on a confusion of offense as a strategy with expansionism as a policy aim, at least as far as the period through the Six Day War is concerned.

In their effort to serve Israel's policy aims, Israel's military chiefs confronted the two basic problems cited above: the enormous disparity of resources between Israel and its enemies and Israel's highly vulnerable geostrategic position. They tried to meet the first of these problems on the structural level by marshaling the totality of Israel's resources into a unique reserve system, and the second by developing the hedgehog-settlement system, intended to provide Israel with some "strategic depth" to compensate for the lack of territorial depth. These organizational solutions, in turn, were necessarily bound up with some strategic concepts of action that constituted the dynamic part of Israel's strategy.

One of these concepts was that in any armed confrontation entailing total or near-total mobilization, Israel had to do everything in its power to make the war as short as possible. This has meant different things at different times but has always involved the idea of striving to reach a quick decision as against trying to gain position by position and win battle by battle. Of course, all states might well favor the principle of a short war and ever since Napoleon many strategists have urged the advantages of seeking a quick decision under any circumstances; however, for Israel these actions were not a matter of preference but of necessity, prescribed by the very nature of its armed forces and the relation of resources between Israel and its enemies. Because its forces were mainly reserve formations that enrolled virtually all the able-bodied population, Israel could not fight a prolonged war without risking the paralysis of its entire economy and life. Moreover, because Israel had no visible and predictable untapped resources to draw on, the prolongation of a war could only deplete its existing forces while giving the enemy the chance to replenish his by drawing on his vast unutilized reserves.

It might be pointed out, incidentally, that the extreme difficulty for Israel of supporting near-total mobilization for any extended period has an important diplomatic corollary, and that is that Israel could not readily sustain not only a long war but also a prolonged crisis, if this involved near-total mobilization. Once such a situation developed, it had to be resolved fairly quickly, either by diplomatic means or by war. This situation was demonstrated in part in 1956, completely in 1967, when Israel went to war, and in the period after the 1973 war, when Israel pressed for quick disengagement by peaceful means.

Another principle of Israeli strategy for the period through the 1967 war was that Israel's forces had to take the offensive and carry the war into enemy territory as soon as hostilities began, if not in anticipation of their outbreak. This principle is partly a logical sequel of the first: if decision had to be reached quickly then only the offensive could accomplish this. In addition, the offensive and carrying the war into the enemy's territory were dictated by the nature of Israel's pre-1967 boundaries and topography. These provided the enemy with so many opportunities for breakthroughs of potentially disastrous consequence that Israeli strategists felt they had to do everything possible to anticipate and foil enemy initiatives by developing offensive threats to his forces and positions. Moreover, because the boundaries and potential front lines ran so close to the centers of Israeli population in so many places, carrying the war into enemy territory was imperative in order to avoid devastation and heavy casualties. In 1948 Israel was compelled by circumstances to fight a strategically defensive war, even though tactically its forces attacked whenever they could; the relatively very high costs it suffered as a result and the extreme precariousness of its position, as Israel saw it, at least in the early stages of the fighting, added an element of trauma to the rational considerations in favor of offensive war.

A consideration that favors a strategy geared to a short, offensive war even if no total mobilization is involved is the realization on Israel's part that international political intervention might stop the fighting a short while after its start. Israel learned from the experience of the 1948 war that political decisions tended to conform to the apparent situation in the battlefield. Therefore, it seemed that taking the offensive was the best way to establish as many advantageous military facts as possible and to deny the enemy any foothold in the little fighting time that might be available before a cease-fire came into effect. The war of 1956 confirmed the lesson of the 1948 war in this respect only as far as the pressure to stop the fighting after a short time was concerned, but not as far as allowing established military facts to stand; however, Israel attributed this to the failure of its British and French allies to do their part in creating rapidly a favorable overall military position.

Israel adopted the principle of the offensive and carrying the war into enemy territory not only for its basic security, but also for its current security problem. To counter Arab acts of sabotage and harassment, Israel relied heavily on raids against targets across the borders carried out by large army units or by the air force. Although this strategy brought many condemnations from the United Nations Security Council and from friendly governments, these never caused Israel to desist from undertaking the same kind of action again. The reasons for its defiance were many, but chief among them was the fear that if it respected frontiers, Arab operations might develop into large-scale guerilla warfare in which the enemy would have several sanctuaries to sally from and withdraw to beyond the armistice lines. Such warfare would compel Israel to use continuously very large forces and would be frustrating, demoralizing, and costly. Israel preferred to suffer the condemnations and to take the risk that its actions might contribute to an escalation into general war, over that prospect.

While the preceding principles concerning the harnessing, distribution, and use of Israel's military forces were held throughout the period up to the 1967 war, their retention in the face of many changes that took place in the enemy camp and at home required far-reaching adjustments and some bold innovations. For example, the whole idea of planning to use a militia-type army in an offensive role with a view to achieving quick decisive results was to begin with highly unorthodox. It was justified only because the kind of equipment and armed forces that the enemy could muster at the time it was adopted allowed Israel's strategists to think that the next war would be essentially an "improved version" of the War of Independence, which had been a war of infantry assisted here and there by some armored and commando formations. In that kind of war, it was not too unreasonable to count on the well-trained standing brigades to provide the offensive punch while the reserve brigades assumed subsidiary tasks. The sudden expansion of the armed forces of Egypt and Syria after 1955 and their acquisition of large quantities of modern Soviet armor, motorized equipment, and jet aircraft abruptly upset Israel's assumptions regarding the character of the next war and raised grave doubts about the applicability of its strategic plans to the new kind of expected war. This was no longer to be a war of infantry but one of large panzer formations moving swiftly on and off roads under the protection of an air umbrella and with the support of first-rate combat aircraft, being able to bypass static defense positions, break through and envelop deployed forces, cut off supply lines, chop up vast areas, and bring about a rapid total collapse. The shock of the sudden change in the image of the next war and the doubt that Israel's militia-type forces could be adapted to that kind of warfare even if they were able to obtain the necessary equipment were as instrumental as any other considerations in impelling Israel's leaders to undertake a "preemptive war" in 1956.

The Sinai campaign, together with the Anglo-French Suez War, brought about the destruction of most of the equipment newly received by Egypt but failed to turn back the wheel as far as the kind of war Israel had to contemplate. For, no sooner did the fighting die down that the Soviets began to replenish the Egyptian arsenal with more and better weapons of the kind that had upset Israel's leaders. Moreover, as Israel began to acquire similar or better weapons, the enemy reacted by acquiring more and better still, and Israel responded again and so on, so that each side forced the other into an all-out arms race that has gone on ever since. Confronted with this inexorable reality, Israel's military leaders had no choice but to undertake the bold attempt of preparing their peculiar armed forces for a war of mechanized maneuver and movement and adjusting their operational strategies and tactics accordingly.

Fortunately for Israel, the 1956 Sinai War provided a quiet interval of ten years during which it could apply itself to this task. By 1966–1967, it was in a position to field some twenty-five first-line brigades, regular and reserve, all motorized; of these, eleven were armored, four were crack paratroop or heliborne brigades. In addition, it could marshal about half that number second-line troops and regional defense forces. In the air it could operate some 300 combat planes of more or less modern vintage. Its enemies together, and even Egypt by itself, had much more, but Israel seemed at least to have made the critical step of inserting the bulk of its reserve forces into formations designed for a war of movement. Whether this was effective remained to be seen.

In terms of strategic doctrine, Israel retained the concept of the short war, but after 1956 its notion of short became even shorter in view of the tremendously enhanced mobility and firepower of its own forces and those of the enemy. Moreover, because of the increased danger of rapid enemy breakthrough and of junction between Egyptian and Jordanian forces across Israeli territory owing to the speed and mobility of armored columns, the principle of taking the offensive as soon as possible became only a second-best alternative to the more desirable one of launching an anticipatory attack when war appeared to be imminent. In air strategy in particular, the vital importance of air power and control of the skies for the success of armored and motorized columns operating in open country made massive attacks on airfields the obvious first move in war for both sides, which in turn made anticipatory attack on the enemy's airfields almost the only way to protect one's own air force. Finally, the combination of all these factors almost ruled out a war of limited aim and made the complete destruction of the enemy's forces the only aim of any war for Israel.

Even while Israel was engaged in making these adaptations and adjustments it strove as much as possible to test and review them in war games, in maneuvers, and in the frequent retaliatory raids and border skirmishes. However, the supreme test of its entire defense planning and preparation did not come until 1967, when it faced alone a challenge flaunted by the united armies of all its neighbors at a time of their choosing. How Israel met that test can be seen in the following concise analysis of the course of that war.

15

The Test of 1967:
The Six Day War

The Six Day War began, predictably, with a series of Israeli air strikes against Egyptian air bases, followed by similar strikes against Jordanian and Syrian airfields. However, unpredictably, these strikes virtually destroyed the air forces of all three countries within a few hours and left their ground forces totally at the mercy of Israel's air force. This stunning outcome was almost universally attributed at the time to unbelievable Egyptian negligence in guarding against the anticipated Israeli attack, but subsequent critical studies have shown that this judgment did less than justice to the Egyptian and the Israeli air forces. The Egyptians thought and acted according to accepted military doctrine and practice; their misfortune was that the Israelis thought and acted in thoroughly unorthodox, almost inconceivable, ways.

The Egyptian air force included some 360 fighter planes and some 70 bombers plus a large number of transport planes, trainers, and helicopters. It was deployed over eighteen air bases, four of them in Sinai, three in the Suez Canal zone, several around Cairo, and the rest all over Egypt. The Egyptian air perimeter was monitored by twenty-three radar stations, and the airfields were guarded by heavy concentrations of antiaircraft weapons and several batteries of SAM-2 (surface-to-air) missiles. Some of the planes were parked behind concrete revetments; others, especially in the forward bases, were dispersed on or near the runways, ready to take off instantly for defensive and offensive missions.

The Israeli air force had about 260 fighter-bombers and 24 light bombers in addition to some 60 jet trainers as well as transport planes and helicopters. It was deployed over eight or nine bases, which avoided crowding in the fields but provided no dispersal of fields because of Israel's small space. Indeed, all but one of Israel's air bases was within the range of enemy artillery fire. The defense of the air force relied on a sophisticated warning system, antiaircraft weapons, a constant air patrol, and rapid scrambling of interceptors; it had proved its worth in many air skirmishes in the interwar period.

The Egyptians, as postwar evidence has shown, had decided for political reasons to let Israel attack first and knew that the first attack would come from the air and would be directed at their air force. They estimated that the Israeli first strike would knock out 20 percent of their air force at the most, after which they would get their chance to strike at Israel's bases and other targets. This estimate was based on calculations that quite reasonably discounted a substantial percentage of Israel's combat aircraft as nonoperational at the time and assumed that another substantial portion would be kept for air defense and ground support. The remaining force, much less than half of Israel's combat aircraft, might concentrate on a few bases for maximum effect or attack a large number for maximum disruption; in neither case, most of it would be detected, intercepted, harassed by ground fire, and decimated. Those enemy planes that would manage to complete their mission would be pursued by Egyptian fighters in what would be the beginning of a counterattack on Israeli air bases.

In actual fact, the Israelis began the war with 90 percent of their planes operational—an extraordinary accomplishment in maintenance. They threw into their first strike every plane they had, including their jet trainers, except for twelve fighters they left for air defense. This was an audacious gamble that the strike would work out as planned: that the Egyptian command would not be able to react and that the Jordanian, Syrian, and Iraqi air forces would react only after some time, when Israeli forces would be free to deal with them. The Israeli planes set out against ten Egyptian bases and began their attack on them at the same instant. Virtually all the planes escaped prior detection by flying below the radar screen through gaps in it previously discovered by Intelligence, or making detours and arriving from unexpected directions. Above all, the Israelis attacked each target in a succession of small waves rather than a single massive wave to minimize crowding and vulnerability and to keep the enemy under prolonged paralyzing attack. While the first wave of four planes was on its target, another was already on its way and a third ready to take off. Moments after the first wave was finished bombing and strafing, the second was ready to begin; and moments after the third wave had completed its mission, the first was already back, having refueled and rearmed at base in record time. Thus the Israelis were able to keep at least the principal bases under constant attack for over two and a half hours, allowing them no chance whatsoever to recover. The first waves concentrated on the Egyptian bombers, which constituted a formidable threat to Israeli cities, and on the best Egyptian fighters; as these were destroyed, the list of targets was extended to all types of enemy planes, radar installations, and SAM-2 sites. Simultaneously, the number of Egyptian airfields attacked was increased until all eighteen were covered. Selected targets were revisited later that day and the next to prevent their recovery and to hit remaining objectives. In this way, the Israelis destroyed on the first day of the war 80 percent of the Egyptian bomber fleet and 55 percent of the fighters in addition to similar proportions of other types of aircraft. They also ravaged all the Egyptian bases, destroyed the radar and communications network, disrupted the command and control structure, and utterly demoralized the Egyptian top command of all forces, in headquarters as well as in the field. The audacity of the Israeli planning, the precision of the intelligence on which it was based, the tight control structure, the faultless execution, and the extremely high proficiency of the ground crews accomplished a knock-out blow where the enemy had expected 20 percent damage. For this the Israelis paid with a total of nineteen planes shot down, mainly by ground fire.

The air forces of Jordan, Syria, and Iraq did not intervene in the war until some three hours after Israel struck—a longer time than the Israelis had anticipated. Syrian planes made some forays against Megiddo, Acre-Haifa Bay, and Tiberias, and Jordanian planes attacked Natanya and an air base near Kfar Sirkin. The attackers caused some slight damage and suffered considerable losses before the Israeli air force was free to turn on them. In a series of raids on Jordanian and Syrian airfields, the entire Jordanian air force of some twenty fighters was destroyed and two-thirds of the Syrian air force was put out of action, the remainder fleeing to distant airfields that placed them beyond the range of effective action in the battlezone. An Iraqi medium bomber was able to penetrate Israeli air space on the second day of the war and to drop some bombs on Natanya. It was shot down on its way back to base and elicited an Israeli attack on the base itself in which most of the Iraqi expeditionary air contingent was destroyed.

Simultaneously with the air strike against Egyptian air bases, Israeli columns crossed the armistice lines at several points to launch a general offensive against Egypt's land forces. In four days of fighting the Israelis overran and occupied the Gaza Strip and all of Sinai—an area six times larger than their country, destroyed the bulk of the Egyptian army, and restored free navigation through the Strait of Tiran.

In Sinai and the Gaza Strip the Israelis faced seven divisions—between 80,000 and 90,000 men—equipped with close to 1,000 tanks and ample artillery. The Egyptian forces were deployed in a defensive-offensive array on three interlinked lines covering the approaches between Israel and Egypt, in a manner that suggested a strategy of absorbing a first Israeli blow and then swinging to the counteroffensive. The first line was held by the Palestinian Division and the Seventh, Second, and Sixth Divisions, all motorized infantry formations with strong artillery and armor support. The Palestinians held the Gaza Strip, while each of the three Egyptian divisions held one of the three east-west axes between the Suez Canal and the Israeli border and the north-south links between them. Behind this line, at a distance of thirty to sixty miles from the Israeli border the Third Division and a Special Task Force under General Sa'd al Din Shazli were deployed in positions from which they could reinforce the first line, block any Israeli breakthrough, and launch a counterattack along any or all of the three approaches to Israel. The Third Division included three motorized infantry brigades and two armored brigades, while Shazli's Task Force included one armored brigade and one motorized commando brigade. Still farther to the west, the crack Fourth Armored Division plus one motorized infantry brigade was deployed in the vicinity of Bir Gafgafa and Bir Thamada near the crucial mountain passes through which the central and southern roads went, twenty to forty miles east of the Suez Canal. The Fourth Division thus formed a third line of defense and was in a position from which it could move quickly in various directions to buttress the defenders of the two previous lines or to follow through any offensive action.

Against this array the Israelis marshaled five task forces, two of reinforced brigade strength and three of divisional strength—a total of some 45,000 men and 650 tanks plus artillery. One of the brigade groups was deployed on the periphery of the Gaza Strip and the other in the area of Kuntila, along the southernmost axis. The former was motorized infantry, the latter armored. The three divisional task forces, identified by the names of their commanders, Tal, Yoffe, and Sharon, were all concentrated at three points on a fifty-mile front facing the two northern axes and their defenders. They comprised among them five armored brigades and two armored "groups" equipped with nearly 500 tanks, six paratrooper or motorized infantry brigades, and several regiments of artillery. Thus, while the Egyptians dispersed much of their armor and concentrated the rest in two lines behind the first, the Israelis concentrated nearly all of theirs in a mailed fist directed at a relatively narrow sector in accordance with their purely offensive strategy.

The Israeli plan involved three phases designed to permit interruption or continuation of the operations according to political and military circumstances. In the first phase the divisions of Tal and Sharon were to attack in coordination the two Egyptian perimeters of Rafah and Abu Egeila, held by the Seventh and Second Egyptian divisions respectively, and thus restrict their capacity to reinforce each other. The Palestinian Division in the Gaza Strip would be cut off by Tal's breakthrough at Rafah and would be dealt with by the independent brigade pressing on the strip from the north. At the same time, even before the Rafah and Abu Egeila perimeters were secured, half of Yoffe's division was to penetrate through the sand dunes between them, deemed "impassable" by the Egyptians, to threaten the second Egyptian line in the vicinity of Bir Lahfan and prevent it from reinforcing the first. The second half of Yoffe's division was to rush through the Abu Egeila perimeter as soon as Sharon's forces had breached it and to fall with its fresh troops upon the Egyptian second line at the nodal point of Jebel Libni, south and west of Bir Lahfan. Meanwhile, the bulk of Tal's forces, after breaking through at Rafah and smashing their way westward to el Arish, would wheel south to

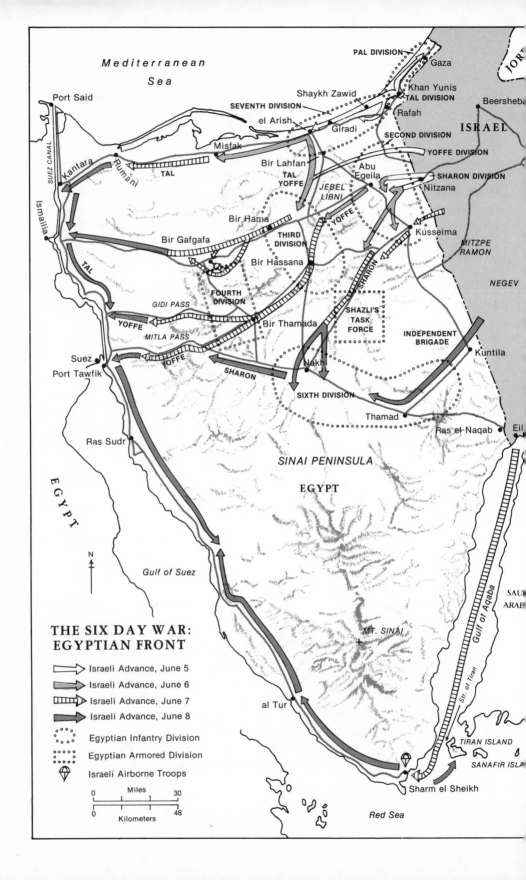

Mediterranean Sea

Port Said

SUEZ CANAL

Kantara

Ismailia

Rumani

TAL

PAL DIVISION

Gaza

Shaykh Zawid

SEVENTH DIVISION

el Arish

Giradi

Khan Yunis

TAL DIVISION

Rafah

Beersheb

SECOND DIVISION

ISRAEL

Misfak

Bir Lahfan

YOFFE DIVISION

TAL YOFFE

Abu Egeila

SHARON DIVISION

JEBEL LIBNI

Nitzana

Bir Hama

YOFFE

Kusseima

MITZPE RAMON

Bir Gafgafa

THIRD DIVISION

Bir Hassana

SHARON

NEGEV

TAL

FOURTH DIVISION

GIDI PASS

YOFFE

MITLA PASS

Bir Thamada

SHAZLI'S TASK FORCE

INDEPENDENT BRIGADE

Kuntila

Suez

Port Tawfik

YOFFE

SHARON

Nakhl

SIXTH DIVISION

Thamad

Ras el Naqab

Eil

Ras Sudr

SINAI PENINSULA

EGYPT

EGYPT

N

Gulf of Suez

MT. SINAI

SAU ARAB

Gulf of Aqaba

THE SIX DAY WAR: EGYPTIAN FRONT

⇨ Israeli Advance, June 5
⇨ Israeli Advance, June 6
⫞⊳ Israeli Advance, June 7
➡ Israeli Advance, June 8

∘∘∘ Egyptian Infantry Division
•••• Egyptian Armored Division
⊕ Israeli Airborne Troops

al Tur

Str. of Tiran

TIRAN ISLAND

SANAFIR ISLA

Sharm el Sheikh

| Miles |
| 0 — 30 |
| 0 — 48 |
| Kilometers |

Red Sea

close one pincer with Yoffe's forces at Bir Lahfan and another with Yoffe's forces at Jebel Libni. These movements should protect Sharon's right flank as he attacked the Kusseima defense network south of Abu Egeila's, thus completing the occupation of the crucial rectangle Rafah–el Arish–Jebel Libni–Kusseima and the destruction or rout of the three Egyptian divisions defending it. The completion of this task was the minimal Israeli objective. In case international pressure forced a cease-fire before their forces could move on to the next stage, they would have at least have completely disrupted the Egyptian offensive threat, placed themselves in a position from which they could threaten the remaining Egyptian forces from several directions, and thus given Israel a strong bargaining position to secure the removal of the Egyptian blockade.

The second phase of the plan was left more flexible since it depended largely on the redeployments of the enemy as a result of the previous actions, but its general idea was clear and the Israeli forces were equipped and conditioned to launch it and the succeeding phase without pause. In this second phase, the forces of Tal and Yoffe were to complete the destruction of the Egyptian second line of defense while rushing westward to block the passes to the Suez Canal and to meet the Fourth Division defending them. A segment of Tal's forces would turn the passes by advancing along the coastal road from el Arish to Kantara on the Suez Canal. At the same time, Sharon's forces would advance south by southwest to protect the flank of the westward advances and intercept Shazli's Task Force and the Sixth Division in their movement either to attack or to flee in consequence of the collapse of the Egyptian lines farther north. The independent Israeli armored brigade at Kuntila would in either case press from the east to meet Sharon's forces.

The third and last phase of the plan was simply to force the remaining Egyptian armor to fight and to destroy it, to march to the Suez Canal, and to mop up the fragments of the Egyptian army left behind the Israeli lines. The capture of Sharm el Sheikh, the root of the whole war, was to be effected by naval units and an airborne contingent at some convenient time as a completely subsidiary, small operation.

Perhaps the most telling comment one could make about the actual course of the military operations is that they went exactly according to plan. The comment is particularly instructive with respect to the operations in the first phase, in which the Israeli forces assaulted a well-armed, well-entrenched enemy, without the benefit of surprise or of air support. Tal's armor attacked, broke through at Rafah in a combination of frontal assault and flanking movement, and made a deep penetration toward el Arish while the Israeli air force was fully engaged in its offensive in the Egyptian air bases. By the time the air force was free, the main fighting in the Rafah perimeter was being done by the paratroopers, who were clearing the trenches in hand-to-hand combat that precluded intervention from the air. Sharon launched his attack on the Abu Egeila perimeter on the night of June 5, after having spent the day in preparatory operations against outlying posts. He might have waited for daylight the next day and assured himself of the support of the air force, but he preferred to attack at night to gain time and to be able to execute some highly complicated flanking maneuvers and helicopter landings in the enemy's rear under cover of darkness. The first half of Yoffe's division churned its way through thirty miles of dunes without encountering any opposition because it was not expected. By the time it reached Bir Lahfan it was already night, and it was then that it engaged an Egyptian armored force many times its size and prevented it from accomplishing its assumed mission of reinforcing the defenders of el Arish and Abu Egeila. After the completion of that phase, when the Israelis had unhinged the enemy's defense line and thrown his plans into confusion, when armored and motorized columns could maneuver in the open spaces and pursue an enemy harassed by an air force that dominated the skies absolutely, it is more understandable that the operations should have gone according to plan. Nevertheless, the Israeli forces might not have achieved quite the results they did without the extraordinary rapidity of action they demonstrated, which depended in turn on a great many qualities of logistical organization, leadership, initiative, improvisation, courage, skill, and, above all, dash. In November 1967 Nasser confirmed earlier Israeli reports that the Egyptian army lost in Sinai 80 percent of its equipment. The losses in personnel were equally high: nearly 12,000 officers and men killed and several times that number wounded, and about 6,000 officers and men captured and several times that number allowed to make their way home rather than being taken prisoner. The Israelis paid for their victory with 275 officers and men killed and 800 wounded. They lost 61 tanks against more than 700 of the enemy's, nearly 200 of them intact.

A few hours after the Israelis began to operate against the Egyptians on June 5, the Jordanians opened an artillery barrage against West Jerusalem and many other points along their border with Israel and seized the strategically located United Nations Headquarters in Jerusalem. The Israelis responded with a counterattack that recaptured the latter position and followed with offensive operations in several sectors that resulted, in less than three days, in the total rout of the Jordanian army and the capture of all the West Bank, including East Jerusalem.

Unlike the Sinai battlefield, the Jordanian front was thickly settled on both sides with hundreds of towns and villages inhabited by hundreds of thousands of people in relatively close proximity. In divided Jerusalem the Jordanian and Israeli positions were actually at most a few hundred yards apart, sometimes within a stone's throw of each other. Also in contrast to Sinai, the terrain was mostly mountainous, could be negotiated by motorized vehicles only along roads and tracks and their sides, contained countless bottlenecks, and was therefore ill-suited for swift, large-scale, wide maneuvers by armor. The West Bank was made up of two bulges hugging the Jerusalem corridor and offering many deadly stategic opportunities to any substantial, determined force. Its main geographic feature is a mountain chain going north and south, on whose spine ran the main north-south road and from which several ribs in the form of roads and tracks descended more or less abruptly to the west and to the east.

On the eve of the war, the Jordanians had concentrated in the West Bank ten of their eleven brigades plus auxiliary and support—some 45,000 men—deployed as follows: in a broad arch in the north, from Tulkarm through Jenin to the Jordan River, three infantry brigades; in Jerusalem itself and in a small arch around it, two infantry brigades. East of these forces and in a position from which they could be reached quickly, were two armored brigades, one near the Jericho crossing of the Jordan River and one near the Damia bridge. An arch beginning to the south of Tulkarm and linking up with the forces in the Jerusalem sector was held by two additional infantry brigades, and the Bethlehem-Hebron area was held by another brigade. Two Egyptian commando battalions, which had been airlifted a few days before the fighting began, were deployed in the vicinity of Latrun, and an Iraqi brigade, the spearhead of three more scheduled to come, was positioned on the east side of the Damia crossing. The eleventh and last Jordanian brigade was deployed south and east of the Dead Sea, looking across the Negev to the Egyptian forces.

It is evident from this distribution of forces that as of June 5, the Arab forces on the West Bank were still basically deployed for defense but were beginning to develop the outlines of an offensive deployment. The emphasis seemed to be on holding firmly the nodal sectors around Jerusalem and Jenin and the rest of the front more lightly, with the two armored brigades poised in the rear to come to the assistance of any threatened area. At the same time the two armored brigades, the Iraqi brigade, the Egyptian commando battalions, and the Jordanian brigade near the Dead Sea pointed clearly to a process of assembling and deploying an offensive force meant to be completed in the days following. The Israeli attack on Egypt interrupted this process and forced the Arab forces in the West Bank to enter the war in the subsidiary role of drawing Israeli forces away to alleviate the pressure on the Egyptian front rather than mounting dangerous offensives.

In actual fact, Jordan's entry into the war drew one Israeli paratrooper brigade from the Egyptian front and three brigades, two of them armored, from the Syrian front. On June 5, the Israeli High Command had deployed against Jordan only three infantry brigades and one armored brigade, in the hope and expectation that, despite the Jordanian-Egyptian treaty, Jordan would stay out of the war. After the beginning of the fighting on the Egyptian front, the Israeli government conveyed to King Hussein, through the chief of the United Nations Truce Supervision Organization, a message to the effect that Israel would not attack if he held back his forces. It was only after the King had given unequivocal indications that he was unable or unwilling to stay out that the Israeli High Command readjusted its thinking and put into operation contingency plans for such an eventuality. Whereas previously it had intended to give the Syrian front second priority after the Egyptian, it now put the Jordanian front in second place and turned on it forces of the Northern Command intended for use against Syria as well as a paratrooper brigade initially meant to be dropped in the vicinity of el Arish.

The total number of forces engaged on the Israeli-Jordanian front was thus more or less evenly matched. However, the Israelis, who relied heavily on their settlements reinforced by second-line units for static defense, had the enormous advantage of being able to concentrate superior forces against selected Jordanian targets. Moreover, to Jordan's misfortune, by the time it decidedly joined the war, the Egyptian air force, which, according to the joint defense plan, was to provide the Jordanian troops with air cover, had already been knocked out, leaving these troops at the mercy of the Israeli air force. On the other hand, the Jordanian troops were entrenched in strong, prepared positions in terrain that was on the whole highly suited for defense and very difficult for the deployment of large motorized forces.

As with the Sinai offensive, the Israeli offensive against Jordan was planned in two continuous phases. The first was intended to secure certain minimal objectives before any possible interruption of the fighting, while the second was designed to capitalize on the achievements of the first phase to secure the maximal objectives if time and circumstances permitted. The objectives of the first phase were three: to push the border back in the Jenin region at the north of the bulge in order to put the Valley of Jezreel, its settlements, and the important air base of Ramat David beyond the range of Jordanian artillery; to lop off the Latrun salient and sit on top of the Latrun-Ramallah road, and thus secure and widen the Tel Aviv–Jerusalem corridor; and to establish a secure link with the Mount Scopus enclave, cut off from the rest of West Jerusalem since 1948, and thus improve the protection of Jerusalem itself. As may be readily seen, the achievement of these objectives would automatically cut off East Jerusalem and place the Israelis is an excellent position to move on against the nodal sectors of the mountain spine in pursuit of the maximal objective of capturing the entire West Bank and routing or destroying the Jordanian army in the second phase.

As in Sinai, the actual course of operations went according to plan almost without a hitch, except that the Israelis had to fight harder, pay a heavier price in casualties, and depend more on the support of their air force to prevail. The principal battles took place in the vicinity of Jenin, on the road leading from it to Nablus and the Jordan River, and in and around Jerusalem. In the first area two of the three attacking Israeli brigades met with stiff resistance and a counterattack by the Jordanian armored brigade initially posted

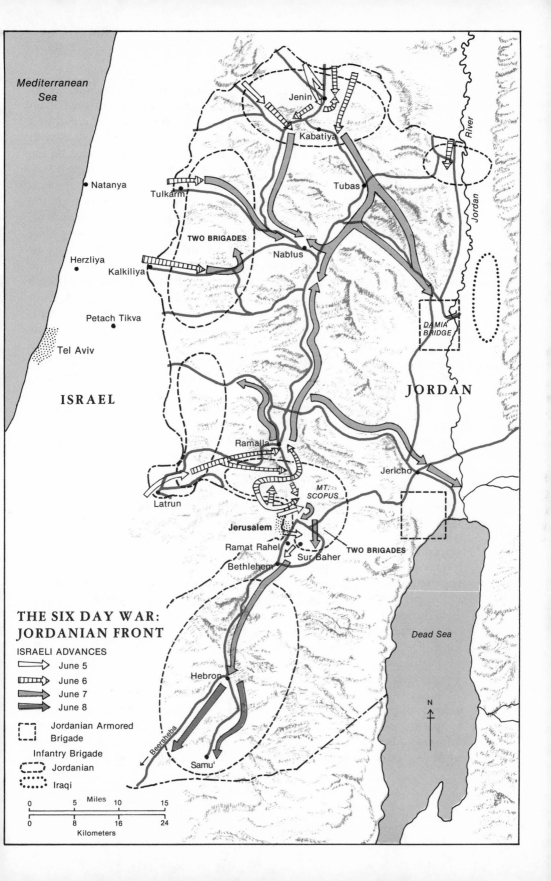

*Mediterranean
Sea*

• Natanya

Jenin

Kabatiya

Tulkarm

Tubas

TWO BRIGADES

Nablus

• Herzliya

Kalkiliya

• Petach Tikva

River

Jordan

Tel Aviv

JORDAN

ISRAEL

*DAMIA
BRIDGE*

Ramalla

Jericho

*MT.
SCOPUS*

Latrun

Jerusalem

Ramat Rahel

Sur Baher

TWO BRIGADES

Bethlehem

THE SIX DAY WAR:
JORDANIAN FRONT

Dead Sea

ISRAELI ADVANCES

⇨	June 5
⬅⬅⬅⇨	June 6
➡	June 7
➡	June 8

Hebron

N
↑

Jordanian Armored
Brigade

Infantry Brigade
Jordanian
Iraqi

Beersheba

0   5   10   15
          Miles

Samu'

0   8   16   24
          Kilometers

near the Damia bridge and prevailed only after repeated interventions by the air force. In the Jerusalem sector two Israeli brigades started out from Latrun and the middle of the Jerusalem corridor and fought their way uphill in a northeasterly sweep toward the area between Ramallah and Jerusalem, with a view to cutting off the northern and eastern approaches to the city. At the same time a third brigade, starting from the southern outskirts, attacked east-ward and then wheeled around in the opposite direction to secure the hills overlooking the city from the south and cut off the Jordanian forces in the Bethlehem-Hebron area. All these attacks, supported by armor, ample artil-lery, or air force accomplished their respective missions without too much difficulty. The real test was faced by the paratrooper brigade that was as-signed the task of assaulting the Jordanian positions in the built-up area just north of the walled old city and breaking through them to link up with the forces that made the sweep around the city. Fighting hand-to-hand, from house to house, mostly at night, without the benefit of assisting armor, artil-lery, or air power, the paratroopers advanced yard by yard in the most bit-terly contested and costly battle of the entire war. After they had finally linked up with the forces operating on the peripheries of the city, they turned around and broke into the old city from the east and took it without encountering much resistance.

While the various Israeli columns were advancing, the Israeli air force struck again and again at the Jordanian armored brigade initially deployed near Jericho and frustrated all the efforts it made to come up the single road to Jerusalem to help its hard-pressed defenders. But for the neutralization and partial destruction of that brigade from the air, the Israelis would have had an even harder time capturing East Jerusalem than they did. In addition to the crucial role that the air force played here and in the battle in the Jenin sector, it continually pounded the Jordanian forces and traffic everywhere else, so that when those two major battles were won and the forces that won them con-verged from the north and south toward Nablus, all Jordanian resistance foundered at once. The Jordanian brigade in the Bethlehem-Hebron area sur-rendered, while the remnants of the brigades that had held the positions west of the spinal road either fled, melted into the population, or were captured.

The exact losses of the Jordanians have not been reliably estimated, but it is clear that the Jordanian army in its entirety was knocked out as a fighting force. The Israelis paid for their success with about 300 killed and 1,500 wounded, considerably more than their losses in the campaign against Egypt. The bulk of the Israeli casualties were suffered in the fighting for Jerusalem.

Shortly after the Israeli attack on Egypt on June 5, the Syrians opened a heavy artillery barrage against all the Israeli settlements within range and at-tempted a few air attacks. The next day relatively small formations of Syrian infantry and armor attacked several Israeli settlements, in the only operations of Arab ground forces inside Israeli territory in the entire war. The Israelis

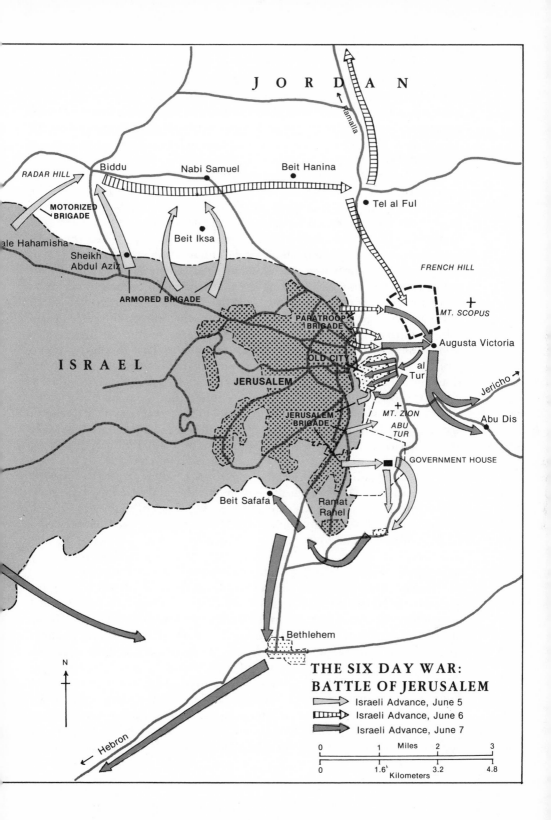

J O R D A N

Jamalla

RADAR HILL

Biddu   Nabi Samuel   Beit Hanina

MOTORIZED
BRIGADE

Tel al Ful

ale Hahamisha

Sheikh
Abdul Aziz

Beit Iksa

FRENCH HILL

ARMORED BRIGADE

MT. SCOPUS

PARATROOP
BRIGADE

Augusta Victoria

ISRAEL

OLD CITY

al
Tur

JERUSALEM

Jericho

MT. ZION

JERUSALEM
BRIGADE

ABU
TUR

Abu Dis

GOVERNMENT HOUSE

Beit Safafa

Ramat
Rahel

Bethlehem

N

THE SIX DAY WAR:
BATTLE OF JERUSALEM

Israeli Advance, June 5
Israeli Advance, June 6
Israeli Advance, June 7

Hebron

0   1   Miles   2   3

0   1.6   3.2   4.8
                  Kilometers

contented themselves on these occasions as in the next two days with defensive operations and with artillery and air strikes until they finished off the Jordanian front. On the morning of June 9 the Israelis, having rushed in reinforcements and redeployed their forces, began an assault on the Syrian heights and, in thirty-five hours of continuous fighting, overran the area and shattered its defenders.

The battlefield between Israel and Syria consisted of the region on both sides of the forty-mile long armistice line between the two countries. The Israeli side of the line was made up of the depression of the upper Jordan River and its tributaries, a basically flat, fertile, thickly settled valley. The Syrian side was constituted by the southwestern extension of the Anti-Lebanon range, known in the Bible as the Golan. Along the northern half of the Syrian side of the frontier the mountains rise steeply at the frontier line itself or very close to it, while along the southern half they tend to rise more gently for a few miles before accelerating their climb. Over most of the length of the frontier the Syrians looked down from the hills on the Israeli plain below, which constituted an easy and tempting target for their artillery. Apart from the few small-scale attempts made by the Syrians to penetrate into Israeli territory, the fighting took place entirely on the Syrian side in a rough rectangle running the length of the border and thirteen to sixteen miles deep.

The Golan Heights as a whole constitute a nodal region traversed by roads linking Lebanon, Syria, Jordan, and Israel. A road coming from Beirut and Saida in Lebanon entered the heights near Banias and ran diagonally along their crest through Mas'ada, Kuneitra, and Rafid before joining the main Damascus-Amman road. This road was intersected at Kuneitra by a road coming from Damascus and going on to Safed, in Israel. In addition, several roads or tracks branched out from the diagonal road in the direction of Israel, the principal of which led to Samakh, south of the Sea of Galilee. Adding to the strategic importance of the heights was the fact that they contain one of the sources of the Jordan River, whose waters have been the subject of dispute, and that the Transarabian Pipeline crossed them on its way from Saudi Arabia to the terminals in Lebanon.

In the course of nineteen years of hostile relations with Israel, the Syrians had converted the heights into a vast fortified camp, comprising three parallel lines of defense dotted with dozens of fortified points with overlapping fields of fire. On the eve of the war the Syrians had deployed in and near the area seven of their nine brigades. Four infantry brigades manned the prepared lines of defense, and an additional infantry brigade, a motorized infantry brigade, and an armored brigade were deployed north, south, and east of Kuneitra in positions from which they could be used for supporting the defense lines or for offense. The infantry brigades were reinforced by battalions of T-34 tanks or SU-100 self-propelled guns and were endowed with vast quantities of artillery and antiaircraft guns—some sixteen battalions in all.

On June 5, the Israelis had two brigades, one armored and one infantry, facing the heights after having diverted other forces of the Northern Command for operations against Jordan. The task of these units was to support the Israeli defense line, which was manned by the settlers in the area reinforced with second line units, as long as the Israeli forces were engaged on the Jordanian and Egyptians fronts. As soon as forces could be transferred from the other fronts, these brigades were to constitute the spearhead of an assault on the heights.

On June 7, General David Elazar, in charge of Northern Command, received orders to prepare for the attack, counting on his two brigades plus all the forces he had detached for operations against Jordan being rushed back to him. He was prepared to move by the next morning, but a delay in the go-ahead order owing to the Arabs' acceptance of a United Nations cease-fire injunction and fears of Soviet intervention held him back. On the morning of the 9th he received his orders and acted immediately.

General Elazar's objective was to capture the Golan Heights up to and somewhat beyond their watershed along a line parallel to the diagonal road and the road descending to Samakh. Like all Israeli commanders, he favored a strategy of indirect approach, mobility, and envelopment, which meant in this case that he had to get onto the main Banias-Kuneitra road in the rear of the enemy, where he could maneuver his motorized columns. However, all the roads and tracks leading from Israel to that road were defended heavily and in depth and it would have required much time and heavy casualties to break through them from below. Elazar's solution was to attempt his principal breakthrough at the northern end of the heights where no roads existed and the terrain was most difficult, but at least the distance from the starting point to the diagonal road was short—only 2.4 miles. Once that axis was secured and a track on it was improvised, Israeli armor could pour through it on the diagonal road, smash its way into the rear of the enemy, and facilitate the opening of new axes of movement by threatening the enemy's reinforcement and retreat lines.

The execution of the plan began with a five-pronged attack along the northern half of the front designed to confuse the enemy about the main attack and to exert assisting pressure. The principal attack was undertaken by two brigades, one infantry and one armored. The armored formation climbed up the roadless mountain behind bulldozers and mine removers who prepared the way for it foot by foot. The entire force moved on a single axis under intense enemy artillery fire. Now and then the Israeli air force temporarily silenced the enemy guns, but they inevitably resumed moments later. Half way up the brigade split in two, one half beginning an enveloping movement while the other plodded its way forward. In the course of the advance, one battalion literally had to run over Syrian positions with its tanks before it could capture them, while another lost all its commanders in battle and was

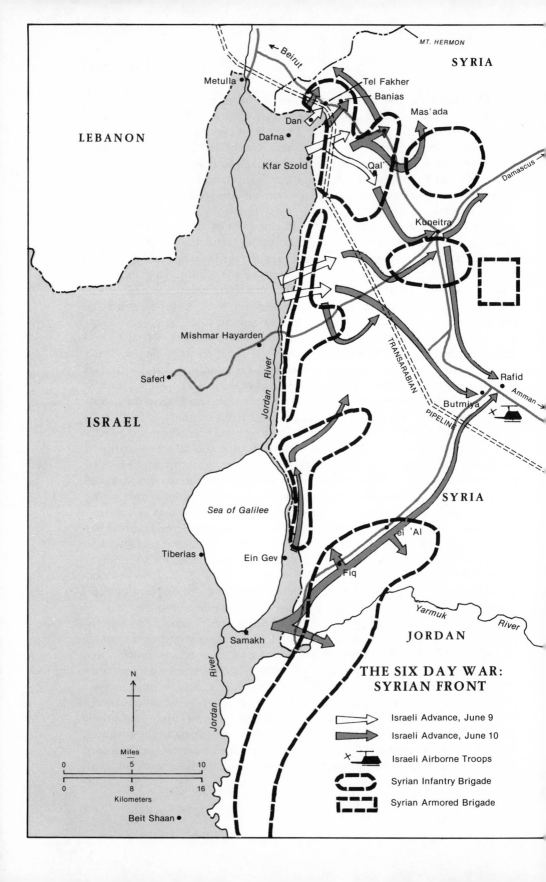

MT. HERMON

SYRIA

LEBANON

Metulla

Tel Fakher
Banias

Mas'ada

Dan

Dafna

Kfar Szold

Qal'

Damascus

Kuneitra

Mishmar Hayarden

Safed

Jordan River

ISRAEL

TRANSARABIAN

Rafid

Amman

Butmiya

PIPELINE

SYRIA

Sea of Galilee

Tiberias

Ein Gev

el 'Al

Fiq

Yarmuk River

Samakh

JORDAN

Jordan River

N

THE SIX DAY WAR:
SYRIAN FRONT

Miles
0   5   10

0   8   16
Kilometers

Beit Shaan

Israeli Advance, June 9

Israeli Advance, June 10

Israeli Airborne Troops

Syrian Infantry Brigade

Syrian Armored Brigade

led forward by a lieutenant. It took the brigade five and a half hours to fight its way through the three miles that separated it from its objective.

While the armored brigade was crawling up, two battalions of the infantry brigade supported by armor started fighting their way up a mile or so to the north with the objective of capturing the Syrian positions on the flanks of the armored brigade and thus securing a corridor for more armor and troops to erupt in the rear of the Syrians. There were thirteen positions to overcome, the principal of which was Tel Fakhir. The battle for that position went on for seven hours and by the time it was over, only four attackers out of one whole battalion were intact. All the rest were killed or wounded while pressing on relentlessly with the assault. The other infantry battalion had an easier time meeting its assignments, but only by comparison with the grueling experience of the first.

While the two prongs of the principal assault thus broke through at the north, the other three prongs, attacking farther south, managed to make preliminary breaches in the first Syrian line in preparation for assaults by larger forces that were arriving from the Jordanian and Egyptians fronts. At the same time a force of two brigades including heliborne troops was assembled at the southern end of the heights, ready to open a new axis for advance as soon as the entire Syrian defense system appeared to be giving way.

Early on June 10 Israeli forces began pressing simultaneously from all directions after a very heavy artillery bombardment and with massive support from the air. The critical developments, however, took place in the northernmost sector. Through the breach painfully effected the previous day by the armored and infantry brigades, a fresh armored brigade rushed in, captured Banias, mopped up the area up to the Lebanese border, and then turned south and east to help the other armored brigade in the capture of Mas'ada. At this point, the Israeli plans called for a carefully concerted effort against Kuneitra, the hub of the Golan Heights and the gate to Damascus, using all the forces that were converging from all the previously opened axes. However, the fall of Mas'ada unleashed a series of developments that made unnecessary any elaborate effort and led to the complete and abrupt collapse of the entire Syrian front.

At 8:45 A.M. on June 10 Radio Damascus, in an apparent attempt to trigger Soviet intervention by suggesting an Israeli march on Damascus, announced the fall of Kuneitra six hours before any Israeli troops had reached it. The news was taken by the Syrian troops throughout the heights to mean that they could not expect any help from the rear and that the Israelis were in a position to move down rapidly from Kuneitra to close all avenues of escape and trap them in death pockets. Without losing a moment they abandoned their positions and started a panic flight. At this point the Israeli High Command ordered a general accelerated advance and even resorted to leapfrogging heliborne units ahead of their troop columns; nevertheless, most of the

Syrian troops managed to get away, leaving behind their equipment. The principal damage at this stage was done by the air force, which kept on the trails of the fleeing Syrians all the way to Damascus. By the evening of June 10 the Israelis were sitting everywhere on the heights, having captured in less than two days what was thought to be an impregnable fortress. They paid for this victory with 115 killed and 306 wounded. The Syrian losses were conservatively estimated at 2,500 killed and 5,000 wounded in addition to 591 prisoners. Half of the seven brigades they had deployed on or near the heights were destroyed as fighting units, fifteen of the eighteen artillery battalions were destroyed or captured, eighty tanks were destroyed and forty captured intact.

The war of 1967 has already been the subject of many studies by military analysts, and all of them have viewed the Israeli campaigns as rare illustrations of nearly perfect application of the classical principles of war—resolve, concentration, utmost maneuver, information, offensive, initiative at the lower levels, training, and, above all, morale. But perhaps the highest compliment paid to Israel's armed forces was that while presenting their performance as models, none of the analysts either noticed or stressed the fact that these forces consisted for the most part of citizens who had been called to the colors on the eve of war—so well integrated were the reserve formations with the conscript units and the permanent cadre. Indeed, the process of mobilizing, assembling, and deploying the reserves presented fewer problems to Israel than the deployment of standing forces did for Egypt. Task forces and brigades composed solely or mainly of reservists were given combat assignments no less crucial and no less demanding than those given to units of the standing army, and they acquitted themselves no less well. Air force teams combining reservists and regulars were able to keep more planes operational and to score more sorties per plane than fully professional air forces are known to have done elsewhere. Senior Israeli staff officers asserted after the war that not one unit of any size had failed to accomplish the particular mission assigned to it. Actually, we know of at least one small naval commando operation that aborted in Alexandria port; however, considering that a war like the one under consideration involves many thousands of particular assignments, even if many more exceptions were found the result would still border on the incredible.

16
National Security, 1967–1973: New Challenges, New Responses

In the wake of their sweeping victory, most Israelis expected at least Egypt and Jordan to sue for peace. Defense Minister Moshe Dayan expressed that feeling when he said that he was waiting for a telephone call from Cairo or Amman any moment. Other Israelis were not so certain about the imminent advent of peace, but they were sure that war, at any rate, had become a very remote prospect. General Sharon voiced that feeling when he said three days after the war that the enemy was not going to be able to fight for so many years, that he, Sharon, and his generation would be too old to participate in the next war. In fact, Dayan did not get his phone call, either then or later, and as for Sharon, he lived long enough to fight not one war but two: the "war of attrition," which followed the Six Day War almost immediately, and the massive October 1973 war.

The persistence of the conflict confronted Israel with a series of grave new security challenges, but thanks to the advantages it had gained in the Six Day War, these challenges were at no stage comparable in nature to those faced before the war. Sheer survival was no longer the issue, at least not directly and immediately. Rather, the problem facing Israel's defense planners was how to frustrate the military efforts made by the Arabs to compel Israel to surrender its war gains on their terms rather than its own.

The Arab efforts to force Israel to yield went through two stages in the 1967–1973 period. In the first stage, they sought to achieve their purpose by taking advantage of political inhibitions preventing Israel from responding with all-out war in order to launch against it a limited war of attrition, where they thought they had the advantage of greater capacity for endurance. Israel defeated that effort, albeit at great cost and not very certainly at the time. In the second stage the Arabs, after modifying their political position somewhat, sought to force Israel to assent to their new terms by a combination of diplomacy and threats of a renewed war. Israel responded first by preparing to resist a new war of attrition. Then taking advantage of a change in the political constellation, it sought to deter even limited hostilities by adopting a strategy of massive retaliation. Throughout the 1969–1973 period Israel had also to face the novel challenge of "feydayeen warfare" in the context of holding a populated, occupied territory.

Israel's Military Posture after the 1967 War

The most immediate and dramatic result of the war was the almost complete destruction of Arab military power. President Nasser, we have seen, admitted that Egypt lost 80 percent of its equipment and fighting units, and while the losses of Jordan and Syria were not so high, they were sufficient to disrupt their armies and air forces as fighting organizations. However, this particular outcome proved to be rather ephemeral, since the Arab countries proceeded immediately to rearm and rebuild their forces with Soviet help (American in the case of Jordan), to the point where within a year and a half they felt strong enough to repudiate formally the cease-fire and declare a war of attrition. The more enduring and most important results of the war were an immense improvement in Israel's position on the two scores where it had been particularly vulnerable and sensitive: geostrategic position and disparity of resources.

On the former score, the change was almost revolutionary. In the north the capture of the Golan Heights gave Israel control of positions from which Syrian guns had been able to harass at will the score or so Israeli settlements in the valley below. More importantly, it denied the Syrians an excellent staging area where they could marshal their forces before descending on Israel in relative safety from Israeli ground forces, which would have had to climb up the difficult slopes to preempt. Instead, it was the Israeli forces that were now in a position to present a threat to Damascus, forty miles of relatively easy terrain away.

In the center, the capture of the entire West Bank foreclosed the possibility of enemy thrusts across Israel's narrow waist and multiple corridors, put enemy weapons beyond the range of Israeli population centers and vital military targets, shortened Israel's front line drastically, and placed Israeli forces in positions along the Jordan River from which they could lunge toward Amman, twenty-five miles away, or cut off Jordan from Syria and Iraq at Irbid-Mafraq as well as from Saudi Arabia at Aqaba.

In the south the occupation of Sinai removed the threat of a rapid junction between Egyptian and Jordanian forces across the narrow part of the Negev triangle—a move that was actually contemplated by the Egyptians on the eve of the war. It gave Israel a relatively short front line along the Suez Canal and the lakes it crosses, an excellent antitank ditch, and a depth of 200 miles of desert behind them. Israel's population centers were placed that much farther from Egyptian forces, while Egyptian population centers on the west bank of the Suez Canal came within range of Israeli light weapons. Cairo itself was only eighty miles away across mainly open terrain. Air bases in the north of Israel fell out of range of Egypt's best combat aircraft, while the arm of the Israeli air force was correspondingly extended to reach every inhabited corner of Egypt. Actual or potential air bases in Sinai added up to fifteen minutes of loitering time to most Israeli combat planes over what they had had before the war while depriving Egyptian planes of comparable margins, thus in effect multiplying and dividing by a considerable factor respectively the combat capabilities of the two air forces. The Egyptian navy, which could maneuver freely before the war between the Red Sea and the Mediterranean through the Suez Canal, was reduced to the same condition as the Israeli navy of having to operate in two independent forces. At the same time, the Egyptian naval bases in Port Said and Suez came within the range of Israeli artillery.

Altogether, although the cease-fire lines multiplied the territory under Israeli control sevenfold, they reduced the length of the prewar boundaries by nearly one-third, while making them much more defensible by resting them on the Suez Canal, the Jordan River, and the crest of the Golan. The coastline was lengthened sevenfold, but only a small portion of the additional length could be threatened by an enemy like Egypt. There was one disadvantage for Israel in the new situation, and that was a substantial extension of its lines of communication and a corresponding reduction in the speed with which it could move troops from one front to another with given means of communication. Another disadvantage, which became tragically apparent in October 1973, was the elimination of the warning time that the Sinai Desert had provided against enemy ground offensives.

With respect to the disparity of resources, the improvement in Israel's position was perhaps as much perceptual as real. It derived as much from a recognition by the antagonists of an already existing situation as from changes in that situation. Israel had attempted to compensate for its comparative weakness in numbers by building its armed forces on a broad foundation of readily mobilizable reserves. However, although Israel found it necessary for purposes of deterrence to stress its full confidence in the system, and its enemies found it necessary for reasons of caution to give credence to it, both of them really entertained some doubts as to how the system would work out in practice. The more the arms race impelled the antagonists to endow their forces with heavy and sophisticated equipment requiring a high degree of technical proficiency, the more serious their doubts became that the reserve formations could effectively master it. The incredible performance of Israel's armed forces as a whole in the Six Day War finally put all these doubts to rest and convinced Israel as well as its enemies that it had actually struck an effective solution to the human resources problem. It showed that the system worked and that the reserves were in fact more proficient at handling modern warfare than the regular armies of the Arab states.

Besides confirming the full value of Israel's reserve resources, the war did give Israel a considerable real resource advantage. Egypt's armed forces were nealy totally destroyed and Syria's and Jordan's were decimated, while Israel's not only remained virtually intact but were enriched by considerable war booty. This particular advantage did not last long since Egypt and Syria rapidly rebuilt their armed forces to prewar levels and beyond with Soviet help, and Jordan did the same at a slower pace with American assistance. However, Egypt's need to replenish its entire arsenal and then redouble it to gain a measure of credibility in its continuing confrontation with Israel put an enormous strain on its resources and made every marginal effort on its part to match new acquisitions of arms by Israel that much more onerous. True, the oil-rich Arab states provided Egypt with substantial subsidies, but these barely covered the resources it lost through the closing of the Suez Canal, the loss of the Sinai oil fields, and the decline in income from tourism. It is also true that the Soviet Union helped by providing some quantities of arms free and others on long-term credit, but the amounts involved in the effort were so enormous that they drained the Egyptian treasury and injected an element of mounting strain in Soviet-Egyptian relations as Egypt kept pressing for more new arms on credit than the Soviets were willing to provide.

The financial penury of Egypt resulting from the war and the continuing confrontation brought to light another reality that had been obscured before 1967. That is that, thanks to a much more rapid rate of economic growth over a long period of time, Israel had in fact reduced the gap in economic resources between itself and its enemies to manageable proportions, and was placed in a position to reverse that relationship in its own favor before too long. This sounds incredible and that is precisely why no one, including the antagonists themselves, had noticed it before the Six Day War. Everyone knew that Israel had a higher per capita product than its enemies and that its economy was growing at a very fast rate, but, in view of the great initial disparity in the absolute size of the economies of the parties, no one bothered to watch and compare the changing picture until after the war. Such comparison showed that whereas in 1950 Egypt had a GNP four and a half times larger than Israel's from which to draw for its defense needs, Israel's more rapid economic growth had reduced that margin to a mere one and a half times by 1967. In the years after the Six Day War, Israel overtook and began to surpass Egypt. Moreover, since Israel's per capita product was always larger than Egypt's and got to be nearly ten times greater, it could, if necessary, draw much more out for defense purposes than could Egypt. As a matter of fact, Israel and Egypt spent more or less the same absolute amounts and GNP percentages on defense in the six years after 1967; but where Egypt's effort left it with such scant resources for investment that its economy fell into stagnation and even regressed, Israel's effort still left it with enough investment resources to ensure a continuing rate of growth of 9 or 10 percent annually.

The addition of Egypt's resources to those of Israel's other active enemies, Syria and Jordan, altered the picture somewhat but did not change it basically. Israel's relative position might have changed only if the total resources of one or two of the oil-rich countries somehow came under Egyptian control, but such a prospect appeared quite remote before 1973. The sudden gushing of oil wealth owing to the quadrupling of oil prices and the diversion of part of that wealth to confrontation countries was altogether unimaginable before it actually happened.

The War of Attrition and Israel's Reactions

The Israelis at first believed their victory to have brought peace very near or at least to have put war very far. These expectations were based on the fact that Israel and its neighbors had this time fought a war without outside interference which Israel had won decisively, but they did not take into account the possibility that the interested outside forces that had been forced by the pace of events to remain passive during the war might reassert themselves after its end to inhibit its consequences. The expectations were implicitly based on analogies with other wars, where the decision of arms left the defeated with no room for further appeal, when in this instance the enemy could and did try to marshal additional means to nullify at least some of the consequences of that decision.

The Arab side, with the help of its Soviet and other friends, tried various diplomatic means to bring pressure on Israel to withdraw unconditionally from the territories it had conquered by war. We need not concern ourselves here with this attempt except to note that it failed, mainly because the United States resisted it. Simultaneously, Egypt's Nasser tried to convince the Soviets to commit their armed forces to fight alongside his own to recover the Arab territories by force, but the Soviets balked and only agreed to help rebuild Egypts's armed forces to give it a measure of bargaining power and capacity for maneuver, while providing it with a protective political shield. Nasser recognized that without the active participation of Soviet forces on his side, his own armed forces could not undertake a campaign to reconquer Sinai and other Arab territories from Israel, but he hoped that these forces, once rebuilt, could inflict enough damage on Israel to force it to accept a settlement that would whittle down its position and place the Arab side in a better condition to try to whittle it further later on. In the meantime the cooperation of the Soviets in rearming and retraining the Egyptian forces might itself embroil them in a more direct involvement in the war against Israel, in the way the American forces became involved in Vietnam.

Nasser defined Egypt's strategy in terms of three stages. The first was what he called the stage of "standing firmly," which meant resisting expected Israeli pressures while rebuilding his armed forces. The second was the stage of "active deterrence," which meant to begin to use the rebuilt armed forces to apply military pressure on Israel to keep the conflict alive and prevent the status quo from congealing. The third and crucial stage, for which the others were merely preparatory, was the war of attrition. This meant an all-out effort to engage Israel in a prolonged but limited conflict in which the Arab side would, he hoped, prevail by imposing on Israel the strain of a continuing high level of mobilization and a hemorrhage of casualties it could not withstand. The war was to take the form of massive artillery bombardments of Israeli positions along the Suez Canal coupled with frequent commando forays across the waterway as a possible prelude to an attempt to cross it in force and establish a firm bridgehead on its Israeli-occupied east side. The Egyptian air force and an extensive SAM-2 and antiaircraft gun defense system were to neutralize the Israeli airforce over the battlezone, and the Soviet political shield was to deter Israel from turning the war of attrition into an all-out war of movement by crossing over to the west side.

For all three stages the Egyptian strategy counted on the assistance of the Palestinian resistance and guerrilla movement that grew rapidly after the Six Day War. Although the Palestinian guerrilla groups proclaimed as their aim the complete dismantling of Israel, which was at variance with the more limited aim formally adopted by Egypt after the war, and although their strategy sought to embroil the Arab states in a losing war with Israel to create the conditions for a massive "popular war of national liberation," Egypt thought it could use them while retaining control of the situation. The function of the guerrillas in Egyptian strategy was to help keep the conflict simmering, to engage large portions of Israel's resources, to contribute to its physical and moral attrition through sabotage and terror, and to arouse world opinion against its repressive actions.

In addition to making use of the guerrillas, Egyptian strategy sought to obtain assistance from an "Eastern Front" composed of the armed forces of Jordan and Syria and an expeditionary Iraqi force stationed on Jordanian soil. The function of that front was to compel Israel to mobilize and pin down large forces, and to assist the guerrillas and the Egyptian front in wearing down Israel economically, physically, and morally.

Application of the Egyptian strategy led Israel to devise new tools and concepts and to develop preexisting ones to meet the new challenges. In the first place, in order to deny and keep denying the Arab states a realistic option of trying to reconquer the territories they had lost in a single-sweep military campaign, it steadily built up its armed forces to counter the growth of the enemy's forces. This effort was partly extensive—creating new formations, building new bases, facilities, strategic roads, settlement-strongholds, and so on. However, because of the limitation of manpower, its main thrust was intensive—upgrading the training and improving and increasing the equipment, mobility, and firepower of its already existing standing forces and reserves. Typifying this effort was the acquisition from the United States of fifty F4 Phantom fighter-bombers—the best weapon system of the kind at the time—development of its incipient capacity for electronic warfare and electronic countermeasures, and expansion of the armored corps by converting infantry units.

While building up a deterrent against an all-out war of reconquest, Israeli strategists had to provide against the kind of alternative war conceived by Egypt and its allies. Initially, during the Egyptian active deterrence stage, the task seemed to be simple and familiar: sporadic Egyptian attacks of whatever form were met by measured retaliation against selected Egyptian targets across the Suez Canal or commando raids behind enemy lines, which led to a temporary subsidence of the fighting. The Egyptians' sinking of the Israeli destroyer *Eilat* in a surprise missile attack, for example, brought an Israeli artillery bombardment of the Egyptian refineries at Suez; a sudden massive Egyptian artillery bombardment of Israeli positions along the canal brought a heliborne commando attack against a Nile dam at Nag' Hamadi in upper Egypt; and so on. However, as Egypt prepared to move to the attrition stage, which entailed a willingness to sacrifice the towns and facilities on its side of the canal after evacuating their population and a readiness to take some blows behind its lines after doing its best to provide protection for potential targets against Israeli commando raids, Israel's strategists were faced with a dilemma: should they try to defend the canal line against the Egyptian attrition offensive at the waterline itself, or should they pull back their forces beyond the reach of Egyptian artillery and counterattack only after the Egyptians attempted to cross the canal? (Invading the other side was barred by the Soviet deterrent.) The latter alternative was more in keeping with the offensive spirit of Israel's armed forces and their armored and mobile character, but it involved the risk that the enemy might succeed in establishing a foothold on the eastern bank of the canal. This might have serious diplomatic implications, would give a tremendous boost to the enemy's morale immediately, and would create a possibility of his subsequently extending the foothold into a bridgehead. On the other hand, defending the line at the waterline meant playing the enemy's game of fighting a static war, in which he could take full advantage of his quantitatively superior standing forces and his better ability to withstand heavy human losses, while leaving unexploited Israel's superior capacity for armored mobile warfare.

The solution adopted by Israel's military chiefs was to try to combine both approaches. They decided to hold the waterline, but only by a relatively small number of troops distributed over a number of strongholds, constructed so as to withstand artillery fire. The gaps between the strongholds were to be covered by mobile patrols, and the entire line (which came to be

264 I The Evolution of Israel

known as the Barlev Line after Israel's chief of staff at the time) was to be backed up by highly mobile armored forces, ready to move swiftly to meet threatening developments at any point on the line. In addition to the shield and sword effect thus provided, commando units were to undertake substanital attacks on selected points on the enemy's flanks and in his rear to force him to spread and thin out his concentrations on the opposite side of the canal.

The practical test of the opposed strategies began in March 1969, when Nasser declared the cease-fire null and void and initiated the war of attrition with massive artillery barrages. In an initial phase that lasted four months the two sides dealt each other heavy blows but the outcome was indecisive. The Barlev Line was battered but held out; the Egyptians executed many raids and ambushes across the canal but failed to capture a single stronghold; the Egyptian air force scored some successes but paid heavily for them and failed to establish a viable presence over the battlezone. On the other hand, Israel suffered heavy casualties; and although the Egyptians suffered more, they showed no sign of exhaustion and were seemingly prepared to go on with the fighting indefinitely. To correct this flaw in the initial Israeli strategy and provide pressure on the enemy to force him to cease fire, the air force was brought into action in a massive way against the Egyptian lines in July 1969. Equipped with new electronic devices to foil the effectiveness of the Egyptian SAM-2 missiles and antiaircraft batteries, Israel's planes proceeded systematically to take apart the Egyptian air defense system and prevent its repair while operating at the same time as a "flying artillery" to batter the exposed Egyptian positions. The intervention of the air force eased the pressure on the Barlev Line, reduced Israeli casualties, and inflicted very heavy losses on the enemy; but after five more months the Egyptians still refused to cease fire and rejected an American proposal presented by Secretary of State William Rogers that would give them back all the territories they had lost in exchange for a binding peace agreement with Israel. In order to bend the Egyptian stubbornness, Israel's air force extended its attacks, starting in January 1970, to military and industrial targets deep inside Egypt, especially in an ever-narrowing circle around the heart of Cairo. These raids exposed Egypt's helplessness in the face of Israel's air force and threatened to bring down Nasser's regime regardless of whether it yielded or continued to resist. But they provoked a new development that confronted Israel with the gravest challenge it faced since the Six Day War.

A few days after the Israelis started their "raids in depth," Nasser secretly flew to Moscow and warned his Soviet allies that he would resign and hand over power to someone who would seek a settlement through the Americans unless he received immediate effective help against the Israeli air attacks. The Soviets responded by rushing in large numbers of new SAM-3 missile batteries along with older SAM-2 missiles and other antiaircraft defense equipment accompanied by Soviet crews with a view to covering all of Egypt with an air defense system. At first, the Israelis treated the injection of Soviet air defense crews as a mere addition to the Soviet "technicians" present since the end of the Six Day War and continued their raids; but then, at the end of March 1970, Israeli air command and control learned that Soviet fighter planes manned by Soviet pilots were sprung up to intercept Israeli planes headed for a mission in the vicinity of Cairo. The Israeli planes were ordered back immediately and Israel now confronted the critical issue of assessing the significance of the Soviet action and determining its own reaction. Clearly, the Soviets had decided to intervene actively in the combat; however, the question was how far they were prepared to go and what should Israel do next. For it to act cautiously and desist altogether from air action over enemy territory would be tantamount to condemning itself to an indefinite prolongation of the war of attrition and to having to fight it on the enemy's terms. On the other hand, to ignore the Soviet intervention and continue as before meant to engage the Soviet air force in a war in which no matter how well the Israelis would do, they were bound to become exhausted by the infinitely greater capacity of the Soviets to replace their losses. Even if the United States were to provide replacements for lost aircraft—which was by no means certain—Israel would soon run out of pilots and would be forced into the inferior military position that was the object of the enemy's war of attrition.

Israel's political and military chiefs decided to follow a middle course. They stopped the bombing in depth but continued and even intensified the bombing in the battlezone—a strip of fifteen to twenty miles wide west of the canal—in the hope of forcing the Egyptians to cease fire. The Soviets did not immediately send their pilots to the battle area, but Soviet-Egyptian teams proceeded systematically to advance a missile defense line in the direction of the canal. By June-July 1970, as they began to penetrate the battlezone itself, the Israeli air force hurled everything at its command in a desperate effort to disrupt their advance and began to suffer heavily in the process. However, the Israelis apparently were causing more damage than they were suffering, for at some point the Soviets decided to send up their pilots to intercept the Israelis. On the first occasion they did so, toward the end of July 1970, they scored a hit against one of the Israeli planes. However, this time the Israelis could not afford to desist or hesitate. They kept attacking the missile sites and when on the next occasion, on July 30, Soviet pilots went up to meet their planes, they engaged them in combat and shot down five Soviet fighters within minutes without suffering any losses themselves.

The combat encounter between Israeli and Soviet pilots did not develop into the feared all-out contest. A few days after the incident Egypt and Israel finally agreed to an outstanding American proposal for a cease-fire and negotiations through United Nations emissary Gunnar Jarring. The cease-fire was supposed to last for ninety days unless progress in the negotiations warranted its extension. However, although the negotiations were delayed and then quickly floundered and although Egypt threatened continuously to resume the fighting, the cease-fire endured for more than three years before being broken by a different kind of war, and thus in retrospect marked the end of the war of attrition. That war and its preliminary and related actions had cost Israel some 600 soldiers and 127 civilians killed and 2,000 soldiers and 700 civilians wounded—a great deal more than the total casualties it had suffered in the entire Six Day War. However, the Egyptians and their Soviet and Arab allies lost so much more that they were compelled to desist without having achieved their objectives. After more than 500 days of combat, it was the practicers of attrition who were attrited and the Israeli armed forces who won in a new type of warfare chosen by the enemy.

The Challenge of the Fedayeen and Israel's Response

Next to the challenge presented by the Egyptian war of attrition and the complications of Soviet intervention that developed from it, the most serious problem faced by Israel after the Six Day War was that presented by the Palestinian guerrillas or fedayeen, as they called themselves. (*Fedayeen,* more accurately *fida'iyyun,* means those who are willing to sacrifice themselves for the sake of their cause.)

The first fedayeen bands were organized by the Egyptian Intelligence from among Palestinians in the Gaza Strip and were sent into Israel on sabotage and terror missions in 1955–1956. Their actions at the time contributed significantly to Israel's decision to go to war in 1956 and was the principal reason for its refusal to evacuate the Gaza Strip until it had obtained some international assurances that fedayeen action would not be renewed. For the next decade there was indeed nearly perfect quiet on that front, as Palestinian energies were channeled by the Egyptians into the formation of regular Palestinian army brigades that were held under tight control. In Syria, however, a new government that came to power in 1965, which believed that Israel could be defeated more readily by a guerrilla strategy than by regular war, gave its support to a small movement of fedayeen, al Fatah, and allowed it to sally from Syria's borders for sabotage action inside Israel. Israeli retaliations led to substantial border skirmishes and air battles with Syrian forces, which eventually led Egypt to make a demonstration of force in support of Syria that escalated into the Six Day War.

Although the Six Day War resulted in a crushing defeat for the armies of the Arab states that participated in it, the fedayeen, who had really provoked it, flourished as a result of it. The war turned them into the only remaining focal point for Arab resistance to Israel at a time of despair and brought to their ranks large numbers of recruits. It induced the governments of the defeated Arab states, eager to prevent Israel from consolidating its conquests, to give them a more or less free hand and provide them with bases and weapons. It opened for them vast sources of funds from oil-rich Arab states, eager to compensate through such support for their inaction during the war and their continuing cooperation with the American and British "imperialist" supporters of Israel. Above all, the war gave rise to an Israeli occupation of thickly inhabited Arab territories, which afforded what seemed like an opportunity for an effective guerrilla-type resistance even while providing a highly credible cause for it. Thus, within a short while, al Fatah itself grew rapidly and new organizations developed, and the fedayeen movement as a whole came to embrace many thousands of active, full-time, well-equipped, and well-provisioned partisans.

The fedayeen proclaimed their aim to be not merely the liberation of the territories conquered by Israel in the Six Day War but also the destruction of Israel and the liberation of *all* of Palestine. Just how they were going to accomplish this was the cause of a great deal of confusion and inconsistency in thought and action, which is partly the reason why their movement was badly divided. Some thought in an altogether nonrational way, which under the inspiration of Franz Fanon saw in violence and resistance a way for an inner psychological revolution that would somehow release the necessary and sufficient forces to accomplish liberation. Others thought in terms of guerrilla and popular liberation war on the analogy of Algeria, China, Cuba, or Vietnam, without regard to the fundamental differences between these situations and Israel's. They did not recognize, for example, that the geography and topography of the territory under Israeli control did not permit the setting up of any guerrilla base that could not be reached by Israeli forces; that the population of these territories (including Israel proper) consisted of a Jewish majority that militantly supported the authorities and an Arab minority whose total size was such (1.5 million including Israel's Arabs) that it could, in the most extreme case, be driven out from Palestine altogether; that the Jews did not depend on the Arabs in any significant way and had themselves nowhere to go; and so on. Still other fedayeen thought in terms of provoking Israel into additional wars with the Arab states in the full knowledge that it would win them, in order to cause it to expand and thus create the "proper" conditions for a war of popular liberation. These fedayeen made light of the possibility that the Arab governments might sooner fight them than become involved in another losing war with Israel, or that Israel might content itself, if it came to war, with destroying enemy forces, and expanding, if at all, only into strategically important but thinly inhabited areas. They overestimated the ability of the movement, riven with dissension and rivalries as it was, to manipulate the Arab states opportunistically for its purposes instead of being so manipulated by them. All these difficulties and deficiencies made the fedayeen's ultimate goal totally unrealistic, but that did not prevent them from presenting Israel with some formidable immediate problems.

As far as Israel was concerned, the fedayeen confronted it with two specific and related problems. The first was the potential ability of the fedayeen to exert pressure on it to quit the occupied territories without obtaining satisfactory settlement terms; the second was their ability to endanger its day-to-day current security, disrupt its orderly life, and weaken its people's morale through acts of sabotage and terror. In this respect, the Israeli evaluation of the fedayeen's role was symmetrical to the Egyptian view of it rather than to the fedayeen's view of their own function and capabilities.

With respect to the first problem, Israel's defense chiefs did not fear that the armed forces at their disposal might not be able physically to hold on to the occupied territories because of fedayeen action and fedayeen-instigated popular resistance. The entire population, fedayeen and all, could be driven out if worse came to worst. What the Israeli chiefs feared was that if resistance in the territories were to develop to an extent that required drastic measures to suppress it, there would be strong pressures within Israel itself to quit; and if these pressures did not suffice, there would be added heavy international political pressures. Since quitting under pressure could jeopardize Israel's long-term prospects of peace and security and would certainly leave unresolved the problem of current security even within the pre-1967 boundaries, it seemed essential to the men responsible for Israel's defense to avert this; and the way to avert this was to prevent the fedayeen from establishing themselves in the occupied areas and from arousing their population to effective, continuous resistance.

The Israeli authorities, led by Defense Minister Moshe Dayan, approached this task with a combination of energetic military measures specifically directed at the fedayeen and bold political measures directed at the population with the aim of minimizing irritants that might encourage cooperation with the fedayeen and maximizing interest in the preservation of peaceful conditions. As part of the latter approach, the Israelis did their best from the outset to keep a low profile in the occupied territories. They kept their armed forces away from populated areas, allowed the continuation of the existing administration and personnel, supported the existing law and law enforcement agencies, rapidly removed curfews and other security restrictions, restored essential services disrupted by the war, and encouraged the local authorities to address themselves to public welfare projects. All these measures constituted a prelude to what came to be known as the Open Bridges policy, which gave systematic expression to Dayan's approach to the problem of the occupation. This policy began by allowing the free movement of people and goods back and forth across the Jordan River in order to avoid the disruption of previous trade relations and family and personal contacts. Next, it was extended to allow Arabs from the occupied areas to move freely in all of what had been Palestine, thus giving these Arabs the first opportunity since 1948 to move about in Israel proper. Then came authorization to Arabs anywhere in the world to visit relatives in the Israeli-occupied areas during the summer, which quickly brought in over 100,000 visitors annually. Finally, Arabs from the occupied areas were allowed to take employment in Israel, a step that initiated a revolution in the life of the areas and their inhabitants.

Three years after the first permissions were granted in 1968, 60,000–70,000 workers, representing about half the wage earners of the territories and, together with their families, one-third of the areas' population, had jobs in Israel. Their wages (formally equal to those of Israeli workers, actually somewhat less but in any case a multiple of the wage rate in their places of origin), added up to one-third the GNP of the territories. Their employment in Israel eliminated unemployment in the territories, caused wages there to rise, triggered a revolution in agriculture, multiplied spending, saving, and investment, stimulated trade, and precipitated many processes of social change. All this did not make the Israeli occupation acceptable, but it did give the majority of the population of the occupied territories directly or indirectly a vested interest in the avoidance of seemingly pointless trouble. Moreover, it increased the pool of individuals who were willing to cooperate with the Israeli authorities in tracking down troublemakers. These results were the exact opposite of what guerrilla strategy normally seeks to accomplish, and in effect turned the tables on the fedayeen.

While the liberal occupation policy was unfolding step after step, Israeli security forces proceeded to break up the underground cells that the fedayeen had been able to establish in the confusion that followed the war or to force their members to flee across the Jordan. This was done not through any massive search-and-destroy operations, but mostly through pinpoint action directed by specific prior intelligence. Among the factors that accounted for the excellence of the Israeli intelligence was the fact that the authorities did not apply the death penalty even to culprits who were caught red-handed. This made it easier for captured fedayeen to speak and for informers to come forth, whether their motives were personal advantage or a desire to be rid of troublemakers. It is true that the Open Bridges policy also made it possible for the fedayeen to send in people to reconstitute some of the cells destroyed, but the Israeli effort was successful overall. This was indicated by the gradual decline in the number and seriousness of the sabotage and terror acts executed in the areas under Israeli control and by the apprehension of the perpetrators sooner or later in almost all instances. In 1971–1973 there were stretches of six or even twelve months without any significant act of sabotage or terror.

The success of the Israeli security forces in checking fedayeen activity inside the occupied territories was closely linked to their effort against fedayeen incursions from across the borders. This effort assumed two forms simultaneously: setting up an ever more elaborate defense system to intercept and destroy fedayeen groups that tried to cross the borders into Israeli-held areas, and reaching out beyond the borders to retaliate against the shelling of border settlements and to hit the enemy in his bases. The latter kind of action was essentially a continuation of the "traditional" Israeli approach which refused almost at any price to recognize political boundary lines as marking a sanctuary for fedayeen. It was an approach that seemingly played into the hands of those fedayeen groups that sought to embroil Israel in another general war with the Arab states; however, besides feeling that it had no choice, Israel estimated that under the post-1967 circumstances the prospect ought to frighten the governments concerned first and impel them to attempt to restrain the fedayeen. As things turned out, Israel's estimate proved to be partly right in the case of Lebanon and completely right in the case of Jordan. In 1969 the Lebanese government tried to bar fedayeen action against Israel from its territory and after severe clashes between the Lebanese army and the fedayeen, a compromise was reached that restricted the latter's freedom of action and confined their operational bases to the southern part of the country, where they were more vulnerable to Israeli counteraction. In September 1970, after Jordan's King Hussein had agreed to a cease-fire along with Egypt and after the fedayeen had proclaimed their intent to force the continuation of the fighting, the King ordered his army to crush them and expel their remnants from the country, which it did after grueling and costly battles.

The setting up of an elaborate defense system along the borders, in contrast to the retaliation policy, was a rather new approach in Israeli defense thinking. It was made necessary by the very large number of fedayeen bands that attempted to cross over almost every night to hit selected Israeli targets, and it was made possible by the immensely increased means at Israel's disposal and the much better borders it controlled after 1967. The Egyptian front was altogether impervious to fedayeen action because of the vast inhospitable desert that separated the front line at the Suez Canal from the populated areas. The Gaza Strip was an isolated pocket, within which sabotage and terror action could be attempted but from which it was not safe to venture far out. The border with Syria was narrow and led mainly to Israeli military positions that were always on the alert. The critical border until 1970 was with Jordan, where the fedayeen had a popular support base among the very large Palestinian population and from which the inhabited parts of the Israeli-occupied areas were not distant. However, here two factors made it convenient for Israel to set up a defense network: the relatively short line of the border, by comparison with the pre-1967 line, and the existence, in the form of the Jordan rift, of a desolate strip between the river and the thickly inhabited plateau of the West Bank.

The system that Israel set up was geared to preventing fedayeen bands from making the distance from their bases to the inhabited plateau in one night, thus forcing them to move or hide in the intervening area by day when Israeli forces could follow their trail and close in on them by land and from the air. Early in the struggle Israeli ground and air forces attacked open or suspected fedayeen bases on the east side of the Jordan, thus forcing the enemy to remove them deeper inland and to disperse them in populated areas, while creating a kind of buffer he had to cross at night before reaching the Jordan. This side of the river, Israel established a string of Nachal settlements that served as fire bases by day and bases for ambushes by night, which barred certain avenues of approach and channeled the enemy to others, longer and more difficult for him. Parallel to the river and at some distance inside, there were electronic fences and other traps that signaled the presence and location of the enemy if he tried to tamper with them, or forced him to lose precious night time if he tried to circumvent them. Once his presence was detected, a number of small mobile units were ready to close in on his estimated whereabouts by daylight, with the assistance of observation and gunship helicopters. When necessary, heliborne units could be instantly called upon to descend in the vicinity of inaccessible spots, and air support could be summoned to blast brush areas or pursue a rapidly retreating unit. The whole system worked as a deadly trap in which many a fedayeen band was caught before the enemy gave up altogether any attempt to maintain fighting contact with the inhabited occupied areas.

The combination of the Open Bridges policy and the military measures adopted by Israel succeeded in meeting the problem of fedayeen pressure to abandon the occupied territories prematurely. It also went a long way toward meeting the related problem of current security, but it did not resolve it entirely. After their expulsion from Jordan, the fedayeen proceeded to intensify their operations from Lebanon, forcing Israel to devise an additional elaborate and costly system to seal that border. Moreover, as their actions in the Israeli-held territories or at their fringes were checked, the fedayeen extended their fight against Israel to the international arena, where they attacked any and every Israeli target they could reach. Israel was still battling with these problems when the October 1973 war broke out.

The Contest of Threat and Deterrence, 1970–1973

The end of the war of attrition can be dated to August 1970 only retrospectively. At the time of the cease-fire and for many months thereafter, Israel confronted the threat of a resumption of that kind of warfare under much worse conditions than those before the truce because of the prospect of Soviet involvement in the fighting and because the Egyptians violated the standstill cease-fire to advance the missile wall to the combat zone. In the absence of choice, Israel endeavored to develop a capacity to fight a costly war of attrition under the changed circumstances. However, after tension between Egypt and the Soviet Union seemed to discount the chances of Soviet intervention, Israel switched to a strategy of total deterrence by threatening to retaliate massively against any enemy combat initiative.

A strategy of total deterrence requires absolute military superiority, which Israel endeavored to develop and maintain in the face of the enemy's buildup of his power. However, the fact that Israel's military power rested heavily on reserves while that of its enemies rested on standing forces left a crack in Israel's military superiority which the enemy decided to exploit, especially since Israel's political posture appeared to leave him with no option other than accepting Israeli dictation. The result was the surprise Yom Kippur War of October 1973.

The August 1970 cease-fire was viewed at the time as a mixed blessing by most Israelis. It provided a respite from the longest period of sustained hostilities Israel had known and halted the murderous process of escalating Soviet involvement in combat, but it was meant to be temporary and was tied to unfavorable political conditions. Moreover, no sooner had the cease-fire come into effect than the Egyptians and the Soviets violated its standstill provisions to advance the missile defense system all the way to the edge of the canal, thus accomplishing overnight and at no cost what they had failed to achieve in three months of bitter warfare. Thus, unless something unexpected happened to prolong the cease-fire, Israel faced the grim prospect of a resumption of the fighting after three months under conditions wherein the entrenched enemy missile defense system and possibly the Soviet air force neutralized the Israel air force and allowed the enemy to resume the war of attrition on his own terms. Israel would not only have to take heavy casualties but the Egyptians might well be able to cross the canal under the protection of the missile umbrella and establish a firm bridgehead on its eastern bank as a prelude to further advance into Sinai.

To meet that new challenge, Israel made preparations to fight on the ground without the customary support of a dominant air force. Working under the pressure of the cease-fire deadline, Israel launched one of the biggest and most intensive construction operations in its history aimed at fortifying the Barlev Line and preparing to meet potential enemy onslaughts. At a cost of over $100 million, the thirty strongholds on the waterline were redesigned and done over to withstand the heaviest possible artillery pounding; a second line of fortifications was built four to six miles inland to back up the first; depots, command posts, communication centers, war rooms, and hospitals were built underground as were fuel, water, and communication lines; and hundreds of miles of road were built to provide maximum mobility and maneuverability for armor and artillery; and so on.

All this effort was not intended to alter the original function of the Barlev

Line but rather to enable it to continue to fulfill it under new possible circumstances of reduced air support. The line was still meant merely to allow small Israeli forces to remain on the waterline and maintain observation despite heavy bombardments, and to obstruct limited crossings in the context of a war of attrition. Major invasion attempts across the waterway were meant to be blocked by standing armored formations deployed within easy reach of the front until the reserve formations were mobilized and thrown into a decisive counteroffensive.

While the army worked feverishly to reinforce and develop the Barlev Line, the air force worked no less intensely on acquiring and developing means to counter the Soviet-Egyptian air defense system. The United States, in reaction to the violation of the standstill cease-fire by the Egyptians and the Soviets, helped by providing additional aircraft and new equipment, notably the Shrike air-to-ground missile designed to home on missile battery radar. However, it was not until February 1971, six months after the cease-fire, that a spokesman for the Israeli air force declared that a "full answer" was found to the missile problem. That answer, he added, involved some losses, but these would be less than those sustained by Israel in the last days before the cease-fire. Evidence of the success would become apparent in the first hours of battle, but the entire missile system would be overcome within two or three days.

Israel's preparations to meet a resumption of the war of attrition were never tested because the war of attrition was never resumed. The three-month cease-fire went on for more than three years, and when it was ended it was by a different, all-out war under different political circumstances. The latter were only remotely the result of Israel's doing, but the fact that the war that broke out in October 1973 was total was the direct result of Israeli strategy.

For reasons analyzed elsewhere in this book, the negotiations for a comprehensive settlement starting with Egypt and Israel did not begin until January 1971, and then quickly reached an impasse. Egypt's President Anwar Sadat, who had succeeded Nasser, upon his death in September 1970, kept the diplomatic process alive by proposing negotiations for a limited agreement through the intermediary of the United States, but by the summer of 1971 these negotiations, too, became bogged down. President Sadat thereupon proclaimed that unless the conflict was on its way to resolution by peaceful means by the end of the year, he would attempt to resolve it by war. The year 1971, he said, was to be "the year of decision."

Israel's defense chiefs believed that Sadat's war threat envisioned an improved version of the war of attrition, taking advantage of the missile umbrella that now covered the canal battlezone. They planned to meet that threat by an improved version of the methods with which they had met the first war, taking advantage of the strengthened Barlev Line and new missile-suppression weapons and tactics. In view of the heavy losses in men and the material costs incurred by Israel in the previous round of fighting, the prospect of another round was rather depressing, especially since the Soviets appeared to be more committed than before and were capable of replacing promptly any materiel the Israelis might destroy. However Israel had no choice but to await an Egyptian move and seek to defeat it locally, since the Soviet political shield barred an Israeli invasion of the west bank of the canal to seek a decisive battle. Indeed, the Soviet shield barred even an Israeli attempt to ease the pressure on the front by repeating the air attacks in Egypt's interior.

The year 1971 passed and Sadat did not go to war even though the diplomatic process was deadlocked. This indicated to the Israelis that the Egyptians probably had their own apprehensions and problems regarding a resumption of the war of attrition, but it did not alter the conception that each held of their respective strategic options. The situation changed abruptly in the middle of 1972, when Sadat decided to expel the Soviet "advisers" and bring into the open the fact that he had been having a long simmering dispute with the Soviets about basic war and peace strategy. The breach between Egypt and the Soviet Union made it possible for Israel to adopt a more active strategy than that of responding in a limited way to an Egyptian war of attrition initiative. Israel could not, to be sure, initiate a general war to end the conflict by imposing its political terms—that might be too provocative to the Soviets and unacceptable to the United States; but it could and did adopt a strategy that sought to deter attrition warfare by threatening and periodically repeating the threat to respond massively to any limited initiatives by the enemy.

A strategy of total deterrence presupposes total military superiority. Israel's defense planners believed that the removal of the Soviet shield gave Israel that kind of superiority, and they strove to maintain and develop it in the face of enemy efforts to contest it. A general indication of Israel's striving is seen in the enormous growth of its defense expenditures. In the three years 1968–1970, Israel was already spending twice as much on defense as in the previous three years; in the following three years, 1971–1973, it redoubled the 1968–1970 expenditures. In the last full year before the 1973 war, defense spending approached $4 billion, nearly ten times the $440 million spent in the last year before the 1967 war.

Israel's defense imports amounted to $1.8 billion in the last three years before the October 1973 war. In addition, ever since 1967 Israel made a determined effort to develop its own military industries to reduce dependence on outside suppliers. By 1973, locally produced weapons included the Kfir supersonic fighter-bomber, self-propelled medium artillery and long-range guns, the Shafrir air-to-air missile, air to ground missiles, the Reshef missile boat, the Gabriel sea-to-sea missile, and most types of ammunition and control systems.

Israel put enormous stress on building up the power of its air force. Among Israel's military leaders there were a few enthusiasts of the famous Italian strategist Douhet who believed that air power by itself could decide wars, but nearly all believed in the omnipotence of the aircraft-tank combination. In addition, the air force was seen as an essential instrument to protect Israel against air attack and permit orderly mobilization and troop movements, and was viewed as a versatile quick-response instrument and a flexible strategic reserve. Thus, in the last budget year before the 1973 war more than 50 percent of the defense allocations were devoted to the air force and 30 percent to the armored corps. Between the 1970 cease-fire and 1973, the Israeli air force nearly doubled the number of its combat aircraft, from 300 to 550. Taking into account the upgrading in the quality of the aircraft, the increase in the power of the air armada in that short time span was much greater. Of course, the surrounding Arab countries and their allies had also increased their air forces and indeed commanded twice as many aircraft as Israel in 1973. However the Arab effort at most kept the numerical ratio of combat planes constant, leaving the Israeli air force vastly superior because of many qualitative advantages. For example, with 127 Phantoms and 170 Skyhawks—four and three times more than it had in 1970—Israel's smaller fleet could carry at least twice the tonnage of the combined fleets of Egypt, Syria, Jordan, Iraq, and Libya. Because of the much greater range of its aircraft, Israel's air force could reach far deeper into enemy territory than the enemy could into its own, or else it had much more loitering time over targets. Superior maintenance kept a much larger proportion of Israel's force serviceable at any given time, and greater turnaround speed made possible twice the number of sorties for each Israeli aircraft. A larger pool of relevant manpower and more effective training endowed Israel with about 50 percent more combat pilots than planes, whereas the Arabs had perhaps that percentage fewer pilots than planes. The quality of the equipment, of command and control, of training and manpower demonstrably assured Israeli fighters of more than ten-to-one kill ratio in air combat. These factors and others added up to an overwhelming superiority for Israel's air force, and what is most important for purpose of Israel's deterrence strategy, the enemy knew it.

On the ground Israel increased by nearly 50 percent the number of first-line brigades over the twenty-five it commanded in the Six Day War, organized most of them in divisional formations and upgraded their training and equipment. Central attention was directed to the armored corps, which was endowed with 2,200 tanks, more than twice the number available in 1967—most of them equipped with a locally produced 105-milimeter gun considered far superior to the gun on most of the enemy's tanks. The number of APCs (armored personnel carriers) was more than doubled, to provide complete mechanization for the entire ground forces. The surrounding Arab countries had somewhat more than twice as many tanks but, even apart from disparities in quality in favor of Israel, that represented a substantial lowering of previous numerical ratios. Artillery, long the black sheep of armor-minded Tzahal, also received a great boost as a result of the war of attrition. The artillery corps was provided with large numbers of the latest United States–built 155-milimeter SP (self-propelled) howitzers and long-range 175-milimeter SP guns, coupled with sophisticated electronic systems to assist in laying precise fire. The Arabs, with 5,000 artillery pieces and missiles of various sorts, still had a 2.5-to-1 numerical superiority over Israel, but that ratio was much smaller than before and its significance was further reduced by the greater mobility and superior quality of much of Israel's new equipment.

On the seas, Israel's navy made a quantum leap after the Six Day War from equipment and vessels that were obsolete and unsuited to their mission to a modern fighting apparatus based upon the needs of the theater in which the navy had to operate. The core of the new navy consisted of eighteen missile boats knows as Sa'ar and Reshef, in addition to two submarines, nine torpedo boats, and thirty-three other vessels. The 250-ton Sa'ar is capable of developing speeds up to forty knots, is armed with automatically radar-controlled 40-millimeter and 76-millimeter guns, and has very advanced means of electronic warfare and Gabriel missile launchers. The Reshef is heavier and has a longer range, but has the same armament as the Sa'ar. The Sa'ar and the Reshef were recognized by world naval authorities as more than a match to the hitherto unrivaled Soviet Komar and Osa missile boats in the possession of Egypt and Syria. Their entry into service starting in 1969 drastically corrected if it did not reverse the relation of naval forces hitherto completely lopsided in favor of the Arabs.

The growth of Israel's military power extended to many other areas and was compounded by many qualitative improvements in organization, training, command and control, and so on, but the examples cited suffice to suggest the extent of Israel's effort to build up and maintain the means to support a strategy of total deterrence. However, as events were to show, the Israeli strategic design had two flaws that proved to be its undoing. The total military superiority necessary to a strategy of total deterrence was almost inherently impossible for Israel to achieve because the bulk of its military establishment depended on reserves while the enemy's rested on standing forces. As long as that was the case there were bound to be moments and situations in which superiority was actually or could be on the side of the enemy. However short the moment and far-fetched the situation, in theory they offered the enemy opportunities and openings that undermined absolute deterrence. Of course, the opportunities and openings might be highly risky in practice, but the enemy's willingness to take risks was a function of the alternatives available to him, which seemed to be highly unattractive. This was where the Israeli strategy had its second flaw.

The Israeli strategy assumed that Israel actually offered the enemy a reasonable political option that made it not worth his while to take grave risks, by inviting him to enter into direct negotiations without prior conditions. However, in the absence of a prior authoritative indication as to what Israel expected to achieve, the invitation to unconditional direct negotiations, which Israel viewed as generous, appeared to the enemy as a call on him to accept Israeli dictation from a position of strength, the more so the greater the military superiority of Israel. This created a situation wherein the enemy thought he might not be worse off taking the risks of going to war even if he were to lose (since he was being asked to "surrender" anyway), and would be better off in direct proportion to the extent he did better than losing completely. This, essentially, is what he did, as he launched a general war on October 6, 1973, designed to capitalize on the gap in Israel's military superiority.

17

Trial by Ordeal:
The 1973 Yom Kippur War

The Yom Kippur War was an effort by an Arab coalition to defeat Israel by breaking through a gap in its security concept. It was an attempt by the vast standing armies of Egypt and Syria to overcome the inferior standing forces of Israel before its reserves could be brought into play, and thus gain a decisively favorable position from which to defeat those reserves as they came into play. The attempt depended critically on surprise so that Israel should be unable to mobilize and deploy its reserves before the Arab forces attacked.

Despite the massive, highly visible preparations that the Arab armies had to make before launching their assault, they, incredibly, succeeded in surprising Israel and thus achieved the most important condition for their strategy. Surprise and a combination of sound planning on the part of the Arabs and poor anticipation and reaction on the part of the Israelis enabled the attacking Egyptians to defeat the standing Israeli forces facing them. The Syrians nearly succeeded in doing the same, but before their failure they contributed to undoing the prepared Israeli plans for containment, mobilization, and counterattack. Henceforth, the war became for the Israelis a confused war of improvisation, with little relation to their tattered defense concept. It became a real trial by ordeal for Israel's armed forces.

In strictly military terms, Tzahal proved its mettle by recovering from the initial setbacks and slowly and painfully turning a near-defeat into a near-victory. However, because of the initial failures Israel emerged from the war in a much weaker strategic-political position than before and had to confront new, most formidable security challenges which had not yet been fully resolved two years later.

The Prelude to the War

The War Concepts of the Opponents

Ever since the end of the Six Day War, Egyptian strategists had pondered and argued among themselves about the kind of war their country eventually launched in October 1973. Already in 1968 *al Ahram* editor and Nasser's confidant Muhammad Heikal had expounded the theory of such a war in one of his weekly columns. Recognizing that Egypt was not then and was not likely to be soon in a position to mount a military campaign for the reconquest of the lost territories, he argued that it could nevertheless transform the political situation sufficiently to force Israel to renounce the territories on Egypt's terms if it could inflict on Israel a substantial limited military defeat—if it could, for instance, cross the Suez Canal in force, establish a solid bridgehead, and destroy one or two Israeli divisions.

Heikal's concept could, of course, cut both ways. Were Egypt to make such an attempt and fail, it would at one and the same time exhaust its military option and expose the limits of the Soviet willingness to provide military support. For this reason and because of Soviet cautionary advice, Nasser resorted instead to the more cautious concept of putting mounting pressure on Israel through a war of attrition that might, if successful, culminate in a massive crossing to seize and hold a bridgehead.

The failure of the war of attrition, the expulsion of the Soviets, and the adoption by Israel of a strategy of massive retaliation to deter partial warfare, on the one hand, and the onset of a diplomatic stalemate and Sadat's strong commitment to go to war if there were no prompt political solution to the conflict, on the other hand, combined to revive active Egyptian interest in the concept of a war for a bridgehead. In October 1972 Sadat proposed such an approach at a conference with his military chiefs, but some of those present, including War Minister and Commander in Chief General Muhammad Sadeq, strongly opposed that view. They advocated instead an all-or-nothing strategy ("all" being a drive all the way to the pre-1967 lines) at a time when it was generally agreed that Egypt was not and would not be for a long time in a position to attempt the "all." Two days later Sadat fired Sadeq and several of his colleagues and appointed General Ahmed Ismail as minister of war and General Sa'd al Din Shazli as chief of staff with instructions to prepare operational plans for a bridgehead war with the forces available to them plus whatever equipment could be acquired before D-day.

The Egyptian planners were acutely aware of Israel's success in cultivating two critical advantages: a far superior air force which could not be crippled by a surprise blow on the Israeli 1967 model because of a proven effective early warning system, and a powerful armored corps highly proficient in a war of movement. But they were also aware of several critical comparative disadvantages of the enemy: long frontiers bordering on four Arab countries and long lines of communication; a small population, making him highly sensitive to human losses, causing the bulk of his strength to be in the form of reserves, and making his economy vulnerable to a prolonged war and warfooting; and finally, proneness to excessive self-assurance because of past successes. The plans they devised were designed to minimize the effects of the enemy's advantages and take maximum advantage of his relative weaknesses. They comprised the following elements:

1. Syria must be brought fully into the operation in order to bring to bear on the enemy a heavier mass and force him to fight simultaneously on two distant fronts. War on the Syrian front would be particularly helpful in reducing Israeli pressure on the Egyptian front because there Israel could not trade territory for time as it could in the south and was therefore bound to direct primary attention to the north first.

2. Jordan should be brought in as a potential associate in order to help pin down enemy forces.

3. The general war plan was for Egypt and Syria to seize rapidly and consolidate strategic territory and then wait for the enemy to bash his head against the Arab lines, thus denying him the opportunity to develop the open warfare at which he excelled and forcing him to fight set battles in which his sensitivity to heavy losses would take full effect.

4. To limit the effect of the enemy's air power, the ground forces would not venture far beyond the missile and air defense system until the enemy's air force was exhausted by attacks on that system, allowing the Arab air forces to contend with what was left of it. The planners feared that if the enemy were to concentrate all his air power on the air defense system he might be able to breach it, but they hoped that the simultaneous threats on the ground on two fronts would distract his air force and prevent it from achieving that concentrated effort.

5. The bulk of the Arab air forces would be preserved as a strategic reserve in order to impose caution on the enemy, to step into possible breaches in the air defense system or on the ground, or to exploit the situation after the weakening of the enemy's air force.

6. In the south, the seizing of a bridgehead would be accomplished in a series of rapid steps. The canal would be crossed along its entire length to confuse the enemy about the main thrusts and disperse the efforts of his air force. Bridgeheads would be established initially by the infantry, and bridges would be swiftly constructed for the passage of tanks so that these should have time to deploy before the first major Israeli counterattack developed. The sand banks, towering thirty to seventy-five feet above the hard shoulders of the canal, would be pierced to allow passage for the armor by teams of engineers using specially developed methods.

In the north, where the Israeli line rested on a series of fortified small hills and antitank ditches, the Egyptian and Syrian planners agreed that large motorized infantry formations would sweep between the hills and clear the way for massive armored formations to rush through and seize the Golan in a continuous succession of sweeps. The advancing forces would be covered part of the way by the fixed air defense system and for the rest by mobile SAM-6 missiles, radar-guided antiaircraft guns, and shoulder-fired SAM-7 missiles.

7. An absolutely critical element in the entire strategy was surprise—enough of it at least to complete the initial phases against the enemy's standing forces alone, before he could bring to bear any significant part of his reserves. Otherwise, the crossing and breakthrough might be aborted at the outset, the enemy could concentrate all his airpower on taking apart the air defense system, the Arab forces would be exposed and off balance as the enemy launched his counteroffensive, and the entire enterprise would turn into a massive disaster. One crucial factor favoring the achievement of surprise was the fact that Egypt and Syria normally deployed massive forces right at the front line, and only needed to complement them and redeploy them for offense before attacking. To accomplish that an elaborate deception scheme was worked out wherein various segments of these forces were to be deployed offensively from time to time in the course of formation training, so as to accustom the enemy to that kind of activity and lower his suspicion when the time for the real moves came.

Except for the possibility of surprise, Israel's defense chiefs anticipated the essentials of the enemy's plans in their own contingency plans. The Intelligence Branch flatly and unequivocally assured the General Staff that it would provide it with at least forty-eight hours warning of any enemy intent to start general hostilities, and on that basis the General Staff worked out operational plans that included the following dispositions:

1. H-hour minus forty-eight hours, the Intelligence warning is received. The standing forces are placed on maximum alert. General mobilization of the reserves is decreed and proceeds in an orderly manner, envisaging the deployment of the first armored reserve formations at the front within twenty-four hours, most available power within forty-eight hours, and nearly all of it within seventy-two hours. The air force is ready at nearly full capacity within hours.

2. At the front, the front-line picket forces are reinforced and the back-up standing armored forces take positions to block enemy attack. In the south, for example, the General Staff normally holds three armored brigades, one in forward deployment and the others some twenty to thirty miles in the rear. As the warning is received, these two brigades are meant to advance to

within range of the waterline and occupy prepared fire positions on dirt platforms overlooking the canal while the third is to be held in reserve to come to
the help of pressed areas. Standing mobile artillery is to be similarly advanced
and deployed in prepared fire positions.

3. H-hour to H-hour plus twenty-four, the enemy makes his thrust and
this is effectively contained by the ground forces alone, without too many casualties or too much loss of ground. The air force is completely devoted to systematically suppressing in thousands of sorties the enemy air defense system,
protecting Israel's airspace, and striking targets of importance and opportunity. The mass of reserve forces reach the front and the armored formations
are ready to swing into counteroffensive operations.

4. H-hour plus twenty-four to H-hour plus seventy-two, the counteroffensive reaches its peak. Large Israeli armored formations which have broken
through the enemy lines are fighting a war of movement and envelopment
deep inside enemy territory; the enemy air defense system has collapsed and
the Israeli air force is wreaking havoc on disoriented and disorganized enemy
formations; the war is now a race to complete the destruction of enemy forces
before the onset of a cease-fire.

Two war concepts—one seeking to establish the conditions for a
grinding defensive battle to achieve offensive purposes, and the other seeking
to achieve defensive purposes by maximum offense—thus opposed each
other, and both depended entirely on the surprise factor. The Arabs counted
on having it on their side, the Israelis on its absence. The Arabs won, with the
consequence that the initial phase of the war went according to their plans
and that the Israeli plans were totally undone and became almost completely
irrelevant.

Surprise Through Self-Deception

The decisive surprise achieved by the Arab side was not due to any dearth of
relevant information in the hands of Israeli Intelligence but to faulty evaluation of the significance of the ample data available. The function of intelligence evaluation and analysis was concentrated exclusively in the hands of
the Research Division of the Intelligence Branch; and, as the Agranat Inquiry
Commission pointed out after the war, the division filtered the abundant
warning information it received through a general "conception" of the situation to which it rigidly adhered. That conception estimated that Egypt would
not go to war until it first secured for itself the capacity to attack Israel's
depth, especially its main airfields, from the air in order to paralyze its air
force, and that Syria would not undertake a major attack on Israel except

simultaneously with Egypt. The origin of that conception probably went back to authoritative information received by the Israelis about the thinking of the Egyptian military chiefs under General Sadeq (who, as we have seen, supported an all-or-nothing strategy), which was not adequately reexamined in the light of subsequent events, including the replacement of Sadeq by Ismail and the acquisition by Egypt of additional weapons systems that gave it the real option of a "bridgehead war." In any case, the analysts of the Research Division, starting from the premises of the "conception," consistently misinterpreted the ample information that came through about intensified enemy activity as indicating greater defensive efforts by the Syrians and preparations for large-scale maneuvers by the Egyptians.

The misinterpretations of Intelligence were accepted as authoritative by all who were in a position to question them (with one exception that made no practical difference), because Intelligence had proved right on several similar occasions in the past and those who challenged it had proved wrong. Everyone remembered particularly an incident that took place in mid-May 1973, only four months before. At that time, too, information was received about Egyptian and Syrian troop concentrations and deployments, indeed about specific attack plans and even about firm orders setting the date for the attack. The Intelligence analysts nevertheless indicated a very low probability of war, but were overruled by the chief of staff and the government. The reserves were mobilized at a cost of $10 million, but nothing happened. If anyone thought at the time that the mobilization of the reserves may have been the reason *why* nothing happened, or that the enemy might have been engaging in a subtle game of crying wolf in order to lull the opponent, he did not stick to these reflections in the critical days of September–October and did not voice them until it was too late.

In the course of the twelve days preceding the outbreak of hostilities, the danger signals multiplied, caused anxious consultations among the responsible authorities, and led to several precautionary decisions; however, in the face of the stubborn adherence of the Intelligence Branch to its estimate of "low" or "lower than low" probability of war, the precautions were less than adequate to the requirements of the situation and were not applied with the necessary strictness and urgency. Thus, on September 24, 1973, United States Intelligence warned its Israeli counterpart of portentous signs of war but was told that the conclusion of Israeli Intelligence was negative. On the same day there was a meeting of the General Staff attended by Defense Minister Dayan at which General Yitzhak Hofi, General Officer Commanding (GOC) Northern Command, expressed anxiety over the Syrian buildup observed from the Israeli surveillance position on top of Mount Hermon, but Intelligence interpreted the evidence to be due to a rotation of Syrian units and to the manning of newly completed and more extensive defensive lines. Fortunately for Israel, Dayan was sufficiently impressed by Hofi's concern to undertake a visit to the front two days later and to press the chief of staff to reinforce the Israeli establishment there despite the complacent evaluation of Intelligence. Not that Dayan rejected that evaluation altogether, but rather like many Israelis, he was inclined to believe that the Syrians were somewhat "crazy" and were capable of attempting to overrun the Israeli settlements on the Golan even though they might subsequently be crushed themselves. Moreover, Dayan had "a thing" about the Russians and did not put it beyond them to let the Syrians make a thrust and then fling themselves between them and the avenging Israeli army. In any case, Dayan came back to the Golan subject with the chief of staff again and again and did not rest until the Israeli armor there was increased from 70 to 177 tanks and the field artillery from four to eight batteries. With regard to the southern front, however, Dayan was content to accept the evaluations of Intelligence at face value and did not question the disposition of forces of the General Staff and Southern Command.

On October 1 the Egyptians and the Syrians completed their front line deployment according to plan. On the next day, Dayan and Chief of Staff General Elazar reviewed the situation. Elazar told Dayan that he had again checked with Intelligence the significance of the Egyptian activity and had reached the firm conclusion that what was happening there was only an exercise. As for the Syrians, there were no signs that they intended to attack, but information had been received of further preparations. The Syrians now had 650 tanks in the first line, 500 artillery pieces, and a missile air defense system that also covered Israeli territory.

Dayan grew more apprehensive about the Syrian front and arranged to have a formal consultation with Prime Minister Meir the next day, as soon as she returned from a diplomatic trip to Vienna. The October 3 consultation was attended by two ministers knowledgeable in military affairs (Chaim Barlev and Yigal Allon) in addition to Golda Meir, the chief of staff, the commander of the air force, and the acting chief of Intelligence (the chief, General Eliyahu Zeira, being indisposed that day). The Intelligence representative pointed out that the Syrian and Egyptian armies were so deployed along the fronts that they were able at any moment to launch an attack, but he did not think that they were about to do so. The chief of staff reported on the strengthening of the Israeli forces on the Golan already achieved and recommended leaving them at their existing strength, fortified by putting the air force on high alert. None of the participants at the meeting questioned the evaluation of Intelligence or suggested further precautionary measures beyond those taken.

During the night of October 4, reports were received that the Soviets were evacuating the families of their advisers from Egypt and Syria. The news, coupled with the accumulating information of activity at the front, alarmed the defense minister and the General Staff enough for them to order early next morning "C Alert" for the army—the highest short of calling up the reserves—and full alert for the air force—including the reserves, but it did not shake the confidence of Intelligence. Later in the morning of the 5th, the Prime Minister summoned members of the Cabinet who were still accessible on the eve of Yom Kippur for an emergency meeting in Tel Aviv to hear reports about the situation and make decisions. The chief of staff and the chief of Intelligence reiterated that the Syrians and the Egyptians were at emergency stations which served equally well for defense and for launching an invasion, but the chief of Intelligence still maintained that an attack was unlikely and the chief of staff supported him. The General Staff assumed that if war were indeed imminent, there would be further indications and specific incontrovertible intelligence reports, presumably from sources that would act only in such contingency. Only if and when these signs appeared would it be necessary to mobilize the reserves and take additional measures. The defense minister said nothing to detract from the reports of the military chiefs, but made the suggestion that the rump Cabinet give the Prime Minister authority to approve mobilization of the reserves if something unusual transpired over the Yom Kippur holiday. This the Cabinet did before breaking off with the feeling that matters were under control.

On the morning of Saturday, October 6, 1973, at 4:30 A.M. the chief of Intelligence received the incontrovertible report he had alluded to the day before and informed the minister of defense that Egypt and Syria were going to start war simultaneously that evening at 6:00 P.M. This warning was far short of the minimum forty-eight hours that Intelligence had "guaranteed" to the chief of staff and was not sufficient to permit the orderly mobilization of the reserves of the land forces according to established timetables and procedures. Moreover, it turned out that even this warning set the time for the start of hostilities four hours later than they actually began, thus further reducing the time available to call the reserves before the enemy opened fire and causing distortions in the deployment of the standing forces available at the front, especially in the south. As if that were not enough, a disagreement between the defense minister and the chief of staff about the extent of the mobilization to be ordered contributed to further loss of precious time.

Upon receiving the Intelligence report, Dayan arranged to meet with the chief of staff at 6:00 A.M. to concert decisions on necessary action. It turned out that the two disagreed on several crucial issues. General Elazar urged near-total mobilization to prepare for the counteroffensive that would follow the blocking of the enemy, whereas Dayan favored mobilizing only the maximal force needed for defense in the opinion of the chief of staff. Elazar recommended a preemptive strike by the Israeli air force to begin at 12:00 noon; Dayan opposed it. Dayan favored giving a warning to the Egyptians and the Syrians that Israel was aware of their plans and was alert to meet them in the hope that this might cause them to desist; Elazar opposed the idea. The two decided to take their differences to a meeting with the Prime Minister scheduled for 8:00 A.M.; and it was not until 9:30, after the Prime Minister decided in favor of the chief of staff on the question of the reserves, that general mobilization was ordered. On the other two questions—warning and preemptive strike—she decided in favor of Dayan. The Prime Minister as well as the defense minister wanted to establish beyond doubt that Israel did not want war and did not start it, even at the cost of forfeiting to the enemy the advantage of striking first. Little did they realize how crucial that advantage would turn out to be.

Initial Forces and Deployments

On October 5, 1973, Egypt and Syria together disposed 500,000 regular troops and a similar number of rear-echelon and supplementary forces, 4,500 tanks, 3,400 pieces of artillery, and 1,080 combat planes. Israel had somewhat over 100,000 regular and standing troops, about 300,000 reserves, most of them of first-line quality and nearly all of them mobilizable within seventy-two hours, 2,200 tanks, about 1,000 artillery pieces, and 550 combat aircraft. The numerical relation of forces was thus heavily tilted toward the Arab side in each item, but in terms of the real balance of forces, Israel was better off than it had ever been, *provided* it was able to mobilize and deploy its forces in time. Since in the war that broke out the next day Israel was not able to do so, the overall balance of forces became of little relevance and what mattered most at that stage and every subsequent stage of the war was the relation of forces actually deployed in the field.

In the opening stage Egypt had massed at the 94-mile front two army corps comprising seven divisions and two independent brigades. The Second Army Corps, including three infantry divisions and one armored division faced the sector between the towns of Kantara and Ismailia; the Third Army Corps with two infantry divisions and one armored division was responsible for the sector from Ismailia to Suez city. The independent brigades deployed in the areas north of Kantara and south of Suez. Behind these forces, in the Cairo area, the First Army Corps was deployed, with one armored and three motorized infantry divisions. The invasion army disposed some 1,400 tanks, half in forward deployment and half within 30 miles of the canal. It was supported by more than 1,000 pieces of artillery. Protecting these forces against air attacks was a network of sixty-two missile batteries. Nearly one hundred additional missile batteries protected installations, lines of communication, and particularly airfields in the interior of Egypt. The Egyptian air force was assigned a strategic reserve role, but stood ready to help with an initial strike, to drop commandos, and to fulfill other special roles.

On the Israeli side, only the air force was nearly totally mobilized and fully deployed by October 5. On the ground, facing the Egyptian invasion army immediately at the waterline were the strongpoints of the Barlev Line manned by 456 troops and 7 tanks. Behind them, within a distance of thirty miles were three armored brigades with 276 tanks under the command of General Albert Mendler (known as Albert), artillery units with 48 field guns, plus a few thousand infantry. These forces, under GOC Southern Command General Shmuel Gonen, may seem pathetically small by comparison with the Egyptian forces but it should be kept in mind that their task was to contain the enemy until the arrival of reinforcements some twenty-four hours later. Moreover the enemy was on the other side of a canal 180 to 240 yards wide and a formidable continuous sand bank 30 to 75 feet high. General Barlev estimated that if the tanks at the disposal of Southern Command were properly deployed according to plan, in the spaces between the strongpoints, on prepared firing ramps and as ready mailed fists, they could defeat an invading force of 1,500 tanks. The trouble was that the force was not deployed according to plan when the fighting started. When General Gonen received the war warning in the morning of October 6, one-third of his armor was deployed in forward positions five to six miles from the canal and two-thirds were at the Bir Gafgafa base, some twenty-five miles from the canal. At this point the defense plans called for him to deploy two-thirds of this total force in the firing positions and to advance the remainder to within easy striking distances of the front, but Gonen decided to hold off execution of these moves to the last moment. Believing he had until 6:00 P.M., he forbade the restless Albert to move until 2:00 P.M., which was exactly when the invasion started. Gonen was later to explain to the Agranat Commission that he wanted to avoid exposing his armor to the initial Egyptian artillery barrage, but the commission rightly rejected the explanation. More likely, Gonen, who was known as an eager warrior, feared that if he deployed his forces "prematurely" the Egyptians might cancel their invasion plans and he would lose the opportunity to give them a drubbing. It was the same kind of reasoning that underlay General Elazar's opposition to giving the Arabs a general explicit warning and it reflected the same spirit of confidence and eagerness to do battle. That spirit may be a healthy mark in an army up to a point, but it could easily degenerate into careless overconfidence, as it did in this instance.

In the north the Syrians had deployed in three forward positions three motorized divisions, each comprising two infantry and one armored brigade, for a total of 1,400 armored vehicles and 600 tanks. Behind them, ready to follow on short notice, were two armored divisions, and, in reserve, three independent brigades, two armored and one motorized infantry, comprising in all over 1,000 additional tanks. Supporting the force were some 1,300 guns, half of them deployed forward and half behind. Protecting it was a dense network of missiles covering the entire Golan, including mobile SAM-6 missiles dispersed among the troops and ready to advance with them.

Facing the Syrians on October 5 was a relatively small Israeli force which might have been even much smaller but for the alertness and caution of General Hofi, the GOC Northern Command, who had seen to it that his force of twelve days before was more than doubled. Perhaps the fact that Hofi had no Suez Canal and sand banks saved him from developing a Maginot Line mentality and thus saved Israel from a certain disaster. For the Israeli Golan defense consisted of a line of fourteen fortified small volcanic hills, each manned by a platoon of soldiers or more, and a fifteenth position on the highest ridge of Mount Hermon. Altogether, there were 5,000 infantry. Between the fortified hills and behind them were 177 tanks assigned to two armored brigades—the 188th and the 7th—and 44 field guns. Tanks and guns had carefully prepared fire positions, and antitank ditches had been dug to channel enemy traffic into killing grounds. As in the south, the task of these forces was to contain the first enemy onslaught until the arrival of the reserve reinforcements, expected to be a short while because of the proximity of Israeli bases.

The Course of the War

The course of the war is best described in terms of four stages, determined by the forces available and the major moves and countermoves of the belligerents on the two fronts. The first stage, lasting from October 6 through October 7, witnessed the initial Egyptian and Syrian onslaughts and the desperate efforts of the standing Israeli forces—abortive in the south, precariously successful in the north—to resist them. The second stage, October 8–10, was marked by major counterattacks by the first concentrations of Israeli reserves on the Egyptian and Syrian bridgeheads, ending in complete failure in the south and complete success in the north. The period of October 11–14 began with an Israeli counteroffensive in the north, which petered out after achieving some success, and ended with an abortive major Egyptian offensive. Finally, the period October 15–25 was dominated by the unfolding of a successful Israeli counteroffensive on the southern front that forced the end of the war, while the northern front remained relatively quiescent.

The First Stage (October 6–7): Facing the Avalanches

At 1:55 P.M. on October 6, some 150 Egyptian planes erupted into Sinai and headed for Israeli airfields, Hawk surface-to-air missile batteries, command posts, radar stations, artillery positions, administration centers, and some strongpoints. Five minutes later more than 1,000 guns opened fire along the entire front and kept it up for fifty-three minutes. Fifteen minutes after the start of the artillery barrage, the first wave of 8,000 infantrymen began crossing the canal in rubber boats and rafts. They brought with them light extendable stepladders which they used to climb the sand ramparts on the eastern side. Some of the attackers immediately engaged the Israeli outposts with flamethrowers, rocket launchers, machine guns, carabines, and grenades while others bypassed the strongpoints and pushed eastward toward the open desert. The first wave was followed by others and then by units of engineers who began to land ferries, build docks, excavate the ramparts, and assemble pontoon bridges.

The object of this activity was to establish three bridgeheads. The Second Army was required to seize two between the towns of Kantara and Ismailia; the Third Army had the assignment of developing a bridgehead opposite the city of Suez. The leading battalions of the Second Army reached the perimeters of its bridgeheads on schedule and began to dig in, siting Sagger antitank missiles on the captured ramps, on the shoulders of low rolling hills, and in scrubs. Teams armed with RPG-7 rocket launchers took up intermediate positions to cover short ranges. The leading units of the Third Army were slightly delayed in doing the same. In the meantime, the engineers were using high-pressure pumps mounted on rafts and sucking water from the canal to produce powerful jets that bored channels through the sand ramparts, which were then tidied up by bulldozers to make passageways for tanks and vehicles. Seven hours after the infantry began their assault, the engineers completed the first pontoon bridge, and by midnight, despite delays in the Third Army area owing to sticky soft sand, ten bridges and fifty medium and heavy ferries were in operation along the canal. The support tanks of the infantry divisions began to cross over.

On the Israeli side, the defense plans had counted on a combination of the Barlev strongpoints, the standing armored formations, and the air force to contain and frustrate a potential invasion. However, when the Egyptians actually attacked, the bulk of the Israeli armor was not deployed in its prepared positions, did not provide the necessary firepower, and did not fill the gaps between the strongpoints. Therefore the enemy was easily able to bypass and isolate the fortified points, turning them into a liability for the Israeli High Command instead of an asset. As for the Israeli air force, its plans had called for concentrating first on carefully and systematically suppressing the enemy air defense system and trying to cripple his air force on the airfields before turning to ground support operations. In fact, it was occupied in the first hour in repelling the Egyptian air attack and hunting down Egyptian helicopters carrying commandos to various points behind the Israeli lines, and when it could finally turn to the offense, it had to divert its attention immediately to attacking the Egyptian forces crossing the canal. The situation was difficult, and only two hours remained before darkness would restrict the scope of air operations; the pilots were therefore instructed to ignore the missile batteries and attack any and all targets. The air force flew some 200 sorties over the canal and lost six planes, five Skyhawks and one Phantom.

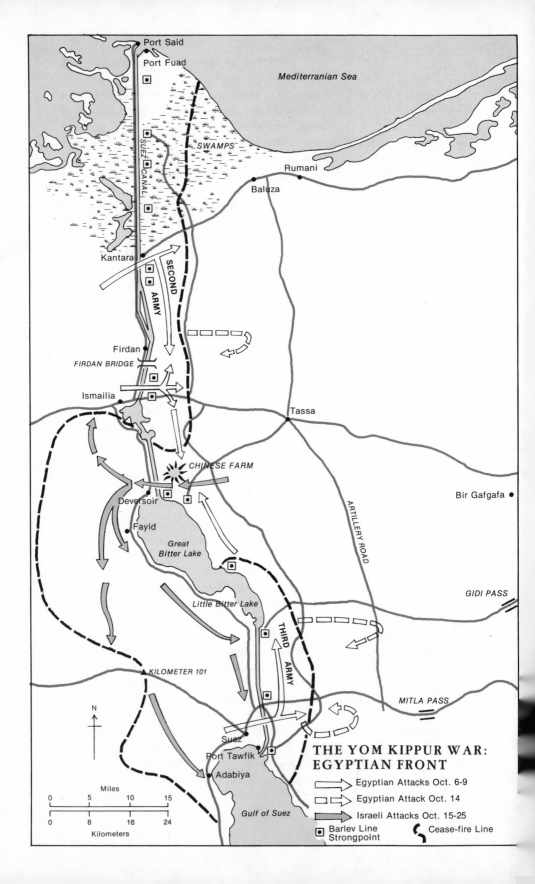

Port Said

Port Fuad

Mediterranian Sea

SWAMPS

SUEZ CANAL

Rumani

Baluza

Kantara

SECOND ARMY

Firdan

FIRDAN BRIDGE

Ismailia

Tassa

CHINESE FARM

Deversoir

Fayid

Bir Gafgafa

Great Bitter Lake

ARTILLERY ROAD

Little Bitter Lake

GIDI PASS

THIRD ARMY

▲ *KILOMETER 101*

MITLA PASS

N

Suez

Port Tawfik

Adabiya

THE YOM KIPPUR WAR: EGYPTIAN FRONT

Miles

0   5   10   15

0   8   16   24

Kilometers

Gulf of Suez

⟹ Egyptian Attacks Oct. 6-9

⟹ Egyptian Attack Oct. 14

⟹ Israeli Attacks Oct. 15-25

▣ Barlev Line
Strongpoint

⟨ Cease-fire Line

We have seen that General Gonen had held back advancing the armored units to their prepared positions according to plan when he received notice of impending enemy attack. Just as the units got ready to start moving, word came of the Egyptian air attacks and artillery bombardments. The forward brigade was then ordered to rush to the canal line and the two rear ones were directed to follow suit and deploy so as to have one brigade in each of the northern, central, and southern sections. By the time the tanks approached the preplanned positions, however, they found them to be already occupied by Egyptian antitank units which received them with hails of RPG shells and Sagger missiles. The tanks charged and suffered heavy losses; they regrouped, maneuvered, advanced, were hit, and came back again and again in a stubborn effort to link up with the strongpoints and regain positions from which they could obstruct the crossings. Indicative of how crucial every hour was in those critical first moments, the Israeli units operating in the southern sector had considerably more success than those in the north because the Egyptian Third Army had been somewhat delayed by technical difficulties in its crossing operations. Overall, however, the Israeli tank forces were cruelly decimated throughout the afternoon while the invaders rapidly increased their strength and consolidated and extended the bridgeheads they had gained.

The Israeli forces had an excellent, highly sophisticated system of communications designed to keep the various levels of command fully informed of all relevant developments and permit maximum coordination; yet, that day and in days to come, the system somehow failed again and again to work as intended. Perhaps it was because too much traffic on it tended to obscure the overall picture; perhaps Israeli commanders were too self-confident to admit to difficulties; or perhaps they were too stoic or mission-minded to report all casualties. In any case, throughout the afternoon and evening of October 6, the divisional command and other higher echelons were under the misconception that the armored counterattacks were succeeding on the whole and had an erroneous impression of the magnitude of the losses they were suffering. Consequently, they decided to continue the ineffective attacks through the night, giving the enemy antitank teams an added edge in their contest with the Israeli tanks, and forfeiting the opportunity to evacuate the strongpoints while there was still a chance to do so.

In the morning of October 7 the alarming results of the fighting up to that point began to dawn on the Israeli command, along with the outlines of a grim picture of the general situation. Albert reported that as of about 6:00 A.M. he had lost two-thirds of the 270 tanks with which he had started. Far from having regained the canal line, he now disposed only some 90 tanks along the entire length of the front with which to face an intense pressure by vast enemy forces (actually five infantry divisions) reinforced by several hundred tanks that had crossed during the night. Albert and Gonen naturally called on the air force to come to the rescue, and this responded as soon as there was enough daylight and the morning mist had lifted. At 6:45 A.M. it began with a number of preparatory strikes against the Egyptian missile system and then proceeded to provide close support. But then suddenly the GOC Israel Air Force, General Binyamin Peled, notified Gonen that he could expect no more air support for a long time because the situation in the north required all the attention of the air force. Gonen checked on the progress of the reserve reinforcements and found that they were still many hours away, although the commanders of two armored divisions, General Avraham Adan and General Ariel Sharon, had arrived with their headquarters in advance of their units.

Bereft of most of his initial armor and deprived of air support, Gonen decided to give up the attempt to restore the Barlev Line for the time being and to take measures to economize his forces and use them in order to gain time. He ordered the evacuation of the strongpoints wherever possible, which proved to be almost nowhere by then and amounted to abandoning them to their fate. He instructed Albert to direct his forces to desist from their general attacks and avoid becoming implicated in big battles. They were to conduct holding operations and trade ground and positions for time if necessary. Gonen's objective was to hang on to a new line along "artillery road," running parallel to the canal six miles inland, until the arrival of the reserves later that day permitted new initiatives. In the meantime, he divided his front into three sectors and assigned them to divisional commanders—Adan in the north, Sharon in the center, and Albert in the south.

Gonen succeeded in his limited holding objective more because the Egyptians did not press their attack than because of the effectiveness of the measures he took. Despite the extraordinary ease with which the Egyptian forces had crossed the canal (they suffered some 200 casualties in the operation while they expected more than fifty times that number), and despite their remarkable success in defeating the first Israeli counterattacks, the Egyptian High Command was not tempted to deviate from its original plans to take advantage of the situation. On the contrary, seeing that its strategy of seizing defensive perimeters and waiting for the Israelis to come charging against them had worked brilliantly against the first Israeli reaction, it now concentrated its effort on preparing as fast as possible a more comprehensive and stronger defense perimeter against the more comprehensive and stronger Israeli counterattack which they knew would come after the arrival of the reserves. Consequently, the Egyptian command applied itself on October 7 not so much to trying to press forward as much as possible as to gaining sufficient depth for the bridgeheads, linking them up into one continuous perimeter, pouring additional armor, troops, and artillery into them, and preparing defense positions to meet the expected Israeli onslaught.

The Syrian attack began simultaneously with the Egyptian on October 6 with a series of very low-level air strikes starting at 1:58 P.M. As the aircraft broke away, some 700 pieces of artillery let off a heavy barrage directed at the Israeli fortified points, presumed artillery sites, headquarters, tank parks, and supply points. Ten minutes after the beginning of the barrage, three motorized infantry divisions comprising 45,000 men, 1,400 APCs and 600 tanks advanced on the Israeli lines. They attacked along the entire front but concentrated their main breakthrough efforts in two sectors, one north and one south of Kuneitra. The task of the infantry divisions and their organic armor was to open gaps through which the armored reserve, consisting of two armored divisions and two independent armored brigades and poised closely behind, might pass on their way to the Jordan River and beyond. Simultaneously, a small Syrian task force of infantry and heliborne commandos began an attack on the Israeli surveillance post on Mount Hermon, which it seized with its precious electronic equipment after subduing its fifty-five defenders.

The Syrian battle plan was simply to overwhelm the Israeli defenders with sheer mass, sweep the Golan, and erupt through the Jordan River bridges before the Israeli High Command could bring the reserves to bear effectively on the battle. The defending Israeli forces, whose task was the exact reverse, included 5,000 infantry, two armored brigades with 177 tanks, and 44 field guns. Unlike the situation in the south, the Israeli forces in the Golan were alert and well-deployed in the face of the enemy attack. The forward armored units were ready on the ramps and met the attackers with effective fire. The advance strongholds, except for the one on Mount Hermon, had been reinforced in time with seasoned troops, and the artillery was arrayed in accordance with contingency plans and covered the entire front with accurate if insufficient fire. All this was not to prevent the Syrians from breaking through, but it was to prove just adequate to prevent a major disaster.

Before the war the Israeli High Command had expected a Syrian offensive to make its main breakthrough effort in the northern sector, and Northern Command had deployed its forces accordingly. In fact, the Syrians mounted a major initial assault with one division in that area, but launched an even greater initial thrust in the center and south with two divisions. The northern sector was held by the crack Seventh Armored Brigade disposing 100 tanks of the 177 available. The brigade covered the approach offering the attacker the greatest space in which to deploy into battle formation, but this approach was stopped short of the strategic road running north from Kuneitra by a chain of foothills to Mount Hermon through which the passes were narrow and in many instances steep. In front of the foothills lay a broad ditch, behind which tanks waited in ambush. The passes were covered by a well-knitted fire system from tanks, artillery, and infantry. In this sector, the Syrian thrust was contained for the first two days and nights, as one assault after another was repelled with heavy losses to the attackers. The fortified points held out and fought back despite repeated massive shelling; Syrian infantry attempting to infiltrate by night with Saggers and RPGs to get to the Israel tanks were fought off by Israeli patrols emerging from the hilltop sites. The principal problem of the defenders was attrition and exhaustion in the face of the astonishing persistence of the enemy and his seemingly inexhaustible resources.

Quite different was the situation in the sector south of Kuneitra. The much larger area was defended by the 188th Brigade with fewer than eighty tanks, which found itself under a two-pronged attack by two Syrian divisions. There were more Israeli infantry in the south than in the north, but they were spread over many more strongpoints and hillposts and were unable to compensate for the shortage of tanks which were extended to the limit of their arcs of fire. In the opening movements of the battle, the Israeli tank gunners firing from their sniping positions at long ranges knocked off many enemy tanks, but little by little the masses of advancing armor pushed the defending tanks from their forward positions. Many Israeli local commanders withdrew to ambush sites from which they continued engagements at closer ranges and scored large numbers of kills, but they could not withstand the tanks following and had lost the advantage in accuracy that they had enjoyed at longer ranges. Forced to move back, they were without supporting infantry on many occasions and were thus vulnerable to dismounted Sagger and RPG teams operating under the cover of darkness. Despite tenacious fighting and impressive kill scores, the 188th was being ground down and reduced to fragments. By midnight of the 6th, its strength had been reduced to fifteen tanks and it ceased to present a serious obstacle to the Syrian advances.

As in the case of the Egyptian front, the Israeli High Command did not have an accurate picture of the grave situation that was developing on the Syrian front. Dayan related in his memoirs that as late as midnight on October 6 the GOC Northern Command as well as his colleague from Southern Command estimated that his forces were containing all the assaults and advances of the enemy. On the strength of such optimistic reports, the General Staff had decided somewhat earlier to change plans and direct the air force to switch its main effort from suppressing the Syrian air defense system to gain more freedom of action against enemy ground forces to doing the same on the Egyptian front. Not that the southern front was deemed to be in danger either, but the situation there was viewed as less satisfactory because the enemy had crossed the canal, whereas in the north the line was thought to be holding.

While the Israeli command was changing plans, the Syrians, sticking to theirs, used the night of the 6th to regroup and pass through the depleted

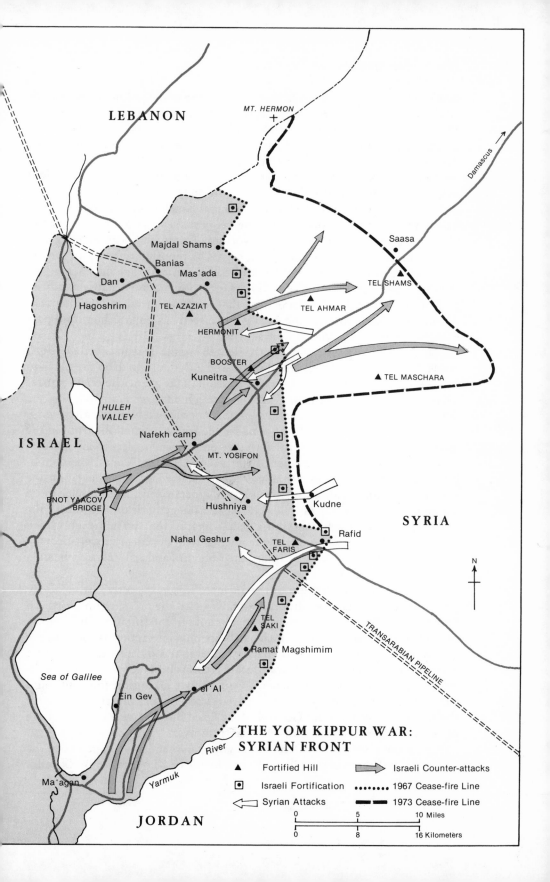

LEBANON

MT. HERMON
✝

Damascus →

Saasa ●

TEL SHAMS ▲

Majdal Shams ●

Banias ●

Dan ●

Mas'ada ●

Hagoshrim ●

TEL AHMAR ▲

TEL AZAZIAT ▲

HERMONIT ▲

TEL MASCHARA ▲

BOOSTER

Kuneitra ●

HULEH
VALLEY

ISRAEL

Nafekh camp ●

MT. YOSIFON ▲

BNOT YAACOV
BRIDGE

Hushniya ●

Kudne ●

SYRIA

Nahal Geshur ●

TEL
FARIS ▲

Rafid ●

TEL
SAKI ▲

Sea of Galilee

Ramat Magshimim ●

Ein Gev ●

el 'Al ●

TRANSARABIAN PIPELINE

N
↑

Ma'agan ●

River

THE YOM KIPPUR WAR:
SYRIAN FRONT

Yarmuk

JORDAN

▲	Fortified Hill	⇨	Israeli Counter-attacks
⊡	Israeli Fortification	······	1967 Cease-fire Line
⇦	Syrian Attacks	▬ ▬	1973 Cease-fire Line

0   5   10 Miles

0   8   16 Kilometers

ranks of their own mechanized divisions and the battered line of the Israelis 300 tanks from their armored reserve in preparation for the next assaults. These began shortly after midnight and before long they jolted the Israeli command into a full crisis and a precipitate change of plans. Dayan reports that he was awakened at 4:00 A.M. on October 7 to be told that the Syrian forces had broken through the Israeli lines in the area of Hushniya, eight miles south of Kuneitra, and were advancing on routes that offered a descent from the Golan Heights to Israel proper. Small Israeli reserve units which had hastily managed to get organized were being rushed to hold the slopes and block the enemy. Dayan hurried to Northern Command headquarters, and by the time he got there at 6:00 A.M., the GOC reported to him that the defense of the entire southern sector had collapsed, and that the enemy had advanced through the southern Golan to a point almost halfway to the Jordan River. The Israeli reserve units that were mobilized and on their way would not be able to meet the enemy and effectively engage him until past midday, six or seven critical hours away.

In order to stop the enemy for that length of time, Dayan called the GOC Israel Air Force, General Peled, directly and asked him to drop the plans to strike the Egyptian missile batteries and send all the planes he could muster against the Syrian tanks that had broken through. He urged him to ignore the Syrian missiles and send his fighter-bombers immediately, wave after wave, into continuous action until sufficient Israeli armor reached the front in the afternoon. Dayan was not entitled to give operational orders to any officers without going through the chief of staff; nevertheless, General Peled complied. He stopped the action that had already started on the canal front (the 6:45 A.M. communication to Gonen already mentioned), altered once more the plans of the air force as well as its basic strategy of dealing first with the missiles, and sent nearly everything he had against the Syrian armor. Israeli tank crews whose vehicles were intermingled with the enemy's were ordered either to leave their tanks or to close their hatches and risk taking a beating from their own pilots.

The massive intervention of the air force was very costly—some thirty planes were lost that day—but it gradually eased the pressure on Northern Command and allowed it slowly to regain hold of the situation. It began to consolidate the reserve units, which had been flung into action as soon as they arrived in dribs and drabs of companies and even troops, into more coherent and substantial formations. It transferred responsibility for the sectors to divisional commanders, with General Dan Lanner taking on the south and General Raful Eitan the north. It prepared to receive and thrust into action a third, crack division under General Musa Peled due to arrive in the evening hours. However, the crisis was still far from over.

At about 1:00 P.M. on October 7, Syrian tanks suddenly appeared at the fences around the camp of Nafekh, southwest of Kuneitra, only six miles from the Bnot Yaacov Bridge across the Jordan. The camp, which served as General Eitan's advanced headquarters, was evacuated and then recaptured, but the Syrians remained in the area and eventually found a gap through which they advanced toward the bridge. The few surviving forces of the 188th Brigade and improvised small units conducted a desperate rearguard action in which the brigade commander and his second were killed, but toward evening substantial reinforcements arrived and stopped the Syrians just three miles short of the bridge. Elsewhere in the southern sector, the Syrian advances were also checked by that time. The Syrian forward units had reached el 'Al, some seven miles from the Sea of Galilee.

The Second Stage (October 8–10): Israeli Counterattacks, Abortive and Successful

The failure of the Israeli efforts to foil the massive Egyptian crossing in the south and the Syrian breakthrough in the north and the heavy losses they suffered in the process threw the Israeli High Command off balance. In the afternoon of October 7, Defense Minister Dayan, after visiting Northern and Southern Commands, went to Operations Headquarters in Tel Aviv to discuss the next moves with Chief of Staff Elazar and his aides. General Elazar was in favor of launching new major counterattacks the next morning in the northern and southern fronts simultaneously. By that time there would be some 500 tanks in the south and 300 in the north, and more would be following after the start of the operations. Although the units were not well organized, their equipment was not complete, and they lacked sufficient artillery support, and although the air force would have to split its effort between two fronts, Elazar thought it essential to attack in order to wrest the initiative from the enemy and spoil his plans. Dayan had altogether different ideas. He was depressed about the failure of the contingency defense plans, the seeming lack of control over the situation by the central and front commands, and above all by the heavy attrition already suffered by Israel so soon after the start of the fighting. Apart from hundreds of casualties and hundreds of defenders in the strongpoints abandoned to their fate, Israel had lost some 300 tanks and 40 planes in the course of the futile efforts to stem the enemy tides in the south and the north. Dayan was afraid, even terrified, that Israel might dissipate its strength in further futile counterattacks to regain lost ground and then find itself powerless when the enemy decided to make his decisive thrust. He therefore advocated pulling back a few tens of miles in the south, to high grounds east of Bir Gafgafa and through the mountains down to Abu Rodeis, and holding that line "at all costs." In the north, he advocated pulling back and holding a do-or-die line on the slopes of the Golan descending toward Israel.

Elazar and Dayan took their disagreement to Prime Minister Meir and

her improvised "War Cabinet". The Cabinet overruled Dayan and authorized Elazar to go ahead with the counteroffensive in the south the next day if,
after visiting Southern Command, he should continue to favor it. It also
authorized the counterattack in the north, although it decided to send former
Chief of Staff General (Reserve) Chaim Barlev to the north to report on the
situation and the prospects. Both reported in favor later that night.

Elazar concerted with Southern Command a plan for a counteroffensive
which called for phased assaults by the divisions of Adan and Sharon on the
flanks of the Egyptian armies with a view to rolling up their bridgeheads and
destroying them in the process. Adan would attack the Second Army from the
Kantara area and proceed southward toward the Bitter Lakes while Sharon
held his forces in reserve in the Tassa area, some fifteen miles to the south. If
Adan's attack went well, Sharon would attack the Third Army from the area
of the Great Bitter Lake southward; if not, Sharon might use his forces to reinforce Adan's attack. Albert's forces would hold in the south and be ready to
support Sharon should he attack. Elements of a fourth division under General
Kalman Magen, which was in process of organization, would follow after
Adan's sweep to mop up. It was agreed that the attacking forces would keep
at least two miles away from the canal in their north-south advance to avoid
the Egyptian infantry missile units positioned on the ramparts, and that if the
opportunity presented itself, they would try to seize some Egyptian bridges
intact and transfer on them small forces to the west bank.

When the time for action came, all the well-laid plans went completely
awry. Adan's three brigades with some 200 tanks began advancing at 8:00
A.M. on October 8 and for a while the attack seemed to be faring well. Some
Egyptian units were overrun and there were signs of panic in the enemy ranks.
Gonen then ordered Adan to direct units of his division to broaden his front in
the vicinity of Firdan, about halfway along his projected line of advance, and
try to seize three Egyptian bridges there. When Adan prepared to execute that
operation, he discovered that his brigades had been advancing much farther
inland than planned, and as he wheeled two of them around to attack the
Firdan area, they came upon their target frontally, where the Egyptians expected them, instead of from the flank, as originally envisaged. The attack
turned into a disaster, as the entrenched Egyptian infantry let the charging
Israeli tanks go through their ranks and then turned on them murderous missiles and RPGs. The two brigades were decimated and the commander of the
lead battalion was blown off his tank and taken prisoner. Immediately after-
wards, the Egyptians started a counterattack along much of the front and
pressed Adan's remaining forces very hard.

In the meantime Gonen, unaware of the real situation, had ordered
Sharon's division to move south to reach the starting point of its attack before
dark. At 2:15 P.M. after realizing what was happening, Gonen ordered
Sharon to turn around and come north again to help stem the Egyptian coun-

terattack. Sharon did so, but his division had to battle its way through territory that had been clear when it moved south and ended up making no contribution to the planned battle. The day ended with the Israeli counterattack a total failure and the Israeli line in some cases farther to the east than it had been in the morning. More importantly, Israel lost some 150 additional tanks bringing the total lost in futile assaults on the Egyptian bridgehead to more than 350. Its air force was also held at bay and was again bled by the Egyptian missile umbrellas.

That night, at a conference of senior commanders with the chief of staff and the defense minister held at Southern Command, a new strategy was worked out for the Egyptian front. There would be no more frontal tank assaults and no more counting on chance. Careful preparations would begin for an eventual systematic effort to cross the canal on Israeli bridges, reach the rear of the Second and Third armies, and conduct a battle of movement and maneuver. In the meantime, Southern Command would conserve its forces, build up additional strength, hold the enemy and try to improve the ratio of forces by allowing the Egyptians to attack and incur losses. An exception to the temporizing approach was made the next day to allow units of Sharon's division to attempt to extricate the defenders of one of the strongpoints. This brought the total number of strongpoints evacuated to six. Of the remainder, five had been overrun at the outset and the rest were given permission to surrender and all did so on the 9th except one which held out until the end of the war.

One of the many ironies of the war was that, in the course of the extricating operation, a patrol from Sharon's forces stumbled upon a gap in the Egyptian line between the Second and Third Armies reaching right down to the water line. Had Sharon's forces attacked in that area the day before, as Sharon himself had urged, instead of spending the time shuttling back and forth, the result of the Israeli counteroffensive might have been quite different. But the discovery of the gap was not altogether wasted and was yet to prove extremely valuable when the Israeli forces got ready to move again a week later.

The counterattack in the north was planned less ambitiously than the southern counteroffensive and fared better, although not without going through some critical moments. In the night of October 7–8, it was agreed that Musa Peled's division was to drive northward on the el 'Al road toward Rafid, at the prewar border line, while Dan Lanner assembled forces and then attacked eastward from the Bnot Yaacov Bridge toward Hushniya and Rafid, converging with Peled's prong. The attacks began with first daylight with strong air support. It was slow, grinding work against strong Syrian forces of armor and artillery, but Israeli aggressiveness and superior tank gunnery were having their effect. Peled took heavy losses but kept advancing steadily, his forces being constantly replenished by convoys of troops and armored equipment moving up from Israel. Lanner's forces, with more room for maneuver, did even better once they got going. At dawn, October 9, a Syrian force of 200 tanks, infantry, and assault guns attempted a counterattack against the converging Israeli prongs, but one part of the Syrian force was thrown back to its original line and beyond, while the other was cut off by the Israeli forces and then cut down during the remainder of the day.

While the forces of Peled and Lanner were closing in on the Syrian forces in the southern sector, the Syrian High Command decided to attack in the northern sector and the area around Kuneitra, still held only by the embattled Israeli Seventh Brigade with scant reinforcements, and thus outflank the Israeli forces advancing in the south. In the course of October 8 the Seventh Brigade held firm, but during the night of October 8–9 the Syrians reorganized, brought in hundreds of additional armored reserves, and in the early hours of October 9 went to the attack after massive artillery preparation. Attempting first to capture the road junction in and around Kuneitra, they were thrown back leaving many tanks and accompanying vehicles burning. At 8:00 A.M. they launched a massive assault on the Seventh Brigade, part of which had been drawn into the struggle around Kuneitra. The Seventh wreaked havoc in the ranks of the attackers for several hours, but more Syrian tanks kept coming. At midday the brigade reached the breaking point. It had been fighting without rest for three days and three nights, it had only forty-five tanks left, and the ammunition for these was nearly exhausted; the Syrians had seized some foothills and were pressing on the weakened line. The point came when Colonel Avigdor, the brigade commander, told Divisional Commander Eitan, "This is it"; he could not longer hold back the enemy. Just then, Eitan received a message from another small unit that it had captured a ridge code-named Booster immediately northwest of Kuneitra on the flank of the attacking Syrians, and that the rear of the Syrian forces was turning around and beginning to retreat. Eitan promptly signaled Avigdor that the Syrians were breaking and urged him to hold on another few minutes. The Seventh Brigade did so, and shortly afterward the Syrian forward tanks also began retreating. The Syrian thrust in the north was definitely defeated.

Not many hours after its grueling test, the remarkable Seventh Brigade took part, along with newly arrived forces, in a concerted pressure from the north and the south with the advancing forces of Peled and Lanner. The converging Israeli forces nearly encircled the First Syrian Armored Division which was forced to withdraw in panic. By the morning of October 10 all the Syrian forces were pushed out of the entire area held by Israel before the war, except for the Mount Hermon outpost which the Israelis failed to recapture in a costly attempt. Out of the 1,400 tanks that the Syrians had committed to the Golan battle, nearly 900 remained strewn in the battlefield, along with thousands of vehicles and hundreds of guns. The Israeli forces lost more than

200 tanks of their own, but their capacity to replenish their losses with fresh forces appeared at the time greater than the Syrians' and the strategic initiative had definitely passed to their hands.

The Third Stage (October 11–14): Israeli Offensive in the North, Abortive Egyptian Offensive in the South

On October 10 the war reached a brief moment of balance. By the middle of that day the Israelis had crushed the Syrian invasion, but the Syrian army still retained much fighting power and held strong lines of defense east of the prewar Golan border. In the south the Israelis had failed to dislodge the Egyptians, but their counterattacks seemed at least to have contained the Egyptians and forced them to spread their forces over a very long and narrow bridgehead, thus restricting their ability to concentrate forces for further offensive operations. All three parties were strained and had used up vital items of ammunition and armament at a rate they could not sustain much longer. A well-concerted political initiative by the superpowers at that point might have brought an end to the fighting.

However, such initiatives as were attempted were hampered by mutual mistrust between the United States and the Soviet Union, and especially by the inability of the latter to persuade the Egyptians, who had done relatively better than either the Israelis or the Syrians, to accept a cease-fire on plausible terms (see Chapter 24 below for a discussion of the diplomacy of the war). Instead, the moment of balance became the starting point for a new phase in the war in which the superpowers became involved as suppliers and new Arab forces joined in the battle. Precisely on October 10 the Soviets began a massive operation to resupply the Syrian and Egyptian forces by air and sea while large Iraqi forces and other Arab contingents rushed to the fronts. On that day, too, Secretary of State Henry Kissinger notified Israel that the President had approved outstanding urgent requests for electronic equipment and additional planes to be delivered immediately, and that he had decided "in principle" on a policy of replacing whatever losses Israel suffered in the battlefield. These developments critically affected the decisions of the belligerents from then on and had a crucial effect on the course of the war.

Late on October 10 the Israeli High Command decided to develop the successful counterattack that had cleared the Golan into an offensive beyond the 1967 line to begin the next day. The decision was neither obvious nor easy. True, the Syrian forces had been cruelly battered and might be vulnerable to a knock-out blow. However, except for one instance of panic in the First Armored Division, which its commander brought under control by ordering artillery fire against his troops, their defeat had not turned into a rout, as the Israelis had expected. Moreover, beyond the prewar border, the

Syrians held very strong and deep lines of defense which they had fortified over a period of six years with a view to just the kind of contingency they now faced. Also, while the overall size of the Israeli forces available for attack was satisfactory, many of the units were utterly exhausted after several days and nights of exertion, and some kinds of ammunition were running short. Nevertheless, the High Command felt impelled by several reasons to go ahead with the offensive. It wanted to take Syria out of the war in order to be able to turn all its efforts against Egypt afterward; it wanted to knock Syria out before it could recover its power through the Soviet resupply and the arrival of Arab reinforcements; it wanted to discourage Jordan, which had been teetering uncomfortably on the edge of nonbelligerency, from joining the war; finally, as an insurance against a cease-fire order before the Egyptians were dealt with, the High Command wanted to seize some positions in the north to use as bargaining counters after the end of hostilities. To serve these aims, the object of the offensive was specifically defined as smashing the Syrian army and bringing Damascus within easy artillery range as quickly as possible. The estimate was that twenty-four to forty-eight hours might suffice to do so.

For a day or two before the offensive, the air force had been mounting exceptionally effective assaults on the Syrian missile batteries as well as on strategic targets in the Syrian interior. The latter were undertaken in retaliation against the Syrians' firing of FROG surface-to-surface high explosive missiles against civilian targets inside Israel and also in order to hasten Syria's exit from the war. Oil refineries, ports, power installations, airfields, the Defense Ministry buildings in Damascus, and other targets were attacked and heavily damaged in the process. When the offensive started it enjoyed unusually effective air support.

The ground assault began at 11:00 A.M. with an advance by Eitan's division in the northernmost sector, using the Hermon slopes to protect its flank and taking the shortest approach to Damascus. Two hours later, Lanner's division, reinforced by units from Peled's, attacked further south, on the Kuneitra-Damascus axis. Eitan's forces, spearheaded by the Seventh Brigade, broke through the relatively thin Syrian defenses facing them, overrunning in the process a Moroccan brigade and forcing a Syrian brigade to retreat hurriedly. Lanner's forces had a much more difficult time in their attacks on the Syrian forces opposing them from dense defense works; nevertheless, at the cost of scores of tanks, they managed to penetrate the Syrian lines by evening and to make a clean breakthrough by early morning. The Israelis had hoped and expected that when that moment was reached, the Syrian front would collapse and they would be able to destroy the disorganized retreating enemy. In fact, however, the Syrians, together with reinforcements from Arab allies that had begun to arrive, continued to offer desperate resistance. The Israeli forces had to chew the opposition bit by bit and battle their way forward slowly at considerable cost and not inconsiderable risk. Thus, on the morning of October 12, Lanner was completely surprised to discover two armored columns approaching his exposed flank from the south. These were elements of an Iraqi armored division that had been known to be on its way for several days but which had managed to reach the front undetected. Lanner, in turn, was able to surprise the Iraqis, ambush their advance units, and destroy a score of their tanks; but the Iraqis pulled back, waited for the rest of their division to join them, and then came back to attack in strength the next day. Lanner was waiting for them with a carefully worked out trap and in the ensuing battle some eighty Iraqi tanks were destroyed against none for the Israelis, but his success did not end the threat to the flank of the Israeli advance. For one thing, additional Iraqi forces were said to be on their way, and for another a crack Jordanian armored brigade had already arrived and taken position in the same area. In the face of these developments, GOC Northern Command Hofi ordered Lanner to stop the advance, protect the Israeli flank, and content himself with operations to improve his position.

Much the same story occurred on the air front. On the eve of the Israeli attack, the Israel air force, employing a combination of saturation attacks, evasion tactics, and countermeasures, had been able to knock out many Syrian missile batteries and cause the remainder to deplete their missile stocks. This made it possible for the Israeli fighter-bombers to give effective assistance to the ground forces in making their breakthroughs. On October 12 the Syrian High Command flung the Syrian air force into the battle in an effort to stem the Israeli ground and air attacks, and paid for its move with twenty-nine planes shot down by the Israeli pilots in one day. On the 13th, however, the Syrian missile batteries were once more firing missiles by the dozens, having had their supplies replenished by the Soviet airlift. Israel's air force continued to support the ground forces but paid for it with six aircraft, all shot down by missiles on October 13.

Already the day before it had become clear to the Israeli High Command that the offensive was turning into a battle of attrition instead of a swift decisive campaign. The Israeli forces could destroy more enemy units and gain some more ground, but such results were not likely to prove decisive and were not worth the cost in casualties and losses that had to be paid for them. This judgment seemed particularly valid because the arms resupply promised by the United States seemed to have bogged down in difficulties and no one knew when they would end. Consequently, the High Command decided to wind up the offensive by midday October 13. The rest of the day and the following days were spent improving the newly gained positions. Except for a successful action to recapture the Mount Hermon strongpoint a week and a half later, this ended the Israeli operations on the Syrian front and established a new defense line. That line was twenty miles from Damascus, ten miles closer than the prewar border at the northern sector of the Golan. At the southern sector the border remained the same.

Viewed in terms of the objectives that had been set for it, the Israeli offensive might be considered as less than a complete success. Some ground was gained, the outskirts of Damascus were brought within reach of the longest-range artillery, two Syrian divisions were savagely mauled, and the Syrian threat was neutralized for some time. But the Syrian forces were not destroyed, Iraqi and Jordanian forces were able to join the battle in time even though their intervention was contained, and Syria was not taken out of the war decisively enough to permit the transfer of substantial ground forces to the southern front. Nevertheless, the Israeli offensive had a crucial effect on the course of the war in a rather unanticipated manner. It forced the Egyptians to change their hitherto very successful war plan and suffer their first major setback, which in turn permitted the Israelis to go ahead with a major move of their own that changed the course of the war and its outcome.

After defeating the Israeli counterattack of October 8–9, General Ismail patiently continued to strengthen his hold on the territory he had captured on the east bank of the Suez Canal. In the following days, there were those in the General Staff and the political leadership who were urging him to strike out at targets such as the passes through the Sinai range some fifteen to twenty miles away, but he refused to get out beyond the air-defense umbrella and indulge in open warfare at which his enemy excelled, pointing to the disastrous outcome of the limited probes he made to advance southward along the Gulf of Suez. At the least, Ismail wanted to repel first the Israeli offensive that he knew was being prepared against him before considering the possibility of venturing out of his perimeter.

The Israeli offensive on the Syrian front did not permit Ismail to maintain this strategy. The Syrian army was fighting a withdrawal action in circumstances where it lacked territory to trade for time. Replacements of war materiel were being flown in by the Soviets, large Iraqi forces were on their way to assist, Jordan was sending in an armored brigade, and Morocco was adding to its contingent in the field; but to use the new materials and the allied reinforcements effectively, it was necessary to have a pause for regroupment, and the Syrians believed that the Israelis would not relent their pressure and provide such a pause as long as the southern front remained quiescent. They desperately urged their Egyptian ally to act and were supported in their pressure by the Soviets. President Sadat yielded and ordered Ismail to prepare a major attack. On October 12 Ismail proceeded to concentrate armored forces on the east side of the canal. In addition to tanks of the Second and Third Armies, he transferred most of the armored elements of the First Army deployed between the canal and Cairo, a step that was to prove fatal in days to come. On October 13 he sent the Egyptian air force to raid and reconnoiter targets east and south of the Sinai range in preparation for the attack. He did not know that on that same day Israel decided to conclude the offensive in the north and let go of the Syrians of its own accord.

The Israelis, for their part, had expected the Egyptians, after having repelled the October 8 attacks, to attempt to advance to the passes. As days passed and the Egyptian attack failed to materialize, some in the Israeli High Command began to worry that the Egyptians might "never" venture out of their bridgehead stronghold and might seek to wage an indefinite war of attrition from it. In order to avert that possibility and force a conclusion, Southern Command, which disposed by then four divisions and 700 tanks, recommended on October 11 a prompt effort to break through the Egyptian lines to the west bank of the canal and on into Egypt. The plan for the operation was presented to the General Staff and the "War Cabinet" by former Chief of Staff Barlev, who had been quietly put in charge of Southern Command over General Gonen after the fiasco of October 8. The War Cabinet found it difficult to decide on the proposal because of differences of views within its ranks and contradictory advice from the General Staff and field officers on several questions, but especially on the matter of timing. Those who doubted that the Egyptians would attack favored immediate action, while those who still expected an attack to come, including the chief of staff, wanted to meet it first and only then attempt the crossing. While the debate was going on in the War Cabinet, information arrived that the Egyptians were making preparations to transfer several hundred tanks to the east side of the canal as a prelude for a major attack. The decision was then reached to delay the crossing operation until after the Egyptian offensive.

Early on the morning of October 14, over 1,000 Egyptian guns bombarded for ninety minutes Israeli positions detected. At 6:00 A.M. the mass of troops began to move. The Egyptian operation was conceived as an advance on a front of fifteen miles. The main body of armor led in the center, followed by infantry and artillery ready for the passage of the Gidi pass, which was the prime objective. On the flanks were formations of armor, infantry in armored personnel carriers, and assault guns. In concert with the ground advance, Egyptian MIGs flew in low to shoot at Israeli positions and were followed by Libyan Mirages. Altogether, the Egyptians committed nearly 1,000 tanks while the Israelis activated 700 in one of the biggest tank battles in history.

The superior range of the Israeli tank guns and the quality of their gunnery quickly influenced the course of the battle. First one Egyptian flank force and then the other was halted. Immediate tank reserves were committed by the Egyptian commanders before 7:00 A.M. as they pressed their attacks in an effort to prevent the Israelis from breaking up the massed center which had advanced. By midday many of these were burning. In the early afternoon Israeli columns, supported by an air force able at last to attack targets removed from the missile network, cut in behind the Egyptian central force en route to the Gidi Pass, struck the mass, and scattered the remnant. At the end of a day of battle, the Egyptians had lost half the armor they had committed that day against fewer than thirty Israeli tanks destroyed.

The Fourth Stage (October 15–25): Israel's Victorious Offensive

The Israelis underestimated the enemy losses, putting them at 250 tanks or less, but even that blow was enough to restore their shaken confidence and to seal their decision to go on the offensive right away. In another irony, the American supplies, which had been held back when the going was most rough for Israel, began pouring in on the day the tide began to turn in its favor.

The Israeli crossing operation was set to start at 7:00 P.M. on October 15. The site chosen was Deversoir, just north of the Great Bitter Lake, in the center of the front. In addition to the advantage of the lake's serving to protect the flank of the crossing, this was the soft area between the two Egyptian armies discovered by General Sharon's scouts a week before. The plan called for two divisions to contain the enemy on the east bank while two others, Sharon's and Adan's, would cross over. Sharon would secure a corridor two and a half miles wide by capturing an important access road as well as a stretch of territory including what is known as "the Chinese Farm." A paratrooper brigade with armor support under Colonel Danny Matt would then cross and secure a bridgehead on the west bank. By morning two bridges would be laid. Sharon's division would cross, clear the area, and protect the bridgeheads on both sides of the canal, and then Adan's division would pass through them and advance on the west bank southward toward the Gulf of Suez in the rear of the Third Army and westward toward Cairo.

The battle began as scheduled, after preparatory bombing of the crossing area. One brigade of Sharon's division attacked from Tassa in the direction of Ismailia while another looped clockwise to attack from the south, thus creating an impression of a calculated assault on the Egyptian bridgehead. Actually these forces sought to contain the enemy while a third brigade drove down to the canal to seize the crossing area. By midnight Sharon had captured the section designated for the crossing, but the road leading to it was blocked by a monster traffic jam and the bridging equipment could not be brought to the water's edge. Hoping that the situation would be sorted out in daylight, Sharon requested and received permission to begin crossing immediately on rafts. By about 9:00 A.M. on October 16, he had transferred to the west bank Matt's brigade and some thirty tanks without encountering any opposition. By that time, however, the Egyptian forces east of the canal were pressing hard against the Israeli corridor and had managed to block completely with their drive the road on which the bridging equipment was being advanced. Undeterred, Sharon ordered Matt's brigade to leave a token force in the bridgehead and send the remainder into the Egyptian rear to raid and destroy, sow confusion in the ranks of the enemy, and disorient his reaction.

In the meantime, Adan's armored division, which had been waiting for the erection of the bridges to cross, was thrown into the battle to clear the corridor. Adan put pressure in three directions—thrusting north to eliminate the Second Army's barrier on the canal access road, south to prevent the Third Army from sending reinforcements to the crossing area, and west to the Chinese Farm to widen the corridor and link up with Sharon's forces which had been battling desperately against determined Egyptian opposition. Adan's forces fought the whole day of October 16 but were unable to dislodge with their armor the well-entrenched Egyptian infantry with their anti-tank weapons and their tank and artillery support. In the evening Southern Command decided to attack the Chinese Farm that same night with infantry, and a paratrooper brigade was flown in from the south for the purpose. The seasoned paratroopers fought fiercely and suffered heavy casualties but failed to drive off the Egyptians and had to be extricated from the battlefield next morning with the help of armor. However, while they kept the Egyptians busy in battle in one area, Adan was able to lever out the forces blocking the road and advance the equipment for pontoon bridges to the waterline. The engineers were supposed to have a bridge up by 11:00 A.M. on October 17, but after the enemy discovered the crossing site and zeroed his artillery on it, the "delivery" time had to be put off to the afternoon hours.

In the afternoon of October 17, with the corridor still insecure, the bridges not up, and Adan's division engaged in battle east of the canal, the Israeli operation was a day and a half behind schedule. Matt's small force on the west bank had been saved so far from the obvious dangers to which it was exposed by its elusive maneuvers and the failure of the enemy to read fully the Israeli intentions. However, now that the enemy, judging by his artillery attacks on the crossing point, appeared to have become aware of what was happening, there was a danger that he might be able to surround and seal the bridgehead on the west bank and thus doom the entire costly and painful Israeli enterprise to failure. To avert that danger, Sharon insistently urged Southern Command and the chief of staff to relieve him partly of the task of widening and securing the corridor and allow him to ferry all the tanks and transfer all the forces he could muster immediately to the west bank to strike preemptively and disrupt threatening enemy projects. Barlev and Elazar turned down Sharon's plea. They were unwilling to commit themselves to a massive crossing before the corridor was secured, bridges for the passage of vehicles and tanks were laid, and Adan's forces disengaged. They only authorized Sharon to ferry enough tanks across to bring the armored force to brigade strength (eighty to ninety tanks) to help Matt hold the area, and in the meantime intensified the efforts to clear and secure the access to the crossing areas and waited for the engineers to complete the first bridge.

As things turned out, Sharon's apprehensions about the bridgehead proved to have been in vain and Elazar's and Barlev's concern about the corridor well-founded. For the remainder of October 17 and part of October 18, the Egyptian High Command continued to believe that the Israeli offensive at this stage aimed at seizing part of the Egyptian bridgehead to make a corridor and it directed all its efforts to defeating that intent by converging counterattacks from the Second and Third Armies. It could not imagine that the Israelis would attempt a serious operation on the west bank while the battle was still undecided on the east bank. Although it was aware of the presence of an Israeli force west of the canal, Matt's constant movement coupled with a breakdown in Egyptian communications led it to believe that it was a matter of a small raiding operation undertaken by the enemy for morale and political reasons. By the time it learned otherwise, the Israeli forces west of the canal were already too strong and too deeply deployed to be amenable to the countermeasures it could take.

In the late afternoon of October 17, the Israeli engineers finally put up the first vehicular bridge. By 10:00 P.M. Adan's division had concluded its operations in the corridor, refueled, and was beginning to cross. By 6:00 A.M. on October 18, it had penetrated six miles on the other side and was advancing in open country westward deeper into Egypt, and southward toward the big Fayid air base. On the same day one of Sharon's brigades crossed over and joined Matt's force in a push northward, while another brigade launched a renewed attack on the Chinese Farm and finally overcame its worn-out defenders. Visiting the place which had been the object of a continuous three-day battle, Dayan described the sight as follows: "I am no novice at war or battle scenes, but I have never seen any such sight, neither in action nor in paintings nor in the most far-fetched feature film. Here was a vast field of slaughter stretching as far as the eye could see. The tanks, armored personnel carriers, the guns and the ammunition trucks crippled, overturned, burned and smoking were grim evidence of the frightful battle that had been fought here" (*Story of My Life*, p. 439).

During the night the engineers put up additional bridges. On the 19th, Magen's division moved through Adan's, headed deeper westward and then wheeled south toward the Cairo-Suez road parallel to Adan's drive. Sharon, for his part, sent another armored brigade across which wheeled northward to the west of Matt's and advanced toward the Cairo-Ismailia road. The Israeli drive to the north went through thick vegetation country which allowed the Egyptians to slow down somewhat the advancing Israeli armor. The drive to the south, however, advanced through open country, and the formidable Israeli armor—air power combination came into its own, at last, and turned the tide of the war.

The Egyptian High Command got the first inkling of the real situation that was developing during the late morning of October 18, more than forty-eight hours after Matt's task force had crossed over and when the Israelis already had several hundred tanks operating on the west bank of the canal. For two days before Soviet Prime Minister Aleksei Kosygin, on a visit to Cairo, had been trying in vain to convince President Sadat that it was time for the Arabs to work seriously for a realistic cease-fire. Kosygin had argued that the Arabs had reached the peak of their military achievements as shown by the failure of the October 14 Egyptian offensive and that henceforth the tide would turn against them, but Sadat continued to express confidence in the effectiveness of the Egyptian "meat-grinder strategy" as shown by what he took to be the futile Israeli assaults on the Egyptians positions. Kosygin had argued that the strategy was already being foiled by the Israeli crossing, but Sadat, still in the dark about what was happening, had maintained that the Israeli operation was of minor importance and was being brought under control. On the morning of October 18 Kosygin came back to the charge armed with satellite photos flown in from Moscow which showed the full extent of the Israeli intent and threat, whereupon the surprised Sadat finally authorized his Soviet guest to start movement toward a cease-fire in place while he reviewed the situation with his High Command.

By the time it was apprised of the Soviet information, the High Command was already beginning to receive reports from units and positions on the path of advance of Adan and Sharon that confirmed the gravity of the situation. It reacted by concentrating all the artillery batteries it could muster against the Israeli crossing and transferring units from the east to the west bank to meet the advancing Israelis. In addition, it hurled into action the air force, which it had hitherto used very cautiously, in a series of continuous desperate attacks against the Israeli bridge and its vicinity. As the Israeli air force sallied forth to meet the Egyptian assaults, there developed air battles reminiscent of World War II in which as many as forty to fifty planes were engaged at one time in a confined area. The attacking Egyptian formations were ravaged but kept coming back again and again. Several times the Egyptians made suicidal attempts to assault the Israeli bridges with helicopters carrying napalm bombs, flying low in the wake of fighter-bomber runs. However, despite the air attacks and the artillery bombardments, the Israelis were able to keep the first bridge in operation and to add another and yet another to it, to transfer a total of three armored divisions to the west bank and to keep them steadily supplied.

While the battle to stem the Israeli breakthrough was going on, Egypt's chief of staff, General Shazli, went on a tour of the fronts on October 19 to ascertain the situation firsthand. He returned to headquarters utterly dispirited and convinced that everything was lost. He believed that the only hope of salvaging part of the Egyptian forces was to evacuate completely the east bank immediately, before the Israelis cut off all ways of retreat. General Ismail and others concurred that the situation was critical but, fearing that a retreat under the circumstances would turn into a total rout, favored instead taking a chance on holding out in place until a cease-fire took effect. There developed an acrimonious discussion and the participants failed to reach an agreed conclusion. Finally, at 1:00 A.M. on October 20, President Sadat was asked to come to headquarters to resolve the dispute, which he did by deciding in favor of Ismail. Shazli, who was in a state of obvious psychological breakdown was relieved of his post, which was given to Chief of Operations General Abdel Ghani Gamassi. The dismissal was kept secret for reasons of morale and in gratitude to the general who had commanded the initial crossing and successes.

Even as this was happening, Secretary Kissinger was on his way to Moscow to discuss a cease-fire at the urgent invitation of Secretary General Leonid Brezhnev. The remainder of the fighting from that time on became a race against time for both Egyptians and Israelis. The Israelis stepped up their operations with a view to reaching the canal north of Ismailia and south of Suez before the cease-fire, thus cutting off and surrounding practically the entire Egyptian army. The Egyptians, for their part, fought desperately to deny the Israelis those objectives and keep open the lines of communication of the Second and Third Armies. By the time the cease-fire was due to take effect at 6:50 P.M. on October 22, neither side had achieved its objective in full. In the north, Sharon had brought the Ismailia-Cairo road under his fire but had not captured the city itself, nor had he cut off the road going north from it to Port Said. In the south, Adan and Magen had crossed and cut off the direct Suez-Cairo road and reached the outskirts of Suez city, but they had not captured the city itself nor had they cut off the indirect road to Cairo running south from it and then west. There were signs of breakdown of organized resistance, especially in the sector of the Third Army where many prisoners were taken, but many units continued to fight on effectively.

The fighting did not stop on schedule but went on for two additional days, during which Sharon consolidated and firmed up his position while Adan and Magen achieved much more. Magen made a broad sweep deep behind Suez and cut off the southern route to Cairo at the small port of Adabiya on the Gulf of Suez. Adan reached the waterline south of Suez city, seized its western suburbs, and attempted to storm the city itself. The latter effort, undertaken for purely prestige reasons, proved to be a costly failure. But Adan and Magen succeeded in closing a solid double ring around the Third Army or what remained of it—20,000 men and 300 tanks.

In the meantime, things had remained fairly quiet on the Syrian front since October 15. On that day the Jordanian armored brigade in ostensible coordination with Iraqi forces mounted an assault on the Israeli flank, which was repelled with heavy losses to the attackers. In the course of the following week the Syrians occupied themselves with building a new line of defense around Damascus and mustering forces for a possible counteroffensive. However, on October 21–22 it was the Israelis who attacked again in the Mount Hermon area. They finally recaptured the surveillance point they had lost in the first days of the war and went on to capture positions the Syrians had always held to the east of it. On October 23 the Syrians agreed to cease-fire and did—at least for a while.

Thus ended the fifth Israeli-Arab war in a quarter of a century. In terms of continuity of action and ratio of forces to battlespace, the war of October 1973 was one of the most intensely fought contests in history. The number of tanks engaged in the armored battles in Sinai and the Golan was exceeded only by the World War II battle of the Kursk salient between the Germans and the Russians. The materiel destroyed was also enormous. Egypt and Syria lost more than 2,000 tanks in roughly equal shares, while Israel lost more than 800. In addition, the Arab side lost some 500 aircraft, two-thirds by Egypt and one-third by Syria, as against 114 for Israel. All but 20 of the Israeli aircraft were lost to Arab antiaircraft defenses, whereas some 400 of the Arab planes were shot down in the air. The losses in personnel were heavy, but perhaps not as high as the losses in equipment might suggest. Moreover, their relative impact was much heavier on Israel than on its enemies. Israel suffered 2,552 dead and over 3,000 wounded, while Egypt suffered an estimated 7,700 killed and between two and three times that many wounded. Syria lost 3,500 killed and a similar proportion of wounded as Egypt's. Israel held some 9,000 prisoners of war, of whom more than 8,000 were Egyptians, while Egypt took about 250 Israeli prisoners and Syria 70–100.

A Note on the War at Sea

As in previous Arab-Israeli clashes, naval warfare played a very marginal role in the Yom Kippur War. Nevertheless, naval operations were of particular interest on this occasion because they involved the first battles in history between missile boats and the first test under fire of the capabilities of these swift attack ships and of tactics in their effective use.

The mission of the Israeli navy is to protect the Israeli coast and keep shipping lanes open. But although the enemy presented no serious threat in these areas, with one exception to be noted below, Israeli missile boat units simply thrust themselves into Egyptian and Syrian naval bases seeking—and finding—opportunities to do battle with enemy missile vessels. Thus, on the night of October 6–7 a formation of five Israeli boats closed in on the Syrian port of Latakia. After sinking an enemy torpedo boat and minesweeper on its way, it came up against three Soviet-built missile boats. Both sides fired volleys, and although the Styx rocket of the Syrian boats has a much longer range than the Gabriel of the Israeli boats, the battle ended within a half an hour with all three Syrian boats sunk and no casualties for the Israelis. That same night a second force of missile boats approached Port Said, destroyed one Egyptian missile ship and chased two others into the port. The following night six Israeli missile boats shelled Egyptian coastal installations. Challenged by four Egyptian attack vessels, they sank three of them. For the remainder of the war the Israeli vessels harassed Syrian and Egyptian coastal installations, including wharves, oil tank farms, coastal batteries, and even air strips with almost complete impunity as the enemy naval forces increasingly chose to avoid battle. Altogether, the Israeli navy destroyed nineteen Arab vessels including ten missile boats, without suffering any loss.

At the outset of the war, Egypt blockaded the Strait of Bab el Mandeb, forming the southern gate of the Red Sea, against Israeli shipping. The Israeli navy, lacking the range to respond directly, reacted by launching a counter-blockade of Egyptian Red Sea ports. Thus, while the Egyptians "proved" that Israeli control of Sharm el Sheikh did not ensure Israeli free navigation to Eilat, the Israelis "proved" that if their vessels were barred at Bab el Mandeb, they could bar Egyptian vessels from the Gulf of Suez and the Red Sea in the vicinity of Sharm el Sheikh.

The Aftermath: The War and Israel's Future Security

The Yom Kippur War demonstrated in the most telling manner both the weakness and strength of Israel's defense endeavor in the years preceding the hostilities. The armed clash revealed many hitherto unsuspected defects of doctrine and practice in Israel's defense preparations which proved to be almost fatal, and it also demonstrated superlative qualities of tenacity, skill, and improvisation under fire on the part of Tzahal which were impressive in proportion to the distance that it had to traverse to go from near-defeat to near-victory. Withal, Tzahal's recovery canceled the consequences of the initial flaws only in the short run. In the longer run, the Yom Kippur War changed fundamentally Israel's security posture and created formidable new challenges which Israel could hope to meet only with massive increases in assistance from the United States.

As the previous description has shown the war revealed many flaws in Israel's defense preparation at the strategic, operational, and tactical levels. Apart from the defects that caused Israel to be caught by surprise by the very outbreak of the war, there was much amiss behind the fact that the Israeli armor was so heavily punished by the enemy's antitank missiles. The relevant Israeli military authorities knew the characteristics of those weapons, were aware that the enemy possessed them in large quantities, and had even devised ways to combat them; but somehow the practical conclusions of this information in terms of the composition of forces and battlefield tactics were not followed up as the Israeli tanks again and again charged the Egyptian infantry in gallant but futile repetition of the 1967 methods.

On the operational level the Israelis failed to anticipate the mass of the initial enemy assaults and their main directions even where, as in the Golan, they were ostensibly prepared to meet them, and consequently did not deploy sufficient forces in the right places. In the south they took a long time to recognize that the assault was taking place along the entire front and they never really guessed the enemy's "meat-grinder" battleplan.

Much more serious was the failure to anticipate the manner in which the enemy made use of his air-defense system in conjunction with the deployment of his ground forces to limit the effectiveness of Israel's air retort. The Israeli air force had developed methods and tactics to suppress the missile defenses and plans to do so, but the plans envisaged a total concentration of effort on the task which was denied to it by the necessity to divert forces to block the enemy's advance on the ground. The air force was eventually able to destroy piecemeal most of the Egyptian missile sites in the battlezone and to suppress many of the Syrian batteries, but the dislocation of its original plans denied to it the opportunity to play a crucial role in the ground battle as planned, in addition to exposing it to very heavy, almost crippling losses.

The most crucial failure, however, consisted, of course, of the structural, conceptual, and attitudinal flaws that allowed the Arabs to gain strategic surprise. As a result the Arabs were able to fight in accordance with their plans, at least in the crucial initial stages, while forcing Israel to fight an improvised and confused war from beginning to end. The process of mobilization and deployment of the reserves was shortened and confused, so that units went to war without their full planned kit, and forces down to the crew of a tank or a gun were hastily and haphazardly combined and thrown piecemeal into battle. Operations were not carried out as planned—from the containment action to the use of the air force for blocking the enemy instead of concentrating first on defense suppression, and from the counterattacks to the crossing of the canal and the subsequent operations. Strategic surprise also caused the war to be prolonged, drew down the stocks of ammunition and equipment, gave time to additional Arab forces to join the battle, and made it necessary and possible for the Soviet Union and then the United States to intervene as arms suppliers. That intervention, in turn, enabled the superpowers to determine the timing for the end of the hostilities so that it should occur before Israel could consummate the victory that came within its reach and had further crucial political effects.

In addition to determining the end of the war, the intervention of the superpowers, particularly of the United States, triggered a resort by the Arab states to the "oil weapon." In the immediate military sense the oil weapon had no effect, but from the moment the fighting ended it began to have an immense bearing on Israel's postwar political-strategic position and its long-term security concerns. These implications are explored fully in the part of this book dealing with diplomacy, but two points need to be mentioned here. One is that the Yom Kippur War ended in a manner that offered improved chances for a settlement of the Arab-Israeli conflict but at the same time contained predictably the seeds of another war if these chances did not materialize. The other point is that in providing against the possibility of another war, Israel had to contend with a potential comprehensive Arab coalition that commanded virtually unlimited financial resources derived from oil revenues, which were quadrupled as an incidental result of the resort to the oil weapon.

The overall military and diplomatic consequences of the Yom Kippur War confronted Israel with a whole array of problems concerning future security. In the very short run Israel needed to correct the mistakes and short-comings in relation to standard military norms revealed by the war and to draw the appropriate lessons regarding fighting doctrines, tactics, performance, optimal use of weapons, and so on. This the armed forces proceeded to do immediately. For the long run Israel needed to assess its political-strategic standing, define anew the specific political ends to be pursued, and devise a proper military strategy to serve those ends. However, since that task relates to the area where the political and military dimensions meet, and because the international situation and Israel's internal politics were rendered highly fluid by the war, Israel was unable to address the problem comprehensively and thoroughly even two years after the war. Instead, it tacitly adopted an operational assumption to the effect that there was to be a prolonged period of confrontation and negotiations, during which the strategic objective was to consist of developing and maintaining a sufficient military capacity to discourage the Arabs from turning away lightly from negotiations to war and of defeating them quickly if they chose to resort to battle—a rather loose and problematic conception, but the best that could be devised under the circumstances.

In view of the experience of the war and the postwar circumstances, the strategy adopted could be translated into three broad specific questions: How to close the gap which the Arabs exploited so well between Israel's standing and mobilizable strengths? How to prevent a possible repetition of long and costly warfare and restore the possibility of open operations and rapid decision right from the outset of hostilities? How to keep a favorable relation of forces in the face of plausible Arab war coalitions endowed with vastly superior resources? Two years after the war Israel was still grappling with aspects of these questions, but the main elements of the responses it essayed were already apparent and included the following:

1. Improvement of the means of intelligence-gathering and diversification of the intelligence evaluation apparatus, according to recommendations of the Agranat Inquiry Commission.

2. Striving to establish through the negotiations for disengagement of forces that took place immediately after the war a variety of tripwire and early warning arrangements, such as limited forces zones, UN buffer areas, and electronic monitoring stations with American participation.

3. Striving to endow the standing forces with a capacity to launch a substantial preemptive strike by themselves, without awaiting the reserves, if necessary, and with the means to undertake prompt counteroffensive operations even while containing an enemy first strike, if he should succeed again in gaining surprise.

4. Expanding the total size of the military establishment to the maximum limit permitted by the size of the manpower pool. Thus, by tightening military service regulations, drawing upon previously exempt categories, and reordering functions and assignments to permit effective use of low qualification manpower in secondary tasks, Israel was able to increase the total size of its mobilizable forces to 600,000 men and women.

5. Raising the level of personnel skills, reducing the differential between second- and first-line formations, and improving command and control in the context of reorganizing the forces in army corps formations.

6. Above all, in order to endow the standing forces with a first strike and counteroffensive capacity and to counter the superior resources of plausible Arab coalitions, striving to extend to the utmost limit the qualitative superiority of the weapons and equipment of all the armed forces. This endeavor is partly reflected in efforts to acquire from the United States and develop locally the finest combat aircraft, the most advanced ECM (electronic countermeasure) equipment, missiles fired from ground and sea platforms, standoff weapons launched from aircraft outside the range of air defense, guided bombs and drones directed from the air or ground launchers, ballistic missiles and varieties of antitank missiles, and so on.

7. Along with all these structural or organizational aspects of strategy, a renewed emphasis on the pre-1967 operational principle of preemption, leaving the notion of second strike only for the case of unwilling forfeiture of first strike to the enemy.

Of course, a strategy of preemption involves an extremely delicate problem of decision for the Israeli leadership, and if the decision is not seen to be warranted, it could entail very severe international repercussions. The problem may not be so severe in four types of situation: (1) where Egypt and Syria effect menacing deployments while infringing on agreements to which they are parties; (2) where they deploy menacingly in Jordanian or Lebanese territory; (3) where large forces of Arab countries of the "second circle" and beyond—such as Iraq, Saudi Arabia, Libya, or Algeria—direct large forces to "front-line" countries; and (4) where Israel obtains specific intelligence of Arab intent to attack, which it could share at least with the United States. All, except perhaps the last situation, can still be fraught with difficulties. Moreover, there is a whole range of conceivable situations where even that much of a case for preemption cannot be made to the outside world and specifically to the United States. However, after the costly Yom Kippur experience it is safe to predict that Israel's decision makers will be most unlikely willingly to allow the enemy to strike first again.

To pursue its postwar defense effort Israel has had to strain its economic resources to the utmost. Direct and indirect defense expenditures in 1974 and 1975 amounted to 36 percent of GNP, nearly double the prewar level. Even so, Israel has had to depend to a decisive extent on increased American assistance. In the first three years after the Six Day War, for instance, American military assistance to Israel averaged about $40 million a year—a very small proportion of its total defense expenditures. In the next three years, it averaged about $400 million—close to 28 percent of total defense expenditures. In 1974–75 the American contribution averaged $1.5 billion—fully 42 percent of Israel's defense spending. In addition, the United States had been virtually the only supply source for the high technology sophisticated weapons that have become the mainstay of Israel's postwar strategy. But the United States' willingness to provide that kind of help has been bound with an evolving conception of shared American-Israeli interests. Consequently, continuation of that aid, and therefore of Israel's ability to pursue its defense strategy, will inevitably be limited by the ability of the two countries to continue to accommodate each other in the face of changing circumstances.

18
The Defense Effort
and the Israeli Polity

In the field of national defense Israel overcame challenge after formidable challenge to secure its existence and to preserve a position from which to insure its future. No outside observer, unless he is blinded by hostility to Israel, can fail to be deeply impressed by the indomitable spirit, the immense ingenuity, and the raw physical courage that made these achievements possible, especially if he recalls the background of the men and women responsible for them. These, one is prone to forget, are the collected fragments of a people that had not fought as a nation for some eighteen hundred years; that had been for most of these years the object of oppression and violence in almost all parts of the world; and that had made the enduring of persecution almost a vocation, justified by a boundless sense of guilt and hallowed as *kiddush hashshem* (Sanctification of the Holy Name).

However, no outside observer, unless he is indifferent to democratic and humanistic values, can refrain from wondering about the possible costs of Israel's epic achievements. With so much of its effort devoted to defense, with so many of its people engaged in the armed forces, and with war so much at the center of its life, has Israel, wittingly or unwittingly, been turning into a militaristic nation? Are its democratic institutions and civil liberties in danger? Are the military getting to shape its politics? Has military power been perverting its values and aspirations? Has its relentless quest for security turned, as Hobbes might have predicted, into a ceaseless striving to accumulate power after power? These would be very difficult questions to address even if one had unlimited scope to pursue them; but, having talked so much about Israel's defense effort, we cannot avoid an attempt to face them, however briefly.

The discussion here will not be concerned directly with the question whether or not Israel might have followed alternative foreign policy courses that might have had different results. We leave this to our subsequent discussion of Israel's options in the face of the international politics affecting it. Our concern here will be with events and effects as they have been, regardless of whether they were "inevitable." I shall only distinguish in this examination among the period up to 1967, the period from 1967 to 1973, and the short time since October 1973 because of the far-reaching impact that the Six Day War and the Yom Kippur War had on Israel's defense posture and activities.

On the question of civil liberties, we find that most of the Arab minority of Israel were subjected for many years after 1948 to more or less stringent restrictions under military government, on the grounds that its members were security risks. The Arabs never lacked very active and vocal champions among some of the Israeli parties who, together with others who opposed military government because they suspected Mapai of using it to extort Arab votes for itself, exerted constant pressure for the abolition of these restrictions, and eventually succeeded in achieving their aim. But the fact remains that nervousness about defense, real or feigned, had led the Israeli government to impose a wholesale curtailment of liberties on a large proportion of the population for fifteen years after the end of the 1948 war. During that period, large parcels of Arab land were sometimes seized on grounds of security, and their owners were given either substitute land or monetary compensation, payments that were more or less arbitrarily determined. This procedure became less frequent with time and virtually ceased long before the abolition of military rule in 1963. However, the spirit underlying it found renewed expression in the refusal of the government to allow the inhabitants of two Arab villages, Bir'am and Ikrit, who were evacuated during the 1948 war, to return to their homes in 1973 on allegedly persisting security grounds, even though they had been explicitly promised when evacuated that they would be allowed to return after the fighting. Here, too, many Israelis adopted the villagers' cause, much of the press criticized the government's decision, and some members of the Cabinet leaked word that they had voted against it, but the decision has so far stood, serving as a reminder that relapses into a harsh and niggardly attitude, justified by its holders on farfetched considerations of security, are still possible.

The overly cautious attitude displayed by the civil government in the Bir'am and Ikrit case contrasts sharply with the approach pursued by the military authorities in the occupied areas. Under the leadership of Moshe Dayan, these authorities have pursued the imaginative Open Bridges policy, even in the face of the real and demonstrated danger of its abuse by guerrilla terrorists. Moreover, reliable inquiries have shown that the Emergency Regulations in effect in the areas have generally been applied in a spirit of moderation, and that the authorities have actively combatted abuses and lapses that took place in the ramified apparatus enforcing them. The one major exception to the more than fair record of the Israeli occupation, assessed in terms of the Geneva Convention on the rules of war applicable there, has been the seizure of land for the purpose of establishing semimilitary settlements or other projects connected with defense. The decisions in all instances were made by the Israeli government, not by the military authorities, but the Defense Ministry under Dayan has usually pressed for them.

For the Jewish population of Israel the only important restriction on civil liberties on security grounds has been censorship of the press and of private correspondence on matters relating to defense. The necessity for censorship has not been questioned by the public and its representatives in the Knesset, but the press has often charged that the law has been applied in an overly restrictive way that infringed on the public's right to know. Legal procedures for appeal do exist, of course, but recourse to them is impractical for a working press except in rare, important instances. For routine reporting on matters relating to security that might be barred by the censor, Israeli newspapers have resorted to citing foreign sources and have sometimes leaked the material to foreign media first, in order to be able afterward to report the story as reported abroad.

Opposition spokesmen have sometimes complained that defense has been interpreted too broadly, so as to protect the government against disclosures and political attacks that might damage its position. However, while it is possible to think of a few instances of delayed disclosure to which this charge might apply, there is no evidence that such practice has been frequent or widespread. Because all governments in Israel have been precariously balanced coalitions of several parties and factions, collusion to abuse censorship for political purposes is bound to be very difficult, if not impossible. During the first few days of the Yom Kippur War, the media were fed highly misleading information by the military spokesmen, but this was due to a combination of communications breakdown, confusion, and wishful thinking rather than to manipulation of information for devious political purposes. Nevertheless, as long as censorship exists, it is susceptible to misuse under circumstances that cannot be foreseen.

On the question of the relationship between the civilian and the military, Israel's record has so far been clean of intrusion of the military into politics in any form remotely resembling the ventures of the armed forces into the politics of Turkey in recent years or of France in the late 1950s, not to speak of the multitude of Third World countries where the military have openly assumed power. No government of Israel has been toppled by military pressure open or discreet, and no decision, as far as is known, has been forced upon the government by the army. An important test was the withdrawal from Sinai and the Gaza Strip after the 1956 campaign. Public opinion generally, including the bulk of the armed forces, was known to dislike it intensely; nevertheless, the army heeded the government's decision to pull back without as much as one officer's publicly voicing his discontent.

An even more crucial test occurred in May 1967, at the height of the crisis that led to the Six Day War. After Egypt closed the Strait of Tiran and massed its forces in Sinai, opinion among Israel's population and among its totally mobilized forces was nearly unanimous as to the necessity of war and was extremely apprehensive about the apparent hesitation of the government to give the order. At a critical moment in the government's deliberations, Prime Minister and Minister of Defense Levi Eshkol held a meeting with a large number of senior army officers to hear their views on the military situation and to report to them the evenly divided position of the Cabinet. In the course of the meeting, one officer after another urged immediate military action, and, in the discussion that followed, harsh words were exchanged between Eshkol and his interlocutors. Yet, the day after this meeting, which came as close as possible to the exertion of pressure by the military, Eshkol felt free to change his own position in the direction opposite to the one that had been urged on him—from supporting immediate military action to joining those members of his government who had been in favor of further postponement of military action. A few days later Eshkol was forced to give up his defense portfolio, which was then assigned to Dayan, but this decision was made by Eshkol's own party leaders who were as anxious as everyone else in the country about his abilities as wartime chief, without any specific connection to the meeting with the military. Finally, in the morning of October 6, 1973, when it had become certain that Egypt and Syria were going to attack that day, Prime Minister Meir felt completely free to turn down the request of the chief of staff to launch a preemptive strike.

Not only have Israel's politics been free from gross intrusion by the military, but the military has been generally kept free from gross political intrusion since the early days of statehood. This is no mean achievement if we recall that at the outset of the 1948 war, there were four different armed groups, three of which were distinctly associated with particular political groups. The Haganah was essentially nonpartisan, but the Palmach—though an arm of the Haganah—was closely identified with the extreme left-wing parties, while the Irgun and Lechi were avowedly and openly dissident armed political groups. David Ben Gurion availed himself of various opportunities to dissolve the Irgun and Lechi by force at the risk of civil war, and pressed for the gradual, peaceful merger of the Palmach into the unified single Defense Army of Israel. For as long as he remained minister of defense, Ben Gurion was accused of injecting politics into the army by excluding from the highest army posts men with a "dissident" or Palmach past; actually, he was inclined for some time to discriminate against such people *as a type,* which included Haganah men as well, in favor of people with a background of regular service in the British army. This was part of his effort to ensure the molding of Israel's Defense Forces into a national army according to established norms, after having eliminated the danger of private armies. The more that goal seemed to be secured, the more he allowed proven talent to become the decisive criterion for assigning the highest command positions.

The same Ben Gurion who applied himself with fanatical single-mindedness to depoliticizing and unifying the armed forces unwittingly nurtured a confusion of authority within the defense establishment and between it and other bodies of the state. The confusion was partly due to the fact that Ben Gurion combined the offices of defense minister and prime minister and held both from the beginning of statehood and for a very long time thereafter. But it was also due to a tendency on his part, which he imparted to the defense establishment as a whole, to circumvent constitutional niceties to get things done. Thus, under his aegis the upper echelons of the Defense Ministry and Tzahal got into the habit of initiating projects that trespassed on the boundaries of other ministries and of pursuing them a long way before seeking the necessary authorization. For example, representatives of the Defense Ministry and the General Staff initiated the contacts and discussions with France that led eventually to Israel's participation in the 1956 war, bypassing the Foreign Ministry entirely; only at the last moment did Ben Gurion submit the intervention project to the Cabinet for approval. The same happened with the project of building Israel's nuclear reactor at Dimona with French cooperation, with the conclusion of several arms deals with West Germany, and with other important undertakings. The implications of the problem remained suppressed during Ben Gurion's tenure of office, but they were to dog Israel for all the years following his retirement.

It is partly because of this problem that Israel has been unable to have a "routine" defense minister ever since Ben Gurion retired. Pinchas Lavon was compelled to resign after a short tenure because of a conflict with the top echelons of his ministry and the General Staff. The exact details of what developed into one of the most serious internal political crises that Israel has faced are not so important in this context as is their general background of constant tension between a forceful defense minister who was determined to assert his authority and an establishment that felt strong enough to resist him. Ben Gurion's second successor as minister of defense, Eshkol, was forced to resign at a time of crisis partly for the opposite reason: for being suspected by his colleagues in the government and in his own party of having yielded entirely to the defense and military chiefs. His reports on the military situation and the policies he recommended on that basis were thought to be a mere echo of the evaluations of the General Staff, and did not command the confidence of politicians who feared that they might be slanted by the General Staff's professional pride and bias for action. Dayan, the fourth minister of defense, was apparently able to achieve both the mastery of the defense establishment that had eluded Lavon and the credibility with the government that had eluded Eshkol, but it is significant that it took a former chief of staff and a national hero to accomplish this.

Moreover, even if we consider Dayan to have been a "civilian" when he assumed the defense portfolio, his tenure was a mixed blessing from the point of view of control of the defense establishment by civilian authorities. On the one hand, partly because Dayan was a member of an opposition party which subsequently became a distinct faction inside the Labor Party, and partly because he had several personal rivals in the Labor Party, there was an enhancement of practices aiming at keeping a close watch on the activities of the defense establishment. For example, the chief of staff was called to appear before the Foreign Affairs and Defense Committee of the Knesset and its Finance Committee more regularly and frequently than ever before; he reported more often to the government as a whole, and sought the approval of the Prime Minister before initiating any significant military action; the state controller continually investigated various aspects of the work of the defense establishment; and so on. On the other hand, because of Dayan's powerful standing in the country and the respect bordering on awe that he commanded in the armed forces and the defense establishment until the Yom Kippur War, his authority in defense matters was rarely questioned. It was almost amusing, for example, to watch the all-powerful minister of finance mercilessly apply the axe to the budgetary requests of all other ministries, and then turn to the Defense Ministry and plead with it to please trim its own budget as much as it thought fit. Thus, although the defense establishment under Dayan was formally subject to greater civilian control than ever before, it was in fact able to have its way more than ever, leaving the question of effective routine civilian control still untested. It is interesting to note that in the wake of the Yom Kippur War Dayan, too, was eventually compelled to resign. He was forced out of office by public pressure in the same way that Eshkol had been, but the public outrage this time was rooted in the muddled definition of the division of responsibility between the office of defense minister and chief of staff.

Another development that gives one pause has been the influx of retired senior military officers into politics and other high public and semipublic posts, especially since 1967. The phenomenon itself is not unusual in countries with the best-established traditions of civilian supremacy, as witness Eisenhower, Grant, George Washington, the Duke of Wellington, and the directories of corporations in the United States and Britain. It is not new in Israel itself, where in the 1950s Moshe Dayan went from being chief of staff to becoming minister of agriculture, Moshe Carmel and Yigal Allon took up various ministries after distinguished military careers, and other generals went on to substantial public and private managerial posts. However, several factors combine to distinguish Israel's situation from that of other countries and the period after 1967 from the period before it, with possibly important consequences.

One important difference between Israel and the United States or Britain derives from the facts that Israel is a small country, that the enrollment of nearly all its able-bodied population in the active or reserve services all the time has necessitated a relatively very large officer corps, that the continuous state of confrontation and the frequent wars have made promotion particularly rapid, and that senior officers have been retired at an extraordinarily young age. All this has meant that the ratio of senior officers becoming available every year to senior positions opening up in the public and private sectors has been much higher than in the United States or Britain, and that the accumulation of military men in senior posts over the years has been relatively much more dense. What this may imply will be considered presently; I need only underscore for the moment that quick comparisons with other countries can be misleading.

The period after 1967 is distinguished from the one that preceded it first of all in terms of the larger number of senior military men gravitating into politics at the same time. This was due partly to the emergence of many generals from anonymity to glory as a result of the Six Day War and the subsequent fighting, partly to the desire of Dayan's rivals in his own party to build up counterweights to his influence, and partly to the eagerness of opposition parties to do the same in relation to Dayan's party as a whole. This sudden expansion of supply and demand for military heroes was also associated with an important change in the heroes' character. With the possible exception of Dayan, the generals who went into politics in the 1950s had actually been politically active people before they engaged in military affairs, and they continued to be politically active when in service before and during the War of Independence. This was still the time before Ben Gurion's "depoliticizing" of the armed forces. Military achievement may have given a fillip to their political advancement, but they would probably have achieved the same political standing over a longer period of time without it. The generals who gravitated into politics after 1967, on the other hand, were strictly career officers whose claim to political standing rested entirely on their military rank and fame. Indeed, the political background of most of these generals was so irrelevant that different parties often sought to draw the same man, and the same man almost impartially weighed joining this or that party. With respect to officers who went into senior management posts rather than politics, the difference after 1967 is that many of the establishments to which they went, be they industrial, financial, construction corporations, or scientific and technological institutes, were by then heavily involved directly or indirectly in defense activities and contracts. This was the result of the immense increase in the amounts spent on defense generally, and of Israel's massive effort to develop its own military industries in particular.

Israeli opinion has been keenly aware of the phenomenon of the increasing prominence of retired military men in public and semipublic life, but the discussion in the media and in political forums has tended to concentrate almost exclusively on the entry of such men into politics and to be somewhat distorted by a polarized perception of the issue. Apologists have resorted to reassuring analogies from the United States without sufficient regard to the crucial differences pointed out above, while critics have evoked exaggerated dangers of a piecemeal take over of the government by the military, disregarding the already patent evidence that, once out of the army and into politics, the senior officers do not necessarily remain solidary but tend to develop rival interests, express diverse views, and incidentally to lose much of their aura in the rough-and-tumble of political warfare. The debate has thus missed the real issue, which goes beyond the sphere of politics and which has to do not just with the military out of the army, but also with the network of relations between the military outside the army and those inside it.

Former military men in politics may not necessarily feel solidarity among themselves, but they do retain connections with colleagues still in the armed forces that may allow them to exert active or passive noxious influences. The prospect of former generals conniving with active officers to use the armed forces under their command to effect a takeover of the government is so remote as not to warrant serious discussion. However, the possibility exists of retired officers' influencing active ones to bend the use of military force in the course of legitimate duty in ways designed to serve particular political convictions that they share. This, though still remote, is not so improbable. Less improbable still is the possibility that active generals on the verge of retirement, in an effort to emulate successful retired colleagues, should of their own accord use their office in ways intended to establish for themselves credit with prospective political patrons. This kind of development appears all the more plausible since there have been actual instances of senior officers still in service taking part in political demonstrations of a kind that would have been unthinkable before 1967.

But the problem extends much beyond the immediate political sphere. The extensive defense effort in which the United States became engaged since the beginning of the Cold War led President Eisenhower, a military man himself, to warn in his farewell address in 1960 against the growth of a "military-industrial complex" with a vested interest in the United States' pursuing courses that require ever higher levels of military preparedness. In Israel, that danger became relevant after 1967 when the government multiplied defense outlays and intensified efforts to develop military industries, and is magnified by the fact that military men, some retired, some in active service, are increasingly found in the top posts in all the relevant establishments—military and industrial as well as scientific-technological and political. These men, sufficiently numerous to be found in nearly all relevant spheres in Israel but few enough to all know one another personally, sharing a substantial common background and conditioned to view defense in the simple terms of "the more the better," may constitute much sooner for Israel the kind of danger Eisenhower feared for the United States. Sometime in 1973, for example, Minister of Trade and Industry and former Chief of Staff Chaim Barlev, speaking apparently in a combination of his former and current capacities, declared that Israel's armed forces were engaged in a long-term program to build up their strength, and that that program was going to proceed as planned *regardless of any political developments*. Even if that declaration was inadvertently imprecise, it is a significant illustration of the kind of danger that might develop and spread.

The question of the impact of the defense effort on the character of the emerging Israeli nation is obviously much more complex than the topics just touched upon, and is more apt to be variously interpreted. One may perhaps confine the limits of possible controversy by drawing an artificial but useful distinction between the impact of defense on the process of nation-building as such and its influence on the moral orientation of the nation. In the first respect, there can be no doubt that the defense challenge and the Israeli response made an enormous contribution to the consolidation of the Israeli nation and its political system. If the Irgun surrendered its private army without serious struggle in 1948, if a Kulturkampf has not broken out between secularists and the religious all these years, if the political warfare of the parties at its height was not extended into open social conflict, and if the antagonism among the various communities, particularly the Oriental and the European, was not inflamed and made the basis of bitter "ethnic" hostilities, thanks are due largely to the general awareness that the enemy was at the gates and that it was imperative to maintain unity in order to confront him.

In a more positive vein, the armed forces have acted as a highly effective melting pot and have assumed educative and social functions not normally undertaken by armies elsewhere. Military service brought together Sefaradim and Ashkenazim, sabras and new immigrants, religious and secularists, men and women, into a proximity that is not easily reached outside the confines of the army. It gave them a chance to know one another and to overcome some of their prejudices and stereotyped ideas; it allowed them to learn and speak the same language and to share a certain amount of common knowledge of the country, its history, its terrain, and its towns and cities beyond the confines of their particular areas of residence. It helped them to acquire some common ethics, values, folklore, habits, and manners and to achieve a common understanding of the nation's condition and its aims. The armed forces addressed themselves specifically to the problem of the intercommunal gap and initiated successful large-scale programs to promote the advancement of Orientals in military as well as civilian careers. Before the establishment of the state, the commitment to the national cause was built up through many years of indoctrination and practical work by the various Zionist groups throughout the world and by their movements in Palestine itself. Since then, the army has become the most important instrument for fulfilling that function among the masses of immigrants who had had no previous acquaintance with Zionism. Although the army's work could not equal that of the

Zionist groups in intensity and thoroughness, it has the advantage of embracing all the population in the prime of life and emphasizing a national rather than a partisan or sectarian perspective.

With regard to the impact of the defense effort on the moral orientation of Israelis, the crucial question is whether that effort has turned or is turning Israel into a militaristic nation. If we take militarism to mean the extension of the outlook conventional among army people to the whole population and the projection of attitudes and dispositions typical of a war situation to all times, then the answer is a qualified yes until 1967, less qualified since. If we understand by militarism something akin to what Germany is reputed to have lived and practiced for long periods of its history and especially in the first half of the present century, then the answer is a slightly qualified no until 1967, more qualified since.

One of the crucial facts about Israel is that it has had no tradition of a military establishment separate from the rest of society. In Yishuv days and since the establishment of the state, the bulk of the armed forces has consisted of masses of citizens clustered around a relatively small core of permanent officers. The absence of a clear-cut separation between civilian and military and the lack of a specialized professional army have prevented the emergence of a caste-like military group with a distinct way of life, a particular collective consciousness, and its own way of looking at things. An attentive tourist can observe that Israel's men in uniform of all ranks outside their barracks look and act less military than most military men elsewhere. On the other hand, the fusion of the military and civilian in a popular army based on reserves has meant that Israel's citizens become involved in military matters more deeply and for longer periods of their lives than most citizens elsewhere. They therefore acquire the habit of looking at certain issues from a functional military perspective to a much greater degree than is usual among civilians in societies with a stricter division of tasks between soldiers and civilians. For example, in March 1973 the Israeli air force chief decided to force down a Libyan airliner that had strayed over Israeli-occupied territory; the plane crashed while attempting to land and about 100 of its civilian passengers were killed. Although most Israelis deplored the tragic outcome, 70 percent of them, according to an opinion survey taken at the time, thought the decision justifed under the circumstances on grounds of military security, against the 25 percent or so who felt the plane should have been allowed to make its way back to its destination. In short, the comprehensiveness of Israel's defense effort has tended at one and the same time to "civilize" the military and "militarize" the civilian.

Unlike Germany in its militaristic periods, Israel has developed no popular ideology glorifying war as such and seeing in the ability to wage it well a mark of inherent national superiority. However, Israelis have taken special satisfaction in saying or hearing it said that the Jews in their homeland have proved themselves to be as good and tough in warfare as any people on earth. Israelis, depending on age and background, may variously take pride in their countrymen's achievements in pioneering, science, learning, piety, enterprise, the arts, and so on; but they are all, without distinction, particularly impressed by military achievement and valor. Until the Yom Kippur War Israelis criticized everybody and everything with total abandon, but the Defense Army of Israel was sacrosanct. This admiration of military prowess and this veneration of the armed forces is, of course, inseparably bound up with the realization by Israelis that their very survival depended on their army and its quality. It also reflects the special appreciation by a people who had seen millions of its members herded into concentration camps and led to slaughter of the fact that it no longer stands in the position of the helpless victim, but can face its enemies weapon in hand and deter or defeat them.

Yet, however justifiable or understandable these feelings may be, they tended after 1967 to spill over into an attitude of relishing power and the instruments of power independently of purpose, almost for their own sake. The quiet pride in the ability of Israel's armed forces that was the rule before 1967 tended to give way to vainglorious boasts that Israel's armored formations, for example, did a better job in Sinai in 1967 than either the British or the Germans in the World War II North African battles; that Israel's air force was the best in the world; that Israel fought down the guerrillas better than the French in Algeria or the Americans in Vietnam; that some weapons produced by Israel were the best in their class; and so on. Some Israeli journalists even took to referring to their country not simply as Israel but as *ha-Otsma ha-Yisraelit* (the Israeli Power). The most disconcerting aspect of such boasts was not so much the applause they elicited from the "average Israelis," but the benign tolerance shown toward them by Israelis who were otherwise alert critics of the shortcomings of their country and their fellow citizens.

The intoxication with power and the exaggerated self-confidence it induced contributed not a little to the failures of the Yom Kippur War, as the Agranat Commission pointed out. On the rebound, Israelis tended for a while to go to the opposite extreme of self-laceration, finding fault everywhere, and mercilessly criticizing senior officers and leaders of the defense establishment whom they had previously adulated. Most disturbing of all, generals who led the country in war joined in the fray with mutual accusations of incompetence, self-serving behavior, and even cowardice. Fortunately for Israel, that masochistic seizure subsided before long, giving way to a more sober appreciation of the country's position and calm recognition of the problems that needed to be faced. Among the important results of the entire experience was an earnest attempt to define the authority and responsibility of the defense minister and the chief of staff vis-à-vis each other, and of both vis-à-vis the Cabinet and the Knesset. At the popular level, one important result was the demythification of Tzahal, the delionization of its generals, and a return to a purposive view of Israel's military endeavor.

Another disturbing phenomenon that first manifested itself after 1967 is the emergence among Israelis of a strong irredentist urge, which found its most typical expression in the development of the Movement for the Integral Land of Israel—a kind of pressure group cutting across existing political parties that seeks to annex the entire West Bank and the Gaza Strip. Enemies of Zionism, who have always depicted it as an expansionist movement that from the outset had set itself the aim of establishing Jewish sovereignty over the entire area from the Nile to the Euphrates, pretend not to be surprised at this phenomenon and to see in it merely a confirmation of what they already believed. A less hostile and more informed observer cannot fail to note that, while Zionism always included a minority that placed its main stress on establishing a Jewish state on both sides of the Jordan by military means, the great majority of Zionists—those that gave the movement its thrust—put their primary emphasis on the functions of gathering segments of the Jewish people in Palestine and molding them into a modern nation and a model society. They were concerned with sovereignty and territory only to the extent that these were necessary for the fulfillment of those goals, and they created an armed force only to defend their labors against those who would disrupt them or deny their continuation. Consequently, the development and growth of irredentism in the wake of the 1967 victory represented a *new* development, which could portend a swing away from the purposeful idealism that had hitherto characterized Zionism and Israel toward the kind of mystical nationalism of manifest destiny that has so often in history proved to be the seedbed of militarism and expansionism. The fact that Israel did not seek the war that gave rise to the irredentist movement may be a refutation of the charges of enemies of Zionism as far as its past is concerned, but it does not give the movement immunity against this kind of mutation. This is particularly true because the steady decline of ideological commitment among Israel's people and political parties has left an immense moral vacuum into which that kind of nationalism could penetrate as an easy substitute. This is why the Yom Kippur War had less of a corrective effect on this problem than on the intoxication with power.

Israel cannot be accused of deliberately cultivating a cavalier attitude toward human life—another mark of militarism. Nevertheless, the constant exercises in fighting, the frequent armed clashes, large and small, and the need to keep army and reserves always ready for war mentally as well as physically could not fail to foster a certain objective recklessness toward life—one's own as well as others'. All nations are familiar with this phenomenon in wartime, but Israel has had to live with it continuously and has suffered its effects more deeply. An exceptionally shocking manifestation of that tendency occurred in the tragic Kafr Kassem incident when, on the eve of Israel's invasion of Sinai in 1956, an Israeli officer ordered his men to open fire on some Arab inhabitants of that village, killing forty-three of them, for violating a curfew they did not know had been imposed. The Israeli authorities were alarmed by the event and brought the officer and his men to trial, giving wide pubilicity to the proceedings in the hope of countering the spirit it reflected. The court rejected the plea of the accused that they had acted under specific orders from their superiors and asserted the principle, very daring to apply to an army, that orders did not exempt soldiers from exercising their own moral judgement and that they remained criminally responsible for patently unlawful action. No comparable incident has occurred in the two decades that have elapsed since, although half of them were years of constant fighting, much of it against guerrillas and terrorists in areas occupied by Israeli forces. However, it is certain that during that period many a life was taken, or laid down, in battle that might have been spared but for prolonged habituation to the idea of killing and being killed. The number of lives thus lost is known only to God, but judging by the recklessness with which Israelis drive their automobiles and the rate at which they kill themselves and others in car accidents, it must be not small.

Other aspects of the impact of defense—especially the impact of what I have called the "militarization of the civilian" on the development of Israeli culture in general—are too intricate to be dealt with fully in a work of this kind. It would be exceedingly difficult in any case to isolate the influence of this factor on Israeli culture from the multitude of other forces affecting it. All that can be said here with certainty is that the defense endeavor has absorbed into its military and civilian establishments a very high proportion of the best minds and energies, as well as large chunks of the country's economic resources, and that to that extent the cultural potential of Israel has not been realized as fully as it might have been. Even if one were to assume that everything that Israel invested in defense was necessary for survival, it would still be tragically ironic that, instead of the dream of many a Zionist that "from Zion the Law shall come forth and the word of God from Jerusalem," the most impressive lessons to emerge from Israel so far have been related to the vocation of Essau, who was told, "By your sword shall you live."

Considering in its entirety the record of the internal consequences of Israel's defense endeavor, one cannot fail to be favorably impressed with the survival of civil liberties and the effective functioning of democracy in Israel so far, despite three decades of intense confrontation and war. Equally impressive is the fact that failures and blemishes in both respects that were noticed were widely discussed and criticized, and that remedial action was sometimes taken as a result, testifying to the vitality of the democratic spirit of the country. On the basis of that record, there seem to be no grounds for fears of a wanton and massive suppression of liberties in Israel in the future under the pretense of defense necessity, nor does it seem likely that the military might some day take over the government as they have done in so many nations, both new and old. On the other hand, there is no escaping the fact that the overwhelming concentration on defense and concern with war have deflected much of the nations's best human and material resources from the cultivation of the good life as visualized by Israel's founders, and that they have sown the seeds of alien growths which began to manifest themselves in dangerous magnitudes after 1967. There exist the beginnings of a military-industrial complex, which, as everywhere, has a natural vested interest in maximizing military investment. This, together with the propensity of Israelis, as part of a people that had been the victim of power, to hoard power for its own sake, threatens to turn the defense effort from a means of survival into an end in itself. At the same time, the development of an irredentist movement feeding on mystical nationalism in connection with territories conquered in war portends the beginnings of a tendency wherein power, even though defensive in origin, generates emotional needs to justify its further application and political situations to justify its further expansion. These interrelated influences make up a vicious circle that could set Israel on a career it neither sought nor consciously embraces, one that is repugnant to its millennial heritage and perilous to its future. The Yom Kippur War may have checked some of these influences at least, but only a durable peace between Israel and its neighbors can definitely neutralize them and reverse the vicious circle. The chances of such a peace can only be assessed in light of the international politics affecting Israel, especially the relations between Israel and the United States.

BOOK TWO

ISRAEL AND AMERICA IN INTERNATIONAL POLITICS

INTRODUCTION

The relationship between the United States and Israel has been exceptional among the respective relationships of the two countries and a most unusual one in the annals of international relations altogether. Formally, this relationship never attained the status of a contractual alliance, yet in practice, it has been as strong as any alliance, written or unwritten, in which either country has been involved, and it has permeated the societies as well as the governments of the two countries as no other relationship of theirs has, with the possible exception of American-British relations.

Any meaningful relationship between two countries involves at least two channels of interaction—one direct, between the countries concerned, and one indirect, going through third parties who affect or are affected by the bilateral relationship. Relations between the United States and Britain, for example, are embedded in considerations of interest and history that are particular to the two countries and in considerations having to do with the role that each country plays in the other's relations with the Soviet Union, Europe, the Old and New Commonwealth, and so on. Relations between the United States and Israel are not exceptional in this respect. What is exceptional is the intensity of the interaction that has taken place through the two channels together, especially in view of the immense disparity in size, power, and international role between the two countries. This intensity is partly accounted for by the fact that the interests at stake in the relations involving third parties have often been crucial for the United States and nearly always vital for Israel. For the United States, these interests have had to do with a many-faceted struggle for control or influence in a highly fluid region of great strategic and economic importance; for Israel they have involved its very existence and national security in an immediate sense. In addition, the intensity of the interaction between the two has been due to a special factor in the American-Israeli relationship relating to the character of Israel as a democratic, Jewish, immigrant, beleaguered state and to the fact that some 6 million American Jews have developed a passionate interest in Israel's security and well-being. This special factor has greatly accelerated American-Israeli relations on the bilateral plane, and has had a very considerable effect on their relations through third parties.

This second part of our study will analyze the evolution of American-Israeli relations from the time of the establishment of the state of Israel until June 1977 (America's role in the emergence of Israel was examined before). Since these relations were embedded in a network that involved other parties and issues, we shall have to dwell on these often and at some length. Moreover, because the stress of this entire book is on trying to further a better understanding of Israel on the part of Americans, we shall analyze American-Israeli relations in very large measure from a perspective that looks outward from Israel. However, the closer the analysis gets to recent years and the more intense the American-Israeli interaction gets to be, the less significant that particular perspective becomes. In any case, we shall cap our historical analysis with a summary analytical overview of American-Israeli relations from a perspective that looks outward from the United States.

19
Striving for Security in the Absence of Peace, 1949–1956

Israel, more than most new nations, began its sovereign career with a very clear conception of the national interest and a clear view of the broad foreign policy aims that flowed from it. Its Zionist vocation and the fact that it had to defend its right to exist in war combined to place clearly before the eyes of its government and people three cardinal objectives: providing for the continued security and integrity of the state, promoting massive immigration of Jews from all parts of the world, and promoting rapid economic development of the country. Each of these national objectives had its own justification in itself and also contributed to reinforcing the others.

Israelis also started with a universally shared recognition that the best way to serve the national objectives was to seek to establish final peace with their neighbors and to cultivate good relations with all the big powers, including particularly the United States and the Soviet Union. In the euphoria of the victorious end of the War of Independence these policy aims appeared perfectly feasible. Had not the United States as well as the Soviet Union supported Israel at crucial moments in the recent struggles? Had not the Arab states, however reluctantly, finally concluded armistice agreements and committed themselves to converting them into final peace treaties? Had not Britain, the only big power whose interests had placed it on the Arab side, finally given up its earlier hostile policy and signified this by recognizing Israel?

In actual fact, Israel's initial policy aims proved to be anything but practicable. Peace with the Arabs failed to materialize, and with this failure went the prospect of Israel's being able to maintain a policy of neutrality or nonalignment in its relations with the big powers. Even as fear of Arab *revanchisme* impelled Israel to seek closer relations with the United States, a greater American involvement in the heartland of the Middle East in the context of a developing Cold War with the Soviet Union compelled the United States to give more weight to Arab sensitivity and correspondingly limited the extent of the support it could give Israel. In the meantime Israel's efforts to reach out to the United States contributed to gaining it the hostility of the Soviet Union, while the United States' effort to reach out to some Arab countries impelled the Soviets to try to undercut this effort by buying the favor of other Arab countries with arms that enhanced their capacity for revenge against Israel.

The impact of these unfavorable basic trends was aggravated by, and in turn aggravated, unfavorable particular developments and turns of events. As a result, by 1956 Israel felt itself so isolated and threatened that it took advantage of a fleeting favorable international conjunction to launch a preemptive war against Egypt in collusion with Britain and France.

These developments in Israel's international political situation and policy unfolded in two distinct though overlapping phases. The first, from 1949 to 1953, saw the evaporation of Israel's initial options and the emergence of adaptations that came in their place; the second, from 1953 to 1956, witnessed the failure of the main adaptations and the rapid deterioration of Israel's situation, leading to the outbreak of the 1956 Sinai-Suez War.

The First Phase, 1949–1953: Propositions and Dispositions

The Failure of Peace and Israel's Arab Policy

Immediately after the conclusion of the 1949 armistice agreements with the neighboring states, Israel's main foreign policy effort was directed toward converting these agreements into final peace. The prospects for such a consummation looked then fairly promising. The Arab governments of the time seemed to have been impressed by the vigorous diplomatic and practical support Israel was getting from both the United States and the Soviet Union and by its ability to protect itself. Though embittered by their defeat, they showed signs of resigning themselves to it while putting the blame for it on one another, on the big powers, or on the United Nations. The common front they had attempted to put up on the Palestine question had patently broken down, and since Egypt led the way in signing a separate armistice agreement, it looked as though each Arab state was going to look after itself and try to live with Israel on the best terms it could work out. Those early months of 1949 presented an opportunity for true statesmanship to apply itself fruitfully to the Palestine question that was not to recur for more than twenty years. Unfortunately, the opportunity was missed, partly through the fault of United Nations agents.

Even as the armistice agreements were being negotiated, the United Nations General Assembly had appointed a Conciliation Commission, composed of representatives of the United States, France, and Turkey, to follow them up by helping the parties to convert them into a final settlement. Instead of following the procedure which had just proved successful in the armistice negotiations and attempting to bring each Arab country face to face with Israel, the commission made the fatal mistake of assembling all the Arab delegations together as one party and thus put them in a position in which none of them would dare make any concession for fear of being accused by the others of being soft on Israel. The first result was that the Arab delegations refused to sit with the Israelis and insisted on dealing with them through the commission. Eventually after months of effort, the commission succeeded in getting the parties to agree on the agenda and the basis for discussion in what came to be known as the Lausanne Protocol of May 12, 1949. The two sides agreed to take the United Nations partition resolution as a basis for discussing the boundaries question, and Israel, for its part, announced its willingness to take back 100,000 refugees as a goodwill gesture prior to any negotiation of the whole refugee question. But this was the limit of the commission's success; from that point on negotiations bogged down beyond retrieving and the two sides tried thereafter to qualify away the Lausanne Protocol.

As the Lausanne negotiations seemed to be heading toward deadlock, the Israelis made an effort to conclude peace with one Arab country separately. In March and April of 1949 they had already made secret contact with King Abdallah of Jordan, during which the terms of the Jordanian-Israeli armistice agreements were actually worked out while the world looked toward the island of Rhodes, where the official armistice teams met. Now, after Lausanne, the two sides got together again and thrashed out slowly but steadily the terms of a peace treaty, which the King undertook to get his government to sign. The agreement was crucial for Israel since it involved a state that had under its control the most threatening strategic feature, the Arab bulge, and contained the majority of the refugees. But by the time negotiations had come near to conclusion, the other Arab states had recovered from their initial resignation and were able to deter any Jordanian leader from putting his signature to a peace treaty. Contacts between the King and the Israelis continued sporadically, but on July 20, 1951, the courageous Jordanian monarch was shot dead in the old city of Jerusalem by a henchman of the former mufti of Palestine, and with him went all prospects of an early peace.

Since those years there was no serious discussion between Arabs and Israelis aimed at achieving peace until after the Six Day War. On several occasions, when changes within one or another of the Arab countries or in the relations among them indicated that there might be an opportunity for a fresh start, Israeli agents made contact with Arab agents to explore the prospects, but these attempts got nowhere. The sad truth was that the Arab governments had very little incentive to make peace and weighty reasons to oppose it. They had concluded the armistice agreements only because of the implied threat of military action to follow if they did not, and they were disposed for a brief while to go further and negotiate peace only because they thought this to be inescapable. But once they sensed that Israel would not dare resume hostilities to compel them to make peace and once they realized the weakness of international pressure, they procrastinated for a time and then balked altogether. The one exception of Jordan really proved the rule. Jordan was the one Arab country that expected to draw important benefits from peace by consolidating its territorial annexation, injecting into its economy large amounts of refugee compensation money, and gaining an outlet to the Mediterranean through free-port rights at Haifa; even so, the attempt to make peace cost the King his life. Egypt and Syria, on the contrary, had reason to fear Israeli competition in their attempts to industrialize. Lebanon would have had to share Beirut's transit trade with Haifa and would have had to share with Israel as well as Syria the benefits from providing passage to oil pipelines. Besides, the Palestine question had become so embroiled in internal Arab politics and inter-Arab rivalries that the Arab governments had become prisoners of the intransigent public opinion they had contributed to arousing.

Once the Israeli government realized that the Arab states were unwilling or unable to make peace, it directed its main foreign policy effort elsewhere, confining itself to an "Arab policy" that amounted to the sporadic assertion of a few principles and an attempt to convey by word and deed certain impressions of its attitude. It reiterated endlessly its readiness to discuss peace with no prior conditions, and at the same time it sought to impress the Arabs with Israel's strength and determination by reacting fiercely against any "encroachment" upon the security and territorial integrity of the country. It made the gesture of allowing over 30,000 refugees to reunite with their families in Israel, released blocked bank accounts of former Palestinians, and declared its readiness to pay compensation for refugees' property and to take back an unspecified number of them in the framework of a general settlement; but it endeavored to stress unequivocally that the bulk of the refugees would not be allowed to return and would have to be resettled elsewhere. It expressed its neutrality in the inter-Arab struggle for unity, but made it plain that it would go to war to prevent the Jordanian bulge from being reinforced by the movement of other Arab troops into Jordan. It declared its opposition to the principle of "preventive war" in order to allay Arab fears and deny them an excuse to launch one themselves, but it initiated a war in 1956 in order to "destroy fedayeen bases" and open the Strait of Tiran and warned that it would do so again in the future if the strait were blocked again.

The prevailing attitude of Israel seemed thus to be: "Talk peace as if you were not acting tough, and act tough as if you were not talking peace." Whatever sense this attitude made to Israelis, to the Arabs the toughness seemed the essential and peace-talk mere deception. To be sure, the position taken by the Arabs themselves left Israel prior to 1967 with no option for a realistic policy aimed at securing peace; however, it is not clear that Israel for its part explored imaginatively all the possibilities for promoting a détente that might have helped the cause of peace. Certainly that cause was not served by such gaucheries as Ben Gurion's inviting Nasser to talk peace on November 3, 1955, while Israeli troops were preparing to attack an Egyptian outpost in Sabha, which they wiped out the next day.

Relations With the Powers: A Brief Venture in Neutrality

While it was still working on a peace settlement with the Arabs, Israel tried to adopt a policy of neutrality in the struggle between East and West and of friendship with the United States and the Soviet Union. Such a policy was not just a reflection of Israel's gratitude for the help it had received from both great powers, but seemed also to be the line best calculated to promote its national interest. It was designed to ensure the continuation of the flow of immigration that was pouring from Eastern Europe and perhaps to win Russia's consent to the emigration of her own Jews, and aimed at the same time at making possible the continuation of the contributions of America's Jews and perhaps getting loans and aid from the American government itself. In the enthusiastic moments to which they were particularly prone in those days, Israelis had visions of their state blissfully immune from the conflicts of the world, quietly gathering its "exiles" from all corners of the globe, developing with the aid of Western Jewry its material and human resources, mending the scars of past hostility with its neighbors, and bringing to them and to humanity at large the home-ripened fruits of the Jewish genius, uniquely enriched by centuries of universal experience. Such visions, alas, did not leave much trace once the Israelis woke up to the reality of the Arab states' unwillingness and inability to make peace. The Israelis not only engaged in marshaling their resources for the "second round" of which the Arabs began to speak, but started on a rapid process of whittling down the neutrality policy in an endeavor to ensure their national security through some diplomatic arrangement with the West.

The process began early in 1950 when Israel's government requested the American government to sell a quantity of arms to it in order to counter the shipments that were being made by Britain to some of the Arab states by virtue of outstanding treaties. The pleas of Foreign Minister Moshe Sharett for approval of the request promptly evoked charges from the Soviet Union that he was "cringing" before the United States. The American government was sympathetic to Israel's needs but feared the development of an arms race in the Middle East that might lead to renewed war. Consequently, it made an effort to coordinate arms sales with Britain and France, the area's traditional arms suppliers, which was reflected in the Tripartite Declaration of May 25, 1950. The declaration, however, went beyond the subject of regulating arms sales to an attempt to lay down a basic policy of the three powers regarding the chief problems of the zone. It proclaimed their determination to act within and outside the United Nations to oppose any attempt to modify the armistice boundaries by force and, while declaring their intention to prevent the creation of any imbalance in armament, promised to supply Israel and the Arab countries with enough weapons to meet their legitimate needs for self-defense, and "to permit them to play their part in the defense of the area as a whole."

The guarantee of its frontiers and the promise to supply it with arms on the basis of a balance of forces between it and the Arab states could not fail to please Israel immensely. The idea of possible participation in a regional alliance, hinted at in the bracketed phrase, was somewhat problematic since it was likely to antagonize the Soviet Union. But this disadvantage seemed to be counterbalanced by the prospect of being included with the Arabs in one defense organization, and by the realization that a worse problem would result if Israel remained outside an organization that promised to reinforce the Arabs militarily. Consequently, Israel's government welcomed the declaration, promptly rejected a warning from the Soviet government against joining any Middle East bloc, and was as promptly denounced as having sold out to the imperialist Western powers.

A few weeks after the Tripartite Declaration, the Korean War broke out. From the beginning of the conflict and throughout its course, Israel supported the United States in every move in the United Nations, including the decision to authorize the forces fighting under the United Nations flag to cross the thirty-eighth parallel and reunify Korea by force. In the world forum and at home, Foreign Minister Sharett explicitly renounced the neutrality policy in favor of a line that, he said, would not align Israel permanently with either bloc. But in December 1950, after the Chinese intervention in Korea had raised the specter of general war, the Israeli government, fearing the disruption of the country's supplies and its isolation in the face of its enemies in such an eventuality, was reported to be studying the possibility of an outright alliance with the West. The outcome of this study and whether it led to any diplomatic initiatives is not known; in any case, the necessity for the move faded as the fighting in the Far East reached a stalemate the following summer and the shadow of world war receded. But Israel's new tendency toward an alignment with the West became increasingly apparent. This tendency was confirmed when, in November 1951, the Israeli government was unofficially reported willing to join the Western-sponsored Middle East Defense Command, a proposal that had been submitted to Egypt the previous month.

From the perspective of subsequent years when neutralism became fashionable and expedient, many friends of Israel criticized its government for surrendering the neutrality policy and seeking to ally itself with the West or with the United States alone. Looking at the matter from Israel's point of view, one may well agree that the government erred in its estimate of the

United States' readiness to meet its wish for such an alliance and therefore made some premature and badly conceived moves. But basically, Israel's neutrality policy became untenable once peace with the Arabs failed and the Cold War encompassed the area. It could not remain indifferent to the efforts of East and West, using weapons as a lure, to win over its declared enemies. Sooner or later it was bound to turn to one of the two camps in search of some guarantee of its security. That it actually turned to the West was not only a logical outcome of the affinity of regimes, the many connections it has with Western Jewries, and of the economic aid it obtained there, but was also a matter in which the Soviet government left Israel little possibility of choice.

American Intervention in the Middle East and First Implications

The Tripartite Declaration and the proposal of a Middle East Defense Command signaled an extension of America's involvement in the Middle East from the Greek-Turkish fringes to the heartland of the area. The extension was of the utmost consequence since it converted what looked to the Soviets like a rearguard British action into a new drive aiming at integrating that part of the world into the global Western containment belt against the Soviet bloc. This necessarily brought the Cold War into the area in an intensive way and thereby complicated all its politics. For although the specific proposal of a Middle East Defense Command submitted to Egypt in October 1951 was stillborn, attempts to draw the area into the Western defense system in one way or another persisted long afterward and America's full involvement in Middle East politics had continued to the present, and so, of course, have their implications. In order to understand this crucial event and subsequent development in the Middle East we must pause for a moment to consider its background.

At the root of the American intervention in the heartland of the Middle East there were three factors: the failure of Britain's postwar policy there, the particular interest manifested by America in Palestine, and the intensification of the struggle between East and West. At the conclusion of the Second World War, Britain emerged as the sole dominant power in the Middle East after having ejected the Italians from Libya and helped ease the French out of Syria and Lebanon. Some time before the end of the war, the United States had begun to show interest in Saudi Arabia and shortly thereafter it began to exert pressure in support of Jewish demands for resumption of mass immigration to Palestine, but these attentions of the American government seemed to be in the nature of lobbying on behalf of some interests of its citizens and did not question Britain's hegemony in the area as a whole. Even after the 1947 Truman Doctrine committed the United States to the defense of the Greek-Turkish fringes of the Middle East and to a policy of containing Communist expansionism everywhere, the American government was on the whole quite content to let the British take care of the Middle East hinterland by themselves. For Britain's interests in the area were known to consist essentially of protecting its vast oil interests, on which it depended heavily for the reconstruction of its economy, and of ensuring the security of its imperial lines of communications; and insofar as these interests required Britain to work for the stabilization of the area as a whole and for its defense against outside threats, they were basically in harmony with America's global policy as enunciated in the Truman Doctrine. The trouble between the two countries over Palestine developed out of the rigidity of Foreign Secretary Ernest Bevin's stand on the question in the context of his varied attempts to realize Britain's broad objectives.

Britain's position in the Middle East at the end of World War II rested on treaties of alliance with Egypt, Iraq, and Transjordan and the Mandate it held over Palestine, and on troops and bases it maintained in all these countries by virtue of those agreements. But even before the war was actually over, nationalists in Egypt and Iraq had begun to agitate for the termination of those treaties and the evacuation of British troops, and Jews in Palestine had launched a campaign of terror and other illegal activities to bring about the repeal of the White Paper of 1939 which restricted Jewish immigration and colonization. Transjordan seemed quite content with its treaty with Britain but was, together with all the other Arab countries, anxious about the future of Palestine. Britain itself, it should be added, was economically exhausted by the war, and its government was under very heavy pressure to reduce the country's overseas commitments as quickly as possible. All this made it quite obvious that Britain needed to revise its entire position in the area.

In going about this task, Foreign Secretary Bevin had one primary object in mind, and that was to secure a few viable bases in the region from which the Suez and overland routes to the East as well as the Iraqi and Persian Gulf oil could be protected. Just where and how these bases should be sought was a relatively flexible question and the foreign secretary had in fact several plans. It might be possible to induce the Arab League to sign a collective treaty to replace the hated treaties Britain had with some of the league's members. It might be possible to help some of the Arab statesmen realize old dreams of a Fertile Crescent or a Greater Syria in exchange for an alliance and bases. It might be possible to induce some Egyptian government and some Iraqi government to sign new, more liberal, agreements to replace the old, while still retaining access to the bases Britain occupied in these countries. There were still other possibilities, but two things seemed to be quite clear to the Labour government's foreign secretary: that any bases that could serve the purpose, if they were to be viable and be held cheaply, had to be held with the consent of the Arab governments concerned, and that the consent of these governments would depend largely on the kind of policy he adopted in Palestine.

We need not concern ourselves here with Bevin's successive attempts to achieve his purpose to highlight some relevant facts. He endeavored, against mounting Jewish defiance and violence and increasing American pressure, to maintain the postwar status quo in Palestine by any means until he could explore with the Arab governments the various possibilities for achieving his purpose. But in the two years during which he was able to withstand the pressure before surrendering the Palestine question to the United Nations, he failed in all his negotiations with the Arab governments, although he had not budged one inch from the White Paper of 1939. Throughout, he saw only shady motives in American pressure on behalf of the Jews and expressed those views in harsh words, thereby permitting a gulf to develop between American and British positions on Palestine. Finally, by early 1948, after the Baghdad mobs had torn up a new treaty he had just signed with the Iraqi Premier, and after the United Nations had already decided to partition Palestine, he was ready to play his last card. This aimed at taking advantage of the chaotic situation that developed in Palestine to gain for his only reliable ally, Transjordan, access to the Mediterranean. Such a move would make that country a suitable alternative site for the bases that existed in Egypt and Iraq. Accordingly, on May 15, 1948, as the Mandate in Palestine formally came to an end, the British-led Arab Legion of Transjordan moved in to seize at least the territory allotted to the Arab state by the partition plan, and perhaps to improve on it by capturing some areas that would make access to the sea more secure. This time however, Arabs, Jews, and Americans coalesced fortuitously to frustrate Bevin's plan. The intervention of Transjordan provoked other jealous Arab countries to send in their armies as much to block its expansion as to fight the Jews, but the Israelis offered unexpectedly successful resistance to all the Arab armies and barred Transjordan's path to the sea; and when the British tried in the United Nations to promote the Bernadotte Plan, which was to give them by diplomacy what their ally had failed to obtain by force, the American President blocked their effort.

The failure of Bevin's endeavors left Britain in a shaky position as the Middle East entered upon an era of turmoil unequalled even in its own long disturbed history. The British still retained bases in Iraq and Suez, but they were clearly on the defensive in both places, especially in Egypt, where a new government led by the veteran nationalist party, the Wafd, was soon to begin a reckless agitation and guerrilla campaign against them. In all the Arab states, governments and political leaders succumbed to waves of assassinations, street riots, and military coups. The peace talks between the Arab states and Israel had failed and the brief moment of sobriety in their relations that followed the war quickly gave way to mutual fears and threats, sharpened by Britain's resumption of arms deliveries to Jordan, Iraq, and Egypt under the terms of treaties with them. It was clear that Britain alone could no longer take new initiatives to stabilize the situation, just as it was clear that such initiatives were crucially needed. For even as the Palestine conflict reached its climax in the war of 1948, the Cold War between East and West had reached new heights as a result of the Communist coup in Czechoslovakia, Tito's defection from the Soviet bloc and Moscow's threatening reactions to it, and the Berlin blockade. The tensions generated by these conflicts made a general war seem very likely and drove the Western powers together in the North Atlantic Treaty Organization at the same time that they impelled Washington to seek to strengthen weak spots at the periphery of the Soviet bloc. Among these, the Middle East heartland seemed so unstable as to invite aggression or encroachment, and since Britain alone could no longer cope with that instability, there was no alternative for the United States but to intervene itself. The first result was the Tripartite Declaration of May 1950.

The immediate aim of the Tripartite Declaration was to freeze the Arab-Israeli conflict after the failure of the peace negotiations and to prevent it from degenerating into another armed clash. But it was also a preparatory step to another measure, forecast in the declaration itself, aimed at providing an outlet for the British-Arab impasse and strengthening the defense of the area by bringing all the parties together into a regional defense organization. The submission of specific proposals for this next measure was delayed by the outbreak of the Korean War a few weeks later which preempted the attention of Washington and the world, but once that war reached the point of stalemate, the need to provide for the defense of the Middle East became more urgent than ever. On the one hand, the Korean War had demonstrated that the Soviet leadership was ready to resort to force to break through at vulnerable spots along the periphery of the non-Communist world; on the other hand, the situation in the Middle East had deteriorated gravely as the Wafdist government broke off negotiations with the British and prepared to abrogate the 1936 treaty unilaterally, and as Iran was thrown into turmoil as a result of the nationalization of the British-owned Iranian Oil Company. Consequently, on October 13, 1951, the United States, Britain, France, and Turkey put forward the proposal for a Middle East Defense Command. The proposal was submitted to Egypt first because the crisis there was nearing its climax, because plans for the defense of the area rested on the Suez Canal base, and because Egypt's acceptance was thought essential to pave the way for acceptance by the Arab countries. When Egypt peremptorily rejected the offer the Middle East Defense Command died. However, other reincarnations of it were still to haunt the area for many years, and the United States was henceforth to be actively associated with them.

Deterioration of Israeli-Soviet Relations

Contrary to earlier expectations, it had become clear to Israel in the course of the many-sided pourparlers concerning the Middle East Defense Command that the proposing powers, while wishing to include Israel in the envisaged organization, were not going to make its participation an essential condition for starting it if the Arab states objected. Therefore, Israel's government was relieved to see the proposal collapse as a result of its rejection by Egypt and tried then to repair some of the damage suffered in its relations with the Soviet Union since it had given its welcome to the Tripartite Declaration. In February 1952 it gave its assurance to the Soviet government that Israel would not join any aggressive alliance against Russia, after having previously rejected several specific Soviet warnings not to join any Western-sponsored regional organization. But the Israeli gesture was futile and relations between the two countries moved soon afterward to the breaking point.

Sometime in the middle of 1952 a wave of anti-Semitism and anti-Zionism erupted throughout the Soviet bloc which, in its emotional fervor and violence, was comparable only to the hysteria that accompanied the Great Purges of the 1930s in Russia. The frenzy soon provided its own justification in a series of sensational events. In December 1952 came the Prague Trials of Communist boss Rudolph Slansky and his associates, which linked the Jewish Secretary of the Czech Communist party with Zionism, Israel, and the "American warmongers" in an unspeakably wicked conspiracy. In the following January came the Moscow Doctors' Plot in which four Jewish physicians were linked with the Joint Distribution Committee, the "well-known agency of the American intelligence," in a satanic scheme to assassinate top Soviet leaders. In February 1953 anonymous infuriated Israelis bombed the Soviet Legation in Tel Aviv and provoked Moscow to retaliate immediately by breaking off diplomatic relations with Israel amid a barrage of vituperation against its government unusual even in the Soviet tradition.

The origin of this frenzied outburst has found no explanation to the present day unless it be attributed to the failing mind of Stalin just before his death. Khrushchev's revelation of other instances of Stalin's odd behavior in his last days, the fact that the fury continued until his death in March 1953 and then stopped abruptly, and the subsequent admission by Soviet authorities that the Doctors' Plot had been contrived seem to point in that direction. But leaving aside the exceptional emotional violence of the eruption, one could think of a few "understandable" reasons as to why the Soviet government should have changed its initial friendly and helpful attitude toward the Jewish state into one of hostility.

First of all, it should be understood that Soviet support of the 1947 United Nations partition plan and of the Jewish state had come against a background of nearly three decades of unrelenting hostility toward Zionism. This hostility had been founded on ideological as well as tactical grounds. Ideologically, Soviet doctrine maintained that anti-Semitism, a chief raison d'être of Zionism, was the outcome of the capitalist system and could be eliminated only by the elimination of that system everywhere. Zionism, by looking for a solution to that problem in the return of the Jews of Palestine, appeared to be a reactionary movement that diverted the attention and great revolutionary potential of the Jewish toiling masses and intellectuals from the class struggle to the pursuit of a romantic idealist dream. Tactically, the Soviet Union opposed Zionism because of that movement's alliance with British imperialism through the Balfour Declaration and the Mandate, and its serving as a whip in the hands of that imperialist power to perpetuate its dominion over the Arab peoples.

After the conclusion of the Second World War, the conflict between the Yishuv and the British on the one hand and the apparent rapprochement between the British and the Arabs, which rested largely on the anti-Zionist Palestine policy of Bevin, suddenly reversed the tactical situation: now it was the Jews who were fighting British imperialism and the Arabs who were lending themselves to its machinations to maintain itself in the area. The appearance of the Palestine question before the United Nations just at that time gave the Russians the opportunity to lend a helping hand to the Jews in their effort to rid that country of British rule. Ideally, the Russians would have preferred to support the federal solution recommended by the minority of the United Nations Special Committee on Palestine, which would have achieved the same purpose of evicting the British without antagonizing the Arabs as much as the partition plan. But a quick survey of the distribution of forces in the United Nations indicated that partition was the only plan that had a chance of getting the required two-thirds majority; consequently, the Soviet Union and its satellites cast their votes for it. When the British and the Arabs made common cause to nullify this decision by force, the countries of the Soviet bloc did a great deal to help the Yishuv and the Jewish state frustrate their effort.

While the Soviets thus supported the Jewish state on tactical grounds, their basic hostility toward Zionism on ideological grounds remained unchanged, or almost unchanged. In his historic speech in the United Nations supporting partition, Soviet delegate Andrei Gromyko went so far as to say that the failure of the capitalist Western powers to protect their Jews against the brutal Hitlerite onslaughts entitled those who survived the massacres to look for protection among their brethren in Palestine in a state of their own. But he left the clear implication that the Jews living in the socialist camp had no need of any Jewish state or any Zionist help. This view was spelled out somewhat later as clearly as it could be for the benefit of the Soviet-bloc Jews by the prominent Russian Jewish writer Ilya Ehrenburg. Writing in *Pravda* of September 21, 1948, at a time when the Soviet government was still giving practical help to Israel, in answer to a question about the attitude of the Soviet Union toward Israel, Ehrenburg noted that the USSR had always supported *all* the oppressed in their struggle against imperialism. After paying tribute to the soldiers and toilers of Israel, he went on to remind his readers that the Jewish state was not heaven, that it was already beginning to be invaded by American capital, and, above all, that the solution of the Jewish question "did not ultimately depend on Palestine and military victories, but on the triumph everywhere in the world of Socialism over capitalism. The citizen of a socialist society. . . ," he concluded pointedly, "looks upon the people of any bourgeois country, including the people of the state of Israel, as upon wayfarers who have not made their way out of a dark forest . . . Soviet Jews are rebuilding their socialist motherland together with all the Soviet people. They are not looking toward the Near East; they are looking to the future."

What happened, then, after the establishment of the Jewish state was that the tactical reasons for supporting it disappeared and were even reversed, and the ideological reasons for opposing it reasserted themselves with more urgency than ever. The tactical reasons disappeared when Israel fulfilled its purpose in Soviet eyes by helping to throw the British out of Palestine and fighting successfully to keep them from reentering it through the back door in the wake of the Arab Legion. They began to be reversed when Israel seemed to be helping to have the "old British imperialism" replaced by the "more youthful and vigorous American imperialism." To Soviet thinking at that time, Israel started to become the tool of American imperialism even before it welcomed the Tripartite Declaration, supported the United States on Korea, and showed its eagerness to join in a regional defense organization; it moved toward the enemy camp when it sought American economic aid and when it adopted a policy of neutrality. For, at that time Soviet foreign outlook was guided by the Zhdanov Doctrine, reminiscent of the later view of Secretary John Foster Dulles, which considered neutrality in the East-West struggle as tantamount to tacit support of the enemy. Naturally, Israel's actual surrender of neutrality and its gradual movement toward the West made matters much worse.

The reversal of the initial grounds for supporting Israel would have been sufficient reason for the reassertion of the ideologically motivated hostility to the Zionist state. As it was, this reassertion was made all the more urgent by a completely unforeseen development of great moment: the reawakening of Zionist sentiment among large numbers of Russia's Jews. In explaining the reasons for Soviet support of the Jewish state Gromyko may have expressed all sorts of implicit caveats about Zionism, but these subtle qualifications were lost on the large number of Russian Jews who had repressed their love for Zion for decades and who now took their government's support of Israel as a license to express their emotions and as a glimmer of hope that they might be permitted to leave for the Promised Land. Was not their government allowing and even encouraging tens of thousands of Jews from the satellite countries to go and join in the defense and development of the new state? Ilya Ehrenburg's letter was designed precisely to warn against such illusions, but so strong was the feeling aroused among Jews that a visit by Israeli ambassador Golda Meir to a Moscow synagogue on the Jewish High Holidays in October 1948 became the occasion for a spontaneous demonstration by thousands of Muscovite Jews expressing their affection for the state she represented. The whole phenomenon of Russian Jews' showing concern for Israel was not merely an intolerable identification with a foreign state; it also reflected, three decades after its enunciation, the fallacy of Soviet doctrine and policy on the Jewish Question, which envisaged its solution by assimilation through the triumph of socialism. Infuriated, Stalin decided to strike back by terrorizing his Jews, by launching a campaign against "rootless cosmopolitans," by destroying all remnants of Jewish culture and eliminating Jewish writers who retarded the process of assimilation, by depicting the state of Israel—the object of his ungrateful subjects' love—in the blackest terms, and leaving no shred of doubt as to how the Soviet government felt about it.

After the death of Stalin in March 1953, the convulsive attacks against Israel calmed down to more routine hostility and, in July of that year, diplomatic relations between the two countries were resumed after Israel had given renewed assurances that it would not join any aggressive pact against Russia. But a few months later, the new Soviet leadership, having given up the Zhdanov Doctrine for a more flexible policy, was engaged in the beginning of a drive to win influence in the Middle East by espousing Arab causes against the West and backing the Arab states against Israel. This was to reach its first climax in the Soviet-Egyptian arms deal in the summer of 1955. For its part, Israel's government became convinced that there was nothing it could do to improve fundamentally the Soviet attitude toward Israel, and resigned itself to taking for granted a relation of subdued hostility between the two countries until a change in the tactical situation in the Middle East or a modification of Soviet policy toward Russia's Jews created more favorable circumstances for friendlier relations.

The Second Phase, 1953–1956: Deterioration and War

After four years of statehood, Israel's government and people may have looked back upon their achievements in the field of international relations with only qualified satisfaction. Israel had gained international recognition, secured American aid, received masses of immigrants from Eastern Europe and the Muslim countries, and was covered by the Tripartite Declaration. But its effort to make peace with the Arabs had failed, and so had its endeavor to consolidate its security position through an international engagement more binding than the Tripartite Declaration. Just then, too, came the icy gusts forecasting the storm that was to blow from Moscow. Yet, from the point of view of Israelis, so bad were the four years following, that from the perspective of the eighth anniversary celebrations, the first four years must have looked to them idyllic by comparison. From 1953 onward event seemed to conspire with event to corner the young state and wreak its ruin until, in 1956, its government seized a fleeting opportunity to strike a daring blow in an attempt to reverse what appeared to be fate's course.

Four Lean Years

The fact that the four lean years of Israel's foreign relations corresponded with the first term of the Eisenhower administration was not entirely coincidental. The Middle East policies and measures adopted by the new secretary of state had much to do with Israel's misfortunes. It was not that Secretary Dulles sought to alter in any fundamental way the American government's moral commitment to the existence and integrity of Israel, as expressed among other occasions in the Tripartite Declaration. In fact, even at the lowest point in Israel's fortunes, he refused to associate the American government with a publicly voiced suggestion by Britain's Prime Minister Anthony Eden that Israel should make some territorial concessions as a price for peace with the Arabs. Rather, Israel's troubles stemmed indirectly from the implications of policies that the United States attempted to pursue vis-à-vis various Arab states. Israel's government saw grave dangers in Dulles' attempt to woo the Arab states into an alliance with the West without due regard for the repercussions on the Palestine issue; it was convinced that the Arabs would use their increased military capacity resulting from the alliance only against Israel. The secretary of state, however, believed that if the Arab states were in the Western fold they could be prevented from taking any warlike initiative against Israel. In effect, Dulles was, as it were, asking Israel to entrust its security to the United States without any formal commitment. This the Israeli government was unwilling to accept if it could help it, especially since the secretary of state, in the course of his efforts to woo the Arabs, tended to speak and act in ways that were bound to arouse misgivings among Israelis.

Israel's apprehensions were aroused by a declaration made by Secretary Dulles as soon as he assumed office to the effect that the United States was henceforth going to pursue a policy of "friendly impartiality" between Israel and the Arab states. For just as the secretary of state was to assert later that neutrality in the conflict between the Free World and Communism was immoral, so the Israelis felt that impartiality as between Israel and the Arab states unjustly and dangerously blurred the distinction between the potential aggressor and his potential victim.

The apprehensions of Israel were reinforced when a request for a $75 million loan was promptly turned down. They became confirmed when, in October 1953, the American government withheld the disbursal of economic aid earmarked for Israel because of its noncompliance with an injunction of the United Nations Truce Supervision Commission to halt work on a hydroelectric project on the Jordan River pending consideration of the issue by the Security Council. These incidents seemed all the more significant to the Israelis since the American government was at the same time making a special effort to be demonstratively friendly to the new government of Egypt and had already outlined the idea of a new regional defense organization which left Israel out of the picture from the outset.

In the spring of 1953 Secretary of State Dulles went on a fact-finding expedition that took him to all the principal countries of the Middle East, preparatory to formulating a New Look in foreign policy. The conclusions he reached confirmed the aim of the Truman administration of trying to reinforce the area against Communist pressure and possible aggression through a regional defense organization linked to the West, but introduced important modifications in the method of pursuing this aim. Instead of trying to build a defense organization encompassing all the area at once, he suggested doing the job piecemeal, starting with the countries of the "northern tier," and then gradually drawing in the others. This approach seemed to the secretary of state to offer the advantage of allowing a start to be made toward the creation of the desired alliance among those countries that had shown some awareness of the Communist danger, without having to wait for a solution of the Anglo-Egyptian problem and the Arab-Israeli conflict. It was probably the hope of the secretary that once the organization got going in the north, it would constitute a pressure on the Arab countries to the south to join it.

The first step toward the realization of the northern tier alliance was taken early in 1954, when Turkey and Pakistan signed a mutual defense agreement that received the blessing of the United States and a promise of military and economic aid. This was of no particular concern to Israel. Two months later, however, the United States awarded military and economic assistance to Iraq with a view toward facilitating the effort of its government to bring that country into the alliance. Israel protested both directly and through its friends in the United States that arms to Iraq endangered Israeli security, since that country, which had participated in the war of 1948, had not even signed an armistice agreement. But Israel was only given verbal reassurances that the military aid given to Arabs would not lead to an arms imbalance or to renewed aggression. At the beginning of 1955, Iraq formally joined the Turkish-Pakistani alliance, in June Britain followed suit, and toward the end of the year Iran too came in, thus converting the Turkish-Pakistani alliance into the Central Treaty Organization, or what came to be known informally as the Baghdad Pact.

The United States, which originated the idea, stayed out of the pact and contented itself for the time being with supporting it economically and militarily. This was hardly a consolation for Israel who knew that the American government's reserve was due to its desire to continue wooing Egypt, whose government was opposed to the pact, and to avoid any premature embarrassment that might result from Congress' choosing to delve into the implications of the pact for Israel. Therefore, as soon as Iraq joined the alliance, Israel's government applied to the United States, Britain, and France to include Israel in the Western defense system through NATO or in some other way; and when this initiative failed, the Israeli government urged the United States formally and openly to conclude a bilateral mutual defense treaty. As Israel itself undoubtedly expected, the American government could not meet this request since it would have doomed American efforts to draw the Arab states into a regional alliance. In August 1955 Secretary Dulles announced the United States' readiness to provide large-scale aid for the repatriation or resettlement of the Palestine refugees and the development of regional irrigation schemes, and its willingness to guarantee any frontiers on which Israel and the Arab states might agree. This generous plan reflected the eagerness of the United States to see the Palestine conflict settled to the satisfaction of all concerned, but from the point of view of Israel and its immediate concern for security, it only begged the question.

Israel's anxiety about its security prospects in the face of these developments was sharpened by the simultaneous deterioration of its position through another chain of events connected with Egypt. In July 1952 a new regime had come into existence there in the wake of a military coup, which brought to power a junta of young officers. The new rulers, fearful of British intervention on behalf of the deposed king, had sought to secure the goodwill and restraining hand of Washington from the outset, and the United States had gladly responded. Relations between the two governments further improved when the new administration in Washington began to turn a sterner countenance toward Israel and exerted a steady "friendly pressure" on Britain to be more accommodating to the Egyptians in the negotiations on the future of the Suez Canal base. The British had wanted to make the surrender of their treaty rights to the Suez base conditional upon the Egyptians' entering into a new defense agreement, but the United States was willing to gamble on the hope, skillfully nurtured by the new Egyptian rulers, that once the Egyptians saw that their country was truly and fully independent, they would then turn around and join a Western-sponsored alliance of their own accord. In July 1954 an Anglo-Egyptian agreement was finally reached envisaging the evacuation of the base mainly on Egyptian terms, and in the following September the agreement was ratified by the British Parliament.

The developments in Egypt were of grave concern to Israel for two reasons. One had to do with the fact that the evacuation of British troops from the Canal base would remove an important buffer between Israel and Egypt and would also place the Egyptians in a better position to enforce a strict blockade of the waterway against Israeli ships and goods; the other had to do with the fear that the elimination of the Anglo-Egyptian dispute would indeed lead to Egypt's joining an American-sponsored alliance that would leave Israel out. So deep was their suspicion by then that the Western powers were bent on going ahead with their scheme to draw the Arab states into their defense network without any regard for the attendant perils to Israel's security, that the Israelis began to react in a reckless manner.

Before the ratification of the Anglo-Egyptian agreement, Israel sent the *Bat Gallim,* flying the national colors, through the Suez Canal in an attempt to test the right of free passage through the waterway. This was the first Israeli ship to seek passage since 1949; in the interim, Israeli cargo had been allowed only in foreign bottoms. By timing the operation as they did, the Israelis sought to accomplish one of two things: if the Egyptians let the ship go by, Israel would have established a precedent of its right to pass; if the Egyptians prevented the ship from going through, then opponents of the new Anglo-Egyptian agreement in Britain might see the incident as evidence that the Egyptians could not be trusted with the physical control of the canal, and might marshal enough forces to withhold ratification of the agreement. In fact, the maneuver failed utterly. The Egyptians impounded the ship and imprisoned its crew, but the treaty was ratified, and Israel reaped only the resentment of the British and American governments for seeking to "embarrass" them. Not long afterward even Israeli cargo on foreign ships was prohibited.

The maneuver with the *Bat Gallim* was awkward but it was at least legitimate, since Israeli ships had the right, confirmed by a United Nations Security Council resolution in 1951, to pass through the canal. But another reaction, the true nature of which was not disclosed for several years, was much less innocent. Toward the end of 1954 the Egyptian authorities announced that they had uncovered an Israel-led ring of spies and saboteurs who had allegedly engaged in bombing and arson attempts against American installations in Cairo with the aim of poisoning relations between Egypt and the United States. The story was generally thought at the time to be a fabrication; Israel declared so explicitly. When the Egyptians hanged two of the thirteen persons involved, Israel retaliated with a raid on Gaza in which nearly forty Egyptian soldiers were killed. Almost six years later it became known unofficially in the course of the Lavon affair that the spying-sabotage adventure had in fact been mounted by Israeli intelligence, if without the authorization of the responsible minister.

Although Israel's efforts to sabotage the prospects of Egypt's joining a Middle Eastern alliance sponsored by the West boomeranged pitifully, Egypt in fact did not join the emerging Badhdad Pact. President Gamal Abdel Nasser, by that time the real boss of Egypt, had come to oppose the pact violently because, while he was busy negotiating an agreement with Britain, the United States had given Iraq military and economic aid and allowed its rulers to become, as it were, the recruiting agents for the pact among the Arabs, pushing Egypt to the sidelines. But Egypt's self-exclusion from the pact was to prove more of a curse than a blessing for Israel, at least in the short run. For Nasser sought to counter Iraq's gains in power and prestige through the alliance with the West and to remedy his own weakness as revealed by the Israelis in their raid on Gaza by turning to the Soviet Union and concluding with it an arms-for-cotton deal, which set in motion a momentous chain reaction in the area and placed Israel in a most perilous situation.

The conclusion of the arms agreement was announced in September 1955, and by then Russian ships were steaming to Alexandria and Port Said carrying the first deliveries. The deal included planes, tanks, guns, warships, submarines, ammunition, and other military equipment of a quality and in quantities hitherto not dreamed of in the area. Russia's purpose coincided largely with Nasser's desire to undermine the Baghdad Pact and deal a blow to the prestige of its Western sponsors. In addition, Russia sought to have a voice in the future of the area and acquire influence among the Arabs as their loyal friend in their struggle against the Western "imperialists" and their "client" Israel. The first consequence of the deal was that Nasser's prestige in the Arab world rocketed overnight. The masses of Arabs everywhere delighted in the Egyptian ruler's defiance of the West, his gaining a powerful ally for the Arabs, and his acquisition of the instruments of revenge against Israel. The other Arab governments, though fearful of Nasser's rising star, could at first only bow to the pressure of their peoples, join in the applause, and think of the best deal they could make with him.

Israel's reaction to the arms transaction was at first one of qualified alarm. Because of the obvious anti-Western implications of the Soviet-Egyptian deal, Israelis expected the United States to react vigorously against Nasser, and, among other things, to reinforce them as a counterweight to the anticipated increase in Soviet influence next door. In any case, there was certainly a widespread confidence among them that the United States would provide them with enough arms to counter Nasser's new acquisitions. One can therefore imagine the Israelis' dismay as they watched the initial shock reaction of the West give way to a frantic endeavor on the part of the United States and Britain to appease Nasser by offering to help him finance the building of the Aswan Dam, at a time when their own request to purchase arms in the United States and other Western countries was meeting with deferment month after month. By the end of February 1956, when Secretary Dulles told the Senate Foreign Relations Committee that Israel should rely for its national defense on "collective security" and the United Nations, not on arms alone, Israel's mood had become one of heavy, brooding, desperate determination. On March 18 Ben Gurion warned that war within a few months could not be avoided unless Israel got the arms it needed to counter Egypt's new weapons. Three days later he repeated the warning, and in the next month he reiterated it from the forum of the Knesset. In the meantime, the Israeli-Arab frontier flared up continuously as Arab fedayeen made deep sallies into Israel to sabotage installations and terrorize the population, and as Israel countered with massive murderous raids against Arab positions.

Thus, as the eighth anniversary of Israel's birth drew near, its government and people might have looked back wistfully at the position they were not satisfied with four years before. In the intervening period they had met nothing but heartaches and failures in their efforts to buttress their security through their foreign relations. Not only were they not able to obtain any firm guarantee or alliance, but several props bolstering their security had been knocked down even as the perils to their country's existence became magnified and immediate. The buffer provided by British troops along the Suez Canal was gone. The arms balance established by the Tripartite Declaration was shattered. Russia was playing a deep game with Israel's most dangerous enemy. Britain was engaged in rebuilding its Middle East position on the foundations of the Baghdad Pact, and its Prime Minister had considered it opportune, after Nasser had concluded the arms deal, to advise Israel publicly to concede some territory in order to make peace with the Arabs. The United States's relations with Egypt continued to be impelled by the momentum engendered by the early hopes of winning that country's rulers to the Western plans for the Middle East, even after Nasser had made it his mission to destroy what little of these plans had already been realized in the north, and had opened the door to Soviet influence in the area. Even France, which had a deep grudge against Nasser for his aid to the Algerian rebels, sent Foreign Minister Christian Pineau to Cairo after the arms deal to try to reach an understanding with the Egyptian ruler so as to avoid his dumping his obsolete arms into North Africa. In the sullen mood that wrapped the country, the ancient Jewish view of the world as divided between the two hostile camps of Jews and Gentiles surged from the subconscious depths of many Israelis, who thought they saw the Christian nations getting ready to look away once more while the Arabs undertook to make the Middle East "Judenrein." The general reaction was a fanatical determination that, whatever happened, the Jews in their own homeland were not going to allow themselves to be tricked into remaining passive.

To War

The low point of Israel's four lean years was reached in the late winter and early spring of 1956, when Nasser's arms deal and its repercussions in the Middle East seemed to conspire with the attitude of the big powers to place Israel in mortal peril. Subsequently, from April–May on, the worst of the crisis from Israel's point of view passed as the Western powers, one after the other, became embroiled with Egypt and mollified their attitude toward Israel, while one of them, France, even began to sell Israel the arms it so desperately needed. But the problem created by the repercussions of Nasser's deal in the area and by his later initiatives continued and became aggravated, so that in the fall Israel confronted a serious and immediate military challenge. Taking advantage of its somewhat improved military position and a favorable temporary international conjunction, Israel decided to strike to remove the military threat facing it and launched its invasion of Sinai.

As far as relations with the Western powers were concerned, the ice had begun to break by about April 1956. The first to come to its aid were the French who, after failing to dissuade Nasser from helping the Algerians militarily, started selling to Israel fairly large quantities of weapons matching, at least in quality, the arms received by Egypt. The Israelis welcomed this help, of course, but continued to press the United States to sell them some arms, mainly because of the political significance of the act. Washington did not quite respond to Israel's demand, but in April and May, partly in response to pressure at home and partly as a reaction against Nasser's continued war against the Baghdad Pact, the State Department let it be known that the United States agreed to relinquish NATO priority over some French military equipment to permit their diversion to Israel. The political results were almost the same as if the United States had sold arms to Israel directly, except that they took a little longer to materialize. For Nasser reacted to the American move by withdrawing recognition from Nationalist China and recognizing Communist China, and this gave the State Department pause. Early in July it was announced that American Ambassador Henry Byroade, whose name had been closely associated with the policy of trying to cultivate Nasser's goodwill, would be recalled from Cairo. Later in the month, the doubts that had been accumulating for some time about the efficacy of that policy, together with complaints from the Turkish, Iraqi, and British allies against favors shown by Washington to the Egyptian ruler in the face of his continued war against the Baghdad Pact, mounting pressure from Congress, and intelligence that the Russians, contrary to Egyptians claims, did not envisage assuming the costs for the Aswan Dam project combined to induce the secretary of state to withdraw in a demonstrative manner the American offer to help build the dam. A few days later, Nasser retaliated by nationalizing the Suez Canal.

The Suez Canal had been built by a French-promoted international company owned for the most part by French and British shareholders. It was the main passageway for most of Western Europe's oil and had been considered by the British, ever since its construction ninety years before, to be the jugular vein of their empire and commonwealth. An international treaty dating from 1884 had prescribed that the canal should be open to the traffic of all nations in peace as in war, but the British, who held physical control of it until 1954–1955, had previously blocked it in wartime against enemy traffic, and now the Egyptians had blocked it against Israeli shipping. One of the main issues in Nasser's nationalization of the canal was the fear that he might use this vital waterway as an instrument of his politics against the West as he had used it against Israel, and as the British had used it against their enemies.

Nasser's action, which had come in direct retaliation for the American withdrawal of the Aswan Dam offer, seemed to throw the three big Western powers together against him. In seeking to evolve a concerted response, however, Britain and France, while ostensibly trying to devise with the United States guarantees against interference with free movement in the canal, pursued in fact an additional aim which the United States wished to avoid. The British, who had lost their control over Jordan the previous March as a result of Nasser's agitation and who resented the trouble Cairo Radio was creating for them in Iraq, the Arabian coast principalities, and Africa, were determined to use the Suez crisis as an excuse to crush, or at least humble and thus render harmless, the Egyptian dictator. So also were the French who had been embittered by Nasser's defiant assistance to the Algerian rebels. Both the British and the French governments had convinced themselves that the Egyptian giant stood on feet of clay and would be easy to topple quickly without any serious consequences in the Arab world. The American government, on the other hand, wedded until very recently to a policy that had estimated highly Nasser's influence among the Arab peoples and had sought to ride on his particular brand of nationalism, was fearful of the repercussions of the Franco-British policy and was disinclined to associate itself with the two "colonialist" powers in any nineteenth-century style gunboat diplomacy. Though wishing to see Nasser go, Secretary of State Dulles rather sought to meet the Suez Canal problem on its own merits, and then work discreetly and slowly to isolate Nasser and render him harmless. The incomplete agreement on aims among the allies made it impossible for them to follow a common course, and although the secretary of state had managed by ingenious maneuvering and a good deal of ambivalent talk to divert the angry partners for a time from the warpath to a diplomatic labyrinth, the difference between them eventually asserted itself and led the French and the British to turn away from Washington and take the road of armed intervention in Suez.

Before the nationalization of the canal, when the French started supplying arms to Israel, they must already have considered and approved the possibility that Israel might use these weapons to fight a war against their Egyptian enemy. At that time, however, the French could expect Israel to fight such a war only if the Egyptians took the initiative to attack, since they were well aware of the weak international position of the Jewish state. In the fall of 1956 the international situation had changed considerably, after the Aswan Dam and Suez Canal episodes had clearly thrown the United States and Britain into the anti-Nasser camp, and as the Soviet Union became involved in trouble with its own satellites. Just who approached whom in that fateful October is not known, but Israel was in any case ready to act for its own reasons. During the preceding few months the cruel thrusts and counterthrusts of Egyptian-sponsored fedayeen and Israeli army units had been resumed after a brief respite arranged by the secretary general of the United Nations and had cast a shadow of violence and terror over the area. Jordan, which had been seething since March, when King Hussein dismissed the British commander of his army, was on the verge of falling completely under Egyptian control. Syria had already placed its armed forces under Egyptian command. Nasser, carried away by the momentum of his enormous popularity with the Arab masses after his arms deal and his Suez coup, boasted about the exploits of his fedayeen and seemed bent on bringing his career to a climax by turning against Israel. The Israeli government seemed, then, to face the alternative of allowing a belligerent Egyptian chief, commanding the combined armies of Egypt, Syria, and Jordan and controlling the Jordanian bulge, to choose the moment of attack, after assimilating the enormous quantities of arms he had received, or to avail itself of the opportunity of Franco-British support and America's involvement in the last stages of a presidential election and Russia's preoccupation with Hungary, and risk an immediate military action to remove the impending threat. Given the recent background of Israel's failures to move the powers to pay heed to its security needs, and the superrealism and toughness exhibited by the men in charge of Israel's national defense, there could be no doubt about the choice. After many long months of uncertainty and tension, it was with a patent sense of relief that the citizens' army of Israel broke forth into war.

Of the torrent of events that burst in the wake of Israel's attack, the following are basic to an understanding of the situation and of subsequent developments:

1. The Israeli invasion of Sinai began on October 29, 1956; the next day the French and the British used it as an excuse for intervening against Egypt.

2. By November 5 Israel was in occupation of the Gaza Strip and the entire Sinai Peninsula, but the French and British forces had occupied only Port Said and a small strip to the south of it.

3. The United States assumed the leading role in marshaling United Nations opposition to the French-British-Israeli action, which expressed itself in a series of quick and overwhelmingly adopted resolutions calling for a cessation of the fighting and for an immediate withdrawal of foreign forces from Egypt.

4. The Soviet Union, while seconding the United States' efforts in the United Nations, sent a series of notes to the attacking powers culminating in one to Israel which questioned its future existence, and one each to France and Britain brandishing the implicit threat of using rockets against them if they did not desist immediately and withdraw their forces.

5. On November 6 Britain and France agreed to cease fire and withdraw as soon as the United Nations Emergency Force, decided upon on November

4, could take over, and by Christmas the Anglo-French forces were out of Egypt.

6. On November 8 Israel, too, agreed to withdraw and had evacuated all the occupied territory by February 1957, except for the Gaza Strip, which it did not consider Egyptian territory, and the tip of the Sinai Peninsula facing the Strait of Tiran, from which the Egyptians had blocked the entrance of the Gulf of Aqaba.

7. A movement developed in the United Nations for adopting sanctions against Israel to force it to evacuate the previously mentioned positions. The United States was about to join that movement but finally succeeded in inducing Israel to give in after assuming a moral commitment to stand by its right of "innocent passage" through the Gulf of Aqaba, and to see to it that the Gaza Strip was not used as a base for renewed fedayeen attacks.

The reasons for the United States' active opposition to its allies and Israel, which has been generally credited with bringing about the cease-fire and the restoration of the status quo ante, are not perfectly clear. Even those who partook of the relevant decisions have given different accounts of the motives behind them. The available evidence seems to suggest that in the immediate sense, the American government's reaction was largely motivated by a strong urge to dissociate itself *actively* from the action of the three attacking powers to prevent the rest of the world from drawing what would seem a natural conclusion that it was in collusion with them. This urge was all the more compelling because it was supported by resentment on the part of the American government at the fact that its allies had kept it in the dark about their plans and Israel had flouted its warnings. Underlying this almost impulsive reaction however, there had been an American predisposition against the type of action undertaken by the French, the British, and the Israelis resting on substantive calculations made months before. These were based on the fear that a direct, open attack against Nasser might set the entire Middle East aflame and imperil all the Western positions and interests in the area, even as it would give Russia a unique opportunity to pose as the sole defender of the Arabs. From such a conflict a general war might ensue.

The results of the military intervention were an unmitigated disaster for Britain and a more qualified one for France. These two once-great world powers were dramatically depicted before the world as incapable of taking action to protect their vital interests against the challenge of an infinitely weaker power without the support of their giant ally. They not only failed to topple Nasser but helped him win a great political victory. They did not secure guarantees of free navigation in the canal but lost whatever concessions to their demands had been proffered before. They did not protect the waterway from Israeli-Egyptian hostilities but provoked its complete blocking and the cutting of the oil pipeline from Iraq, which plunged Europe into a prolonged oil shortage. The collapse of their prestige encouraged the intensification of pressures against their remaining interests in the area. Thus Britain's 1954 treaty with Egypt was repudiated, its installations and depots in the Suez base were seized, and its position in the Persian Gulf principalities and in Iraq was shaken. France, already out of the Middle East, had less to lose; nevertheless, its cultural influence and institutions in Egypt and Syria, built over many generations, were practically wiped out.

As for Israel, the outcome of the war was quite different. In the immediate sense, Israel gained only few and limited advantages, but these were sufficient to place it in a position in which it could afford to sit back and let the other actors in the Middle East drama fight each other to a stalemate that suited its interest fairly well, at least for a while. To understand Israel's position fully, one must turn to the unfolding and results of the power struggle that took place in the area as a whole in the months and years following the Sinai-Suez War.

20

A Decade of Consolidation and Hope, 1957–1967

Even before the rubble from the Sinai-Suez War had been cleared away, the United States was impelled to take the final step in the process of its involvement in the Middle East and assume practically the sole responsibility for defending the Western position in the area. That position seemed at the time to be challenged by a formidable double threat. One was the threat presented by the tremendously enhanced appeal of Nasser and his brand of Arab nationalism which appeared to Secretary Dulles to be firmly committed to an anti-Western line. The other was the threat of further Soviet penetration powered by the credit that Russia had gained among the Arab masses through its energetic and drastic verbal interventions on the side of Egypt. With the loss of British power and prestige in the Middle East, Washington feared that the last friendly Arab governments, together with the remaining Western bases and the enormous Western-controlled oil reserves, might be overrun by a continuation of the drive of Nasser and the Soviets, each using the other. Blocking that drive and reversing it wherever possible became the immediate target of the United States.

Largely as a result of American initiatives, the Middle East became from the beginning of 1957 to the end of 1958 the arena of a brink-of-war diplomatic struggle between the United States, backed by some Arab governments, and Soviet-supported Arab nationalism of the variety identified with Nasser. The struggle reached its peak in July 1958, when American marines landed in Lebanon and British paratroopers in Jordan following a revolution in Iraq that brought down its pro-Western regime. When these operations were over, the balance sheet of two years of struggle appeared to be highly unfavorable to the United States. American diplomatic and military maneuvers had succeeded in retrieving Jordan for the Western camp, but had completely failed in the effort made to retrieve Syria. Lebanon, formerly pro-Western, and Iraq, previously the mainstay of the Western position in the Arab East, were lost to the West. Had those setbacks been in equal measure the gains of

Nasser and Russia, the outcome would have been sheer disaster. Fortunately —though from no virtue of American policy—this did not turn out to be the case. For the elimination of the Western position in Iraq triggered a struggle in that country among Communists, Nasserists, and independents which ended in a victory for the last group, but not before it had set Moscow at odds with Cairo for the first time since they formed their tacit alliance in 1955. These events gradually led to a subtle diplomatic realignment resulting in a situation in which all the participants in the Middle East struggles checked one another into a delicate balance that held more or less precariously until June 1967.

Throughout these events, Israel played a passive but important role. Its very presence served to tie down the bulk of Egypt's armed forces, restrict Nasser's freedom of action, and thus prevent most of the struggles in the area from assuming the character of military conflicts which might have entangled the big powers. The United States learned to recognize this balancing role of Israel for the first time when it engaged in confrontation after confrontation with the Egyptian-Soviet bloc, and appreciated it all the more and began to count on it deliberately when its incentive and willingness to follow an activist policy declined after the demise of the Baghdad Pact. The new American interest in Israel that was thus discovered was to lead in the course of the years to the development of a strong entente between the two countries. But even while this relationship was gradually maturing, Israel cultivated the unwritten alliance with France contracted on the eve of the Sinai-Suez War, explored and knitted additional diverse relationships, and broke out of the relative isolation in which it had been confined in the prewar years. The decade following the Suez-Sinai War was thus for Israel a time of consolidation and growing confidence in the future.

The Powers' Struggle, 1957–1958

The diplomatic offensive of the United States, designed to stem the tide of mounting Soviet influence and of Nasser's anti-Western nationalism, was launched with the promulgation of what came to be known as the Eisenhower Doctrine. This was a public law, approved by Congress in March 1957, by means of which the government sought: to serve notice to the Russians that the United States would fight to prevent them from overruning the Middle East, to strengthen friendly governments menaced by Nasser and his followers, and to provide a means other than treaties and alliances which governments that feared either the Soviet or Nasserist threat could use to associate themselves visibly with the United States. It is true that the doctrine spoke of providing protection only against overt aggression, and only hinted at the Nasser threat by speaking of aggression on the part of "a nation controlled by international communism." But these, as events were to prove, were merely diplomatic phrasings designed to facilitate the aim of openly rallying friendly governments behind the doctrine; they did not restrict the freedom of action of the American government, which was, after all, free to interpret as it wished the meaning of its own doctrine.

As soon as Congress approved the doctrine, President Eisenhower sent Special Ambassador James P. Richards to the Middle East with the mission of rallying the area's governments behind it. Richards obtained warm endorsement for the doctrine from Iraq, Lebanon, and Libya, and more reserved support from Saudi Arabia, Yemen, and Israel. Significantly, he was not received in Egypt and Syria. His plan to go to Jordan was upset by the outbreak of a crisis in that country, which provided the first practical test of the American policy outlined in the doctrine.

In March 1956, following the outbreak of violent demonstrations against Jordan's impending adherence to the Baghdad Pact, King Hussein had dismissed General Glubb, long-time British commander of Jordan's army and influential adviser to its rulers, and attempted to embark on a course more attuned to the wishes of the nationalist admirers of Nasser within his own country. In the following October, elections produced a government which committed itself to liquidating Jordan's treaty with Britain and signed an agreement placing the Egyptian, Syrian, and Jordanian armed forces under the command of an Egyptian commander in chief. In March 1957, after the Sinai-Suez War, the British and Jordanian governments agreed to terminate the treaty between the two countries, and Saudi Arabia, Egypt, and Syria jointly undertook to provide Jordan with the annual subsidy of about $35 million that Britain had hitherto supplied. By then, the young King was having second thoughts about the course he was taking. He had sought to enhance his own position by following a pan-Arab nationalist line but actually found himself pushed aside by his own government, which was bent on pursuing Nasser's lead to the point of turning the country into an Egyptian protectorate. On April 10 the King marshaled his courage and, using as an excuse his Premier's declared intention of establishing diplomatic relations with Russia, denounced the machinations of international Communism and dismissed his government. This act plunged the country into weeks of confusion, plots and counterplots, riots and repression. At several points in the crisis, the American President and the secretary of state expressed the desire of the American government to "hold up the hands of King Hussein," invoked the Tripartite Declaration of 1950 and the Eisenhower Doctrine to warn all of Jordan's neighbors to keep their hands off, and declared the independence and integrity of Jordan to be "vital" to the national interest and world peace. To give weight to these statements, the Sixth Fleet was ordered to the eastern Mediterranean. With this vigorous support, with help from Iraq, which kept troops poised on the frontier ready to move in if Syria did, with backing from King Saud, who placed Saudi Arabian troops previously stationed in Jordan at the disposal of King Hussein, and with courage and some luck the young Jordanian monarch mastered the crisis. A little while later the United States took over and increased the subsidy which Egypt, Syria, and Saudi Arabia were supposed to provide to Jordan, and the country was safely brought back into the Western camp.

Whether American or other friendly intelligence services had been involved in planning Hussein's royal coup d'état is not known. But in the next test of American policy, in Syria, there is some evidence that something like the combination of moves that had detached Jordan from the Nasser camp was *deliberately* planned. Syria had been the one Arab state that had showed unflagging solidarity with Egypt's ruler and had followed him in seeking ties with Russia. During the French-British-Israeli attack on Egypt, President Shukri of Kuwatly had dashed off to Moscow to seek Soviet support; and, while there he had arranged for Syria to receive large arms shipments, which were followed later on by agreements for trade and aid. Within the country, there was fierce maneuvering among half a dozen political groups in which the pro-Nasser (at the time) Ba'thists and the Communists had the upper hand. The plan for detaching Syria from the Moscow-Cairo axis seemed to call for a coup by some opposition factions supported by a few army officers inside Syria, to be backed by supporting military maneuvers on the Turkish, Iraqi, and Jordanian sides of the frontier, and perhaps by another movement of the Sixth Fleet. But during the first half of August the plan was foiled by the discovery of the Syrian plotters, together with some evidence implicating American, British, and Iraqi intelligence groups. The American government's hasty attempts to improvise an alternative move boomeranged.

On August 13, 1957, the Syrian government requested the immediate departure of the American military attaché and two members of the American diplomatic mission, and followed this move by retiring ten senior army officers and replacing the conservative chief of staff by Brigadier Afif al Bizri, an alleged Communist. The United States reacted by declaring the Syrian ambassador in Washington persona non grata and sending Loy Henderson, undersecretary of state, on a flying visit to the Middle East to consult with governments of the countries neighboring Syria, except Israel. On his return, Henderson reported the "deep concern" of these neighbors over the buildup of arms and increase of the Communist threat in Syria, whereupon the President expressed his intention to carry out the policy expressed in the Eisenhower Doctrine to help the threatened nations. Orders were given to speed up arms deliveries to Jordan and other countries of the area, the Sixth Fleet held maneuvers off the Syrian coast, and the President called upon the Syrian people "to act to allay the anxiety caused by recent events." All of this amounted to an invitation to the Syrian people to revolt and a promise of backing Syria's neighbors should they decide to take action to "protect themselves." But the Syrian people did not rise, and the only country among Syria's neighbors that made some move was Turkey—the one least plausibly threatened—which concentrated troops on its Syrian frontier. Lebanon and Jordan, which had received hurried shipments of American arms, presumably against the Syrian danger, acted to the contrary by expressing their devotion to Arab solidarity and making it clear they wanted no conflict from which only Israel could benefit. King Saud, who had lent a helping hand in Jordan, said he saw no threat. And the Iraqi Premier, whose intelligence service was implicated in the discovered plot, visited Damascus where he announced that "full understanding" had been reached. The strong impression created in the Arab world that the United States, with the help of Turkey, was out to crush Syria made it impossible even for the Arab governments most loyal to Washington to take a public stand that could be understood as supporting this move.

As the American government sensed that it had overplayed its hand, it endeavored to beat as graceful a retreat as it could. But the Soviet Union and Egypt, once they realized that the danger of war was over, did their best to capitalize on the American government's miscalculation and to make its retreat as embarrassing as possible. The Soviet Union, which spoke at the beginning of the crisis in terms of "not being able to remain indifferent to what goes on in the Near East," now whipped up a real war scare, sent the Turkish government note after note of warning couched in the most vigorous terms, and spoke of contributing armed forces to crush the aggressors. Nasser, who had watched impotently while the Syrians went into a real panic over the initial American reactions, now made bold to send two Egyptians battalions to Syria, presumably to help stem the impending Turkish invasion. The crisis petered out in November 1957, but not before Russia and Egypt had forced the United States to pass to the defensive, having "proved" that the Eisenhower Doctrine was just another instrument of imperialist domination. Substantively, the American moves not only failed to detach Syria from its alignment with Nasser, but they precipitated a chain of events in that country which resulted, in February 1958, in its complete merger with Egypt.

The formation of the United Arab Republic out of Egypt and Syria gave Nasser a dramatic, tangible success in his drive for Arab unity, and endowed him with a prestige in the Arab world that seemed well-nigh irresistible. Yemen immediately joined in a confederation with the new state. King Saud, whom the Americans had tried to build up as a counterweight to Nasser, was forced by an intensive Egyptian propaganda campaign against him to hand over active direction of domestic and foreign affairs to his brother Feisal, known to be less disposed to adventurism. Iraq and Jordan tried to deflect the Nasserist tide by forming a federation known as the Arab Union, which was promptly recognized by the Arab masses as the union of two frightened governments that it was. In May 1958 an intricate internal political struggle in Lebanon became converted, under the impact of Nasser's success in neighboring Syria, into a civil war that threatened to sweep away the country's pro-

Western government, headed by President Camile Chamoun. The United States rushed arms shipments to the beleaguered government, ordered the Sixth Fleet to the Lebanese waters, and increased the available marine units in the Mediterranean, without producing any effect. As the American government pondered what to do next a revolution broke out in Iraq, on July 14, 1958, which swept away the government that had brought that country into the Western alliance.

The United States, like all other nations, believed the Iraqi revolution to be another Nasserist coup and reacted immediately by landing the Marines in Lebanon, after having elicited an invitation to do so from President Chamoun. Simultaneously, Britain responded to a call from King Hussein and landed paratroopers in Jordan in concert with the American action. The minimal object of the Anglo-American military moves was to protect the friendly governments of Lebanon and Jordan from being submerged by the revolutionary tide. At the same time, however, they were designed to place troops close to the Iraqi scene in case the opportunity presented itself to redress the situation there. This possibility so alarmed Nasser, himself surprised by the revolution but believing it to favor him, that he dashed off to Moscow and came back declaring he would fight to defend the revolutionary government. At the same time the Soviet government thundered against "imperialist piracy" in Lebanon and warned against any move on Iraq. For a few days the world seemed to be perched on the brink of war, but it soon became clear that no member of the "legitimate" government of Iraq remained alive or free to invite outside help, and that the new leaders held the whole country under firm control. From then on it was all anticlimax. The Lebanese reached a compromise agreement that restored their country's traditional balanced position, and Hussein was saved; the problem now was to find a way that would allow Britain and the United States to withdraw their troops with as little embarrassment as possible. After long and bitter debates in the United Nations, the Arab states themselves produced the formula. This took the form of a resolution sponsored by all of them reminding themselves of their obligation to respect one another's system of government, and asking the secretary general to help in making practical arrangements that would uphold the principles of the UN Charter and facilitate the early withdrawal of foreign troops from Lebanon and Jordan. The resolution was unanimously approved, and the American and British troops were out by November 1958.

As the United States completed the withdrawal of its troops from Lebanon, two years after Britain, France, and Israel had begun to withdraw theirs from Egypt, the record of the intervening period must have looked dismal indeed. It had attempted to stem the tide of Nasserism, check Soviet influence, and rally the governments of the area around itself; but in fact, Nasser was entrenched in Syria, the Baghdad Pact was dead and buried, together with the friendly Iraqi government that had supported it; Lebanon, recently an ally, now became neutral; friendly King Saud, on whom great hopes had been placed, was striving to become inconspicous; and Jordan, rescued temporarily, was as insecure as the life of its King. All the credit America had gained in the Arab world by opposing its allies in 1956 had been dissipated, while Soviet influence had continued to increase and seemed now deeply entrenched on the shores of the Tigris as well as the Nile and the Orontes. What must have seemed worst of all to the American government, there was little if anything it could do to alter this outcome.

The Shaping of a Stalemate, 1959–1964

Just when the United States' effort to shape the diplomatic-strategic map of the Middle East had been acknowledged a complete failure, the area itself began to develop the elements of a balance of power that was to check Nasser's drive, slow the Soviet advance, and give the United States an opportunity to regain some of the influence it had lost. The key to the new balance was Iraq. The new regime began its career by proclaiming its allegiance to Arab solidarity and establishing close relations with the Soviet Union and countries of the Soviet bloc. Its advent also released a number of popular forces that had been oppressed under the previous regime, chief among which were the Ba'thists, the Istiqlal right-wing nationalists, and the Communists who, though never a large group, were able to build up new mass organizations very quickly. As soon as the danger of outside armed intervention receded, the popular forces, each of which could count on some support among the army officers who had made the coup, began to contend for determining Iraq's course. The Ba'thists and the Istiqlalists pressed for immediate merger with the United Arab Republic and had the support of Colonel Arif, the second in command in the new regime. The Communists, fearing Nasser would suppress their party as he had done in Syria, were anxious to keep Iraq free to steer its own course. They found a receptive ear in General Abdel Karim Kassem, the leader of the new regime, who for personal reasons as well as for reasons rooted in Iraq's economic interest and its ethnic and religious diversity, was opposed to a merger. The struggle between the two tendencies produced the usual plots and counterplots which resulted, four months after the revolution, in the arrest of Arif and Ba'thist and Istiqlalist leaders in and out of the army, an open break between Kassem and Nasser, and the strengthening of Communist influence. In March 1959 a pro-Nasser revolt by an army unit and tribesmen in the Mossul province, adjoining Syria, led by a certain Colonel Shawwaf, was suppressed by Communist partisans and loyalist forces with much slaughter. By that time, relations between Iraq and the United Arab Republic had degenerated into a cold war worse than the hostility between the two countries under the previous Iraqi regime, and the Iraqi Communists, having wiped out or silenced most of their enemies during the months of upheaval, seemed to have the country virtually in their power.

In the course of the widening conflict between the two countries, Nasser, for very good reasons, had singled out Kassem's collaboration with the Iraqi Communists as a special target for his attacks. The Communists had not only been instrumental in foiling the efforts of his partisans in Iraq and destroying many of them, but presented a threat to his own position in Syria. Nasser knew that there had been many in Syria who had favored merger with contiguous, oil-rich Iraq rather than with his own country, but had been handicapped by Iraq's monarchic regime and its alliance with the West. Now that Iraq was under a republican, nationalist, anti-Western regime, its attraction became very strong, and Kassem, along with the Iraqi and the Syrian Communists, tried to enhance it by playing on the discontent of the Syrians with the high-handedness of the Egyptians. In December 1958, soon after the arrest of Arif and other pro–United Arab Republic leaders in Iraq, Nasser extended his attacks beyond the Arab Communists to the interventionist policies of the Soviet Union. By the spring of 1959, after the Mossul debacle, he was charging the Communists with having hatched a plot at the Twenty-first Congress of the Soviet Communist Party in Moscow to break up the United Arab Republic and create "a Red Fertile Crescent [the territory comprising Iraq, Syria, Jordan, and Palestine], with Baghdad as a command post of the counterrevolution against Arab nationalism."

Nasser's use of the Soviet and Communist threat in his power struggle with Kassem brought several sharp retorts from Moscow, including a humiliating public rebuke by Khrushchev himself. Although the most severe verbal clashes were smoothed over each time by vague formulas and did not stop Soviet economic aid to Egypt, it became quite obvious that in the new situation that was emerging in the area, the interests of the Soviet Union and of Nasser had begun to diverge. To get rid of Western power in the Middle East, the Russians had been willing to support Nasser's effort to extend his hegemony over Syria, Iraq, and Jordan, even if this meant the suppression of the local Communists. But once the revolutionary government of Iraq proved it could serve the same purpose while using the help of the Communists, the Soviets had every reason to favor it over Nasser. To be sure, the Russians were loath to drive the chief of the United Arab Republic into the arms of the West, and expected him to render further service in areas such as Saudi Arabia, Jordan, Libya, and Israel still under Western influence; for this reason, they refrained from pushing their quarrels with him too far and continued to provide him with economic and military aid. But they made it quite clear that they were not going to allow him to use them purely for his own self-aggrandizement, and that they would oppose any effort he made to extend his power over areas that had already been pulled from under Western influence.

As Nasser understood better the terms of his relations with the Russians, he began to seek to improve his relations with the West in order not to be too dependent on Moscow. The United States was favorably disposed toward such moves for the same reason, especially since Nasser's drive in the area as a whole had come to a standstill after his failures in Iraq. These failures, paradoxically, were also decisive in leading to the weakening of the position of Iraq's Communists. For, as Nasser's agitation against Kassem's "collusion" with the Communists subsided, the Iraqi chief felt more secure and no longer needed to rely heavily on Communist support. He therefore took every opportunity to whittle down the power of Communist organizations and succeeded eventually in undermining the party by splitting it and setting up a "national" Iraqi Communist party. At the same time, in an effort to retain a bridge to the West, Kassem used the fact that his army was equipped with British materiel as an excuse to seek British weapons, and the British government, after consulting the American, eagerly met this request in an effort to salvage some shred of influence in Baghdad.

By the summer of 1960, five years after the inauguration of the Baghdad Pact and the Soviet-Egyptian arms deal had transformed the Middle East into one of the main arenas of the Cold War, and two years after the Iraqi coup, the dust of these turbulent years had settled down to a general stalemate that continued for the next four years before beginning to show serious cracks. Having failed to rally any bloc of Arab countries into the Western camp, the United States became more reconciled to seeing these countries neutral. It sought to maintain friendly relations with even the radical Arab governments and helped them economically so as to prevent them from becoming too dependent on the Soviet Union and to keep the way open for a more positive association. The Soviet Union, fearing that too bold a move to bring any one country unequivocally into its camp might drive the others into the camp of the enemy, was content with denying the West control over the area, and it too sought to keep its key countries from falling into American hands by means of a policy of friendship and aid. As for Nasser, having been denied the prize of Iraq by Kassem and the Russians, he did not wish to antagonize the West by turning to some secondary target like Libya (before the discovery of oil), a complex one like Jordan, or a very difficult one like Saudi Arabia. Moreover, since his pan-Arab drive had lost its momentum through the Iraqi setback, he found himself falling increasingly on the defensive in Syria itself, where in September 1961 a military coup finally succeeded in pulling the country out of the United Arab Republic, thus reversing the most important achievement of Nasser's pan-Arab movement. Perhaps no clearer illustration of the general wariness of all concerned lest the delicately balanced stalemate become upset can be found than in the mildness of the repercussions caused by this last event. Washington, Moscow, Jerusalem, and all the Arab capitals were intensely interested, but nobody mobilized any troops, moved any fleets, apprised the United Nations, or exchanged angry warnings and sharp threats. Nasser sent 150 paratroopers to Latakia who were immediately captured and sent back home; Cairo and Damascus had some violent exchanges over the airwaves, and the broadcasts of other countries in the area were gleeful; but nothing more happened.

Israel's Improved Position after Sinai

Throughout the years in which the events just described unfolded, Israel was only rarely impelled or called upon to make an important move. That it could afford to remain relatively passive while the future of the area around it was being contested is an indication of its greater sense of security and of the great improvement in its strategic and diplomatic posture that took place after Sinai, largely though not entirely as a consequence of it.

At first glance, Israel's tangible gains from the 1956 war seem rather limited and hardly worth the military risks and the international condemnation it incurred. It was forced to disgorge all its territorial conquests, including the Gaza Strip, which the Egyptians claimed on no basis other than the frequently violated armistice agreement dating from seven years before. True, Israel was able to destroy or capture large quantities of Egyptian equipment, to rout and disorganize two Egyptian divisions, and to put the Egyptian military base in Sinai out of commission by ruining fortifications and facilities in that peninsula; but all this meant at most setting the Egyptian military effort back a year or two and inflicting some financial losses on Egypt. For immediately after the war, Egypt started rearming and reorganizing its forces with Russian help and rebuilding or replacing the destroyed installations in Sinai. Another apparent gain was the posting of a United Nations force on the Egyptian side of the frontier to prevent border incursions, but this was equally advantageous to Egypt, providing a screen behind which it could reorganize militarily with greater safety. In any case, the existence of that force depended explicitly on the continued willingness of Egypt to let it remain on its territory. The only lasting tangible gain deriving directly from the Sinai War was the opening of the Gulf of Aqaba for navigation, although even this achievement depended in the final account on Israel's continued capacity to deter Egypt from resuming the blockade rather than on Israel's having obtained any diplomatic or strategic guarantees capable of securing its freedom of navigation. To these gains some observers add what they believe to be the salutary effect of disabusing Nasser and the Arabs about Egypt's real strength and about the prospects of liquidating Israel, but the fact that Israel scored its military success at a time when Egypt was under attack by two big European powers could be, and was, construed in ways that supported opposite conclusions.

The real gains derived by Israel from Sinai were for the most part indirect, unforeseeable, and not immediately visible. They may be credited to that campaign only in the sense that they occurred in the situation that emerged after it and were unlikely to have materialized if the campaign had not taken place. They can therefore be detected only by looking at the Sinai War in the context of the situation that preceded and the events that followed it.

First of all, the war disrupted the movement to tighten the Arab semicircle around Israel that was under way before the hostilities began. It forced the postponement of Egypt's assumption of effective command of Jordan's troops, hampered the efforts of Nasser's supporters in that country to consolidate their position, and gave King Hussein the opportunity to launch his coup d'état in April 1957 without fearing military intervention from an Egypt still preoccupied with recovering positions it had lost in the war. Jordan's successful escape from Egypt's control became all the more crucial for Israel after the Egyptian-Syrian merger a year later. It not only denied the very large armed forces of the United Arab Republic control of the strategically important Arab bulge in Palestine, but also deprived Nasser of a position from which he might have been able to foil Syria's secession from the United Arab Republic in 1961. The fact that the United States committed itself in very firm terms to the preservation of the independence and integrity of Jordan in the course of Hussein's struggle to escape Egyptian domination only enhanced the value and significance of the Jordanian countercurrent.

Second, the war provided the occasion for the formation and consolidation of a tacit Franco-Israeli alliance that lasted until 1967. This alliance was of vital importance for Israel in that it secured an enduring source of first-rate military equipment to counterbalance the armaments received by the Arabs from Russia and added an advocate of its cause in the councils of the big powers. Initially an ad hoc affair, the Franco-Israeli cooperation developed a momentum of its own and spread to many areas. When the French began selling arms to Israel in the spring of 1956, their purpose was strictly limited: they wanted to exert pressure on Nasser to cease helping the Algerian rebels militarily. When that effort failed and Nasser went on to nationalize the Suez Canal in the summer of 1956, the French government started to think of Israel as a partner in an eventual military action against him and to arm it accordingly. It would be surprising if, when that partnership was sealed and plans for the campaign were worked out, the French and the Israelis did not also agree on projects for consolidating the anticipated gains from the military campaign through far-reaching political and territorial revisions in the area surrounding Israel.

Many, including people in Israel and France, thought that the failure of the Sinai-Suez War would be the prelude to the dissolution of the marriage of convenience between the two countries. In actual fact their relations only gained in strength and scope during the following years. For one thing, once direct retaliation against Nasser was tried and failed definitively, support for Israel became all the more important as the only means left to France for exerting indirect pressure on him in connection with Algeria. Second, Nasser's seizure of French property and his liquidation of the vast French cultural establishment in Egypt after the war brought France closer to Israel not only because of greater resentment against him, but also because there was nothing more to lose from a thoroughly hostile policy toward him. Third, as is usual among highly articulate democratic societies, the fact of Franco-Israeli cooperation and "brotherhood in arms," however Machiavellian might have been its origins, called forth torrents of literature and oratory on both sides justifying it morally and dwelling on the transcendent ties underlying it, which contributed an added momentum to their tacit alliance while giving it a more positive character. Thus, various projects of economic, technical, political, cultural, and scientific cooperation were started that went on expanding over the years. One such project alone brought hundreds of French scientists and technicians to Israel where they worked with Israelis on the erection of a 22-megawatt nuclear reactor at Dimona. Finally, the espousal of Israel, especially supplying it with arms, was viewed by France as giving it the right to have a say in any big-power discussion of the Middle East.

The French were bitterly resentful of the fact that they had been completely left out of the Anglo-American plans in connection with the Baghdad Pact. The two powers had assumed, quite rightly, that it would be difficult if not impossible for any Arab state to associate itself with France while it was suppressing the Algerians, but that they did not even consult it about the pact was taken by France both as an insult and as a design of the Anglo-Saxons to exclude it altogether from an area in which it had had an important say for nearly two centuries. With the loss of all its positions and influence in the Arab countries as a result of Suez and Algeria, the alliance with Israel became the most important means for asserting the *présence française* in the Middle East. The French position in Israel meant that any potential big-power scheme for settling Middle East problems had to have French support or risk being made unworkable. Such schemes were never attempted in fact before 1969, but they were always being urged from many quarters and seemed the logical thing to do. But more important than this consideration was the desire to force France on the attention of the Arab countries as a power to be reckoned with. While the Algerian War lasted, the reckoning the French wished the Arabs to make was the probability of suffering damage at their hands, through Israel, in retaliation for further aid to Algeria. After the settlement of the Algerian conflict, in 1962, the desired reckoning was that the Arab states should seek to appease a power that could harm them from an invulnerable position. This the Arab states eventually began to do, and France eventually found it expedient to reverse course, choosing the critical moment of total Arab-Israeli confrontation in 1967 to do so. However, by that time the alliance had done much to enable Israel to stand on its own feet militarily, and by that time Israel had found a new source of support in the form of enhanced understanding and cooperation with the United States.

A further gain that Israel derived indirectly from the Sinai War was a greatly improved understanding with the United States. In a certain sense

Israel's involvement in the Sinai adventure could be viewed as the outcome of a loss of confidence on its part in the intentions of the American government. As has been said before, the records that have come to light so far show that the Eisenhower administration continued to uphold the United States' commitment to resist any attempt to alter by force the territorial and political status quo between the Arab states and Israel; however, the manner in which Secretary of State Dulles had pursued his Middle East policies until the Sinai-Suez War, and his apparent willingness to accept the disruption of the balance of armaments that resulted from the Soviet-Egyptian arms deal had aroused strong suspicions among Israelis that he was taking excessive risks with their security if he was not actually working deliberately on a policy aimed at putting them in a position in which they could be forced to make concessions.

The root of the trouble lay in a basic difference in the assessment of Arab attitudes and the possibility of modifying them. The secretary of state no less than the Israelis recognized the importance of solving the Palestine problem for the stability of the area. He was inclined to believe, however, that American military and economic cooperation with the Arab states was the best way of placing the West in a position in which it could exercise a restraining influence on them and perhaps induce them in due course to come to terms with Israel. In the meantime it would be in the Israelis' best interest if they would keep quiet, stop trying to press the United States to identify itself openly with them and protesting against every Western gesture toward the Arabs, and refrain from any action that might exacerbate Arab feelings against them. The Israelis, on the other hand, believed that the main motive of the Arabs in cooperating with *any* power was precisely to get arms and strengthen themselves for an eventual showdown with them. They did not share the secretary of state's confidence in the American government's ability to influence the Arabs decisively on the Palestine question except through determined use of its power, and were convinced that American efforts to court the Arabs would be interpreted by them as an abandonment of Israel and would therefore encourage them to persist in their intransigence. So sure were the Israelis of their assessment of the situation that they were inclined to suspect that, in taking a different view, Secretary Dulles was only rationalizing his wish to woo the Arabs into the Western camp regardless of the perils to Israel's security involved in this process. Therefore, when the Arab menace had seemed to assume dangerous proportions, and when an opportunity for taking action to remove it had presented itself, they saw no alternative but to act.

The shock of the war and the acute international crisis it provoked impelled the American government to take Israel's anxieties about its security more seriously. The secretary of state came to a clearer realization that whether or not these anxieties were justified, it was important to try to give them greater consideration because the Israelis would ultimately act on them, and this might lead to another dangerous international crisis. This new approach found its clearest expression in the Israeli-American discussions on the withdrawal of Israeli troops from the Gaza Strip and the part of the Sinai Peninsula controlling the entry to the Gulf of Aqaba. The Israelis feared that these territories would be used again by the Egyptians to launch raids against Israel and to block passage to its ships, and they therefore refused to withdraw unless they were given some international guarantee against such eventualities. The American government did not believe that Israel's fears would materialize and was not, at the same time, prepared to give any formal guarantee which might unnecessarily antagonize the Arabs and appear as a reward for aggression. As the American government prepared to support a United Nations resolution for sanctions against Israel, it seemed that the difference in estimating the situation was about to lead once more to a grave crisis. This time, however, a way out was found at the eleventh hour. An exchange of correspondence was arranged in which the United States government stated that it was its belief that the Gulf of Aqaba "comprehends" international waters and that no nation has the right to prevent free and innocent passage in it and through the strait giving access thereto. The American note added that in the absence of an overriding decision to the contrary, as by the International Court of Justice, the United States was prepared to exercise, on behalf of vessels of United States registry, the right of free and innocent passage and to join with others to secure general recognition of this right. As for the Gaza Strip, the United States pledged to exert itself on behalf of an impending United Nations resolution that would deploy the United Nations Emergency Force on the boundary between the strip and Israel in order to prevent infiltration and reprisal. This arrangement, pretending that the United States merely adhered to legal "realities," helped to restore the confidence of the Israelis in American intentions and established a pattern for subsequent relations between the two governments. From then on there was closer consultation on all Middle East issues affecting Israel's security based on a renewed commitment on the part of the United States to Israel's integrity and independence and an earnest endeavor not to allow a gap in the assessment of events and possibilities to widen to a point that might lead to an open clash of positions.

This improved understanding between the United States and Israel was greatly enhanced by the course of events in the years after the Sinai-Suez War. In 1957–1958, the United States gave up the effort to please Nasser and developed instead a policy aimed at containing his influence and rolling it back, which created an obvious harmony between America's immediate objective and Israeli interests. This harmony was reflected in the welcome accorded by Israel's government to the Eisenhower Doctrine—the first American diplomatic initiative in the Middle East that sought openly to enlist the cooperation of several Arab states as well as Israel—and allowed that government to take a more sophisticated view of the American moves in the

Middle East. Not only did it not embarrass the American government with the usual representations every time it rushed arms or economic aid to some Arab country, but it actually did what it could to facilitate the American efforts to create a loose pro-Western Arab bloc to counter the Cairo-Moscow axis. Thus, when Iraq and Jordan formed the Arab Union with Western blessing in order to counter Nasser's United Arab Republic, the Israeli government warned against the introduction of Iraqi troops into the West Bank of the Jordan but otherwise refrained from making further difficulties on this issue which it had always considered as vital. A few months later, when the Iraqi revolution brought about the almost complete encirclement of Jordan by hostile states, Israel allowed British paratroopers to fly over its own territory to bring succor to King Hussein's embattled regime. It also allowed American tanker planes to use Israeli air space in order to replenish Jordan's exhausted fuel reserves after the "brotherly" Arab government of Saudi Arabia had refused to allow help to come from its side.

In the situation that developed after the Iraqi revolution, the agreement of American and Israeli immediate objectives became ever more pronounced and gave rise to ever more enhanced cooperation between the two governments. Ever since 1950 the United States had attempted to pursue a Middle Eastern policy that included an inherent contradiction: it had tried to separate the Arab-Israeli problem from the East-West struggle in the area and to take a conservative position in regard to the former and a revisionist position in regard to the latter. Whatever ultimate theoretical unity may be thought to exist between the two courses, in practice they proved irreconcilable and hampered each other. The American commitment to preserve the status quo on the Palestine issue tended, by identifying America with Israel's interest, to handicap the effort to rally the Arab countries into the Western camp. At the same time, the effort to lure these countries into a Western alliance with diplomatic, economic, and especially military inducements tended, both directly and indirectly, to undermine the foundations of the status quo on the Arab-Israeli conflict, and to raise doubts in the minds of Israelis about the strength of the American commitment to them. The decisive collapse, after the loss of Iraq, of the American government's effort deliberately to organize the Arab East, and its conversion to a position that accepted the status quo in the area as a whole as well as in Palestine, finally removed that contradiciton and eliminated a source of friction between the United States and Israel. America's initiatives after that time to gain the friendship and promote the economic development of the Arab countries no longer appeared so threatening to Israel; on the contrary, to the extent that they tended to perserve the general balance in the area, they rebounded to its benefit by helping to maintain the status quo between it and its neighbors. Similarly, the commitment to Israel ceased to appear as burdensome to the United States as when it was trying to build an alliance with the Arabs; indeed, to the extent that this commitment meant supporting the balance of forces between Israel and its neighbors, it could not fail to contribute to the general balance by helping to deter one neighbor from overrunning a weaker one in the name of Arab unity and thus perhaps upsetting the general balance.

The new American-Israeli understanding was clearly illustrated in the course of the attempt made by the Kennedy administration to take a new approach in the Middle East after the collapse of the policy based on the Eisenhower Doctrine. This approach sought to take advantage of the rift that developed between Egypt and the Soviet Union to associate the United States with Nasser's Arab Socialism and, by helping to make it a success, built it up as an alternative to the Soviet model for economic and social development of the Arab countries. This approach, which in earlier years might have caused alarm in Israel, gave rise only to a mild concern which was itself fairly promptly dissipated. For the administration was careful not only to reassure Israel that the rapprochement with Nasser was not to be at its expense, but actually took steps to reinforce Israel as a counterweight to Nasser in case he misused or abused American assistance to him. Thus President John Kennedy told Foreign Minister Golda Meir in the course of a visit to Washington in 1963 that the United States viewed Israel as an ally even though there was no treaty to this effect between the two countries; and when Nasser in fact accelerated Egypt's arming in connection with his involvement in war in Yemen, the President publicly approved for the first time the sale of American weapons (Hawk antiaircraft missiles) to Israel and, on that occasion, hinted for the first time that the United States thought of Israel and its neighbors in terms of a balance of power.

The Yemen War and the American military support of Israel set in motion a process of increasing friction between the United States and Egypt which gradually terminated the experiment in cooperation between the two countries and replaced it with a relationship of barely suppressed mutual hostility. By 1965 the Johnson administration had phased out economic aid to Egypt and gone over to a more pronounced conservative approach that had as its main objective keeping the peace in the area and thus avoiding the danger of military confrontation with the Soviet Union, while maintaining an American presence and protecting specific American interests. In pursuit of that aim the United States explored with the Soviet Union and Egypt the possibility of stopping the arms race in the Middle East and consolidating the status quo; when this effort failed, it strove more openly and consciously than ever before to accomplish the same objective by maintaining a multiple balance of military power between Israel and the Arab countries taken together, and between Egypt and Arab countries friendly to the United States. Indicative of the position that Israel came to occupy in the United States' policy at that stage was the decision of the Johnson administration to provide Israel with large quantities of "offensive" weapons, such as tanks and fighter-bombers, as distinguished from the "defensive" weapons that the previous administration had sold to it. The public announcement of these decisions was no less indicative of the development that had taken place than the acts themselves.

Further Consolidation of Israel's International Position after Sinai

Besides initiating a Franco-Israeli alliance that lasted for a decade and beginning a process of closer understanding between the United States and Israel, the Sinai-Suez War enabled Israel to break out of its previous isolation and establish new relations or improve old ones with many other countries and regions of the world. Some of these relations involved substantial diplomatic or military gains; others were of moral or psychological importance. Together, they helped to project Israel as a prominent and frimly established member of the community of nations and to enhance its own confidence in its future.

The partnership between Israel and Britain in the Sinai-Suez War did not, as in the case of its partnership with France, continue after the failure of that venture, because Britain still retained an interest in the Baghdad Pact and in the Arab principalities of the Persian Gulf that could be damaged by too close an identification with Israel. However, the protection of these interests against the persistent pressures of Nasser's Egypt impelled Britain to take discreetly an increasingly supportive attitude toward Israel because of its strategic position and the natural role it played as a check on Nasser. Thus, much as the British government tried to blur the record of its collusion with Israel in the Suez venture after the debacle, it was forced within less than two years to seek Israel's assent to the flying of British paratroopers above its territory on their way to assist the Jordanian regime at the time of the 1958 Iraqi revolution. After the collapse of the Baghdad Pact, Britain found itself involved in a conflict with Iraq over Kuwait and with Egypt over Aden and South Yemen. In handling these situations, the British played mainly on the opposition of interests between the Arab states themselves, but they also found it useful to support Israel as an added lever, especially by providing it with naval equipment which they hoped would hamper Nasser's ability to maneuver in the Red Sea, the Arabian Sea, and the Persian Gulf. In short, after Sinai-Suez the British learned to look upon Israel as an important power factor in a fluid situation that can be useful to them, rather than as a destabilizing element that only upset their efforts to maintain a position for themselves in the Middle East or parts of it.

In addition to the gains scored in the relations with France, the United States, and Britain in the years after 1956, Israel made a breakthrough in its relations with West Germany. In the early 1950s, when the Federal Republic was beginning to make its way into the West European alliance against heavy emotional resistance, it had thought that establishing diplomatic relations with the Jewish state could greatly facilitate the effort by confirming the image of a new Germany it was trying to project. However, Israel would not hear of the idea at the time, and its assent to the reparations agreement negotiated mainly by the president of the World Jewish Congress was the most it could psychologically manage. Over the years, Bonn's increasing acceptance as a member of the Western community of nations and its meticulous execution of the reparations agreement, which incidentally flooded Israel with German products, made Israel more willing to formalize and extend relations with it; but by then Germany had become reluctant. It feared that changing the status quo of its relations with Israel might provoke the many Arab states with which it had in the meantime established diplomatic relations to retaliate by recognizing East Germany—an issue about which Bonn was extremely sensitive. Nevertheless, Bonn could not afford to incur the hostility of Israel either, for obvious moral reasons as well as because of Israel's close relations with the United States, France, and other European countries. Consequently West Germany was prepared to compensate Israel's government in other ways.

In 1958 German Defense Minister Franz Joseph Strauss, on a visit to Israel, agreed with Israeli Deputy Defense Minister Shimon Peres secretly to supply Israel with arms. Two years later Israeli Prime Minister Ben Gurion met German Chancellor Konrad Adenauer in New York and sought and obtained assurances from the German leader that he knew about the arms deal and approved of its continuation. In addition, Adenauer agreed to a request from Ben Gurion for a $500 million loan on easy terms for developing the Negev. German arms as well as the German credits flowed to Israel regularly for four more years, until their secret was discovered early in 1965. The revelation immediately led to a crisis between Bonn and the Arab states, and when Bonn announced the termination of the arms deliveries, a crisis ensued with Israel. The upshot of the affair was that West Germany agreed to establish formal diplomatic relations with Israel and compensate it financially for the termination of the arms agreement, while several Arab states severed their relations with Bonn. Given the situation of total confrontation between Israel and the Arab states surrounding it, the latter's loss of contact with a major European power that was also a source of substantial economic assistance to them was Israel's gain, in addition to the direct gain that Israel achieved by normalizing its relations with a power that had deep reasons to try to please it.

The enhancing and development of relations with West Germany had only a most indirect connection with the aftermath of the Sinai War. Not so was the case with another, most visible and unexpected change in Israel's international standing: the development of a whole network of relations with a multitude of Asian and African nations through an imaginative program of technical assistance. Israel's efforts in that sphere had their beginning several years before the Sinai War, but it was not until after that campaign that they assumed the dimensions of a deliberate, large-scale program. For one thing, these efforts could not have prospered without opening the short route to East Africa and Asia through the Gulf of Aqaba. For another thing, the overwhelming preoccupation with the immediate Arab threat had claimed all of Israel's attention, and it was not until that threat abated after Sinai that it could devote some of its means and energies to activities that bore no *immediate* relevance to security.

Israel's first venture in foreign assistance began almost accidentally in Burma. In 1953 Foreign Minister Sharett, while representing Mapai at the First Asian Socialist Conference in Rangoon, managed to persuade the Burmese government to exchange diplomatic representation with Israel. Up to that time Israel had failed to induce any Asian country except Turkey to establish normal diplomatic relations with it. The Muslim countries of Asia had avoided such a step out of solidarity with the fellow-Muslim Arab states, and the non-Muslim ones had lacked any positive inducement, moral or material, to establish connections with Israel. Non-Muslim Asian peoples had had for the most part no contact with Jews, no real appreciation of the problem of anti-Semitism and Jewish persecution, and were unaware of the strong Jewish ties to Palestine, which was stock knowledge among the Western peoples brought up on the Bible. Asian intellectuals who had heard something about Zionism were on the whole inclined to consider it as an instrument of Western imperialism aimed at imposing an alien people on the indigenous population, rather than a genuine nationalist movement. This indifference or antipathy of the Asians was reinforced by the fact that up to the mid-1950s Israel had had almost no commercial intercourse with any Asian country but Turkey. In view of all this, Israel considered the breakthrough achieved in Rangoon as of some importance and sought to consolidate it. Since the conventional motives for close, friendly relations among nations—such as cultural affinity or community of political or economic interest—were lacking in this instance, Israel endeavored to create artificially some tangible bonds between the two countries. Shortly after the establishment of diplomatic relations, Israel sent to Burma teams of medical personnel, engineers, conservation specialists, and various technicians of which that country was short. This reinforced the friendship between the two countries and led to the acceptance by Prime Minister U Nu of an invitation to visit Israel in the spring of 1955, which in turn led to an expansion of the cooperation program. Scores of Burmese ex-servicemen and their families were brought to Israel to spend extended periods in cooperative and collective villages to learn advanced agricultural techniques and to assimilate the Israeli experience in setting up settlement-outposts for application in Burma's jungles. After the opening of the Gulf of Aqaba, cooperation between the two countries was further extended into new areas. Burmese enterprises, such as the Five-Star Shipping Line, were established under Israeli management, Israeli enterprises entered into agreements to market Burmese products in Asia and Africa, and joint Burmese-Israeli companies were established in Burma, such as the public construction company formed in partnership with Solel Boneh.

The idea of using technical assistance and economic cooperation to justify and cement friendly diplomatic relations, first applied by Israel in Burma, and the patterns of cooperation developed in the course of its application there were extended after 1957 to several other Asian countries. Thailand, the Philippines, Nepal, Laos, Cambodia, South Vietnam, and Japan established diplomatic relations with Israel and all but the last participated in greater or lesser degree in various aid and cooperation projects.

These achievements were, however, overshadowed by the successes attained through the same methods in Africa. Among the emerging nations of that continent, Israel did not have to contend with any of the prejudices it encountered in several Asian countries. Most of the black states of Africa had had no special bond with the Arabs (some have known them only as slave traders) and were ready to view Israel on its own present merits. The first black African state to achieve independence, Ghana, accepted the Israeli offers of aid and exchange of diplomatic representation, and the success of this experiment in cooperation set an example for the other countries. Henceforth, the arrival of Israeli diplomatic missions and technicians became almost an integral part of the independence ceremonies marking the birth of each new African state. By the end of 1962 over 900 Israeli experts in a score of fields were engaged in technical assistance projects throughout Africa, while 1,000 Africans were undergoing training in Israel and 3,000 had already completed courses of varying duration and returned to their respective countries. Altogether, Israel was lending assistance of one sort or another to sixty-five countries in Africa, Asia, and Central and South America.

Because Israel's aims in engaging in the aid program included a diffuse combination of hopes and expectations, it is difficult to determine the extent to which the results met them. Insofar as economic benefit was one of the hopes, the returns it actually obtained were rather modest. Except for the special case of Iran, its trade with the Third World countries, although it developed substantially in the course of the 1957–1966 decade, remained an inconsiderable proportion of its total trade. Political support for its cause, which was certainly part of its expectation, fared only a little better. African and Asian recipients of assistance did not always give to their relationship with Israel the same significance that Israel assigned to its with them, and while they sometimes acted in the United Nations and other forums in ways that justified Israel's expectations, at other times they disappointed them rather cruelly. Israel nevertheless persisted in its efforts and even intensified them continually, partly because of a sense that things might be much worse otherwise, but above all because it felt a profound urge to break into the open, to overcome the Arab efforts to isolate it morally, to combat the attempt of its enemies to depict it in the eyes of the majority of the nations of the world as an offspring of Western imperialism thrust forcibly upon the Middle Eastern nations. In this respect Israel's effort paid off handsomely. Where in the first decade of statehood, for example, the establishment of diplomatic relations with one non-Western country was considered an achievement, in the next five years Israel was able to establish diplomatic relations at ambassadorial level with two dozen countries. And where U Nu of Burma was the only chief of state to pay an official visit to Israel in the first ten years of its existence, ten heads or chiefs of state came on official visits to Israel in the course of one year in 1961–62.

A special case in Israel's relations with African and Asian countries was its connection with Turkey, Ethiopia, and Iran. Unlike other Third World countries, these nations shared with it significant potential diplomatic-strategic interests. All four nations belong to the Middle East or its immediate periphery but are not Arab. All four have grounds for actual or potential conflict with Arab countries (Turkey with Syria over the Alexandretta district and over Syria's alliance with Egypt and the Soviet Union in opposition to the Baghdad Pact; Ethiopia with Egypt and sometimes the Sudan over their support of Somali irredentism; Iran with Nasser for his hegemonial aspirations in the Persian Gulf and with Iraq after the latter left the Baghdad Pact, over Shatt el Arab, control of the Persian Gulf, and other issues). All had reasons to fear the emergence of a strong Arab national power and to resent Soviet support of their enemies, all four maintained particularly close relations with the United States, and all border on or are near very important strategic international waterways.

Because of the potential common interest latent in this situation, Israeli diplomats discreetly explored the possibility of some form of combination among the four countries in the course of the diplomatic realignments that followed the demise of the Baghdad Pact. Evidently, these explorations produced no formal collective engagement, but the interest shared between Israel and each of these countries underlay the development of especially close relations on a bilateral basis. Turkey was for a long time the only Muslim country to recognize Israel and to exchange diplomatic representatives with it; in addition, they consistently had substantial commercial relations. Ethiopia exchanged ambassadors, received many and diverse Israeli assistance missions after 1957, and was partner in a joint enterprise to supply Israel with meat, in addition to maintaining other trade relations. Iran has not formally exchanged diplomatic representation with Israel to the present day because of the Shah's concern for the Muslim sensitivities of his subjects, but it has had more extensive and fruitful connections with Israel than any other Asian or African country. Iran received various Israeli assistance missions. After the opening of the Gulf of Aqaba in the wake of the 1956 war, Israel obtained most of its oil requirements from Iran through Eilat, where a 16-inch pipeline carried it to the refineries in Haifa. In the early 1960s a project was broached to build an additional pipeline of a 42-inch diameter from Eilat to Ashdod to provide an alternative outlet for Iranian oil in case the Suez Canal were closed; after the Six Day War the project was promptly executed to the benefit of both countries. In the 1950s and 1960s, when Nasser was pressing his pan-Arab drive, the Shah saw Israel as an important counterpoise to him. After the collapse of the Baghdad Pact, of which Iran was a member, Iran and Israel were useful to each other in dividing Iraqi energies and preventing their exclusive concentration on either of them. Since the withdrawal of the British from the Persian Gulf in 1971, Iran has had added reason to appreciate Israel's role in keeping Egypt occupied on the Suez Canal front, thus leaving it in no position to contest Iran's aspiration to fill the vacuum left by the departure of the British itself.

In sum, by the time Israel was separated from the 1956 war by as much time as that war was separated from the moment of the country's birth, its diplomatic-strategic position was better than it had ever been before. The borders had been almost completely quiet since the end of the Sinai campaign. The Arab ring around it had been loosened by the defection of Jordan and then of Syria from the Egyptian camp, and Egypt itself was bogged down in a compaign in Yemen it could neither win nor terminate. The alliance with France had survived the end of the Algerian War and gone on prospering under the Fifth Republic. The struggle between East and West, one supporting Nasser's pan-Arab drive and the other endeavoring to build an Arab bloc allied to itself, had abated after 1958, reducing the danger of the emergence of threatening combinations against Israel, and was replaced by a competition between the United States and the Soviet Union centered on the protection of existing positions, which corresponded much more with Israeli interests and orientation. Relations with the United States had constantly improved as the immediate objectives of the two countries became more and more compatible, and issued in an implicit adherence of the United States to a policy of maintaining a military balance of power between Israel and its neighbors through direct provision of offensive as well as defensive arms. Britain, too, had come to have an interest in a strong Israel, and West Germany had joined France, the United States, and Britain as provider of arms and economic and political support. Withal, Israel was able to avoid becoming identified exclusively as the protégé of Western powers thanks to an imaginative and highly successful effort to cultivate relations with scores of new and developing countries in Asia, Africa, and Latin America—an effort that projected Israel as the self-assured, successful, dynamic, and idealistic new nation it actually was.

21

The 1967 Eruption

On May 14, 1967, Israel celebrated the nineteenth anniversary of its independence. Israelis, taking stock of the state of their nation, as is their wont on such occasions, had some reasons for concern and ample grounds for satisfaction. Immigration in the previous year had reached the lowest point in fifteen years, and the economy was experiencing the first break in the process of rapid growth it had sustained since independence owing to a government "go slow" policy that seemed to have slipped. Unemployment had also reached a disturbingly high level after years of labor shortage. However, the fact that the principal concerns of the Israelis on that occasion were internal was an indication of the extent to which the international standing of their nation, and particularly its security position, were deemed to be good. True, the borders with Syria and Jordan had recently been troubled, and the Arab chiefs had held a series of summit meetings in the previous two or three years in which they attempted to concert plans for military action against Israel; but the outcome of both summits and border encounters had, if anything, only confirmed the effectiveness of Israel's deterrent power and the solidity of its international support. Thus, when Independence Day began, war and the thought of war were as far from the minds of Israelis as they had ever been.

Yet, before that day was over, the news broke out that President Nasser had put Egypt's forces on maximum alert and had begun marching troops into Sinai, in a move that proved to be the first in a series of steps that issued in general war three weeks later.

The Six Day War, as that clash came to be known, was radically different from the previous two Arab-Israeli wars in its scope, the conditions under which it was fought, its outcome, and its consequences. Moreover, the war and the crisis that led to it brought into play all the ingredients that had become tangled in the Arab-Israeli conflict in the course of the years: it put into dramatic focus the bewildering interaction between the real and perceived military relationship between the belligerents themselves, the mercurial fluctuation of inter-Arab relations between fierce rivalry and close association, the competition among the big powers and the contest between the United States and the Soviet Union as played in the Middle East arena, and the subtle endeavors of "clients" to manipulate their super-power patron and vice versa, and, finally, the intricacies of the internal politics of the belligerent countries as well as some of the outside powers as they bore on their foreign policies.

The Remote Background

Although the explosion of 1967 was neither expected nor planned in advance by any of the belligerents involved, its remote origins may in retrospect be traced to a gradual process of erosion of the balance that had developed in the Middle East in the wake of the 1958 Iraqi revolution. That balance had accounted for the region's relative quiescence in the ensuing years, when Nasser cooperated with the United States as well as the Soviet Union, the Soviet Union worked with Kassem as well as Nasser, and the United States maintained friendly relations with Nasser as well as the conservative Arab countries (Saudi Arabia, Kuwait, Jordan, Lebanon, Tunisia, and Morocco) and Israel. Each of these relationships involved elements of discord and tension as well as shared interest, but for several years after 1959 each party to them was willing and able to suppress the former and stress the latter, thus making possible a general relaxed situation. As time went on, however, fortuitous events put increasing strains on this system of relationships, eventually upset it altogether, and produced another system fraught with enhanced mutual suspicion, fear, and hostility, ever the necessary prelude to war.

The first strains in the system developed between Egypt and the United States over Nasser's military intervention against Saudi Arabian–backed royalists in Yemen in 1962. Initially, the United States had tried not to rock its relations with Egypt over the issue, but as the fighting dragged on and the Egyptians poured in more and more troops without being able to gain a decision, they sought to get at Saudi Arabia itself through subversion and air attacks against alleged royalist bases in Saudi territory. Since the Saudi rulers were traditionally friendly to the United States and since American oil companies had an immense stake in Saudi Arabia's enormous oil reserves, the United States felt compelled to come to that country's aid. When an American-sponsored agreement between Cairo and Riyad on the cessation of all outside intervention in Yemen collapsed amid mutual accusations of bad faith, American-Egyptian relations began to deteriorate.

The Yemeni conflict also contributed indirectly to damaging American-Egyptian relations through its effect on the Israeli question. At the outset of the American-Egyptian rapprochement, each side had entertained hopes of altering the other's position on Israel, but after these hopes proved illusory, both sides agreed to put the issue "on ice" and not allow it to interfere with their developing relations. The Yemen War made this agreement unworkable. As the war dragged on, the Egyptians accelerated their plans to strengthen their armed forces and, by the end of 1963, had formed at least two new divisions equipped with Soviet weapons. The Israelis reacted by turning to the United States for arms and diplomatic support. Although the United States had never before provided Israel with substantial quantities of weapons directly, it agreed on this occasion to supply Israel with Hawk surface-to-air missiles, reaffirmed its commitment to support Israel's integrity and independence along with all "other" Middle East countries, and hinted at the desirability of keeping a balance of power in the region. The Egyptians dared not react immediately for fear of jeopardizing the flow of American aid, but their resentment of the United States deepened and the link between the two countries became further strained. By 1965, after Nasser had taken some further initiatives in the Congo and elsewhere that displeased the United States, and after the United States had provided Israel with "offensive" weapons and terminated its economic assistance to Egypt, relations between the two countries were back to square one. Although the United States expressed no overt hostility to Nasser, he was nevertheless convinced that it was in fact trying to isolate and destroy him and his regime.

While American-Egyptian relations were deteriorating under the direct and indirect impact of the Yemen War, Soviet-Egyptian relations were moving in the opposite direction, mainly as a result of the collapse of Kassem's Soviet-backed regime in 1963. That event not only removed a major stumbling bloc in the way of closer Soviet-Egyptian relations, but also gave rise to a new Soviet policy that was to contribute much to the atmosphere that nurtured the war.

The Soviets' decision to support Kassem's regime had embroiled them in the internal and inter-Arab politics of the Arab countries with almost calamitous results. It had brought them into a clash with Nasser that injected in their relations a new element of mutual suspicion. It had implicated them in Kassem's use of the Communist party of Iraq to suppress his opponents with great violence, only to see him turn next against that party and outlaw it. It had led them to provide Kassem with vast amounts of arms, only to see him use them in a savage war against their traditional Kurdish protégés. It had impelled them to recognize hastily the secessionist regime in Syria, and thus caused them to betray their hostility to the cause of Arab unity (except under their own aegis) in the eyes of the Arab public. It had led them to support Kassem's claim to Kuwait and placed them in a position of isolation against all the Arab countries. In the end, all the damage they suffered on account of Kassem proved to have been in vain, as he and his regime were finally overthrown in 1963 by a military coup led by the Ba'th party, which naturally vented its rage on the Soviet Union and the Iraqi Communists.

The collapse of their position in Iraq led the Soviets almost instinctively to cling more tightly to their position in Egypt. Secretary General Khrushchev himself lent his weight to the effort by undertaking a long visit to Egypt in the spring of 1964, during which he committed the Soviet Union to another big dose of economic assistance to help in the industrialization of Egypt. The overthrow of Khrushchev shortly thereafter momentarily put in doubt the entire Soviet commitment in the Middle East, but a review of that commitment by his successors reconfirmed it while putting it in the context of a more coherent policy.

Pondering over the lessons of the disastrous experience with Kassem, the new Soviet leadership drew several lessons. One was the necessity for the Soviets to seek an insurance for their political and material investments in individual Arab countries by striving to bring about the creation in these countries of a broad base of support for the Soviet Union, beyond the particular ruler and his immediate associates. A related lesson was that the Communist parties and front organizations in the Arab countries were not yet in a position to provide that base by themselves, and that the desired support had therefore to consist of an alliance between Communists and nationalists. A third lesson was that the Soviet Union must never again get caught in a cross-fire between rival client states. In practice, these conclusions indicated a policy of trying to promote the formation of "popular fronts" embracing Communists and other "progressive" and "anti-imperialist" forces within the various Arab countries, and of endeavoring to create a coalition of client states, especially Egypt and Syria, which had been at odds since the breakup of the United Arab Republic in 1961. To accomplish these aims it was necessary to drum up a common external danger that dictated the necessity for unity, and such a danger the Soviets readily found in the form of American "imperialism" and its Israeli "stooges." Indeed, from the end of 1964 on, the Soviets regularly circulated stories about a global American imperialist offensive against progressive forces which, in the particular Middle East region, used Israel as its chief instrument and had the Syrian and Egyptian regimes as its targets.

The Soviet effort in the 1960s to build up a coalition of client Arab states on the basis of opposition to imperialism at a time when the United States contented itself with support for individual friendly countries was a curious reversal of the roles that the two superpowers had attempted to play in the 1950s. But the destabilizing effect on the region was the same, and in some respects even worse. For, at least in the 1950s, the United States sought to insulate the Arab-Israeli conflict from its alliance schemes and the Soviet Union exploited that conflict only marginally and indirectly in its efforts to frustrate the American aims, whereas in the 1960s, the Soviet Union deliberately made Arab hostility to Israel the hub of its policy objective while the United States relied in large measure on Israel to check and balance the pro-Soviet Arab states. Thus the rivalry between the superpowers in the Middle East, which in the mid-1950s focused on the inter-Arab arena and stimulated inter-Arab conflicts, focused in the mid-1960s on the much more dangerous and explosive Arab-Israeli conflict and stimulated it. A series of such stimulations, for which the Soviet Union was mostly responsible, had much to do at least with initiating the course of events that led to war.

The first major occasion for the application of the new Soviet approach of exploiting the Arab-Israeli conflict to promote a union of friendly Arab forces occurred in late 1964 and 1965. In mid-1964 Israel completed and inaugurated the National Water Carrier, which drew waters from the Jordan River and the Sea of Galilee and pumped them to the south of the country. The sources of the waters used by Israel are found in Syria and Lebanon as well as Israel, and a major tributary comes in from Jordan. Israel had based its project on the exploitation of its share of the waters, as determined by the American-sponsored Johnson Plan of a decade before, in the preparation of which Arab as well as Israeli engineers had cooperated. But the Arab governments had refused to ratify the plan because it was premised on Israel's right to exist, and Israel had gone ahead to develop its part of the plan alone.

The completion of the plan led the new Ba'thist government of Syria to issue a belligerent call for an Arab response, which implicitly challenged and condemned President Nasser, the foremost Arab leader, for doing nothing. Partly to silence his Syrian rivals and partly to create an opportunity and an excuse for pulling honorably out of his Yemen entanglement, Nasser responded by inviting all the Arab chiefs to a summit meeting which set up a committee to study and report recommendations to another summit meeting. At the second summit, the committee submitted concrete plans to divert Jordan River sources in Arab countries, but recommended applying them only after the Arab countries had made the various military preparations to deter and counter the anticipated Israeli military reactions. The Syrians deemed the recommendations to be a formula for evading the issue and urged instead immediate action. However, Nasser was able to isolate his rivals and to have the summit endorse the committee's recommendations. The oil-rich Arab countries agreed to finance the reinforcement of the armies of Syria and Jordan and the assembled leaders agreed to create a Palestine Liberation Army and a Palestine Liberation Organization. Also in ostensible fulfillment of these recommendations, Nasser concluded with Crown Prince Feisal of Saudi Arabia an agreement that would permit him to pull his forces out of Yemen in order to deploy them against Israel.

Although the Arab states were openly preparing to go to war with Israel over the Jordan waters and although the Arab position on the issue was premised on the denial of Israel's right to exist, the Soviet Union publicly supported the Arab position. The Soviets may have estimated that nothing would come of the Arab war plans, and may have therefore thought their support to be of no immediate practical relevance, but the Arab leaders themselves could not have failed to read in the Soviet stance a tendency on the part of the Soviet Union to rally to the radical Arab position that sought nothing less than the complete destruction of Israel. Some Arab leaders at least took that possibility seriously and looked for further evidence for it, which the Soviets did not fail to provide.

The big war plans of the summits did indeed come to naught, but they generated a number of developments that contributed directly or indirectly to the situation that produced the 1967 war. The summit deliberations underscored the fact that eight years of nearly perfect quiescence of the Arab-Israeli conflict had not altered by one iota the Arab position with respect to it and their insistence that its resolution lay only in the destruction of Israel. The result was a heightening of tension and a general acceleration of the arms race in the area. The deliberations also gave the Syrians reasons to take action to terminate the quiet that had prevailed on Israel's borders. Partly to force the hand of the Arab leaders and partly to play up to the gallery that the summit meetings created, the Syrians proceeded on their own with preliminary work to divert the waters of the Banias source near the Israeli border. Israel, as expected, tried to stop the work by force and the result was a prolonged chain reaction of border violence that linked directly to the events that led to war. Finally, the summit and the border clashes brought together the Syrian authorities and a newly founded Palestinian guerrilla organization, al Fatah, which arose in reaction against the "established" Palestinian leadership, in a plan to launch a systematic campaign of sabotage inside Israel. Israel's retaliations resulted in serious combats (including an air battle on April 6, 1967, in which six Syrian planes were shot down and Israeli fighters buzzed Damascus) that undermined the authority of the Syrian government, and the Israeli threats of more serious retaliation unless the Syrians desisted was the immediate ground for the Egyptian mobilization that started the movement toward war.

The Soviets' drumming up the danger to "progressive" Arab regimes from an American-Israeli campaign to destroy them fell on receptive ears in Egypt and in Syria. For one thing, relations between these regimes and the United States had in fact been deteriorating steadily. For another thing, these regimes were experiencing internal difficulties in which they suspected the CIA had a hand. Above all, they were pleased to hear the Soviets themselves tell them how noxious a role Israel was playing in the area because this forecast to them an eventual Soviet repudiation of Israel's right to exist. But the two regimes did not quite draw from the Soviets' warnings the conclusions they had wanted them to draw. As a matter of fact, instead of uniting in the face of the impending danger, they found in that very danger new grounds for indulging their rivalry, and instead of mobilizing all the progressive forces on their home fronts, they redoubled their vigilance to preserve their exclusive hold on power.

Finally, in February 1966, a new regime suddenly came to power in Syria as a result of an intra–Ba'th coup which was prepared to associate Communists in power formally and openly and was willing to be more cooperative with Nasser. The Soviets were so thrilled at this first apparent success in the area in many a year that they went to great lengths to try to secure it. In May 1966 Soviet Premier Kosygin visited Cairo and made it one of his principal objectives personally to bring about a Syrian-Egyptian reconciliation and alliance. His effort bore some fruits in that Egypt and Syria concluded a joint defense treaty in November of that year, but the two governments immediately developed differences over the applicability of the treaty. The Syrians, and the Soviets too, wanted to read it as committing Egypt to come to Syria's help in case of border incidents and limited skirmishes such as were taking place continually, in the hope that this would deter or restrain Israel; whereas the Egyptians insisted that the treaty applied only to the threat of large-scale invasion of the territory of one of the parties to it. Since the border incidents went on and went mostly quite badly for the Syrians, and since the Soviets wanted to enlist Egypt's deterrent power on behalf of the Syrian regime, they kept accusing Israel and its imperialist backers of actually planning a massive invasion of Syria. Finally, on one occasion, on May 13, 1967, they put out a warning of an impending Israeli large-scale invasion of Syria which Nasser *chose* to believe. He mobilized his troops and marched them into Sinai, warning Israel to keep its hands off Syria. Within three weeks this act developed into war.

The Immediate Causes of the War

In the immediate sense, the 1967 war, like so many others, was the result of a whole series of miscalculations and misjudgments on the part of all the interested parties, but especially on the part of President Nasser who took the initiative into his hands and maintained it until the fighting broke out.

Ever since the end of the 1956 war, Nasser had repeatedly warned zealous Arab interlocutors against the dangers of taking action against Israel that might set in motion an uncontrollable drift toward war before Egypt was prepared and circumstances were right. Yet, although he acknowledged more than once not long before May 1967 that these conditions were not ripe, he did precisely what he had cautioned against. He initiated one move and allowed the situation created by it to dictate to him the next and then the next until he found himself practically begging for a showdown. By that time he had convinced himself that his swift tactical maneuvers had created within the span of two weeks the necessary strategic and diplomatic conditions that he had previously indicated would require many years of many-faceted efforts to bring about. Among the factors that had prompted him to press his initiatives to the brink and over, probably the most important was the nature of Israel's responses to his moves. The timidity and hesitation that characterized these responses, in stark contrast with his own and everyone else's expectations, encouraged him to believe that he had indeed seized and created the opportune moment, and emboldened him to press on to the point of leaving Israel with no choice but capitulation or war.

Chronology of the Crisis

To understand the intricate interplay of forces that produced the war, it might be useful to start with a brief chronological review of the main events:

May 14, 1967: Egypt's armed forces are suddenly put in a state of "maximum alert" and Egyptian combat units are demonstratively marched into Sinai. The Egyptian press explains that these measures are taken in view of reliable information that Israel planned to attack Syria and were meant to warn Israel that Egypt would enter the battle if Israel did attack.

May 16, 1967: As the Egyptian troop buildup in Sinai continues, the Egyptian chief of staff, General Muhammad Fawzi, sends a letter to United Nations Emergency Force Commander, General Indar Jit Rikhye, asking him to withdraw immediately the UN forces from "the observation points on our frontier."

May 18, 1967: Egyptian Foreign Minister Mahmud Riyad writes to UN Secretary General U Thant informing him of the decision of his government "to terminate the existence of U.N.E.F. on the soil of the U.A.R. and the Gaza Strip." The secretary general immediately signifies his compliance with the Egyptian request.

Israel, which had previously mobilized some reserve units, calls in more reserves for active duty.

May 22, 1967: In a speech at an Egyptian air base in Sinai, Nasser announces the closing of the Gulf of Aqaba to Israeli ships and to all ships carrying "strategic material" to Israel. He adds: "The Jews threaten war; we tell them: Welcome. We are ready for war."

In a speech made the same day but before Nasser's speech, Israeli Prime Minister Levi Eshkol disclaims any aggressive intentions on the part of Israel and calls for the withdrawal of Egyptian and Israeli forces to their previous positions.

May 23, 1967: In a speech to the Knesset, Eshkol says that "any interference with freedom of shipping in the Gulf and in the Strait constitutes a gross violation of international law, a blow at the sovereign rights of other nations, and an act of aggression against Israel."

In Washington, President Lyndon Johnson declares in a nationally televised statement that "the United States considers the Gulf to be an international waterway and feels that a blockade of Israeli shipping is illegal and potentially disastrous to the cause of peace. The right of free, innocent passage of the international waterway is a vital interest of the international community."

On the same day, the Soviet government issues a formal statement that reviews the origins of the crisis without making any specific reference to the blockade and warns that "should anyone try to unleash aggression in the Near East, he would be met not only with the united strength of Arab countries but also with strong opposition to aggression from the Soviet Union and all peace-loving countries."

In New York, the Security Council meets in an emergency session at the request of Denmark and Canada. The debate trails off in the following days without reaching any conclusion. Efforts of the United States to obtain a resolution essentially requiring Egypt to refrain from blockade action while the council discusses the issue is blocked by Soviet opposition.

May 26, 1967: Israeli Foreign Minister Abba Eban confers in Washington with President Johnson and Secretary of State Dean Rusk after having conferred with President Charles de Gaulle in Paris and Prime Minister Harold Wilson in London.

Egyptian Defense Minister Shams Badran arrives in Moscow and confers with leaders of the Soviet government.

May 28, 1967: Following Eban's report on his trip to Washington, Prime Minister Eshkol declares in a speech to the nation that the Cabinet had decided on "the continuation of political action in the world arena" to find ways to reopen the Strait of Tiran, and had drawn up policy lines "to obviate the necessity of Israel having to use armed forces for her defense."

May 29, 1967: President Nasser declares before the Egyptian National Assembly that "the issue today is not the question of Aqaba or the Strait of Tiran, or UNEF. The issue is the rights of the people of Palestine, the aggression against Palestine that took place in 1948, with the help of Britain and the United States. . . . [People] want to confine it to the Strait of Tiran, UNEF, and the right of passage. We say: We want the rights of the people of Palestine—complete." The President adds that Defense Minister Badran brought him a message from Soviet Premier Kosygin "in which he says that the Soviet Union stands with us in this battle and will never allow any state to intervene until things go back to what they were before 1956."

May 30, 1967: King Hussein of Jordan suddenly visits Cairo and signs with Egypt a treaty of joint defense that places Jordan's armed forces under Egyptian command in case of war. On the same occasion, Jordan allows the entry of Iraqi troops into its territory and King Hussein reconciles himself with the leader of the Palestine Liberation Organization, Ahmad Shukairy, who flies back to Amman with him.

May 31, 1967: The United States is reported to be engaged in efforts to bring Western maritime powers into a scheme of action to counter the Egyptian blockade. The Soviet Union is reported to be sending additional naval units to the Mediterranean.

June 1, 1967: A reshuffling of the government in Israel brings in a "wall-to-wall" coalition including all parties except the Communists. General Dayan, chief of staff during the 1956 war, takes over the defense portfolio from Prime Minister Eshkol.

June 2, 1967: Prime Minister Wilson confers with President Johnson in Washington. It is reported that the talks dealt with the project of issuing a declaration on freedom of navigation in the Gulf of Aqaba to which Western maritime powers would subscribe.

June 4, 1967: It is announced that Egyptian Vice President Zakariya Muhieddine would visit Washington and American Vice President Hubert Humphrey would visit Cairo shortly to hold talks on the crisis.

A conference of eleven Arab oil-producing countries opens in Damascus on Iraq's initiative to consider prohibition of sale of oil to countries that would support Israel.

Iraq adheres formally to the Jordanian-Egyptian joint defense agreement. Elements of an Iraqi expeditionary force have already entered Jordan.

An airlift continuing throughout the day brings Egyptian equipment and men into Jordan.

Algeria, Libya, and the Sudan are reported to be preparing to send contingents to Egypt. Kuwait's forces have already arrived.

June 5, 1967: Hostilities begin at about 8:00 A.M. Tel Aviv time with an Israeli air strike against Egyptian airfields and several armored thrusts into Egyptian positions. Syria immediately begins bombarding Israeli settlements. Two hours later, Jordan opens heavy artillery fire along its entire front with Israel.

June 8, 1967: Cease-fire on the Jordan-Israel front

June 9, 1967: Cease-fire on the Egypt-Israel front

June 11, 1967: Cease-fire on the Syria-Israel front.

The Dynamics of the Crisis Viewed from Cairo

A perusal of the chronology clearly indicates that Nasser held the initiative throughout and suggests four questions: (1) Why did Nasser mobilize his troops and concentrate them in Sinai? (2) Why did he demand the withdrawal of UNEF? (3) Why did he go on to proclaim the blockade of the Gulf of Aqaba? and (4) Why did he escalate the issue from the strait question to the entire Palestine problem?

The answer to all these questions would be greatly simplified if one were to suppose that Nasser had deliberately sought a military showdown with

Israel from the very outset. His moves would then constitute a logical succession of steps toward such a showdown and the only question would be about his choice of time. However, all the evidence runs against such a supposition and everyone, including Nasser and the Israelis, as well as interested and neutral observers, rightly rejected it. Rather, evidence and personal testimony concur that Nasser made at least his first move with a limited objective in mind, and that it was the repercussions of that move and the circumstances in which he made it that suggested to him the next step and then the next.

Nasser himself indicated on various occasions after the beginning of the crisis that he had made his first move only because he had received intelligence from the Russians, which his own sources confirmed, that the Israelis were planning an attack on Syria, and he wanted to deter them from carrying out their intent. Thus, on May 22 in the speech in which he proclaimed the blockade, he said: "The sequence of events determined the plan. We had no plan before May 13 [the day he received the intelligence] because we believed that Israel would not dare attack any Arab country and would not dare make such an impertinent statement [threatening Syria]." He repeated the same point in a letter to President Johnson about a week later, and he reiterated it in his resignation speech on June 9, 1967, and in the address he gave on the anniversary of his regime, July 23, 1967.

On all these occasions, Nasser also pointed out that the Soviets had specifically indicated to him that Israel had concentrated eleven to thirteen brigades for the attack that was planned for May 17, that the Syrians had reported to him that they had identified eighteen Israeli brigades in their sector, and that his own intelligence sources had ascertained the fact of very heavy Israeli troop concentrations. All this, if true, would suffice to explain Nasser's decision to mobilize and deploy his troops. One could then say that, in view of the large size of the Israeli forces in question, the Israelis were bent on executing an invasion of Syria rather than a mere retaliatory raid, and that he could not "sit out" such an operation without forfeiting any claim to Arab leadership, especially since he had recently concluded a joint defense agreement with Syria.

It happens, however, that the alleged Israeli troop concentration did not take place. The United Nations Truce Supervision Organization, which had many times in the past checked on similar allegations and submitted reports that obtained the credence of Arabs, Israelis, and United Nations organs, explicitly reported this time that it had failed to detect any Israeli troop concentration. More important, Egyptian Defense Minister Badran testified in the course of the trials of several high officials that were held in early 1968 that the Egyptian chief of staff at the time of the crisis, General Fawzi, flew to Syria after the Russians had reported about the Israeli troop concentrations and reported back that there was no sign of any unusual Israeli activity and that the Russians must have been having hallucinations. It was pointed out in the previous section that the Soviets had an important interest in making the Egyptians believe that Israel was intent on invading Syria; but why did Nasser agree to adopt what he knew to be false information and act on it as if it were true?

Two related reasons suggest themselves. The first is that the Soviet initiative in conveying to him specific "intelligence" about an Israeli invasion plan amounted in fact to an invitation to him to take some substantial military measures against Israel that he could not resist. For many years before, Nasser and other Arab leaders had endeavored to win the Soviets over to the thesis that Israel must be forcefully dismantled or cut down to harmless proportions, but had encountered staunch opposition on grounds of ostensible principle and practicality. More recently, the Soviets seemed to have implicitly relented a bit on the principle when they supported the Arabs in the Jordan waters dispute, but they continued to be cautious about the possibility of an Arab armed encounter with Israel on the practical grounds that it might lead to a big-power confrontation. Now, with their invitation to Nasser to act, they seemed to be willing to take another step forward and contemplate, indeed urge, a large-scale Arab military initiative, albeit of limited scope; this opened too good a prospsect for Nasser to let go, especially since the manner in which the Soviets conveyed their desire was sufficiently vague to allow him to stretch its scope and perhaps take the Soviets further than they intended to go.

The second reason why Nasser decided to act as if the Russian information were true is that in a certain sense he believed it to be *essentially* true. Israel may not have been concentrating forces for an invasion of Syria just then, but Nasser was convinced that an American-supported Israeli large-scale attack on Syria was very likely to take place sooner or later. Ever since the United States terminated its economic assistance to Egypt he had held the belief that the United States was out to destroy him, and as he looked upon the mounting tension between Syria and Israel, he saw it as offering a good opportunity for the United States, acting through Israel, to hit him indirectly by hitting at Syria. In other words, Nasser had reached through his own independent thinking conclusions that were quite similar to those that the Russians were voicing. But although, as Nasser himself was to point out later, his suspicion of the United States went back at least two years before the crisis, he had not dared do anything to ward off the expected American-Israeli blow for fear of finding himself confronting the United States alone. Now that the Russians themselves seemed to be urging him on and promising him their implicit support, he gladly availed himself of the opportunity to strike first and try to throw his enemies' plans into confusion.

In addition to the desire to capitalize on the Russians' coming forward on Israel and the concern with the threat of an American blow, a number of factors contributed to driving Nasser on the course he took. There was, first of all, the very difficult economic conditions at home. The ten-year plan to double Egypt's national product, on which Nasser had pinned his hopes for Egypt's future, had run into great trouble. The first five-year plan, completed in 1965, had fallen short of its targets and had brought on severe shortages and inflationary pressures. The second five-year plan, begun immediately after, encountered in addition a great dearth of capital and had to be prolonged, then altered to switch the emphasis from heavy to consumer industries, and finally was scrapped altogether as Egypt failed to meet its payments to foreign creditors. Compounding Egypt's difficulties, and incidentally lending all the more weight to Nasser's suspicions, was the cessation of American wheat shipments, which had saved Egypt an average of $150 million in foreign currency every year since 1960. As the prospect for the growth of what Nasser called "organic strength" thus appeared to be dim, the temptation to look for short cuts through political maneuvers must have been very great indeed. Moreover, Nasser, who was well aware of the arguments administration spokesmen often used in their efforts to secure Congressional approval for aid to Egypt, might well have hoped that by "making trouble" he would press the United States into resuming wheat shipments.

Another factor affecting Nasser's behavior was the decline in Egypt's standing in the Arab world and the apparent collapse of the drive for Arab unity, which were related in turn to the economic difficulties at home, the failure to win the Yemen War or bring it to an honorable conclusion, and the loss of room for maneuver in the international political arena as a result of the decline in the role of the nonaligned group of countries. A dramatic move against Israel, particularly one undertaken to bail the Syrians out of a situation they could not handle by themselves, promised therefore to put him back in the Arab limelight and restore to him the prestige and stature that he knew were convertible into concrete political benefits.

Still another factor affecting Nasser's thinking was the doubt that was beginning to shake his grand strategic concept toward Israel. Nasser, like everyone else, knew that Israel won the 1948 war and established itself because it mobilized its resources to the utmost for that struggle, whereas the Arabs threw into it only a tiny portion of their potential power. To reverse the 1948 decision, the Arabs seemingly needed only to exert themselves to realize their potential superiority and to resist the temptations and provocations to engage in a premature fight. In the years following the 1956 war, when that grand strategy was finally crystallized, things seemed to work according to plan. By the mid-1960s, however, the grand strategic objective seemed to have receded and the assumptions underlying it appeared very dubious indeed. On the one hand, the development of Egypt's economy ran into serious difficulties after what seemed to be a promising start, and the drive for Arab unity, which had received a tremendous impetus by the union of Egypt and Syria, bogged down completely after the Syrian secession, the aborting of the

1963 union between Egypt, Syria, and Iraq, the interminable war in Yemen, and so on. On the other hand, Israel developed its capacities so fast that the gap in the relative size of the gross national product of Egypt and Israel was reduced from a ratio of about four and a half to one in 1949 to one and a half to one in 1967. By 1967, too, the actual *quantitative* relation between the armed forces of the two was, overall, as close as that between their respective GNPs. In other words, time, which was supposed to be Egypt's main asset, had in fact worked in favor of Israel.

The collapse of the hope of eventually achieving a sufficient margin of conventional military superiority to win a decisive offensive war required a change of strategy if Egypt were to stick to its objective of overcoming Israel. There are sufficient indications that Nasser was wavering between a number of alternatives, including one that would attempt to tip the balance against Israel by means of an ad hoc unification of Arab forces, another that would seek to give full play to massive human numbers rather than sophisticated equipment, a third that would be geared to a guerrilla-type war of liberation, and perhaps others. But it was at any rate clear in his mind that the previous grand strategy of waiting and preparing was of no avail, and that if an opportunity presented itself to try out some of the other alternatives or at least to prepare the ground for them, it was not to be missed. The mobilization of his forces and their deployment in Sinai on May 14, 1967, in the circumstances indicated above, appeared to Nasser as serving the additional purpose of deterring, or at least making more difficult and less frequent, Israeli retaliatory actions against guerrilla operations and thus giving these a better chance to develop. When this initial purpose appeared to have been served, other opportunities for more decisive gains seemed to have opened up.

The next question was the removal of UNEF. This subject has stirred much unnecessary controversy because its various elements have been confused by the disputants for purposes of ex post facto self-justification. To begin with, Egypt's intentions and motives should be perfectly clear. There is no doubt that the Egyptian government initially wanted the UN troops removed *only* from the Egyptian border with Israel and concentrated in the Gaza Strip. This is quite clear from the letter of General Fawzi to General Rikhye. The reason for this Egyptian request was to make the message of the mobilization credible to all concerned, after that move had been derided in Israel as everywhere else as an empty show.

However, when General Rikhye conveyed General Fawzi's request to UN Secretary General U Thant, the latter ruled that the request was made by the wrong person to the wrong person and was therefore invalid. The Secretariat was later to avail itself of this point in order to argue that U Thant had received only one Egyptian request and that was for a complete removal of UNEF from Sinai and the Gaza Strip. "Legally," the claim is, of course, correct, and it would have been equally correct substantively if the secretary general had in fact not reacted to the message at all. In fact, however, U Thant responded by inquiring from Egyptian Foreign Minister Riyad about the precise intentions of his government and by indicating to him that while he, U Thant, considered Egypt to be perfectly entitled to ask for a complete removal of UNEF, he did not think it had a right to order how and where the UN force should be deployed. Perhaps he meant to bluff Nasser into canceling the original demand for a partial UN pullout. If so, the secretary general must have been incredibly ill-advised about Nasser's character and his motives for marching his troops into Sinai, especially since General Fawzi's request, whatever the standing assigned to it in the UN Secretariat, had already been made public in the Egyptian media and had committed Nasser beyond recall. In any case, on May 18, 1967, Foreign Minister Riyad wrote back conveying his government's request to "terminate the existence of U.N.E.F. on the soil of the U.A.R. and in the Gaza Strip," U Thant complied forthwith, and the crisis took a more serious turn.

Why did Nasser go on to prolcaim the blockade of the Strait of Tiran?

In the speech in which he proclaimed the blockade as well as on several occasions afterward, Nasser argued that the closing of the Gulf of Aqaba followed inexorably from the occupation of Sharm el Sheikh by Egyptian troops in place of the UN forces. However, although the world has tended to accept this view as evidenced by the widespread attempts to shift all the blame back to U Thant, in Egypt itself the issue was not by any means seen as predetermined, as is evident in press comments at the time and in subsequent high-level Egyptian testimony.

Probably the most important consideration underlying Nasser's decision was the weakness manifested by Israel in its response to his previous moves. The Israelis had not been preparing an invasion of Syria but they *had* been envisaging some kind of action against it in retaliation for its support of a campaign of sabotage inside Israel. This was apparent not only from the warnings they were voicing and from the effort they were making to prepare world opinion, but was also part and parcel of their well-established strategy for dealing with incursions from across the borders. In preparing for the action, the Israelis had not counted at all on any serious Egyptian intervention, since Egypt had not intervened on similar occasions in recent months and had indeed explicitly indicated that its joint defense treaty with Syria left the responsibility for local border defense to each of the parties alone. Therefore, when Nasser marched his troops into Sinai, the Israelis were completely taken by surprise. For a few days, they tried to "protect" their initial judgment by characterizing Nasser's move as an empty demonstration; but when he demanded the withdrawal of UNEF and thus upset entirely an important security arrangement that had worked for ten years, all skepticism vanished. Caught off balance, the Israelis began to beat a hasty retreat. Clearly, they had not bargained for a showdown with Egypt, and much as the press and government officials had previously talked about the "impossibility" of remaining passive in the face of Syrian provocations, they nearly all abruptly changed their tone now and began to talk about the need to defuse the crisis. The reversal reached its climax in a speech Prime Minister Eshkol made before the Knesset on May 22, 1967, in which he disclaimed any intention of launching any kind of attack against either Syria or Egypt, warned of the danger of troop concentrations and urged the mutual withdrawal of forces; and, instead of the previous sharp warnings that he and others had voiced, expressed merely the "expectation" that the Arab countries would reciprocate Israel's innocent intentions.

Eshkol's speech occurred after Nasser had already decided on the blockade and could not therefore have influenced it, although it did influence Nasser's posture thereafter. But the appeasing mood expressed in the speech was already quite evident before, and it had a crucial influence. It encouraged Nasser, as he himself later admitted, to believe that Israel under its existing leadership might not fight, especially if it did not receive encouragement and support from the United States. As he revealed in a speech on July 23, 1967, and as was confirmed by others, he told the Supreme Executive Committee, which he had convened in his house to decide on the question, that he estimated the chances of war as a result of the closure of the gulf at not more than 50 percent.

Given this low estimate of the chances that Israel would respond with war, the closing of the gulf had a great appeal to Nasser. His expulsion of UNEF after marching his troops into Sinai and his successful intimidation of Israel had already restored him, as if by a miracle, to the position of the undisputed hero of the Arab world that he had occupied more than once before. He knew, however, from his past ups and downs that as soon as his opponents in the Arab world recovered from the first gust of his regained popularity, they would seek to minimize his political victory over Israel by taunting him about Israeli shipping going through waters he controlled. To retain the gains he already achieved he was impelled, given his relatively low estimate of the risk involved, to seek more gains by closing the gulf.

Nasser's success in forcing Israel to back away from its retaliatory threats against Syria dealt a severe blow to its "current defense" strategy, which had been specifically designed to frustrate the development of a guerrilla campaign against it by retaliating against the countries from which incursions originated. Given his low estimate of the probability that Israel would respond with war, closing the gulf appeared to offer excellent chances of consolidating this gain against possible Israeli recovery. For if Israel did not, indeed, go to war in the face of a challenge it had solemnly vowed to resist, that would be an indication of a total collapse of will and of demoralization that would permit further massive inroads without much risk. But even if Israel decided after all to go to war, Nasser thought there would still be time, while his troops delayed the Israelis in Sinai, for world pressure to develop and force an Israeli withdrawal—as it had in 1956. Nasser would then end up with the gulf still under his control, and closed. And this time he would be in a position to pursue Israel further, by means of guerrilla units and in other ways.

If on May 22 Nasser proclaimed the blockade while wishing that it should not lead to war, a week later he seemed to be doing almost everything to goad Israel into war. After having escalated the crisis once by removing UNEF and a second time by closing the Gulf of Aqaba, he went on in the last week of May to escalate it still further by proclaiming that the issue at stake was not simply navigation in the gulf but the entire Palestine question, by stating that if war broke out his objective would be the destruction of Israel, by asserting unequivocally that the Palestinians had the right to fight for their homeland regardless of consequences, and by declaring that he was not content with restoring the situation to what it was before 1956 (when the gulf was closed), but sought to restore it to what it was before 1948 (when Israel did not exist). He thus deliberately placed the government of Israel before the dilemma of risking the state's existence by fighting right away or risking it by facing blockade and generalized guerrilla warfare together with internal demoralization and possibly political collapse. In the course of that week, Nasser told his associates that the chances of war had risen to 80 percent. Why did he escalate the issue at stake and press the crisis?

The short answer is that Nasser convinced himself that his moves had created a unique opportunity for dealing Israel a decisive blow that could bring about a fabulous payoff. At the least, the reward would be Egyptian hegemony in the area. At best, it could mean the fulfillment of the dream of integral Arab unity under Egyptian aegis in a very substantial part of the Arab world.

Nasser, according to his closest confidant, believed there were three conditions that needed to be met before Egypt could initiate a war against Israel: (1) the concentration of superior military power, (2) diplomatic isolation of Israel, and (3) Arab unity. On the eve of the crisis, on May 13, none of these conditions seemed to Nasser to obtain, but such was the course of events unleashed by his moves, so rapidly did the situation develop, and such was his incredible daring to draw swiftly far-reaching conclusions and to act on them, that it appeared to him during the last week in May that all three conditions were met. His tactics, he thought, had changed the strategic picture at least momentarily.

Regarding the concentration of superior military power, three factors combined to cause Nasser to revise his views. The first was the purely psychological one of becoming intoxicated by the sight of the enormous quantities of men and equipment he had deployed in Sinai. The second factor was a downward revision of the impression he had of Israel's might as a result of the sheepish reaction of its government to his expulsion of UNEF and its relatively mild response to his blockade move. Everyone involved in Arab-Israeli affairs had expected a blockade of the Gulf of Aqaba to bring a swift and drastic Israeli counteraction, especially in a situation in which Israel's armed forces were already mobilized and deployed on the Egyptian frontier. This is why President Johnson, for instance, found it necessary to go on the air within hours of Nasser's blockade declaration to make clear the United States position, why he characterized Egypt's action as potentially disastrous to the cause of peace, and why he discreetly asked Israel to give him a 48-hour delay before taking action. Yet, although there were many in Israel who urged an immediate military response, the government's reaction was mild under the circumstances. In a speech delivered by Eshkol to a packed Knesset on May 23, the Israeli Prime Minister admonished Egypt by saying that "any interference with freedom of shipping in the gulf and the strait constitutes a gross violation of international law, a blow to the sovereignty and rights of other nations, and an act of aggression against Israel." He reminded the world that this was a "fateful hour" not only for Israel but for the world too, and called on the major powers and the United Nations to act without delay in maintaining the right of free navigation to Eilat. "If a criminal attempt is made to impose a blockade on the shipping of a member of the United Nations . . ." he said in his punchline, "it will be a dangerous precedent that will have grave effects on international relations and the freedom of the seas." The contrast between this kind of talk and the reaction generally expected, particularly the appeal to the world and to an obviously paralyzed United Nations to act on behalf of international order as well as Israel, could only convey the impression that Israel itself judged its strength to be inferior to the task of picking up the gauntlet thrown down by Egypt. The days that followed saw a toughening of the vocabulary used by Israeli spokesmen, but this only made the weakness of the next authoritative decision of Israel stand out all the more clearly. On May 28, 1967, Prime Minister Eshkol announced that the Cabinet had decided the previous day to allow more time for "the continuation of political action in the world arena."

The third factor leading Nasser to believe that the condition of concentration of superior force had been met was much more real, although it too contained a psychological element. As soon as Egypt mobilized on May 14, Nasser's chief of staff had flown to Damascus to bring into operation the terms of the joint defense agreement with Syria. This brought a considerable addition to the forces at Nasser's disposal as well as the strategic advantage of being able to open a second front to the north of Israel. A much more important accretion of force and a truly crucial strategic advantage were gained after the blockade move, when King Hussein of Jordan signed a joint defense agreement with Egypt that placed under Egyptian command Jordan's small but tough armed forces and put at the disposal of that command the Jordanian bulge with its invaluable strategic potentialities. Nasser and Hussein also made arrangements for bringing considerable Egyptian forces and an entire Iraqi division into Jordan.

The Egyptian-Jordanian treaty was signed on May 30, but according to the authoritative *al Ahram,* Nasser knew that it was forthcoming at least four days before and had the agreement at the back of his mind when he made some of the declarations that escalated the crisis. Thus, within two weeks of his initial mobilization move and a week after his blockade proclamation, Nasser saw the forces at his disposal increased or about to be increased by the addition of all the Syrian, all the Jordanian, and a sizeable portion of the Iraqi armed forces, and his strategic posture immeasureably improved by the prospect of being able to press Israel on three fronts and from many critical directions out of the Jordanian bulge. A little time and some coordination and these changes could indeed make Egypt's military posture formidable; but, the swirl of events apparently blurred in Nasser's mind the distinction between the potential and the actual and led him to act as if he already effectively commanded advantages that were only partly secured.

Regarding the second condition that had to be met before initiating a showdown with Israel—isolating Israel from its friends—the decisive moment in Nasser's eyes seems to have been reached on May 28, when Premier Kosygin reassured him—as he revealed in a speech the next day—that the Soviet Union would neutralize the United States in the event that Israel went to war. The significance of this development in Nasser's eyes and in terms of the attitude of the big powers would be better appreciated if we recall the background against which it took place. I have argued that the Soviet Union had practically incited Nasser to move his troops into Sinai in order to deter the Israelis from hitting Syria in a big or limited action and to cement the Syrian-Egyptian alliance. The Russians had not counted on the complications that developed with UNEF any more than Nasser had, but, in view of the circumstances under which Nasser asked for the removal of that force, they went along and supported his move after the fact. Nasser's further initiative in proclaiming the blockade, however, startled them and caused them to pause. For one thing, they had already achieved their objective of forming a broad Arab deterrent to Israeli attacks and had no interest in this additional move. For another thing, they, as everyone else, knew the gravity with which Israel had looked upon such an eventuality and feared that war might ensue that would face them with difficult dilemmas. Above all, they were concerned about the reaction of the United States in view of its sympathy, indeed, its suspected collusion with Israel and its specific commitments to Israel on this particular issue, especially after President Johnson responded to Nasser's blockade immediately and forcefully with his May 23 statement. This is why the Soviet government, in *its* statement on the same day, had gone into a long diatribe against Israel and those backing it, specifically supported Nasser's mobilization and removal of UNEF, but had been conspicuously careful not to make any explicit reference to the closing of the Strait of Tiran.

As long as the Soviet Union maintained its reserve on the issue of the strait, Nasser feared that the chances of a strong American intervention on behalf of Israel were very high. But when the Soviet Union committed itself to opposing American intervention, the act seemed to Nasser to be significant not only in itself but also as a reflection of a lowered Russian estimate of the probability of American intervention. These evaluations appeared all the more trustworthy because Nasser knew that the United States and the Soviet Union had been in touch through the "hot line" at the highest levels in an effort to prevent a misunderstanding of each other's intentions, and because the overt behavior of the United States appeared to confirm them.

The United States, we have seen, began by reacting quite strongly to Nasser's blockade proclamation. Besides the President's prompt and forceful statement on May 23, a strong verbal note was delivered the next day to the Egyptian government by the newly appointed American ambassador to Cairo in which the United States government essentially insisted on a return to the status quo ante pending negotiations and made it clear that it did not rule out the use of force if Egypt insisted on applying the blockade. The administration persisted in this position until May 26 in order to give Israel reason to hope that a settlement might be achieved without its having to resort to arms. After that date, it began to waver.

On May 26, in the course of discussions with Israeli Foreign Minister Eban, President Johnson stated that he intended to use any or all means to keep the Strait of Tiran open and referred specifically to plans to organize a concerted action by the Western maritime powers to break the blockade, by force if necessary. However, he asked Israel to abstain from any forceful initiative for about two weeks until he could obtain the necessary Congressional and international support to bring his plans to fruition. The President summed up his position by saying that "Israel would not be alone unless it decided to go alone," a statement that left Israel free to act or accept his request for delay and therefore was viewed in the administration as a real test of Israel's mood. When the Israeli Cabinet, after hearing Eban's report, decided two days later to accede to the President's request, most people in the administration concluded that "the worst of the crisis was over." The fact that the Israeli government had accepted the American thesis of a *collective* initiative of maritime powers, even more than its acceptance of the delay, persuaded the administration's officials that Israel must have deemed the cost of war prohibitive, and that, consequently, if a formula could be found that would save everybody's face, the crisis would be "licked." For notwithstanding the various references made by American spokesmen to the Gulf of Aqaba as an international waterway, the fact was that the United States had no crucial interest of its own in the issue as such, but was most concerned about it only because it could lead to war with all its unpredictable consequences. Once it appeared that Israel was not prepared to go to war, the problem lost most of its urgency for the United States. It did not take the Soviet Union long to detect the resultant weakening of America's position on the issue and to exploit it to undermine any possibility of collective action by firming up its support of Egypt.

It should be mentioned, for the sake of a fuller understanding of the American position, that President Johnson himself started with a strong inclination to take forceful action not only in order to prevent war but also to fulfill what he deemed to be existing commitments to Israel on navigation in the gulf. However no sooner did he reveal this inclination in the May 23 statement than a groundswell of opposition began to build up in Congress and outside it against any unilateral American intervention. The President, taking account of this mood, switched to the idea of a collective initiative but remained quite earnest about forceful action, which is probably why he was able to persuade the Israelis to wait. Once he succeeded in this however, the sense that the crisis had eased, pressures at home, and lack of response abroad blunted the remaining edge of this position and led him to go along with efforts to "patch things up." On the one hand, there was continuing strong opposition to the use of force, even in a collective setting, in Congressional circles weary of another Vietnam, among officials who feared for the American position in the Arab world, and among those who maintained that such action was not really needed since compromise was possible. On the other hand, all but two or three of the potential partners of a collective action first balked at making any threat to use force, and then shied away even from a simple declaration asserting the right of free passage for ships of all nations in the Gulf of Aqaba for fear of endangering their interests in the Arab world or suffering Arab sanctions.

While the United States thus appeared to be engaged in a repeat of the Dulles performance of 1956—when the secretary of state started with tough talk in connection with Nasser's nationalization of the Suez Canal and then proceded to paralyze Britain and France with ingenious schemes and verbal acrobatics, the Soviet Union went on to give Nasser and the world a token of its earnestness by moving additional naval units to the western Mediterranean. The reinforced Soviet squadron was no match for the American Sixth Fleet, but the Soviet naval units could serve as a tripwire to hamper and restrict the American fleet and were therefore usable as an indication of serious intent to oppose American intervention. The Soviet fleet also helped to deter other maritime powers from joining the United States in any collective demonstration of force or action.

With the United States practically neutralized, Nasser did not need to worry about other friends of Israel. De Gaulle had already made it clear to Foreign Minister Eban and to the Egyptian side that he opposed the use of force and favored a Big Four effort to solve the crisis. Prime Minister Wilson had initially assured Eban that Britain was willing to join the United States in any action to reopen the Strait of Tiran, but the position of France, the increasingly hesitating position of the United States, the reticence of other maritime nations, the firming up of the Soviets, his concern with the fate of British oil interests, and the impression that Israel might not go to war after all, led him to pull back thereafter. Essentially, then, despite continuing noises to the contrary, the incredible seemed to Nasser to have happened: in a week of tactical maneuvering, Israel was effectively isolated from the West.

The third and last condition that Nasser had set for himself before seeking a showdown with Israel was Arab unity. The kind of unity Nasser had in mind in the years before the crisis was integral unity—that is to say, a merger of at least several critical Arab countries—and, of course, such unity did not take place in the week following the proclamation of the blockage. However, the crisis he unleashed had precipitated symbolic as well as real manifestations of Arab solidarity of such scope and intensity as to lead him to expect that solidarity to fulfill, at least for the moment, the same function of pooling the Arabs' military, diplomatic, and economic resources as full Arab unity. At the same time, he saw these manifestations as preparing the ground for culminating a victory over Israel with the realization of the longed-for integral Arab unity. The extent to which the course of events led Nasser to readjust quickly his evaluations and objectives is nowhere indicated better than in his change of attitude on this question. On May 21, the day before he announced the blockade, *al Ahram* reported that Egypt had refused a proposal made by some conservative Arab countries to assemble the Arab Common Defense Council, on the grounds that "only those can confront Israel who can confront imperialism. All other talk is illusion and deception." Five days later, with the secret knowledge that Jordan was about to throw its lot with him and with other manifestations of Arab solidarity, Nasser could barely control his enthusiasm in addressing a delegation of the Arab Workers' Congress:

> If Israel began with any aggression against Egypt or Syria, the battle against Israel will be total and its object will be the destruction of Israel. We can do this. I could not have spoken like that five years ago or three years ago. . . Today, eleven years after 1956, I say these words because I know what we have in Egypt. And what Syria has. I know that the other countries too—today Iraq has sent troops into Syria; Algeria will send us forces; Kuwait too will send up forces. . . This is Arab power; this is the true rebirth of the Arab nation, which had previously been feeling rather hopeless.

Nasser's feeling that he had triggered a rebirth of the Arab nation must have been strengthened even more in the days that followed. Literally every single Arab country offered to contribute or actually began to contribute troops. Even a symbolic force committed the contributing country to the confrontation with Israel and served notice upon the world that they would jointly react against the interests of any nation that supported Israel. Naturally, the fact that the oil-producing countries—Libya, Kuwait, Iraq, Saudi Arabia, and Algeria—joined in the act lent a particular weight to this collective diplomatic Arab deterrent. Indeed, this deterrent had much to do with frustrating the schemes of collective action by the Western maritime nations.

Two questions remain concerning this Egypt-centered analysis of the evolution of the crisis: If it is true that Nasser escalated the issue at stake in the crisis from the problem of navigation to that of Israel's existence, and that he did so because the repercussions of his earlier moves had convinced him that the conditions for a showdown with Israel had materialized at last, why then did he agree on June 4 to send Vice President Muhieddine to Washington and receive Vice President Humphrey in Cairo to hold talks on the crisis? And why did he not take the initiative to attack Israel first and thus gain for himself the military advantages that might be had from striking the first blow?

The answer to the first question is that Nasser thought that there was much to gain from the talks and little risk in them. Nasser revealed after the war that he had told his Executive Council on June 2, 1967, that the chances of war were by then 100 percent and that Israel was going to strike on June 5, but he also said on the same occasion that he thought the talks with the United States might delay the outbreak of war as long as they lasted. A delay was advantageous to Nasser because it would give him time to complete his preparations and would especially give the Iraqi troops the chance to deploy themselves on Jordan's West Bank, while it would only increase the psychological and economic pressure on Israel, whose life was completely disrupted by total mobilization. Moreover, the talks offered the chance of trying to split the United States from Israel by a show of moderation on the gulf issue and thus further isolate his enemy. The risk he ran was that of giving the American administration the chance to trap him into a position of appearing to be intransigent and defiant and thus to allow it to press Congress to support a forceful response. However, the preliminary talks with the American special envoy, Charles Yost, that had led to the idea of the exchange of visits, and Nasser's reading of the administration's mood at that point had rightly persuaded him that the risk was negligible.

As to the second question, the answer is simply that the isolation of Israel, which was one of the essential conditions for seeking a showdown with it, was operative only if he did not strike the first blow. Nasser well knew that the Soviet commitment to neutralize the United States depended on a prior Soviet assessment that the American inclination to intervene was weak, and the American inclination was weak as long as the issue appeared to be free navigation in the Gulf of Aqaba. Were Nasser, by attacking Israel first, to convert the issue formally and openly into an assault on Israel's existence, the whole situation would be altered. The odds for American intervention would then leap to near certainty, and this in turn might well scare the Soviets into a passive position. Evidence that these were the kind of thoughts Nasser had in mind was revealed, in fact, in the postwar trials of high Egyptian officials. Former Minister of Defense Badran testified that after he returned from Moscow on May 28, he went to General Headquarters where Nasser was having a conference. Nasser pointed out that the chances of war had risen from 80 percent to 100 percent, but that political considerations dictated that Egypt should not strike the first blow because the Americans would intervene. General Sidki Mahmud, commander of the air force, objected that he could not risk being paralyzed by an Israeli first blow, whereupon Marshal Abdel Hakim Amer asked him whether he preferred to strike the first blow and face the Americans, or be hit first and face Israel only? Sidki Mahmoud immediately agreed that the latter was preferable. Asked what losses he expected to suffer from an Israeli first blow, he said 20 percent.

The Dynamics of the Crisis as Viewed from Israel

If in analyzing the crisis from the perspective of Egypt there were four key questions corresponding to Nasser's rapid moves, in looking at the crisis from the perspective of Israel there is only one: why was there such a timid public reaction on the part of the government until June 1 and then a diametrical reversal in the following days?

In attempting to answer the questions about Nasser, it was necessary to range far and wide into various economic, diplomatic, and military spheres. In trying to answer the question about Israel, however, one need not go too far away from its own internal politics and problems of decision-making. The reason for this difference is that Israel, unlike Egypt, did not have much room for maneuver to alter the overall situation. It had no kindred nations to rally, alliances to activate or fashion, or untapped resources to mobilize, but could only throw its own weight in the scales. Even the limited room for exertion it had with a view to bringing the United States to intervene on its behalf depended, as it appears in retrospect, on the impression conveyed by the Israeli government about its disposition to act militarily. For, as pointed out before, the principal reason the United States had for intervening was to prevent the outbreak of war, which in turn depended on the extent of Israeli determination to resist the blockade.

The initial timidity of the Israeli government is partly explainable by the character of the Israeli government system. Once taken by surprise, Israel's government could not by its very nature react as swiftly and as decisively as Egypt's. In Egypt, an authoritarian system permitted one man to make quick decisions or to arbitrate decisively between the views of advisers and assistants who did not question his supremacy. In Israel, on the other hand, an effective democracy and one based on a coalition of minority parties at that, dictated the necessity to arrive at new decisions by a near-consensus of eighteen Cabinet members, a strongly dissenting minority of whom could bring down the government. Such a system naturally fostered compromises and encouraged equivocal stands.

This structural factor and the element of surprise do not, however, suffice to account for the indecisiveness displayed by Israel's government between May 15 and June 1. After all, the same structure did not prevent the government from promptly adopting fateful decisions in the past, nor was it to prevent it from acting with incredible boldness in the days and weeks that followed. One must therefore look for the answer to the question beyond governmental structure, to the particular leadership of Israel at the time and the specific circumstances under which it operated.

All the evidence that has come to light suggests that the key to the evolution of the situation in Israel lay in the development of a "credibility crisis" regarding Eshkol's role, in his capacity of minister of defense, as a link between the military and the government. This thesis should not be confused with others that may sound somewhat similar, which view the military in Israel as tending to intervene in politics to foil the moderate policies of men like Sharett and Eshkol and force on them aggressive, adventurous lines. The military leaders did have their own evaluations of Nasser's intentions and capabilities and their own estimates of the capabilities of Israel's armed forces that differed, sometimes rather sharply, from those of members of the government, but there was nothing unusual or illegitimate in that. The question is whether they attempted to force their views on the government by some devious ways, and on this there is no evidence whatsoever, with one possible exception to be noted below. Furthermore, neither in the past nor in this particular occasion was Eshkol himself the "moderate" man besieged by intransigent military leaders. One may indeed say that half the problem of credibility was precisely due to the fact that for several years Eshkol had worked so closely with the military that some members of his government came to suspect that he had surrendered to them his judgment in defense matters. The other half of the problem was that some of his political opponents had been constantly accusing him of disastrous shortcomings in managing the defense affairs of the country by not doing enough.

The roots of this problem went back to Eshkol's quarrel with Ben Gurion centering on the second phase of the Lavon affair, which led to the breakup of Mapai in 1965. After that time, Ben Gurion and his supporters, including men with a great deal of experience in various aspects of defense such as Moshe Dayan, Shimon Peres, Issar Harel, and others, periodically made vague charges of negligence on Eshkol's part in matters relating to national security. Partly in reaction to such attacks, Eshkol had tended to lean over backward and respond favorably to requests made by the professional heads of the defense establishment concerning budgetary allocations, permission to undertake retaliatory actions, and so on. Indeed, during Eshkol's three years of tenure as defense minister the Israeli armed forces improved and increased their equipment faster than in any comparable period before. At the same time, they tried out new and more dangerous types of military action in the repeated border clashes with Syria, such as using air power to attack Syrian gun emplacements and to penetrate deep into Syrian territory in pursuit of enemy planes. All this did not, of course, silence Eshkol's critics or assuage the doubts they raised, but it did have the effect of sowing the seeds of distrust among some of his partners in the government that he might have gone too far the other way and fallen under excessive influence of the military. In "normal" times, Eshkol was able to tread carefully between the two opposite suspicions and use them to offset each other. However, as the crisis set in, Eshkol shared with the military an unfortunate but understandable misjudgment of Nasser's intentions, and when this became apparent he began to doubt himself and to allow now one kind of suspicion now another to assail him and jostle his reactions. By the time he settled into a firm position, he had already forfeited the confidence of his colleagues in his judgment both with regard to the situation and to the capacity of Israel's armed forces to execute what action seemed to be needed. Only a man of trusted military capacity and total independence from Eshkol could resolve the Cabinet's doubts, and when such a man was found in the person of Dayan and was foisted upon Eshkol, Israel moved.

I have already intimated that the Israelis definitely contemplated some kind of action against Syria in the course of the month of May. Syrian-supported guerrilla activity had become more serious in the preceeding weeks, and the Israelis considered it a matter of cardinal importance to nip it in the bud by denying to the terrorists any sanctuary in the Arab states across the border. The scope of the envisaged action had not apparently been determined by May 14, but it seemed clear from the declarations of responsible Israelis that the alternatives under consideration included an air attack or an unusually large-scale raid by land forces against Syrian military bases. Eshkol himself had threatened an air strike, but his chief of staff, General Rabin, had hinted publicly that a different type of action might be taken. Whether Rabin spoke with Eshkol's approval or whether this was an instance—the only one on record up to that point—of the military trying to force his hand is not known. It is generally known, however, that Eshkol had excellent working relations with Rabin, and this suggests the possibility that the two types of threat might have been deliberately orchestrated. In any case, the military leaders were certain that whatever action was contemplated, Egypt would not react, and had imparted that conviction to Defense Minister (and Prime Minister) Eshkol, who must have conveyed it to the Cabinet as his own judgment.

The assessment of the military rested on good grounds and was shared by experts everywhere. It was based on the relative strength of Egypt and Israel, the presence of a large number of Egyptian troops in Yemen, the poor state of inter-Arab relations which were at their nadir just then, the known positions of the big powers, and last but not least, Nasser's own highly cautious behavior in the preceding eleven years and even since he concluded his joint defense agreement with Syria. But it was, as it turned out, neither the first nor the last time that the vaunted Israeli intelligence establishment made a mistake in political evaluation. That the assessment proved wrong might not have mattered much under different circumstances, but in the atmosphere of suspicion surrounding Eshkol's stewardship of defense, it was to have crucial consequences.

The military were so sure of their initial expectation that Egypt would not react that they stuck to it even after Nasser made his first move. They explained away the Egyptian troop movement as a poor bluff, and although they were careful to take precautionary measures after obtaining the necessary authorization, they maintained that Israel was still free to act aginst Syria. Eshkol, who considered himself to be politically responsible for what appeared to be a wrong forecast of Egyptian passiveness, had a psychological interest in going along with the view of his military chiefs. Judging by his subsequent action, however, he must have begun to wonder whether he was not following them too uncritically.

Nasser's demand for the removal of UNEF caused the first divergence in the views of the military and the government as a whole, and the first manifestation of indecisiveness on Eshkol's part. There was no disagreement at this stage or at any other that precautionary measures should be taken on the basis of the worst assumptions, and consequently Israel's mobilization and deployment of troops proceeded automatically with the Arab military moves—unlike what was to happen in 1973. The divergence was about the implications of the new situation. The military now became convinced that Nasser meant to intervene in case of an Israeli attack on Syria and were inclined to explain this unexpected behavior on his part by referring to the Russian factor. Furthermore, they clearly saw that, by removing UNEF, Nasser served notice that henceforth his side of the frontier would no longer remain inactive in guerrilla operations, but precisely for these reasons, they thought it was crucial for the future of Israel's security not to be intimidated and to respond forcefully to the next act of guerrilla warfare even if this meant risking a large-scale encounter with Egyptian forces.

The government accepted the revised interpretation of Nasser's intent and agreed that the removal of UNEF created a new security problem but refused to follow the conclusions of the military chiefs, who seemed to be advocating action for one reason and its opposite. The government's concern with international repercussions, its suspicion of the role of the Soviet Union, and its disappointment with the forecast previously given to it led it to attempt to meet the new security problem not by asserting Israel's deterrent power in a certain clash with Egypt, but by diplomatic action designed to defuse the immediate crisis and to restore as much as possible a semblance of the status quo ante. The government was not unaware that its line would concede an important diplomatic and psychological victory to Nasser that would enhance his standing in the Arab world, but it comforted itself with the hope that once this particular crisis blew over, the Arabs would be "back at each other's throats." Clearly, the difference between the military and the government was the difference in the perspective of those whose business is to prepare for war and are therefore psychologically ready for it when it comes, and those whose concerns are with the labors of peace and need time to get used to the idea of having to go to war.

The position taken by Eshkol personally at this juncture is not known, but the character of the speech he delivered before the Knesset on May 22 suggests that he sought to take as much distance as possible under the circumstances from the views of the military. In that statement, it will be recalled, Eshkol forgot almost entirely the "unbearable" situation with Syria and renounced any intent to attack Syria, Egypt, or any other Arab country, without making any conditions except for indicating that Israel "expected" to be treated on the basis of reciprocity. Having identified himself publicly with this extremely conciliatory position, Eshkol could not very well speak tough on the very next day before his colleagues in the Cabinet, his countrymen, and the world at large, after word came of Nasser's closing of the Strait of Tiran. This does not mean that the proclamation of the blockade was taken lightly by Eshkol, the government, or anyone in Israel. It rather suggests that, within the context of the heightened crisis, there was an already established disposition to take a more pragmatic, limited view of the situation and to think in terms of dismantling the immediate crisis at hand, instead of taking a broader theoretical-strategic view of the blockade as a basic challenge to Israel's security and respond accordingly. The difference between these two approaches was clearly illustrated by the contrast between the positions of the government and the military leaders.

In an emergency Cabinet session held on May 23, everyone agreed that Israel confronted a grave crisis and that the Strait of Tiran must be reopened. There was some discussion of the possible broad implications of the issue, but for practical purposes the problem was put in terms of the specific question of how to restore free navigation. After a discussion of the means that might be used to achieve this objective, it was decided that since other nations had an interest in the question and since the United States in particular had given some specific assurances on the subject, an urgent and intense effort should be made to achieve this objective by diplomatic means. The outcome of this decision was Eshkol's speech of May 23, in which he merely "admonished" Egypt and called on the big powers and the United Nations to remove the blockade, as well as Eban's going on mission to Paris, London, and Washington.

As for the military, their first preoccupation after the blockade proclamation was to keep track of new military developments on the enemy side and to order the expansion of the mobilization and the deployment of troops according to the new situation. By May 24 they had already done this and were prepared with a new evaluation and a plan of action which they submitted to the minister of defense. As they saw it, Nasser's latest move was to be viewed not as a mere act of blocking navigation to and from Israel's southern port, important as this may be, but as a challenge to Israel's deterrent power. Consequently, unless Israel *itself* nullified Nasser's action, his challenge would prove successful, and it would be a signal for further encroachments and harassments that would sooner or later lead to war but under more unfavorable conditions. Israel, they argued, was capable of acting alone, and they presented a plan for operations against the Egyptian concentrations in Sinai which, they expected, would compel Nasser to desist from his blockade.

Eshkol, it appears from the subsequent course of events, was persuaded by these arguments, but since the Cabinet had already decided on diplomatic action and since Eban had accordingly made plans for his trip to Paris, London, and Washington, there was little he could do except to press his foreign minister for speed and to instruct him, halfway through his mission, to stress the broader issue of the threat to Israel's security as well as the specific problem of navigation. To the military Eshkol explained that Israel needed in any case to win the support of its friends to its position so as to avoid a repetition of 1956, when the United States turned against it and forced it to relinquish its gains.

With regard to the last question, Eban's trip to Paris turned out to have an opposite effect. President de Gaulle not only refused to commit his government to action on behalf of Israel's navigation right, but he took the opportunity to extend to it a "friendly" warning not to start shooting on penalty of forfeiting French sympathy and support. Thus, instead of securing French understanding, Eban's initiative elicited "advice" from de Gaulle that tied Israel's hands in the measure it cared about possible penalties for ignoring it. In London, as pointed out above, Eban received a promise from Prime Minister Wilson to join the United States in action to secure free navigation, which was subsequently given rather innocuous interpretations. In the meantime, though, the promise disposed Eban to think that collective action, which President Johnson was to propose, had already one important adherent and was not therefore so far-fetched.

We have already examined Eban's mission to Washington and the considerations underlying the American position as far as the problem of navigation is concerned. I should add here that the anxiety of Eshkol about the broader question of Israel's security, which was aroused by the reports of the military chiefs, resulted in a certain amount of confusion that vitiated the effectiveness of Eban's effort in the American capital. Upon arriving in Washington, Eban found instructions awaiting him to elicit the American position on the broad question of Israel's security as well as the navigation problem. Eban accordingly raised the question with President Johnson and received the reply that the United States meant to stand by its commitments to defend Israel. The President added, as an encouraging opinion, not a qualification, that his advisers were convinced that Israel alone could defeat the Arabs if they went to war.

After leaving the President, Eban found a message from Tel Aviv to the effect that Israel's Intelligence had obtained specific information that the Egyptians planned to attack on May 27 and was instructed to convey this information urgently to the American government. The American officials to whom Eban conveyed the message were skeptical and the episode created an impression of a frightened Israel that ran counter to the previously held impression about Israeli self-confidence and determination. American officials waited for confirmation of one or the other from the decision of Israel's Cabinet. When that decision came out in favor of continuing diplomatic action rather than going to war, the conclusion was more readily drawn that Israel must have thought the cost of war to be prohibitive and had no recourse on the navigation question other than what the United States was prepared to do.

What went on in the Israeli Cabinet meeting on that May 27 and on the following day was actually somewhat different. The decision in favor of diplomatic action was taken under circumstances that contained the seeds of its undoing a few days later. Two themes underlay the long and agonized discussions: the validity and desirability of President Johnson's plan and the costs to Israel of the alternative of military action. Taking everything into account, Eban argued in favor of holding back until the outcome of the President's project became apparent. He found support for his view among some Cabinet members. A second group voiced something akin to the view of the military chiefs, doubting the effectiveness of the President's plan even if it could be realized. Members of this group wondered how long the maritime powers would keep naval units in the Gulf of Aqaba just to insure Israeli free navigation, and argued that even if such freedom were secured indefinitely, the fact that it would depend on others would imply a failure of Israel's independent deterrent that would have ominous consequences. This group therefore urged immediate military action, and was confident of its outcome. It was less confident about the costs but was willing to pay the price anyway. Between these two groups there was a third whose views were critical for the outcome of the discussion. This group strongly doubted that the President would be able to deliver on his promises and saw the logic of those who urged immediate military action, but its members mistrusted the evaluations that were presented about the outcome and the costs of such action and demanded that Moshe Dayan be brought into the government as defense minister before they would contemplate military action. When the question of immediate military response was finally put to a vote, the result was a tie, with nine ministers for and nine against. But among those who voted against were members of the third group, mostly from the National Religious Party, who did so only because they mistrusted Eshkol's competence as minister of defense and were intent on having him replaced.

After the Cabinet meeting broke up inconclusively, Eshkol attended a special meeting of the General Staff to report on what happened. It was now the turn of the military chiefs to question his leadership and determination and to argue again before him that the issue was no longer, if it ever was, simply the blockade but the very existence of Israel. The Egyptian army had changed from a defensive to an offensive deployment, and every day that passed without a riposte would increase the casualty rate in the war by 200. Nasser had thrown the gauntlet in Israel's face; failure to respond would certainly invite new pressures and eventual war.

Shortly after these painful meetings, Eshkol was awakened in his home by the Soviet ambassador to be handed an urgent message from Premier Kosygin that included a warning to Israel to refrain from any aggressive action against the Arab countries. But, contrary to expectations, the message was couched in comparatively moderate tones and even hinted that the Soviet Union might be open to a less one-sided position in the future if Israel exercised self-restraint. Eshkol, who had for years dreamed of a rapprochement with Russia, was induced by the hint to propose to go to Moscow for further talks with the Soviet government. Naturally, the surprised ambassador could only reply that he would refer the proposal to Moscow. But the episode indicated that the faintest trace of hope from Moscow was sufficient to detract Eshkol and counter whatever effect his discussions with the military leaders had had on his determination.

Hours after the nocturnal visit of the Russian, the American ambassador appeared in the dawn of a Sunday morning to deliver a message from President Johnson. The note reiterated the promise made to Eban, spoke in hopeful terms about progress of the project of collective action by maritime powers, and urged Israel to refrain from hurried military action. The urgent American plea for restraint appeared to Eshkol to be an ominous change in the position reported by Eban, which had essentially left the choice to Israel whether to act alone or to wait until the United States could help. This, together with the Soviet warning and the hint of more promising relations with Moscow, helped sway Eshkol to change position and go along with those who opposed immediate military action and favored continued diplomatic efforts. Little did he know that the origin of the two messages from the chiefs of the superpowers was nothing other than the alarm Israel itself had raised in Washington two days before about an impending Egyptian attack. The United States government had reacted by cautioning the Egyptian government and asking the Soviet government to do likewise. The Soviets had agreed, on condition that a similar message be directed at Israel.

Eshkol's apparent inability to stick to one clear conception as to just what the issue at stake was, whether it was possible or desirable to rely on the big powers for keeping the strait open, what was the likely outcome of war and its likely costs, whether it was essential to act immediately or it was possible to wait, ended up by causing the mistrust in his judgment to spread from his coalition partners to many of the leaders of his own party. Feeling in the country at large also flowed in the same direction in torrential strength after Eshkol went on the air on May 28 to report on the decision of the government. By that time, the paralysis of the United Nations, the barrage of broadcasts from Arab capitals voicing dire threats, reports of ever greater Egyptian troop concentrations, and the tension naturally fostered by a state of total mobilization had built up a climate of unbearable suspense that sought relief in the words of the Prime Minister. It so happened that Eshkol had to read his speech in bad lighting from hurriedly handwritten notes and while he was in a state of near physical and mental exhaustion. Consequently, besides reporting what was taken as a "do nothing" decision, his delivery was painfully faltering. The nation which had been sitting on edge for so long and expected from its leader a speech of Churchillian quality got instead what was dubbed "the mumbling speech" in which it was given nothing to hold on to. For the first time Israelis began to fear that their unquestioning faith in their armed forces might not have sufficient "cover."

Acting under the impact of the enormous wave of popular disgruntlement, the parliamentary party of the Maarakh, including Eshkol's own Mapai and Achdut Haavoda, urged at a meeting held with Eshkol on May 29 that the defense portfolio be handed over to Dayan or to Minister of Labor Yigal Allon, a hero of the 1948 war and member of Achdut Haavoda. Overwhelmed, Eshkol resigned himself to handing the defense position to Allon. But when he proceded to convey this decision to his coalition partners, he encountered determined opposition from Moshe Shapira, who suspected that Allon would be beholden to Eshkol and not sufficiently independent. Shapira threatened to hand in the resignation of his party from the government and thus bring it down unless Dayan was appointed without delay. After another day of wrangling, the Secretariat of the Prime Minister's own party voted for Dayan as defense minister as well as for a "wall-to-wall coalition" excluding only the Communists. The die was cast.

While this was happening, the events discussed above were taking place: the fizzling of the project of collective action, the spreading of the notion in American government circles that the Israeli Cabinet decision of May 28.

marked the passing of the worst of the crisis and opened the door for compromise, the mounting intransigence of Egypt, the rallying together of the Arab countries, and the conclusion of the Jordanian-Egyptian agreement. These developments, especially the beginning of an airlift that brought Egyptian troops and materiel to Jordan and the movement toward that country of sizeable Iraqi troops, disposed even the most hesitant members of the Cabinet to think that military action could no longer be postponed. What the presence of Dayan and other new ministers in the government did was not so much to influence the decision whether or not to act as to help set the aim of action boldly as destruction of the principal enemy forces—and make it possible to make that decision with an easier heart.

22

New Options, Alignments, and Tribulations, 1967–1970

The Six Day War overturned the previous power relations in the Middle East and marked the beginning of a new configuration in which both the issues at stake in the diplomacy of the region and the intensity with which the contenders fought for them were vastly different from what they had been before the war. Essentially, the war gave rise to a "bargaining situation" between Israel and its Arab neighbors, previously conspicuous by its absence, and thus made a settlement of the conflict possible *in principle* for the first time since 1949. In reality, however, the war caused a substantial modification of the perceptions and aims of the belligerents and of the superpowers in the direction of seeking a more stable order, but the change only marked the starting point of an intense and complex struggle over the nature of that order. The principal struggle pitted an American-Israeli partnership against one associating the Soviet Union and Egypt and related Arab forces. However, the course of that struggle also generated frictions within each of the partnerships, the effects of which rebounded on the principal struggle, and so on. In the course of the contest, arms races and limited warfare, troop deployments and threats of general war supplemented the conventional means of diplomacy.

The struggle for the postwar order went through three stages in the period 1967–1973. The first stage lasted from the end of the war in June 1967 to the beginning of the war of attrition in March 1969. During it, the various parties sorted out their positions and the principal partnerships were formed, and the issue between the rival partnerships came to focus on divergent interpretations of UN Security Council Resolution 242. The second stage was dominated by the war of attrition, which lasted from March 1969 till August 1970, and by its effect on the partnerships and the parties. The strains it placed on all brought about a cease-fire and an agreement to negotiate, which set in motion events that shaped the next stage, stretching from August 1970 to the outbreak of the war of October 1973.

This chapter will be devoted to the struggles in the first two of these stages. In order to facilitate discussion, the historical examination will be preceded by a concise analysis of the basic considerations affecting the position of each of the parties concerned and the dynamics of the two principal partnerships.

Basic Considerations Affecting the Parties

Israel

The war transformed Israel's strategic-diplomatic position and opened before its eyes new perspectives and options such as it had not had since the end of the War of Independence. Ever since the failure of the 1949 peace efforts, Israelis had lived with the proposition that the Arab states would never make peace with their state as long as they could entertain a reasonable hope of being able to crush it one day in the battlefield. Now that the principal Arab states challenged Israel at a time of their choosing after long years of preparation and were decisively defeated, many Israelis believed, by a simple reversal of that proposition, that the Arabs would be ready to contemplate promptly the conclusion of a peace settlement.

Enhancing this expectation was the fact that the war left Israel in control of substantial territories belonging to Egypt and Syria proper and of Palestinian lands annexed by Jordan in 1948. These territories not only gave it a vastly improved strategic position which was apt to further discourage any enemy military ventures, but they also provided it for the first time since 1949 with valuable assets it could offer to the enemy as an inducement to make peace, or that it could withhold from him if he refused to do so. One concern initially marred these prospects in the Israeli view, and that was fear of a repetition of 1957, when Israel was forced to surrender the assets it had gained in the 1956 war without any visible political returns, but this concern was soon dissipated when the United States indicated publicly and unequivocally that it would oppose any attempts to compel Israel to withdraw without a peace settlement.

Consequently, Israel now set for itself two new operational national goals: seeking a formal, final peace with its neighbors and redefining the 1949 boundaries. Technically, the latter objective was justified by the fact that the 1949 borders were only armistice lines, and that the 1949 Armistice Agreements had been invalidated by the 1967 war. Beyond that, however, Israel sought certain modifications of the prewar territorial status quo on historic-national grounds and for security reasons. Israel did not define formally and specifically the exact changes it sought, but simply invited the Arab states to enter into unconditional direct negotiations aimed at settling all questions and establishing lasting peace. Until the Arabs agreed to that proposition, Israel intended to retain and defend all the captured territories.

This stance of refraining from defining territorial objectives made a great deal of sense on tactical grounds in the immediate postwar circumstances. As long as the Arabs did not indicate their willingness to enter into peace negotiations, there was no point in stating territorial demands that might galvanize Arab resistance, draw international opposition, and above all embarrass and possibly alienate the United States. However, if Israel's basic postwar position is to be properly understood, it is essential to recall that Israel's posture was not merely the result of tactical international political considerations but was also the consequence of a deep internal division of opinion in the government and among the public, which made it very difficult anyway to agree on the desirable and possible territorial changes. In other words, the stance was not part of a broader strategy designed to achieve a well-defined goal, but was rather a means of postponing the definition of goals and the elaboration of a strategy to advance them until such an undertaking became either feasible or inescapable. The trouble was that by the time circumstances favored or pressed for such undertaking, the prolonged postponement had further fragmented opinion so much as to make agreement almost impossible and allow only ad hoc improvisations.

It has been pointed out in the discussion of Israel's internal politics that at first the division of opinion among the leadership and public was almost entirely a function of historical-national aspirations and centered mainly on the West Bank, or what Israelis called Judea and Samaria. A small but vocal minority viewed the area as part of the historical homeland of Israel and wanted to annex it in its entirety, but the majority, mindful of need to induce Jordan to make peace, entertained more limited aspirations. All were at one in seeking to "unite" the old city of Jerusalem to the new and make it part of Israel's capital, but for the rest they were divided as to what else was desirable and possible to achieve without jeopardizing the chances of peace.

Initially, security considerations played only a minimal role in influencing the territorial aims of Israelis. After having destroyed Arab military power in the war, Israel felt sufficiently confident and secure to be willing to contemplate returning all the captured Egyptian and Syrian territories in exchange for peace and various security arrangements such as demilitarization, buffer zones, and so on. However, after the Arabs rapidly rebuilt their military power with Soviet help to an extent that enabled them to launch a war of attrition, and after the guerrilla movement developed into a serious threat to current security, the need for substantial territorial changes on grounds of security became widely and strongly felt and complicated all the issues. It injected new conditions for a settlement with Egypt and Syria, it combined with emotional considerations to magnify the expectations from Jordan, and it further divided opinion as to the extent of the necessary changes and their compatibility with the possibility of achieving peace.

In principle, the circumstances favoring or making necessary the delineation of specific territorial objectives and a calculated strategy to achieve them could take one of three forms. They could be an inducement, in the form of an expressed willingness on the part of the Arabs to negotiate peace, which would cause the crystallization of a position on desirable and achievable aims. They could take the form of intense pressure—economic, military, or international—which would narrow the scope of differences and compel agreement on minimum requirements. Or they could be a combination of elements of both. In practice, as we shall see, such circumstances never quite developed in the years between 1967 and 1973, with a possible partial exception in the summer of 1970 which tended to prove the rule. Consequently, the tendency to greater fragmentation of opinion in the government and among the public went unchecked, making a comprehensive policy decision ever more difficult to achieve.

Of course, in principle there was yet a third possibility for Israel to develop a clear conception of ends and means, and that was through self-generated initiative. Had Israel had at the helm a man of the stature of Ben Gurion in his prime days, for example, he might have been able to seize the essentials of the situation, formulate goals, devise an active strategy to pursue them, and might have pressed his views on the leadership and the public against hesitation and opposition. However, Israel's government after the war happened to be headed by Levi Eshkol, a kind and decent person, but a pragmatist and compromiser by nature, and a man who had just been removed by his own party from the leadership of the nation's defense because of demonstrated hesitancy and weakness. He was followed early in 1969 by Golda Meir, a woman of boundless determination and real strength, but whose entire career and life conditioned her to place the highest priority on the preservation of formal party unity, and who therefore sought to avoid as much as possible any deliberate high policy decisions that might precipitate divisions. Any departure from the initial formal Israeli stance remained therefore dependent on the interplay between external circumstances and the continually changing internal configuration of divided Israeli opinion.

The United States

Like Israel, the United States had not anticipated the situation that developed as a result of the Six Day War. However, unlike Israel, its government was able after a brief period of uncertainty to improvise a basic policy appropriate to the new circumstances. On the face of it, the new American policy appeared to be as formal and limited as Israel's; however, underlying it was a more comprehensive perception of the situation and of the American interest, which gave the American government a greater capacity to adapt the basic policy to changing circumstances. The adaptations may not always have been fortunate, but they at least avoided rigidity, allowed the exploration of options, and provided useful experience.

The United States had long suffered from the exploitation of the Arab-Israeli conflict by Nasser and the Soviets in order to undermine its position in the Middle East. It had made repeated attempts to promote a settlement of the conflict but all had failed because of the lack of any real bargaining situation between Israel and its neighbors, and it had made diverse efforts at least to contain or stabilize the conflict so as to restrict its damage, but these efforts were frustrated by action on the part of Nasser and the Soviets. The collapse of the American effort to stabilize the situation through a military balance that occurred as a result of the crisis triggered by Soviet and Egyptian actions in May 1967 was only the latest and most ominous of these instances. Had the coalition formed by Nasser won the war, or had it even scored only a political victory akin to the one gained in 1956, Nasser and his Soviet supporters might have been placed in a position to wipe out the American position in the Middle East in the same way they did the British and French. Israel's swift victory not only averted that danger but also provided an opportunity to turn the tables on the Soviets and to apply enormous pressure on their Arab friends to agree, at last, to settling the conflict. The United States decided to avail itself of that chance by declaring its intent, in fact, to support Israel in its newly gained position until a final peace was concluded between it and the Arabs.

Because it relied on what Israel had accomplished by itself, the new American policy had the rare merit of being bold in aim and conservative in means. It sought a radical solution to the Arab-Israeli conflict, but needed only to oppose diplomatically efforts that were being made to compel Israel to withdraw unconditionally. Of course, the new policy could be a source of trouble if the Soviets chose to react rashly, of if they and their Arab friends could convert the American open association with Israel into an effective weapon for renewed assault on the American position in friendly Arab countries. However, the Johnson administration estimated in the aftermath of the war that the Soviets were in a chastened frame of mind, that Nasser had been too weakened by defeat to be able to mount a serious campaign against the American positions in the Arab world, and therefore that its objective was attainable without great risks, complications, or costs.

Subsequent events were to impel the Johnson administration to provide Israel with massive arms as well as diplomatic support. This, coupled with a change of administration and of personnel dealing with Middle East policy, was to bring about a reevaluation of the risks involved in the situation, a considerable revision of tactics, and a generally much more active American role. However, throughout these developments the new American strategy remained unaltered. It persistently sought to utilize the assets gained by Israel in the Six Day War to achieve a final peace settlement and put to rest a conflict that had long bedeviled American interests.

The Soviet Union

Because of their conspicious failure to protect their clients from dire defeat, the Soviets lost in six days most of the credit in the eyes of the Arab publics and Third World countries they had painfully accumulated over the previous twelve years. Beyond this blow to their prestige and image, the Soviets were confronted with two immediate problems and a dilemma. One problem was the effect of the war on their concrete positions in the Middle East, and the other, no less serious, was the demonstrated willingness and ability of Nasser to implicate them in dangerous courses they had not been prepared to follow. The first of these indicated urgent action in support of Egypt and Syria; the latter indicated great caution. Hence the dilemma.

In an immediate sense, the outcome of the war involved the danger of a collapse of the Egyptian and Syrian regimes on which the entire Soviet position in the Middle East rested. Beyond that, there was the danger that even if the two regimes survived, they, and especially the Egyptian, might sue for terms from the United States, if not from Israel, that could only lead to a settlement at the expense of the Soviet position. To ward off these dangers, the Soviets had to be prepared to provide massive assistance, which they could ill afford, to help put their defeated clients on their feet again. But much more serious than the ruble and kopek costs was the danger that either regime, and particularly Nasser, should use their help to implicate them once again in situations in which the choice for them would be between risking confrontation with the United States, or seeing billions of their investments go up again in smoke, together with their Middle East position.

In an effort to steer a course between these two anxieties, the Soviets decided on a basic policy of helping their clients rebuild their armed forces up to the point where they would be in a position to *bargain* for a settlement rather than submit to one, but not so much that they might be tempted to contemplate reversing the outcome of the war by another war. As a further protection against dangerous unilateral initiatives by Egypt or Syria, and as an added insurance for their new investments, the Soviets sought to make their help conditional upon their clients' undertaking internal "reforms" to broaden the base of support of their regimes, the point of which was to strengthen pro-Soviet elements in the two states.

The new policy was broached to the Syrians and the Egyptians by President Nikolai Podgorny personally in a special trip to the area. Nasser reluctantly agreed after the proposal he preferred of a joint Soviet-Egyptian military campaign to reverse the outcome of the war was turned down. The

Syrians refused to contemplate a political settlement altogether, and the most they would commit themselves to in exchange for Soviet aid was to refrain from interfering with the Soviet-Egyptian efforts in the direction of a settlement. The Soviets had no choice but to content themselves with this outcome. However, the Syrians' reticence and Nasser's reluctance left their fears of becoming embroiled in dangerous situations through actions of their clients barely assuaged, and this fear was to prove of crucial importance at several junctures in the subsequent course of events.

Egypt

On June 4, 1967, Nasser felt that he stood within striking distance of achieving hegemony in the Middle East; five days later, his country had been reduced to powerlessness and he, a shattered man, had tearfully abdicated. Yet, despite this stunning turn of fortune, Nasser promptly recovered his personal balance, regained control of the situation, and, within two weeks, came up with a policy to deal with the new circumstances in which he and Egypt found themselves.

On the face of it, Nasser faced three broad options in the wake of the war: suing for peace, living with the postwar situation as Egypt and the other Arab countries had done after the 1949 defeat, and preparing for a resumption of the war. In fact none of these options appeared to Nasser to be feasible by itself, and he ended up adopting a policy that combined elements of all three.

The peace option appeared to Nasser to be out of the question not only for personal emotional reasons, but also because of weighty real-political considerations. To the United States and Israel, asking Egypt to agree to peace may have seemed to be simply asking it to renounce its former hostile and aggressive behavior and commit itself to act like a good neighbor. To Nasser, however, peace, even one that involved returning to Egypt all its lost territories, appeared as ceding to Israeli military power and as consecrating Israeli military and political dominance in the Middle East, with far-reaching implications for the future of Egypt, Arab nationalism, and Middle East–world relations. As he proclaimed in a play on the relevant Arabic words, peace (salam) was tantamount to surrender (istislam). That he had done much to bring about the situation he deplored was, of course, irrelevant to the reality he faced. And that Israel might not necessarily behave as a bully after peace, and might, indeed, dismantle much of its military machine were optimistic assumptions he was not prepared to build on after twenty years of relentless Arab-Israeli hostility.

Living with the postwar situation appeared to be as impossible as making peace. In 1949 the Arab states had adopted that alternative to peace because they could tolerate a stalemate and because they trusted that in the long run the balance of power was bound to turn in their favor and give them chances to revise the outcome of the war. In 1967, however, neither premise seemed to be valid. On the one hand, defeat had generated enormous political, economic, and psychological pressures that Egypt, and Nasser's regime, could not bear for any length of time, and, on the other hand, the chances of reversing the power balance against Israel in the foreseeable future appeared extremely dim in view of the negative trend of that balance between 1949 and 1967. Moreover, this time, unlike in 1949, Israel was in occupation of Egyptian national territory, and the longer it remained in undisturbed control of it, the greater were the chances that it would ultimately take possession. Therefore, a stalemate, far from being an option Nasser could choose, was one he felt he had to do his utmost to prevent.

The war option had a strong, immediate appeal to Nasser on obvious psychological and political grounds, and he went to great lengths to make it a viable policy immediately and in the following years. In the wake of the Arab debacle, Nasser became convinced that no Arab coalition, much less Egypt by itself, could hope to marshal the military power needed to defeat Israel in the foreseeable future. Consequently, he believed that the much-desired war option depended on the participation of the Soviet forces in future fighting alongside the Arabs. In order to induce the Soviets to take on a fighting role, he offered to conclude with them a mutual defense treaty, despite Egypt's bitter experience with a similar treaty that had served as a cover for a lengthy British occupation of the country. Alternatively, he offered to place Egypt's air force under Soviet command, as a way of luring Soviet forces into the fighting. However, the Soviets, tempted as they may have been, refused the bait and proposed, instead, an alternative policy, which Nasser adopted with some arrière pensées.

That policy, as seen in the discussion of the Soviet position, was to rebuild Egypt's armed strength so that it could bargain for a political settlement and not have to turn to the United States to plead for terms. From the point of view of the Soviets, the latter was the essential point, whereas for Nasser the crucial point was twofold. The first was that he got the Soviets to subscribe to a distinction between a "political settlement," by which he understood recovering his territories in exchange for some quid pro quo short of peace, and peace proper, which he associated with surrender and viewed as destructive of his role as leader of Arab nationalism. The other crucial point for Nasser was that he obtained from the Soviets a commitment for large-scale military assistance including hardware and advisory personnel, coupled with an understanding that his rebuilt armed forces would be used as a means of pressure for achieving an acceptable settlement. This left open the possibility of eventually implicating the Soviets into military action, either in the course of applying military pressure, or in case the kind of settlement he would accept should prove to be unattainable.

Syria, Jordan, and the Palestinian Guerrillas

If the basic policy orientation chosen by Nasser was influenced by considerations pertaining to Egypt's relations with other Arab countries, the orientations adopted by the other principal Arab belligerents hinged entirely, in fact if not in principle, on Egypt's position.

For Syria's leaders the theoretical option of peace was even more repugnant than it was for Nasser, partly because of Syria's traditional stance in the forefront of Arab hostility to Israel and partly because its losses in men, materiel, and territory were much less drastic than Egypt's. For the same reasons, as well as because its leadership had faith in the effectiveness of a strategy of "popular war of liberation", Syria viewed the option of renewed war against Israel less pessimistically than Nasser. Where Nasser saw a successful war as being dependent on Soviet active involvement in the fighting, the Syrians saw it as being dependent on active commitment by Egypt and other Arab forces, with the Soviets merely providing an insurance against Israeli seizure of Damascus or other substantial Arab territories. Finally, because the territory they lost was small and of only symbolic importance, the Syrians could bear a prolonged stalemate and indecisive hostilities much more readily than the Egyptians.

Consequently, when the Syrians were approached by the Soviets to adopt the same course as Egypt, they balked, and agreed only not to oppose Egypt's pursuit of a political settlement publicly. Their reasoning was that if Egypt's search for a settlement short of peace were to prove successful, they could always follow its lead, as they had in 1949 in connection with the armistice agreements. If, however, the search failed and matters came to stalemate or war, they would then have their way without having "compromised" themselves by expressing a willingness to reach a settlement of any sort with Israel.

Jordan's King Hussein had had fewer illusions than Nasser about the chances of the Arabs in the Six Day War and was therefore even more pessimistic than he was about their chances in another war. The possibility of Soviet participation in any future fighting, which redeemed the war option in Nasser's eyes, only made it more tragic in the view of the King, who expected to lose either way. Similarly, a stalemate was repugnant to Hussein for the same reasons that it was to Nasser, with the added consideration that, because Israeli emotional-national aspirations centered mainly on the territories he lost, the longer the occupation lasted the more likely the chances that Israel would take possession of them, or of parts of them.

Partly because he had nothing to gain from war and much to lose from stalemate and partly because the relation of forces between Israel and Jordan made accomodation more obviously necessary and excusable, King Hussein was prepared to contemplate peace with Israel on reasonable terms. The problem, however, was that he, mindful of the sad experience of his grandfather (who was shot by a Palestinian back in 1951 for seeking to make peace with Israel), was extremely reluctant to break ranks with his fellow Arabs and negotiate a separate peace. He believed that if he could get a prior Israeli assurance that he would recover substantially all his lost territories in exchange for peace, he might be able to secure Nasser's approval for the deal; and with that approval he was prepared to face other Arab opposition. But Israel was not prepared to show its hand in advance and Nasser was not prepared to sanction any move toward peace on Hussein's part before Israel agreed to return all the territories.

The Palestinian guerrillas, consisting of a large number of movements of different sizes and inclinations loosely federated in the Palestine Liberation Organization (PLO), became a factor to be reckoned with about a year after the war. The PLO was committed to the replacement of Israel by a Palestinian "secular democratic state," and was therefore opposed to any settlement with the Jewish state. Its strategy, to the extent that it had a generally shared one, was to embroil the Arab states in renewed war with Israel regardless of outcome, in the belief that even Arab defeat would only create better conditions for a "popular war of liberation."

The PLO's position was thus strongly opposed to Egypt's and Jordan's with respect to aim and to strategy. However, as long as Jordan's position depended on Nasser's and as long as Nasser's idea of a political settlement short of peace was rejected by Israel and the United States, the Arab states found themselves in fact engaged in a political-military struggle with Israel as much as was the PLO, and the theoretical differences among them were suppressed. The position of the PLO became distinctly and specifically relevant only after Egypt, followed by Jordan, took a step forward in its policy in 1970 that seemed to give peace a greater chance than before. When that point came, the PLO clashed openly with Jordan and Egypt and the paths of all three diverged.

The Dynamics of the Principal Partnerships

The preceding review points out explicitly or implicitly a number of relationships in the positions of the various parties. Two of these, however, need to be underscored and elaborated because of their critical significance for the course of events: these are the relationship between the Soviet Union and Egypt and that between the United States and Israel.

We have seen that the Soviet Union and Egypt had a joint interest in rebuilding Egypt's military capability and using it to enhance Egypt's bargaining power in the pursuit of a political settlement. However, the two had different dispositions as to the *limits* of the military means to be used in the course of seeking a settlement. The Soviet Union, concerned about possible confrontation with the United States and about the possibility of another Arab debacle that would be ruinous to its position in the area, was bent on stopping the military effort short of general war, whereas Nasser was prepared to cross that threshhold if he could embroil the Soviets in the fighting. Similarly, the two partners had different conceptions as to the *limits* of an acceptable settlement. The Soviets were not ultimately averse to a full peace agreement provided it could be achieved under their aegis or otherwise secure for them their positions in the area, whereas for Nasser, peace under any foreseeable circumstances had a connotation of surrender to Israel and involved a risk of undermining Egypt's standing in the inter-Arab and international arenas. The potential differences between the two could—and in fact did— remain irrelevant as long as they both believed that the kind of settlement sought by Nasser could be achieved by the means sanctioned by the Soviets. They were apt to become troublesome the moment that belief ceased to hold, as it in fact did in 1970. Nasser then pressed for escalating the extent of Soviet military support, whereas the Soviets pressed Nasser to scale down the aim he had set for himself. The result of the clash, as we shall see, was a compromise that met the immediate tactical needs but contained the seeds of future, more serious, conflict.

The relationship between the United States and Israel was essentially similar though somewhat more complicated. The United States and Israel, we have seen, had a common interest in denying to the belligerent Arab states the territories they lost in the war until they were prepared to conclude a final peace. However, the two had different conceptions as to the terms of the desired settlement. The United States was interested chiefly in liquidating the Arab-Israeli conflict and had an interest in boundaries only to the extent that this question was relevant to its main purpose, whereas Israel was bent on achieving certain modifications of the prewar boundaries in addition to formal peace. Moreover, the two had different conceptions as to the methods to be used in advancing their goals. Israel, partly unwilling, partly unable to define its territorial demands, favored unconditional negotiations and believed that a combination of deterrence and a passive diplomatic posture was the best way to impel the Arabs to assent. The United States, on the other hand, anxious about the consequences of a possibly unnecessary prolongation of the conflict for its relations with friendly Arab countries and the Soviet Union, was inclined to seek, and to be seen to seek, a settlement in every possible way. These differences could—and did—have a limited relevance as long as the Arabs refused to make peace and as long as Israel carried the burden of military deterrence unaided. Once either of these conditions changed, the differences over the terms of peace or the methods of advancing a settlement were apt to manifest themselves and become troublesome and in fact they did, in 1969 and in 1970.

The Shaping of Positions and Alignments: 1967–1969

When Nasser first decided to risk war by closing the Strait of Tiran and then to court a showdown, he had imagined that if the war did not go so well as he hoped, Israel might manage to make some territorial gains after paying heavily for them, but then the world community would press it to withdraw in the interest of stopping the fighting or avoiding its resumption and averting the dangers to world peace. The Soviets, too, had counted on such "worst case" calculations when they decided to support Nasser on the blockade question. The totality and speed of Israel's victory all but destroyed such prospects by removing the possibility of immediate resumption of fighting. However, since the Egyptians and the Soviets had no other apparent option, they tried to pursue this one for all it was worth while thinking of a better alternative.

Already in the second day of the war, when it became apparent to the Soviets that their Egyptian friends were in serious trouble as a result of the destruction of their air force and that they were headed for worse, they pressed hard in the Security Council for a resolution calling for an immediate cease-fire and the return of all troops to their original positions. This time, however, unlike the time after the 1956 war, the United States was in no hurry to go along, but, on the contrary, frustrated the Soviets' efforts until developments in the battlefield forced them to vote for an unconditional cease-fire. In supporting that resolution, the Soviets hoped to salvage whatever was possible from the Egyptian wreckage, and particularly to save the Syrians, who had not been seriously hit up to that point. When the Israelis, nevertheless, availed themselves of excuses provided them by the Syrians to launch a massive assault on their positions, the Soviets resorted to making their boldest threat since 1956, when they implicitly brandished rockets against Britain and France. The episode is worth dwelling upon because it is highly instructive about the Soviet diplomatic style in times of crisis.

As President Johnson related it in the memoirs he wrote after leaving office, on June 10, 1967, the sixth day of the war, at 9:05 A.M., the "hot line" between Moscow and Washington, which had already been used a few times in the course of the crisis to establish agreement that the two superpowers should not intervene in the war and should strive for a cease-fire, suddenly came alive with a message from Soviet Premier Kosygin. The Premier accused Israel of ignoring all Security Council resolutions and said that "a crucial moment had now arrived" involving the possibility of an "independent decision by Moscow." Kosygin foresaw a "risk of a grave catastrophe," and stated that "unless Israel halted operations within the next few hours, the Soviet Union would take all necessary action, including military."

The President commented that he thought the Soviet communication to be a "grave message," and responded to it with two "messages" of his own. On the "hot line", he told Kosygin that the United States was pressing Israel for full compliance with the cease-fire and that he hoped these efforts would be successful soon. At the same time, he ordered the Sixth Fleet, which was at that moment cruising some 300 miles west of the Syrian coast, to head east to within 50 miles of the coast in sight of the Soviet naval units that were trailing its movements. In this way, he sought to convey to the Soviets in terms he thought they well understood that "the United States was prepared to resist Soviet intrusion into the Middle East." The effect of the latter move, according to the President, was that subsequent Soviet communications became much more tempered, and a cease-fire came into effect later that day without any further complications.

It is hard to believe that, as President Johnson implies, the Soviets envisaged military intervention to try to reverse the course of the war or at least to repel the Israeli attack on Syria. Even apart from the question whether they had the logistical capacity to do so at that time, the pattern of their past (and subsequent) behavior suggests a different interpretation. Thrice before the Soviets had made threats in connection with Middle East crises—in 1956 during the Suez-Sinai war, in 1957 during the Syrian war scare, and in 1958 in connection with the Iraqi coup and the American military intervention in Lebanon; and they were to make additional threats again in 1970, at the end of the war of attrition, and in 1973, at the end of the October war. In all these instances, the Soviets waited until the crisis passed the peak of danger and just then made their threats. The idea in each case was to create without undue risk the double impression that the denouement of the crisis was the result of their move and that they were prepared to take strong action if their position in the postcrisis dealings was not respected. So, the likelihood is that on June 10, 1967, they hoped that sheer threat, coupled perhaps with the dispatch of symbolic forces, would force the Israelis to wind up their military operations in Syria promptly. They could then claim to have brought about the termination of the fighting and saved the Arabs from worse disaster than they suffered, they would score a point against the United States, and they would establish for themselves and their friends a better bargaining position in the postwar diplomatic struggles. If that was the case, the President's order to the Sixth Fleet did not ward off an intervention by the Soviets but surely spoiled their game.

As soon as the fighting ceased, the Soviets successfully initiated a move to call an emergency session of the United Nations General Assembly, in which they made an all-out effort to push through a resolution condemning Israel as an aggressor and enjoining it to withdraw its forces from the territories it occupied in the war. The Soviets must have known that, in view of the opposition of the United States to this kind of move in the Security Council, the passage of such a resolution by the General Assembly was unlikely to have much practical effect. Nevertheless, they proceeded with their initiative in the hope of embarrassing the United States and putting pressure on it to limit its support for Israel. Moreover, they engaged in that campaign in order to give a sop to their Arab friends and gain time to sort out their own tattered position in the wake of the war.

While Premier Kosygin was in New York conducting the campaign in the United Nations, President Podgorny, accompanied by Chief of Staff Matvei Zakharov, went to Egypt and Syria to try to reach an agreement on policy with their governments. In Cairo, they encountered an embittered Nasser who was prepared to go to any lengths to have his revenge on Israel while playing on the theme that Egypt and the Soviet Union were fighting the same anti-imperialist cause. In the course of the discussions that went on for four days, Nasser proposed to conclude with the Soviet Union a mutual defense treaty and, on that basis, to prepare for a joint military campaign to reverse the Israeli-American victory and recover Egypt's national territory. The Soviets balked, invoking the grave international consequences of such a plan. Instead, they urged Nasser to give first priority to the preservation of the "Egyptian revolution" through a combination of internal reforms and defensive buildup. They specifically proposed to help Egypt rebuild its armed forces to enable it to resist Israeli-American pressure and to establish a bargaining position that would permit the Egyptians, with Soviet help, to recover their territories through an "honorable" political settlement. Nasser agreed, but not before making another attempt to embroil the Soviets by proposing to place the Egyptian air force under a Soviet commander, as part of the reconstruction of Egypt's forces. Podgorny and Zakharov were inclined to agree, but, after consulting Moscow, gave a negative reply.

In Damascus, the Soviets failed to obtain from the Syrian government even the guarded and skeptical commitment to seek a political settlement that they had elicited from Nasser. The most the Syrians would concede in exchange for Soviet military aid was to refrain temporarily from any military initiatives of their own and from obstructing Egypt's attempts to reach a political solution.

Even before they had obtained Nasser's reluctant agreement and Syria's grudging tolerance, the Soviets began to skirmish ahead in search of the elements of a political settlement. Their attempt to obtain a resolution in the General Assembly in favor of an unconditional Israeli withdrawal having been foiled by the United States, they proceeded to explore with it the conditions of a settlement it was prepared to accept. At that time, the United States' position was sufficiently fluid and the Soviets were willing to depart sufficiently from their extreme public stance that Foreign Minister Gromyko and Secretary of State Rusk were able, at meetings they held at the margins of the United Nations session, to reach an agreement on the outlines of a settlement.

However, several of the Arab countries that were not directly involved in the conflict, led by Algeria, raised such a cry of protest that the Soviets quickly backed away, realizing that they had moved too far too soon. Subsequently, they continued their explorations at the Glassboro summit that brought together Premier Kosygin and President Johnson in late June, 1967; but since the Arab states had not yet sorted out their positions among themselves, the Soviets preferred to confine themselves to probing the thinking of the Americans and to conveying to them, if only by their mere presence, that they were open to negotiations at the appropriate time.

The appropriate time proved highly elusive in this instance as in many others since. After the fiasco of the initial Soviet-American attempts at an agreement, Nasser tried to assemble the Arab chiefs in a summit to coordinate the position of the Arab states and line up maximum support for his own policy. However, because of various inter-Arab rivalries, especially Nasser's conflict with King Feisal of Saudi Arabia over the still unsettled Yemen problem, and because of Nasser's battered prestige as a result of the war, he was unable to realize his project for some two months. By the time a summit finally convened in Khartoum in late August, 1967, and gave Nasser more or less what he wanted, the American position had settled into a policy that ran counter to the Egyptian-Soviet conception of a political settlement. The Khartoum summit "authorized" the Arab countries that had been directly involved in the war to seek, if they wished, a political settlement of all the issues involved in the crisis; but it insisted that such a settlement must involve no negotiations with Israel, no peace with it, and no recognition of it. Tough as it was, this formula, if advanced during the General Assembly debates or at the Glassboro conference, might have made possible a Soviet-American agreement and elicited massive international support. This might not have brought about a settlement, but it would have certainly greatly helped the Arab cause and driven a wedge between the United States and Israel. At the time the Khartoum resolution was adopted, the United States was no longer prepared to accept it.

Even before Israel's victory had been fully consummated, the United States had sensed that the success of Israel's arms provided an opportunity for more promising attempts to settle the Arab-Israeli problem. For this reason, and also because of a strong suspicion that the Soviets had been at the root of the whole trouble and because of resentment at the way they had paralyzed all efforts to contain the crisis before it broke out into war, the United States had foiled the intense Soviet attempts to obtain a Security Council withdrawal order, and had stalled for time to allow the Israelis to complete their military operations. However, the United States was uncertain and vague as to the kind of solution to the conflict it should insist on in the wake of the war. Some Middle East specialists, accustomed to thinking in terms of containing rather than trying to solve a conflict that seemed to them intractable, urged that the United States should seek to end the military confrontation between Israel and its neighbors on the basis of a series of ad hoc arrangements regarding specific problems. Others, unencumbered by either past experience or prejudice regarding the area, argued that the United States should seek to achieve a complete, "once and for all" peace settlement. The President came down clearly in favor of the latter position in a statement outlining American policy on June 19, 1967. While serving notice that the United States would not press Israel to pull back its armies until the Arabs joined it in a peace effort, he stated that the United States was committed to a peace that is based on five principles: the recognized right of national life, justice for the refugees, innocent maritime passage, limits on the arms race, and political independence and territorial integrity for all. The President also asserted that ultimately the parties to the conflict must be the ones to make a settlement in the area, but that in the meantime, the United States was willing to see any method of peacemaking tried.

Although the President's statement was quite clear, adherents of the alternative position apparently viewed it as an indication of preference or maximal desire rather than a firm and precise definition of policy that overruled their own proposals. The President himself, judging by what could be learned about what he said at the Glassboro meeting, was not, it seems, very clear in his own mind at that time about the distinction between peace as the end of active confrontation, and peace as the juridical liquidation of a dispute. This is why even after his statement of the "five principles of peace" Secretary of State Rusk was able to reach a tentative agreement with Gromyko that was based on ending belligerency rather than formal peace. The American position settled on insistence on peace in the technical juridical sense only in the course of the following weeks, and it did so as a result of encounters with the Israelis.

The Israelis had been completely unprepared to deal politically with the situation they faced as a result of their military victory and were deeply divided in the views they improvised after the event. Faced with the necessity to take a stand in the face of the Arab-Soviet campaign in the United Nations, the only platform they could advance that commanded general agreement among themselves was one that called for peace between Israel and its neighbors to be achieved through direct negotiations. The more apparent the divergence of views among themselves became in the course of the following weeks and months, the more emphatic and specific became their insistence on these two points, which they conveyed to the United States through the many channels that exist between the two countries.

The emergency session of the General Assembly failed to muster the required majority in support of any resolution on the conflict, except for one opposing unilateral change in the status of Jerusalem and one that passed the entire problem on to the next, regular session. When that session convened in the fall of 1967, the matter was taken up in the Security Council. By that time all the parties had, finally, sorted out their positions, defined them, and coordinated them among partners, allies and friends so that effective negotiations could take place. The Arab-Soviet side, anxious to avoid leaving the situation in the field completely unregulated and cognizant of the play of the American veto power, was eager to obtain any resolution that could be interpreted in any way to accomodate its position. This made it possible for the United States, working directly and through third parties, to exact concessions that accomodated its own and Israel's views. The result was Resolution 242, that masterpiece of ambivalence, adopted on November 22, 1967.

The resolution speaks in the preamble of "the inadmissibility of the acquisition of territory by war and the need to work for a just and lasting peace in which every state in the area can live in security." It then

> affirms that the fulfillment of the Charter principles requires the establishment of a just and lasting peace in the Middle East which should include the application of both the following principles:
> i) Withdrawal of Israeli armed forces from territories occupied in the recent conflict; ii) Termination of all claims or states of belligerency and respect for and acknowledgment of the sovereignty, territorial integrity, and political independence of every state in the area and their right to live in peace within secure and recognized boundaries free from threats or acts of force

The resolution goes on to affirm the necessity for guaranteeing free navigation through international waterways in the area, for achieving a "just settlement of the refugee problem," and for guarantees of security and territorial inviolability including the establishment of demilitarized zones. Finally, it calls on the secretary general to designate a special representative to establish and maintain contact with the states concerned "in order to promote agreement and assist efforts to achieve a peaceful and accepted settlement in accordance with the provisions and principles of this resolution."

Although the resolution was unanimously adopted and received the specific approval of Israel's United Nations representative and the Egyptian and Jordanian governments, it did very little, in fact, to advance a settlement, since each party read into it exactly what it wanted. Egypt took it to enjoin Israel's withdrawal from *all* the occupied territories on the basis of a timetable to be worked out through the UN representative, after which belligerency would be ended; while Israel read it as calling for negotiations to establish "secure and recognized boundaries" as part of a comprehensive peace treaty. Nevertheless, the resolution proved to be important in two respects. On the immediate level, it provided everybody with a respite each needed for his own reasons while the secretary general's representative, Ambassador Gunnar Jarring of Sweden, shuttled between the capitals of the countries concerned in a vain effort to turn the verbal bridge between the positions of the parties into a real one. For the longer term, the resolution provided an agreed frame of reference that was sufficiently ambiguous to allow now one party now the other to shift its position in response to changing political and military realities without appearing to be yielding to pressures and while pretending to consistency.

By the time Resolution 242 was adopted, the Soviet Union had gone a long way toward replenishing the arsenals of Egypt and Syria destroyed during the war. In the course of the following year, while Jarring plodded through his hopeless mission, the military buildup continued even as President Nasser and other Arab spokesmen stated frequently that renewed warfare was inevitable and as armed skirmishes erupted periodically. These developments on the Arab-Soviet side helped produce two important reactions on the American-Israeli side. As the Arab buildup began to reach levels that threatened Israel's military superiority, President Johnson decided to accede to an Israeli request for the purchase of fifty Phantom fighter-bombers and other equipment. The size of the transaction and the quality of the planes involved were dramatic, but no less important was the fact that the transaction represented the first move by the United States to support by military means, not just diplomatic action, the thesis that Israel should hold on to the conquered territories until the Arabs were prepared to make peace. Second, even as Israel proceeded to protect its military edge to retain its bargaining counters, it began to tilt increasingly toward a "tougher" conception of an acceptable bargain. Leaders and segments of the public who had been prepared to return all or most of the territories in exchange for peace when Israel's superiority was unchallenged, now felt that the restored military capability of the Arabs made it necessary for Israel to insist, in addition to peace, on some territorial changes in order to place it in a better position to defend itself against possible Arab bad faith.

In this climate of deepening stalemate, sporadic violence, and sharpened confrontation between the Israeli-American and the Arab-Soviet alignments, the American presidential elections took place. They brought about a change of the guards and a change of approach that combined with developments in the area to produce a new diplomatic situation.

The Diplomacy of the War of Attrition, 1969–1970

President Johnson's decision to provide Israel with fifty Phantoms had stirred latent anxieties of the Soviets, who saw it as a setback to their design to place the Arabs in a bargaining position that would permit them to seek an "honorable settlement." Merely to respond to it in kind entailed accelerating a costly arms race by proxy with the United States, playing perhaps into Nasser's intent to embroil them, and the risk of the heightened tensions' exploding into a general war. Consequently, while discreetly taking account of the American-

Israeli deal in determining the level of supplies they provided to their friends, they had approached the United States with a proposal for a political settlement and an invitation to discuss it with them. The proposal, sent on December 30, 1968, suggested a timetable for the application of Resolution 242, allowed room for "contacts" among the belligerents to discuss details, and contemplated an indefinite presence of United Nations forces and demilitarized areas. On January 15, 1969, in one of the last acts of the Johnson administration, the United States had answered in a note rejecting the Soviet proposal. The note reiterated America's opposition to any Israeli withdrawal before a settlement, insisted on a peace agreement to be reached by the parties themselves, expressed strong opposition to an imposed solution, urged an agreement to limit the supply of arms, and indicated willingness to discuss the conflict with the Soviets within that framework.

A few days later, President Richard Nixon assumed office, bringing with him a substantially different attitude from the one evident in the previous note. Shortly after his election, he had sent former Governor William Scranton on a fact-finding tour of the Middle East, and Scranton had announced publicly that the new administration intended to follow an "even-handed" policy in the Middle East, presumably in contrast with the previous administration's bias in favor of Israel. In his first press conference after assuming office, the President voiced his belief that the Middle East situation was a "powder keg" that could explode into general war involving the risk of big-power confrontation unless it was promptly dampened. Consequently, he was not at all disposed to continue his predecessor's approach of merely upholding Israel's military superiority and sitting back until the Arabs indicated their willingness to negotiate peace. Rather, President Nixon believed that if the United States was going to be involved in the business of providing arms to one of the parties in the conflict, it was incumbent on it to play a much more active role in seeking to control the situation and advancing a settlement.

Nixon, therefore, reversed the position taken in the January 15, 1969, note and agreed, early in 1969, to enter into talks with the Soviet Union aimed at working out "guidelines" for a settlement based on Resolution 242. In addition, in order to satisfy a demand that French President de Gaulle had insisted upon since the 1967 crisis, the President agreed to talks among the Big Four at the United Nations level to run parallel to the Big Two discussions. Israel objected to the proposed talks on the grounds that they undercut the principle of direct negotiations and portended an imposed settlement, but the President overrode those objections by maintaining that the United States did not view the aim of the talks to be an imposed solution and promising that they would leave ample room for negotiations.

For some six months before the start of the big power talks, the Egyptian-Israeli front had erupted periodically in large-scale fighting as

Nasser engaged in what he called "active deterrence" and Israel countered with deterrent retaliation. Shortly after the talks began, Nasser formally repudiated the 1967 cease-fire and launched his war of attrition. Initially, the negotiators in the two sets of talks did not pay much heed to what seemed to be different words to describe the same previously existing reality. Before long, however, the war of attrition began to make itself felt, and its course determined in large measure the course of the negotiations, particularly those between the United States and the Soviet Union, by far the more important of the two sets.

The American-Soviet talks proceeded amiably between Assistant Secretary of State Joseph Sisco and the Soviet Ambassador to the United States, Anatoly Dobrinin. On May 26, 1969, the United States formulated some "concrete ideas" about a settlement that appeared to the Soviets to be worth exploring with Egypt at a high level. The ideas centered on an Egyptian-Israeli settlement involving a "contractual agreement," frontiers that "do not reflect the weight of conquest" (meaning: that allowed for some adjustments), and negotiations between the parties to determine the specific boundaries. On June 10, 1969, Soviet Foreign Minister Gromyko went to Cairo to discuss these ideas with President Nasser, and the results were reflected in a Soviet note of June 17, responding to the American proposals. The note rejected any notion of a separate Egyptian-Israeli deal and insisted on a package including all the Arab parties. It insisted on a timetable for Israeli withdrawal from all the conquered territories and opposed any discussions on the subject of boundaries. It refused to contemplate a contractual agreement and envisaged only a declaration of "end of belligerency," to be given after the completion of the Israeli pullback. It demanded satisfaction of the "political rights" of the Palestinians, not merely of their claims as refugees. In short, the note took matters back to square one, if not beyond.

Underlying the toughness of the Egyptian position that the Soviets reflected in their note was the fact that the war of attrition seemed to be going quite well for the Egyptians. Up to that time, the Israelis had given as well as they received, but their casualties had reached the rate of eighty killed a month, an alarming level for a small, tightly knit, extremely sensitive society. The Egyptian General Staff felt that it had succeeded at last in imposing on Israel the kind of warfare in which its side enjoyed a distinct advantage, and Nasser proclaimed on July 23, 1969, the anniversary of his regime, that the "stage of liberation of the occupied territories had begun."

Three days before Nasser made that declaration, the Israelis passed to the offensive, throwing their air force against the Egyptian positions to make up for their weakness in artillery and number of standing forces. Using new tactics and electronic devices, they proceeded to take apart systematically the Egyptian air defense system and then to wreak havoc on the Egyptian artillery positions. Within two months, Egypt lost one-third of its first line combat aircraft and most of its SAM defenses in the canal zone. By late September 1969 the effect began to tell on the Egyptian diplomatic position and was reflected in a suggestion by the Foreign Minister Riyad that the "Rhodes format" might be an acceptable way to seek a settlement. (Rhodes was the site of the 1949 Egyptian-Israeli armistice negotiations. These began with the two parties dealing with each other through a mediator and ended up with them dealing directly with each other in the presence of the mediator. Also, the Rhodes formula implied separate talks between Israel and each of the Arab parties.) Since the issue of negotiations was a central bone of contention between Israel and Egypt, Riyad's suggestion hinted at a general toning down of Egypt's position and provided renewed momentum for the American-Soviet talks.

During the month of October 1969 the American and Soviet negotiators hammered steadily at the outlines of an Egyptian-Israeli settlement. On October 28, 1969, the agreed results were summarized by the American side in a brief, which the United States government, for some unknown reason, submitted under its *sole* sponsorship to the governments of the Soviet Union, Britain, and France as well as Israel, Egypt, and Jordan. The brief envisaged essentially a binding peace agreement and an Israeli withdrawal to the 1967 boundaries, except for the Gaza Strip, which was to be subject to discussion between Israel, Egypt, and Jordan. The Palestinian refugees were to have the right to either repatriation on the basis of an agreed annual quota, or resettlement outside Israel with compensation. Other principles included free navigation, security provisions to be worked out by the parties, and international assurances. The final agreements were to be negotiated under the aegis of Ambassador Jarring according to the Rhodes formula. The United States also indicated that it was preparing a brief on a Jordanian-Israeli settlement, which it submitted in the following month. The same basic principles were applied there, too, except for a reference to "insubstantial" boundary alterations which may be required for mutual security, and for the treatment of the Jerusalem question. The status of the city was to be determined by an agreement between Israel and Jordan; the city should be united and administrative arrangements should reflect the interests of the three religious communities concerned.

The American note shocked the Israeli government, who saw in it a confirmation of its worst fears of the big-power talks. In its view, the note spoke of negotiations but left little worth negotiating about after it set down the final borders in advance. It envisaged a contractual peace, but took no account of Israel's need for secure boundaries. The principles regarding Jerusalem portended a redivision of sovereignty over the city, while the provisions concerning the refugees were seen as a threat to the continuation of Israel's character as a Jewish state. The government made these points and others in its reply to the note, and, in order to marshal support against it in the United

States and undermine the whole idea of big-power talks, it leaked its content to the press and drummed up its objections.

The Arab response to the note was hardly more encouraging. Jordan was discreetly pleased, but Nasser rejected it vehemently and promptly, announcing on November 9, 1969, that after seeing the American peace plan, he had come to the conclusion that "the United States is the number one enemy of the Arabs." Yet, despite this highly unpromising reception by Israel and Egypt, Secretary of State Rogers made a public declaration on December 9, 1969, in which he proclaimed the substance of the October-November notes to be America's formal policy. Why did the secretary of state launch a plan (henceforth known as the Rogers Plan) one month after it had been foredoomed by Israel's and Egypt's emphatic rejections?

The clue to the answer lay in Nasser's previously cited declaration. Having gone to war and incurred enormous sacrifices in order to resist peace settlement, negotiations, and "the liquidation of the Palestinian problem," Nasser felt it impossible to turn around now and agree to these ideas, especially since the war of attrition was obviously going badly for him. Doing so under these circumstances was viewed by him as the beginning of a process of surrender that was bound to continue as Egypt negotiated from a position of confirmed weakness. On the other hand, Nasser realized that the American proposals departed from the Israeli positions and gave rise to friction between the two countries, and he guessed that the Americans took the step they did to demonstrate their goodwill to friendly Arab countries. He therefore concluded that if he could arouse and marshal Arab hostility against the United States, he would at one and the same time strengthen his weak bargaining position and widen the fissure that developed between the United States and Israel by playing further on the former's anxieties about losing its Arab friends. Thus, the declaration that the United States was the Arabs' foremost enemy was in fact the opening shot in a campaign launched by Nasser to assemble an Arab summit, whose avowed objective was to concert an assault on the interests and position of the United States and to mobilize the Arab resources for a "total war" against Israel. The fact that two months before, in September 1969, the conservative, pro-American monarchy of oil-rich Libya was overthrown by a group of radical army officers gave Nasser's campaign a threatening edge in the view of the surviving pro-American Arab regimes and an added measure of credibility to the dangers feared by the United States.

Nasser's campaign produced an agreement among the Arab chiefs to assemble in a summit at Rabbat, Morocco, on December 20, 1969. The secretary of state made his declaration on December 9 with a view to undercutting Nasser's design by showing the United States to be "fair-minded," and establishing publicly a clear distance between it and Israel for the benefit of the pro-American Arab countries. Given this purpose, the fact that Israel had responded to the Rogers Plan with bitter public denunciation and that this had led to an acrimonious polemic between the two partners was more welcomed than regretted by the secretary of state, since it lent added credence to the point he sought to make.

In actual fact, the Rabbat summit broke up in complete, open disagreement that disarrayed Arab ranks for the next four years, but that result owed little to the American maneuver. Indeed, the debacle occurred because Saudi Arabia, the leading country "friendly" to the United States, played one-up on Nasser and accused him of being insufficiently intransigent toward Israel and of working in collusion with the Soviet Union to achieve a settlement. Without defending the United States, the Saudis countered Nasser's aim to denounce it and to mobilize Arab resources for continuing war with proposals for an all or nothing, purely Arab military effort against Israel. Nasser walked out of the conference before it was formally closed, stopping on his way for a consolatory triumphant visit in Libya.

Israel's anxiety about the American position and Nasser's frustration in Rabbat spurred both of them to seek to change the situation through action in the battlefield. At the beginning of January 1969, the Israelis escalated their counter-attrition by launching their air force on a systematic bombing campaign against military targets in the Egyptian rear, in which their aircraft closed rapidly around Cairo and occasionally caused substantial civilian casualties when missing or mistaking its objectives. The Israelis sought to topple Nasser by showing him to be incapable of protecting his people, or at least to compel him to renounce the war and to cease fire, thus terminating the situation that, in their judgment, had brought about the undesirable developments in America's policy.

Nasser, for his part, had only the Soviet card to play after the Arab card had missed in Rabbat, and the Israeli escalation only added urgency and gave a focus to his move. As soon as the scope of the Israeli raids became apparent, Nasser hurried secretly to Moscow to confer about his deteriorating position. It has since been learned that Nasser urgently asked the Soviets to provide him with improved weapons and long-range aircraft that would allow him to hit Israel's depth as it was hitting his. The Soviets refused, citing the inability of the Egyptians to use the weapons in question without extensive training and expressing fears that matters might escalate into general war and dangerous superpower confrontation. They urged, instead, a switch to political initiatives. Nasser pointed out that it was necessary first to restore his weakened bargaining position by reinforcing Egypt militarily, and threatened that if the Soviets were not prepared to help, he would resign, publicly explain why, and give way to someone who would seek a settlement through the Americans. The Soviets, taken aback, arranged emergency consultations at the Politburo and Central Committee levels and came out with a crucial decision: they would provide Egypt with a comprehensive sophisticated air defense system including missiles and aircraft as well as the personnel to man them while the

Egyptians received training in their use; in exchange, they demanded from Nasser that once Egypt's bargaining position was sufficiently restored, he would make an earnest effort to seek a political solution on terms akin to those of the Rogers Plan. Nasser agreed, but, once again, not without *arrière pensées*. Now that he achieved an escalation of the Soviet military involvement, matters might develop in a manner that would obviate the need for him to redeem his political pledge.

These facts about the strain and compromise between Cairo and Moscow became known only years later. At the time, the outcome of Nasser's Moscow trip appeared to outsiders, particularly to Israelis, in a much grimmer light, which the Soviets, in a bid to get the maximum political mileage out of it, did very little to dispel. To the extent that they found it necessary to justify their actions formally to the United States in order to avert a reaction in kind on its part, they made sure to do so in a way that did not completely allay all anxieties.

As far as the Israelis are concerned, the first indications of the results of Nasser's trip came in the form of intensified shipments of Soviet arms. In late February it became apparent that these included large numbers of MIG-21 fighters and new SAM-3 antiaircraft missiles designed to counter the kind of tactics and measures that the Israelis had used effectively against the SAM-2s. Worse still, it became known that Soviet crews were arriving with the new weapons in addition to many more thousands of Soviet "advisers." In March, the number of advisers exceeded 10,000, making possible the staffing of the Egyptian army with them down to company level. In addition the Israelis gained preliminary evidence that Soviet pilots were flying Soviet planes on operational missions over Egypt. On April 18, 1970, the evidence was confirmed as a group of eight Soviet-piloted MIGs attempted to intercept a pair of Israeli aircraft on their way to a mission deep inside Egypt. The Israeli authorities recalled their planes and ran tests in the next few days only to find out that Soviet aircraft scrambled up in combat formation at almost every approach of Israeli planes. Finally, as the Israelis stopped their raids in depth altogether, the Egyptian forces resumed the offensive along the canal front while Soviet-advised Egyptian crews made systematic and persistent efforts to advance the new missile defense system toward the front line in order to nullify Israeli's air superiority.

The Israelis saw these developments as part of an open-ended Soviet intervention in support of Nasser's proclaimed objectives. They were convinced that unless the United States acted decisively to stop them, the Soviets would go on next to provide air protection for the crews advancing the missiles to the front line and thus create a mobile air defense umbrella that would permit the Egyptian forces to attempt a crossing of the canal and an invasion of Sinai. The Israelis made their point to the United States, indicated that they would resist further Soviet action, and pointed out the disastrous consequences that might ensue; but the American response was not reassuring—indeed it seemed calculated to encourage Soviet boldness.

Already on January 28, 1970, before the influx of new Soviet weapons and personnel to Egypt had become apparent, Israel had sought to buy from the United States some forty-five Phantom and eighty Skyhawk fighter-bombers and additional equipment to reinforce and replenish its heavily strained arsenal. The White House immediately let out unofficially that the request was viewed with favor, and the President announced publicly in mid-February that he would make a firm decision on the question within thirty days. It was evident that both announcements were intended to warn the Soviets to restrain their support for the Arab side or else the United States would increase its for Israel; yet, on March 23, 1970, after the dimensions of the Soviet arms and personnel sent to Egypt had become apparent, Secretary of State Rogers (not the President) announced that the President had decided to "hold in abeyance for now" decision on Israel's arms request. Rogers added that the United States would continue to watch the military balance in the area and would review its decision if necessary, and backed up this indication of concern by announcing a $100 million loan to Israel to help it defray the costs of past arms deliveries. However, these gestures were scant consolation to the Israelis, who were further befuddled by the explanation given of the President's decision. The secretary of state said that the United States hoped thereby to win Soviet support for the limitation of the arms race in the Middle East, as if the Soviets had not done enough damage already.

In early April 1970, shortly after the secretary of state's statement on arms, Assistant Secretary of State Sisco went out to the Middle East to assess the position of the parties in the wake of the Soviet and American moves. Apart from the fact that Nasser had agreed to receive him, Sisco found the Egyptian leader as bellicose as ever, the Israeli government no less determined to maintain maximum pressure on Egypt, and the Jordanian government so hamstrung by the Palestinian guerrillas that he had to cancel a planned trip to Amman because of hostile demonstrations. Sisco had barely returned home when it became known that Soviet pilots were scrambling up to meet Israeli planes. The Israelis believed this escalation to be directly related to the "timidity" demonstrated by the United States, and pressed harder for the arms they had requested, as much for the political significance of a favorable decision as for the military value of the weapons. By this time many American influential commentators and personalities, including people not known for their sympathy for Israel, were expressing dim views of the Soviets' intent and urging a firm response, and the President's assistant for national security affairs (Henry Kissinger) was reported to believe that the Soviets had drastically upset the balance of power in the Middle East through their actions in the single month of March. Reflecting these concerns, the President announced that he had ordered an "immediate and full" evaluation of the reports of the expanded role of the Soviets in Egypt in order to see what new actions or initiatives might be needed.

Before the evaluation work got very far, the President and the bulk of the foreign policy–making apparatus became absorbed in the "incursion" into Cambodia and its domestic aftermath and remained so throughout the month of May. Although the President, in announcing and defending the intervention in Cambodia at the end of April, linked his decision to the Middle East, the domestic storm of protest released by the Cambodian venture raised a real question as to whether the show of determination in southeast Asia did not preempt, rather than portend, similar determination in southwest Asia. In the meantime, on May 21, 1970, the President told visiting Israeli Foreign Minsiter Eban that the United States was prepared to provide Israel with a small number of planes but would do so only quietly. At the same time, the President forewarned his guest that the United States was contemplating some new diplomatic initiatives to try to check the very dangerous situation that had developed in the Middle East. In view of the Israelis' sad experience with American initiatives undertaken under pressure (the big-power talks, the Rogers Plan, the attempt to limit the arms race by "holding in abeyance"), Eban must have been as apprehensive about the forewarning as he was disappointed by the American insistence on discretion about the arms provision.

The behavior of the United States in the face of the expansion of the Soviet role in the conflict reflected a substantial long-standing difference of perspectives and judgments among the President's foreign policy advisers. Henry Kissinger and some members of the defense and intelligence establishment had their view sharply focused on the Soviet Union and tended to suspect it of seeking to exploit the Middle East conflict to establish predominance in the area. They believed that the Soviets could be deterred only by firmness in the shape of strong support for Israel, and were inclined to explain away or attribute lower priority to the effect of such a policy on friendly Arab countries. Secretary of State Rogers and his department, on the other hand, considered that a complete American identification with Israel not only hurt the American interests in friendly Arab countries but was precisely calculated to give the Soviet Union the best opportunities to score against the United States. Altogether they were less suspicious of the Soviets and believed that they were interested in a settlement, although they might have problems with the Arab partners. In any case, after having gone through the trouble of establishing some distance between the United States and Israel through the Rogers Plan, they were loath to reidentify the American position with Israel's through such moves as open large-scale arms supply as long as this was not strictly necessary. The President himself was temperamentally more attuned to the views of his adviser on national security affairs, but for reasons of intraadministration human relations he had assigned the Middle East to his secretary of state and was inclined to let him have his way especially in public, while intervening occasionally, in private, to give the secretary of state's approach a harder edge toward the Soviets and a softer one toward Israel. This context helps explain the American reactions to the Soviet moves in the wake of Nasser's visit to Moscow, which unfolded as follows.

On January 31, 1970, some three weeks after the conclusion of Nasser's visit, Premier Kosygin sent President Nixon a personal note in which he denounced Israel's "barbaric raids" against Egyptian cities and warned that, unless the West restrained Israel, the Soviet Union would have to supply Egypt with new arms. Kosygin deliberately refrained from explaining whether by "new arms" he meant additional arms, new types of arms, defensive or offensive weapons. This letter came not long after the Soviet Union had sent to the State Department its belated formal reply, dated December 23, 1969, to the American note of October 28, which had served as the basis for the Rogers Plan, in which it had gone back on the agreement of its representative in the Big Two talks with respect to several crucial points. Kosygin's message and the December 23 note appeared to the President to add up to a tough line and a determination on the part of the Soviets to press the military confrontation in the Middle East rather than try to terminate or mitigate it, and he promptly responded in kind. On February 4, 1970, he answered Kosygin's letter by asserting that the United States was not responsible for the escalation of the war and inviting the Soviet Union to cooperate in restoring the cease-fire. The President also called for discussions to limit the supply of arms to the belligerents, and indicated that otherwise the United States would have to supply Israel adequately. On the other hand, the President reaffirmed his belief in the fairness of the Rogers Plan and his continued support for it. Two weeks later, the President struck a similar note in public in his State of the World Message, prepared by Kissinger and his staff. He cautioned the Soviets not to try to manipulate the tensions in the Middle East to gain predominance, noted the dangers of the situation, and pointedly stressed that the interests of outside powers are greater than their control. He expressed America's opposition to an imposed settlement, and reiterated its willingness to provide friendly states with arms as they were judged necessary.

Kosygin did not reply to the President's letter, but on March 11, 1970, the Soviets discreetly indicated through diplomatic channels that they were providing Egypt with weapons for antiaircraft defense only and that they had gained political concessions from Nasser in exchange. Circumstantial evidence suggests that they did not spell out the actual concessions they obtained, that they did not dwell on the fact that antiaircraft defense could make possible Egyptian offense by other means, and that they did not set a limit on the area in which the new weapons might be deployed. Nevertheless, the indication by the Soviets that they were exercising restraint and were pressing Egypt in the direction of moderation was apparently sufficient to enable the secretary of state to persuade the President to "hold in abeyance" the supply of arms to Israel until the Soviet assertions were further explored. It was partly to do that exploration that Assistant Secretary of State Sisco went to the Middle East in early April 1970.

Sisco did not detect any softening in the Egyptian position, and shortly after his return to the United States it became known that Soviet pilots were flying combat missions over Egypt. The President was inclined to suspect Soviet deception, while the State Department tended first to cast doubt on the Israeli assertions about a new Soviet role and then to minimize its significance. It was then that the President ordered a "comprehensive review" of the subject. By early May 1970, when it had become clear that the Soviets had taken over the air defense of Egypt's interior, that they were helping to advance the air defense system toward the front, and that their contribution had enabled the Egyptians to resume and intensify their offensive along and across the Suez Canal, even the State Department was prepared to go along with the idea that the United States had to respond with arms provision to Israel. However, in their tenacious concern about repercussions in "friendly" Arab countries, the secretary of state and his staff insisted that the United States should give only minimum publicity to its intent by announcing only that it is "reconsidering" the arms question, that the quantity of arms to be supplied be minimal, and that it should be coupled with a new diplomatic overture to impress upon all parties that the United States was not seeking confrontation and escalation but a fair settlement. The overture, which came to be known as the "Rogers Initiative," took the form of a proposal for a limited cease-fire and resumption of negotiations under the aegis of Jarring on the basis of Resolution 242, which was submitted to Egypt, Israel, and Jordan on June 19, 1970. It eventually succeeded in part, bringing about a long truce and short-lived abortive negotiations, but it did so only because the President and Kissinger provided some stiff inputs that altered its dangerous resemblance to appeasement.

Perhaps the greatest merit of the Rogers Initiative was that it was launched at a time when the belligerent parties themselves were looking for a way out of a situation that had become extremely strenuous. After the Israelis had been forced by the intervention of Soviet-manned fighters to stop their raids in Egypt's interior, the Egyptian forces had intensified their action dramatically in the front-line zone. While their artillery resumed a daily barrage against the Israeli lines, their commandos staged daring attacks across the canal, and their air force ventured large-scale raids on Israeli positions, their Soviet-advised air defense crews made persistent efforts to advance their newly acquired SAM-3 and SAM-2 missile batteries closer to the canal. The Israeli air force responded with redoubled attacks, seeking to destroy the missile sites as soon as they were set up and to punish the massed Egyptian ground troops and artillery batteries. By June 19, 1970, when Secretary Rogers conveyed his proposal to the parties, the battle had reached fearful proportions. The Israelis were launching more than 150 air attacks daily and the Egyptian forces, as Nasser subsequently revealed, were suffering casualties at the rate of nearly 1,000 a week. The Israeli losses were far fewer, but they were much more strongly felt in the small, closely knit, and open Israeli society. Moreover, the Syrian front had become intensely active in the previous months, and the Palestinian guerrillas were exerting constant pressure from Jordan and Lebanon. All this required the Israelis to keep large numbers of reserves under arms, disrupted normal life routine, and created a sense of war all around, rendered much worse by its seeming endlessness. The strains of this situation had begun to tell on both sides albeit in different forms. In Egypt, Nasser's speeches and the controlled press alternated between boastful promises, strident menaces, and shows of reasonableness culminating in an outright statement by Nasser on June 13 that he was prepared to contemplate a limited cease-fire to give diplomacy a chance. In Israel, there had been frequent rumblings among intellectuals, academicians, and segments of the public, including high school students, that the government had not done enough to advance the chances of peace, and the government had taken a few cautious steps to meet the point of its critics while denying their criticism. The most important of these steps was Prime Minister Meir's formal announcement in the Knesset on May 26, 1970, that Israel accepted Resolution 242 and the Rhodes formula. To the outside layman, the announcement was hardly news, but to the Israelis and better-informed outsiders, who knew that hitherto only the Israeli representative at the United Nations had endorsed Resolution 242 and that the Israeli government had since carefully avoided reference to it, Golda Meir's statement was a significant policy departure. Because it was, the Gachal faction of the coalition successfully insisted on being allowed to abstain in the Knesset vote that followed the Prime Minister's presentation.

If the judgment underlying the Rogers Initiative that the time was ripe for a move to end the fighting and resume diplomacy was correct, the specific substance of the proposal and the manner in which it was handled by the State Department almost doomed it and nearly caused the opposite of what was intended. In the first place, the proposal was formally submitted to Israel and the Arab side without prior exploration or discussion. Presumably, the secretary of state wanted to avoid repetition of the experience of the Rogers Plan, when the "ideas" submitted to the Israeli government on October 28, 1969, were leaked to the press the next day. But in a situation in which Israel looked almost desperately to the United States to relieve its fears of further Soviet intervention, the abrupt way in which the proposal was submitted appeared like a peremptory American decision taken in panic. Prime Minister Meir, who received the document from American Ambassador Walworth Barbour, observed immediately that the proposed ninety-day cease-fire seemed to legitimize Egypt's resumption of the fighting after the truce and invited Israel to negotiate under the gun. She inquired about the supply of arms in that period, and was told that it would be suspended if it interfered with the negotiations. At the same time, the ambassador had nothing reassuring to say as to what would happen if Egypt took advantage of the cease-fire to advance the missile sites toward the Suez Canal, which is what the Israelis suspected to be Nasser's prinicpal aim when he publicly indicated his willingness to accept a limited cease-fire a week before. In view of all this, the Prime Minister concluded in her own mind that the entire initiative was almost calculated to use the Soviet pressure to press Israel against the wall and force it to accept the original Rogers Plan. She told the ambassador then and there that her government would reject the proposal, and two days later her Cabinet confirmed her prediction with a unanimous vote. The Cabinet also decided to convey its decision and the grounds for it directly to the President rather than to the secretary of state—a measure of the extent to which the dualism in American policy had become obvious.

The next few weeks were among the most anxious that Israel had hitherto known. Despite the fact that Nasser, too, had at first promptly turned down the Rogers Initiative, the secretary of state refused to take either Israel's or Egypt's no as final and, in an effort to keep his proposal alive, continued to play down the scope and significance of the greater Soviet involvement, to play up Nasser's reasonableness, and, most relevant to Israel, to oppose any dramatic American action such as openly providing Israel with large amounts of arms. In the meantime, as the fighting continued to rage fiercely, the Israelis learned that Soviet-piloted planes were extending their protective umbrella to the Egyptian flank at the Gulf of Suez. And while they wondered when the Soviets would cover the front itself and visualized nightmarish scenarios about the consequences of such an act, they discovered that their planes were no longer safe even before any such additional Soviet intervention. At the outset of July, 1970, the Soviet-assisted Egyptian missile crews finally succeeded in stealing a march on the Israeli air force and installing several missile sites in the battle zone, with the result that the Israelis lost several of their precious Phantoms within a few days. On July 6, 1970, Israeli Chief of Staff Chaim Barlev declared that this development upset the balance of power in the canal, and in the following days responsible, and probably officially inspired, press comments suggested that it may have become necessary for the Israeli ground forces to invade the other side of the canal in order to yank out the missile sites. At the same time, the foreign press engaged in one of the flurries of speculation about Israeli nuclear capability which mysteriously erupt whenever Israel feels itself to be in a tight situation. Responsible Israelis were saying in private that the country would go "all out" rather than yield to the combination of Soviet military and American political pressures.

The dark forebodings of the Israelis found some relief in occasional words and deeds emanating from the White House that ran counter to the premises if not the line of the State Department. For instance, on July 1, 1970, the President gave a television interview that had the effect of a cool breeze on the stifling Israeli summer. The President reaffirmed the interest of the United States in keeping a balance of power in the Middle East and asserted that Israel was entitled to "defensible borders." He accused the Arabs of being the aggressors who wanted to "throw Israel into the sea" and castigated the Soviet Union for supporting them. He depicted the Middle East situation as graver than Vietnam because it could lead the United States and the Soviet Union into a conflict neither wanted. A few days before, Henry Kissinger, in a briefing to the press, had provided a background that gave the President's remarks an even sharper edge. The adviser to the President had depicted the Soviets as possibly engaged on a pursuit of Mediterranean predominance and let out that the United States was out to "expel" them from the Middle East. Both sets of remarks were softened or counterbalanced in the following days and weeks, but they did keep alive among Israelis the hope that the United States would "see the light" before it got to be too late, and thus helped to restrain them. Even more effective was the decision of the President in mid-July to accelerate previously scheduled arms deliveries to enable Israel to compensate in some measure for the losses and wear and tear of its air force.

The reticence of the State Department was explainable in part by some evidence that Soviet and Egyptian policies were being reconsidered in the wake of the Rogers Initiative. To Nasser, the Rogers proposal was basically attractive for almost the same reasons that it was repulsive to Israel—a limited cease-fire, the possibility of improving his military position, negotiating while Israel was under pressure, and the indication that the proposal itself gave of American nervousness. However, Nasser still disliked the idea of a contractual peace, which was still part of the American thinking, and he was suspicious that the United States might be maneuvering to split up the Arabs and gain territorial concessions for Israel under the guise of "insubstantial modifications." In any case, he was convinced that matters had developed favorably that far thanks to the increased Soviet intervention and Egyptian persistence, and believed that more could be accomplished if the Soviets could be induced to deal more of the same medicine. Therefore, he gave an initial negative response to the Rogers proposal and set out for Moscow to try to persuade his partners.

Nasser spent two weeks in the Soviet Union, starting on June 30, 1970, in which he underwent medical treatment while pursuing negotiations. Circumstantial evidence and scattered bits of information that have come out since suggest that Nasser urged the Soviets to allow their pilots to intervene in the battle zone long and strongly enough to permit the Egyptian forces to establish a missile defense system. This would enable him to enter into negotiations from a position of strength and seek a settlement that avoided a contractual agreement—for instance, through simultaneous unilateral declarations of end of belligerency—which in turn would preserve the unity of Arab ranks. He argued that Israel was unlikely to defy the Soviet fighters without American support, and that American behavior since the Soviets had increased their support and involvement indicated that such support would not be forthcoming, or in any case would not be prompt and decisive. The Soviets, long suspecting that Nasser was bent on embroiling them in the war, argued that further military intervention on their part was dangerous and unnecessary, and demanded that Nasser live up to the promise he had made in his previous visit in January to seek a political solution along lines similar to the Rogers Plan. They explained that Egyptian valor and their own help had already placed Nasser in a good bargaining position, shaken Israel, and forced the United States to assume a moderate stance; but they added that Israel was getting desperate, that important voices in the United States were clamoring for tough American action, and that President Nixon was unpredictable and inclined to take sudden adventurous decisions as he had done recently in Cambodia. Additional Soviet intervention was bound to provoke undesirable reactions and result in losing the present favorable conjunction.

It so happened that while this debate was going on in Moscow, Nixon and Kissinger made the tough statements previously cited, and that the Israeli Phantoms started falling to the fire of missiles successfully installed in the combat zone. The Soviets used both events to support their arguments and Nasser found himself in the unusual position of trying to tone down the American danger, underreport the Israeli plane losses and underestimate their significance in order to defend his argument that a further strengthening of his position was safe and necessary. The result of the prolonged deliberations was a compromise of sorts, which, however, failed to meet Nasser's principal demand. According to a story that came to light several years later, Anwar Sadat, who was vice president at the time, met Nasser at the Cairo airport on his return from the Soviet Union, on July 17, 1970, and on the way home, asked him how things had gone. Nasser replied briefly, in English, "It's a hopeless case," and added dejectedly that he had decided to accept the Rogers proposal, which he in fact formally did on July 22, 1970.

While the Soviets covertly resisted every effort of Nasser's to embroil them further in the fighting, overtly they tried to convey the opposite impression to retain maximum bargaining power for him and protect their image in Arab eyes. The commiqué issued at the conclusion of Nasser's visit called for a political settlement of the crisis, but it also asserted that Israeli attacks had made the situation dangerous and added that peace can be assured "through measures to end Israeli aggression." One meaning of that threatening clause became apparent shortly thereafter, when at the end of July, Soviet-piloted fighters for the first time challenged Israeli planes over the combat zone. They did so on two separate occasions, thus barring the hypothesis of accident. In the first encounter the Israelis broke off the engagement, but in the second they sustained it and shot down five Soviet planes against no losses for themselves. Although the incident was not repeated despite the fact that Israeli planes continued to operate for several more days before a cease-fire came into effect, the Soviets achieved part of the effect they wanted. Long after the event, Israelis believed that if the fighting were resumed, the Soviets would probably take part in it. It was a perfect case of the Soviets playing on the dire expectations of their opponents, although unforeseen circumstances were to make that psychological success largely irrelevant.

Nasser's acceptance of the Rogers Initiative immediately triggered American demands on Israel to follow suit. Israel repeated and expanded on its objections—the failure of the proposal to commit Egypt to direct talks even at a later date, the limited duration of the cease-fire, the danger that it would be used by the Egyptians and the Soviets to strengthen the missile defenses, further delays in American sale of planes, and Nasser's and Jordan's refusal to take responsibility for terrorist attacks against Israel while the cease-fire would protect them against Israeli retaliatory raids. Beneath and beyond all these objections Israel feared that the Rogers Initiative was only a device to bring about an imposition of the Rogers Plan. The State Department responded to Israel's arguments and concerns selectively, lamely, and impatiently, urging it, for instance, to agree to the Rogers proposal first and then discuss negotiating procedure and substance, or pointing out that the cease-fire provided for a standstill of forces but evading a direct answer to the question of what would happen if the provision were violated. The discussion was saved from degenerating into a confrontation only by a timely intervention of the President that put the talks on a different track. On July 24, 1970, he sent Prime Minister Meir a note that addressed itself to the issues of basic concern for Israel beyond the immediate Rogers proposal and provided important assurances about them. These included: (1) American recognition of the need to preserve the Jewishness of Israel—to allay Israeli fears about the refugee provisions in the Rogers Plan and recent statements on the subject by Nasser; (2) American acknowledgment that Israel's borders would not be the same as those of June 4, 1967—a more favorable rephrasing of Rogers' "insubstantial modification" clause; (3) an assurance that the United States would not be a party to an imposed solution—allaying a long-standing Israeli fear and unequivocally rejecting a long-standing Egyptian demand; (4) support for a peace settlement based upon secure and recognized boundaries as the outcome of negotiations between the parties to the conflict; (5) agreement that Israeli troops would remain on the cease-fire lines until a contractual peace agreement was signed; (6) a pledge to maintain the military balance in the Middle East core and to continue the supply of arms to Israel; and (7) a promise of continuing large-scale American economic aid.

The Prime Minister responded appreciatively to the President's note, but asked for further reassurances and clarifications. One of these was a request for a formal affirmation that his note constituted American policy toward Israel and the Arab-Israeli conflict, which the President granted. Another, ostensibly following from the first, was an assurance that the Rogers Plan would be withdrawn, which the President refused to give. Further exchanges secured an American assurance of support for Israel in case the standstill cease-fire was violated or the Soviets intervened in battle.

While these exchanges were taking place, the Israeli leadership engaged in a continual tense debate and intense political maneuvering to determine Israel's final answer. The President's note of July 24, 1970, coupled with the enormous pressures built up by the course of events in the previous months and with gloomy perceptions of the alternatives ahead, finally broke down the previous unity of the government based on a platform of unconditional direct peace negotiations and forced on it the necessity for choice. On July 31, 1970, the debate finally came to a close in a vote to accept the American proposal, which was supported by all parties in the coalition except Gachal. The Gachal ministers resigned, bringing to an end the National Coalition Government that had led Israel since the eve of the Six Day War. It is indicative of the extent to which the Israeli public was sick of war that Gachal insisted on going on record as being in favor of the cease-fire although it turned down the other elements of the American proposal.

The cease-fire came into effect on August 8, 1970, and terminated what Nasser called the "war of attrition" and the Israelis the "Thousand Day War." One of the principal results of that prolonged, costly contest was that Egypt gave up its insistence on Israeli withdrawal from the occupied territories without prior negotiation and ultimate contractual agreement, while Israel gave up its insistence on unconditional direct negotaitions and firmly endorsed Resolution 242. Another result of the war was to bring into play the divergent interests of the belligerents and their respective superpower partners and place the two partnerships under very heavy strain. Although the strain was more apparent in the American-Israeli than in the Soviet-Egyptian partnership, the subsequent course of events was to show that the American-Israeli relationship was more solid and better able to overcome the strains.

23

The Prevailing of the Israeli-American Partnership, 1970–1973

Despite the assurances given by President Nixon, Israel's government had accepted the Rogers Initiative only with great reluctance and grave apprehensions. The difference between the Gachal ministers who resigned over the issue and many, perhaps most, of their colleagues who voted in favor was not so much over the quality of the American proposal and what it portended as it was over timing and tactics. Both groups were convinced that the envisaged Arab-Israeli negotiations would become stalled quickly and that Israel would come under American pressure to make dangerous concessions to get them going again. Israel would then face the choice of either yielding, to its own detriment, or engaging in a confrontation with the United States against a background of resumed fighting, probably with Soviet participation. The principal difference was that Gachal favored a firm Israeli stand then and there without compromising Israel's position through concessions, whereas the others were prepared to pay a certain price in the present to postpone as long as possible a crisis with the United States and find temporary relief from an extremely onerous immediate situation.

What actually happened was something that no one in Israel, or for that matter anywhere else, had even vaguely anticipated. In the first place, the cease-fire which was scheduled to last for three months unless the progress of negotiations warranted its extension, persisted in fact for over three years notwithstanding the lack of any such progress. In the meantime, American-Israeli relations, which were seemingly headed for confrontation in August 1970, evolved in the opposite direction in the remainder of that year and during the course of 1971, as the White House perspective increasingly encroached upon and then prevailed entirely over the State Department approach. At the same time, relations between the Soviet Union and Egypt underwent a reverse process of mounting strain and friction, which culminated in the expulsion of the Soviet advisers from Egypt in the summer of 1972. By that time, American policy in the Middle East became completely oriented on

Israel, sharing with it not only basic goals but also an almost identical evaluation of the situation and a common conception of means and ends.

This unexpected evolution unfolded through a complex and tortuous process before issuing in a consistent clear-cut pattern. At the heart of it all was Washington's changing perception of Soviet intentions and dispositions in the Middle East as well as in the global arena. In an initial phase, the White House found it necessary to take exceptional measures to buttress Israel's military position and to plan a major joint action with it to counter what seemed to it to be a series of challenges calculated to erode the American position in the Middle East. For a while the White House actions severely undermined but did not stop altogether the simultaneous efforts of the State Department to advance an Arab-Israeli settlement in accordance with its conception of the situation, with the result that American policy appeared sometimes to be working against itself. Eventually, however, the configuration that emerged in the area and the onset of détente on the global arena made the endeavor of the State Department appear unnecessary as well as futile and led it to desist. The stage was set for the emergence of a single American conception which, generalizing from what had taken place, viewed Israeli military predominance as apt to prevent war in the area, check the Soviets, and impel the Arab side to agree eventually to negotiate unconditionally.

The Erosion of the Rogers Policies

Within hours after the cease-fire came into effect, the Rogers Initiative ran into difficulties as a result of a massive violation of the truce's standstill provisions by the Egyptians and the Soviets. While that crisis was being debated, a civil war broke out in Jordan which decisively affected the issue of the debate as well as subsequent American-Israeli relations. Before the Jordanian crisis was resolved, President Nasser suddenly died and was succeeded by Anwar Sadat, who took Egyptian policy through some abrupt twists and turns to a dead end before making a desperate effort to break out. These three events and their repercussions dominated the post–cease-fire diplomacy and determined the fate of the Rogers Initiative and other related State Department moves.

As soon as the cease-fire came into effect, Egyptian missile crews and their Soviet advisers violated its standstill provisions by rebuilding and rearming destroyed missile sites and establishing new missile sites in the combat zone. Within forty-eight hours, thirteen *new* missile batteries with ninety launchers were deployed. The Israelis immediately notified the United States discreetly of the violations and asked it, as initiator and guarantor of the cease-fire, to see that the status quo ante was restored before the negotiations proceeded. The State Department, suspecting Israeli intent to stall the negotiations, reacted by casting doubt on the Israeli reports while ordering an

American U-2 plane to start reconnaissance flights over the battlezone two days after the start of the cease-fire. Since the United States had no independent intelligence of the missile deployment at the time the cease-fire came into effect, the U-2 could only detect violations occurring after the start of its reconnaissance. By that time the violations were no longer very substantial, and the State Department therefore urged Israel to ignore them. Infuriated, the Israeli government reacted on August 12, 1970, by making the charges public, thus forcing the issue.

The State Department voiced displeasure at Israel's action, but, in order to save the negotiations, offered to compensate it for the military disadvantage it had incurred by accelerating the delivery of a small number of Phantoms, and providing it with airborne Shrike antimissile missiles. Prime Minister Meir was inclined to accept the American offer, but Defense Minister Dayan opposed it as inadequate and insisted that Israel should refuse to participate in the negotiations until the missiles were removed. While the government debated the issue, reports came of a second wave of violations, involving the installment of ninety additional missile launchers in the period between August 15 and 27, 1970. The reports promptly ended the debate in Israel, but the State Department, which now had its own evidence, waited until September 3, 1970, before acknowledging publicly that large-scale violations had taken place and announcing increased military assistance to Israel. Two days before, the Senate had voted unlimited funds to provide Israel with weapons to restore the military balance that had been upset by the Egyptian-Soviet moves. Thus the attempt of the Egyptians and the Soviets to improve their bargaining position by reinforcing Egypt's military capacity had the ironic effect of practically committing the United States to maintaining Israel's capacity to hold on to the cease-fire lines, blurring the previous distinction carefully cultivated by the State Department between American support for the defense of Israel proper and the defense of its conquests.

In its acknowledgment of September 3, 1970, the State Department called on the parties to abstain from further violations and resume negotiations in good faith. The Israeli government, however, responded three days later that the situation created by the violations had to be rectified *in fact* first—that is to say that the missiles had to be removed or Israel had to take actual possession of sufficient weapons to restore the disturbed military balance. Besides its unwillingness to negotiate from a diminished military posture, Israel's government feared that assent to the State Department's proposal might encourage it to press for further "accommodations" that would erode the Israeli position entirely. Naturally, the State Department thought the Israeli stance to be unduly hard and unhelpful. An argument ensued that began to strain American-Israeli relations when fateful events suddenly erupted in Jordan and altered the entire situation.

Jordan's King Hussein had been eager to negotiate peace with Israel since the end of the Six Day War but his hands were tied by Nasser's opposition and the Palestinian guerrillas who were strongly based in his territory. During the long war of attrition, the guerrillas had grown in popularity, numbers, and strength and had established themselves as a virtual state within the Jordanian state. From time to time, the King had made efforts to reassert his control which resulted in open fighting with the guerrillas, but he dared not press his efforts very far for fear of Egyptian and general Arab reaction. On July 25, 1970, three days after Nasser agreed to the Rogers proposal, King Hussein announced the agreement of his government too and looked forward at last to the chance of achieving a peace settlement. The PLO, however, viewed the Egyptian and Jordanian assent to the American plan as a prelude to the liquidation of the conflict to their detriment and vowed to sabotage the peace project.

In pursuit of that intent, the Popular Front for the Liberation of Palestine, one of the movements in the PLO, launched on September 6, 1970, four simultaneous attempts to hijack commercial airliners over Europe. One of the attempts, directed against an Israeli El Al jet, was foiled by the security crew on board, but the three others, involving TWA, Pan Am, and Swissair liners, succeeded. The hijackers caused one of the planes to land in Cairo airport and after evacuating its passengers, blew it up as an act of protest, defiance, and threat. The other two planes were directed to an abandoned airstrip in the desert northeast of Amman, where they were joined on September 9, 1970, by an additional hijacked plane belonging to BOAC. The guerrillas held the planes and their 425 passengers, mostly American, hostages in the baking summer desert and threatened to kill the ones and blow up the others unless all the Palestinians held prisoner in West Germany, Switzerland, and Israel as a result of previous guerrilla actions were released. Deadlines were set and extended but Israel, backed by the United States, refused to yield. Finally, on September 12, 1970, the guerrillas, partly because they apparently got wind of what was coming and sought to prepare for it, partly for logistical reasons, blew up the planes and released most of the hostages, retaining only some 50 of them whom they trasnferred to a refugee camp under their control.

In the hectic week before this happened, the King had been made to look completely helpless by all the world's media focused on the little desert strip, and questions were raised about the value of any agreement concluded by a ruler who was so obviously not the master of his own house. Consequently, on September 15, 1970, after the bulk of the hostages had been removed to safety, King Hussein, now covered on his Egyptian flank by Nasser's anger at the Palestinians' defiance of his policy, decided to act. He placed the country under marital law, appointed a government of generals, and launched an all-out campaign to crush the guerrillas. The guerrillas fought back fiercely, but as the tide began to turn against them, large Syrian tank units crossed the frontier on September 19, 1970; to help them in their avowed aim to overthrow the regime. Soviet advisers accompanied the Syrian units up to the frontier but did not cross it with them.

The Israelis were naturally concerned about the possibility that the guerrillas should win and establish in Jordan an intransigent regime under Soviet patronage. They conveyed their apprehensions to the United States government as soon as hostilities broke out only to discover that the American government, at least the White House part of it, was even more concerned than they. In the White House conception, Jordan under King Hussein was not only a force for moderation in the Arab-Israeli conflict but constituted also an important buffer separating the pro-Soviet radical regime of Egypt from those of Syria and Iraq, and all three of them from oil-rich, friendly Saudi Arabia and the Persian Gulf principalities. The fall of the Jordanian regime would bring about a solid pro-Soviet bloc from the Euphrates to the Nile which would upset the inter-Arab balance as well as the Arab-Israeli balance, exposing to danger all the American positions and interests in the Middle East.

Already on September 16, 1970, President Nixon had told a group of midwestern editors in an off-the-record briefing that was promptly reported by the *Chicago Sun-Times* that the United States might have to intervene in Jordan if Syria or Iraq (which had some 18,000 troops stationed in Jordan) threatened Hussein's regime. On the 17th, reports that Syrian tank forces moved closer to the Jordanian frontier prompted urgent consultations between Nixon and his advisers as to what the United States should do if the Syrians crossed the border, and these brought up the point that it could not do much by itself for technical reasons, and that any effective intervention had to involve the Israelis. On the next day, September 18, 1970, the President met with Prime Minister Meir who had come to the United States to plead her case in the dispute over the Egyptian-Soviet violations of the cease-fire. Recalling the discussion with his advisers from the previous day, the President was very forthcoming and informed the Prime Minister that he had decided to give Israel $500 million in military assistance, and to supply it with thirty-six additional fighter-bombers as well as other equipment before the end of the year. He urged her to consider the advantage of starting diplomatic talks with Egypt, but did not press his point when Meir refused to contemplate any negotiations until complete rectification had been put into effect.

On September 19, 1970, after the Syrian tanks crossed into Jordan, the President ordered a partial but conspicuous alert of American airborne units stationed in the United States and West Germany, reinforced the Sixth Fleet with a third carrier task force, issued a warning to the Soviets to restrain the Syrians, and conveyed an assurance to King Hussein not to worry about the Israelis, who had quietly effected partial mobilization and deployed their forces for possible intervention. The next day more Syrian troops poured into Jordan and engaged the King's forces. The secretary of state now issued a statement denouncing the Syrian "invasion" as an "irresponsible and imprudent" action and demanded a Syrian withdrawal, while Assistant Secretary of State Sisco privately warned the Soviet chargé d'affaires about the possibility of a direct Israeli or American intervention.

In warning about an Israeli intervention Sisco was playing the same game he believed the Soviets were playing. While the Syrian troops were massing at the border, the Soviets had assured Kissinger that "rumors" to the contrary notwithstanding, no "invasion" was going to take place (hence Secretary Rogers' pointed use of the term in his statement). After the Syrians had crossed, the Soviets denied any involvement on their part and supported the Syrian official story that it was a question of Palestinian units using Syrian equipment, as "demonstrated" by the fact that the Syrian air force took no part in the action. In serving his warning, Sisco pretended to be reporting a judgment as to how the Israelis might act, when in fact the United States was prodding Israel to act.

In the evening of September 20, 1970, National Security Adviser Kissinger telephoned Israeli Ambassador Rabin, who was accompanying Prime Minister Meir at a dinner of Jewish organizations in her honor, and informed him that he had just received an urgent request from the Jordanians asking him to arrange for an intervention of the Israeli air force against the Syrian tanks. Kissinger asked Rabin if Israel was prepared to do so. After additional phone calls and hurried consultations among Rabin, Meir, and Tel Aviv, Rabin met Kissinger in Washington and told him that Israel was prepared to act, but wanted to know what the United States would do if the Egyptians and the Soviets intervened. Kissinger recognized the validity of Rabin's question and promised him a reply soon, after taking up the matter with the President.

While the President pondered Israel's question the Syrians captured Irbid, an important junction of roads linking Jordan, Syria, Iraq, and Israel, and King Hussein sent additional urgent appeals for American and British help. Consultations with the British, who had sent paratroopers to Amman in 1958 while the American marines landed in Lebanon, revealed that they not only refused to intervene militarily this time but strongly counseled against American intervention. Similar opposition was expressed by other European allies. The President ordered Kissinger to work out with Rabin contingency plans for a joint American-Israeli intervention, which were transmitted step by step to American military commands overseas, particularly the Sixth Fleet; but he held up his reply to Israel's question to await some specific developments in the battlefield.

Late in the afternoon of September 21, 1970, the Soviet chargé d'affaires had indicated that the Soviet Union was urging restraint on Syria and asked the United States to urge similar restraint on Israel. At the same time, evidence was beginning to arrive that the Jordanian armor had managed to block the Syrian advance, although it had failed to retake Irbid. The question on the President's mind was whether the Syrians would throw in their air force or additional armor to overcome Jordanian resistance or would demonstrate restraint, as the Soviets had led the Americans to expect. The answer came later that night: the Syrians threw in a small additional tank force that could be the vanguard of larger forces. The President made up his mind.

Rabin and Kissinger had worked out a two-stage contingency plan for an Israeli air strike and armoured assault on the Syrian forces in coordination with an American airborne descent on Amman airport. Israel was to open with a massive air strike against the Syrian armor to help the Jordanian forces. If that did not suffice to turn the tide, Israeli armored columns would advance in a pincer movement from the Golan and the Jordan Valley farther south to cut off and destroy the Syrian intervention forces. Additional operations were to be undertaken in Syrian territory to protect the flank of the Israeli left thrust. At the same time, an American paratrooper battalion was to seize the airport of Amman, to be followed by another airborne battalion with heavier equipment, and the two were to hold and secure the area pending the arrival of additional reinforcements. Israel was thus to bear the sole burden of the first stage, the main burden of the second, and was to provide the ready reserves in case the American operation ran into difficulties. The question that Israel raised regarding the American role in case it ran into complications was therefore crucial for the whole undertaking. Late on September 21, 1970, the President answered it unequivocally: if the Egyptians or the Soviets intervened, the United States would intervene against both. The initial force to do so would come from the three carrier task forces of the Sixth Fleet, elements of which were conspicuously cruising not far from the Israeli coast.

King Hussein was apprised of the essentials of the American-Israeli plans, and the order to go ahead with them now depended on the outcome of a battle that raged between the Jordanian and Syrian forces. The Syrian command ran the battle with the knowledge that the Americans had been threatening to intervene, that their fleet was concentrated within striking distance, and, above all, that large Israeli forces were poised on their flanks; and it must have wondered, therefore, whether victory might not be worse than defeat. The Jordanian King, on the other hand, reassured by the American-Israeli decision, was able to throw into the battle everything he had, including his small but efficient air force, which he now dared to engage without fear of provoking the Syrian air force to intervene. The outcome became apparent in the afternoon of September 22, 1970, when Syrian tanks began to pull back across the border. By evening, the Soviet representative in Washington was telling Kissinger that the Soviet Union was doing everything to have Syria desist and was making lame excuses about how matters had gone that far in the first place. The next day the Syrian retreat continued and the King was able to turn his full strength against the main centers of guerrilla forces. An episode was thus closed which Kissinger was to recall several times later as having brought the United States extremely close to war with the Soviet Union.

The Jordanian episode had a far-reaching effect on the American attitude toward Israel and the Arab-Israeli conflict. On the immediate psychological level, the President, who had taken personal command of the crisis, was deeply impressed by the determination shown by the Israelis at a time when America's formal allies had quit on him. He also appreciated the speed, efficiency, discretion, and trust with which the Israelis acted through their gifted ambassador, Yitzhak Rabin. Because events moved too fast for paperwork, the crucial American-Israeli coordination was worked out entirely on the basis of a verbal understanding. Two years later, the President was to express his feelings in a highly unconventional fashion when at a farewell party at the end of Rabin's ambassadorial mission, he publicly told Prime Minister Meir that Rabin was one of the best ambassadors ever to serve in Washington and that Israel should make good use of him, adding jocularly that if Rabin were ever out of a suitable job, the United States would be glad to engage him.

Apart from its effect on Nixon's personal attitude toward Israel, the Jordanian episode drove home to the President and some of his advisers a crucial point which they previously saw only in the abstract. The crisis and its denouement demonstrated to them in a concrete and dramatic fashion the value for the United States of a strong Israel. At a time when the regional balance among the Arab states, between the United States and the Soviet Union, as well as between Israel and the Arab states was seen to be imperiled and when the entire American position in the Middle East appeared, as a result, to be in jeopardy, the United States was able to retrieve the situation and turn it around only through the effective cooperation of a powerful Israel.

More specifically, for some time before the crisis the President had been harboring mounting suspicions that the Soviets were using the Big Two talks as a screen to cover an effort to exploit the Arab-Israeli conflict to achieve predominance in the Middle East and the eastern Mediterranean. Their role in the Syrian invasion appeared to him to be the high point of a pattern that had begun with their rejection of the Rogers Plan and continued with their refusal to contemplate measures to limit the supply of arms to the belligerents, their despatch of "advisers" in massive numbers to Egypt and Syria, their creation of naval and air bases in these countries, their assumption of a combat role in Egypt, and their collusion with the Egyptians in violating the cease-fire agreement. The American action in the Jordanian crisis was therefore seen by Nixon as the first successful attempt to call a halt to the Soviet drive and begin to reverse it by forcing the Soviets to back down in view of their friends, and the key role of Israel in that action was particularly appreciated.

In addition to helping to check the Soviets, the President and his advisers could not fail to notice that Israel's military power had also helped defend the Jordanian regime directly, and other friendly Arab regimes indirectly, even while deterring the resumption of general war in the area. That observation became the basis of a new formal conceptualization of American political strategy in the Middle East which Kissinger was to work out in a year or so and implicitly incorporate in the elaborate State of the World document submitted to Congress.

In the meantime, the Jordanian crisis had the effect of substantially tilting the balance of influence in Middle Eastern matters within the administration in favor of Kissinger and against Rogers. In the course of the marathon consultations he held among his staff, the President had again and again espoused his national security adviser's analysis of the situation and his recommendations for action rather than those of his secretary of state. Moreover, he had assigned to Kissinger the key role of coordinating the intervention plans with Rabin and keeping in touch with the situation in Jordan, thus breaking the previous division of labor that had left the Middle East as Rogers' nearly exclusive domain. Henceforth, although the secretary of state remained formally in charge of Middle East policy, his role was to be checked much more seriously and often than before by interventions from the President, acting on Kissinger's advice.

A first test of the new dispositions in the American government occurred shortly after the situation in Jordan subsided. In the latter part of October 1970, Prime Minister Meir was back in the United States in quest of aid and arms for the next year. The White House gave her assurances of assistance to the tune of $500 million dollars and a favorable response to her arms request for 1971, while the secretary of state sought to take advantage of the occasion to induce Meir to return to the negotiations. Meir, however, insisted that the arms deliveries promised for the remaining months of 1970 must first be received, and the secretary of state felt obliged to desist.

Many other tests, some much more serious, were to follow in each other's heels in the next year or so, and, although they were all eventually resolved in the same direction, not all of them were disposed of so simply. The reasons why so many occasions for friction arose reverted ultimately to one major change in the Middle East scene that took place while the fighting in Jordan was still going on. That was the sudden death of Egypt's President Nasser on September 28, 1970, and the accession to power of Anwar Sadat.

Nasser, we have seen, had accepted the Rogers Initiative after having failed to get the Soviets to escalate their participation in the combat. His next gambit was to enter the negotiations envisaged by the American plan from as strong a position as possible by playing three cards: the *threat* of increased Soviet intervention if the negotiations failed, which his adversaries did not know was unreal; the threat of resuming the fighting from a vastly improved military position, achieved by the rapid deployment of missiles after the cease-fire; and the old standby of threatened pressure on Arab countries friendly to the United States. Sadat, a member of the original junta that took over in 1952 and one of two or three out of some fifteen officers who had survived purge or death for eighteen years, was inclined to follow his predecessor's strategy but with two important modifications. Since a peace agreement appeared to be inescapable, as Nasser himself had privately conceded, Sadat sought to trade that concession for American support for the territorial and other demands of Egypt; and, since a trade-off was to be attempted, he thought he might as well pursue it directly with the United States, rather than through the intermediary of the Soviet Union.

Sadat's strategy was to be reduced to shambles by the course of events, and before he was able to devise a viable alternative in the summer of 1973, he was to be reduced to having to resort to a succession of wild and inconsistent improvisations simply to keep alive and in power from month to month. Nevertheless, his initiatives and moves repeatedly put pressure on America's new relationship with Israel, and directly or indirectly challenged the two to define it more specifically.

One of the most crucial of Sadat's moves occurred in February 1971. Sadat had previously agreed to a renewal of the cease-fire for another three months on the understanding that Israel would return to the negotiations in December, which it finally did. In January 1971 Jarring resumed his mission and this time quickly brought it to a head. On February 8, 1971, he sent Egypt and Israel similar formal notes designed to find out if there was a basis for agreement between the two. He asked Egypt if it was prepared to sign a binding peace agreement with Israel embodying a final settlement, assuming it would recover sovereignty over Sinai, and Israel if it was prepared to return Sinai, assuming Egypt would sign a peace agreement including satisfactory security arrangements. On February 15, 1971, Sadat answered in the affirmative, marking the first time that Egypt formally and authoritatively agreed to a contractual peace. On February 25, 1971, Israel replied with a categorical negative, marking the first time it formally and authoritatively indicated that it sought modification of its boundaries with Egypt in the context of a peace settlement. This brought Jarring's mission to a final halt, amid charges by Israel that he had exceeded his mandate in the first place by submitting proposals of his own.

Sadat's reply had been viewed by the State Department as a major breakthrough in the conflict, and it had strongly urged Israel to give a positive reply for its part, or at least to answer the inquiry directed to it in a way that kept the negotiations open. When Israel did the reverse, the State Department asked it to reconsider and when it refused, Secretary Rogers castigated it in public while implicitly siding with Egypt. In a news conference he gave on March 16, 1971, he expressed continuing American support for Jarring's mission, and, in impatient didactic tones, urged Israel to seek security in satisfactory political arrangements and guarantees by an international peace-keeping force rather than by the acquisition of territory. The very next day Israeli leaders answered in public with equally blunt and argumentative words. Prime Minister Meir recalled the terms of the President's July note, asserted that the borders of Israel must be defensible, and vowed that "there are certain things beyond which Israel would not go." Defense Minister Dayan, responding to the tone taken by the secretary of state, said in effect that it was time Mr. Rogers began to understand that he does not understand the Arab view. Minister Without Portfolio Yisrael Galili, Meir's most influential adviser, urged his countrymen to be prepared for a "bitter argument" with the United States. The secretary of state took his case to the Senate in an effort to forestall the customary resolutions to force the hand of the administration in cases of open friction with Israel. The post-September honeymoon between the United States and Israel appeared to have come to an end.

For its part, the Israeli government had been prompted in its reply to Jarring by several considerations. First, there were the perennial internal political considerations. Before leaving the government, Gachal had argued that the Rogers Initiative was an opening wedge to reintroduce the abhorred Rogers Plan, while the ministers who finally voted for the initiative had relied on the assurance in President Nixon's note that Israel was entitled to "defensible borders." The Jarring inquiry seemed to confirm Gachal's prediction and therefore made it particularly important for the government to take a firm stand in order to forestall charges that it had engaged on the slippery slope of yielding to pressure. Second, February-March 1971 was a very bad time to ask Israel to put its trust in political arrangements and outside guarantees. By that time, the United States had already "compensated" Israel for the Egyptian-Soviet violation of the cease-fire with additional military assistance and weapons, but the memory of the argument that preceded the corrective action was still vivid in the minds of the Israelis, as was their sense that the correction would not have taken place if they had not stood firm. Finally, President Nixon *had* given a promise to support "defensible borders" in July, which he confidentially reaffirmed in the months after the Jordanian episode, and the Israeli government thought that the time had come to force the United States government to decide "once and for all" which of the two voices it was speaking with effectively counted, that of the secretary of state or that of the President.

It is indicative of the state of the American-Israeli relationship after the Jordanian episode that, despite Israel's rejection of points of substance and procedure vital to Secretary Roger's diplomatic conception and strategy, the State Department did not even attempt to apply pressure on Israel by manipulating the supply of arms to it, as it had done for much less reason in the past. Indeed, the administration went out of its way to announce on April 20, 1971, that the United States was supplying Israel with additional Phantoms and considering a new request for more, under its pledge of the previous fall to maintain the balance of power. The sharpness of the secretary of state's *verbal* reaction to Israel's response to Jarring was in a sense a measure of his frustration in the face of a developing tendency in the administration as a whole to view military assistance to Israel mainly as a function of meeting the Soviet challenge in the area and deterring war, thus largely taking it out of the play of immediate Arab-Israeli diplomacy.

The "bitter argument" between the secretary of state and Israeli leaders was interrupted before it went very far by another move of President Sadat. On April 2, 1971, Sadat revived a proposal he had voiced before the failure of Jarring's initiative to reopen the Suez Canal in exchange for a partial Israeli withdrawal. Since Israeli Defense Minister Dayan had made a similar suggestion in November of the previous year, the secretary of state seized the opportunity in order to get away from the controversy over a comprehensive settlement by offering the United States' good offices to advance what came to be known as a "partial" or "interim" settlement.

In his eagerness to take advantage of this unexpected way out of stalemate and to use the opportunity of Sadat's agreement to American mediation in order to improve American-Egyptian relations, frozen since 1967, Secretary Rogers promptly set out personally to the Middle East in the first week of May 1971 to promote an agreement. In Cairo, he found Sadat to be receptive to the idea of improving American-Egyptian relations, but his discussions there and in Jerusalem revealed, to his disappointment, the existence of a wide gap between Egypt and Israel on two crucial points. Egypt insisted that the interim agreement should be designated a first step toward complete Israeli withdrawal from Sinai, and that Egyptian forces should take possession of the area east of the canal to be evacuated by the Israelis, whereas the Israelis objected to the latter demand and insisted that the envisaged agreement should stand on its own and not be linked to the question of further withdrawals. The positions of the two parties were, not surprisingly, consistent with their positions on a general settlement, but since the Egyptian conditions were in line with the conception of the Rogers Plan, the secretary of state was inclined to support them against Israel's views. The ground was laid for another "bitter argument," although it was some time before the dispute broke into the open because of yet another move by Sadat.

Ever since Nasser's death, a silent struggle for power had been taking place in Egypt, which had pitted a number of Nasser's lieutenants against Sadat. Sadat's opponents were headed by Ali Sabri, a former Prime Minister, the head of Egypt's only political organization (the Arab Socialist Union) and a man known to be close to the Soviet Union. The struggle finally came to a showdown on May 12, 1971; the ostensible grounds for it included Sadat's overture toward the United States as well as an agreement he had concluded with Libya and Syria to join the three countries in a federation. (Incidentally, the latter agreement was one of the reasons for Sadat's turning away quickly from the issue raised by the Jarring inquiry to the idea of an interim agreement, since Syria and Libya remained vehemently opposed to the notion of a peace agreement with Israel.) On May 15, 1971, Sadat emerged victorious from the struggle, having arrested in the process Ali Sabri, his associates, and their followers. The Soviets, who had been concerned about Sadat's acceptance of exclusive American mediation, became alarmed when their supporters within the Egyptian regime lost out and were purged. On May 25, 1971, ten days after the showdown, President Podgorny rushed to Cairo at the head of an impressive delegation to try to shore up their position in Egypt. Podgorny pulled out a prepared draft of a Soviet-Egyptian treaty of "friendship and cooperation" and made Sadat's acceptance of it a test of his proclaimed continuing dedication to good and strong relations between the two countries. Caught in a weak moment after the recent shake-up, and fearful that the Soviets might withhold military supplies and thus incite the armed forces against him if he refused, Sadat felt compelled to sign on the dotted line on May 27, 1971.

The real significance of the Soviet-Egyptian treaty—that it was more a symptom of a crisis of confidence than of greater closeness between the Soviet Union and Egypt—was not to become apparent until a year or so later, when Sadat ordered the expulsion of the Soviet advisers. At the time the treaty was concluded, however, and for sometime thereafter, it was generally thought to mark the climax of a persistent process of Soviet entrenchment in Egypt. One immediate effect was that it led to the suspension of the American mediation effort until the situation became somewhat clearer. Another was to cause Israel to approach the United States with an emphatic request to put the supply of arms to it on a long-term basis, as the Soviets had done with Egypt, instead of the year-to-year basis which hampered sound defense planning.

Israel's request was received with sympathy in the White House and other parts of the American government. The State Department, however, making virtue out of apparent necessity, sought to bargain a favorable American response on this question for a more accommodating Israeli position on the subject of interim settlement. On July 30, 1971, Assistant Secretary of State Sisco went to Tel Aviv to discuss with Prime Minister Meir a three- or four-year arms agreement linked to a softening of Israel's stand. The Prime Minister showed some willingness to compromise on various aspects of the proposed interim settlement, but on the crucial question of linking a withdrawal from the canal to a general withdrawal, she remained adamant.

For the next two months or so, the State Department was caught in a paralyzing dilemma. On the one hand, Sadat was getting restless and doing things that threatened to produce a military explosion or to undermine the American position in the area. On July 23, 1971, the anniversary of the Egyptian Revolution, he solemnly proclaimed 1971 to be the "year of decision," in which the conflict had to be settled by peace or by war. In August he tried to call an Arab summit to endorse his decision and put pressure on the United States, and when that project failed, he assembled a "mini-summit" of radical Arab countries to put pressure on conservative countries, friends of the United States, who had balked at the larger summit. In September, he publicly charged the United States with deception and procrastination in the endeavor to promote a settlement and announced that he had decided to take the entire issue back to the United Nations General Assembly the following month. All the while he kept reiterating his "year of decision" slogan, and in early October he announced that he was going to Moscow to coordinate with Egypt's ally the strategy of peace or war. All these developments put heavy pressure on the State Department to take some initiative to break the stalemate.

On the other hand, considerations having to do with suspicions of the Soviet Union caused President Nixon and his advisers to tie its hands. In the first place, the White House took a much more dim view of the Soviet-Egyptian treaty than the State Department. More importantly, on July 9–11, 1971, Kissinger undertook his famous secret trip to China, which ostensibly wrought a revolution in the world diplomatic balance. The White House was uncertain how the Soviets would react—whether they would become more accommodating or more truculent. As it looked to the Middle East for signs of the answer, the indications it found were not reassuring. There was Sadat's proclamation of the "year of decision," which he seemed to link to the recently concluded Soviet treaty. There were reports in August that the Soviets had considerably reinforced their own squadrons in Egypt and were flying reconnaissance over Sinai and the Sixth Fleet from bases in Egypt. And there were the attacks of Sadat against the United States just mentioned. These developments inclined the President to think that now was not the time to do anything that might suggest a weakened American support for Israel and thus encourage Soviet-Egyptian boldness. On the contrary, despite the inconclusive outcome of Sisco's July mission to Israel, the President had it announced in late August that the United States was going to help Israel in a long-term program to "modernize" its armed forces.

The State Department finally broke out of its inertia in early October 1971, on the occasion of the General Assembly's debate on the Middle East issue at the Arabs' request. The United States had to take a stand on the subject, and the secretary of state decided to use the occasion to launch a renewed American effort to advance an interim settlement in order to forestall the deterioration of the situation toward war, or, at least, to secure some protection for the American position in the area by demonstrating once more America's fairness. In a major speech delivered on October 4, 1971, Rogers explained the advantages to all parties of an agreement to reopen the Suez Canal, described the positions of the parties up to that point, delineated six points in which these positions differed, called for a determined effort to narrow these differences, and expressed continuing American support for renewed efforts by Jarring to achieve a comprehensive settlement.

The main feature of Rogers' "Six Point Program" was that, while urging compromise on all six points of disagreement, it implicitly gave strong public support to the Egyptian position that a partial settlement must be linked to an agreement on a general settlement. This appeared to Israel to be an attempt to apply the obnoxious Rogers Plan by installments, and undercut the attraction of a related proposal made by the secretary of state to hold "proximity talks" between Egyptian and Israeli negotiators, with an American as a go-between. Worst of all from Israel's point of view, the secretary sought to persuade it to adhere to his program by reverting to the pressure tactic of withholding the supply of arms already promised.

The fate of Rogers' program recapitulates neatly the nature of the complex forces that had entered into play since the Jordanian episode and the way in which these resulted in Israel's having its way with the United States. While the State Department pursued the secretary's initiative in discussions with Israel and Egypt, President Sadat went on his much heralded "war or peace mission" to Moscow. Some four years after the event, Sadat was to reveal that the results of his talks were extremely disappointing to him. One understands from the remarks he made then that the Soviets not only would have nothing to do with his "year of decision" slogan, but that they severely reprimanded him for proclaiming it without prior consultation, as required by the Soviet-Egyptian treaty. In any case, they urged him to drop the war talk, refused to provide him with the arms he felt necessary to pursue his objective, and agreed to supply him only with a limited amount of second-rate materiel for face-saving purposes. At the time of the visit, however, the impression created by Sadat's mission was quite different. The Joint communiqué issued on October 13, 1971, did speak of the agreement of the parties to seek a peace settlement based on complete Israeli withdrawal from all the occupied territories, but it added that the Soviet Union had agreed to new measures to bolster Egypt's military capacity, thus preserving the notion Sadat needed to maintain at home and abroad that the Soviets supported his "war or peace in 1971" idea. This impression was further strengthened by the fact that Sadat stopped in Damascus on his way home from Moscow, where he and the Syrians announced that the Syrian armed forces had been placed under supreme Egyptian command in preparation for coming military tests.

On October 14, 1971, the day after the Soviet-Egyptian communiqué was issued, Israeli Foreign Minister Eban held a meeting with Secretary Rogers, in the wake of which Rogers felt it necessary to issue a public statement deploring the Soviet pledge to bolster Egypt's military strength and cautiously warning that the United States would have to "carefully reconsider" its military commitment to Israel in light of President Nixon's commitment to maintain the Middle East balance of power. The next day, October 15, 1971, seventy-eight Senators voted in favor of a resolution calling on the administration to resume the shipment of Phantoms to Israel and to refrain from using the supply of arms to it for policy bargaining. On October 25 Meir brought her dispute with the State Department into the open in the course of a speech in the Knesset, in which she specifically attacked Rogers and Sisco by name, charging them with going back on their previously expressed support for Israel's position and embracing Egypt's on the question of the link between an interim agreement and further Israeli withdrawals. She announced that Israel would not take part in any proximity talks until the embargo on arms deliveries was lifted, the secretary of state dropped his Six Point Program, and agreed that it was not part of the task of the American go-between to make proposals of his own.

In an effort to justify and defend its policy before critics at home, the State Department, on November 4, let out to the press that American Intelligence sources reported a sharp drop-off in Soviet arms shipments to Egypt since the previous July. The report added that the estimate of American officials in touch with Soviet affairs was that the Soviets would give Sadat only a limited amount of arms in the wake of his October visit in order to bolster his internal position, and that the Soviet Union wanted a limited agreement on the canal before President Nixon's scheduled visit to Moscow in May 1972. Two weeks later reports from unidentified sources appeared in the American press to the effect that the Soviets had just provided Egypt with a number of TU-16 medium bombers equipped with air-to-ground missiles, enabling it to strike at Israel's depth. This forced the State Department to qualify its previous statement that the Soviet Union had shown restraint in its dealings with Egypt. On November 22, 1971, the Senate voted 81–14 half a billion dollars in military credits to Israel, specifying that half the amount was to go for the supply of Phantoms. On the same day the State Department indicated that the United States decided to halt its efforts to promote an interim agreement.

The termination of the State Department's endeavor on behalf of Roger's Six Point Program marked the end of an entire phase in American Middle East diplomacy, which had begun with the Big Two and Big Four talks and proceeded through the Rogers Plan, the Rogers Initiative, and the Rogers mediation. Although these policies achieved some important tactical successes, including most notably the ending of the war of attrition and facilitating Sadat's agreement to the idea of a contractual peace with Israel, they failed in their ultimate goal of advancing a settlement or even starting a viable movement toward it. Officials in the State Department and outside observers have blamed this failure on an insufficient American willingness to exert pressure on Israel to comply with those policies owing to American internal political considerations. The preceding analysis clearly suggests that, while such considerations did have some effect, particularly as far as Congress is concerned, the erosion of the Rogers policies was ultimately due to an inherent contradiction in their underlying conception. Essentially, the principal asset enabling the United States to aspire to a settlement in the first place was Israel's hold on the conquered territories, its strength, and its resultant ability to deny to the Arabs and their Soviet partners the alternative option of recovering the lost territories by means of war and pressure. The application of heavy American pressure on Israel was bound to undermine that asset of American policy by suggesting that Israel might be isolated or sufficiently weakened to enable the Arabs and the Soviets to pursue the option of war, pressure, and threats. This contradiction had eluded the secretary and his State Department staff, who were still accustomed from pre-1967 days to view the United States as a more or less independent outsider in the Arab-Israeli situation, free to dispense or withhold favors and support to the parties. Once experience began to reveal that conceptual flaw in the spring and summer of 1970, the United States was forced to make pragmatic adaptations that ended up by eroding the Rogers policies. The adaptations happened to produce for a while a pattern wherein the State Department continued to pursue the Rogers policies while the White House intervened increasingly to ensure a continual supply of arms to Israel and to qualify occasionally the substance of the State Department policies; but that dichotomy was not intrinsically necessary, and the pattern itself could not last very long in the face of its diminishing effectiveness and the friction and mistrust it generated between the United States on the one hand and Israel and Arabs on the other.

The Merging of American and Israeli Conceptions

In the course of opposing the successive Rogers policies, Israel naturally presented to the United States alternative assessments of the situation and urged it to adopt alternative policies that ostensibly served better the interests of both countries. These arguments and theses met with increasing receptivity on the part of the White House and other segments of the American government the more the Rogers premises and policies were buffeted and eroded by events. By the time the State Department gave up on the last of Rogers' initiatives, the United States was in fact ready to give the Israeli approach a try.

In contrast to what had happened to Rogers' approach after it had been adopted, almost every major event following the new American disposition tended to confirm its validity and thus enhance the American commitment to it. December 31, 1971, saw the end of Sadat's "year of decision" and although the stalemate was more deeply set than ever, Egypt did not go to war and did not seem to be about to do so, thus "proving" the Israeli thesis that a strong Israel firmly backed by the United States was the most effective way to prevent war. In July 1972 Sadat ordered the expulsion of the Soviet advisers from his country and the termination of Soviet base rights in it. This major crisis in Soviet-Egyptian relations and setback to the Soviets apparently confirmed another key Israeli thesis to the effect that a strong Israel unequivocally backed by the United States was the best way to check and roll back Soviet power and influence in the area. This same event, coupled with the disarray that prevailed in inter-Arab relations, seemed to prove a third Israeli thesis to the effect that unequivocal American support for Israel would not, in the long run, undermine the American position in friendly Arab countries and benefit the Soviets there, because those countries needed American support against their Soviet-supported, radical, sister Arab countries as much as the United States needed their friendship.

In view of the apparent brilliant confirmation of the Israeli propositions, the United States finally adopted their policy sequel of upholding the status quo until the Arabs were prepared to enter into negotiations with Israel without prior conditions. To be sure, the United States was aware that the longer the status quo endured the higher the Israeli expectations from a settlement might rise, thus making the achievement of any settlement extremely difficult, and for this reason, it periodically urged the Israeli leadership to come forward with "constructive proposals" and initiatives to advance peace. However, partly because the United States itself felt comfortable with the status quo, it did not press its urgings as hard as it might have even without resorting to the discarded type of pressures; and, in the absence of any urgent incentive to do otherwise, Israel made essentially pro forma responses to the American requests. What it did seriously attempt was to undertake or contemplate moves designed to make the status quo even more unbearable to the Arabs in order to press them to negotiate. But that gambit helped precipitate war sooner than it produced negotiations.

On November 22, 1971, when the State Department announced the halt of its efforts on behalf of Rogers' Six Point Program, it also indicated that there were no signs of any special Egyptian military buildup along the Suez Canal, and ventured the opinion that Sadat's threatening rhetoric was, more than anything else, designed to influence the forthcoming General Assembly debate on the Middle East. This cool estimate of Arab threats, so contrary to the rather alarmist previous tendency of the State Department, was partly meant to counter the pressure that was building up in Congress and parts of the administration in favor of providing Israel with additional large amounts of weapons on an urgent basis. However, it tacitly acknowledged the validity of the main premise of those who were in favor of strong support for Israel, which was that a militarily superior Israel was an effective means to prevent war. State Department objections to any particular arms transaction thus became arguments over degree and technical details which could be easily overridden or countered once the principle was conceded.

Confirmation of the efficacy of the Israeli deterrent came shortly thereafter from authoritative Arab sources. On November 28, 1971, the Arab League's Joint Defense Council met in Cairo to coordinate Arab military and diplomatic action. The meeting started in a heavy mood owing to the assassination of Jordan's chief delegate, Prime Minister Wasfi al Tal, by Palestinian fedayeen. In the course of it, the Egyptian chief of staff, General Shazli, prepared the ground for Sadat's backing out of his "year of decision" commitment by arguing that the Arab states collectively were not prepared for war with Israel and must devise a "new strategy" to achieve their objectives. Two weeks later, Jordan's King Hussein revealed that point in public during a visit to Washington, adding that Jordan would not be drawn into an armed conflict. On December 13, 1971, Sadat, in an interview with the New York Times' C. L. Sulzberger, tried lamely to save face before Western audiences by saying that his "year of decision" meant a commitment on his part to *decide* by the end of 1971 which way Egypt was going to go, not a commitment actually to go to war if there were no promise of peace. As to the question of what that decision was going to be, the answer had already been given in the shape of an Egyptian-sponsored motion in the General Assembly instructing the secretary general to reactivate the Jarring mission and calling on Israel to "respond favorably" to the latter's memorandum of February 8, 1971, which suggested Israeli withdrawal from all of Sinai.

The statements, actions, and inactions of the Arab leaders did not add to the substance of what was already known about their capabilities and intentions at that juncture, but they provided a clear, tangible vindication of the administration's decisions on arms to Israel which ran counter to the State Department's reticence. In this respect there was an interesting symbolism, whether or not it was intended, in fact that on the day Sadat's deadline expired, press reports indicated that President Nixon had agreed, in the course of discussions he held with Prime Minister Meir in the first week of December 1971, to supply Israel with forty-two Phantoms and twice that many Skyhawk fighter-bombers over the next three years. In addition to this approval of Israel's long-standing request to put the provision of arms on a long-term basis, the reports added that the United States had also concluded an agreement with Israel on November 1, 1971, to help it in developing its own military industries.

Sadat's failure to live up to his slogan greatly detracted from the limited credibility he had in his own country and was the cause of the outbreak of violent student demonstrations against him—a rather rare occurence in tightly policed Egypt. In trying to meet his problems on the home front, Sadat resorted to desperate improvisations and more empty threats which had the effect of providing additional justification for a more Israel-oriented American policy. For example, after denouncing the new American-Israeli arms deal and accusing the United States of deceiving him with insincere peace endeavors, Sadat flew to Moscow at the beginning of February 1972 for the proclaimed purpose of obtaining more weapons and assistance from the Soviets and fixing with them the zero hour for the resumption of the fighting. American observers, however, promptly learned, probably from Soviet sources, that there was no cover at all for Sadat's claims. The Soviet authorities, eager at all costs to avoid even giving the impression that they supported war on the eve of President Nixons's historic visit to China, turned down categorically the Egyptian's requests for offensive weapons and for endorsement of a threatening posture. The most the Soviets were prepared to do to help Sadat save face vis-à-vis his own people was to agree to send Defense Minister Andrei Grechko to Cairo to "review Egypt's needs," and even that promise they did not fulfill promptly.

While waiting for Grechko, Sadat explained to his people in a speech he gave on February 16, 1972, that the reason why he did not go to war at the end of 1971 was that the United States had strengthened its commitment to Israel to compensate for the loss of prestige it suffered as a result of Pakistan's defeat at the hands of India in the December 1971 war. While all the evidence clearly indicates that Sadat was merely grasping for excuses, the particular argument he used provided additional reinforcement to the thesis that enhanced American support for Israel helped to deter war. The point was particularly telling because Sadat could not at the same time state to his people that the increased American support for Israel was being matched by increased Soviet support for Egypt.

Before Grechko got to Cairo, Sadat was back in Moscow on April 27–29, 1972. The explanation he gave to his people for this second trip to the Soviet Union within less than three months was that he wanted to coordinate positions with the Soviet leaders prior to the American-Soviet summit due to meet the following month, which had the Middle East problem on its agenda. Shortly after he returned to Cairo, Sadat declared in a May Day speech to his nation that he now had "a guarantee that within a reasonable time we shall have the means to liberate our land." Actually, his achievement in Moscow fell far short of that. The Soviets merely agreed to provide Egypt with a modest additional amount of military aid and went on record, in the joint communiqué, as believing that, in view of the continuing frustration of a political settlement, "the Arab states have every reason to use other means to regain Arab lands." Even that gain over the previous February was due in large measure to the desire of the Soviets to establish a stronger bargaining position vis-à-vis the Americans in the forthcoming talks, and was achieved only in exchange for Sadat's giving them additional base rights in Egypt.

Shortly after Sadat spoke of the "guaranteed means" to liberate the Arab lands, the Moscow summit was concluded with a whole series of accords between the United States and the Soviet Union, including an agreement on the need to avoid armed clashes in the Middle East. Sadat, whose remaining card vis-à-vis the United States and Israel consisted of the tattered prospect/threat of Soviet military backing, and who had just paid a considerable price to obtain the Soviets' subscription to the statement about using "other means" to liberate Arab lands, felt deeply betrayed. After a period of brooding and consultation with other Arab leaders, he reacted by ordering, on July 18, 1972, the immediate withdrawal from Egypt of all Soviet military advisers and experts and placing all Soviet bases and equipment on Egyptian soil under the exclusive control of Egyptian forces. The impact of this bombshell on the Soviets was barely cushioned by a simultaneous call by Sadat for a "Soviet-Egyptian summit" to be held in Cairo to discuss the "new stage" in the relations between the two countries.

The reasons Sadat gave for his act in the announcement were that the Soviets had refused to supply Egypt with the necessary weapons to enable it to go to war in 1971, that they had tried to impose conditions on the use of Soviet weapons, and that they were too cautious and had agreed with President Nixon to avoid clashes in the Middle East. In the next three months Sadat provided additional information on the promptings for his decision, which put Soviet-Arab relations in an entirely different light from that of the public communiqués and declarations in which they had hitherto been seen. By far the most important additional information was the revelation that he had acted on the advice of King Feisal of Saudi Arabia, reputed among the Arabs to be a friend of the United States. Feisal ostensibly explained to Sadat that the growing American support of Israel had been due to the increasing Soviet military penetration of Arab countries, which did not even help the Arabs in achieving their goals. By eliminating or weakening the Soviet factor, Sadat would encourage the United States to take some distance from Israel and attempt earnestly to advance a settlement that the Arabs could accept.

The above analysis of American policy and action in the previous years, especially in 1970–1971, indicates that Feisal's insight was sound and his advice shrewd. However, the manner in which Sadat acted on them and the timing of his action were faulty, depriving them of the efficacy they might have otherwise had. For example, shortly before issuing the anti-Soviet decree Sadat had been denouncing the United States and pinpricking it through such acts as demanding that it should cut by half its small diplomatic mission operating under the Spanish flag since the break of diplomatic relations in 1967. These indications of hostility obscured the message that the action against the Soviets was also an opening to the United States.

More importantly, to the extent that that message was sensed, the United States was not prepared to avail itself of it just at that time. Having just concluded with the Soviet Union a series of agreements giving expression to détente, and having come to an understanding that pledged the parties to refrain from attempts to undercut each other and avoid exacerbating the Middle East situation, the United States was not inclined to rush into any action that might be construed by the Soviets as taking advantage of their troubles in Egypt to advance its own position. This self-abnegation seemed particularly appropriate after the humiliation recently inflicted by the United States on the Soviet Union through the mining of Haiphong, and was meant to encourage the Soviets to exercise similar restraint in Vietnam and other parts of the world where they were in a position to take advantage of American difficulties.

Most important of all, Sadat's expulsion of the Soviets was seen in the United States as the major payoff of a policy of close support for Israel rather than as a possible ground for changing that policy. The combination of Israeli military strength and unequivocal American backing had already proved its efficacy in deterring war and preserving a balance between friendly and hostile Arab countries; now that same combination seemed also to be effective in checking and rolling back Soviet influence and diminishing the danger of a superpower confrontation. It was that policy, Washington believed, that caused the Soviets to despair of the Arabs' capacity to alter the situation by war without their own participation, maximized their fears of such participation, and impelled them to adopt the cautious course that led to the crisis between them and Egypt.

Some analysts have seized on the fact that Sadat's move came in the middle of an American election year as the explanation for the United States' failure to respond positively to it. Although it is generally true that an election year is not a propitious time for initiating an adverse change in American policy toward Israel, the preceding analysis suggests that, on this occasion, there were good substantive reasons for not doing so—indeed, for reaffirming a policy course that had seemed to work so well. This is why the United States persisted in that course *after* the elections and even went further by adopting Israel's thesis regarding the content of a peace settlement, despite the fact that Sadat repeated his overture in a more direct and explicit fashion.

Sadat himself tended to attribute America's failure to react as he had expected to the election year explanation, and he looked forward to 1973 as a more suitable time to try to elicit the kind of response he hoped for. However, if he were to play the Soviet card at that later date, he had to retrieve it first. Moreover, he needed to mend his relations with the Soviets to ensure a minimal flow of arms and spare parts for his Soviet-equipped armed forces. Consequently, after having waited vainly for the Soviet leaders to come to Cairo, he decided to send his Prime Minister, Aziz Sidki, to Moscow to begin discussion of the "new stage" in Soviet-Egyptian relations. The Soviets, fearing that a complete break with Egypt might undermine their entire Middle East position, agreed to receive Sidki in mid-October 1972.

Sidki and the Soviets were able to repair the immediate consequences of the crisis from their respective points of view. Egypt agreed to "invite" back several hundred Soviet advisers and to renew the right of the Soviets to use some military facilities on its soil. In exchange, the Soviets agreed to provide

Egypt with massive amounts of military equipment including the advanced SAM-6 mobile antiaircraft missiles (Sadat was to say a few months later that he was "drowning in Soviet weapons"). With respect to basic issues of strategy and policy, however, the two parties were only able to define the differences between them rather than resolve them. Essentially the Soviets reiterated their willingness to help Egypt seek a satisfactory settlement by all means short of joining it in war, while Sidki expressed Egypt's readiness to make every effort to seek a solution by political means but reserved its right to go to war if all else failed. Outwardly, the two sides agreed to project an impression of reconciliation, and the joint communiqué announced that the top Soviet leadership accepted in principle Sadat's invitation to visit Egypt.

After he patched up his relations with the Soviets, and after Nixon was reelected and reinstalled, Sadat picked up the American gambit once more. In February 1973 he sent his national security adviser, Hafez Ismail, to Washington to explore the United States position and possibilities of a settlement. But before doing so he sent Ismail to Moscow, on February 7–8, partly to soothe possible Soviet anxieties about the forthcoming Washington trip and partly to try to take advantage of these anxieties to press for a more forthcoming attitude on their part, which could be of help in the bargaining with the United States. In Moscow, Ismail was able to get the Russians to subscribe publicly to a promise to "facilitate the strengthening" of Egypt's armed forces and to reiterate their declaration that the *Arabs* have the right to use every means to liberate their territories. In private, however, the Soviets continued to resist Egypt's demands for large quantitites of offensive weapons beyond a few air-to-surface and surface-to-surface missiles, or to hint that they themselves might be involved in renewed fighting. They persisted in pressing for greater effort toward a diplomatic settlement and specifically urged Egypt to strive for an interim accord to reopen the Suez Canal.

In Washington, Ismail met with President Nixon and Secretary Rogers, but, significantly, the real discussions took place during three long secret meetings with Henry Kissinger in the course of a weekend the two spent together in a private mansion in Connecticut. Ismail quickly discovered that the United States, far from being prepared to do more for Egypt than it did in the past owing to Egypt's demonstrated willingness and ability to break away from the Soviets, was in fact disposed to do less. Kissinger, speaking for the President, indicated that, while the United States was eager to advance a settlement, it saw no use in taking any new, open diplomatic initiative, and considered that a solution must ultimately result from a dialogue between the parties themselves. The United States was prepared to help start such a dialogue by holding separate, secret discussions with the parties, like the ones Ismail was engaged in then. Kissinger rejected the notion, asserted by Ismail, that the United States could impose a settlement on Israel; it might at best be able to exercise a measure of effective influence on it, if the Arabs could accede to some kind of formula that reconciled their own concern with sovereignty with Israel's security needs. A settlement by stages spread over a number of years might resolve that equation, but, in any case, a return to the pre-1967 borders was not possible. In short, Ismail gained the very strong impression that the United States, while pursuing its own interest, had come to adopt a view of the Middle East situation and a conception of the way to resolve the crisis that were virtually identical to Israel's.

The failure of Ismail's mission to Washington was confirmed by the subsequent course of events. Even while he was holding his secret talks with Kissinger, Prime Minister Meir arrived in the United States for what had become a traditional periodic top-level consultation. If Ismail's attempt to trade on the Soviet position in Egypt had any impact on Kissinger and Nixon, it did not reflect itself in the visible outcome of their discussions with the Israeli Prime Mininster. Meir left the United States amid public reports that the United States had agreed to enter into a new contract to provide Israel with large amounts of additional high quality weapons, including Phantom and Skyhawk aircraft.

Ismail and Kissinger had agreed to keep in touch through secret channels, but whatever views they exchanged in the following months did not seem to bring the American-Egyptian positions any closer or to alter American-Israeli relations. On the contrary, one month after Ismail returned to Cairo, President Sadat delivered a major speech in which he heaped scorn on the American views conveyed to his adviser, and announced a major reshuffling of his government (in which he assumed the prime ministership in addition to the presidency) in order "to prepare the country for total confrontation with Israel" on the diplomatic and military levels. Shortly thereafter, Sadat called on the Arab countries to use oil as a weapon in the struggle against Israel and, after getting a favorable public response, caused the initiation of a Security Council debate to review Resolution 242. Sadat hoped either to press the United States to go along with an attempt to give the resolution a more specific content in line with Egypt's position, or else to force the oil-producing countries to threaten or apply sanctions against it if it refused. The maneuver boomeranged: the United States espoused publicly *Israel's* interpretation of the resolution, and the oil threat was shown to be empty—at least for the moment.

At the outset of the debate, on May 29, 1973, the American representative, John Scali, served notice that the United States would oppose any effort to push through the council any new resolution that differed from 242, and argued that progress toward peace in the Middle East could be achieved only through direct or indirect negotiations between the parties. On June 14, 1973, Scali went farther and, for the first time, implicitly but firmly repudiated one of the main principles of the Rogers Plan. While emphatically rejecting the Arab demand that Israel .commit itself to withdrawal to the pre-1967 borders as a precondition to any negotiation, he unequivocally supported the Israeli position that *new* boundaries had to be defined, and that agreement on these could be reached only through negotiations by the two sides. The next day, the council decided to postpone the conclusion of its debate because of the impending meeting of the second Soviet-American summit, in Washington. When it met again, the United States used its veto to block a resolution voted on July 26, 1973, which "strongly deplored Israel's continuing occupation of Arab lands occupied during the 1967 war." This was the second time in ten months that the United States used its veto in favor of Israel.

During the summit discussions of the Middle East, the United States took on an even stronger position on the question of negotiations than the one taken by Scali in the Security Council and made it a point to make that position publicly known. On June 23, 1973, in the course of reporting to the press on the work of the summit, Kissinger stated that the Middle East proved to be the toughest issue on the agenda, and that the United States insisted that Arabs and Israelis had to negotiate directly while the Soviets' position was that negotiations had to be undertaken through Jarring, as Egypt demanded. Two days later, the President and Kissinger together, while elaborating on the final-joint Soviet-American communiqué, reaffirmed that difference between the American and Soviet positions but expressed their satisfaction that despite the disagreement, the two sides concurred on the need to avoid big-power conflict in the area.

This last point was the capstone of the Nixon-Kissinger Middle East policy that had been emerging since the end of 1970, and was virtually identical with Israel's. That policy demanded that the Arabs agree to "unconditional negotiations," knowing that Israel would not return to the pre-1967 borders. Until they did so, Israel's military strength, coupled with the manifest caution of the Soviets, would deter them from going to war. If they, nevertheless, irrationally went to war, then the pledge of the two superpowers to avoid involvement in the conflict would at least keep the clash localized. The only remaining concerns of the United States were that if the Arabs did go to war and were, as expected, quickly crushed by Israel, their defeat was as likely to produce political chaos as a change in their disposition toward a settlement, and that in either case there might be a serious disruption of the flow of oil. Because of these concerns, remote as they appeared, the United States was somewhat uneasy about sitting completely passively until the Arabs turned around and agreed to unconditional negotiations, and prodded Israel from time to time to think of ways to induce the Arabs to negotiate seriously.

For its part, Israel had recognized for some time that the changed Middle East situation since 1970 created room for maneuver in several directions. Its government as a whole had been particularly impressed by Sadat's expulsion of the Soviet advisers, and had initially seen that act as not only removing the incubus of possible Soviet military intervention against Israel, but also as a change in the strategic-political configuration that improved the prospects of some sort of settlement. Beyond that, however, the government was divided as to what might be specifically done to take advantage of the new situation. One month after Sadat's move Defense Minister Dayan, typically, seized the initiative and, on August 17, 1972, publicly proposed an interim peace agreement with Egypt along a line cutting across the middle of the Sinai Peninsula. When Sadat ignored the proposal and went on to try to repair his relations with Moscow and to pursue the various initiatives described above, Dayan, typically again, swung to the opposite extreme and asserted, on April 3, 1973, his conviction that peace was not in the horizon for the next ten to fifteen years and urged Israel to act accordingly in its handling of the occupied territories.

In the meantime, the government as a whole went through a similar process but in a more cautious and ambivalent manner. In August 1972 it decided to explore the possibility of "proximity talks" through an American intermediary to ascertain possible change in Egypt's disposition, but in September it backed away in the heat of the emotions raised by the massacre of eleven Israeli athletes in Munich and declared that it would not negotiate until terrorism was eradicated. In February 1973, during a visit to the United States, Meir relented from that position and assented to two American proposals. She discreetly agreed to a suggestion by the President to attempt to foster a secret Arab-Israeli dialogue through the intermediary of Kissinger, and she publicly agreed to a proposal by Secretary Rogers to hold formal "proximity talks" with Egypt through the intermediary of himself or Sisco. However, as the former attempt led nowhere and as the secretary of state's suggestion was turned down by Egypt, the government began to entertain ideas to take advantage of Israel's highly favorable situation through unilateral action "on the ground."

The impetus for the project was provided by Dayan. Having reached the conclusion that a settlement was not in the offing for the next ten or fifteen years, the defense minister started a campaign in Israel designed to lead to the adoption by the government of measures that would amount in fact to an annexation of the West Bank, the Golan, and parts of Sinai. In his usual style, Dayan not only forcefully advocated his ideas verbally, but also stretched the considerable authority of his office to create facts (such as settlements and resettlements) and generate concrete plans (such as the proposal to establish a port city to be called Yammit astride the former Egyptian-Israeli border) that practically began the application of his ideas.

As pointed out in the discussion of Israeli politics, Dayan's immediate objective was to have his plan adopted as the program of the Maarakh in connection with the general elections scheduled for October 1973. His campaign began to polarize his party as his opponents, led by Deputy Prime Minister Yigal Allon, Foreign Minister Abba Eban, and the powerful Finance Minister Pinchas Sapir, bestirred themselves to resist it. The latter three differed a great deal among themselves in temperament and thinking but they all shared the view that Dayan's proposals would foreclose the chances of peace, which they believed still existed, would saddle Israel with a "demographic nightmare," and would undermine its social order and endanger its democracy. Meir herself was sympathetic to the views of the trio, but she and others in the Labor party had to reckon with the fact that Dayan commanded substantial support inside the party, and with the possibility that, unless he was given some satisfaction, he and his followers might defect to the opposition. Since there was no group to the left of the Maarakh that could be rallied to compensate for the loss of Dayan and his supporters, the result could well be the triumph of a rightist coalition and an outright annexationist program, along with the termination of the forty-year-long rule of Labor.

To avert that danger, it will be recalled, the Labor party ended up by adopting, in August 1973, the "compromise" plan known as the Galili Document as part of its election platform. The plan envisaged permitting public and private bodies to purchase land in the occupied territories, and called for the creation over the next four years of a large number of publicly supported settlements in addition to private investments and enterprises. The rationale of the plan was that if the Arabs were prepared to seek a settlement through unconditional negotiations, then the envisaged action would put pressure on them to do so promptly; and if they were determined to avoid doing so, then the contemplated actions would be justified by that very refusal. In other words, the Arabs' will to settle was to be tested by means of a gradual process of foreclosing or at least restricting the chances of an eventual settlement.

To the United States, the Galili plan appeared as a drastic departure from the previous Israeli policy of "sitting tight" until the Arabs were prepared to negotiate, to which it had adapted its own policy. It so happened that the debate in Israel that resulted in the adoption of the plan coincided with mounting concern in the United States about an impending "energy crisis," with renewed warnings by Saudi Arabia that it would not increase its oil production unless the United States modified its policy toward the conflict, and with increased Arab pressure on American oil companies, culminating in the nationalization by Libya of the companies operating on its soil. In view of all this, President Nixon indicated in early September 1973 that he was giving highest priority to achieving a Middle East settlement and implied that the United States contemplated some new moves after the Israeli elections due the following month. The evolution of American-Israeli relations in the course of the preceding years and contemporary evidence (such as the remarks made by the newly confirmed secretary of state, Henry Kissinger, to a group of Arab leaders advising them not to expect any dramatic movement), suggest that the President probably had in mind nothing more than a variant of the proposal for a mediated Arab-Israeli dialogue. Be that as it may, events made this issue irrelevant. Before the Israelis went to the polls and before the President could do anything, Egypt and Syria went to war and forced an upheaval in the entire Middle East diplomatic and military configuration.

24

The Cataclysm
of October 1973

If in the case of the Six Day War one had to range far and wide to discover and analyze its remote and immediate causes, in describing the origins of the Yom Kippur War one need only make a simple summary statement and recapitulate some points already made in support of it.

Basically, Egypt enlisted Syrian participation and went to war in October 1973 to break an unbearable stalemate and reactivate diplomacy. After having made many sincere but fumbling attempts to prevent the onset of that stalemate and failed, President Sadat finally decided to try to alter the diplomatic-strategic configuration that supported it by going to war. Of course, Sadat might have tried to end the oppressive no-war—no-peace situation by conceding more to Israel's demands than he did rather than gambling on war against a militarily superior enemy—which is what everyone expected or hoped he would do. However, the general expectation overlooked several considerations that were foremost in the minds of Sadat and Syria's President Assad and that made the war option appear preferable to the option of concessions. In the first place, because Israel refused to define what it expected them to yield and because of their deeply ingrained suspicion borne by long hostility, the Arab leaders had a highly exaggerated notion of the concessions they would have to make to achieve a settlement. On the other hand, they had hopes that the adverse balance of military power they faced might be sufficiently altered to their advantage to make war less hazardous if they could capitalize on Israel's "defense gap" (see above, Chapter 17) by launching a surprise attack and pursuing some particular strategies and tactics. Moreover, the Arab leaders thought they might be able to achieve their objective of breaking the stalemate and forcing diplomatic movement even if they failed to win the projected war, provided only they did not lose too quickly and drastically. The international concerns that would be stirred by the war itself, coupled with threats to the supply of oil which Saudi Arabia promised to brandish, might suffice to precipitate efforts by the United States and other powers to press for movement beyond the stalemate. Finally, the Arab leaders felt that if yield they must, considerations of national honor, internal politics, and psychology dictated that they should put up a fight before doing so. All these considerations still left a very large element of fatalism and gamble in the Arabs' decision to go to war, but the gamble paid off, proving once more the adage that war is, par excellence, the province of chance.

Like the Six Day War, the Yom Kippur War overturned the previous diplomatic-strategic configuration and transformed Israel's position. As in 1967, the revolution in Israel's external standing was accompanied by a great internal political upheaval. However, whereas the 1967 commotion was essentially due to the sudden opening up of options that did not exist before, that of 1973 was caused by the sudden collapse of options that seemed to have crystallized in the intervening years, along with many related perceptions and expectations. The war affected seriously Israel's standing in the Third World, the European, the Middle Eastern, and the superpower arenas, but in 1973 as in 1967, the most critical factor was the evolution of its relationship with the United States. That evolution gave expression in the most substantive and dramatic ways so far both to the American-Israeli alliance and to the latent differences of perspective between the two countries. The process began with the first shot of the Yom Kippur War, proceeded through the war's convoluted course, and continued in its intense aftermath.

The Diplomacy of War

The Arabs' decision to go to war took everybody by surprise because it seemed to be utterly irrational. The United States, Israel, and for that matter the Soviet Union and much of the rest of the world were convinced that the war would end quickly with a decisive Israeli victory. The Arabs might score some initial successes under the effect of surprise, but once Israel completed the mobilization of its reserves and committed them to the battle, the tide of the war, so ran the general belief, would be promptly turned and Israel would duplicate its 1967 feat. That initial expectation, its subsequent evident failure, and then its sudden, belated coming close to fulfillment dominated the diplomacy of the war, which, in turn, set the stage for the postwar diplomacy.

When Golda Meir went on the air to announce the war to her people, she characterized the Egyptian-Syrian attack as "suicidal." That evaluation of the odds was shared not only by nearly all Israelis, but also by the United States and the Soviet Union and served as a premise for their first reactions. Then as later, the reactions of the superpowers unfolded on several levels: what they respectively believed, what they conveyed to each other, and what they conveyed to the parties to the conflict. It will be some time before the resulting intricate pattern can be fully described, but enough information has already come to light to permit a drawing of its main outlines.

On the surface, the outbreak of the war seemed at first to cause remarkably little diplomatic reaction. In contrast to the 1967 crisis, for example, nobody rushed to issue any momentous declarations, violent condemnations, or solemn warnings, and nobody even bothered to summon the UN Security Council, let alone submit a cease-fire resolution. Instead, the United States and the Soviet Union engaged in rather leisurely consultations during the first two days of the war which came to a rest in a loose agreement. On October 7 President Nixon had sent a letter to Secretary General Brezhnev reminding him of the commitment assumed by the two powers in the Moscow and Washington summits to avoid situations that could lead to conflict between them, and urging that they work together to contain the conflict and bring it to a rapid end; and Brezhnev had responded late that same day indicating his agreement to consider a cease-fire through the United Nations and expressing the hope that the fighting could be contained. It looked as though détente was working out in the Middle East and that the previous effort of the superpowers to "quarantine" the Arab-Israeli conflict and insulate themselves from its dangers was succeeding.

In reality, the initial easy agreement between the United States and the Soviet Union and their relaxed behavior were deceptive. Yes, they were both interested in avoiding a clash between themselves and in putting an early end to the fighting, but each of them wanted the war to be stopped at the most favorable moment to itself, which also meant at a moment favorable to the party or parties it supported. This difference, coupled with the failure of calculations on both their parts, was to strain their initial relative concord, embroil them in mutually opposed action, and eventually bring them face to face in perilous confrontation.

From the moment the war broke out, Kissinger, who presided entirely over American policy as secretary of state and head of the National Security Council at a time when the President was completely absorbed in the Watergate affair, wanted the fighting stopped after Israel reversed the initial Arab gains but before it inflicted a total defeat on its enemies. His opinion of Israel's military capability was so high that, in the first few days of the war, his concern centered much more on the latter aspect of the problem than the former. A total Israeli victory raised, in his view, the spectre of chaos, leftist coups, and Soviet intervention in the Arab countries on the one hand, and additional Israeli conquests and the foreclosure of any chance of settlement on the other; whereas if Israel could be held to a limited military success— enough to persuade the Arabs of the futility of the military option, but not enough to suggest to Israel that it might dictate terms—then the chances of a settlement would be substantially improved over what they had been before the war. The problem was how to achieve this finely tuned result. At the outset of the war, Kissinger estimated that Israel would need two days to mobilize and commit its reserves, and two or three more days to defeat the Arabs completely. He therefore wanted the cease-fire to take effect sometime in the fourth day, October 10, and was satisfied when he obtained the Soviets' agreement in principle late in the night of the 7th, just before the expected Israeli counteroffensive was to come into full swing.

The Soviets, for their part, shared entirely Kissinger's estimate of the capacity of Israel's armed forces, down to the time they would need to mobilize and to defeat the Arabs totally; however, precisely for this reason, they wanted the fighting stopped sometime in the second day or early in the third at the latest, while the Arabs held their initial gains and before the Israelis were able to launch their counteroffensive. Shortly before the start of the war, they had agreed with Syrian President Assad that they would begin moves aimed at a cease-fire the day the hostilities began with a view to actually achieving it the next day or shortly thereafter. When it was time for them to move, however, they ran into unexpected trouble.

In the evening of October 6, a few hours after the fighting started, the Soviet ambassador in Cairo met President Sadat in an emergency audience and sought his assent to a cease-fire in place, after informing him that the Syrians had already given theirs. Sadat rejected the suggestion indignantly. He had not been apprised by his Syrian ally of such an agreement with the Soviets and suspected that the latter were deceiving him, especially since the move did not fit with the agreed Syrian-Egyptian strategy. The central feature of that strategy was not the capture of maximum territory, but to cause maximum bloodletting to the enemy by seizing and holding a line and forcing him to bash his head against it. This had not yet come to pass. The Egyptian forces had effected a successful massive crossing of the Suez Canal and had stemmed the first Israeli countermoves, but they had not yet established a solid, continuous line; nor had the enemy attempted as yet the expected major counteroffensive. Moreover, for all Sadat knew, the Syrians themselves were doing well up to that point and things were working according to plan in the Golan Heights, too.

The next day, October 7, the Soviet ambassador came back to the charge after having evidently checked with Moscow and received confirmation that the Syrians approved an initiative for a cease-fire. In the meantime, Sadat had sent an urgent inquiry to Assad about his alleged assent, but had received no reply when the Soviet ambassador came to see him again, despite the lapse of a considerable time. The delay in Assad's answer caused Sadat to suspect that there might be some truth in what the Soviet ambassador was saying; nevertheless, he again refused to go along with a cease-fire initiative. It was against this background that Brezhnev wrote his reply to Nixon's letter, in which he expressed his "agreement to consider" a cease-fire move through the United Nations. In its late timing and reserved language, the reply reflected the difficulties the Soviets were having with their friends; in its affirmative content, it reflected their real wish, based on their evaluation of the situation.

The Security Council met on October 8, but its deliberations only reflected the divergent intentions and positions of the parties and the superpowers. The United States proposed a cease-fire and a return to the prewar lines; the Soviet Union opposed any return to the prewar situation and called for Israeli withdrawal to the pre-1967 lines. After an hour and a half of rhetoric, the council adjourned with no decision, and everyone looked to the battlefield for developments to break the deadlock.

On October 8 and 9, the Israelis launched their expected counteroffensives on both the Egyptian and the Syrian fronts. In the south, we have seen, the counterattack turned into a disaster; in the north, it succeeded in stemming and beginning to roll back the tide of Syrian armor while inflicting catastrophic losses. This ambivalent outcome, achieved at enormous cost and coming on top of previous setbacks, jolted the Israelis but did not overly disturb Secretary Kissinger. He continued to believe that the Israelis would be able eventually to rout the Arabs, but he now revised his estimate of the time they would need to do so by extending it two more days and adjusted his tactics accordingly. The critical time to achieve a cease-fire that would consecrate a limited Israeli victory now became October 12–13, which meant that action aimed at achieving a cease-fire by that date had to be undertaken in about three days. Until then, he had to parry the Soviets, invoking Israeli resistance in order not to provoke them.

The Soviets read the outcome of the battles of October 8 and 9 in the same way as Kissinger, but they, of course, drew different conclusions from their reading. The success of the Egyptians in repelling the Israeli counteroffensive averted the immediate disaster they expected and feared, but they remained convinced that the critical moment was postponed by only two or three days. The Syrians had lost over 600 tanks, their air defense system was collapsing, and total defeat appeared imminent. Once the Israelis knocked out the Syrian forces, they would concentrate all their power against Egypt and knock it out. If a cease-fire were to be of any use to the Arabs, the Soviets believed, it had to be initiated immediately. Even so, measures had to be taken to shore up the situation until the cease-fire could take effect and to make certain that it did take effect before it got to be too late.

Already on October 8, after they failed to persuade Sadat to agree to a cease-fire in place and when it looked as though the fighting was going to go on longer than they had expected, the Soviets had decided to provide their friends with arms and ammunition to replace their losses in order to stiffen their morale and their capacity to hang on. Immediately thereafter, Soviet ships loaded with arms were reported to have gone through the Turkish straits. On October 9 they urged Arab countries that had not taken part in the war to rush to join the fighting, specifically called on Iraq to transfer to Syria 500 tanks, promising to replace them later, and undertook to seek assurances from the Shah of Iran not to press Iraq from the east in order to permit it to send substantial forces to the west, to Syria. By the night of the 9th, these measures did not appear to the Soviets to be sufficient to avert the disaster they feared and they decided to take additional measures.

Late on the 9th, the Soviet ambassador had another emergency meeting with Sadat in which he explained the strategic situation as the Soviets saw it, and urged him, once more, to assent to proceedings aimed at a cease-fire in place and to launch an offensive on the Egyptian front to ease the pressure on the Syrians until the cease-fire could take effect. Sadat refused to alter his strategy, preferring to consolidate his line east of the Suez Canal and wait for the next Isreli counterattack rather than preempt, but he agreed to have the Soviets work for a cease-fire in place coupled, however, with a commitment by Israel to withdraw from all the occupied territories. In the meantime, he called on the Soviets to take emergency measures to assist Syria and Egypt to hold out until the United States was forced to agree to such cease-fire and Israel to abide by it. The Soviets acted accordingly. On the next day, the 10th, they notified the American representative in the Security Council that they were prepared to co-sponsor a resolution for a cease-fire in place; at the same time, giant transports began a massive airlift of military supplies from Soviet-controlled areas to Syria and Egypt. That same evening, it was learned that they put three of their seven airborne divisions on alert.

The battles of October 8–9 confronted Kissinger, too, with a problem of arms supply. Already on the 7th, Israel had asked the United States to provide it with quantities of ammunition that was running out fast, and Kissinger had given his assent for Israeli cargo planes to pick them up, provided they painted over their markings to avoid recognition. Early on October 9, after the failure of the Israeli counteroffensive on the Egyptian front, Israel put in an urgent request for all kinds of arms and ammunition, including notably jet planes and tanks, of which Israel had lost more than one-quarter of its inventory. To underscore the urgency of the request, Meir proposed to leave Israel in the midst of the war and come secretly to Washington to explain the situation.

Kissinger continued to believe that Israel could win unaided and was afraid that providing it with massive amounts of arms would encourage it to prolong the fighting until total victory, besides provoking the Soviet Union and the oil-producing Arab states. He therefore politely turned down the suggestion of a visit by the Prime Minister and tried to play for time, not by questioning Israel's arms needs, but, on the contrary, by expressing his full sympathy while resorting to various dilatory maneuvers.

On the same day the Israeli ambassador, Simcha Dinitz, brought the arms request and the visit proposal, Kissinger sought and obtained a presidential decision "in principle" to replace all of Israel's war losses. He informed Dinitz and referred him to the secretary of defense and his staff to work out the specific supply list and the modalities of delivery. For the next three days the distraught ambassador encountered all sorts of problems about quantities of available supplies, the chartering of commercial transport planes to carry them, the destination to which American planes would take the supplies, and so on. Each time he came back to complain to Kissinger, and each time the secretary of state resolved one difficulty, another suddenly emerged. Whether the problems were real or contrived, Kissinger made no special effort to cut through them decisively as he could and did when he felt that the situation as *he* saw it called for immediate action.

That kind of situation built up over the next three or four days. On the one hand, the Soviets seemed to indicate by their incitement of hitherto non-belligerent Arab countries to join the war, by their massive airlift, and by the alert of their airborne divisions, that they were intent on going a long way to ensure an Arab victory, unless they were checked. On the other hand, the Israeli counteroffensive in the north, which had begun promisingly and had continued beyond the prewar line on the 11th, began to lose momentum and bog down in the following days, without producing the expected Syrian collapse that would have permitted Israel to shift all its weight to the southern front. That the Soviet resupply operation and the intervention of substantial Iraqi forces at Soviet instigation may have contributed to that outcome only made matters worse and suggested the possibility of further deterioration of the situation. Instead of the limited victory that Kissinger thought Israel should have achieved by that time, Israel seemed to be in danger of being overcome through exhaustion and attrition.

The reality of that danger and its horrendous implications were driven home to the secretary of state by three Israeli initiatives, all taken on October 12. First, Israel asked him to promote through a third party—the British or the Australians—a resolution for a cease-fire in place linked to Resolution 242. The fact that Israel was now advancing a proposal similar to the one it had turned down two days before, when the Soviets had broached it, was an ominous indication of the deterioration of its situation.

While Israel's foreign minister and its Washington ambassador were discussing the terms of a possible cease-fire with Kissinger, Prime Minister Meir reached out to President Nixon personally with a direct message of truly critical import. The exact contents of the note are not yet known, but its substance can be fairly assessed from circumstantial evidence. The Prime Minister pointed out that Israel had suffered very heavy casualties and its resources were running very low. Israel found itself in this situation because it had refrained from preempting at the outset out of consideration for the United States, and because the Soviets had subsequently intervened to replace the Arabs' losses in crucial items. The United States had expressed ample appreciation of Israel's condition but had done little to help. Things had now reached a point when Israel's very existence was endangered. If the United States did not begin immediately to resupply it on a massive scale, it might soon be forced to use every means at its disposal to ensure its national survival.

The gist of the Prime Minister's message to the President was also implied in a formal note that Ambassador Dinitz delivered to the secretary of state late in the night of October 12. Dinitz reiterated his country's case and needs, complained bitterly about the runaround given to its arms request, and concluded with the ominous warning: "If a massive airlift to Israel does not start immediately, then I will know that the United States is reneging on its promises and policies, and we will have to draw very serious conclusions from all this." Some analysts have interpreted the warning to mean a threat that Israel would "go public" and arouse its friends against the administration. While this sense was probably included in the "very serious conclusions," it was far from being the most crucial component of them.

Kissinger, along with a few people at the top government echelons, had long known that Israel possessed a very short nuclear option which it held as a weapon of last resort, but he had not dwelt much on the issue because of the remoteness of the contingency that would make it relevant. Suddenly, on October 12, 1973, the scenario of an Israel feeling on the verge of destruction resorting in despair to nuclear weapons, hitherto so hypothetical, assumed a grim actuality. The secretary of state, whose policy had been inspired by the desire to preserve détente and by fear of the chaotic consequences of a total Israeli victory, did not need much pondering to imagine the catastrophic consequences of Israel's taking that road.

The Israeli messages also alerted the secretary of state that while trying to prevent an Israeli total victory, he may have brought Israel to the verge of defeat, and that while seeking to protect détente he may have allowed the Soviets to exploit it to their advantage. Quite apart from the nightmare of the nuclear issue, the principal aims he had set for himself at the outset of the war appeared to be near defeat. Consequently, after the Israeli ambassador delivered his "ultimatum," Kissinger once again promised to do his best, and this time he did. Very late that same night, he met the President and reviewed the situation with him. The next morning, the President summoned his principal advisers to an emergency conference at the White House and ordered them to start immediately to provide Israel with all the arms it needed, to draw if necessary on American forces' stocks, and to deliver the arms to Israel proper in American air force planes. All the previous seemingly insuperable problems vanished like a morning mist, and by the dawn of the next day the first flights of a massive airlift were on their way to Israel.

On October 14, the day the airlift started, the Egyptian front, which had been relatively quiescent since the 10th, came suddenly alive. In response to repeated pleas by the hard-pressed Syrians that were strongly endorsed by the Soviets, the Egyptians launched a second offensive designed to relieve the pressure on their allies and reach the Sinai passes, some twenty miles from their lines. Whether the Egyptians did so also in anticipation of the American decision to resupply Israel is not known. In any case, the offensive was easily repelled by the Israelis at a very heavy cost to the Egyptian armor. More importantly, since the Egyptians had committed their strategic reserves to the abortive operation, the *west* bank of the canal was left denuded of sufficient mobile forces, and the Israelis could now attempt to cross over and start a flanking operation in the rear of the enemy. The operation took the Egyptians by surprise, the effect of which was compounded by a grave failure of communications. By the time the Egyptians finally realized what was happening, the entire military picture had changed beyond recognition.

At midday on October 16 President Sadat, for the first time since the beginning of the war, delivered an address to the People's Assembly in which he gave an optimistic report on the course of the war and indicated that Egypt was prepared to accept a cease-fire provided Israel withdrew forthwith from all the occupied territories under international supervision. Once these withdrawals had been carried out, he added, Egypt was prepared to attend a peace conference convened by the United Nations, and he would do his best to persuade other Arab leaders involved and the representatives of the Palestinian people to take part in it. He further added that Egypt was willing to start work on clearing the Suez Canal immediately in order to reopen it for international shipping. When Sadat made his speech, in which the only "soft" point was the agreement to a peace conference *after* a complete Israeli withdrawal, he already knew about the failure of the Egyptian offensive of the 14th, but he had no idea of the Israeli crossing to the west bank which was already nearly forty hours old and was quite menacing by that time. Indeed, the Egyptian President first learned about an Israeli military presence on the west bank of the canal from the mouth of the Israeli Prime Minister, during an address she gave to the Knesset a few hours after he gave his own speech. Even then, he put the news down to psychological warfare and political maneuvering, preferring to believe the answer his military staff gave to Meir's revelation to the effect that it was a question of three Israeli tanks that had infiltrated to the west bank under the cover of night, and were being hotly pursued.

Even while Meir was speaking, Soviet Premier Kosygin secretly arrived in Cairo with the mission to coordinate political moves with Egypt in light of the military situation. The Russian leader, it turned out, was far better informed than the Egyptian, and had infinitely better communications. Kosygin began by telling Sadat that the Arabs had reached the peak of their military achievement as shown by the failure of the second Egyptian offensive and Syria's state, and that it was therefore time for them to work seriously for a realistic cease-fire before the situation turned further against them. The terms enunciated by Sadat in his speech were not apt to achieve that objective, and Egypt had better drop its demand for an Israeli withdrawal and content itself with a cease-fire in place and a reiteration of Resolution 242. Sadat resisted, pointing out that his strategy of causing the Israelis to break their head against the Egyptian line was working in the battles going on at the time. Kosygin came back to the charge the next day with the argument, based on information he had apparently acquired in the meantime, that the Egyptian strategy was already being foiled by the Israeli crossing; but Sadat, still in the dark as to what was happening at the front, minimized the importance of the Israeli operation. Finally, late on the 18th, Kosygin was able to produce satellite photos flown in from Moscow that showed the real extent of the Israeli penetration and threat, whereupon Sadat empowered Kosygin to begin working for an immediate effective cease-fire on the terms the Russians had suggested, subject to confirmation after reviewing the military situation with his General Staff. Kosygin flew back on the 18th, and on the 19th Brezhnev sent an urgent message inviting Kissinger to come to Moscow for "consultations on the Middle East," and asking him to receive Foreign Minister Gromyko in Washington if he could not come.

Late on the 19th, Sadat was called to a meeting of his General Staff to resolve a difference of view that had developed among his chief commanders regarding the military situation, following an exhaustive tour of the front by the chief of staff. It turned out that the difference was not over whether it was time for a cease-fire, but whether and how the Egyptian armed forces could be saved before a cease-fire came into effect. The chief of staff believed that everything was lost and that the only hope of salvaging part of the Egyptian forces was to evacuate the east bank immediately, before the Israelis cut off all ways of retreat, whereas the minister of war and others were in favor of taking a chance on holding out in place until a cease-fire took effect. Sadat agreed with the latter view and then and there replaced his chief of staff who was in a state of visible collapse. There was hardly a question of terms any longer, as Sadat's chief concern now centered entirely on looking for means to save his armed forces by obtaining a cease-fire resolution as quickly as possible, and seeing that it was enforced before it got to be too late.

The breakdown of Egyptian communications regarding the Israeli crossing affected in some measure the American perception of the situation, too. The secretary of state, of course, had access to his own sources of intelligence, including satellite reconnaissance, to inform him about the general picture of the fighting. But he also looked to the behavior of the belligerents and the Soviets for additional signals to help him interpret the situation, and these signals did not quite jibe with the intelligence evidence. Sadat's speech of the 16th gave no inkling of nervousness. On the contrary, his public insistence on an explicit Israeli commitment to withdraw from all the occupied territories represented a toughening of the position conveyed through the Soviets on the 10th. As for the Israelis having been chastised by the failure of their initial sanguine expectations, they too were playing the reports of their crossing operations on a very low key, which suggested that they might indeed be of limited significance. Since the secretary of state and his intelligence analysts had already proved wrong at least twice in forecasting prompt Israeli victory, it was not surprising that this time they lent greater weight to the political signals they received than to evidence of the military intelligence. The result was that Kissinger almost missed his aim of stopping the Israelis short of total victory, and that the American position was variously misunderstood by all sides at various times.

On October 16, one day after the Israeli crossing, Kissinger had had a talk with the Saudi foreign minister in which he intimated that two or three weeks of additional fighting were likely before the two sides were sufficiently exhausted to accept a cease-fire that would be conducive to settlement. The next day, he and President Nixon had met a delegation of Arab foreign ministers for discussion of the situation, during which the secretary conveyed to his interlocutors the impression of being in no hurry to do anything about the Middle East, and that he was thinking of tackling the problem only after his return from a trip to China, scheduled to *start* in ten days. On the 19th, before receiving Brezhnev's invitation, he had sent through to Congress a request for $2.3 billion to cover the cost of military assistance to Israel, of which only one-fourth accounted for arms already shipped up to that point.

Brezhnev's urgent invitation to Moscow was therefore the first intimation Kissinger had that developments in the battlefield may have begun to affect the Arab-Soviet position. Even then, however, he did not realize the extent to which matters had come to a head. Shortly before receiving Brezhnev's invitation, he had expressed to Israel's foreign minister the opinion that a cease-fire had to entail Israeli political concessions. Shortly after receiving the invitation, he told the Israeli ambassador that he did not believe any agreement would be achieved in Moscow, and that he was going there mainly to keep the Russians from hardening their position or escalating their intervention.

On the plane taking him to Moscow, Kissinger received the news that Saudi Arabia had joined the other Arab oil producers in declaring a total embargo on oil shipments to the United States in retaliation for the aid bill submitted that day. In the days and weeks that followed, the embargo was to play a crucial role in Kissinger's calculations. Whether it already affected significantly his position and behavior in Moscow is not known.

Kissinger met Brezhnev in the evening of the 20th and found him in a grim mood. The Soviet leader spoke of the necessity to salvage détente but gave a grim assessment of the situation and stressed the danger of superpower confrontation it entailed. He concluded by saying that it was high time to call for a cease-fire in place linked to Resolution 242 immediately, and to see that it was promptly and effectively heeded. Kissinger agreed that the situation was extremely dangerous, but basing himself on recent discussions with

Israel, he insisted that the cease-fire had to be linked to peace negotiations, not only to a mere repetition of 242, or else it would break down all over again. Brezhnev rejected the proposed linkage, but the two agreed to meet the next afternoon.

In the interim, Brezhnev submitted Kissinger's proposal to Sadat and urged him to accept. Sadat, who in the meantime had had his dramatic meeting with his generals, agreed, after extracting assurances from the Soviets that they would do everything to ensure that the cease-fire was respected. Therefore, when Brezhnev met Kissinger again in the afternoon of the 21st, the Soviet leader surprised the secretary of state by agreeing promptly to his formula and dwelling mostly on the need to achieve prompt compliance. The two then formulated a draft of what came to be known as Security Council Resolution 338, which was unanimously adopted on October 22. On his way back to the United States, Kissinger stopped in Israel at the request of its government to provide "clarifications and explanations."

Kissinger's agreeing to an immediate cease-fire came as a shock to Israel's government. Not only was the action contrary to what he had led it to expect on the eve of his departure to Moscow, but it was taken by the secretary without prior consultation with it—unlike what Brezhnev did with Sadat. The Israeli government might have suspected at this point that Kissinger was seeking different objectives from its own; however, the "explanations and clarifications" he provided, coupled with his impeccable cooperation since the start of the airlift, suppressed any doubts and continued to obscure from its eyes the changes that had begun to occur in the American conceptions and policy.

Altogether, Israeli diplomacy throughout the war was rather sparse, simple, and essentially reactive rather than deliberately conceived. On October 5, one day before the outbreak of hostilities, the Israeli government sent a cable to the secretary of state informing him of the massive Egyptian and Syrian deployments and asking him to convey a message to the two Arab governments: if the deployments were for defensive reasons, Israel wished to assure them that it had no aggressive intentions. If they were related to offensive intentions, Israel wanted to warn them that it would respond forcefully and massively to any kind of attack. The cable to Kissinger added that this initiative was only precautionary, since the Israeli Intelligence believed that the probability of war was low.

Because of technical reasons—Kissinger was in New York and the responsible officials in the State Department did not think the cable was urgent—the secretary of state did not receive the Israeli communication until midday the next day, when it had become certain that the Arabs were definitely going to attack. During the hassle that developed later on over the question of American arms to Israel, Meir was to argue publicly that, but for the negilgence of the United States, war might have been averted altogether. The argument was dubious because it ignored the fact that the Israeli communication indicated that war was unlikely, and because in any case it was probably too late for Egypt and Syria to call off the campaign at that point, especially since they saw no evidence of Israeli preparedness in the field to back up any Israeli warning. On the other hand, the effort to prevent war, however badly conceived, does clear the Israeli political leaders of the suspicion subsequently voiced by some people that they welcomed war.

The next major policy act immediately before the war was the decision made by Meir on the morning of October 6 on the advice of her defense minister *not* to authorize a preemptive Israeli air strike, as her chief of staff recommended. In retrospect, that decision was criticized as politically futile and militarily disastrous. Meir, however, vigorously defended it even with the benefit of hindsight on the grounds that it made it unmistakably clear to the Israelis who were asked to risk their lives that they were repelling aggression, because it avoided embarrassment for the United States, and because it entitled Israel to demand American aid and understanding, which might not have been forthcoming had it chosen to preempt.

From the time the fighting started until the October 22 cease-fire, Israeli diplomacy went through three stages. During the first two to three days of the war, Israel's principal concern was to secure the time necessary to mobilize its reserves and let them have a go at the enemy, but that proved to be no problem, since no one was rushing to halt the fighting as far as Israel knew. On the contrary, from the very close contact its Washington ambassador and its foreign minister kept with Secretary Kissinger, it knew that the United States was also interested in gaining time for it and that the Soviets were not pressing for any prompt cease-fire. The problem that did develop in those days was totally different and entirely unexpected.

At the start of hostilities, Israel had defined its war aims to be simply "to overwhelm" the aggressors, as Meir said in an address to the nation. After three days of fighting, it appeared that it was Israel that was in danger of being overwhelmed, and the critical task of Israeli diplomacy at that stage became one of securing American military assistance to avert that danger and to avoid alternative, desperate measures to respond to it. From the very first moments of the war, the reports from the front to Israel's improvised "War Cabinet" had been far worse than expected. However, the nerve-wracking stream of bad news reached a critical point on October 8. In the morning of that day, the commander of the northern front reported that he did not know how much longer his forces could hold out. After a bitter, costly, and uncertain battle that went on throughout the day, the situation was barely saved in the north; but then reports came from the south that the Israeli couteroffensive launched earlier that day had ended in disaster. Sometime during that period, Defense Minister Dayan told Prime Minister Meir that "the Third Temple is going under" (meaning the state of Israel). Meir herself confessed shortly after the war that there was a moment in the course of it when she, too, had feared that Israel might be overwhelmed and destroyed. It is most probable that the time in question was late on October 8th, and it is perfectly plausible to assume (as *Time* magazine reported years later) that preparations to turn the nuclear option of Israel into usable nuclear weapons were initiated at that time.

It was in that grim mood that Prime Minister Meir proposed to go to Washington in secret to explain Israel's position, its immediate need for arms, and presumably, hint at the desperate alternative it contemplated if it did not get help. Kissinger's objections to the trip, coupled with his assurances that the arms would be forthcoming, kept the Prime Minister at home, but all of Israel's diplomatic effort continued in the next four days to center passionately and exclusively on actually getting the promised American arms into the hands of the Israeli fighters.

In the first three days of that period—the 9th through the 11th—Israel's situation improved dramatically on the Syrian front and became less critical on the Egyptian. This and the expectation that American arms would be arriving any moment led Israel to brush aside the idea of a cease-fire in place linked to 242 which the Soviets broached on the 10th. Israel's objection could kill the idea that easily because the Soviets were not pressing hard for it, and because Secretary Kissinger, seeking a limited Israeli victory, was not yet interested in it.

The exhaustion of the momentum of the Israeli advance in the north, the influx of Soviet arms to the Arab side and the entry of Iraqi and Jordanian forces into the battle, the failure of American arms to arrive, the terrible attrition suffered by the Israeli forces, and the ominous concentration of the largely intact Egyptian forces on the east side of the Suez Canal combined to form a grim new picture before Israel's eyes. Instead of the sudden collapse feared a few days before, the prospect now seemed to be one in which Israel's forces were gradually exhausted by an enemy who was continually replenishing his own, until the moment came when it would have no forces left and could be dealt a coup de grâce. To meet that situation, Israel took on October 12 the three initiatives mentioned above. On the one hand, it indicated its willingness to accept a cease-fire in place linked to 242 as suggested by the Soviets before, provided the resolution was introduced by a party other than the United States. The idea was not to betray indirectly Israel's sense of weakness and to keep the hands of the United States entirely free to help with arms. On the other hand, Meir wrote a letter to President Nixon, and Ambassador Dinitz delivered a note to Secretary Kissinger in which Israel hinted that unless American arms started to flow immediately, it might find itself compelled to resort to nuclear weapons. The first initiative failed to get off the ground, as Sadat replied negatively to a preliminary inquiry by British Prime Minister Edward Heath. The other two, we have seen, helped produce immediate results. Not only did the United States launch the airlift, but Secretary Kissinger and President Nixon went out of their way to show solicitude toward Israel and followed the despatch of arms with a request to Congress for massive financial assistance.

From October 14 when the airlift started until October 21 when Kissinger concluded the Moscow agreement, Israeli diplomacy reverted to the quiescence of the first stage, or nearly so. As the tide of the war turned, Israel gradually altered its views of the acceptable terms as well as the desirable timing of a cease-fire. It did not, however, exert itself to try to secure the conditions it wanted and contented itself with making its wishes known to the United States. On October 16 Meir said, in the speech in which she announced that Israeli forces were fighting on the west side of the Suez Canal, that Israel had received no cease-fire proposal and offered none, thus wiping clean the slate of previous probes. On the 17th, Foreign Minister Eban who was in Washington, reacted to a new Soviet probe for a cease-fire coupled to 242 by suggesting to Kissinger that any mention of 242 should be coupled with a reference to negotiations for peace. In the following day or two, the Israeli government instructed Eban that it wanted no reference to 242 at all, and that it desired a simple resolution for a cease-fire coupled only with an immediate exchange of prisoners. On the 19th, on the eve of Kissinger's departure to Moscow, Eban and Dinitz merely asked the secretary of state to play for time for Israel to develop its operations and were assured by him that he would do so.

Partly because of Kissinger's assurances, partly because the Arabs had given no sign of relenting from their proclaimed conditions for a cease-fire, Israel's leaders did not feel the need to rush their military commanders to accomplish all they could before a resolution was issued to end the fighting. On October 20, when Kissinger was already in Moscow, Defense Minister Dayan told a conference of Israeli press editors that he saw no prospect for a cease-fire on the horizon. On the 21st, the day Kissinger concluded the agreement with Brezhnev, Deputy Prime Minister Allon assured the commanders of the Israeli forces on the west side of the Suez Canal that they had ample time to develop their operations and that there was no need to hurry. Later that day, Foreign Minister Eban was telling the Security and Foreign Affairs Committee of the Knesset that the Kremlin talks did not involve more than an exchange of opinions when he was interrupted by a messenger calling him to the Prime Minister to discuss a crucial message from Washington. The message turned out to be a letter from President Nixon to Meir informing her of the Moscow agreement and urging Israel to announce its acceptance immediately.

Meir assembled the Cabinet at midnight to discuss the President's message. Most members expressed disappointment at the timing of the Moscow agreement and shock that it was concluded without prior consultation, but they all agreed that, after the American airlift, Israel was in no position to turn down an explicit request by President Nixon. Everyone was aware that American military help would be needed well beyond the cessation of hostilities and that badly needed financial assistance was being processed in Congress right then. Moreover, the Israeli leaders were wary and still shaken by the early failures and by the level of casualties suffered, were highly attracted by the provision about negotiations for peace, and saw it as representing a hope for an end to wars. The Cabinet discussed the possibility of insisting that an immediate exchange of prisoners be made part of the cease-fire, but in the end it decided not to do so on the grounds that Nixon and Kissinger would view it as a rejection of the Moscow agreement. So, in the early hours of October 22, the Cabinet empowered Prime Minister Meir to send a message to President Nixon agreeing unconditionally and merely asking that Kissinger should stop over on his way from Moscow to give "explanations and clarifications."

In Jerusalem, Meir and her colleagues received Kissinger more warmly than he expected but asked him four questions: Why did he agree so promptly to a cease-fire? Why did he not consult or notify Israel in advance? Why did he agree to a reference to 242 when he knew Israel objected to it? And why did he not insist on including a reference to an immediate exchange of prisoners as he knew Israel wanted? Kissinger answered that the Kremlin had started from a very rigid position and then suddenly swung around and agreed to his terms without prior haggling. At that point, he did not want to delay things for fear that the Soviets might pass over to intimidation and threats. As for alerting Israel, he explained lamely that he could not do so because the Soviets engaged in electronic jamming that disrupted the American communications system. Similarly, he explained that his agreement to 242 was done according to a presidential decision that he could not gainsay. As for the exchange of prisoners, insistence on an explicit linking of the issue to a cease-fire, he pointed out, would have torpedoed the agreement and pushed Moscow against the wall. Instead, he added, he obtained a personal commitment from Brezhnev that such an exchange would take place immediately after the cease-fire.

It is interesting to note that even at that point, the Israelis did not suspect that Kissinger might have been acting on the basis of policy calculations different from their own. The very way in which they formulated their questions suggested, on the contrary, that they continued to believe in a complete community of aims between them and him and were only puzzled about the tactical decisions he had made in serving them. Even more interesting, the secretary of state made not the slightest effort to correct their assumptions, and, indeed went out of his way to appear to confirm them.

After his discussion with the Prime Minister and her associates, Israel's military chiefs were brought in to brief Kissinger about the battlefield situation. Kissinger realized for the first time how close Israel was to destroying or encircling the entire Egyptian army, and probably understood better why Bezhnev had been so edgy and why he had conceded to his terms so readily. Kissinger asked how many days were needed to encircle the Egyptian Second and Third Armies and was told that that would take seven days, but their destruction, especially from the air, would take only two or three more days. At this point, the secretary of state, instead of struggling to contain his relief that the cease-fire was to take effect before this could happen, puzzlingly exclaimed: "Two or three days? That's all? Well, in Vietnam the cease-fire didn't go into effect at the exact time that was agreed on."

The Israelis, who had launched and concluded their entire Syrian campaign in 1967 after the appointed cease-fire time, hardly needed to be instructed about the time difference between agreement and application; consequently, the secretary's remark in their presence and in that context could only be taken by them as an invitation to disregard the cease-fire and go on to try to destroy the Egyptian forces. Why did Kissinger convey that idea when it was contrary to his entire policy? And if he had changed his mind, why did he subsequently apply the heaviest pressures on the Israelis to desist?

Conceivably, the Vietnam remark was a slip that betrayed a weakness of Kissinger to please his interlocutors of the moment rather than any deliberate intent. It is also possible that, after learning about the real situation in the battlefield, Kissinger felt that he did not get as good a deal from Brezhnev as the situation "entitled" him to and wanted to play the hand over. Perhaps he felt that he had allowed Moscow to gain the credit for saving the Arabs when it was he, Kissinger, who stopped the Israelis; and consequently, he egged the Israelis to go on in order to stop them again and be seen to be the one who did so, thus placing himself in the position of a credible mediator. Finally, it is possible that the entire maneuver was designed to repair what he sensed to be damage to his credibility with the Israelis as a result of his Moscow agreement by showing them that he was "with them" and then telling them that he felt *compelled* to ask them to desist. Be that as it may, the Israelis hardly needed the encouragement to go on and attempt to achieve the maximum they could before a real cease-fire could take effect.

Kissinger was barely back in Washington, early in the morning of the 23rd, when he was approached by Soviet Ambassador Anatoly Dobrynin with frantic complaints that Israel was violating the cease-fire on a massive scale, and with reminders that the Soviet Union had guaranteed to Egypt prompt and effective compliance with the cease-fire. The secretary of state acted as if he knew nothing of the matter. He asked the Israeli ambassador for explanations, and the latter said that it was the Egyptians who violated the cease-fire in an effort by the Third Army to capture certain menacing Israeli positions. Kissinger then checked with his own intelligence sources, and these confirmed the Israeli's story but added that the Israeli forces took advantage of the Egyptian violations to carry out offensive operations designed to encircle the Third Army. Kissinger reported the Israeli explanations to Dobrynin and proposed that the Soviet Union and the United States should draft a second cease-fire resolution that would include enforcement provisions. In the meantime, Israeli forces reached the outskirts of the city of Suez, nearly completing the encirclement of the Third Army.

The Israeli operations were just what Sadat had feared and had sought to guard against by seeking a Soviet "guarantee" of immediate Israeli compliance. Disappointed by the Soviets, he now asked for an American guarantee before agreeing to another cease-fire. That was just what Kissinger had been looking for. He had President Nixon assure Sadat in a secret message that the United States would not allow the destruction or starvation of the Third Army, and proceeded to do everything to deliver on that promise. He joined the Soviets in sponsoring Resolution 339 which called for an immediate cease-fire to be supervised by United Nations personnel in the area, and a return of the forces to the lines they held on October 22, at the time the first cease-fire was to come into effect. Resolution 339 was passed at 1:00 A.M. on October 24, but as the fighting continued, Kissinger applied intense pressure on Israel to comply immediately. He summoned the Israeli ambassador and told him that if the fighting continued as a result of Israeli actions, Israel should not count on military aid from the United States. He informed him that American Intelligence had learned that the Soviets had placed seven airborne divisions on alert and added that the United States was not prepared to go to a Third World War so that Israel should have the Third Army.

Before Kissinger's pressure could have its effect in the battlefield, Sadat sent an urgent message to Nixon and Brezhnev at 3 P.M. on the 24th, in which he accused Israel of continuing violations and asked them to send American and Soviet forces to the Middle East to enforce the cease-fire, in accordance with the assurances they had separately provided. Kissinger advised the President to reject the appeal immediately while assuring the Egyptian leader that the United States was endeavoring to achieve the same purpose by other means. He also warned the Soviets that the United States was opposed to the idea of sending big-power troops to a volatile area. For a moment, these steps seemed to be effective, but later that afternoon, several Third World nations picked up Sadat's appeal and prepared to submit a resolution to the Security Council for a big-power truce enforcement force. The Soviet representative first held back, but then seemed to turn around and support the proposal. Finally, at 9:25 P.M. on October 24, the Soviet ambassador delivered to Kissinger an urgent note from Brezhnev to Nixon which brought to a head the Soviet-American competition for position in connection with the Middle East war.

The note denounced Israel for "brazenly" challenging both the Soviet Union and the United States and for "drastically" violating the cease-fire.

Echoing Sadat's appeal, the Soviet leader then said: "Let us together . . . urgently dispatch Soviet and American contingents to Egypt . . . I will say it straight, that if you find it impossible to act together with us in this matter, we should be faced with the necessity urgently to consider the question of taking appropriate steps unilaterally. Israel cannot be allowed to get away with the violations."

Kissinger noticed, of course, the hedges in the critical passage— "consider the question" and "appropriate steps"—but the tone of the note as a whole, coupled with the known Soviet military preparations, left no doubt in his mind that the reservations meant that the Soviets intended to act unless they met with a most determined American reaction. He well knew that the United States could not possibly comply with the request to send troops to enforce a cease-fire in a combat zone—not so soon after Vietnam, not alongside Soviet troops, not against Israel. On the other hand, allowing the Soviets to send troops unilaterally meant letting them take all the credit for stopping the Israelis and saving the Arabs immediately and establishing a powerful military presence in the area which could have enormous consequences in the longer run. With the entire future of the Middle East and its vital resources at stake, he felt he had to act firmly and quickly.

After hurried consultations with the President and a rump National Security Council, Kissinger obtained approval for an American response in two parts. First, American forces all over the globe were placed on heightened degrees of alert. The alert included the Strategic Air Command, containing nuclear strike forces, as well as the 82nd Airborne Division at Fort Bragg, North Carolina. In addition, a task force including the aircraft carrier *John F. Kennedy* was despatched to the Mediterranean to join the two task forces operating with the Sixth Fleet. The second part of the response was a message to Brezhnev signed by the President in which the United States reaffirmed the terms of the Kissinger-Brezhnev understanding that the two powers would cooperate in the search for peace and disputed Brezhnev's claim that Israel was brazenly violating the cease-fire. The note asserted that the situation did not warrant sending American or Soviet forces to the Middle East and indicated that the United States could not accept unilateral Soviet action. The entire pattern of American-Soviet relations and the future of détente was at stake. Instead, the United States urged the Soviet Union to support the despatch of United Nations observer and peacekeeping forces drawn from countries without veto power or without nuclear forces. Simultaneously with the note to Brezhnev, Kissinger sent renewed urgent warnings to Israel to desist immediately, and this time Israel complied promptly.

The note to Brezhnev was sent in the early hours of October 25, Washington time, by which time the alert was in full swing and evidence of it had been picked up by Soviet Intelligence. Several hours later, the CIA reported to a White House conference that a Soviet ship carrying radioactive material had just docked in Port Said, Egypt, which suggested that the Soviets might be preparing a nuclear backup for their intervention troops. The tension persisted until the early afternoon, when the Soviet representative in the Security Council finally stopped pressing for the inclusion of the superpowers in the peacekeeping force and yielded instead to the American view. The Soviet retreat was made easier by the inclusion in the resolution of a provision authorizing the two superpowers to send in a small number of unarmed "observers" alongside the United Nations force, and by the fact that by that time the shooting had effectively ceased.

The net outcome of the hectic developments in the three days since the October 22 cease-fire resolution was an extraordinary success for Kissinger's diplomacy. Whether he had planned matters that way or not, Israel was able to improve its military position a great deal and was grateful to Kissinger, even though he had barred it from complete vicotry. The Egyptians saw him as the one who saved them from total defeat, even though he had helped place Israel in a position to put them under such threat. Finally, although these additional gains were scored at the expense of the Soviets, the structure of détente remained essentially intact.

Israel's Position in the Wake of the War

The war transformed almost entirely Israel's diplomatic-strategic position. From the perspective of Israel's prewar standing and conceptions, the change was completely for the worse. But from the perspective of the theoretical prospects of a resolution of the Arab-Israeli conflict in a manner that would meet Israel's need for peace and security, the change had its positive as well as negative sides and was not unfavorable on balance. The postwar problem for Israel was to recognize and assess accurately the new situation and adapt its policy and action accordingly—a difficult task under any circumstances, made even more difficult by the immediate postwar conditions in which it found itself.

Diplomatic Isolation in the World Arena

The most visible effect of the war on Israel's international position was its nearly total diplomatic isolation at least in the short term. The most dramatic though not necessarily the most important manifestation of this phenomenon was the rapid succession of declarations issued by countries of black Africa condemning Israel for its continuing occupation of Arab lands and breaking off diplomatic relations with it. This process had begun sometime before the war, but the war turned what looked like instances of stray sheep into a real stampede. Thus, whereas in the twenty months preceding the war only seven African countries followed the example first set by Uganda's Idi Amin, twenty countries severed relations within one month of the start of the war. By November 25, 1973, only three out of forty-two black African countries still retained diplomatic relations with Israel. Among the countries that dropped Israel, many were beneficiaries of past and ongoing Israeli technical assistance and mutual cooperation programs. Several were headed by leaders who had demonstrated a particular interest in Israel, such as Haile Selassie of Ethiopia, or had shown special appreciation and sympathy for it, such as Kenya's Jomo Kenyatta and Senegal's Leopold Sedar Senghor. More than half the countries that ruptured relations in 1973 had refused to support a United Nations draft resolution condemning Israel as an aggressor after the 1967 war.

Israelis have attributed this sudden massive desertion to pressure by Arab and Muslim countries in the Organization of African Unity, but this only begs the question, since Arab-Muslim pressure was constant. The success of that pressure in 1973 was probably due to a combination of reasons: a growing skepticism among African leaders about the sincerity of Israel's professed desire for peace, especially after the failure of an OAU mediation mission headed by President Senghor in November 1971; a recession of African fear of Arab political power in Africa since the death of Nasser and the diffusion of Arab power centers; and the newly gained capacity of mostly conservative Arab countries to reward and punish economically through their oil-derived affluence.

The action of the African states, coming on top of the long-standing ostracism of Israel by nearly all the Soviet bloc and the much larger Muslim bloc created a massive anti-Israel coalition in all international forums, which often drew in additional states eager to court its favors or avoid its wrath. The result was a guaranteed overwhelming majority for any anti-Israeli resolution regardless of substance or fairness, and sometimes regardless of the competence of the particular bodies concerned to deal with the issues voted upon. It is true that few of these resolutions had significant practical consequences and that their moral significance was increasingly impaired by their complete one-sidedness and by the very massiveness and certainty of the majorities by which they were adopted. Nevertheless, this development undoubtedly restricted Israel's room for maneuver and reversed the practical and psychological benefits it had gained through the imaginative endeavors of the 1950s and 1960s to reach out to the Third World.

While the African countries were breaking relations with Israel in droves, the Western European governments were falling over themselves in a scramble to please or appease the Arab side and take some distance from Israel. If in the case of the African countries considerations of principle and Third World solidarity at least gave some cover to self-interest and timidity in the face of pressure, in the case of the Europeans, the strong popular sympathy for Israel only underscored the cynicism and loss of backbone of the governments in their indecent rush to do anything to escape Arab oil sanctions.

European governments had long been highly sensitive to the danger that an Arab-Israeli explosion presented to their oil supply, half of which came from the Middle East by 1970. For this reason, several of them had tried after the 1967 war to explore ways in which they, individually or collectively as the European Community, might help advance a settlement of the conflict that would protect them against that danger. However, as these efforts bore no fruit and as the conflict seemed to subside into an indefinite stalemate, the European governments gradually fell back on an approach that tried to secure their interest by insulating themselves from the conflict. They gave symbolic or nominal support to the Arab side but abstracted themselves from any significant practical role, leaving the management of the conflict entirely to the superpowers. In this way they hoped to "quarantine" the conflict and protect themselves from its dangers.

The Europeans' expectation rested implicitly on the unrecognized assumption that the superpowers themselves would be able to stay out of a potential war, in accordance with the general spirit of détente and the particular understandings to that effect which they reached in the Moscow and Washington summits. When that assumption proved wrong, and particularly when the United States began supplying Israel with arms on a massive scale in response to Soviet help to the Arabs, the European governments suddenly found themselves confronting a very painful choice they had not quite anticipated: whether to permit the United States to draw on equipment stocks it kept in Europe and use some NATO facilities in its effort to help Israel, and thus become its accomplices and risk Arab oil sanctions; or to oppose it and thus put an immense added strain on already difficult NATO relationships. In varying degrees and at a different pace, they all chose the latter, except for authoritarian Portugal. Some, like Greece and Turkey (joined by Spain, an ally of the United States but not a member of NATO) drummed up their opposition in order to score maximum credit with the Arab side—Turkey actually went so far as to let Soviet planes overfly its territory on their way to the Arab countries while barring the United States from using its bases on Turkish soil to help Israel. Others, such as Holland, West Germany, and Italy, winked at some violations of their proclaimed rules restricting the United States as long as these remained undetected. Britain formally proclaimed a policy of neutrality and declared an embargo on arms to the Middle East, which in practice affected only Israel, whose armored forces relied heavily on the British-made Centurion tanks. France announced that there would be no change in its previous, avowedly pro-Arab, policy, and conspicuously refrained from protesting the transfer by Libya to Egypt of French-supplied Mirage fighter-bombers in volation of the terms of the original sale contract.

The strain that developed between the United States and its Eruopean allies over the issue of aid to Israel was greatly exacerbated by the United States' sudden declaration of a global alert to meet the threat of Soviet military intervention. The Europeans complained bitterly that the United States took an action that had an immense bearing on their fate as its allies without consulting them beforehand, while the United States complained that its own allies had let it down at a critical moment and had pursued shortsighted policies that sabotaged its own attempt to manage the war so as to create a favorable framework for a settlement. The nearly total breakdown of communication and understanding between the two sides gave rise for a while to a sense of "each for himself" among the Europeans, which manifested itself in a rush of each and all to subscribe to political formulations demanded by the Arabs and a scramble to conclude with Arab countries whatever bilateral or multilateral deals they could. Eventually, the panic subsided and gave way to a more sober appreciation of the situation, but this provided only a little comfort for Israel.

The war taught the Europeans that they could not evade the Middle East issue but had to tackle it directly in a considered manner. On November 6, 1973, the foreign ministers of the nine members of the European Economic Community began this process by formulating a common stand on the problem. That stand asserted the urgent need for a settlement on the basis of Resolutions 242 and 338, interpreted almost entirely according to the Arab views. The territorial question was slightly fudged, but, on the other hand, the "legitimate rights of the Palestinians" was added to the conditions spelled out by the Security Council resolutions.

The Europeans also learned that whatever position they took, they could not be entirely independent from the United States. This was so not only because their national defense was involved in a possible American-Soviet clash over the Middle East, but also because they could not effectively insulate themselves from future Arab oil sanctions by their own independent effort. Once the mechanism of the Arab oil weapon began to be understood, it became apparent that, regardless of what Europe did to please the Arabs, the imposition of sanctions on the United States at any future date would necessitate also the reduction of supplies available to Europe in order to prevent reallocations and diversions to meet America's needs. An American-Arab confrontation was therefore most likely to have a "fallout" effect on Europe's economy in the same way that an American-Soviet confrontation was bound to have a similar effect on its national defense. Consequently, it was clear that if the Europeans were to advance a Middle East settlement that would obviate the inevitable dangers and problems of war, it was necessary for them to work with and through the United States. From Israel's point of view, this conclusion checked the haphazard drift of European countries toward the Arab side, but it also created a solid bloc interested in a settlement on any terms which was ready to exert constant pressure in that direction on the United States.

Changes in Regional Power Relationships

The Arabs' use of the oil weapon with such effectiveness was itself a reflection of another major change brought about by the war, namely a new pattern of inter-Arab politics and solidarity. On the surface it may seem that Arab solidarity in 1973 was no different from that manifested in 1967 or on other occasions, but careful examination would show some basic differences fraught with far-reaching implications.

One of the differences was the much greater involvement of more remote Arab countries in the conflict. Whereas Jordan, one of the countries immediately surrounding Israel, played a greatly reduced role in the 1973 war, several countries of the "second circle," and even of the Maghreb, played a much more meaningful role in the 1973 conflict than in 1967. Iraq sent very substantial forces to the front, as it had in 1967, but this time they took an active part in the fighting. Kuwait, Saudi Arabia, and the Arab Emirates contributed vast amounts of money to the war chest, while Libya contributed money as well as Mirages acquired from France. Morocco had a significant force in the Syrian front from the outset, while Algeria sent a large armored formation to help Egypt contain the Israeli bridgehead in addition to buying vast amounts of arms for it from the Soviet Union.

A second and much more important difference was that Saudi Arabia took the lead in putting the Arab oil weapon into play. Of course, in 1967, too, oil-rich countries including Saudi Arabia formally applied sanctions which seemingly went even farther than in 1973 by placing a total embargo on oil shipments to Britain as well as the United States. However, in 1967 Saudi Arabia proclaimed the embargo involuntarily, under pressure by Nasser, and therefore did not enforce it strictly and canceled it as soon as possible; whereas in 1973 it introduced the weapon of its own accord, set up a staff to use it, and adopted a systematic, subtle strategy to maximize its effect in direct and indirect ways. This in turn created circumstances that allowed Iran to force up the price of oil dramatically, and thus unwittingly provided an additional dimension to Arab power.

The significance of the enhanced Arab solidarity and the use of the oil weapon becomes fully apparent if one looks at the reasons underlying them. The more active role assumed by countries of the second circle was probably a direct consequence of the vast growth of Israeli power in the years after 1967. As the military capabilities of Israel multiplied in those years, the "radiation" of that power began to be felt directly by countries that had previously felt completely immune. Their concern with Israel and their support for countries of the first circle ceased to rest solely on pan-Arab considerations and came to be a matter of national interest and an investment in their own security. In a sense, this development was merely a continuation of a process that went back to the very beginnings of the Zionist endeavor in Palestine. The Zionist movement and then Israel had to cope with ever larger segments of a reservoir of Arab forces. Each time they defeated one segment, the very power they mustered to do so activated previously quiescent Arab forces and impelled them to join the defeated forces in a new attempt, and so on. Thus the over-coming of the sporadic Palestinian Arab outbursts of the 1920s by the Jewish settlers helped bring about the general revolt of 1936–1939. The insuffi-ciency of that revolt brought the general Arab resistance supported by Arab League volunteers and funds in 1947–1948. The collapse of that brought the intervention of the surrounding Arab states in 1948. The decisive defeat of that combination in 1967 brought, in 1973, the coalition of the first circle countries backed by countries of the second circle.

Saudi Arabia's deliberate use of the oil weapon is explainable partly by this enhanced concern about Israel and partly by a change in the configura-tion and dynamics of inter-Arab relations. Many times after 1967, Nasser and Arab radicals had urged Saudi Arabia to use oil as an instrument in the service of the Arab cause, but Saudi Arabia had refused. King Feisal, in partic-ular, had flatly ruled that "oil and politics should not be mixed." At that time, Feisal feared that once he agreed to make the oil weapon available, a popular Arab leader such as Nasser might arrogate to himself the effective right to decide when and how it was to be used. Moreover, since Saudi Arabia itself depended in those days on all the revenues it was getting for its own needs, the oil weapon was only of limited use and could indeed be turned around to hurt the Saudi regime itself. This situation changed radically in the few years before the October War. On the one hand, the enormous in-crease in oil revenues far beyond current needs gave the Saudi ruler much more leeway in handling the oil weapon; on the other hand, the death of Nasser and the failure of a comparable personality to emerge in the Arab world meant that King Feisal could be sure to retain control of the weapon himself. The one possible exception was Colonel Muammar Qaddafi of Libya, who considered himself Nasser's heir and the custodian of Arab nationalism and the pan-Arab cause, but Qaddafi could become a real threat only if he could succeed in the endeavor he was making to extend his limited base by uniting with Egypt. Since Libya's oil was the principal attraction for Egypt of Qaddafi's proposed union, Feisal believed he could forestall that union and the threat it presented by being prepared to help Egypt finan-cially and use the oil weapon on its behalf.

These developments had several crucial direct and indirect implications for Israel. One direct implication was that *if the Arab-Israeli confrontation continued,* Arab countries of the second circle and the Maghreb were apt to become more and more involved in it alongside the first circle countries, to the point where the two might constitute one single fomidable war coalition, with enormous territorial, human, financial, and political resources. At worst, such a development could eventually present such a threat to Israel's existence as would drive it to seek unconventional means of defense, which in turn would give the whole conflict a truly apocalyptic potential. At best, it could mean that Israel would remain indefinitely engaged in a conflict it could never hope to win. Perhaps the possibility of a decisive Israeli victory, in the sense of its being able to impose its will on its enemies, was never very real; but in any case the October War drove home the point that the very persistence of the conflict generated and galvanized an ever greater Arab strategic depth which was ultimately beyond Israel's capacity to overcome. Israel could win another war and another, but each victory would gain it only another spell until its enemies recovered and came back for another round.

Apart from these discouraging long-term prospects, the alignment of first circle Arab countries with the fabulously enriched countries of the second circle presented Israel with severe problems in the short and intermediate time ranges. As long as the confrontation continued, such an Arab coalition could sustain an arms buildup beyond Israel's capacity to match out of its own heavily strained resources. Although from a strict military point of view several years at least would be needed before the Arab coalition could convert its potential into actual power, the political consequences of the Arab potential were apt to become apparent much sooner. The mere accumulation of arms by the Arabs at a much faster rate than Israel was likely to weaken its relative bargaining position and to impel it to seek ever larger injections of American aid. Such injections were bound to depend on the extent to which Israel's policy and behavior fitted with the United States' conception of the situation and its objectives and policies, which, as we shall see, themselves underwent a great deal of change as a result of the war.

One favorable consequence of the war in the regional arena was that Egypt and Syria agreed to enter into peace negotiations, the former unconditionally, the latter with some qualifications. This development appears to be at odds with the notion of enhanced and potentially ascending Arab power just presented, and many observers have therefore questioned the validity of one or the other of the two propositions. However, the paradox disappears and the consequences remain compatible if two points about the situation on the Arab side are kept in mind.

The first is that the potential Arab power-advantage depends on a continuation and consolidation of the Arab coalition of first and second circle countries which itself depends on a continuation of the Arab-Israeli confrontation. But continuation of the confrontation after the October War was not in itself in the interest of countries of either circle. The Egyptian and Syrian leaders realized even before the war that the destruction of Israel had ceased to be a practical objective regardless of any possible conventional power relationship because of the high probability that Israel had a "last resort" nuclear option. Consequently, they had to scale down their aim to the still feasible objective of seeking to recover their lost territories and gaining some satisfaction for the Palestinians. Since that objective, unlike the destruction of Israel, appeared to be achievable by negotiations in the wake of the war, there was no point in continuing the confrontation without first exploring that possibility.

For the oil-rich countries of the second circle, continuation of the confrontation made even less sense than for countries of the first circle if there was a way of avoiding it. The conservative rulers of Saudi Arabia and the rich Persian Gulf principalities had long been wary of the Arab-Israeli conflict because it entailed the growth and consolidation of the power of radical Arab forces and Soviet influence in the first circle Arab countries, which they viewed as presenting a more clear and imminent danger to their regimes and way of life than Israel. Worse still, the persistence of the conflict created pressures on them to help bankroll the development of those hostile forces, and to take their distance from the United States, their natural and historical ally against those forces.

After the Six Day War, they had hoped and expected that the United States would use the possibilities opened by that war to advance a settlement that would relieve them of those pressures, but the onset of a stalemate after 1970 bid fair to prolong the confrontation indefinitely with all its nefarious consequences for them. In order to break that stalemate and particularly to press the United States to revise its position and resume seriously its efforts on behalf of a settlement, they decided to throw their financial and political weight behind the military effort of Egypt and Syria. Once that result was achieved, or seemed to be, the chief interest of the oil-rich countries came to center on discreetly using their resources to promote the termination of the conflict rather than prolonging a confrontation that endangered them. Altogether then, the effect of the Yom Kippur War in the regional arena was to make a settlement more possible in principle by making continuation of the confrontation a highly unattractive option to contemplate for any of the parties involved.

Effect on the Israeli-American Relationship

Important as were the changes in Israel's position in relation to the Third World, Western Europe, and the Arab arena, they were overshadowed by the change in its position in relation to the United States. The war invalidated nearly all the previous American assumptions and expectations regarding the Middle East conflict and gave way to others which dovetailed much less closely with Israel's. In principle, the two still retained basic shared interests and the differences between them were not irreconcilable, but the adjustment of positions was bound to be difficult in practice and could give rise to serious misunderstandings and painful encounters.

By the time the war was over, few of the premises of the United States' prewar policy remained intact. (1) The United States had counted on Israel's military superiority, coupled with unequivocal American political support, to deter the Arabs from going to war and force them to be more forthcoming in seeking a settlement; instead, they chose to fight. (2) In considering the remote contingency of war, the United States had anticipated that Israel would defeat the Arabs decisively and quickly, and had only worried about the possible effects of the defeat on the Arab countries; instead, the Arabs did well enough in the war to place Israel in jeopardy and embroil the United States in an altogether different set of complications. (3) The United States believed it had maneuvered the Soviets into renouncing policies that exacerbated or exploited the conflict; instead, the Soviets intervened in the war to such an extent that the United States itself felt forced to intervene, and that the two superpowers ended up in dangerous confrontation. (4) The United States had believed the oil-rich Arab countries to be vitally interested in avoiding confrontation with it on account of the Arab-Israeli conflict despite the tentative warnings they had sounded, and was skeptical about the effectiveness of the sanctions they threatened; in fact, these countries dared challenge the United States and used the oil weapon with telling effect. (5) Finally, the United States had tacitly assumed that Western Europe had taken itself out of the picture as far as the conflict was concerned; in fact, key European countries became deeply implicated in it and took on the role of critics and antagonists of American policy and action. In short, the United States had believed that the Arab-Israeli conflict had been effectively defused, contained, and insulated by a combination of diplomacy and balance of power; instead, it proved to be as explosive as ever and the repercussions turned out to be more far-reaching and dangerous than ever.

Well before the full effect of the war had become apparent, Secretary Kissinger had started the process of revising American policy necessitated by the failure of previous assumptions. We have seen that the mere fact that the Arabs chose to go to war already led the secretary of state to pursue an objective different from Israel's, and to seek to have the war end in a situation conducive to fruitful negotiations rather than in total Israeli victory. This divergence was first deliberately concealed and then appeared to be irrelevant as the United States had to help Israel to avert possible disaster; however, once the tide of war turned decisively in Israel's favor, the secretary reverted to his original intent with redoubled insistence. For if he had initially feared that some complications *might* result from a total Israeli victory, by the time such a victory was within reach of the Israelis, worse complications than he had anticipated had actually begun to take place. The oil embargo was on,

Europe had demonstratively dissociated itself from the United States, the Soviets had intervened and were threatening further intervention, and the United States had become a party to the war and was therefore seen as largely responsible for its outcome and consequences.

The implications of that situation were horrendous to contemplate. Were the United States to have allowed Israel to score a total victory after having helped it, the Middle East might have become polarized, with the Soviet Union in the position of the exclusive supporter of an embittered united Arab front opposing isolated Israel and the United States. This would have given the Soviets indirect and remote but effective control over the flow of oil, which they could use to break up NATO and "Finlandize" Europe while punishing the United States. Of course, the United States would be in a position to react through Israel in the Middle East, and perhaps through China at the other end of the Eurasian landmass, but the stakes of such a contest would be so high for all sides that the danger of a disastrous superpower conflict would be enormously heightened.

Preventing a total Arab defeat was only one crucial step in the secretary of state's unfolding new policy conception. Another no less crucial step was to prevent the Soviets from usurping the credit for that outcome and thus pose as the saviors of the Arabs and place themselves in a position where they might exploit the confrontation and prolong it at will. To achieve that aim he went as far as calling for a global alert to face down the Soviets. These two steps, in turn, were only necessary prerequisites for the main goal that Kissinger set for himself, which was to advance a settlement of the Arab-Israeli conflict. That, the secretary came to believe, was the only way to snap the dangerous triangle revealed by the war entangling the superpowers, Western Europe, and the Arab-Israeli problem.

In principle, the commitment of the United States to advancing a settlement was not problematic for Israel since it coincided with its real and avowed aim. Nor was there any problem regarding the two countries' perceptions of some key features of the situation which sustained a strong sense of their need for each other. The United States was quite aware that Israel's impressive military recovery, albeit with American help, was the factor that salvaged the possibility of negotiations altogether. It recognized that Israel's strength and its continuing control over territories wanted by the Arabs made the option of continuing confrontation highly unattractive for the Arab states and their Soviet supporters, forced the Arabs to turn to the United States in pursuit of the alternative option of seeking settlement, and contributed essential assets for the United States' chances of being able to achieve one. Israel, for its part, was more than ever aware of the indispensability of the United States as a provider of the arms and financial assistance needed to maintain its own strength, and it recognized the crucial role of the United States in shielding it from international pressures and particularly in neutralizing the

Soviets' renewed willingness to intervene and threaten demonstrated in the course of the war. The potential problems between the United States and Israel latent in the new American conception lay in differences between the two regarding the degree of urgency of a settlement, the proper timing for it, the short-term implications of failure to settle, and, ultimately, in their respective conceptions of the essential content of a settlement.

Because of the global complications and implications revealed by the war, a settlement became for the United States a matter of imperative necessity; whereas for Israel, it was only a desirable consummation, subject to many qualifications. For the United States, the international political pressures made it essential to start on the road to settlement immediately; for Israel, the timing was conditioned by a different set of considerations including internal conditions and perceptions of the military balance, and the global situation was to it a factor only to the extent that it reflected itself in the American attitude. For the United States, the alternative to an immediate start toward a settlement was a continuation of the confrontation with all its horrendous potential consequences; for Israel, continuation of the confrontation for some time longer entailed no unacceptable penalties and could be viewed as potentially beneficial to its bargaining position. Underlying these differences there was a revival of a general, latent difference between the two countries regarding the content of an envisaged settlement, which had manifested itself in the clashes over the Rogers policies but was later suppressed as the United States increasingly deferred to Israel's stance. The United States was vitally interested in a settlement as such—in the effective termination of the conflict—but had no interest at all in the question of the particular territorial terms it should comprise, except insofar as that question was relevant to the attainment of an agreement. For Israel, on the other hand, the priorities were almost reversed: it was interested in a settlement only to the extent that it would satisfy certain undefined territorial demands that it deemed essential for its national interest.

Altogether, the changes in the American position wrought by the war revived or created serious potential differences between the United States and Israel in a context in which the two continued to share basic interests and key perceptions. In principle, that situation allowed mutual accommodation and conciliation of differences. In practice, because of the pressures under which the two had to labor, the adaptation was bound to be stormy and painful.

25
Readaptations and Step-by-Step Diplomacy, October 1973–May 1974

The guns of October had barely fallen silent when a multilateral diplomatic engagement began that continued at an intense pace for eight months and produced a series of Arab-Israeli limited agreements before coming to a pause. The driving force behind that activity was Secretary of State Kissinger, who was himself impelled by the enormity of the stakes involved (America's future in the Middle East, oil flow, détente or confrontation, NATO) and by the ambition to follow through an intricate policy design he had begun to apply.

Initially, Kissinger's agenda comprised two points in the given order: (1) consolidation of the cease-fire by resolving certain urgent impending issues (lines of demarcation, the fate of the Third Army, prisoners of war) that threatened to plunge the area into renewed fighting and undo the American position achieved so far; and (2) preparing a peace conference to work out a comprehensive settlement as provided in Resolution 338, which all the parties had accepted. However, the course of the negotiations he conducted with the parties on the cease-fire problems showed that order to be highly unpromising and suggested instead an alternative approach. That approach called for trying to work out a series of partial agreements that would be broad enough to make the immediate issues more tractable, yet limited enough to avoid coming up at once against the very difficult questions involved in a total settlement. This essentially pragmatic adaptation to the situation was turned into a specific diplomatic approach to peace dubbed "step by step" after it produced two "disengagement agreements," one between Egypt and Israel in January 1974 and one between Syria and Israel in May 1974.

The efforts of Kissinger to deal with the cease-fire problems in the context of his initial agenda brought the Israeli government face to face with the new American conceptions and perceptions for the first time. The shock of the encounter, the strains it provoked, and the dangers it evoked had much to do with the subsequent successful endeavor of the secretary of state to explore an alternative approach. The pursuit of limited agreements was not itself by any means easy in terms of American-Israeli relations, as the negotiations with Syria showed and as the failure of a second round of negotiations with Egypt was to show later on. However, it undoubtedly averted unnecessary head-on clashes between the two countries at a difficult moment for both, gave them time and occasions to sort out their common interests and their differences, and provided opportunities to bridge the differences on a gradual basis.

Cease-Fire Problems; Israeli-American Strains

The final cease-fire found the Israeli forces occupying some 600 square miles of Egyptian territory west of the Suez Canal, surrounding entirely the Third Army, and holding 7,800 Egyptian prisoners of war. The Egyptians held a 5- to 7-mile-deep bridgehead east of the canal along its entire length except in the area where the Israeli corridor to the west pierced it. They also held about 250 Israeli prisoners of war. The Syrians held an estimated 127 Israeli prisoners, while the Israelis held 368 Syrian soldiers and occupied 165 square miles of Syrian territory beyond the prewar line.

Right after the war Israel hoped to trade off the "assets" it held vis-à-vis Egypt for a return of prisoners and a withdrawal of the Egyptian forces east of the canal. With regard to Syria, Israel hoped for a simple exchange of prisoners, "sweetened" perhaps by renunciation of some of the freshly conquered territory. Such a transaction would nullify the military results of the war, restore the status quo ante, and leave it in a good bargaining position on the eve of the expected peace negotiations.

Precisely because the trade-off would eliminate all traces of Arab achievement, Syria and Egypt were determined to oppose it. The Syrians, knowing how terribly anxious the Israelis were to recover their prisoners, were determined to hold them back until Israel was prepared to pay a price for them in *prewar* territory. The Egyptians, too, were aware of the value of the Israeli prisoners they held but they could not afford to sit back until Israel was prepared to "pay" for them because their own Third Army was in imminent danger of collapse through starvation. They wanted the siege lifted immediately and demanded the withdrawal of Israel's forces to the lines they occupied in October 22, as enjoined by Security Council Resolution 339. They, of course, held back the prisoners pending Israeli compliance, but they also used other means. On the one hand, they agreed to hold negotiations with Israel at the military level on enforcement of United Nations cease-fire resolutions. On the other hand, they sought American mediation and threatened to call on Soviet assistance to supply the Third Army or resume the war unless Israel relented.

The Israelis were not too surprised by the Arabs' initial opposition to their design, but they were confident they held the means to overcome it. Egypt's prompt agreement to direct negotiations at the military level—the first such instance since the 1949 armistice talks—seemed to them to confirm their expectations. They were, however, surprised and even flabbergasted when the United States began to undercut their bargaining position by pressing them very hard to open promptly a supply line to the Third Army independently of any other issue. Very reluctantly, they agreed in principle to allow one convoy of food and nonmilitary supplies to pass through their lines, but then proceeded to stall in the execution and bargain for a list of prisoners and International Red Cross visits in exchange for greater dispatch. The Israelis had not realized up to that point the extent to which the American perspective had changed, and that the United States was much more interested in this instance in laying the foundations for negotiations and establishing a dialogue with Egypt than in seeing Israel extract every advantage from a favorable tactical situation.

The Israeli Prime Minister was confronted with the new American perspective and its implications for the first time in the course of a visit to Washington starting on October 31, 1973. Meir had taken the initiative for the visit partly to try to straighten out what seemed to her to be some inconsistencies in the American actions, partly to seek American agreement to a long shopping list of equipment to rebuild Israel's armed forces. She was therefore startled to learn during a meeting she had with President Nixon on November 1 that the seeming inconsistencies were actually consistent aspects of a new American overall conception of the situation. Far from endorsing the Israeli trade-off scenario, the United States sought to trade off the Israeli assets for the establishment and reinforcement of American influence in Egypt in order to advance peace, avert war, and remove the Arab oil embargo. Israel was not only expected to let go of the Third Army shortly, but had also to be prepared to let go of territories under its control later on, not so much on the basis of specific quid pro quos as to help the United States advance a total settlement. The President was particularly emphatic on the question of the Third Army, asserting that the United States could not allow Israel to starve it out and thus risk Soviet intervention. He could not, he said, go through the October 25 alert exercise with the Russians every day. Moreover, he informed Meir that Egypt had a project for a Security Council resolution calling for a return to the October 22 lines, and he warned that the United States would use its veto to block it only if Israel had opened a corridor to the Third Army.

The position taken by the President reflected an understanding that Kissinger had reached with Sadat. On October 27 Kissinger had written to the Egyptian President asking if he would receive him in Cairo on November 6 for a full day of discussions. Sadat had not only agreed immediately but had also promptly sent to Washington a high-ranking emissary, Mahmud Fahmi (soon to become foreign minister), to prepare the ground for the Cairo talks. Fahmi held important talks with the President and the secretary of state on October 29–30, as a result of which it was agreed that Egypt would subsume its demand for a return to the October 22 lines under broader negotiations to start soon. These negotiations would seek the withdrawal of Israeli forces by stages across the canal and into Sinai as part of a settlement process, which would relieve the Third Army and remove altogether the embarrassing Israeli military presence west of the canal. In the meantime, the United States would endeavor to obtain a secure supply corridor to the besieged army through the Israeli lines.

Kissinger was convinced that Israel's position west of the canal was untenably overextended and had to be given up sooner or later. By holding up to the Egyptians right then the prospect of an Israeli withdrawal later on, he thought he could circumvent the thorny issue of the cease-fire lines, engage the parties in the actual process of negotiations, and increase America's credit with Egypt and the Arabs. This approach, he believed, would work in the long run for the benefit of Israel as well as the United States. The problem was how to convince the Israelis to relinquish their own approach of seeking to restore the status quo ante by means of military pressure before entertaining any negotiations, and particularly how to get them to relinquish their hold on the Third Army right away. He attempted to tackle this problem in a series of meetings with Meir.

Meir was totally unprepared psychologically to absorb the new American thinking, partly because it ran counter to the belief she liked and needed to hold that Israel had won the war and was "entitled" to have its way. Furthermore, Kissinger had hitherto done little to suggest to her and other Israelis that the United States' views had ceased to coincide completely with Israel's and had rather done much to encourage their belief that they continued to do so. Therefore, when she was first confronted sharply with the American ideas, Meir viewed them as indications of an erosion of American support for Israel rather than as attempts to adapt continuing support to changed circumstances. The more Kissinger dwelt on the need to take into account those circumstances—the oil boycott, Europe's defection, the dangers of polarization in the Middle East and confrontation with the Soviet Union, the long-term balance of power—the more he confirmed the apprehensions of the Prime Minister. Small Israel, she felt, was being asked to sacrifice itself and risk its own future for the interests and convenience of big others. Nothing was more apt to stimulate her resistance.

Meir did not mind subsuming the question of the cease-fire lines under a broader effort to disengage the opposed forces when Kissinger broached it. But she rejected any notion of unilateral Israeli withdrawal and reiterated her view that the Egyptians should pull back from the east side of the canal in exchange for the Israelis' pulling back from the west side. However, she reserved her fiercest resistance to Kissinger's ideas regarding the Third Army. Kissinger demanded a supply corridor to the besieged army under United Nations control; Meir insisted on an exchange of prisoners before she would let go. Kissinger assured her that the exchange would take place immediately after the corridor was opened; she vehemently stood on a reverse order. Israel was entitled by right, according to the Geneva Convention, to have its prisoners back, and Kissinger had assured her on October 22 that it was understood by all that an exchange of prisoners would take place within seventy-two hours. Meir added that she could not explain to her people giving supplies to the Egyptian army while Israeli soldiers were arbitrarily held in Egyptian captivity. Kissinger pleaded with her to look at substance rather than right, to take the longer view and help him advance the peace Israel needed; he invoked the spectre of Soviet helicopters flying supplies to the Egyptians and threatened to have American helicopters do the job, but Meir would not budge. Finally, after the secretary had thoroughly and absolutely pledged himself to a prompt return of the prisoners, and after it had been made clear to an Israeli delegation that the extent of American military aid to Israel depended on its willingness to cooperate politically with the United States, Meir relented, partly. She would open a corridor to the Third Army and allow one United Nations inspection post at its starting point, but the corridor must remain under Israeli control, both in order not to split the Israeli forces at either side of it and in order to retain the option of closing it again if necessary. Kissinger pressed for a bigger United Nations role, indicated that the President expected it, and had Vice President Nelson Rockefeller intercede to urge it, but all to no avail. In her deep apprehension as to where America was headed, Meir would not go beyond that one provisional concession.

Kissinger had pressed for a firm corridor in order to take to Sadat an earnest of America's willingness and ability to move Israel and help advance a settlement, but the limited concession made by Meir proved to be quite sufficient. The secretary of state arrived in Cairo in the evening of November 6, after stopovers in Rabbat and Tunis, and met Sadat for the first time on the morning of the 7th. After three and a half hours of discussions he emerged with the main elements of a draft agreement to stabilize the cease-fire to be proposed to Israel, as well as an agreement to restore diplomatic relations between Egypt and the United States (broken since 1967) and to exchange ambassadors within two weeks. Beyond these specific conclusions, Kissinger and Sadat were also able to achieve a measure of understanding on a number of other issues, including the next steps toward peace, Egyptian assistance in lifting the oil embargo, the general nature of an eventual Arab-Israeli settlement, and the potential position of the Soviet Union and the United States in the area. To his surprise and delight, Kissinger discovered in this first meeting that Sadat was at least as eager to cooperate with the United States as he himself was with Egypt. Moreover, Sadat's disposition was not premised on any expectation that the United States should abandon or betray Israel. The Egyptian leader was resigned to accept the special American-Israeli relationship and did not demur when Kissinger told him in the course of the discussion that if the war were renewed, the United States would inevitably find itself again on Israel's side. All Sadat wanted was that the United States should press and steer Israel toward a settlement that the Arabs could accept.

The draft agreement on the cease-fire issues comprised six points:

1. Both sides would "observe scrupulously" the cease-fire.
2. They would "immediately" begin talks to settle "the question of the return to the October 22 positions in the framework of agreement on the disengagement and separation of forces under the auspices of the UN."
3. The city of Suez would receive "daily supplies of food, water and medicine."
4. There would be "no impediment" to the transfer of nonmilitary supplies to the east bank.
5. UN checkpoints would be established along the Cairo-Suez road and Israeli officers could check that cargoes going to the east bank were nonmilitary.
6. As soon as the UN checkpoints were established, there would be "an exchange of all prisoners of war, including the wounded."

In the evening of November 7, Sisco (now under secretary of state) flew to Tel Aviv to obtain Israel's consent to the agreement. Kissinger, basing himself on the discussions with Meir in Washington a few days before, was so certain of Israel's prompt approval that he arranged to meet Sisco the next day in Amman and fly together on to Riyad, Saudi Arabia. After all, the six-point proposal gave Israel practically everything it wanted and even a little more—prompt return of the prisoners, immediate direct negotiations on disengagement which subsumed the issue of return to the October 22 lines, and continuation and legitimization of Israeli control over supply to the Third Army. He was, therefore, flabbergasted to learn the next day that Sisco had run into difficulties. The Israeli Cabinet was reacting the same way Meir had when she was first exposed to the new dispositions of Washington, and several of its members resisted, picking at various points in the draft agreement. The proposal spoke of three United Nations checkpoints instead of one, it included a reference to the October 22 lines, there was no specific timetable for execution especially in connection with the prisoner exchange, there was no reference to lifting the Egyptian blockade on the Strait of Bab el Mandeb, and so on. Kissinger responded by providing reassuring clarifications regarding some points and coupling these with a strong message from himself and another from President Nixon urging Israel not to make difficulties and warning it again of the dangers and consequences of renewed fighting. Finally, the Israeli government consented and the agreement was signed on November 11 by Israeli and Egyptian generals at kilometer 101 on the Cairo-Suez road.

The Six Point Agreement, as it came to be known, was a crucial landmark for American postwar policy. It consecrated the acceptance of the United States by the Arab side as a broker or intermediary, defused a highly explosive situation, at least temporarily, and laid the ground for further movement away from war and toward peace under American aegis. This enabled Kissinger to go to Riyad and begin to press for the lifting of the oil embargo, and gave the secretary some leverage in his attempt to reinfuse some confidence in the United States among the panicked governments of Western Europe.

For Israel, too, the agreement was a turning point. Until the moment Sisco brought the Kissinger-Sadat proposal, Israelis generally, including members of the government and the opposition, were convinced that the war would be resumed at any moment. For one thing, Egypt was concentrating and deploying large forces around the Israeli salient after having refused the trade-off Israel had proposed. For another thing, they had been informed by an alarmist press about the demands made by the American leaders and the war warnings they had voiced during Meir's visit to the United States, and since Meir resisted the demands they expected the warnings to come true. Altogether, they had revised their initial views about the amenability of the enemy and had come to feel that while the Egyptians were in a dire predicament, they were too self-assured and belligerent to agree to Israel's terms without a fight; and most Israelis did not mind that prospect, seeing it as an opportunity to finish the job left undone and turn the political situation around. In this context, the Kissinger-Sadat draft agreement came as something of a surprise and gave rise to ambivalent reactions. On the one hand, the accommodating spirit shown by Sadat seemed to augur well for the prospects of an eventual settlement; on the other hand, the accommodations might be only a bait to lure the United States into an American-Egyptian partnership from which Israel could expect no good. This was one reason why the government procrastinated and tried to find fault with the proposal. However, once the majority led by the Labor Alignment finally agreed, it felt impelled to justify its act in large measure as a deliberate investment in a policy of peace.

This policy turn on the part of the Israeli government generally and the Labor Alignment in particular, crucial as it was for Kissinger's purposes, was, however, severely constrained by the prevailing internal political circumstances. Ever since the first days of the war, Israelis had been nurturing deep resentments against the leaders in charge of the country's defense and foreign policy for the failures that led to the initial disasters and subsequent heavy losses. However, as long as the war was going on or as long as its resumption appeared to be imminent, they held back on expressing their feelings for the sake of national unity in the face of peril. Once the government had accepted the Six Point Proposal and the chances of war appeared to have receded, the pent-up feelings burst forth in torrential strength through many channels. While the right-wing Likkud opposition fiercely attacked the agreement as capitulation to pressure and blasted the government for mismanaging the war, large leftist groups within the Labor Alignment attacked their own leadership for its lack of a clear peace policy then as before the war. Adding to the turmoil, General Sharon just then provoked the "war of the generals" with charges that timidity and failures of judgment on the part of the top military leadership were responsible for causing Israel to miss the chance it had had to achieve a truly decisive victory and to suffer far heavier casualties than was necessary. The government's decision on November 18 to appoint the Agranat Inquiry Commission helped quiet spirits somewhat, and the Alignment's moderating of its election platform temporarily assuaged the rebellious groups within its ranks. However, as public opinion polls taken at the time showed, mistrust of the government and perplexity remained very high. One such poll taken by the daily *Haaretz*, for example, showed more than half the sample interviewed to feel that Meir should resign; at the same time, another poll showed that as many as 39 percent could not name an alternative Prime Minister. In these circumstances, the ability of the government to act significantly in accordance with the assent it gave to Kissinger's peace design was severely limited.

Preparations for Negotiations; Improved Israeli-American Climate

The Six Point Agreement was signed at kilometer 101 by General Aharon Yariv for Israel and General Abdel Ghani Gamassi for Egypt on November 11, and the two officers and their aides immediately proceeded with discussions to implement it. The talks began on arrangements for supply to the Third Army and the exchange of prisoners and remained stuck there for four tense days before a resolution was finally achieved. After the arrangements were executed, the negotiators addressed themselves to the much more difficult next item: "the question of the return to the October 22 positions in the framework of an agreement on the disengagement and separation of forces." Yariv began by proposing a return to the prewar lines and Gamassi began by demanding an Israeli withdrawal to the el Arish–Ras Muhammad line, halfway across the Sinai Peninsula; although the two generals subsequently "informally" modified their positions a great deal, no agreement could be reached and the talks were suspended sine die on December 2.

Kissinger, now the recognized diplomatic prime mover, was not surprised by the stalemate at kilometer 101. The Israeli government had told him already on October 22 and again before accepting the Six Points that it would be unable to make any important substanive move before the elections scheduled for December 31, and he had accepted that position even before the outbreak of political turmoil in Israel made it inescapable. He had therefore viewed the generals' talks as a means to gain time with the Egyptians, and before these talks broke down he was already engaged in new initiatives aimed at gaining more time and sustaining the momentum for peace.

After mediating the Six Point Agreement Kissinger had flown on to China and Japan; but as soon as he returned home he began consultations with Israel, the Arab parties, and the Soviets on plans to assemble a Middle East peace conference at Geneva, in accordance with Resolution 338. Kissinger realized, of course, that even apart from the hiatus imposed by the Israeli election schedule, the conference could not possibly begin to tackle the basic issues in dispute without long advance preparation; nevertheless, he sought to assemble the conference promptly because it would gain him time, because of the enormous symbolic and psychological significance of getting Arabs and Israelis around a peace table for the first time in the history of the conflict, and because he believed that the event would help him in his endeavor to have the oil embargo terminated. To serve these ends under the circumstances, he devised the following scenario: The conference would open with all the participants for a brief ceremonial and introductory session. This would be followed by a brief working session which would establish procedures and direct the parties to take up discussion of disengagement and separation of forces as the first order of business. The conference would then adjourn until the first week of January, when it would take up the actual negotiations.

Kissinger discussed these ideas with the parties, starting with Israel's Eban in Washington on November 20, 1973. Eban indicated Israel's general agreement to the main outlines of the plan, since these were obviously designed to accommodate it, but raised certain reservations concerning the role of the United Nations and the question of Palestinian representation. He also reiterated his government's insistence that the Syrians must deliver a list of prisoners of war and allow Red Cross visits before the conference convened. The Soviets, too, readily assented in principle, but added some observations. Fearful of Kissinger's recent solo performance and anxious to assume an active role themselves, they eagerly agreed to cosponsor the conference and insisted only that it be convened as soon as possible and that it be kept in continuous session once assembled. As for the Egyptians, they had their own reasons to favor an early convening of the conference—Sadat wanted to convince critics at home and in the Arab world that his opening to the United States and his endeavor to move things toward a settlement were working; however, they were disappointed with the notion that the discussion of the disengagement of forces was to be put off until January. They had previously agreed to subsume the question of Israeli withdrawal to the October 22 lines under broader disengagement talks, but now they were being asked to subsume the disengagement talks under the Geneva conference. Inspired Egyptian press comments complained that Kissinger had misled or deceived Sadat, and the Syrians, who were more suspicious than the Egyptians to begin with, echoed and magnified that theme.

In an effort to restore and protect his credibility with the Egyptians, which he deemed essential for his entire postwar design, Kissinger began to address himself seriously to the question of facilitating a disengagement agreement even while working on his plans for a conference. Shortly after the talks at kilometer 101 were terminated, he invited Israeli Defense Minister Dayan to Washington to discuss the subject. Dayan had always doubted the political and military wisdom of Israel's sitting right at the waterline of the canal and had made no secret of his views. Already in the summer of 1971, in the course of Sisco's discussions with the Israelis of the possibility of an interim agreement, Dayan had sought to persuade his colleagues to agree to an Israeli withdrawal from the canal line in exchange for Egyptian political concessions and agreement to keep only limited forces east of the canal. Kissinger knew that and also knew that as defense minister, Dayan was apt to be more keenly aware than his colleagues that the Israeli positions west of the canal were overextended and that they were becoming ever more vulnerable the more the Egyptians had the chance to rebuild their air defenses and reinforce their troops around the Israeli salient. Therefore, the secretary of state thought Dayan would be the best member of the Israeli government with whom to try to reach an understanding on disengagement, and in this he proved right.

Dayan met Kissinger on December 7, 1973, and presented to him the official Israeli government position on disengagement, based on a return to the pre-1973 lines. However, the defense minister also added his own "personal" views, which he thought might eventually win acceptance on the part of the government. These envisaged an Israeli withdrawal to a line ten kilometers west of the Mitla and Gidi Passes—some thirty kilometers east of the canal—in return for Eyptian agreement to substantial demilitarization of the forward areas, obligation to reopen the Suez Canal and rebuild the canal cities, and lifting the blockade of Bab el Mandeb. Kissinger believed the essentials of Dayan's ideas would be eminently acceptable to the Egyptians. He was planning to leave the next day for another round of the Middle Eastern capitals to work out the remaining details of the Geneva conference and press further for the lifting of the oil embargo, and he was highly pleased to have Dayan's ideas and to be able to use them in his talks with Sadat as evidence of his own good faith, dedication to progress on disengagement, and successful handling of Israel.

Kissinger arrived in Cairo on December 13 into a rather uncertain atmosphere. Two weeks before, an Arab summit meeting in the Algerian capital had cautiously endorsed efforts at settlement but had opposed lifting the oil embargo until Israel began to withdraw. A few days before, Sadat had met with Syria's President Assad and the two had agreed to go to Geneva, but only after the conclusion of disengagement agreements. Sadat himself appeared more ready now than six weeks before to move forward on the road to settlement, but he also seemed somewhat more suspicious of Kissinger for his support of Israel's dilatory tactics on disengagement. The Egyptian President was obviously embarrassed by the continuing existence of the Israeli salient seven weeks after the war and one month after the Six Point Agreement. It belied his claim to victory and undermined the miraculous turn of fortune he enjoyed. He wanted an Israeli agreement to withdraw and was prepared to be reasonable to facilitate it, but he hinted that if he did not get what he wanted by negotiations, he would have to get it by force.

Kissinger cautioned Sadat again that if Egypt renewed the war the United States would find itself again on Israel's side. On the other hand, he explained that military action was unnecessary as well as risky, and presented an outline of Dayan's ideas as evidence that an agreement was readily attainable after the Israeli elections, and that the United States had not been sitting idly by. Kissinger was thus able to obtain Sadat's agreement to attend the Geneva conference even without a prior disengagement agreement, and a promise to help persuade Syria to do the same. He also obtained from the Egyptian leader proposals on disengagement which were not very far from Dayan's ideas, and a promise that he would discuss with other Arab states a possible lifting of the oil embargo.

Kissinger flew from Cairo to Riyad on December 15 in pursuit of that latter objective. Before setting out on his Middle East trip, the secretary and other administration officials had made noises about tough countermeasures that might be taken if the embargo continued "unreasonably and indefinitely." Now he tried to alternate those threats with inducements in the shape of a forthcoming peace conference and the prospect of an Israeli withdrawal in order to obtain a Saudi commitment to an early termination of the sanctions against the United States. The Saudi King appeared somewhat more responsive this time than he had on Kissinger's previous visit, but he still insisted on seeing concrete achievements before lifting the embargo.

From Riyad Kissinger flew the same day to Damascus where he conferred with President Assad. Kissinger knew that Assad had agreed with Sadat to go to Geneva after the conclusion of disengagement agreements, and he wanted to persuade the Syrian President to agree to a reversal of the order as he had the Egyptian. However, he had no "Dayan ideas" with which to tempt Assad to go along, nor was Syria's bargaining position such as to permit Assad to hope for Israeli concessions later on. Israel's salient west of the canal was at least distant and exposed, making its renunciation likely, whereas its salient east of the prewar line in Syria was much better shaped strategically and lay close to supply centers. Assad had only two weak cards to bargain with, his assent to Geneva and the Israeli prisoners of war, and he was not prepared to give away either without getting something in return. So after discussions that lasted six hours, Kissinger left for the next leg of his trip without Syria's agreement to attend the peace conference, but with the hope that he might still prevail on Assad to change his mind with the help of Egypt, the Soviet Union, and even Israel.

Kissinger arrived at Jerusalem on December 16, after a stopover in Beirut in which he obtained the blessing of the Lebanese government for his peace mission, and another in Amman, in which he secured the Jordanian government's agreement to attend the Geneva conference even if Syria did not go. His immediate task in Israel was twofold: to remove remaining obstacles in the way of the conference and to turn Dayan's "personal" views into a position supported by the Israeli government. Beyond these aims, however, Kissinger also wanted to explain adequately his policies to the Israeli government and try to regain from it a measure of confidence in himself, after the battering his reputation in Israel had recently suffered.

One remaining obstacle in the way to the conference was the problem of Palestinian participation. Kissinger had tentatively worked out with Sadat a proposal wherein the invitation to the conference would say that the question of Palestinian participation will be taken up at the first stage of the conference. The Israeli government strongly opposed any specific reference to the Palestinians and wanted it stated that invitations to any other countries or groups could be sent only with the agreement of all the primary participants—in other words, it wanted a veto power over any invitation to the Palestine Liberation Organization. Kissinger realized that the issue was fundamental for Israel and therefore made a special effort to accommodate it. He cabled Jerusalem's position to Soviet Foreign Minister Gromyko and asked him to seek a modification of position from Sadat. The Egyptian President responded by dropping reference to the Palestinians, but refused to grant Israel the right to veto an invitation at a later stage. Kissinger then proposed and Israel accepted, the following solution: the invitation would say that "The sides agreed that the question of participation of other factors in the Middle East will be *discussed* [emphasis added] at the first stage of the conference." At the same time, the United States would give Israel a written private assurance that it would oppose, to the point of veto, any invitation to the PLO without Israel's consent.

Another serious obstacle was the problem of Israeli prisoners in Syrian hands. Some members of the Israeli government, including Dayan, held that Israel should not go to Geneva unless Syria first gave a list of the prisoners and allowed Red Cross visits. Others, including Meir, argued that Israel should go in order to avert charges of torpedoing the conference, but should refuse to sit in the same room with the Syrians until they met Israeli conditions. Kissinger, without questioning Israel's right or justifying the Syrians, argued that if Israel wanted the prisoners it should be interested in Syrian participation in the conference; and if it wanted Syrian participation, it should make some conciliatory move in that direction as it had toward Egypt when it agreed to discuss disengagement. The Israeli leaders were galled by this logic, but Kissinger exhorted them to keep their eyes on their objective and reminded them that even the United States had to pay a price to get its prisoners back from North Vietnam. At the time these discussions were taking place, the ruling Labor Alignment was running its entire electoral campaign on the theme that, whatever happened in the recent past, Labor was the only force that could lead the country toward an honorable peace. To allow the projected peace conference to fail at this point would have deprived it of the one plank that might save it from electoral disaster. So in the end, the government not only agreed to drop its conditions, but also authorized Kissinger to have a general declaration made in Damascus that Israel was willing to enter negotiations for separation of forces with Syria, and that its position in the talks would be "logical."

As things turned out, the Syrians decided to boycott the Geneva conference all the same, but the willingness of the Israeli government to heed Kissinger's urgings was significant. Together with Kissinger's effort to accommodate the Israeli government on the Palestinian question, it reflected the beginning of a new understanding between the two, which extended also to the question of disengagement of forces.

Kissinger brought from Cairo ideas on disengagement that were considerably more moderate than the Israelis had expected. During Kissinger's previous visit to the Egyptian capital, Sadat had insisted on an Israeli retreat to the el Arish–Ras Muhammad line, more than midway across Sinai. Although General Gamassi had informally suggested to General Yariv at kilometer 101 that that position was negotiable, he had still left the strong impression that Egypt would want to end up on a line east of the Mitla and Gidi Passes. Moreover, since those discussions took place, Egypt had made strenuous efforts to reinforce its military position in the battlefield, concentrated vast forces of armor and artillery around the Israeli salient, and substantially rebuilt its air defense system, leading the Israelis to believe that the Egyptians meant to press for their terms to the point of possible resumption of hostilities. Now Kissinger indicated to the Israelis that Sadat's *opening bid* was for an Israeli withdrawal to a line east of the passes. Moreover, Sadat was now amenable to the idea of a limited-forces zone and substantial restriction of armaments, which he had previously opposed; he was prepared to start work to reopen the Suez Canal immediately after the conclusion of an agreement; and he was ready to allow Israeli cargo through once the canal was reopened. The Israelis responded by dropping their own idea of an exchange of banks and proposing instead a line between the passes and the canal. They also wanted a greater degree of demilitarization and more specific Egyptian commitments regarding navigation in the canal and reconstruction of Egyptian cities on its bank. These ideas were still some distance from Dayan's "private views," let alone Sadat's, but they established sufficient common principles between Israel and Egypt to lead Kissinger to believe that a disengagement agreement would be readily attainable after Geneva. He left Israel satisfied that he had achieved the specific objectives of his visit.

Kissinger also left with the feeling of having gone a long way toward his more general aim of reversing the mistrust toward him among members of the Israeli government. He accomplished this partly by explaining the relation of the specific moves he sought to an overall strategy to deal with the postwar situation, and even more by the mood and tone in which he delivered his explanations. Kissinger argued that the oil embargo had isolated Israel internationally and placed it in a precarious situation. The Third World had joined the Soviet bloc in screaming for an immediate Israeli withdrawal to the pre-1967 boundaries. Western Europe and Japan were exerting pressure in the same direction. In the United States itself, dozens of officials in the State Department and the Pentagon were waiting for the opportunity to turn American policy from an Israeli orientation to an Arab orientation. Sadat was in a good position to use the international situation to try to achieve a general agreement on his terms, but fortunately he happened to be particularly interested at that very moment in removing the Israeli presence from the canal area. This made possible the idea of a disengagement agreement, which could help see Israel out of its present very difficult situation.

The aim of the disengagement talks, Kissinger pointed out, was to circumvent the need to talk about final borders and arrangements at this time. Moreover, success of the talks could lead to the lifting of the oil embargo, which in turn would ease the pressure of Europe and Japan and keep the pro-Arab forces within the American bureaucracy in check. Once the embargo was lifted, it would not be so easy to impose it again if negotiations did not go well. Besides, the West would be better prepared to deal with such an eventuality than when it was caught by surprise. On the other hand, should the disengagement talks fail, there would be created immediately a climate of international crisis that would break open the dam holding back the pressures on Israel. For all these reasons, and considering that Israel's forces on the west bank of the canal were overextended anyway, it made very good sense for Israel to do its best to ensure the success of the disengagement talks.

Kissinger's hosts took exception to his "disregard" for justice and argued several of his points, but they could not fail to notice that he talked to them not as the distant secretary of state of a big power, but as a man who was in touch with their feelings, shared many of their aims, and placed himself on their side in opposition to a hostile world and even to segments of his own government. They particularly took to heart his suggested strategy of playing for time in the expectation that things would get better later on. In the short run, that lesson helped Kissinger's purpose. In the somewhat longer run, it was to prove troublesome.

Peace Rendezvous at Geneva

On December 21, 1973, the foreign ministers of Israel, Egypt, Jordan, the United States, and the Soviet Union gathered at the Palais des Nations, once the headquarters of the League of Nations, under the chairmanship of United Nations Secretary General Kurt Waldheim, for what came to be officially known as the Geneva Middle East Peace Conference. None of the participants expected any substantive results from the conference at that stage and none was achieved. Nevertheless, the very fact that Arabs and Israelis formally got together around a peace table for the first time in a quarter century of conflict constituted a true symbolic and psychological breakthrough. Moreover, the conference provided a ready framework for future use for partial or comprehensive peace negotiations.

The conference proceeded essentially according to plan. In the first day each of the participants delivered a formal speech, and in the second the conference "instructed" Egypt and Israel to begin forthwith their talks on a disengagement of their forces. There were a few minor surprises: there was a hassle over the table arrangement, apparently part of contemporary diplomatic protocol; the Israeli and Arab representatives delivered tougher speeches than expected for the occasion; Egyptian Foreign Minister Fahmi unexpectedly gave a tough rejoinder to Eban's presentation, in which, however, he occasionally addressed his remarks to the Israeli foreign minister directly, instead of speaking to the chairman; on the other hand, the Arab delegates refused to "fraternize" with the Israelis by objecting to a cocktail party under United Nations auspices; and so on. The only significant unplanned event associated with the conference was a private meeting between Soviet Foreign Minister Gromyko and Israeli Foreign Minister Eban arranged through Secretary Kissinger. In the long and surprisingly cordial meeting, Eban pointed out that now that the Soviet Union was a cochairman of the conference, it might be appropriate for it to restore its diplomatic relations with Israel, broken since 1967, and to modulate its attitude toward Israel. Gromyko indicated that diplomatic relations would be renewed after some "meaningful progress" had been achieved in Israeli-Arab negotiations. He went on to urge Israel to keep the Geneva conference formally going by participating in a nominal "continuing working group" until the conference could reassemble at the ministerial level. At the behest of Kissinger, Israel later agreed.

Besides creating a formal framework for peace negotiations, the Geneva conference served some particular purposes, temporary or lasting, for each of the participants. For Sadat, it served to demonstrate to his people and to the Arab public that he had succeeded, through the war, in breaking the stalemate in the conflict and activating promising diplomatic processes aimed at prompt Israeli withdrawal and eventual settlement. For Jordan, the conference acknowledged it in the role of at least the custodian of the West Bank and the interlocutor empowered to negotiate its future. For Israel, the conference broke the Arab resistance to face-to-face negotiations aimed at achieving peace, and for the ruling Labor Alignment specifically it provided a badly needed peace platform to counterbalance its responsibility for the disastrous failures of the war. For the Soviet Union, the conference legalized and institutionalized its role as a Middle East power, formally on a par with the United States. For the United States, it provided another visible "accomplishment" in its role as intermediary in the conflict, a framework for possible further advances in its endeavor for peace, and an added argument in its effort to have the oil embargo lifted.

Israeli-Egyptian Disengagement; American Engagement

The disengagement negotiations between Egypt and Israel were supposed to start in earnest at Geneva on January 7, 1974, one week after the Israeli elections. This plan never materialized. Instead, Secretary Kissinger went to the Middle East on January 10, and, in a week of shuttling between Aswan and Jerusalem, successfully mediated an agreement between the two countries which was signed at kilometer 101. The agreement was a real turning point in the history of the Middle East, and the manner in which it was reached was even more significant than its content in making it so.

Strangely enough, the change of venue and approach was initiated at the suggestion of Israel, which had long suspected mediation and insisted on direct negotiations. On January 3, 1974, the Israeli government dispatched Dayan to Washington to discuss disengagement with Kissinger. In the course of two long meetings on the 4th and 5th, Dayan argued before the secretary of state that Geneva was not an effective forum for negotiations and urged him instead to come back immediately to the Middle East and personally get the disengagement talks going. Dayan repeated before Kissinger his "personal" views concerning an agreement, and expressed the opinion that, with a "push" on Kissinger's part, these views would be accepted by the Israeli government as a whole and a quick agreement could thus be reached. Kissinger checked with Sadat and found the Egyptian President to be as interested as Israel in a mediation effort forthwith.

The eagerness of the Israeli government to achieve a disengagement agreement promptly and in the most expeditious way was the result of complex considerations. For weeks after the cease-fire, Israelis had been torn by two powerful currents of thought and emotion. One inclined them toward drawing lessons from events as they actually happened to break previous rigidities and look for new approaches that would give compromise and peace a better chance; the other riveted them to previously held notions as to how events should have unfolded, and inclined them toward seeking to alter the situation even by war to bring it into conformity with those preconceptions. The Labor Alignment, as the most representative grouping, typically harbored and expressed both currents, but the approach of the elections and the fact that the opposition preempted the tough, unyielding perspective forced its leadership to suppress its own ambivalences, renounce the war option, and take its stand on the platform of accommodation and seeking ways to peace. Once it did so, and once it received from the public a diminished but still effective backing, various pressures impelled it to seek the quickest and most effective way to achieve a disengagement agreement.

By the time the elections were over, the Israeli reserves had been mobilized for nearly three months. Although the Israeli economy proved to be much more resilient than anyone had expected, the scope and duration of the mobilization were straining it immensely. The reservists had to be paid living salaries and their families had to be taken care of; factories and fields were severely hampered by the absence of key personnel and managers; businesses were threatened with ruin. Despite substantial demobilization, the labor force still averaged only 75 percent of normal in November and 80 percent in December. Moreover, while Israel was forced to reduce its total forces, the Egyptians and the Syrians were able to increase theirs and to draw substantially upon the reserves of other Arab countries. The imbalance was particularly dangerous in the southern front, where the Israeli salient lay at the end of a long line of communication which passed through a narrow bottleneck at the canal crossing. Finally, the cease-fire on either front was so ineffective that a small-scale "war of attrition" was actually taking place, in which the Israelis suffered a constant trickle of casualties that was all the more painful for being seemingly purposeless. For all these reasons, once the government laid aside the war option and committed itself to seeking a partial settlement, which meant withdrawal from the canal area, it sought to achieve an agreement as fast as possible. Such an agreement, notwithstanding the previous almost mystical expressions of faith in direct negotiations, appeared in January 1974 to be more readily achievable through the mediation of Secretary of State Kissinger than through Geneva.

When Kissinger set off for the Middle East on January 10, 1974, he still thought of Geneva as the ultimate forum for the conclusion of an agreement because of a presumed need to bring the Soviets into the picture. He considered his mission to be one of helping the parties to frame their ideas in the form of proposals that afforded a reasonable chance of success. However, after he got to Aswan and had two working sessions with Sadat, matters suddenly changed. Kissinger started by presenting Dayan's "ideas" to his host and getting his reactions to them. The two went carefully over the whole array of issues involved: the line to which Israel would withdraw, the kind and quantity of armament that would be allowed in the evacuated territory, the size and mandate of the United Nations force that would be interposed between the belligerents, the reopening of the Suez Canal to Israeli navigation, the rebuilding of the canal cities, and the relationship between a disengagement agreement in Sinai and one in the Golan, as well as between two such agreements and an overall peace settlement. By the time they finished their review, Sadat, sensing that his own ideas and Dayan's were not so far apart and eager to avoid complicating things by bringing in the Soviets, surprised Kissinger by proposing that, instead of limiting himself to having the parties formulate and exchange proposals in preparation for Geneva, he should try to finish the negotiations then and there while he was in the area. Kissinger said he was prepared to make the attempt, but he needed to find out how quickly the Israelis were prepared to move.

Sadat's proposal reflected an understandable eagerness on his part to achieve agreement as quickly as possible. The war had done marvels to his political position at home and in the Arab world, but the more time passed with the Israelis sitting sixty miles from Cairo and with an army corps and Suez city dependent for survival on Israeli goodwill, the more the claim to victory on which his new position rested appeared to be hollow. An Israeli withdrawal that would leave him in control of both banks of the canal would confirm his claim and stem the erosion of his gains. Also, the war had opened up the first prospects in years of reviving the Egyptian economy, choked by a bureaucratic incubus and starved of investment by isolation and ruinous defense spending; but the climate of uncertainty and probability of war generated by the presence of Israeli forces west of the canal prevented the initiation of reforms and stemmed the flow of potential investment funds from abroad necessary to realize the new prospects. But while all this argued for seeking prompt agreement, Sadat's proposal to Kissinger went further. By suggesting that Kissinger should try to work out an agreement then and there, Sadat in effect also deliberately proposed to bypass Geneva and the Soviets openly, and openly espoused the United States as the sole trusted mediator. The significance of this act in terms of the relative position of the superpowers in the Middle East is readily apparent. What may be less apparent is that it also represented a bold policy choice on the part of Sadat, in fact a gamble that renounced a credible war option, for which association with the Soviet Union was essential, for the option of seeking a peaceful settlement through exclusive cooperation with the United States. That choice was to manifest itself with full clarity later, when Sadat would formally terminate the Soviet-Egyptian Friendship and Cooperation Treaty.

Israel's government, for reasons already cited, was also eager for a quick agreement, and Sadat's willingness to bypass Geneva and the Soviets made it even more so. Matters therefore moved ahead fast. Kissinger landed in Israel at 6:00 P.M. on January 12, 1974, and immediately plunged into discussions with an Israeli team of negotiators. Before the evening was over, he had obtained the Israeli Cabinet's agreement to submit a formal Israeli disengagement proposal to Egypt, and had worked out with the negotiating team the outlines of such a proposal, which incorporated Dayan's ideas and took into account Sadat's views and position as interpreted by himself. The next day, Israeli and American working groups filled in the details, and by evening Kissinger was off to Aswan with the full Israeli proposal, including maps. Three hours later he was conferring with Egyptian Foreign Minister Fahmi in preparation for a meeting with Sadat scheduled for the next morning.

Sadat, who had wanted the Israelis to withdraw east of the passes or at least to the middle of them, accepted the Israeli offer of a withdrawal to a line twenty kilometers from the canal which would leave their forces west of the passes, after Kissinger asserted his conviction that the Israelis would go no further. On the other hand, the Egyptian President insisted on a further Israeli withdrawal at the southern end of the line, which he considered to be too close to the southern entry of the Suez Canal. He was also prepared to thin out Egyptian forces and firepower east of the canal beyond his previous suggestion, but not as much as Israel proposed. He was prepared to give private assurances that the canal would be reopened and the cities along it rebuilt, and he might even allow Israeli cargo to go through, but he would not explicitly commit Egypt to such steps as Israel demanded, because that would be a diminution of its sovereignty. Altogether, Kissinger felt that Sadat's position was substantively reconcilable with Israel's but that the Egyptian leader found it difficult to accept terms that were labeled "Israeli proposal." Such an act appeared to Sadat, and might be characterized by his opponents, as "yielding" to Israel.

To get around that difficulty, Kissinger proposed to incorporate the mutually agreed features of the Israeli and Egyptian positions in an "American proposal" for the disengagement of forces, and to put down the private assurances that Sadat was prepared to give in a "memorandum of understanding" between Egypt and the United States. The latter would serve as a basis for assurances that Kissinger, in turn, would give to the Israelis. Sadat agreed, and for the rest of the day Egyptians and Americans worked on drafting the "American proposal." Late in the evening, Kissinger was off again to Jerusalem.

That same night Kissinger briefed senior officials of the Israeli Foreign Ministry about the results of his mission to Aswan, and the next morning at 7:00 A.M. Israel's political leaders met to consider them. The idea of "American proposals," and especially Kissinger's triangular approach to the political quid pro quos that Israel demanded in exchange for withdrawal presented an important issue of principle. Israel had always insisted on a direct trade-off of political for territorial concessions because, like direct negotiations, it implied recognition of Israel and of the principle of give-and-take with it. However, in the face of Israel's own need for a prompt disengagement agreement and in view of the critical importance of preserving good relations with the United States, the Israeli government agreed that morning to the triangular approach and even welcomed it, just as it had previously favored Kissinger's intercession over the direct negotiations of Geneva. Under the test of reality, Israeli leaders were discovering that empirical adaptations were more helpful than abstract preconceptions.

The next sixteen hours witnessed feverish activity at a variety of levels as Kissinger conferred alternately with the Prime Minister, the negotiating team, and the foreign minister while the Prime Minister met alternately with her close advisers and the Cabinet and American-Israeli teams worked on details, formulations, and maps. The principal substantive issues at that stage were the forces and armaments that the sides would be allowed to deploy at their new front lines, and the size, composition, and mandate of the United Nations forces to be deployed in the buffer zone between the lines. Kissinger was able to satisfy Israel on some points and persuade it to yield on others, and he agreed to seek a modification of the Egyptian position on still other points. The next morning, January 16, he tied up some loose ends and was off again for Aswan for the third time. The indefatigable secretary of state spent some nine hours in the sunny temporary Egyptian capital and was back the same night in a storm-bound Jerusalem with most of the modifications he sought. The next morning he met with Meir and the last remaining problems were overcome. That afternoon the Israeli Cabinet met and unanimously approved the terms of the disengagement agreement.

The agreement was signed by the Egyptian and Israeli chiefs of staff on January 18, 1974, at kilometer 101 on the Cairo-Suez road—not in Geneva. It comprised four brief sections. Section A pledged the two sides to observe scrupulously the cease-fire and to abstain from all military or paramilitary (that is, guerrilla) action against each other. Section B divided the area between the Suez Canal and the western end of the Gidi and Mitla Passes into an Egyptian and an Israeli zone of limited forces separated by a zone of disengagement in which United Nations forces drawn from nonpermanent members of the Security Council were to be stationed. The zones of limited forces were to be open for inspection by United Nations forces, to which Israeli and Egyptian liaison officers were to be attached, and the air force of each country was to be permitted to operate without interference from the other up to its respective line. Section C provided for the application of the

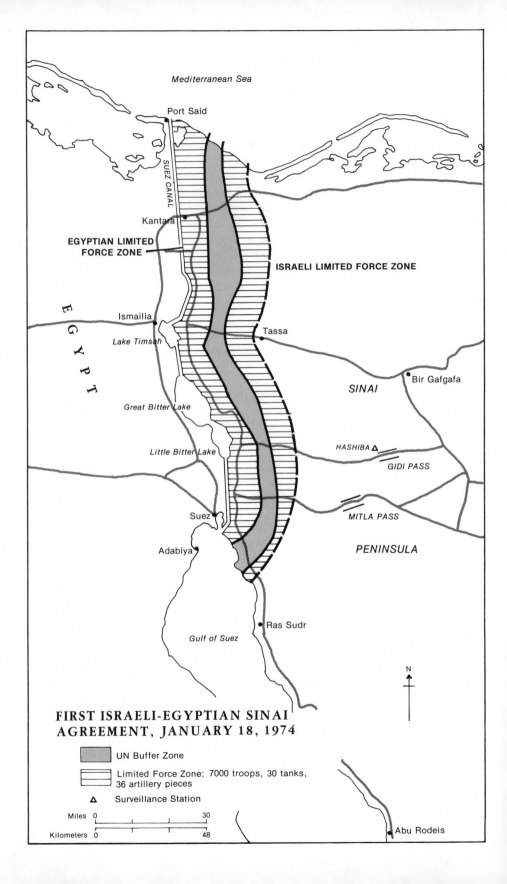

Mediterranean Sea

Port Said

SUEZ CANAL

Kantara

EGYPTIAN LIMITED FORCE ZONE

ISRAELI LIMITED FORCE ZONE

E G Y P T

Ismailia

Lake Timsah

Tassa

Great Bitter Lake

SINAI

Bir Gafgafa

Little Bitter Lake

HASHIBA △

GIDI PASS

MITLA PASS

Suez

Adabiya

PENINSULA

Gulf of Suez

Ras Sudr

N

**FIRST ISRAELI-EGYPTIAN SINAI
AGREEMENT, JANUARY 18, 1974**

UN Buffer Zone

Limited Force Zone: 7000 troops, 30 tanks,
36 artillery pieces

△ Surveillance Station

Miles 0   30

Kilometers 0   48

Abu Rodeis

agreement by stages to be worked out by military representatives of the two countries in accordance with a defined timetable, which set forty days for the completion of the entire process. Section D stated that neither country considered the agreement to be a final peace agreement. It rather defined it as "a step toward a final just and durable peace according to the prescriptions of Security Council Resolution 338 and within the frame of the Geneva Conference."

The details of the thinning out of forces and arms restrictions were spelled out in an addendum in the form of a letter from President Nixon to President Sadat and Prime Minister Meir which the two signed. This set a limit of 7,000 men, 30 tanks, and 36 artillery pieces on the forces that each side was permitted to deploy in its limited-forces zone. In addition, Egypt agreed not to deploy SAM antiaircraft missiles in an area reaching back twenty kilometers *west* of the Suez Canal.

Finally, the formal agreements were supplemented by a series of triangular and bilateral "memoranda of understanding," all involving the United States. In one set of memoranda, Egypt and Israel agreed to have American aircraft and satellites regularly monitor compliance with the provisions on the deployment of forces. In another, the United States indicated to Israel its understanding, on the basis of a memorandum it received from Egypt, that the blockade of Bab el Mandeb would be lifted, that Egypt would reopen the Suez Canal, allow Israeli cargo to pass through it, and rebuild the canal cities. In a third set, the United States reasserted its support for Israel in one note and in another promised Egypt help in clearing the Suez Canal and in rebuilding its economy. All these provisions, while not making the United States a formal guarantor of the agreement, certainly assured its involvement in case of serious violation by either side in the future. This began a process of increasing American engagement toward Israelis and Arabs that went parallel to the process of increasing Israeli-Arab disengagement from conflict.

For the United States and Israel, the Disengagement Agreement represented the first real attempt on the part of the two since the beginning of the Yom Kippur War to accommodate mutually their interests and aims. Unlike the Six Point Agreement, which was largely the result of unilateral American pressure, and unlike even the American airlift to Israel, which was undertaken on the basis of American calculations that differed greatly from what the Israelis assumed, the Disengagement Agreement was promoted by Kissinger on the basis of prior and concurrent thorough discussion of the overall situation, and explicit efforts to work out a political strategy apt to serve equally the American and the Israeli interest. Because of this, the agreement reversed the process of mistrust of the United States generally and of Kissinger in particular that had been taking place in Israel since the last days of October; and because of this, the achievement of one agreement helped prepare the ground for achieving another, much more difficult one.

Israeli-Syrian Disengagement; Greater American Engagement

The United States and Israel as well as Egypt were acutely interested in following the Egyptian-Israeli agreement with a similar accord between Syria and Israel. All three parties recognized that without a disengagement and separation of the Syrian and Israeli forces, the situation in the north could explode in a general war that could drag in Egypt and other Arab countries and undo everything achieved so far. Syria, too, was keenly interested in an agreement, if only because it feared that Egypt might go on to conclude a separate peace and leave it to face Israel by itself. However, despite this convergence of interests in a Syrian-Israeli accord, the difficulties of achieving one proved to be enormous and required many times the effort invested by Kissinger in achieving an Egyptian-Israeli agreement. Whereas the latter accord necessitated one week of preparatory talks and one week of shuttle diplomacy to bring about, the Syrian-Israeli agreement required more than a month to get the preparatory stage started, more than two months for the preparatory discussions, and fully twenty-seven days of shuttle diplomacy to consummate!

Kissinger began to prepare the ground for a Syrian-Israeli disengagement immediately after the signing of the Egyptian-Israeli agreement. On January 20, 1974, he flew to Damascus for a long meeting with President Assad and picked up the discussion where he had left it in mid-December, on the eve of the Geneva Conference. The United States, Kissinger argued, had shown its willingness and ability to persuade Israel to make significant withdrawals on the Egyptian front and was prepared to exert itself to the same end on the Syrian front; but, in order to get the negotiations going, it was essential that Syria should provide a list of the Israeli prisoners of war and permit Red Cross visits. Without this, there was no hope of engaging the Israeli government in talks. Assad remained as adamant as before that Israel must first submit a serious disengagement proposal and only then he would give the list and allow the visits. However, he agreed this time to send a Syrian representative to Washington to continue the discussion—the only indication of enhanced Syrian interest in the wake of the Egyptian-Israeli agreement.

It was more than five weeks before Kissinger was able to get the parties to agree to a formula that broke the deadlock on this very preliminary issue. Syria and Israel would simultaneously exchange documents through Secretary Kissinger; Syria would hand him a list of prisoners and its proposal for disengagement to transmit to Israel at the same time that he would receive from Israel for transmittal to Syria a proposal for disengagement. After receiving the Israeli document, the Syrians would allow visits to the prisoners by the Red Cross. On February 27, 1974, Kissinger flew personally to Jerusalem and Damascus to perform this transaction and to arrange for a follow-up to the negotiations in Washington.

In the plans exchanged, the Israelis proposed a disengagement and separation of forces to take place entirely within the bulge conquered by them in
the October War, wheras the Syrians demanded half the Golan. As in the case
of the Egyptian-Israeli disengagement, Kissinger tried to narrow the gap
between the two positions in discussions in Washington before going back to
the area for a final stage of intense exchanges; only this time he made very
little headway. He knew that Dayan favored ceding Kuneitra—the ruined
principal town of the Golan just within the prewar line—as an inducement to
the Syrians, and he tried again the gambit of getting Dayan to express that
view as his "private" idea. But this time the Israeli defense minister, his position at home greatly weakened, was not prepared to do so, and Kissinger had
to be content with his own estimate that such a concession on Israel's part
was achievable. This and the agreement of the two sides in late April 1974
that he should come to the area for another round of shuttle diplomacy was
all that the secretary of state was able to accomplish in two months of desul-
tory exchanges. In the meantime, incidents at the front line had developed
into a real war of attrition, in which artillery exchanges were gradually supplemented by encounters of ground troops, interventions by the air forces,
and air battles.

Three reasons accounted for the slowness and difficulty of the Syrian-
Israeli negotiations up to that point. In the first place, relations between Syria
and Israel had always been particularly bitter, and the fact that the Syrians
were using the Israeli prisoners of war and a war of attrition as their principal
bargaining cards only exacerbated the feelings of hostility. Second, the secretary of state did not initially attach the same degree of urgency to achieving a
Syrian-Israeli agreement as he had to an agreement between Egypt and Israel.
Until the war of attrition threatened to get out of hand, the configuration of
the cease-fire line on the Syrian front did not seem to be as menacing of war as
did the interpenetrating Egyptian and Israeli deployments. Moreover, Syria
did not appear to Kissinger to be as important and accessible a political prize
as Egypt. Most importantly perhaps, in early March, 1974, Kissinger
achieved his major immediate political objective without a Syrian agreement,
as the Arab states finally lifted the oil embargo against the United States. The
third reason was that Israel was caught during that period in a succession of
political storms that severely limited the capacity of its government to act on
anything. The acceleration of demobilization after the signing of the
Egyptian-Israeli agreement sparked new waves of demonstrations spearheaded by war veterans which demanded the resignation of Moshe Dayan.
Shortly after the defense minister yielded to the pressure, a storm broke out
inside the Labor Alignment over the old guard's hold on the leadership which
caused Golda Meir to give up her attempt to form a new postelection government. Then, after Meir came back and constituted a new government that included Moshe Dayan, the publication of the interim report of the Agranat

Commission on April 2, 1974, released another storm in the country at large as well as inside the Labor Alignment which brought about the final resignation of Meir and her government on April 11. Kissinger could not do much until the political winds began to subside after April 22, when Yitzhak Rabin was nominated by the Central Committee of the Labor Party to form the next government. As Rabin engaged in that complicated task and while the Meir government was acting in an interim capacity, Kissinger arrived to conduct his shuttle negotiations.

The basic situation confronting Kissinger at the outset of his mission was far less promising than the one he had faced at the beginning of the Egyptian-Israeli negotiations. To be sure, Israel wanted its prisoners of war back very badly and was anxious to turn its attention to healing the still raw wounds of the war; but militarily, it was not under the same pressure to reach an agreement as it had been on the eve of the Egyptian negotiations. Whereas the Israeli salient in the south was precarious and its defense required Israel to maintain a very onerous level of mobilization, the bulge in the north presented no special problems and could be held indefinitely if need be. Syria's leadership, for its part, wanted very much to recover the territory lost in 1973 and especially some of the territory lost in 1967 in order to vindicate its claim of victory in the war and justify the risks and sacrifices incurred; but, in the final account, the entire territory occupied by Israel was of no great practical importance to Syria and certainly bore no comparison with the enormous significance for Egypt of the Suez Canal and the canal zone. To wrest an agreement out of such a weak bargaining situation, Kissinger had to introduce substantial innovations in the strategy and tactics he had pursued in the previous shuttle. One key point in Kissinger's strategy was to exploit, now bluntly, now subtly, the uncertainty of Egypt's position in case of failure of the negotiations in order to press the Israelis and the Syrians to come forward. Before the Israelis, he repeatedly expressed his conviction that if no agreement with Syria were reached, the war of attrition would escalate into general war and Egypt would be forced to come in. The Soviets would then be back in Cairo, the entire world would gang up against Israel, and the United States would be hard pressed to take a distance from Israel—in short, everything accomplished so far would become unraveled and Israel would be far worse off. With the Syrians, however, he played on the suspicions they harbored that Egypt, backed by Saudi Arabia, Jordan, and other Arab countries, had made a deal with the United States for a separate settlement with Israel and would leave them in the lurch if matters came to war. Throughout the negotiations, Kissinger shuttled among the Arab capitals to keep friendly Arab leaders apprised of the situation and to urge them to intercede with Damascus, but this also helped nurture the suspicions of the Syrians.

While seeking to convey to the Israelis and the Syrians opposite impressions about the consequences of failure to reach an agreement, Kissinger himself apparently believed that a third outcome was possible between the two extremes. Twice in the course of his endeavors, for example, when it appeared that negotiations had come to a dead end, he began working on a formula for leaving the door open for another round of negotiations at a later date, which suggests that he thought postponement might forestall either of the "predictions" he sought to convey to the parties. The parties did not seem to detect the contradiction between his prognosis and his fallback position.

Besides taking advantage of the ambivalences of the "Egyptian connection" to add to the incentives of the parties to agree, Kissinger also found it necessary to increase considerably the American input into the negotiations. Apart from the obvious much greater investment of time and effort, the secretary modified his role in the negotiations subtly but significantly. Whereas in the Egyptian-Israeli negotiations he played primarily the role of intermediary, who transmitted and explained the parties' ideas to each other, in the Syrian-Israeli negotiations he slid increasingly into the role of moderator, who advocated strongly some of the positions he conveyed, and even of mediator, who advanced positions of his own. The shift in role was translated almost exclusively into additional pressure on Israel, but the pressure was mitigated by a climate of "arguing among friends" that Kissinger was able to maintain, thanks to the credit he had built up with the Israeli negotiators.

But the most important additional American input into the situation took the form of strong, written assurances offered to Israel to compensate it for concessions it was asked to make. These further converted the United States from being a broker of the agreements to being a party to them. One of the assurances was a promise by the secretary of state to try to place the supply of arms to Israel on a long-term instead of a year-to-year basis. Another, more important because it left the initiative in Israel's hands, was a commitment that the United States would support politically Israeli reaction against possible guerrilla action originating from Syrian territory. Virtually at the last moment, after agreement on all issues had been painfully worked out, the Syrians had objected to inclusion in the final draft of wording that would commit them to bar guerrilla action against Israel originating from their territory. Such wording had been included in the Egyptian-Israeli agreement, but Syria absolutely refused to agree formally "to act as a gendarme for Israel" against the Palestinians, even though in practice it always exercised strict control over action originating from its territory. Israel was equally vehement on the issue. Ten days before, in the very midst of the negotiations, Palestinian guerrillas infiltrating from Lebanon had undertaken an action in the village of Maalot which resulted in the death of twenty-four Israeli youngsters and the wounding of sixty-three, and a month or so before a similar action of theirs in Kiryat Shmona had resulted in many victims. To break the deadlock that threatened to undo the whole agreement, Kissinger gave Israel the crucial commitment. The secretary of state hoped that his move would help deter the kind of action Israel wanted barred, but he had no illusion about the Israeli reaction if the deterrent failed. Israel's response to Maalot and Kiryat Shmona with massive air raids against targets in Lebanon was fresh before his eyes.

The final agreement initialed on May 29, 1974, and formally signed in Geneva on May 31 followed the same general outlines as the Egyptian-Israeli agreement with a few sometimes significant differences. Israel was to withdraw from the entire salient captured in the October War plus Kuneitra and a few strips of territory conquered in 1967; a disengagement zone was to be created where United Nations troops were to be stationed; on either side of that zone two areas of thinned out and limited forces were to be created. Since, unlike the Egyptian-Israeli case, prisoners of war had not been exchanged prior to the disengagement, the agreement also included provisions for the consummation of that exchange.

The document included a clause to the effect that the agreement was a step toward a just and durable peace, but the wording was somewhat different from that of the Egyptian-Israeli agreement. The latter said, "This agreement is not regarded by Egypt and Israel as a final peace agreement," whereas the Syrian-Israeli document simply stated, "This is not a peace agreement." The former went on to say that the agreement was a first step toward "a *final*, just and durable peace *according* to the provisions of . . . 338 (emphasis added)"; the latter did not include the word *final* and said "on the basis of . . . 338" instead of "according to." The Egyptian agreement added after 338 "and within the framework of the Geneva Conference"; the Syrian agreement omitted that addition. On the other hand, the Syrian-Israeli agreement was formally signed in Geneva, whereas the Egyptian-Israeli was signed at kilometer 101. Finally, whereas the Egyptian-Israeli agreement was negotiated and concluded in a way that completely excluded the Soviets, the latter were associated symbolically in the Syrian-Israeli agreement. Besides the fact that it was signed in Geneva, Foreign Minister Gromyko made an appearance in Damascus in the course of the negotiations and went on to Cyprus for consultations with Kissinger.

The Syrian-Israeli agreement was universally viewed at the time as a turning point in the Arab-Israeli conflict, away from war and toward peace. Even the PLO, which had done its best to wreck the negotiations through outrageous provocations as in Maalot and Kiryat Shmona, believed for a moment that a peace settlement had become inevitable and prepared itself to join the bandwagon. The Palestinian National Council, the PLO's representative assembly, met in Cairo in July 1974 and decided, among other things, to establish Palestinian "national authority" in any piece of "liberated" territory, thus enabling the organization to play a role in a possible disengagement in the West Bank.

For the United States, the agreement seemed to consummate a miracu-

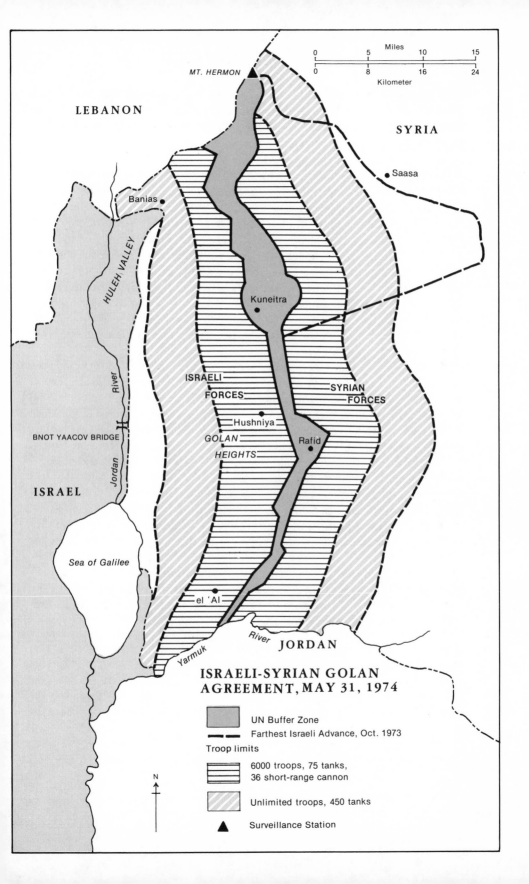

Miles
0   5   10   15
0   8   16   24
Kilometer

MT. HERMON

LEBANON

SYRIA

Saasa

Banias

HULEH VALLEY

River

Kuneitra

ISRAELI
FORCES

SYRIAN
FORCES

BNOT YAACOV BRIDGE

Jordan

Hushniya

GOLAN

Rafid

HEIGHTS

ISRAEL

Sea of Galilee

el 'Al

Yarmuk   River   JORDAN

ISRAELI-SYRIAN GOLAN
AGREEMENT, MAY 31, 1974

UN Buffer Zone

Farthest Israeli Advance, Oct. 1973

Troop limits

6000 troops, 75 tanks,
36 short-range cannon

Unlimited troops, 450 tanks

Surveillance Station

N

lous turnabout in its Middle Eastern and international position. A few
months before, as its Middle East policy came crashing down in war, the
United States confronted an oil embargo, the prospect of entrenched hostility
of all the Arab countries, Soviet predominance in the Middle East, defection
of Western Europe and breakdown of NATO solidarity, end of détente, reversion to the Cold War, and enhanced chances of superpower confrontation. Now, in the spring and early summer of 1974, the Middle East seemed
to be coming under a pax Americana and the international position of the
United States seemed better than it had been before the crises. Not only were
traditionally friendly Arab countries brought back into the fold, but also formerly hostile countries, which had not even had diplomatic relations with the
United States since 1967, were turned into willing partners or cooperating interlocutors. Soviet influence in the area and Soviet capacity for mischief-
making were greatly reduced, and Western Europe began to recognize that
the remedy to its demonstrated vulnerability to oil pressure lay in part in
greater cooperation with the United States rather than in taking greater distance from it.

Many factors combined to make this brilliant reversal of fortunes possible, not the least of which was the personality of the American secretary of
state. But perhaps the most important ingredient was the success of the
United States in conveying to the Arab side *at one and the same time* the sense
that it was able to move Israel and that such a feat was by no means easy. That
double impression set limits on the expectations of the Arabs from the United
States and disposed them to make concessions as well as to seek them; at the
same time, it caused them to appreciate the contribution of the United States
to the achievement of agreement and to understand, rather than resent, whatever compensations it provided Israel in order to overcome its resistance.

For the United States and Israel, the Syrian negotiations were a far more
stringent test than the Egyptian of their ability to adjust their respective conceptions, priorities, and immediate interests in a manner that served their
shared overall objectives. The successful outcome showed that the adjustment could be accomplished, but the labor and difficulties entailed in the
process showed, or at least should have shown, that further successful adaptation was not to be taken for granted.

26
Faltering Steps, Reassessment, Realignment, Pause, June 1974–May 1977

Kissinger's achievements up to that point, for all their vital importance, were still largely precarious. They had turned a potentially disastrous situation for the United States into one that held brilliant prospects and had fashioned in the process a structure of relationships that favored the realization of those prospects. However, nothing that was accomplished was secure against reversal, and everything depended on further forward movement. Kissinger realized that and endeavored to maintain the diplomatic momentum after the Syrian agreement by seeking a Jordanian-Israeli agreement and then attempting a diplomatic expedition to achieve a second Egyptian-Israeli agreement. However, several developments combined to defeat both endeavors and put in question his entire design and all his achievements up to that point.

Some of these developments had to do with the emergence of a new group of leaders in Israel and with changes in Israel's objective position in the wake of the conclusion of the Egyptian and Syrian disengagement agreements. Although other developments contributed to the failure of Kissinger's endeavors, including the resignation of President Nixon, changes in inter-Arab politics, and an incipient Soviet-Egyptian rapprochement, the secretary of state initially pinned the responsibility on Israel and relations between the two countries plunged into a subdued but real crisis which lasted several months. The crisis drove home to both sides the extent to which the pursuit of their respective interests depended on mutual accommodation, and this, coupled with changes in Sadat's perception of his own position largely related to the crisis, made possible the conclusion through Kissinger's mediation of a second Egyptian-Israeli agreement. As with the previous agreements, the successful conclusion of what came to be known as the Sinai II Agreement required a substantial American input. This time, however, the input was so extensive that it made the United States a virtual guarantor of the Middle East peace and turned the American-Israeli relationship into a virtual alliance.

Disagreement on Jordan

Barely two weeks after he returned to Washington from his month-long Syrian-Israeli mediation, Kissinger was back in the Middle East. His mission this time was to accompany President Nixon on a triumphal tour of the scene of his accomplishments which the President thought might help him stem the tide of Watergate. However, the secretary took advantage of the occasion to start promoting a disengagement agreement between Israel and Jordan. Already in January 1974, after the conclusion of the Egyptian-Israeli agreement, Jordan's King Hussein and Prime Minister Zeid Rifai had presented to Kissinger a map for a proposed Jordanian-Israeli disengagement which envisaged an Israeli phased withdrawal of eight to ten kilometers from the Jordan River, demilitarization of the area, and United Nations presence. Kissinger had transmitted the proposal to Israel and was inclined to pursue it at the time because it seemed to him to offer relatively better prospects of success than a Syrian-Israeli disengagement. However, both Israel and Egypt gave a much higher priority to a Syrian agreement, and Kissinger went along, promising King Hussein to take up the matter later on. Now, after the Syrian agreement, Kissinger suggested to the Israelis that the time had come for an agreement with Jordan and enlisted President Nixon's weight, which counted very heavily in their eyes, to support his suggestion.

Kissinger felt he needed to use presidential as well as other pressures on Israel because he realized by then that the Jordanian-Israeli situation was not very promising—not because it was too problematic but because it did not present enough problems for the two parties! King Hussein did need an agreement badly to keep alive his claim to speak for the West Bank and on behalf of its population in the face of a mounting PLO challenge, but Israel was under no pressure to make any partial deal with the King. It had no large forces entangled on the Jordanian front as it had had on the Egyptian, nor was it engaged in any war of attrition with Jordan as it had been with Syria. Jordan had taken only a limited part in the war on the Syrian front, and its participation had raised no issue of prisoners or new territorial problems. True, Israel had some interest in keeping King Hussein as the interlocutor for the West Bank and forestalling PLO assumption of that role, but its new leaders were not altogether convinced of the imminence of that danger and were divided as to the best tactics to meet that problem as well as the entire future of the West Bank.

Underlying the division in the government was, of course, the fact that many Israelis considered the West Bank—Judea and Samaria—to be an integral part of the national homeland which must be retained in its entirety, while many others thought that substantial parts of it, including particularly most of the strip along the Jordan River, had to be kept under Israeli control for reasons of security. Further complicating the situation, Prime Minister

Rabin had, rather gratuitously, tied his own hands by committing his government to go to the country before finally concluding any agreement involving the surrender of any West Bank territory. Several months before, Meir had given such a commitment while trying to form a government in order to draw the religious parties into the coalition and undercut the demand being voiced at the time for an all-inclusive national government; Rabin had automatically reiterated Meir's commitment even though his government did not include the religious parties. In view of the very high emotions attached to the issue, the fact that the Labor party itself was divided on it, and that the government rested on a very slim majority; and considering, on the other hand, that Rabin was a completely new, untested, and not yet popular political leader, who lacked any personal charisma and persuasive power with the public, the chances were high that if Rabin went to the country with a Jordanian disengagement agreement he, and the Labor party, might fail to be returned to power.

Kissinger and the President left Israel with a commitment from its government only to study the whole Jordanian question; yet, in Amman, the Americans told King Hussein that his turn for a disengagement had finally come. Kissinger did not yet understand Rabin's problem and thought that a certain amount of gentle pressure and persuasion would bring him around. The secretary must therefore have been surprised to see Rabin maneuver in the following weeks on behalf of another agreement with Egypt and steer his Cabinet toward making a decision, on July 21, 1974, to "act for negotiations for a peace agreement with Jordan." The decision was a formal acknowledgment of the United States' interest in Jordan but was in effect meaningless, since it was clear that King Hussein was not ready to assent to Israel's minimal demands for a comprehensive peace agreement and vice versa. The Israeli leaders knew this from their many secret meetings with the King over the years, and because only a few months before he *had,* in fact, turned down a comprehensive settlement proposal based on the Allon Plan, submitted to him by Israel.

At the end of July 1974 Foreign Minister Yigal Allon went to Washington for a general review of the situation and determination of the next diplomatic moves. Kissinger strongly criticized the decision of the Israeli Cabinet and warned that, by not agreeing to take a step with Hussein now, Rabin was making it impossible in the future to talk to the King about anything because the PLO would become the only interlocutor. He cautioned Allon that an agreement with Egypt would not be easy and raised before him the spectre of reconvening the Geneva Conference, where Israel would come under heavy pressure to return to the pre-1967 lines on all fronts. Allon, for his part, explained to the secretary of state Rabin's dilemma and the danger that a premature election, before the Prime Minister had had a chance to consolidate his political position, could well result in a Likkud-dominated government, which would foreclose the chance of any settlement at all with Jordan. Allon suggested that he personally favored an interim agreement with Jordan and pleaded for time to find a way out. In the end, it was agreed that Rabin himself would come to Washington in early September to continue the discussion, and that in the meantime the United States would consult Israel before making any additional move on Jordan.

Before Rabin got to Washington, President Nixon finally broke down under the weight of Watergate and resigned, and Kissinger lost a very valuable buttress for his Middle East policy. Nixon had enjoyed a very high standing and influence with the Israelis, and Kissinger had skillfully used him to intervene at crucial moments to overcome difficulties in his dealings with the Israeli government. The secretary had been particularly hopeful about the prospects of Nixon's influence with Rabin, because of the special relationship that had developed between the two from the days when they together handled successfully the Jordanian crisis of 1970. Nixon's departure upset this expectation as it did many other things.

The prospects of Rabin's talks were also marred by an incident that proved to be the first manifestation of a basic incongruence in the operating styles of the secretary of state and the new Israeli Prime Minister. In mid-August 1974 King Hussein visited the United States and held talks with President Gerald Ford and Secretary Kisssinger, at the conclusion of which a joint statement was issued that said, "It was agreed that consultation between the United States and Jordan will continue, in order to take up at an early and convenient date problems that are of special concern to Jordan, including an Israeli-Jordanian agreement for a disengagement of forces." Kissinger clearly intended the statement to provide Hussein with as much support as possible to help him face the challenge of the PLO, and to put some pressure on Israel on behalf of disengagement while keeping all options open. Rabin, on the other hand, viewed the statement as a breach of the promise given by Kissinger to Allon only a few weeks before to consult Israel before making any move on Jordan, and was particularly aghast at the specific mention of disengagement. He reacted by making public statements scornfully denying the urgency of the Jordan problem ("Hussein won't run away") and forcefully reiterating the priority of an Egyptian agreement, which clearly committed him on issues that were still under discussion.

In Washington, in September, Kissinger tried to enlist the prestige of the new President and the fact that he had just responded favorably to a massive Israeli arms request to induce Rabin to change his position on Jordan; but Rabin stood his ground, and would only agree to keeping open the discussion of the Jordanian as well as the Egyptian options. Kissinger was to come to the area the following month to see what could be done on the spot.

Kissinger's October 1974 trip proved to be a total failure as far as the Jordanian question was concerned. In Jerusalem he tried hard to advance various ideas for a disengagement but, in the face of strong resistance, was forced to content himself with an agreement to continue the discussion in Washington in December. In Cairo he pleaded with Sadat for support for King Hussein at the forthcoming Arab summit in Rabbat and received the Egyptian President's promise to do his best. Kissinger's aim at that point was simply to keep the Jordanian option open at both the Arab and Israeli ends in the hope that time might provide the opportunity to activate it, but that aim was decisively defeated at the Rabbat Arab summit two weeks later. In the face of seemingly equally theoretical claims by Hussein and the PLO for responsibility for recovering the lost Palestinian territories, the summit decided unanimously to divest Hussein of any role and to invest it all in the PLO, which was recognized as the sole legitimate representative of the Palestinian people. This decision paved the way for the recognition of the PLO by the United Nations and the formal appearance of its leader before the General Assembly not long after, and killed *any* Jordanian option for any foreseeable time. Rabin had prevailed over Kissinger, but only at a cost that Kissinger had predicted Israel would have to pay.

Falling Out of Step on Egypt

The collapse of the Jordanian option automatically brought the alternative of a partial Egyptian-Israeli agreement to the center of attention of all the three parties directly concerned. American policy and everything it had achieved so far depended on continuous motion, and a second Sinai accord now offered the only prospect of movement under American control. The Rabbat summit had implicitly endorsed a different approach by enjoining the Arab confrontation countries against making any separate political agreements, but that made it all the more necessary for the United States to pursue an Egyptian-Israeli partial accord. A comprehensive, Geneva-type conference had no chance of even getting started because of the problem of PLO representation, and the mere attempt to convene one at that time would play into the hands of the Soviets and undermine the leading role that the United States had assumed.

For Sadat, too, another partial agreement had a great deal of appeal notwithstanding the Rabbat injunction. He had been severely criticized, discreetly at home and loudly in the Arab countries, for relying excessively on the United States and for allowing himself to be persuaded by it to trade off the assets gained by the Arabs in the October War for some minor returns. He needed another substantial Israeli withdrawal mediated by the United States in order to rebut his critics and vindicate his policy. Moreover, since the execution of the disengagement agreement, Egypt had proceeded energetically to clear the Suez Canal, rebuild the canal cities, and return to them many of the one million refugees that had left them, as part of a general effort to turn the canal zone into a takeoff platform for the moribund Egyptian economy. These developments represented a clear and substantial diminution of Egypt's option for war, and Sadat wanted an equally visible if not equally substantive reduction of Israel's option by having it give up the strategic Sinai passes.

For Israel a move with Egypt was diplomatically inevitable since Rabin had been urging it for some time in preference to a Jordanian disengagement. Beyond that, however, such a move fitted into a comprehensive conception that Rabin had developed as a guide for his policies and actions in the years ahead. As he was to expound it in an interview with a correspondent of *Haaretz* on December 3, 1974, that conception started from the premise that Arab oil power, Europe's economic dependence on oil, and the continuing rivalry of the superpowers in the Middle East had created an international constellation that was highly unfavorable for Israel. That constellation, however, was not permanent. Within seven years at the most, it was apt to change as Europe and the United States reduced their dependence on Arab oil. Israel's objective should therefore be to gain time and endeavor to emerge "safe and sound" from those "seven lean years." The realization of that objective in the existing circumstances suggested a number of instrumental aims, including cooperation with the United States in the step-by-step approach to peace, trying to weaken the Egyptian-Syrian military link, and preventing Egypt's return to the Soviet sphere of influence. The pursuit of these aims in the aftermath of Rabat indicated that Israel should seek another agreement with Egypt, and should be prepared to pay a certain price to get it.

It will have been noticed that the main elements of Rabin's conception were virtually identical to the concepts that Kissinger had tirelessly preached to the Israeli leaders on many occasions over the previous year or so. That much conceptual sharing had developed between the United States and Israel, or at least between the American secretary of state and the Israeli Prime Minister. However, Rabin also introduced several modifications and refinements that Kissinger did not share and which were to be the source of some difficulty between the two. One was that Rabin believed Syria to be fundamentally opposed to peace, by stages or otherwise, and therefore wanted to drive a wedge between it and Egypt and place himself in a favorable position to deal with it forcefully. Another was that he applied the imperative of gaining time across the board to include the United States and meant to keep the pace of the step-by-step movement as slow as possible. A third was that he was determined to ration the price Israel had to pay to buy time and other advantages in a much more precise and specific way than the secretary of state anticipated.

Kissinger had begun preliminary explorations of a possible Egyptian-Israeli agreement several months before Rabat. However, throughout that period his heart had been set on a Jordanian agreement, and he had discussed the Egyptian alternative mainly because the Israelis were constantly advancing it and because he thought he might bring them around to his view if he could show them that an Egyptian agreement was not so simple as they imagined. Now, after the Arab summit, Kissinger took the initiative into his own hands and began to look earnestly for a way to an agreement. His first move was to go to Cairo in November 1974 to explore Sadat's position and intentions.

Kissinger discovered that the Egyptian President was willing to attempt another accord with Israel despite the Rabbat injunction against separate political agreements. However, in order to defend his defiance of the injunction before the Egyptian and Arab public, Sadat insisted on two points: he wanted the Israelis to evacuate the Sinai passes and hand over to him the Abu Rodeis oil fields, on the Sinai shore of the Gulf of Suez; and he wanted the agreement to have a purely military character, at least in appearance, involving no overt political concession to Israel. Sadat viewed the very fact that he was willing to make a separate partial deal with Israel through the United States as ample concession for what he asked for, and he backed up his view with the threat to go to Geneva otherwise and to bring the Soviets back into the picture. The Egyptian President had been concerned that the fall of President Nixon might entail a diminished American willingness or ability to "deliver" Israel and had intensified his attempts to patch up his relations with the Soviet Union. As a result of these efforts Party Secretary Brezhnev was due to visit Cairo in January 1975.

Early in December 1974 Foreign Minister Allon presented to Secretary Kissinger and President Ford Israel's position. He delivered the outlines of a proposal for submission to Egypt that included a public commitment by Egypt to end the state of belligerency, demilitarization of the areas to be evacuated by Israel, and other specific terms, the effect of which would be to take Egypt out of the war legally and practically. In exchange, Israel was prepared to withdraw thirty to fifty kilometers along various parts of the front but without giving up the passes and the oil fields. Allon explained that the proposal was only an opening bid and asked Kissinger to convey that impression to Sadat. Kissinger, however, refrained from doing so and the result was, as he expected, that Sadat turned it down promptly and categorically.

Kissinger did not bother to soften the Israeli proposal partly because he wanted to impress Sadat with the toughness of Israel's position in order to get all the more credit for whatever changes he could induce it to make. But the principal reason was that Israel's formal proposal seemed to have been invalidated by none other than Israel's Prime Minister. On December 3, 1974, Rabin gave the *Haaretz* interview referred to above. Besides revealing his objective of gaining time, his interest in splitting Egypt and Syria, and his willingness to pay a price for the mere conclusion of a limited agreement with Egypt, Rabin had gone out of his way to suggest that "nonbelligerency" was not essential and that any other political commitment by Egypt might acceptably be given to the United States, rather than to Israel. In giving short shrift to Israel's formal proposal, Kissinger knew, as did Sadat, that more "reasonable" Israeli proposals would be forthcoming.

The damage caused to Israel's negotiating position by Rabin's extraordinary disclosures was compounded by Allon's effort to repair it by reconciling Rabin's terms with those of the proposal he submitted. Allon argued in effect that Israel defined its position in terms of a sliding scale, with what it was prepared to give being dependent on what Egypt was prepared to give in return. What Rabin was speaking about was a limited agreement involving modest concessions in exchange for modest returns, whereas the proposal he submitted envisaged a more ambitious trade-off. Allon conceded that the proposal may not have been sufficiently balanced, but he gave it as his "private opinion" that if Egypt was prepared to agree to nonbelligerency, Israel would be prepared to give up the passes and the oil fields. To Kissinger, and perhaps to Sadat too, the subtleties of sliding scale and implicit contest appeared to be quite secondary; what mattered was that the Israeli Prime Minister seemed to be willing to forego nonbelligerency, and the foreign minister the passes and the oil fields.

The impression was further strengthened when in the following month Allon appeared again in Washington with an invitation to Kissinger to come to the area himself to conduct "exploratory talks" with the parties. The Israeli government had authorized that step partly for fortuitous reasons (Allon had to be in the States to launch the annual United Jewish Appeal campaign and he needed to have something to tell the secretary of state whom he could not fail to call on), partly because it realized that the multiple positions taken by Israel—the sliding scale—had caused some confusion all around and needed straightening out. Kissinger, however, understood the invitation differently. He had repeatedly and forcefully conveyed to the Israelis his conviction that an agreement was possible only if they were prepared to give up the passes and the oil fields in exchange for "elements" of nonbelligerency but no formal declaration of such. Since they invited him to come to the area and conduct talks, he concluded that this could only be because they were prepared to come around to his position. Believing an agreement to be within reach, he decided to make the "exploratory trip" an explicit prelude to another round of shuttle diplomacy, and announced the former for February 10, 1975, and the latter for early March.

After five days in the Middle East, during which he held discussions in Israel, Egypt, Israel again, Syria, Jordan, and Saudi Arabia, Kissinger realized that the gap between Israel and Egypt had not narrowed at all, and that, if anything, his trip seemed to have brought to the fore problems he had not anticipated. Nevertheless, having already committed himself to a shuttle in March, he put a brave front on the inconclusiveness of his February expedition and claimed that it helped prepare the ground for a solution.

The mere announcement of Kissinger's two-phased expedition had led the Soviets, the Syrians, and the PLO to intensify their pressure on Egypt not to conclude another separate agreement with Israel and to seek instead a re-convening of the Geneva Conference. This had led Sadat not only to reem-phasize publicly that he would only contemplate a military agreement with Israel, but also to commit himself to linking the envisaged agreement with a similar agreement between Israel and Syria. Kissinger in turn had tried to assuage the apprehensions of the Soviets, the Syrians, and others by stating that the Egyptian-Israeli agreement would be followed by a reconvening of the Geneva forum. But the Israeli negotiatiors, for whom buying time and the hope of separating Egypt from Syria and the PLO were among the principal attractions of an agreement with Egypt, viewed the linkage with either Geneva or with a Syrian agreement as unacceptable and emphatically rejected it in their first meeting with Kissinger. In addition, the Israelis outlined clearly their sliding scale concept and insisted that for any extent of Israeli with-drawal Egypt had to make public concessions in return, not mere under-standings whispered to the United States.

In Egypt Kissinger found Sadat to be as intent as ever on getting nothing less than the passes and the oil fields, and no less opposed to a formal ending of belligerency as long as Israel occupied any Arab territory. He was prepared to discuss other possible means by which Egypt could make its policy of peaceful intentions more explicit, such as giving assurances to the United States, but such assurances would have to be contigent on continuing progress toward an overall settlement and would be invalid if Israel should refuse to follow up with agreements on other fronts. Thus, the February expe-dition yielded no progress except an improved understanding of positions and issues by Kissinger and the parties themselves, and that understanding showed that the gap between Egypt and Israel was wider than had been sup-posed by all before the secretary of state's visit.

In the interim between the exploratory trip and the shuttle, Kissinger de-cided that the first step in his forthcoming mission should be to try to find out the general extent of the concessions that Egypt was prepared to make in ex-change for the passes and the oil fields. He assumed that Egypt would not grant, and Israel would not ultimately insist on, a formal declaration of non-belligerency; the specific objective he set for himself was to try to work out a package of elements of nonbelligerency that would be sufficiently substantial to satisfy Israel yet disconnected enough to meet the Egyptian objection to ending the state of war while Israel remained in occupation of Arab territory. This conception did not pay sufficient attention to the importance of the re-lated factors of linkage and time for Israel and proved to be altogether too simple in fact.

Kissinger began his shuttle with a trip to Aswan on March 8, 1975, in which he was able to obtain Sadat's agreement to two important points of principle. In exchange for Kissinger's assurance that an Egyptian-Israeli agreement would be followed by a Syrian move or an initiative aiming at Geneva, Sadat agreed to drop any formal linking of the agreement under negotiation to those other questions. Also, contrary to the position Egypt had previously taken, Sadat now agreed to the principle of making a political gesture to Israel itself in exchange for what he wanted to get. The next day Kissinger went to Jerusalem and tried to obtain the Israelis' agreement in principle to exchanging the passes and the oil fields for elements of nonbelligerency, but the negotiating team (composed of Rabin, Allon, and Peres) told him that it was authorized by the Cabinet to agree only to a more limited withdrawal, and that before it could discuss the kind of withdrawal Kissinger was asking, it needed to know specifically how far Egypt was willing to go. To help Kissinger find out the answer, the Israeli negotiators gave him a list of possible elements of nonbelligerency which included: movement of third parties between Israeli and Egyptian territories, direct transit of air and maritime traffic between ports of the two sides, abstention from hostile propaganda, suspension of economic boycott, joint Egyptian-Israeli commissions to supervise the agreement, fulfillment of all commitments assumed in the previous disengagement agreement, allowing Israelis to serve on crews of ships moving through the Suez Canal, and so on.

In the next few days, Kissinger tried to work out the best package of elements that could be obtained from Egypt but found it difficult to get the Egyptians to move as far as he thought possible without being able to tell them explicitly what territory they would receive. So, at the end of the first week, he insisted that the Israelis state their willingness to give up the passes and the oil fields. The Israelis obliged, but, to Kissinger's surprise, they firmly insisted on a nonbelligerency declaration plus the elements of it in return. Sadat rejected Israel's demand but made some further minor concessions to keep the negotiations going.

By March 19 Kissinger confronted the Israelis with what he thought was the best package he could achieve and urged them to agree. The package included the following elements in exchange for the passes and the oil fields: A joint "nonuse of force" document would say that the conflict between Egypt and Israel could not be solved by military means but only by diplomacy. Egypt would not resort to threats of use of force and would settle the dispute with Israel by negotiations and other peaceful means for the duration of the agreement. The agreement would remain in effect until superseded by another agreement—Kissinger told the Israelis they could expect the accord to last for two years. The Egyptians would reaffirm the language of the January 1974 disengagement agreement pledging nonuse of military or paramilitary action. The mandate of the United Nations peacekeeping force would be renewed every year instead of every six months as at present. The Egyptian forces would move a few miles eastward, but would not enter the passes, which would be placed under United Nations control. Kissinger also reported that the Egyptians, as a gesture, would relax the economic boycott against five American companies that do business with Israel, and that Sadat promised to look for ways to tone down anti-Israel propaganda.

The negotiating team took the package and Kissinger's recommendation to the full Cabinet. After deliberations that lasted for fourteen hours, the Cabinet came out with a counterproposal: in exchange for the package offered, Israel would withdraw its forces only halfway through the passes, except for an electronic early warning station, and would transfer the oil fields as an enclave to the Egyptians. The withdrawal proposal was explained to Kissinger in a way that left open the possibility of bargaining on the distance of the pullback, if the electronic warning station was accepted. Kissinger took the offer to Sadat and returned on March 21 with a completely negative reply. Unless the Israelis were to change their mind, Kissinger pointed out, failure of the negotiations was certain.

In a last-minute effort to save his mission Kissinger resorted to a device he had used with success more than once before. On March 21, 1975, the President of the United States sent Rabin a very tough message in which he warned the Prime Minister that if Kissinger's mission failed because of Israel's refusal to be more flexible, there would be a drastic "reassessment" of American policy and American-Israeli relations would suffer as a result. This time, however, the presidential intervention boomeranged. Rabin upbraided Kissinger for trying to apply pressure on Israel, and when Kissinger denied having anything to do with the President's message, Rabin told him flatly that he did not believe it. Rabin then summoned the Cabinet for an emergency session for the next day, although it was the Sabbath, to formulate Israel's response, while Kissinger went off on a visit to Massada.

The Cabinet supported the negotiating team and reaffirmed its refusal to give up the passes in their entirety in the absence of nonbelligerency. In order to avoid responsibility for saying that final no, it offered to give up some northern part of Sinai and to allow a United Nations road to connect the oil fields with the Egyptian positions, but Kissinger did not bother to take the new proposals to Egypt. He communicated them by telephone and, as he expected, received a final Egyptian refusal.

In the evening of Saturday, March 22, 1975, Kissinger had two relatively short final meetings with the Israeli negotiating team. Excerpts of the exchanges that took place were subsequently leaked by State Department sources to an American journalist, Edward Sheehan. Because they convey the drama of the meetings, sum up Kissinger's thinking neatly, and touch upon the principal concerns of the Israelis, they are worth citing at length.

Allon: We'd still like to negotiate an interim or overall agreement, but not on the basis of an ultimatum from the other side.

Kissinger: There was no ultimatum. In the absence of new Israeli ideas, we received no new Egyptian ideas.

We have no illusions. The Arab leaders who banked on the United

States will be discredited. Step-by-step has been throttled for Jordan, then for Egypt. We're losing control.

We'll now see the Arabs working on a united front. There will be more emphasis on the Palestinians and there will be a linkage between moves in the Sinai and on Golan. The Soviets will step back onto the stage . . . The Europeans will have to accelerate their relations with the Arabs.

If the interim agreement in 1971 had succeeded there would have been no war in October 1973. The same process is at work here. We just don't have a strategy for the situation ahead. Our past strategy was worked out carefully, and now we don't know what to do.

There will be pressures to drive a wedge between Israel and the United States, not because we want that, but because it will be the dynamic of the situation. Let's not kid ourselves. We've failed.

Allon: Why not start up again in a few weeks?

Kissinger: Things aren't going to be the same again. The Arabs won't trust us as they have in the past. We look weak—in Vietnam, Turkey, Portugal, in a whole range of things. Don't misunderstand me. I'm analyzing the situation with friends. One reason I and my colleagues are so exasperated is that we see a friend damaging himself for reasons which will seem trivial five years from now—like 700 Egyptian soldiers across the canal in 1971.

I don't see how there can be another American initiative in the near future. We may have to go to Geneva for a multilateral effort with the Soviets—something which for five years we've felt did not offer the best hope for success . . .

Allon: The Egyptians really didn't give very much.

Kissinger: An agreement would have enabled the United States to remain in control of the diplomatic process. Compared to that, the location of the line eight kilometers one way or the other frankly does not seem very important. And you got the "non-use of force." The elements you didn't get—movement of peoples, ending of the boycott—are unrelated to your line . . .

Peres: It is a question not just of the passes, but of our military (intelligence) installations that have no offensive purpose and are necessary. The previous government could not overcome the psychological blow that the Syrians and the Egyptians launched a surprise attack. We need an early warning system. We need 12 hours of warning. Under the proposed agreement we'd have only six. If there had been any Egyptian concessions regarding the duration of the agreement and the warning system, then what you've said would be very touching. But then we would have faced new negotiations with Syria . . .

Kissinger: This is a real tragedy. We've attempted to reconcile our support for you with our other interests in the Middle East, so that you wouldn't have to make your decisions all at once. Our strategy was to save you from dealing with all those pressures all at once. If we wanted the 1967 borders we could do it with all of world opinion and considerable domestic opinion behind us. The strategy was designed to protect you from this. We've avoided drawing up an overall plan for a global settlement.

I see pressure building up to force you back to the 1967 borders; compared to that 10 kilometers is trivial. I'm not angry at you, and I'm not asking you to change your position. It's tragic to see people dooming themselves to a course of unbelievable peril.

Rabin (wryly): This is the day you visited Massada.

As soon as Kissinger returned to Washington, a bitter controversy developed within and between the United States and Israel over the question of who was responsible for the failure of Kissinger's third shuttle. This analysis suggests that the fiasco was the result of a combination of three factors: the circumstances affecting the inclinations of Egypt and Israel, the development of divergences in conception between Rabin and Kissinger over secondary policy objectives, and mistakes of tactics and judgment on the part of the Israeli leaders and the secretary of state. Both Egypt and Israel had a strong interest in a second agreement; however, unlike the situation at the time of the first agreement, neither party was under any specific pressure to reach one just then, or had any particular reason to fear risking the failure of that particular round of negotiations. This encouraged inflexibility on both sides, which was, naturally, inimical to compromise and accord. The situation was rendered more difficult by the fact that Prime Minister Rabin had actually developed a conception which, starting from the premises and overview that Kissinger had strongly impressed on the previous government, went off to deduce guidelines that put a high premium on delaying the achievement of any agreement that did not effectively take Egypt out of the war. Conceivably, Rabin and Kissinger might have been able to adjust and reconcile their different guidelines if they had engaged in the kind of extensive dialogue that the secretary was wont to have with former Prime Minister Meir. However, Rabin's personality and the distribution of power among the new Israeli leadership team made that kind of discussion difficult. That Rabin chose to air his views in public only made matters worse and almost forced Kissinger to act in a manner that stressed his dissociation from them to preserve his own credibility with the Arab side. In addition, the Israeli leadership erred by adopting the complicated sliding scale negotiating position, and then speaking of different options with different voices at different times. This gave rise to a certain amount of confusion about what Israel would eventually accept, which Kissinger wrongly sought to exploit rather than clarify. The secretary gambled on the notion that once the Israelis were committed to another shuttle, they would be unwilling to risk being charged with the responsibility for its failure. In this, as in his last-minute effort to save the situation by invoking blunt presidential pressure, he proved to have miscalculated the odds.

Reassessment and Realignment

One day after Kissinger returned to Washington, President Ford made a solemn public announcement that he had ordered a "total reassessment" of United States policy toward the Middle East. One reason behind the President's announcement was simply the desire to gain time. The collapse of Kissinger's mission created an atmosphere of crisis that could precipitate rash moves by one party or another, starting perhaps with Egypt or Syria making problems in connection with the renewal of the mandate of the United Nations forces, due to expire in April on the Egyptian front and in May on the Syrian. The announcement sought to forestall such developments by telling all concerned that the United States, the acknowledged key actor in the situation, needed some time before coming up with some fresh approach.

Another reason had to do with American-Israeli relations specifically. Although before boarding his plane for home Kissinger had gone out of his way to declare publicly that he did not blame Israel for the failure of his mission, privately he and the President were convinced of the contrary. They were deeply embittered at the inflexibility of Israel's new leaders and deemed their attitude to be shortsighted and ungrateful. At a time when Indochina was collapsing, Portugal was in danger of slipping under Communist rule, and Turkey was ordering American bases closed, the President and his secretary of state badly needed a success in the Middle East to redeem the record; instead, the Israeli leaders administered to them another dramatic failure. In his last minute message to Prime Minister Rabin, President Ford had specifically threatened a "reassessment" of American policy toward Israel if it caused Kissinger's mission to fail; in making the public announcement, the President was in fact serving notice to Israel that he was proceeding to deliver the punishment.

Reassessment in this sense took several forms, the most important of which was restriction of arms supply and suspension of consideration of economic assistance. While American government spokesmen repeatedly asserted that the supply of arms to Israel was continuing, a selective embargo was in fact imposed. The United States had often used this kind of informal sanction in the past to induce Israel to take some specific action; this time, however, the sanction appeared to be almost purely vindictive since it came after the fact. Moreover, the action was particularly painful and potentially damaging to American-Israeli relations because it came only a short time after Kissinger had committed the United States to *increased* and more regular military assistance to Israel in connection with the conclusion of the first Egyptian agreement and especially the Syrian agreement.

Reassessment in the plain sense of reviewing concepts and policy plans in light of the situation that developed after the failure of the negotiations was the least significant of the reasons for declaring a "reassessment." Kissinger and his staff may have needed to recollect their thoughts, seek advice, consider available options, and reach conclusions. But this kind of activity, which is a normal part of policy-making, hardly needed to be solemnly announced. Nor did it require all the theatrics that followed, as week after week prominent individuals and small groups from the foreign policy establishment, the Congress, and the academic world were summoned with great fanfare to take part in perfunctory consultations. That part of "reassessment" was almost entirely meant to serve the purposes of gaining time and putting psychological pressure on Israel to soften it up for whatever next move might be made. It stimulated a flow of leaked information, stories, and articles, most of them tending toward the idea that the United States should go to Geneva and publicly announce a position in favor of a settlement based on a return to the 1967 borders, with strong security guarantees for Israel.

The real substantive reexamination of the situation by Kissinger and his staff actually pointed out fairly quickly that the option of going to Geneva and announcing an American plan was unpractical and unwise in the existing circumstances. In the first place, it was doubtful whether a Geneva conference could be convened at all because of the problem of Palestinian representation. The Arab states collectively were firmly committed since Rabat to the notion that the PLO was the only authorized representative of the Palestinians and had to be present in any general peace conference, whereas the Israeli government was no less firmly committed to a refusal to deal with what it called a "terrorist organization." Even if that problem were somehow overcome or circumvented, assembling several Arab delegations together to deal with an overall settlement was a sure prescription for eliciting and stimulating competition in extremism among them. This would doom the prospects of fruitful negotiations while offering the Soviets opportunities to fish in troubled waters. Whatever position the United States might take on general or particular issues, the Soviets would be able to outbid it by taking one more favorable to the Arabs. Sooner or later the United States would find itself facing the choice of either taking a stand that would antagonize the Arabs, drive them into the Soviets' arms, and create a dangerous polarization in the area; or else going all the way in support of the Arab demands, antagonizing and confronting Israel, and perhaps driving it, in despair, to resort to a nuclear strategy. Either situation would destroy or greatly diminish the leverage that the United States would be able to exercise over the Middle East situation in the long run: the former by undermining its position with the Arabs, the latter by making it entirely dependent on their goodwill. In the short run, either would also greatly increase the chances of war which the United States wanted to avoid.

Because the prospects of Geneva were so unattractive, and because it was necessary to do something before long, the secretary of state and his staff soon reached the conclusion that the only hopeful course was to try once more for a limited Egyptian-Israeli agreement. For various reasons, however, they continued to uphold the Geneva option in public at least as one of three choices—in addition to seeking a limited Sinai accord and the complete nonstarter alternative of a final, separate Egyptian-Israeli settlement. One reason for keeping the Geneva option alive was to blur the fact that the secretary of state was coming around to the view expressed by the Israelis in the last stage of the previous negotiations when they suggested a new attempt at a limited agreement after a while. Another reason was to keep up the pressure on the Israeli government to impel it to soften its terms for a partial agreement. A third reason was that the Geneva option was turning into a cause of contention both between the Soviet Union and the Arabs and among the Arabs themselves, a contention which allayed the dangers Kissinger had feared most and helped create an atmosphere favorable to another attempt at a partial Egyptian-Israeli agreement.

Kissinger had warned the Israelis that the failure of his March mission would lead to the formation of a united Arab front, more emphasis on the Palestinian question, a linkage between Sinai and Golan, Soviet reentry into the stage, and enhanced danger of war. The last of these predictions was promptly proven to be wrong, as President Sadat announced one week after the collapse of the talks that he had decided to renew the mandate of the United Nations forces due to expire a month later, to continue rebuilding and developing the canal zone, and to reopen the Suez Canal for navigation on June 5, 1975. The Egyptian leader, recognizing that he had no realistic war option in view of the Arab-Israeli balance of forces at the time, shrewdly moved promptly to prevent the development of a war scare that might be magnified by the Syrians and the PLO to embroil him in conflict. The other predictions of Kissinger appeared for a moment to be materializing but then they too began to fall apart. At the end of March 1975 the previously feuding leaders of Egypt, Syria, and the PLO, brought together in the Saudi capital by the funeral of King Feisal (assassinated on March 25 by a young member of his family), began an effort to work out a common political and military strategy in light of the situation after the fiasco of the Sinai negotiations. At the same time, the Soviet capital suddenly began to come alive as the Soviets invited a succession of Egyptian, Syrian, and PLO officials to discuss with them the modalities of Geneva. However, by the end of April or early May it became apparent that the Arab parties could not agree on a common policy among themselves, and that the Soviets were unable either to reconcile the differences among them or to heal their own ailing relations with Egypt (Brezhnev's visit to Cairo never took place). The heart of the disagreement was the insistence of Syria and the PLO that the Arab parties should go to Geneva all together or not at all, and that if Geneva did not materialize or failed to make progress, they should all, together, engage in confrontation with Israel and, if necessary, with the United States too. To Sadat, such a strategy appeared to be playing completely into the Israelis' hands. It would allow them, first, to engage in procrastination, and then would help them to recreate a solid front with the United States which the Arabs would have difficulty facing. Sadat urged, instead, agreement on the principles of no surrender of Arab territory, no separate settlement, and no final settlement without securing the Palestinians' rights, while leaving ample flexibility in tactics and method. In short, he sought to preserve the option of another attempt at a limited agreement as well as to keep open the American connection.

As the inter-Arab and Soviet-Arab policy reassessment failed to produce agreement on a new approach, Sadat took the initiative to reactivate the old one. He arranged to meet President Ford and Secretary Kissinger in Salzburg, Austria, at the beginning of June 1975 to review the situation and discuss the next move. Sadat tried to take advantage of the chill in American-Israeli relations to get President Ford to agree to make a public commitment to the pre-1967 borders, but the President and the secretary of state demurred on the grounds that any public commitment to a particular plan would detract from the ability of the United States to act as a mediator and secure gradual Israeli withdrawals. Kissinger reviewed the three options that the United States thought were available, and after discussing them all Sadat opted for a resumption of negotiations for an interim agreement while contributing a thought that was to prove crucial. He continued to insist that Israel must give up the passes and the oil fields, but suggested that the United States might itself man the electronic early warning station that the Israelis insisted on retaining in the passes. This provided an opening for a resumption of American-Israeli specific discussions on a new interim agreement.

Israel's reaction to the failure of Kissinger's mission, like the American, had unfolded on two levels—one demonstrative and public, the other studied and discreet. The tone of the reaction on the first level was set by an overwhelming vote in the Knesset approving the government's stance in the negotiations and by universally favorable comments on it in the media and opinion polls. Since the formal end of the October War, Israelis had again and again heard their government solemnly vow to stand firmly on this or that issue only to see it repeatedly back down after an American intervention, intercession, mediation, or whatever. This time, the government took a strong position and, for once, stuck to it and dared say NO to Kissinger. That pleased them immensely and the Prime Minister responsible for taking that stand, hitherto viewed as a dullard and a fumbler, became a national hero overnight.

Buoyed by the public's support, Rabin and his colleagues responded to the open American pressures with continuing open defiance. For example, Defense Minister Peres was due to go to Washington in early April to discuss Israel's arms needs; as officials in the Pentagon let it be known that his visit was not opportune because of the ongoing policy review, Israeli officials let it be known that Israel had no intention of softening its negotiating strategy until the "Ford Administration" agreed to resume the talks on Israel's pending arms requests. As the administration's showy part of the reassessment unfolded, with its insinuations that Israeli intransigence was responsible for the failure of the talks and its implicit threats of going to Geneva and of supporting the pre-1967 borders, Israel's government responded by mounting a countercampaign in the United States to refute the allegations of inflexibility, by announcing that it was not afraid to go to Geneva, and by calling upon Israel's friends in Congress to support its basic position and needs. The fact that the administration was not doing very well in the field of foreign policy generally, and particularly that Kissinger's deals in Indochina were coming apart, provided a receptive climate for Israel's argument that it was being pressed to make a fragile and dangerous settlement. On May 21, 1975, no fewer than seventy-six senators addressed a letter to President Ford in which they endorsed Israel's demand for "defensible" borders and favored massive economic and military assistance to it.

While in public the leaders of Israel took a determined and combative posture in the face of the American pressures, in private these pressures forced them to make their own policy reassessment. Rabin and his colleagues had allowed the March negotiations to collapse in the belief that these could and would be picked up again before long without any undue damage and possibly with important benefits. The refusal to yield to Kissinger's urgings and pressures would have demonstrated to him that there were limits to what he could get Israel to accept, and this, in turn, would impel him to put as much pressure on Sadat to go toward Israel as he did on the Israeli government to go toward Sadat. In the meantime, Sadat himself might come to expect less from the United States, develop a more realistic view of his bargaining position, and be more accommodating when the negotiations resumed. Kissinger, we have seen, had tried to dissuade the Israelis by depicting to them a bleak picture of what would happen if the talks failed, but the Israelis remained unmoved.

The actual situation that unfolded after March 22 showed the Israelis to have been right in some of their expectations and wrong in others. Sadat did not revive the war option or turn toward the Soviet Union, and the Arabs failed to close ranks or agree on a common strategy, contrary to what Kissinger had predicted and more like what they had sensed. However, before all that became quite apparent, the secretary of state had committed the United States to a posture that castigated and penalized Israel and praised and supported Sadat's position. Whatever the reasons for Kissinger's behavior—I have argued that they comprised an element of vindictiveness as well as an effort to ward off developments that he feared—the effect was to undercut the grounds for the Israelis' hope that another round of negotiations might give them what they wanted. Consequently, they faced the necessity of either renouncing the option of seeking a limited agreement with Egypt in favor of another approach, or else of modifying what they wanted to achieve from a limited agreement in the light of what was possible.

As that situation became more or less apparent, the Israeli government informally split as to the best direction to be taken. Some, including members of the Independent Liberal Party and Mapam, were in favor of announcing a comprehensive, moderate peace plan and indicating Israel's readiness to go to Geneva to discuss it. They reasoned that if the Arabs went along, a comprehensive settlement might well be achieved, and if they did not, Israel would be in a strong position to gain American support and international understanding. Others, including some of the reputed "hawks" in the Cabinet, favored the Geneva option, but without a previously announced Israeli plan, in the expectation that nothing would come of it either because it would not be possible to assemble the conference or because the conference would break down after a while. This would gain time for Israel until the American presidential election year set in, paralyzing any serious diplomatic movement and stimulating a climate favorable to Israel. Prime Minister Rabin, with the support of others, viewed the tactical Geneva move as a possible fallback position if the Geneva option were somehow forced on Israel, but he much preferred to stick to his original conception, with suitable modifications to take account of the new reality: if Israel could not gain the time it wanted by means of "buying" Egypt's exit from the war, then it should try to gain that time by "buying" a strongly enhanced Israeli deterrent power. Stated differently, since the United States was so interested in an Egyptian-Israeli agreement and was pressing Israel to give up the passes and the oil fields without getting the end of belligerency in return, it should itself provide Israel with the compensating security margin it needed.

Toward the end of April 1975 Foreign Minister Allon visited Washington where he learned that the secretary of state, contrary to the impression that was being publicly conveyed at the time, had not renounced the possibility of trying for another Sinai agreement if a promising negotiating approach could be found. This helped Rabin to neutralize pressures on behalf of other options within the Cabinet until he got a more definite American commitment to the option he favored. This happened in early June 1975, during a visit of the Prime Minister to Washington following President Ford's meeting with President Sadat in Salzburg. The American President was still under a strong impression of his meeting with the Egyptian leader, whom he believed to be eager to retain and develop the American connection and to move toward settlement. He had also just received the message of the seventy-six Senators calling for "defensible borders" for Israel and large-scale economic and military assistance. The President therefore put before Rabin a clear-cut choice: if Israel altered its March position enough to give another round of negotiations a reasonable chance of success, it could definitely count on much

American assistance and support; if it did not, the United States would decide to go to Geneva and he, Ford, would announce an American plan and pursue it regardless of any considerations of internal American politics. Rabin may have had his doubts about the second proposition in view of what had transpired since March, but he was not about to quibble, since the first proposition was just what he wanted to hear.

After Rabin reported to his colleagues in Jerusalem, the Cabinet set up several task forces to formulate the commitments that Israel expected from the United States in exchange for agreement to give up the passes and the oil fields. The results served as a basis for negotiations between the United States and Israel, with the United States informing Egypt of their progress and receiving from it relevant inputs and approvals. By the early part of August virtually complete agreement was reached on all points, and Kissinger was ready to start another round of shuttle diplomacy on August 20, 1975. The secretary of state had learned the lesson of the failure of the previous round, and had practically secured the success of his mission before he started.

The second Sinai Agreement was initialed on September 1 and formally signed at Geneva on September 4, 1975, after twelve days of negotiations, more of which were devoted to the American-Israeli than to the Egyptian-Israeli part of the accord. Although most of the features of the new agreement had been foreshadowed in the first Sinai Agreement, many of these were carried so far further in the second that they assumed a qualitatively different character. In addition, the second agreement included some entirely novel features regarding the United States role vis-à-vis the agreement itself, and especially vis-à-vis Israel.

As far as Israel and Egypt are concerned, the agreement involved the following trade-off: Israel agreed to pull out of the passes, the oil fields, and the territory between the oil fields and the Egyptian positions to the north of them with two exceptions. It was to retain some hills at the eastern end of the Gidi Pass, mainly so that its government could claim that it did not give up the passes without getting nonbelligerence. Far more important, Israel was to retain a sophisticated electronic strategic early warning station inside the passes which was to be matched by a similar Egyptian station, and the two were to be part of an American-controlled system including an American-manned tactical warning station. The passes and the oil fields area were to be part of demilitarized buffer zones under the control of United Nations forces, according to the pattern set by Sinai I.

In exchange, Egypt subscribed to several clauses committing it not to resort to force and to seek a settlement by peaceful means and agreed in addition to several elements of nonbelligerency:

> The conflict between them [Egypt and Israel] in the Middle East shall not be resolved by military force but by peaceful means. [Article I]

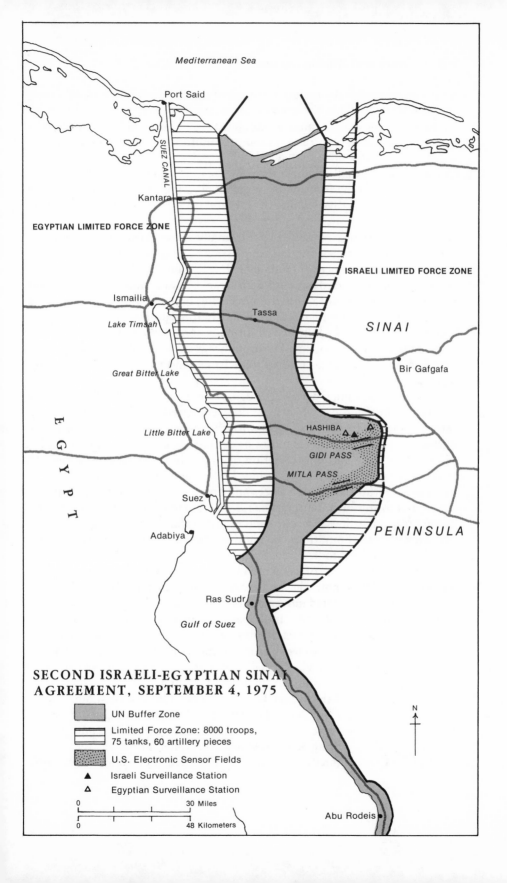

Mediterranean Sea

Port Said

SUEZ CANAL

Kantara

EGYPTIAN LIMITED FORCE ZONE

ISRAELI LIMITED FORCE ZONE

Ismailia

Lake Timsah

Tassa

SINAI

Great Bitter Lake

Bir Gafgafa

Little Bitter Lake

HASHIBA

GIDI PASS

MITLA PASS

E
G
Y
P
T

Suez

Adabiya

PENINSULA

Ras Sudr

Gulf of Suez

SECOND ISRAELI-EGYPTIAN SINAI AGREEMENT, SEPTEMBER 4, 1975

UN Buffer Zone

Limited Force Zone: 8000 troops,
75 tanks, 60 artillery pieces

U.S. Electronic Sensor Fields

▲ Israeli Surveillance Station

△ Egyptian Surveillance Station

N

0   30 Miles

0   48 Kilometers

Abu Rodeis

The parties hereby undertake not to resort to the threat or use of force or military blockade against each other. [Article II]

The parties shall continue scrupulously to observe the cease fire on land, sea and air and to refrain from all military and paramilitary actions against each other. [Article III/1]

The parties shall continue their efforts to negotiate a final peace agreement within the framework of the Geneva peace conference in accordance with Security Council Resolution 338. [Article VIII/2]

In addition to nonuse of force, Egypt formally agreed to permit "nonmilitary cargoes" destined for or coming from Israel to pass through the Suez Canal (Article VII), to renew the mandate of UNEF annually (Article V) instead of every six months, and to establish with Israel a joint commission to deal with problems that might arise from the agreement under the aegis of a UN official (Article VI). The agreement was to remain in force until superseded by a new agreement (Article IX), but it was informally agreed that it was to be valid for at least three years. Also, Egypt informally agreed to relax the boycott of several American companies trading with Israel, and to ease anti-Israel propaganda.

An integral Annex defined the deployment lines, areas of limited armaments, and buffer zones which essentially emulated on a larger scale the pattern of Sinai I. In the areas of limited forces and armaments, the parties agreed to restrict themselves to not more than 8,000 men, 75 tanks, and 72 pieces of artillery and not to station or locate in these areas weapons that could reach the line of the other side. The last limitation applied also to the areas beyond those of limited forces and armaments. In addition, the parties agreed not to station antiaircraft missiles within ten kilometers east and west of their respective lines. The parties agreed that the UN would supervise compliance with these limitations. In addition, their own reconnaissance aircraft could fly up to the middle of the buffer line, and the United States would fly periodic reconnaissance of its own every week or so or at the request of either party or the UN commander and make its findings available to all three.

The Annex regulated movement of personnel in the buffer zones and of civilians in the oil fields area. It obligated Israel to leave intact installations and infrastructures in that area. Representatives of the parties were to meet at Geneva within five days to work out the details of implementation and complete them within two weeks; actual implementation of the entire agreement was to be completed within five months of signing.

As in the case of the Syrian-Israeli agreement and the first Sinai Agreement, the achievement of Sinai II necessitated American inputs of various sorts; only this time these were more concrete and far-reaching and more essential to realizing the agreement. One novel contribution was the commitment of the United States to station American civilian personnel in the buffer zone to supervise and participate in manning the electronic surveillance system. This step was taken to facilitate acceptance by Egypt of the Israeli strategic early warning station, but it also had the effect of turning the United States into a designated, compulsory, on-the-spot witness of any violations of the agreement or of threatening force deployments by one side or the other. In a strategic context in which preemption may be of critical importance and in which the American judgment as to whether preemption was called for might be crucial, the American "testimony," explicit or tacit, could be vital. It could justify the action of the would-be preemptor and for this reason it might deter the would-be attacker in the first place. Because of this importance of the American presence, the Israeli government made it an indispensable condition for acceding to the agreement, and insisted on holding back application of the agreement until that presence was approved by the United States Congress.

The United States also facilitated agreement by giving assurances to Egypt that it would make a serious effort to help bring about further negotiations between Syria and Israel, that it would consult with Egypt in the event of Israeli violation of the agreement "as to the significance of the violation and possible remedial action by the United States," and that it would provide technical assistance to Egypt for the Egyptian early warning station and by reaffirming the American policy of assisting Egypt in its economic development, the specific amount to be subject to Congressional authorization and appropriation.

The most important American contribution, however, took the form of a whole array of assurances, undertakings, and commitments given to Israel to induce it to make the concessions that made the agreement possible. Some of these, as Secretary Kissinger was to point out before Congress, were legally binding while others were in the nature of assurances about American political intentions; some were entirely within the purview of the authority of the President of the United States while others depended on existing or prior authorization and appropriation by Congress; some were formal reaffirmations of existing American policy while others referred to contingencies that might never arise. Nevertheless, the package as a whole was quite impressive and, but for the fact that it bore the label of Executive Agreements, it exceeded in many ways many a formal treaty signed by the United States.

The undertakings were expressed in two documents called "Memorandum of Agreement" (not of "Understanding," as in the case of the disengagement agreements) and one document called "Assurances from USG to Israel" which "augmented" one of the memoranda. One Memorandum of Agreement comprised sixteen articles and covered a wide range of subjects. It began by pledging the United States government "to make every effort to be fully responsive, within the limits of its resources and Congressional authorization and appropriation, on an ongoing and long-term basis to Israel's military equipment and other defense requirements, to its energy requirements and to its economic needs." It then went on to spell out some specific commitments in each of these areas. For example, the United States agreed to periodic consultations between representatives of the United States and Israeli defense establishments to discuss Israel's long-term military supply needs with a view toward turning the conclusions agreed upon into specific particular American-Israeli agreements. The first such study was to begin within three weeks and include Israel's 1976 needs; in the course of the study the United States undertook to consider sympathetically Israeli requests for sophisticated weapons. The "Assurances" document augmented this clause by obligating the United States to provide Israel with F-16 aircraft and to study "with a view to giving a positive response" high technology and sophisticated items, including the Pershing ground-to-ground missile with conventional warheads.

In the sphere of energy, the United States committed itself for a period of five years to help meet Israel's needs for oil in case it is unable to meet its requirements through normal procedures; to help it do so within certain limits even if the United States was itself subject to "quantitative restrictions through embargo or otherwise"; to help finance Israel's additional oil costs as a result of its giving up the Abu Rodeis oil fields; and to help Israel expand and stock its reserve oil storage facilities from their existing capacity of up to six months' needs to a capacity of up to twelve months' needs. In addition to the promises of financial aid implicit in all the preceding, the "Assurances" obligated the administration to submit annually for approval by the United States Congress a request for military and economic assistance in order to help meet Israel's economic and military needs.

The Memorandum included a dozen additional articles, most of them specifying American policy regarding issues closely related to the agreement, but several of them expressing American stances on basic or long-range questions. Among the former were articles that obligated the United States to consult with Israel and consider possible remedial action in case of Egyptian violation of any of the provisions of the agreement; to vote against any Security Council resolution which "in its judgment" adversely affected or altered the agreement; and not to join in, and seek to prevent efforts by others to bring about, consideration of proposals which "it and Israel agree are detrimental to the interests of Israel." In the same category of articles the United States government expressed the position that the Egyptian-Israeli agreement did not depend in any respect on any act or development between Israel and other Arab states, but stood entirely on its own; it agreed with Israel that the next agreement with Egypt should be a final peace settlement; that "under existing political circumstances" negotiations with Jordan would be directed toward an overall peace settlement; that the agreement with Egypt should not enter fully into effect before approval by the United States Congress of the United

States role in connection with the surveillance and observation functions; and so on.

Among the articles of longer-term relevance, one pledged the United States government to conclude with the government of Israel at the earliest possible time, "if possible within two months," the contingency plan for a military supply operation to Israel in an emergency situation. Another stated the position of the United States government that the Strait of Bab el Mandeb and the Strait of Gibraltar were international waterways and committed that government to "support Israel's right to free and unimpeded passage" through these straits. Similarly, the United States government recognized Israel's right to freedom of flight over the Red Sea and the straits, and pledged to "support diplomatically" the exercise of that right (notice the difference between the unqualified support for navigation and the qualified support for flight). But probably the most important article in the long-term category was one that implicitly but clearly sought to reassure Israel about the Soviet Union It said:

> In view of the long-standing United States commitment to the survival and security of Israel, the United States Government will view with particular gravity threats to Israel's security or sovereignty by a world power. In support of this objective, the United States Government will in the event of such threat consult promptly with the Government of Israel with respect to what support, diplomatic or otherwise, or assistance it can lend to Israel in accordance with its constitutional practices.

The second Memorandum of Agreement addressed itself entirely to the Geneva Peace Conference. It obligated the American government to coordinate with Israel the timing of the reconvening of the conference and the strategy to be pursued, and particularly to make every effort to ensure that at the conference all substantive negotiations would be on a bilateral basis. Most importantly, the memorandum specifically committed the United States to continue to adhere to a policy of not recognizing or negotiating with the PLO so long as that organization did not recognize Israel's right to exist and did not accept Security Council Resolutions 242 and 338, and to oppose and if necessary to vote against any initiative in the Security Council to alter adversely the terms of reference of the Geneva Conference or "to change Resolutions 242 and 338 in ways which are incompatible with their original purpose."

The assurances, undertakings, and commitments given by the United States to Israel in connection with Sinai II were criticized in some American quarters as being far too excessive in relation to what Israel was required to give up. If so much was given to induce Israel to withdraw some thirty kilometers, it was asked, how much more would have to be given to it, how much indeed could be given it, to secure its withdrawal to anywhere near the pre-1967 boundaries? This analysis of the post–October War diplomacy suggests that in the first place, this criticism errs by measuring what the United States granted against what Israel gave up. A more relevant equation would weigh the price the United States agreed to pay against the consequences for its interests and position that were likely to ensue if it had failed to secure an agreement, and against the benefits it could expect to reap by having achieved one. Beyond that, however, the American assurances, undertakings, and commitments were not merely part of a deal relating to the particular agreement between Egypt and Israel. They were also an expression of the underlying basic relationship between the United States and Israel, which was hastily and rather sloppily committed to paper because of the strains of adaptation the two had recently endured. And that relationship, despite its ups and downs, has been one of enduring friendship enhanced by an evolving but firm, if unwritten, alliance.

Diplomatic Pause and Prospective Trials

The conclusion of Sinai II brought about a pause in the hectic diplomatic movement triggered by the Yom Kippur War which lasted until the advent of the Carter administration in January 1977. During the intervening sixteen months or so, however, the conditions affecting the parties involved in the Arab-Israeli conflict and Israeli-American relations did not remain stagnant. Sinai II caused a rift between Egypt and Syria, and as the latter began to build a military coalition to compensate itself for Egypt's "defection," the Arab forces began to polarize. The conflict between Damascus and Cairo spilled over into the simmering strife in Lebanon and stimulated its development into a full-fledged civil war, which brought about indirect and then direct Syrian military intervention that threatened to ignite a large-scale armed Arab-Israeli encounter. Thanks largely to the Israeli deterrent, which the United States supported, restrained, and exploited all at once in quiet mediation efforts, the latter danger was averted and the Syrian intervention evolved into a stabilizing rather than disruptive factor.

While Israel's role as a balancer in the Middle East was once more proving its value to the United States, the progress of the American election campaign brought forth the seasonal renewed expressions of American friendship toward Israel and dedication to its survival and well-being, confirming and enhancing the letter and spirit of the obligations and commitments assumed by the Sinai II executive agreements. Previous promises of economic and military aid were fulfilled generously, while new ones for the future were extended by the candidates.

In Israel itself, however, these favorable external developments were not matched by a similar internal evolution. On the contrary, economic difficulties coupled with weaknesses in the political configuration and instances of corruption at the highest political levels undermined the authority of the government and led to its downfall in December 1976 and the scheduling of early elections for May 1977. The Israeli election campaign unfolded at a time when the newly installed American administration was engaged in preliminary explorations aimed at resuming the negotiations for a Middle East settlement, in the course of which President Carter made a series of policy statements about the nature of the peace settlement he envisaged that stirred widespread anxiety in Israel. While there is no evidence as yet about the extent to which the President's statements may have contributed to the almost revolutionary outcome of the Israeli elections, it seemed likely that if a Likkud-led government were indeed formed, the views expressed by the President and the known views of Likkud leader and presumptive Prime Minister Menachem Begin would set the United States and Israel on a collision course. Conceivably, the two leaders might be able to avoid a collision by shifting the stress to issues on which they could agree and putting the onus of further change in position on the Arab side, especially with respect to the question of Palestinian representation. Possibly, a clash between Carter and Begin might take place but have salutary results, the way the "reassessment" crisis ultimately produced Sinai II. But it is also possible that the clash could stimulate a deterioration of the Middle East situation toward confrontation and war, with consequences that defy speculation.

Secretary of State Kissinger had promised Egypt's President Sadat in the course of the negotiations leading to Sinai II that once the agreement was consummated, he would try to promote a second agreement between Syria and Israel. He had, however, committed himself in writing to Israel that the Sinai II Agreement stood on its own and did not depend in any respect on any act or development between Israel and other Arab states. This obligated the United States to defer to Israel's views regarding the possibility of an agreement with Syria, and as Israel took the position that there was room in the Golan only for "cosmetic changes" in the disengagement lines in connection with a limited agreement and as Syria showed no interest in that kind of change, negotiations for a second Israeli-Syrian agreement never got off the ground.

The Syrian government suspected that the intent of the United States was to isolate it and allow Israel to deal with it by force, in accordance with the scheme voiced by Rabin in the famous *Haaretz* interview of December 1974 (see above, this chapter). It was particularly furious at Egypt for lending itself to that ostensible plan and publicly denounced its leader and the Sinai Agreement in terms that created a breach between the two countries. At the same time, the Syrian government took a series of diplomatic-strategic initiatives designed to enhance the country's defensive capacity in case of a military encounter with Israel. Suspecting that in such an encounter Israel would seek to score a quick victory by striking through Syria's flanks to envelop the very strong lines facing the Golan, the Syrians sought to form a political-military alliance with Jordan and the PLO, which commanded the only significant forces in Lebanon, to provide for that contingency. Jordan went along because it believed the scenario depicted by the Syrians to be highly plausible and thought that coordination with the Syrians would benefit its own defense. Moreover, Jordan welcomed the opportunity to gain some leverage with the Syrians in connection with its own underground struggle with the PLO. The PLO, for its part, resented the Egyptian "defection" even more than the Syrians and welcomed the opportunity to build up their political and military position in Lebanon that closer cooperation with the Syrians offered. The latter consideration was particularly important because the latent tensions between Christians and Muslims in Lebanon over various issues, including the standing and behavior of the PLO in the country, had exploded in sporadic warfare in which the Palestinians were deeply involved.

Even as they excoriated the Egyptians and endeavored to strengthen their flanks, the Syrians sought to score some diplomatic success to match Egypt's gains in Sinai II by calling for a Security Council discussion of the conflict shortly before the mandate of UNDOF (the UN forces in the Golan) was due for renewal, and seeking specifically to promote recognition of "Palestinian rights" and of the PLO as sole Palestinian spokesman. The United States, anxious to avoid being cast in a negative role that would embarrass Egypt for its association with it, made some attempt to give the Syrian initiative a constructive turn. Before the Security Council's debate, a high State Department official testified before a congressional committee that the "Palestinian issue was at the heart of the Middle East problem" and gave it as his view that the PLO position was susceptible to evolution in a moderate direction. During the Security Council's discussions, the United States sought to have the proposed Arab resolution on Palestine modified in a way that would allow it at least not to oppose it. When it failed in that attempt, it cast a veto against the resolution on January 26, 1977; but on the same day, President Ford took advantage of the occasion of a state visit by Rabin to stress publicly, after confirming continued American support for Israel, that the United States thought it was urgent that further steps be taken to advance peace negotiations. Two days later Rabin responded to what he believed the President had had in mind by stating in an address to a joint session of Congress that Israel's government was ready for negotiations with any Arab state but would not cooperate in national suicide by meeting with the PLO.

In a continuing concern to help Sadat face muted opposition at home and increasing isolation in the Arab arena, the administration notified Congress on March 3, 1976, that it intended to sell Egypt six C-130 military transport planes—the first transaction of military equipment with that country in over twenty years. By that time, however, the difficulties encountered by Egypt in the wake of signing Sinai II were already easing, as a result of Syria's increasing involvement in the Lebanese civil war and the consequences of that involvement in the Arab camp as well as on the Syrian-Israeli front.

In January 1976 Syria had sent into Lebanon three battalions of the Palestine Liberation Army, which owed allegiance to it. Their intervention in the fighting checked the advances that the Christian-rightist forces were making without tipping the scales decisively against them; nevertheless it gave rise to strong, open or discreet, expressions of disapproval from several Arab countries who feared the establishment of Syrian hegemony in Lebanon and the international repercussions that a victory of the leftist-PLO coalition might produce. The disapproval became more sharp and open after regular Syrian troops took positions three miles inside Lebanon on April 9. Five days later Israel's Prime Minister warned Syria against overstepping "a definite red line" in its involvement in Lebanon. The same day, Secretary Kissinger declared before the Senate Appropriations Committee that Syrian military movements into Lebanon were "getting very close to the borderline of Israeli tolerance," and added that the United States was in constant touch with Syria and Israel in an effort to avoid confrontation between the two.

Partly because of unwillingness to extend their front line by taking over full responsibility in Lebanon, partly because of fear of provoking American-supported Israeli intervention at a time when the Arab states were increasingly at odds with one another, the Syrians sought to bring about a termination of the war on the basis of a program of constitutional reform that would award the Muslims of Lebanon important but moderate gains. The Christian-rightist alliance was willing to go along, but the Muslim-leftist coalition led by Kamal Jumblat and supported by the PLO rejected the Syrian plan and insisted on imposing its goal of a secular, democratic state dominated by it. As the leftist-PLO forces launched an offensive that threatened to overwhelm the Christian-rightist forces, Syrian troops advanced en masse on June 1, 1976, to halt them. While Syrian armored and motorized columns overran the main leftist-PLO positions and decimated their principal forces, the Christian militias launched successful attacks everywhere else on the weakened and isolated enemy garrisons. And as the PLO forces normally deployed in southern Lebanon in proximity of Israel were redeployed to fight the Syrians farther north, Israel helped the Christian forces there take over and create a buffer zone under their control.

The open, massive clash between Syrian troops and the PLO brought about a complete disruption and fragmentation of the Arab ranks. Egypt and Syria recalled their diplomatic missions in each other's capitals amid violent mutual recriminations. Iraq moved troops toward Syria's border, and Syria pulled out large units from the Golan front line to face the buildup of Iraqi forces. Libya, Iraq, Egypt, and other Arab states poured in money, arms, volunteers, and ostensibly Palestinian personnel on one side or the other and engaged in a war of each against all in the media. The Lebanese civil war was thus turned into an all-Arab civil war which lasted until November 1976 when Saudi Arabia was finally able to bring Egypt and Syria together and engineer an Arab League agreement that in effect authorized Syria to enforce in the league's name a cease-fire and the restoration of law and order in Lebanon.

In the meantime, the absorption of the Arabs into the Lebanese conflict and the divisions in their ranks removed all pressure from the United States to even pretend to keep the momentum of Middle East peace diplomacy alive and allowed it to turn its attention fully to the election campaign. As voting time approached, the presidential contenders vied with each other in demonstrating their support for Israel and dedication to its welfare. On July 1, 1976, for example, President Ford signed legislation providing Israel with $4.3 billion in aid and credits for the period June 1975 to September 1977, after working out a compromise with a previous congressional authorization measure that would have provided even more. On the same day, candidate Carter declared that he would continue economic and military aid to Israel indefinitely, while making annual judgments as to the amount. On September 30 Carter denounced Ford for agreeing to sell a large number of Maverick air-to-ground missiles to Saudi Arabia and a week later he said in a nationally televised debate with Ford that he would consider another Arab oil embargo against the United States as an "economic declaration of war" and would not ship anything to those countries. Ford came back a few days later with an announcement that the administration had agreed to lift the ban on the sale of some sophisticated military equipment to Israel and speed up delivery of other equipment already approved, and on October 20 Deputy Secretary of Defense William P. Clements revealed that the United States was exploring with Israel coproduction arrangements for F-16 jet fighters and confirmed reports that Israel would get new kinds of bombs.

Presidential elections have almost always been good seasons for Israel, but the climate of the 1976 campaign was particularly favorable. The Entebbe rescue operation of July 3 stirred up widespread feelings of admiration for Israeli courage and skill, while the spectacle of the civil war in Lebanon generated greater understanding for Israel's tough stance toward the PLO and for its suspicion of the value of commitments and obligations that might be given to it by Arab leaders when they were violating those they had assumed toward their own brethren and allies. Among those who follow international affairs and strategy closely, Israel's role in imposing caution on the Syrians and compelling them to opt for limited objectives promotive of stabilization in Lebanon was also noted. Nevertheless, the United States was not about to revert to any pre-1973 policy of exclusive orientation on Israel or expose its newly gained standing in Arab countries to undue risk. A reminder of this came on November 11, 1976, shortly after the elections, when the

United States joined the Security Council in a unanimous resolution deploring the establishment by Israel of settlements in occupied territories as unhelpful to the cause of peace, and declaring "invalid" the unilateral absorption of east Jerusalem. Evidence that this dual approach was not merely a partisan stance came soon after, with the accession of the Democratic administration of Jimmy Carter.

By the time President Carter was inaugurated, it had become a truism in American foreign policy circles that the time was never more ripe for a comprehensive Middle East peace settlement. This notion had become established partly as a result of self-serving declarations by leaders of the outgoing administration and partly as a result of a "peace campaign" that Arab leaders launched to impress the President-elect after having patched up their quarrels. But the notion also had substantial foundations in the realities of the strategic situation "on the ground" and the diplomatic configuration that Secretary Kissinger had helped shape, which were reinforced by the events in Lebanon. On the one hand, the PLO had been cut down to size by the Syrians, who also demonstrated a hitherto unsuspected sense of restraint and responsibility. Moreover, the Syrian-PLO clash entailed also a certain degree of estrangement between the Syrian government and the Soviets, who were caught once more in a conflict between two clients, and this was expected to have a further moderating influence on the Syrians. On the other hand, the events in Lebanon themselves demonstrated once more how easy it was for the open wound of the unsettled conflict to become infested by its surroundings and infest them in turn, giving rise to unexpected complications and dangers. As if to confirm that point, large-scale riots broke out in many parts of Egypt in the last week of January 1977, owing to the country's economic penuries and the strains of the defense burden, which presented a real threat to Sadat's government and all he stood for.

The combination of a sense of urgency and opportunity led the Carter administration to place the resumption of efforts to advance a Middle East settlement at the top of its list of priorities. Regarding the method of promoting a settlement, the President and his new foreign policy advisers were strongly set against the step-by-step approach and favored instead an early reconvening of the Geneva Peace Conference to push for a comprehensive agreement. As to the substance of the settlement to be promoted, the administration was inclined in favor of a model recommended in a report by a Brookings Institution study group published in December 1975. The group consisted of academic experts, former diplomats, and laymen of diverse sympathies and experience, and included Zbigniew Brzezinski, who became President Carter's national security adviser, as well as other individuals who took on important posts in the new administration. The report advocated a set of interrelated ideas for a settlement to be promoted by the United States, including the following: (1) Seeking an Arab-Israeli agreement in principle on a gradual Israeli return to the pre-1967 boundaries (except for mutually agreed changes and the special case of Jerusalem) in exchange for peace and normalization of relations among the parties. (2) The actual process of withdrawal and normalization of relations should proceed in a succession of stages defined in advance and spread over a number of years, with movement to each new stage dependent on satisfactory execution of the previous one. (3) In the case of the West Bank and Gaza, the application of the same interrelated principles of withdrawal and normalization by controlled stages should somehow make room for the exercise of Palestinian self-determination, which might take the form of either an independent state or an autonomous entity federated with Jordan. (4) The final boundaries would be safeguarded by supervised demilitarized zones and other security arrangements. (5) The entire settlement would be buttressed by unilateral or multilateral guarantees to some of or all the parties, coupled with large-scale economic aid and military assistance, pending the adoption of agreed arms control measures. As may be seen even from this brief summary, the Brookings report left a great deal of latitude with respect to many important issues, such as the definition of normalization, the duration of the stages, the nature of the security arrangements, the scope of external guarantees, and so on, and it more or less begged the question on a number of others, such as the modalities of Palestinian self-determination, the status of Jerusalem, and the possible modification of the pre-1967 boundaries. Nevertheless, the report was seen by the administration as a useful frame of reference for the explorations that were planned before the formulation of a definite policy and the initiation of attempts to carry it out.

The administration's initial plans envisaged a number of steps before going to Geneva. In the second half of February, Secretary of State Cyrus Vance was to visit the principal Middle Eastern countries involved to hear the views of their leaders and explore with them questions of procedure for reconvening the Geneva conference, especially the problem of overcoming the obstacle of Palestinian representation. The secretary of state was also to arrange for the leaders of Israel, Egypt, Jordan, Syria, and Saudi Arabia to meet successively with the President and his advisers in the course of the following three months for comprehensive exchanges of views on all issues involved in a settlement. The administration would consolidate its views in the light of these exchanges and sometime in the early summer of 1977, after the Israeli elections, the secretary of state would go out to the Middle East once more, this time to engage in the practical business of securing a modicum of agreement on procedure and substance among the parties to give the peace conference a chance to succeed, or at least to prevent its breaking down in failure too soon.

For reasons that are not yet altogether clear, the administration did not quite follow its own script. Secretary Vance did play his part as planned: he went out to the area, listened to the parties, reaffirmed American opposition to dealing with the PLO until it recognized Israel's right to exist and accepted Resolution 242, and elicited from President Sadat the potentially helpful suggestion that a link be established between the PLO and Jordan before the reconvening of Geneva, which could allow the latter to act as surrogate for the former, thus overcoming Israeli objections to PLO participation. The President, however, began with what seemed like an ad lib, then added another and yet another, and ended up enacting a completely improvised script that spelled out American positions on key issues and seemed to inaugurate a new kind of "diplomacy by public statements."

The process began on March 6, 1977, during Prime Minister Rabin's visit to Washington for the first of the series of planned consultations with Middle East leaders. In welcoming Rabin, the President stated amid the routine remarks appropriate to the occasion that he wanted Israel to have "defensible borders." That phrase, as we have seen, had a very definite meaning in the lexicon of Middle East diplomacy, indicating substantial modifications in the pre-1967 boundaries in favor of Israel. Its use by the President that early in the play caused an immediate stir in the media and rang the alarm in Arab capitals. Three days later the President used the occasion of a press conference to correct the impression he had created and clarify his intent, but in the process of doing so he spelled out new positions on several additional crucial issues. He distinguished between "legal borders," agreed and recognized, and "defense lines," presumably what he meant when he spoke of defensible borders, which may not conform to the legal borders for some time. He outlined the idea of stages which may last two to eight years or more. He elaborated on the quality of the peace to be sought in a settlement, stating that it should include open borders, free trade, tourist travel, cultural exchanges, and so on. And, finally, he "guessed" that Israel would have to withdraw ultimately to the pre-1967 borders with "minor adjustments," and added "but that still remains to be negotiated."

The President's statement of March 9, 1977, came out in a rather confused and disconnected fashion which invited misunderstandings and selective attention to particular points. In Israel, for example, Prime Minister Rabin expressed satisfaction that the United States had come to accept Israel's concept of the nature of peace and favored defense borders but demurred at the idea of return to the pre-1967 boundaries, whereas his political opponents ignored the first two points, denounced the third, and attacked the Prime Minister for not taking stronger exception to the entire scheme, which they equated with the abhorred Rogers Plan. In Arab countries, on the other hand, the reaction was somewhat the opposite. The "moderate" sector, including Egypt, Jordan, and Saudi Arabia, was delighted that a President of the United States had finally come out publicly in favor of return to the pre-1967 borders—a step that President Sadat had failed to induce either President

Nixon or President Ford to take—but took exception to the notion of defense borders and dismissed with ridicule the idea of the nature of peace ("how can we be forced to trade with Israel?"). Other Arab sectors either reversed the stress or attacked the whole scheme, especially for failing to say anything about the Palestinian problem except to mention that it must be solved.

The fact that the President defined American positions on such important issues so early in the process of consultation, the disordered manner in which he did so, and the reactions his statements provoked aroused concern among officials and foreign policy analysts in the United States who much preferred the systematic, quiet diplomacy envisaged in the original plan. Others, however, claimed to see merit in getting the parties concerned "used to" some concepts even before the start of serious negotiations, and related the President's pronouncments to his "populist" style generally and his campaign commitment to "open diplomacy" in particular. At any rate, the President himself was not deterred by either reactions or criticisms, and within eight days he used the platform of a town meeting in Clinton, Massachusetts, to make an additional important statement on the Middle East. This time he spelled out in an orderly fashion three "requirements" for a Middle East settlement. The first was full peace for Israel—here the President reiterated the terms of his previous statement after describing the creation of Israel as "one of the finest acts of the World's nation [sic] that has ever occurred." The second requirement was the establishment of permanent boundaries for Israel—here the President merely stated the positions of the parties without repeating the idea of the pre-1967 boundaries. The third requirement was dealing with the Palestinian problem—and here the President referred to the Palestinians' commitment to the destruction of Israel which must be overcome and then added that "there has to be a homeland provided for the Palestinian refugees who have suffered for many, many years." That was the first time that an American official of any rank, let alone the President, had come out publicly in favor of a Palestinian homeland. As the statement came out then, the qualifier "for refugees" left a certain amount of ambiguity which was seized by optimists in Israel and pessimists in the Arab camp, but the President removed the qualifier in subsequent pronouncements and only left a slight ambiguity as to the territorial scope and character of the homeland.

In the course of the next two and a half months, as Arab leaders came and went and the Israeli elections approached and passed the climactic moment, President Carter made another dozen statements on the Middle East which seemed to be intended primarily to sustain a sense of tension and impending movement. Most of them either reaffirmed points already made or sought to foster a favorable disposition toward the United States by complimenting visiting Arab leaders about their wisdom and courage and restating in very strong terms the United States commitment to the peace and welfare of Israel. However, two of these statements, made after the results of the Israel elections became known, portended the difficulties that were apt to develop between the Carter administration and Israel's new regime.

On May 25, 1977, in an informal question and answer period upon the departure of Saudi Crown Prince Fahd ibn Abdel Aziz, the President said that so far as he knew, there were "no disturbing differences at all" between the United States and Saudi Arabia. In answer to another question, he said that his views were not yet firm on what the composition of the Palestinian homeland might be and added "but all the United Nations resolutions have contemplated a homeland for the Palestinians." On the same day, the President gave an interview to *U.S. News and World Report* in which he said that United Nations resolutions generally as well as 242 were "the premise" for negotiations "in the past and the future," and the next day at a press conference he asserted that United Nations resolutions "coming from the Security Council" included the right of the Palestinians to have a homeland and to be compensated for the losses they had suffered. These assertions, especially the last, were not only inaccurate or completely wrong, but were also apt to undermine the foundations of Arab-Israeli negotiations which rested only on Security Council Resolutions 242 and 338.

Inaccuracies apart, the President seemed to be clearly intent on bringing into the discussion General Assembly resolutions which have no binding character and which have been overwhelmingly unfavorable to Israel, and the point of his so doing was apparently to hint to Begin, who had begun to make ominous statements of his own about settlements in the "liberated" territories, that if he wanted to start from a tough stance, the United States could do so just as well. Confirmation of this point may be found in the interview Carter gave to *U.S. News and World Report* the day before, in which he said, in what he described as a carefully devised and accurately expressed answer, that American friendship for Israel is based on two premises. One is respect for human freedom and the other a common commitment to find a permanent and lasting peace in the Middle East. The implication was clear: if the new government of Israel faltered on the commitment to find a permanent peace, it would undermine one of two premises of American friendship for Israel.

The oft-repeated positions of President Carter, the positions taken by Begin and the National Religious Party in their election platforms (see above, chap. 12), and the verbal skirmishes already begun made a severe confrontation between the Carter administration and the new regime in Israel seem highly likely. As of the end of May 1977, President Carter expected before long to receive prospective Prime Minister Begin in Washington, after the latter had formed his government, for extensive discussions. In that meeting, the two leaders would have the choice of addressing themselves pragmatically to certain limited questions with a good chance of reaching at least a temporary agreement on them, such as reaffirming adherence to Resolutions 242 and 338, agreeing to go to Geneva, and putting off discussion of the future of the West Bank until the question of the interlocutor on that subject, an issue for the Arabs to sort out, was settled at least in accordance with the American stance. But the two leaders would also have the choice of going instead to the heart of the matter and addressing then and there the big issues dividing them, on the theory that this had to be done sooner or later and was better done sooner.

If they should take the second approach, or if they should come to it after trying the first one, a severe confrontation between the United States and Israel was highly likely to ensue. One result of the confrontation would certainly be an enormous strain on Israel's supporters in the United States which might either weaken them all or stir many of them to redouble their efforts, depending on the exact posture taken by the administration. Other results are much less certain. Possibly, American pressure on an Israel that has become highly dependent on it might force Begin himself to alter his views enough to permit the United States and Israel to strike a bargain related to a general settlement after the example of Sinai II. In that case, Begin would be best placed to have the bargain accepted by Israel. Alternatively, the pressure might cause defections from Begin's coalition that would bring down his government and make way for another that would strike the bargain and also be in a reasonable position to put it across. A third, equally probable possibility, however, is that an American-Israeli rift would tempt some Arab party or parties, with possible encouragement from the Soviets, to try to add military pressure to the American squeeze, and this could trigger a chain reaction that would explode quickly into general war. Whatever the outcome of the war, it would probably raise more problems than it would solve, if indeed it would solve any.

27
American-Israeli Relations: An Overview

America's relations with Israel, this study has shown, have undergone a profound and complex evolution in the less than three decades since Israel came into existence. That evolution has been determined primarily by the changing role that Israel occupied in the context of America's changing conceptions of its political-strategic interests in the Middle East. However, the evolution took place within the framework of a "special" American connection with Israel based on an interplay between a general American moral interest in and sympathy for that democratic Jewish state and the particular attachment to it and concern for its welfare on the part of the near totality of America's 6 million Jews. This "special connection" has secured for Israel a modicum of American support even when that seemed to be a burden on the perceived American political-strategic interests, and has encouraged a higher level of support when Israel seemed to be playing a useful role in the context of the perceived American "real" interest. It has maximized to the utmost America's favorable disposition when Israel came to be seen as playing the central role in advancing American interests in the region, and it has cushioned the shock when America and Israel fell out on particulars of perceived interests and facilitated the resolution of the differences. This final chapter will examine briefly the elements of the American special connection with Israel, review the main stages of American-Israeli relations in light of the changing conception of America's interests in the Middle East and Israel's role in them, and conclude with a few observations on the future of American-Israeli relations.

America's Special Connection with Israel

The United States has had an abiding moral interest in Israel that has been articulated in various ways by every American government since the birth of the Jewish state. On an abstract plane, that interest may be viewed as a logical progression from the proposition that the supreme interest of the United

States is the preservation of its free way of life. For the American free way of life to persist and prosper in the face of the temptations of alternative forms and the challenge of antithetical systems, other free societies must exist and prosper. This is necessary so that the United States and these other societies may mutually sustain their faith in the possibility of free government, which, as Lincoln indicated in the Gettysburg Address, is essential for the survival of free government. Israel's existence and success as a genuine democracy therefore helps sustain faith in the democratic way of life in the United States as in other free societies.

On a more palpable and observable plane, the United States has had a long tradition of sympathy for peoples striving for nationhood and independence generally and for persecuted peoples in particular, which inclined it to look with favor on the aspirations of Jewish nationalism. And while it is true that Jewish nationalism conflicted with Palestinian nationalism which might also be entitled to sympathy on this score, Americans have tended to give priority to the Jewish aspirations to national restoration because these aspirations still left room for the Palestinians to realize theirs, whereas the Palestinians' aspirations negated Israel's entirely at least until very recently. Moreover the Jewish claims received a far wider hearing because of the presence of millions of Jews in the United States, and encountered far greater receptivity because of their association with the Biblical record and prophecies.

The idea of a Jewish state elicited special sympathy from Americans because of the terrible holocaust suffered by the Jews in our time. Support for Israel was seen as a kind of amends by the world, the Western nations, and the Christian peoples to the people who suffered that terrible ordeal and as providing a place of refuge for the individuals who survived it.

Americans have also felt a strong sympathy for Israel as a democratic nation and a society imbued with the libertarian values and humanistic culture of the West. The United States has had to associate itself with and support many an authoritarian country and regime out of strategic necessity. But it could hardly fail to respond to calls for support and aid from a truly free small country and still maintain its claim to lead the Free World against the forces of tyranny. Israel evoked all the more sympathy on this score because it has been one of the rare working democracies among the scores of new nations that came into being since the end of World War II, and because its experience evoked echoes of America's own experience. Like the United States, Israel is a nation of diverse immigrants who left inhospitable lands for new shores where they endeavored to build a new just and free society, and experimented in the process with new forms of human association. Also, the pioneering spirit that built Israel is reminiscent of America's youthful days, and its drive and accomplishments in the economic, social, scientific, and military spheres have been strongly appreciated by an America dedicated to the cult of achievement and progress.

The general American sympathy for Israel has been greatly enhanced by the deep and active interest in that country manifested by America's Jews. I have already referred to the process wherein organized American Jewry had moved from supporting various "nonpolitical" aspects of the Zionist endeavor in Palestine, through supporting the Zionists' struggle to keep that country open to large-scale immigration, to supporting vigorously the recommendation of the United Nations commission to terminate the Mandate and create a Jewish (and an Arab) state. In the course of the years since, the feeling of American Jews toward Israel has evolved under the impetus of their practical relations with it and the impact of threats to its security and existence to the point of becoming all-embracing. The old distinctions between Zionists and non-Zionists vanished entirely and gave way to a generally shared attachment to Israel and willingness to help it which has encompassed virtually all Jews regardless of background, class, age, or denomination (opinion polls over the last decade have consistently shown 90 percent of American Jews to be supportive of Israel). Identification with Israel became in a very real sense the most important and most universal identifying principle of American Jews.

The attachment of American Jews to Israel has worked in various ways to create an "organic" connection between the United States and Israel. The financial aid of American Jews has been essential for Israel's survival and development and had very early on turned any Israeli foreign policy option other than a Western orientation into a purely hypothetical possibility. The magnitude of that aid has been well-nigh incredible. Starting with $200 million during the year in which Israel struggled for its birth, the level of assistance has tended to taper off in relatively quiet years, shoot up in times of crisis, and ease down again but to ever higher plateaus. Thus, in the crisis year of 1967 the amount of aid in donations and loans jumped six or sevenfold over the level of previous years to attain nearly $600 million; and, after settling down to roughly half that amount annually in the following six years, it shot up again sixfold in the year of the 1973 war to the fabulous level of $1.8 billion.

By the kind of aid they have given and by their own visits American Jews have brought a sense of American "presence" into every corner of Israeli life. There is hardly an important educational, cultural, scientific, or philanthropic institution in Israel today which is not supported in some significant way by American Jewish (as well as governmental) aid, including all seven institutions of higher learning and research, the main museums, the Israel Philharmonic Orchestra, the Hadassah Medical Center and other facilities, the Histadrut, almost the entire vocational school system, and scores of religious schools, orphanages, and culture and sports centers throughout the country. American Jewish tourists have flocked to the country at an annual rate that exceeded 200,000 in recent years and have not only spent money that was helpful to the economy but have also brought to the masses of Israelis an awareness of the ties between their country and the United States.

Indirectly, the relations of American Jews with Israel have been instrumental in bringing to the country from the United States a constant stream of movie, theater, and sports stars, artists, scientists and scholars, journalists, politicians, and other VIPs. In a reverse direction, they have brought to this country virtually every member of the Israeli political, military, economic, cultural, scientific, and educational establishments in addition to the scores of thousands of students, trainees, and plain tourists who have come on their own. Together with the impact of American movies, which have a near monopoly in that country of avid moviegoers and television viewers, American books, magazines, and records, which are consumed at rates comparable to those of parts of the United States, the impact of American Jews had been to make Israel easily one of the most "Americanized" and America-conscious countries in the world today.

American Jews have affected American-Israeli relations not only by serving as a bridge between the two countries but also through their impact on American politics and policy. Before assessing that impact, it is important to put the question of Jewish influence in some perspective because the subject has often been distorted in innocence or out of malice aforethought.

In the first place, there is no doubt that American Jews have endeavored in many ways to promote American policies and actions favorable to Israel. American Jews have been influenced in their voting behavior by the attitude taken by candidates and officeholders on matters relating to Israel, and the latter have often taken a stand on such matters with this fact in mind. For although the 6 million American Jews constitute only a small minority of the American electorate, they tend to go to the polls in larger percentages than the average for all Americans and they are concentrated in such large cities as New York, Chicago, Philadelphia, and Los Angeles which often swing the votes of the pivotal states they are in. Moreover, American Jews have been important financial contributors to election campaigns of favorably disposed candidates even in constituencies that do not have substantial numbers of Jewish voters, and this, before the recent campaign-financing reform legislation, tended to enhance their political weight. There is, in addition, an official Israeli lobby registered with the United States government which has endeavored very effectively to influence legislation affecting Israel. Much of the success of AIPAC (American Israel Public Affairs Committee) has been due to its ability to enlist the cooperation of various Jewish and non-Jewish organizations in demonstrating broad grassroots support for the positions it has sought to advance in Congressional bodies.

Second, the Jews have not been the first or the only ethnic or religious group in America to try to influence American policy in favor of kinsmen or coreligionists abroad. From the 1794 Irish-American opposition to the Jay Treaty, through the efforts of Catholic opinion in favor of nonintervention in the Spanish Civil War, to the successful endeavors of Greek-Americans to promote an arms embargo against Turkey on account of Cyprus, there is a long record of similar activities which suggests that ethno-religious politics have been an important feature of American political life. The exertions of American Jews on behalf of Israel have undoubtedly been more prolonged, massive, and tenacious, but then no other group has been haunted by the kind of memory and prompted by the kind of fear for their brethren that have motivated American Jews.

Third, the efforts of American Jews on behalf of their interest in Israel comes under the constitutional right of peaceful assembly and petition. More relevant perhaps, the endeavor of various groups to promote their particular interests and views and the efforts of politicians to organize a variety of such views and interests into a winning majority are essential features of the American democratic process in modern times. In a society so diverse that there is no longer any obvious majority interest, the aggregation of a variety of minority interests and views around platforms and positions they can all support is one of the two principal methods of making the system work.

Fourth, the other method to make the system work is for the policymakers to propose platforms and policies and seek to enlist public and Congressional support for them, or to use the prerogatives afforded them by the separation of powers and checks and balances to modify, filter, and resist if they can propositions of interest groups, even if these are aggregated into majorities, in the name of alternative conceptions of the national interest. This provides a measure of insurance against hasty policy or action whatever its source. The upshot of the process as a whole is that to the extent that American Jews have been able to advance their interest in Israel, their success has depended on the sympathy or at least lack of opposition on the part of their coalition partners and the public at large, and on the willing or reluctant disposition of the policymakers to go along with the propositions advanced by them and their supporters. Opinion studies and the historical record strongly support this conclusion.

Over the last decade, for example, opinion polls have shown that somewhat less than 50 percent of Americans have had no opinion on the Arab-Israeli conflict and that of the more than 50 percent who did have a view, those who favored Israel outnumbered those who sympathized with the Arabs by more than ten to one. The Yom Kippur War, the Arab oil embargo, and the rocketing of the price of oil substantially increased the percentage of Americans concerned about the conflict and presumably galvanized the potential opposition to supporting Israel on the grounds of self-interest. Yet, a Louis Harris poll that confronted the public with a choice between continuing to support Israel with military aid and getting Arab oil in sufficient quantities and at lower prices discovered that 64 percent of Americans opposed stopping aid to Israel against only 18 percent who preferred enough and cheaper oil. Conceivably, the public was reacting in pique and most probably it was influenced by the fact that the United States was actually giving massive aid to Israel on the grounds of presumed national interest, but that is just the point here.

Historically, the combination of general American sympathy for Israel and the endeavors of American Jews had an almost qualitatively different impact on American policy and action vis-à-vis Israel before 1967 and since. Before 1967 a clear distinction is discernible as between the diplomatic-strategic sphere and the economic and other fields. In the latter area, the impact of the combination led to a uniformly and unequivocally friendly and helpful attitude toward Israel. During Israel's first nineteen years of existence, the United States awarded it nearly $1.5 billion of aid in various forms, mostly outright grants of one kind or another. On a per capita basis of recipient country, this was the highest rate of American aid given to any country. As part of the American foreign aid programs, Israel also received all sorts of benefits on a scale proportional to its share of economic assistance. Thus, hundreds of American technicians and Israeli trainees were exchanged, dozens of Israeli cultural, educational, and philanthropic institutions enjoyed American assistance from counterpart funds, and the Israeli public was allowed to buy American educational and cultural material payable in Israeli currency at the official rate. No sooner had the United States launched the Atoms for Peace program than Israel began building a small nuclear reactor within the framework of that program. In short, any benefit the United States granted to other countries was extended to Israel promptly and on a generous scale.

In the diplomatic-strategic sphere, however, the impact of American Jews and general American sympathy on American policies was not nearly so successful before 1967. That combination played a vital role in inducing the United States to support the United Nations partition plan. (This support was eminently justifiable in terms of the Palestine problem as it presented itself at the time, but it was not on those grounds that the support was given.) It was also important in bringing about the immediate recognition of Israel, in inducing President Truman to oppose any suggestion to alter the partition plan against Israel's interest, and in prompting the American government to issue, together with Britain and France, the Tripartite Declaration. Under the Eisenhower administration, the combination contributed to preserving the American commitment to the existence and integrity of Israel at a time when greater American involvement in the Middle East threatened to undermine it. But at no time during the pre-1967 period was Jewish influence and general American sympathy sufficient to induce the American government to give Israel what it wanted most at that time—a bilateral or multilateral formal alliance that would guarantee its security. Moreover, on many specific issues the strongly expressed wished of American Jews did not prevail with the American government. Thus, American Jews were unable, for instance, to move their government to exert pressure on the Arab countries to lift their economic boycott of Israel or desist from blocking the Suez Canal to Israeli shipping and trade. They failed to dissuade the American government from providing some Arab countries with military and economic aid despite their hostile practices against Israel, and to prevent American formal condemnations of Israel for its retaliatory raids across the armistice lines. During the crisis that began with the 1955 Soviet-Egyptian arms deal, an incredibly intense campaign of persuasion and lobbying failed to move Secretary of State Dulles to allow the sale of American arms to Israel to counter the Arab threat. Later, when Israel launched its attack on Egypt in October 1956, the American government did not hesitate to initiate a condemnatory resolution in the United Nations Security Council although its own fate was about to be decided in national elections, and in the following months it prepared to join other members of the United Nations in voting sanctions against Israel unless it withdrew from positions it had occupied in the war. In subsequent years of that pre-1967 period United States policies and actions did not clash as often with the desires and actions of Israel, but this was not so much due to any reassertion of Jewish influence or changes of administration as it was to changes of circumstances in the Middle East that altered the conception of the United States' interest in the area and Israel's role in relation to it.

The further change in American conceptions after 1967 turned the United States into a virtual ally of Israel. That evolution has been analyzed in great detail in the previous six chapters and will be recapitulated in the section that follows. One need only note in this context that within the new framework of joint American-Israeli diplomatic-strategic interests, the combination of Jewish interest in and general American sympathy for Israel attained its maximum effectiveness. Initiatives taken by the administration to provide Israel with economic and military assistance and to support it diplomatically were promptly and enthusiastically endorsed by vast majorities in Congress and by organs of public opinion. When the administration diverged from Israeli views on some particulars of policy or was slow in meeting Israeli arms requests, Congress and organs of opinion exerted often effective pressure to "rectify" the administration's positions. One notable reflection of the post-1967 configuration is that the United States became Israel's sole supplier of arms on a grand scale. Another is seen in the fact that in the last six years only the United States allotted to Israel more than $7 billion in economic and military assistance and loans, over four times the total amount of assistance awarded to it in the entire pre-1967 period.

The Stages of American-Israeli Relations

From the perspective of the interplay between America's "special connection" with Israel and its "real" interests in the Middle East, American-Israeli relations have gone through several periods, stages, and phases, all determined by the changing position occupied by Israel in the context of changing

American perceptions of its real interests in the area. The Six Day War of 1967 was a watershed which clearly demarcated the period before it, in which Israel played at best a useful role in the prevailing conceptions of the American interest in the Middle East, from the period after it in which Israel came to play a central role in the conception of American Middle East interests. Within each of the two periods there were important differences in the degree to which that major distinction applied. In the pre-1967 period, for example, there was one stage, extending from 1948 to 1957, in which the moral interest in Israel was viewed as a burden on the real interests as perceived at the time, and another, encompassing the years 1957 to 1967, in which the strain between the two kinds of interest was greatly eased as Israel began to play an increasingly useful role in the context of new perceptions of the real American interests in the area. Similarly, in the post-1967 period, after Israel assumed a central role in the conception of American Middle East interests, there was a stage, from 1967 to 1973, in which the real American interests corresponded at some point almost entirely with Israel's, and another stage, from October 1973 to the time of writing (June 1977), in which the perceived real interests of the two were more interdependent than identical. Each of the four stages was itself marked by secondary variations that could be thought of as distinct phases. These will be identified and described in the course of an outline by stages of the evolution of American-Israeli relations.

The First Stage, 1948–1957

During this first stage the United States sought to bring the Middle East into its global system of containment and deterrence directed at the Soviet Union. That endeavor was deemed vital to the interest of the United States because of the geostrategic location of the Middle East at the right flank of NATO and to the south of the Soviet heartland at a time when such location mattered greatly. The American strategic deterrent at the time relied on strategic bombers and intermediate-range ballistic missiles (IRBM) as the principal means of delivering nuclear and thermonuclear weapons. Therefore, access to bases in the Middle East could give the United States potential staging areas from which to reach crucial power centers in the Soviet Union and thus make its deterrent more effective.

Bringing the Middle East into the Western defense system required, among other things, courting the Arab countries and drawing them into the Western camp. This requirement inevitably clashed with the American moral interest in Israel and resulted in strained American-Israeli relations.

In addition, through most of this stage, Middle East oil appeared to have a crucial *strategic* importance because it was an indispensable resource for the reconstruction of Europe at a time when Europe seemed unable to secure it itself. The American moral interest in Israel somehow appeared to make the

American efforts to secure the flow of oil to Europe more difficult if not to endanger those efforts outright.

While this stage as a whole was thus characterized by a strain between the real American interests in the Middle East at large and the United States' moral interest in Israel, the degree of strain and its outcome differed as between two phases.

Phase 1, 1948–1952. During the first phase the strain between the two sets of interests was felt, but the moral interest in Israel by and large prevailed. Although the Cold War was already on and the effort to bring the Arab countries into the Western defense system was in full swing, the fact that Britain had the primary responsibility for lining up the Arab countries allowed the United States to continue to stress the moral interest that had led it to support Israel at the moments of its birth. The United States saw to it that the first plans for a Middle East alliance included Israel, and prepared the ground for that by the role it played in issuing the 1950 Tripartite Declaration.

Phase 2, 1953–1957. As Britain's effort faltered, the United States increasingly assumed the primary role in trying to build a Middle East alliance. The United States initiated the Northern Tier–Baghdad Pact project and ran afoul of Egyptian-Iraqi rivalry and Soviet backing of Nasser. Nasser and the Soviets used the American sympathy and support for Israel as a weapon to embarrass the United States' Arab friends and to frustrate its alliance plans. In reaction, the United States, under the aegis of Secretary of State Dulles reacted at first by demonstratively playing down its connection with Israel.

The resultant strain between the United States and Israel reached one climax after the 1955 Soviet-Egyptian arms deal, when the United States refrained from providing Israel with arms to counterbalance Nasser's in accordance with the spirit of the Tripartite Declaration and in effect urged it to turn to the United Nations for its security. Another climax was reached when Israel went to war in 1956 in collusion with Britain and France, and the United States threatened it with sanctions to compel it to retreat from Sinai and Gaza.

The Second Stage, 1957–1967

This stage was marked by the failure of the attempts made by the United States to bring Arab countries collectively into some form of association with the Western defense system, America's subsequent renunciation of that aim, and its replacement by one that sought to preserve American positions in the area and check the spread of Soviet influence through a policy of stabilization and regional balances of power.

Underlying this basic change of orientation was a change in the global strategic situation. As the United States came to base its deterrent increasingly on intercontinental ballistic missiles (ICBM) stationed on American soil and in Polaris-carrying submarines in and under the high seas, foreign bases generally ceased to be crucial. Concomitantly, foreign alignments became important not so much for the contribution they made to the American deterrent capacity as for their political significance in the context of a global contest stimulated by the decolonization movement and Chinese global strategic conceptions that centered on competition for friends and influence in the Third World. In that contest the Middle East was significant because of its nodal location in relation to the Soviet Union and the Third World, and because the Soviets had acquired a firm footing there in the previous stage, but it was no longer so vital as before. It was important for the United States to retain and if possible to extend the positions of influence it had there, but it was no longer necessary for it to try to convert these positions into formal alliances or alignments.

The fact that the United States no longer needed to court the Arab countries to bring them into a Western defense system eliminated a serious source of strain on the American moral interest in Israel. Moreover, since formal groupings and alignments were no longer necessary for the United States, it could openly cultivate friendly Arab countries as well as Israel on an individual basis in its effort to protect and advance its positions against opposite Soviet efforts. Finally, because Israel was politically stable and militarily powerful, it could be a particularly valuable asset in the context of the American design to achieve a favorable stability and balance of power in the area.

A similar development affected the American interest in Middle East oil during that stage, reducing considerably its significance as a *strategic* issue. It was not that Europe's dependence on Middle East oil decreased—on the contrary, it increased. Rather, a recovered and self-assertive Europe increasingly took over from the United States most of the responsibility for securing its oil supply and did so in many ways in competition with the United States. Taking advantage of the disentanglement from Third World conflicts they achieved with the progress of decolonization, European countries sought to secure their oil supply through direct diplomatic and business deals with the Arab countries. In this context, the American interest in Middle East oil centered mainly on protecting American companies against wanton seizure of their profitable business, and residually on preventing interruption of the flow of oil through political subversion and military action. Since Nasser's Egypt was directly or indirectly the main source of such threats, and since Israel pinned down most of Nasser's forces and absorbed much of his attention and energy, Israel became an asset in relation to the American oil interest, although the American oil companies continued for the most part to think of it as an embarrassment if not a curse for their position.

These broad changes in the course of the years between the 1956 and

1967 wars unfolded gradually, and three phases may be clearly discerned in the course of that evolution.

Phase 1, 1957–1960. After the seeming collapse of British and French influence in the Middle East in the wake of the 1956 Sinai-Suez War and the upsurge of Soviet influence in the area, the United States assumed alone the task of trying to check the Soviets by attempting to isolate and bring down Nasser, who was viewed as their principal vehicle and ally. This was the period of the Eisenhower Doctrine and the crises resulting from its pursuit that broke out in Jordan, Syria, Lebanon, and Iraq. Insofar as the United States identified Nasser, rather than Israel, as the principal obstacle in the way of rallying a Middle East grouping behind the Eisenhower Doctrine, the strain between the United States' interests in the region and its moral interest in Israel began to ease. Moreover, in the course of the frequent crises that the American efforts precipitated, the United States began to appreciate the fact that Israel's sheer presence and strength helped to constrain the anti-American forces, and facilitated the limited successes it was able to achieve in Jordan and Lebanon.

The ultimate failure of the Eisenhower Doctrine after the 1958 Iraqi coup marked the last effort by the United States to set up a pro-Western grouping in the Arab world. It was followed by a spontaneous stalling of the anti-American pan-Arab drive led by Nasser and the emergence of a spontaneous quiescent stalemate in the area. In the meantime, developments in weaponry and strategy made Middle Eastern alliances and bases unnecessary for the United States' defensive posture.

Phase 2, 1961–1963. The drive for a Middle East alliance or alignment had embittered all relations in the area: American-Israeli, American-Arab, American-Soviet, Arab-Arab, and Arab-Israeli. The Kennedy administration sought to take advantage of the end of that drive and its related strife to consolidate a temporary balance that had developed spontaneously in the area and to regain some of the influence lost to the Soviets in the previous phase. In the process, it initiated a policy of rapprochement with Nasser, but simultaneously enhanced the eased relations that had developed with Israel. It gave large-scale economic aid to Egypt, but engaged the United States as a provider of arms to Israel for the first time by selling to it Hawk antiaircraft missiles. In the many-sided network of relations that replaced the previous polarization, President Kennedy tentatively but explicitly referred to balance of power as a guiding principle of American Middle East policy, publicly allowing for the first time for a strategic role for Israel in the context of American policy.

Phase 3, 1964–1967. Kennedy's attempt to protect the American positions through a balance of power while trying to roll back Soviet influence stumbled eventually against Nasser's involvement in the Yemen War. Kennedy had hoped to induce Nasser through economic assistance to turn his attention to the development of Egypt, but the Egyptian leader could not resist intervening in Yemen in what seemed to him an opportunity to revive his pan-Arab drive. As the intervention turned into a long and indecisive war, it presented a grave threat to the friendly regimes of Saudi Arabia and the Persian Gulf principalities, diverted Egypt's scarce economic resources to armament and war, and accelerated the arms buildup throughout the region. The United States, especially under the new Johnson administration, switched in disappointment to a more hard-nosed policy of containing Egypt through balance of power, phased out economic assistance to it, and provided Israel with "offensive" weapons such as tanks and Skyhawk fighter-bombers.

The longer the Yemen War lasted and the more violent it became, the more apparent became Israel's role as a "balancer," pinning down the bulk of Egypt's forces that might have otherwise reinforced the expeditionary force in Yemen and endangered even more Yemen's neighbors. This role was all the more appreciated after Nasser persuaded the Soviets to support his Yemen War financially and with additional weapons, and as the Soviets endeavored to form a grouping of radical Arab states under their aegis.

The Watershed of the 1967 Crisis and War

Israel's role as a check on forces and potential developments detrimental to American Middle East interests reached a high point in the 1967 crisis. During the three weeks that preceded the Six Day War Nasser had created a situation in which the entire Middle East was staked on the outcome of the crisis. A military victory for Nasser would not only have crippled or destroyed Israel, but would also have put him in a position to establish his hegemony in the Middle East and sweep it clean of any remaining American positions, including the oil-rich Arab countries with the principal of which he was still engaged in war in Yemen. Even just a political victory would have placed Nasser in a strong position to venture a new confrontation with Israel later on, and in the meantime would have put him in a perilously powerful position in the entire Arab world, to the detriment of the United States and the benefit of the Soviet Union. The United States would have then faced the dilemma of taking direct drastic action to check and reverse these outcomes at a time when the Vietnam War was sapping its national unity and will and absorbing a vast portion of its military resources, or resigning itself to them with incalculable consequences for its global position.

Israel's complete and swift victory, achieved "cleanly" through its own unaided forces, dispelled these spectres, brought immediate relief to threatened friendly Arab countries, and in many ways turned the tables on the Soviets and their clients. It was the United States that was now in a position to use its client's victory to check and roll back the Soviet position in the Middle East, to promote a new order in the area that protected and advanced its own interests, and to use its Middle East position as a leverage to influence the Soviets' behavior in the global arena.

Because the 1967 crisis and war raised so much the stakes at play in the superpower rivalry as well as in the conflict between Israel and its enemies, the period since has been marked by very intense many-sided diplomatic activity punctuated by frequent threats, limited warfare, and sharp general war. This, coupled with developments in the global arena, naturally led to fluctuations in the American policy conceptions and courses that sometimes corresponded and sometimes clashed with those of Israel. Throughout the fluctuations, however, the basic American interest and strategy in the Middle East remained heavily centered on Israel, reinforcing and being reinforced by the abiding moral interest in the democratic Jewish state.

The Third Stage, 1967–1973

The collapse of the previous American attempts to stabilize the Middle East situation through a military balance and the record of repeated attempts by the Soviets and their Arab friends to exploit the Arab-Israeli conflict to undermine and try to destroy the American position in the Middle East impelled the United States to attempt to use Israel's victory to achieve a "final" settlement of the conflict. It accordingly decided to help Israel resist all diplomatic and military pressures to pull back from the territories it had captured during the war and conversely to maintain the pressure of the Israeli occupation on its enemies until the latter concluded with it a comprehensive peace agreement. This decision marked a crucial turning point in American-Israeli relations in that it wedded America's real interests in the Middle East to Israel's and brought the real American interest into complete harmony with the moral interest in Israel.

However, although the United States and Israel came to share the same basic objective of a peace agreement and the same basic strategy of denying to the belligerent Arab states recovery of any of their lost territories by any means other than movement toward peace, the two also had particular interests of their own that did not always coincide or harmonize. The United States had additional interests in friendly Arab countries and global concerns related to the Middle East situation, and Israel had particular territorial demands it wanted to achieve in a peace settlement and was subject to internal constraints that entailed at times different tactical conceptions. In the course of the years 1967–1973, these differences sometimes came into play, creating strain between the two countries; sometimes they were suppressed or subsumed under their joint interests, making for harmony in their relations. The interplay between their common basic interests and their respective particular concerns may be reviewed in terms of three phases.

Phase 1, 1967–1968. During this phase the United States shaped its basic postwar position in a manner that corresponded almost entirely with Israel's views at the time. While foiling the Soviet-Arab campaign to force Israel to withdraw unconditionally after the pattern of 1956, the United States proclaimed through President Johnson the "Five Principles" of its policy which in effect sought to use Israel's victory to achieve a comprehensive peace settlement on terms that met the basic interests of the two countries. For a moment the administration explored the possibility of tempting the Soviet Union with American collaboration in working out a Middle East settlement in exchange for Soviet collaboration in facilitating a Vietnam solution, but as the Soviets seemed to show little interest in the exchange, the administration continued to play its strong Middle East hand independently. It acceded, along with the Soviets, key Arab states, and Israel to Security Council Resolution 242, but it read it as incorporating Johnson's Five Principles and in the same spirit as Israel's reading. When the Soviets rebuilt the Egyptian and Syrian arsenals to a point that might tempt them to contemplate war as a means of recovering their territories, Johnson decided to sell Israel fifty Phantom fighter-bombers, virtually doubling the capacity of its air force, to help it negate that option to the Arabs and discourage the Soviets.

Phase 2, 1969–1970. The almost complete identification of American policy with Israel's under the Johnson administration had caused apprehensions among members of the foreign policy "establishment" within and outside the government bureaucracy, especially after Johnson decided to provide Israel with Phantoms toward the end of his term. The apprehensions were partly due to substantive concerns about the implications of America's massive military support for Israel; but they were also due in large measure to a lag in perception, involving a failure to recognize the extent of the convergence that had taken place between the real interests of the United States and Israel and a view of the action of the Johnson administration as motivated by political and emotional considerations. There was therefore an expectation that the advent of a new Republican administration headed by a combative President who owed no obligation to Israel's friends at home would bring about a far-reaching policy change.

In fact, although President Nixon was predisposed to believe that his Democratic predecessor might have excessively indulged Israel, after sober consideration of the situation he quickly came to the same basic conclusions as had President Johnson. He recognized that the United States' fundamental interests in the Middle East hinged on a final resolution of the Arab-Israel conflict, that the territories held by Israel provided the essential means to bring the Arab states and the Soviet Union to agree to such a settlement, and that it was necessary to maintain Israeli military superiority to deter war and deny the Arabs and the Soviets the alternative of recovering the territories by force. However, the Nixon administration was anxious to further two particular aims while advancing an Arab-Israeli settlement. It wanted to protect the regimes of friendly Arab countries, which were believed to be exposed to added pressure by a complete American identification with Israel, and it wanted to promote détente instead of confrontation with the Soviet Union in the hope of facilitating a solution to Vietnam and a limitation of the strategic arms race. The pursuit of these particular objectives led the administration to adopt during the first two years of its tenure courses and positions that clashed with Israel's views and preferences and periodically strained relations between the two countries.

As part of the new approach, the United States engaged in the Big Two and Big Four talks aimed at elaborating Resolution 242 into an outline of a Middle East settlement to be pressed on the parties by the big powers. The United States and the Soviet Union arrived at some agreed conclusions which were turned down by Egypt and Israel, but while the Soviets reneged on the conclusions after Egypt rejected them, the United States adhered to them despite Israel's opposition and proclaimed them as its plan for resolving the conflict. Indeed, the point of the Rogers Plan was precisely to establish a distinction and a distance between the United States' position and Israel's in order to ease the pressure on friendly Arab governments.

As part of the same approach, the United States "held in abeyance" an urgent Israeli request for arms at the height of the war of attrition, even while reasserting the principle of "balance of power" and giving Israel financial assistance. It wanted to induce similar restraint on the part of the Soviets with respect to their clients and to avoid embarrassment to friendly Arab governments. When the Soviets refused to agree to limit arms shipments and on the contrary went on to accelerate their supply of arms and advisers and even to commit their personnel to combat in Egypt, the President agreed to provide Israel with a limited quantity of arms, but he insisted on doing so discreetly out of regard for friendly Arab countries and in order not to jeopardize a new political move by Secretary Rogers aimed at achieving a limited cease-fire and a resumption of negotiations under United Nations emissary Gunnar Jarring.

Each of these episodes involved more or less sharp and open disputes between the United States and Israel, in which the protagonist on the American side was Secretary of State Rogers rather than the President. The last of these, the Rogers Initiative, raised the dispute to the level of acute crisis and Israel finally adhered to it only after the President secretly qualified the Rogers Plan to support "defensible borders" for it and promised it additional weapons.

Phase 3, August 1970–October 1973. When the Nixon administration started out on its new Middle East policy, the particular aims of promoting détente and protecting American positions in friendly Arab countries while pursuing an Arab-Israeli settlement seemed to go hand in hand in suggesting a position of distance from Israel and restraint in supplying arms to it. By the spring of 1970, Soviet behavior in the international arena generally and in the Middle East in particular was raising strong suspicions that the Soviet Union viewed American moderation as an indication of weakness to be exploited rather than as a factor facilitating cooperation. After reneging on the agreed conclusions of the Big Two talks, the Soviets had gone on to reject an American proposal to limit the supply of arms to the Middle East, increased the supply of weapons to Egypt and multiplied the number of "advisers" there, and finally committed their personnel to combat. The President's principal foreign policy advisers were sharply divided as to what the United States should do in response. Kissinger, the architect of the détente policy, stressed the need to respond to Soviet truculence in the Middle East by standing firmly and more closely behind Israel and meeting pressure with counterpressure. Secretary Rogers, fearing the repercussions in friendly Arab countries, advocated continuing to maintain a distance from Israel and trying to check the dangerous situation that led to increased Soviet intervention through a new political initiative to end the fighting. The President was temperamentally inclined to the views of his national security adviser but decided to adopt a forceful stance in Vietnam (the incursion into Cambodia), while in the Middle East he tried to straddle the positions of his principal advisers. He gave secret encouragement to Israel while publicly supporting the Rogers Initiative. The success of that initiative seemed to vindicate the secretary of state, but the further course of events undermined Rogers' position and brought the President down firmly on the side of Kissinger's.

The first relevant event was the Soviet connivance with the Egyptians to violate the standstill cease-fire to gain a strategic advantage over Israel they had failed to gain by war. This led the United States, with the reluctant assent of the secretary of state, publicly to promise Israel additional arms to right the military position and keep Israel committed to negotiations. Before that issue was definitely settled, the crucial events of the September 1970 Jordanian civil war occurred. The intervention of Syrian troops on the side of the PLO was generally seen as inconceivable without Soviet connivance, and its consequences were deemed potentially disastrous. Were the Syrian-PLO coalition to succeed in overthrowing King Hussein's regime, the entire American peace endeavor would be disrupted, friendly regimes including the oil-rich countries would be exposed to hostile regimes by the removal of the Jordanian buffer, and the chances of general war in the area would be immeasureably increased. This latest instance of Soviet "treachery" not only justified Kissinger's apprehensiveness in the eyes of the President, but also pointed to the need to adopt the kind of response recommended by him. This became particularly clear when consideration of possible American reactions by the military chiefs led to the conclusion that the only effective moves that could be undertaken required Israeli participation in the planning and execution.

The success of the actual plans for graduated Israeli and then American-Israeli intervention worked out by Kissinger and Israeli Ambassador Rabin in compelling the Syrians to withdraw and saving King Hussein's regime after the mere deployment of Israeli forces marked a turning point in

Nixon administration policy. Henceforth, the President allowed his secretary of state to continue exploring new initiatives aimed at promoting a partial or comprehensive settlement, but he did not permit him to put into question for any length of time the United States' commitment to massive military support for Israel—all the more so since that policy not only did not produce an escalation of Soviet support for their Arab clients but rather seemed to combine neatly with the American overture to China and incredibly forceful initiatives in Vietnam to impel the Soviets at last to respond positively to the American call for détente in many areas. In the meantime, the Soviets' more cautious behavior after the Jordanian episode discouraged plans for warlike initiatives by Egypt and generated friction between the two countries which reached a climax in the expulsion of Soviet advisers from Egypt and the closing down of Soviet bases in that country in July 1972.

By that time the policy of the Nixon administration as articulated by Kissinger in the State of the World Message had been turned on its head. The objectives of advancing a settlement while promoting détente in an area of confrontation and protecting oil-rich Arab countries remained the same, but these objectives were now seen to be best served by a policy of unequivocal military support for Israel and increasing identification with its policy conceptions rather than by taking a distance from it and severely rationing the supply of arms to it. The reversal found a symbolic expression in the second Soviet-American summit in Washington in the early summer of 1973. Whereas the original policy began with Soviet-American talks to work out a settlement, now the President and his national security adviser insisted before Party Secretary Brezhnev that the Arab-Israeli conflict could be settled only by direct negotiations between the parties, and rejected his plea that at least Jarring should renew his intermediary role.

Two minor concerns qualified the otherwise complete satisfaction of the United States. One was that the longer the status quo lasted, the more Israel seemed to expect from a settlement and the more "facts" it established that might hamper eventual agreement. The other was the restlessness that friendly oil-rich Arab countries were beginning to manifest about the stalemate because of fear that it might lead to radical upheavals in the area and a reassertion of Soviet influence. These concerns led the United States to reiterate periodically its interest in a settlement and to explore occasionally ways in which it might help advance one. But neither appeared to be sufficiently urgent to upset through any drastic initiative the almost complete convergence of American and Israeli conceptions and interests.

The Fourth Stage, October 1973–September 1975

The Yom Kippur War provided an occasion for the most vivid expression of the American-Israeli alliance that had been developing since the Six Day War. For the first time in the war-studded record of the Arab-Israeli conflict, the

United States intervened openly and dramatically on Israel's side, providing it with massive amounts of arms and financial assistance to help it repel its assailants and win. At the same time, however, the war undermined or over-turned virtually all the calculations and assumptions that underlay the almost complete orientation of American Middle East policy on Israel in the last few prewar years. Contrary to expectations, the Arabs were not deterred from going to war, Israel did not win quickly and easily, and the Soviet Union, despite détente, did not stay out of the conflict. In addition, "friendly" Arab countries used the oil weapon against the United States and Western Europe, Western Europe broke ranks with the United States, and the United States and the Soviet Union came to open confrontation. The United States believed that the Arab-Israeli conflict had been defused, contained, and insulated; instead it proved to be as explosive as ever, and the repercussions of the explosion proved to be more far-reaching than ever. They thrust the conflict into a critical pattern of intertwined relationships in which the fate of the Middle East, the viability of NATO, and the future of superpower relations were at stake.

The fact that America's prewar conceptions turned out to be invalid and the reality that emerged in their place naturally called for a new policy direction. Already before the full ramifications of the new situation became apparent, Secretary of State Kissinger (now formally and fully in charge of American policy) had come to the conclusion that it was necessary for the United States to use the war to advance a settlement of the conflict, and had tried to foster what he deemed to be propitious conditions for such an endeavor. He had helped place Israel in a position to check the Arabs militarily and secured the agreement of the Soviets and the Arabs to peace negotiations as a condition for the cease-fire, and he had prevented Israel from achieving the decisive military victory that came within its reach and made certain that Egypt gave the United States the full credit for saving its forces from destruction. Immediately after the war, Kissinger sought to widen the overture he had made toward Egypt in order to propel the United States and himself into the role of a credible peace broker, and thus short-circuit the perilous intermeshing of superpower, European, and Middle East issues that had developed by then.

The new American policy of reaching out to the Arab side and urgently seeking to promote a settlement continued to involve a decisive measure of interdependence between American and Israeli interests and conceptions; but it also created substantial potential differences between the two. On the one hand, the two countries had an interest in achieving a real peace that was only heightened by the experience they had, the one of the risks of war and the other of its ordeals as well. In addition, the secretary of state keenly realized that Israel's strength was the factor that preserved the possibility of negotiations (having supported Israel for that very end), and that that strength had to be sustained to keep the possibility open. Kissinger was also aware that

Israel's continuing control of territories wanted by the Arabs provided the assets that gave negotiations a reasonable chance of success, and that America's support of Israel contributed no less than the gestures it made toward the Arabs in making them receptive to the overture it made to them. Israel's government, for its part, realized that Israel's much increased dependence on the United States for the arms and money it needed to maintain its strength and for protection against possible Soviet military intervention required it to bend a great deal to accommodate America's particular concerns.

On the other hand, the new direction also entailed substantial differences of views between the United States and Israel regarding the degree of urgency of a settlement, the proper timing for it, the short-term implications of failure to settle, and above all regarding the essential terms of a settlement. For the United States, a settlement had become a matter of imperative necessity, for Israel it was still only a desirable consummation; for the United States, the oil embargo and the international complications made it necessary to start on the road to settlement immediately, for Israel the shock of war and internal political conditions made it difficult to do so right away. For the United States, the alternative to prompt movement toward settlement was continuing Arab-Israeli confrontation and possibly war with their horrendous possible consequences, for Israel continuation of the confrontation for a while longer and even resumption of the fighting could be helpful rather than damaging to its bargaining position. Most important of all, the United States' vital interest in a peace settlement as such tended to overshadow its concern for the terms of a settlement, while Israel continued to be interested in a settlement only if it met certain conditions relating to its national security and aspirations.

Immediately after the war, these differences between the American and Israeli perspectives came into play and led to a very strained moment in American-Israeli relations. Secretary Kissinger pressed Israel very hard to relinquish its stranglehold on the Egyptian Third Army, and President Nixon justified that move not just by reference to the need to consolidate the ceasefire but also by placing it in the context of a general view of American policy which envisaged far-reaching Israeli withdrawals without any particular quid pro quos other than helping the United States to advance a total settlement on the best terms achievable. However, the very strain that developed as a result of the clash of perspectives helped underscore the reality of the interdependence of the interests of the two countries and impelled their leaders to explore and adopt a gradual, open-ended approach to peace, "step by step." This approach did not guarantee agreement between the United States and Israel, let alone between Arabs and Israelis, as events were to show, but as events were also to show, it did make it possible for the two to effect a successful transition through the critical postwar period, to overcome their respective immediate problems, and to work out gradually an understanding on basic principles and particular issues centrally relevant to future progress toward a Middle East peace settlement.

In the course of the two years following the Yom Kippur War, the United States made six attempts to promote limited agreements between Israel and several of its neighbors. Only four of these were successful, but all were significant landmarks in the endeavor of the United States and Israel mutually to adapt and adjust their postwar policies and interests. The attempts and their significance are summarized as follows:

1. *The Six Point Agreement, November 8, 1973.* This agreement between Egypt and Israel settled the questions of supply to the beleaguered Egyptian Third Army and exchange of prisoners of war, and subsumed the problem of demarcation of the cease-fire lines under the broader question of disengagement of forces which the two parties agreed to negotiate.

The agreement began to turn Egypt and Israel away from war and laid the foundation for the concept of gradual movement toward peace by defining a limited agenda for the next step. It began to establish Kissinger as a peace broker with Egypt and reassure the Israelis that the American overture toward Egypt did not need work to their detriment.

2. *The Egyptian-Israeli Disengagement Agreement, January 18, 1974.* This agreement disengaged the forces of Egypt and Israel, involved the first significant Israeli withdrawal from occupied territories, and saw the first formal and practical Egyptian commitments to a process of peace-seeking. It definitely established the concept of step-by-step movement toward peace even while retaining the framework of the Geneva Peace Conference, and it definitely established Kissinger as an effective peace broker between Israel and its neighbors.

The agreement made it possible for the United States to have the Arab oil embargo removed. It undercut the danger of Soviet exploitation of Arab grievances to put pressure on the United States and NATO, and it began to restore the shaken confidence of Western Europe in America's leadership. The United States achieved these crucial gains while reinforcing, rather than weakening, its understanding with Israel, for whom the agreement was beneficial both in itself and because it began to engage the United States as a guarantor of the peace.

3. *The Syrian-Israeli Disengagement Agreement, May 31, 1974.* This accord settled pending dangerous cease-fire problems while repeating the pattern of the Egyptian-Israeli disengagement agreement. It consolidated the achievements gained through the latter by bringing Syria into the gradual peace process and extending America's broker role to all the countries directly involved in the Arab-Israeli conflict.

Because of objective circumstances and the record of particularly bitter hostility between Syria and Israel, the completion of the agreement required a greater American input than the Egyptian accord, not only in terms of the time invested by the secretary of state in promoting it but also in terms of specific obligations assumed by the United States toward Israel to induce it to agree to its terms. One obligation was to endeavor to place American supply of arms to Israel on a long-term basis. Another was to support politically Israeli military reactions against possible guerrilla action originating from Syrian territory.

4. *Failure to Start Negotiations for a Jordanian-Israeli Disengagement, June–October 1974.* Between June and October 1974 the United States endeavored to persuade Israel to conclude a limited agreement with Jordan to bring it into the picture as a party to the negotiations and undercut the rival claim of the PLO to be the exclusive spokesman for the Palestinians. Israel's government resisted for internal political reasons, preferring to seek next another limited agreement with Egypt. In October the issue was foreclosed for the foreseeable future as the Arab summit in Rabbat unanimously endorsed the claim of the PLO and Jordan's King Hussein officially bowed out of the scene.

The episode was significant as an indication of the disposition of the American leadership to bend its best judgment to accommodate Israel, especially where, as in this instance, there was no clear and present penalty for doing so.

5. *Failure of the Attempt at a Second Egyptian-Israeli Agreement, February 10–15 and March 8–22, 1975.* In this third campaign of shuttle diplomacy Secretary Kissinger tried and failed to achieve an agreement involving Israeli withdrawal from the Sinai passes and oil fields in exchange for Egyptian political concessions to Israel. Although unpropitious bargaining circumstances as between Egypt and Israel, change of leadership personnel in Israel and the United States, and tactical errors on the part of Kissinger and the new Israeli leadership team contributed to the aborted negotiations, the failure was ultimately due to a renewed expression of the difference of perspectives between the United States and Israel regarding the degree of urgency of a settlement and the essential conditions it must meet. The ensuing crisis in American-Israeli relations served once again to underscore, but in a very concrete and specific context, the extent to which the interests of the two countries were interdependent. It also drove home to both the necessity for mutual accommodation, which bore relevance not only to a limited Egyptian-Israeli agreement but also to any future overall settlement.

The United States under President Ford badly needed a Middle East success to compensate for foreign policy setbacks in Vietnam, Turkey, and Portugal and applied heavy pressure on Israel to make the concessions necessary to secure agreement. When Israel resisted, the administration blamed it for the failure of the negotiations and declared a "reassessment" of its entire Middle East policy while restricting the flow of arms and economic aid to

Israel. The reassessment centered on exploring the alternative to the step-by-step approach of convening the Geneva Peace Conference and seeking a comprehensive settlement, but the exploration demonstrated fairly soon the futility and dangers of that option under the existing circumstances.

In the first place, there was the problem of Palestinian representation, on which the United States for its own reasons opposed the Rabbat stance to which the Arabs were committed. Even if that hurdle were somehow overcome, the United States would find itself caught in the conference between Israeli positions over which it would have little influence, and Arab positions which inter-Arab outbidding and Soviet support would very likely make unyielding. Sooner or later the United States would be forced to choose between coming down entirely on the Arab side, or drawing a line beyond which it would not go against Israel. The latter would precipitate a polarization that would pit the United States and Israel against the Soviets and the Arabs and undo everything American policy had accomplished so far; the former would precipitate an all-out confrontation with Israel that would certainly arouse massive opposition from Congress and public opinion, might drive Israel to take desperate courses, but above all would greatly diminish the leverage that the United States would be able to apply to the Middle East situation in the long run, leaving its position there entirely dependent on Arab goodwill.

The reassessment thus brought out in a very specific and concrete context that while the United States had a vital interest in a Middle East settlement, that interest could be served only by a settlement that preserved a strong American-Israeli connection and therefore a settlement to which Israel could be induced to agree. This meant that the United States should go to Geneva only in a context of a cooperative relationship with Israel, and the immediate implication was that the United States should first attempt to revive the negotiations for a limited Egyptian-Israeli agreement, seek to expand the concessions Egypt was prepared to make, and compensate Israel for the ones required of it to make an agreement possible.

Interestingly enough, Egypt and Saudi Arabia saw the situation in a similar light. They feared that Geneva might never convene because of the Palestinian representation problem. Even if they compromised on this issue, they did not believe that the interests of the United States would allow it to go through with an all-out confrontation with Israel, and they did not like the prospect of polarization and tying the Arab cause once more exclusively to the Soviet Union any more than did the United States. They realized that the ability of the United States to "deliver" Israel lay precisely in the very close connection between them and did not mind if the United States had to compensate Israel to make it accede to Arab demands. This is why they, too, put aside the Geneva conference idea and sought to facilitate a new attempt at a limited agreement.

The crisis led Israel's government, too, to make its own reassessment and come out with conclusions that converged with those of the United States. Israel had engaged in the step-by-step process to gain time and avoid having to negotiate a comprehensive settlement in circumstances where its diplomatic-strategic position was comparatively weak because the impact of Arab oil power was at its height. That strategy, however, depended on retaining the diplomatic, military, and economic support of the United States, and the suspension of that support in the months following the failure of the March negotiations drove that point home. In those negotiations Israel had specifically sought to trade off the Sinai passes and oil fields on which Egypt insisted for particular concessions that would effectively take Egypt out of the war at least for a number of years. Since it could not obtain those concessions from Egypt, and since the United States nevertheless evinced a very strong interest in an agreement, the Israeli government decided to seek from the United States security compensations to make up for those that Egypt would not concede. Since the United States had come to the same conclusion and since Egypt did not object to the idea, the basis was laid for the resumption of negotiations for a partial agreement with greatly enhanced chances of success.

6. *The Second Sinai Agreement, September 4, 1975.* By virtue of this agreement, Israel assented to evacuate the Sinai passes and hand over intact to Egypt the Sinai oil fields. In exchange, Egypt committed itself not to resort to force and to seek a settlement of the conflict by peaceful means, to leave the areas evacuated by Israel demilitarized and under United Nations control, to observe reciprocal limitations of armament and military presence beyond the United Nations buffer zones, to permit nonmilitary cargo destined for or coming from Israel to pass through the Suez Canal, and various other measures. The agreement was to be valid for three years unless superseded by another.

In order to make the agreement possible, the United States assumed several obligations which made it virtually a formal arbitrator and guarantor of it. It committed itself to position American civilian personnel in the passes to supervise an electronic warning system consisting of an Israeli and an Egyptian strategic early warning station and an American-manned tactical surveillance station. In addition, the United States agreed to continue aircraft and satellite reconnaissance to ascertain compliance with the terms of the accord, and undertook to consult with either party in case of violation of the agreement by the other "as to the significance of the violation and possible remedial action by the United States."

As far as Israel was concerned, the United States balanced the exchange it made with Egypt with a whole array of assurances, undertakings, and commitments expressed mainly in a Memorandum of Agreement which amounted to a virtual alliance in all but the name. The memorandum included several clauses that pledged the United States generally and specifically to help Israel on a long-term and ongoing basis to meet its requirements for arms, economic assistance, and energy. Other clauses committed the United States to support Israel's right to free and unimpeded navigation in the Strait of Bab el Mandeb and the Strait of Gibraltar and its right to fly over them. The United States also undertook to conclude promptly contingency plans for arms supply to Israel in an emergency. One clause reiterated the "long-standing commitment" of the United States to the "survival and security" of Israel and asserted that the United States government would "view with particular gravity threats to Israel's security or sovereignty by a world power." In the event of such threat, it would "consult promptly with the government of Israel with respect to what support, diplomatic or otherwise, or assistance it can lend to Israel in accordance with its constitutional practices."

Besides these long-term obligations, the United States subscribed to several commitments designed to reassure Israel about American policy in the next diplomatic stage. These included notably a pledge not to recognize the PLO or negotiate with it as long as it did not recognize Israel's right to exist and did not accept Resolutions 242 and 338, to oppose to the point of using the veto any initiative in the Security Council to alter adversely these resolutions or the terms of reference of the Geneva Conference, and to coordinate with Israel the timing of the reconvening of the conference and the strategy to be pursued there.

The Next Stage in American-Israeli Relations

The conclusion of the Sinai II Agreement marked a high point in the endeavor of the United States and Israel to accommodate each other's perceived interests in the postwar circumstances which bode well for the prospects of further cooperation on their part in connection with the pursuit of a general peace settlement. These prospects were further enhanced by the success of the leaders of the two countries in weathering the difficulties stirred by the inter-Arab strife that followed in the wake of the agreement, and by their effective handling of the much more threatening problems raised by the Lebanese civil war. Yet, by May 1977 relations between the United States and Israel were under the shadow of greater uncertainty than they had known in a very long time, and the air was thick with speculation about an imminent crisis.

Ironically, the reasons for the abrupt change in atmosphere go back to the workings of democracy in the two countries. In the United States the November 1976 elections placed in the White House a President who was deeply committed to open diplomacy and was a firm believer in the power of the spoken word. From the moment he assumed office, President Carter gave top priority to the need to advance a comprehensive peace settlement in the Middle East and proceeded to work toward that objective by making declaration after declaration stating his views on critical issues of substance and procedure and conveying feelings and judgments about countries and leaders involved. Although the substantive positions he adopted did not differ much from the known private convictions of his two predecessors and of former Secretary of State Kissinger, the public enunciation of these positions in advance of negotiations and even of serious bilateral consultations created an atmosphere of tension and a situation in which the President appeared to be gambling on either a quick breakthrough or prompt confrontation with one party or another.

If the Carter approach had a reasonable chance of being effective with leaders of Israel's Labor government, it had only a minimal chance of working on the new Likkud regime made possible by the May 17, 1977, elections. The Labor leaders had at least had ample opportunity in their dealings with American leaders to anticipate American intents and to think of possible ways to accommodate their own with them, whereas the Likkud leaders, especially its chief, Menachem Begin, were disposed both by inclination and by habit acquired in the course of three decades of opposition to be guided by ideological conviction and always to think that more could be sought and achieved than the Labor government allowed was possible. And so a situation developed in May 1977 wherein President Carter, who had pronounced himself publicly in favor of the pre-1967 boundaries with "minor adjustments" and in favor of a Palestinian homeland, was expecting to receive in Washington Prime Minister Begin, who had vowed not to retreat from "liberated" Judea, Samaria, and Gaza and to consider a territorial compromise in Sinai and the Golan only in the context of complete peace.

Although a confrontation between the United States and Israel appeared highly likely to follow the leaders' meeting, the resolution of the confrontation before it did irreparable damage seemed to lie in recognition by the two of three interrelated principles, or rather imperatives, which emerge from the realities of the Middle East situation and the experience of the two countries since the Yom Kippur War. These imperatives are: the United States and Israel must strive to advance a settlement in every possible way; United States policy must have a dual orientation, on Israel as well as on Arab states; and the United States must be prepared to inject major "inputs" to make possible Arab-Israeli agreement.

Striving to advance a settlement has become imperative because the Arab-Israeli conflict has proved to be impervious to long-term stabilization by any other means, and because a new explosion of it in war could cause devastating damage without holding any promise of improved chances of settlement no matter what outcome the war had. In general, the conflict has proved impervious to stabilization because too many critical variables have become entangled in it to make control of all of them possible. More specifically, balance of power and Israeli military superiority failed to deter the Arabs from

596 / *Israel and America in International Politics*

going to war in October 1973 in order to break the political stalemate and are less likely to do so in the future. For one thing, trying to maintain Israeli military superiority indefinitely is bound to prove enormously costly in the face of the virtually unlimited financial resources available to potential Arab coalitions. Even now, before the Arab resources have been put into full play, the effort to maintain a provisional Israeli deterrent capacity is costing the United States some $2 billion a year in assistance to Israel and is taxing to the utmost Israeli resources. But even if the problem of cost and other bottlenecks were somehow overcome, the deterrent would not be effective as long as the Arabs could profit diplomatically even from a war they might lose militarily, and that kind of situation is almost certain to persist in the foreseeable future because of the Arabs' command over oil resources needed by the Western world, their command of finances deriving from oil, their great potential strategic depth, and the normal play of big-power rivalries.

Even before the outbreak of any future war, the political alignments and military preparations preceding it could undo everything the United States managed to accomplish since the October 1973 war and could wreak havoc in the relative positions of the United States and the Soviet Union in the Middle East and in American–West European relations. With so much at stake, the war could easily lead to a disastrous superpower confrontation. Against these enormous potential costs, the potential benefits of even a swift and "clean" Israeli military victory would not be very substantial. Such a victory might gain some time before the Arabs recovered and rebuilt their forces, and might even induce Arab leaders to moderate their terms for a settlement; but as long as the Arabs are not reduced to a condition of complete helplessness, which is out of the question in view of the basic disparity of resources between them and Israel, there is no assurance at all that the new terms of the Arabs would be acceptable to Israel. This is not necessarily because Israel's "appetite" might grow, but simply because the experience of the conflict might well increase its needs—just as happened after the 1967 war.

The argument was recently made that if Israel were to adopt a nuclear strategy—that is, to declare possession of nuclear weapons as a deterrent—a stable framework for the Arab-Israeli conflict might be created. That argument is deeply flawed and fraught with disaster. If the nuclear strategy is intended to deter a war aiming at the destruction of Israel, then it is unnecessary. The strong *suspicion* that Israel has a "last resort" nuclear capability coupled with its conventional military capacity and American commitments to its survival are ample to take care of such a threat, and all the evidence suggests that the Arabs have indeed drawn the appropriate lesson. If the nuclear strategy is aimed at deterring the Arabs from undertaking general or limited war for more limited objectives, then the deterrent will not be credible and therefore will not be effective. In the meantime, Israel's declaring possession of nuclear weapons would cause the Arabs to seek from one or more of the world's nuclear powers extension of a nuclear umbrella over them according to the terms and spirit of the existing international treaty against nuclear proliferation, and would precipitate frantic collective efforts on their part to acquire a nuclear capacity of their own. This would give rise to a transition period of great uncertainty and explosiveness; and even if this were successfully traversed and both Israel and the Arabs ended up with second-strike capabilities, the balance of terror would be highly unstable. Each side would still endeavor to preserve its own second-strike capacity against perceived efforts by the other to negate it; and this would add the costs of a nuclear arms race to those of a conventional one while giving rise to frequent occasions in which one side or the other might be tempted to strike first.

It has sometimes been argued that strategic depth and the resources commanded by the Arabs, which were cited above as contributing reasons barring stabilization through deterrence and making war highly unprofitable from either an American or an Israeli point of view, ought to make the Arabs unwilling to settle and should therefore cast doubt on the sincerity of their proclaimed desire to achieve a lasting peace. This argument erroneously assumes that what is bad for Israel is necessarily good for the Arabs and vice versa (a zero-sum game in the jargon of conflict theory). It specifically ignores the other considerations cited that make it highly unrealistic for the Arabs to aspire to the destruction of Israel and compel them to limit their aims. It also overlooks the point that continuing confrontation entails heavy costs and dangers to the regimes of key Arab countries too, and that only the lack of any other alternative and the pressures of stalemate are apt to force them into incurring these costs.

The second imperative is closely related to the first but also stands on its own grounds. It is crucial to keep in mind that what we call "dual orientation" has nothing to do with the inane slogan of "evenhandedness," which suggests images of the United States as a kind of Olympian power above the Arab-Israeli fray, free to dispense favors evenly or unevenly. It means rather that there must be recognition that the United States has crucial interests in Arab countries as well as in Israel, and that the pursuit of these interests in the years ahead requires it to endeavor to cultivate good relations with the ones as well as the other and to seek to accommodate their principal respective concerns. Apart from the highly detrimental consequences of confrontation and war, the United States has a very substantial diplomatic-strategic interest in preventing the reassertion of Soviet influence in Egypt and its recovery in Syria. It has a vital strategic-economic-political interest in ensuring the uninterrupted flow of Arabian oil to itself and its NATO allies. And it has a crucial interest in securing the cooperation of Saudi Arabia in restraining the rise of oil prices, and a very important financial interest in exporting goods and services to oil-rich Arab countries. The American moral and strategic-political interests in Israel have already been examined and it is only necessary here to point out that the successes that the United States has encountered in advancing its interests in the Arab countries have rested decisively on its especially close relationship with Israel, as President Sadat himself often avowed. Preserving that relationship is important both in itself and in order to make it desirable for the Arab countries to continue to seek the goodwill of the United States. It is also useful as a safeguard against possible future unfavorable winds that may sweep the Middle East area. Doing this while cultivating the American interests in Arab countries can be realized only in the context of striving to achieve a settlement of the Arab-Israeli conflict.

The third imperative derives from the first two and from a judgment based on the record about the possibilities of resolving the Arab-Israeli conflict. It seems obvious from the history of the conflict since 1967, but especially since 1971, that Israel's demands for territorial changes to meet its critically sensed security needs and the Arab demands to recover all the lost territories in the name of national sovereignty and honor cannot be reconciled in terms of the existing elements of the situation. Ingenious schemes such as the one proposed in the Brookings report might narrow the differences between the parties considerably; but ultimately, the equation of the parties' crucial concerns cannot be completely balanced without an additional external input. Since the United States is vitally interested in a settlement and since it is bound to pursue a dual orientation, it must be prepared to provide that external input to make possible a settlement acceptable to both parties.

Sinai II demonstrated that point in every way. The failure of the first try in March 1975 showed that American mediation endeavors could narrow the gap between the parties' positions but could not close it entirely. The "reassessment" crisis showed that trying to close the gap merely by applying pressure and threat to one side (in this case Israel) to force it to move forward could be self-defeating from the point of view of broader American interests. The resolution of the crisis became possible after the United States succeeded in inducing Egypt to take another step forward and then induced Israel to close the remaining gap by providing it with the added security and other assets it sought in exchange for the passes and the oil fields but did not get from Egypt. In the context of a comprehensive peace settlement, the American input on the Arab side is likely to take the form of massive economic and technological assistance. On the Israeli side, it will probably require nothing less than turning the present tacit alliance into a formal American-Israeli mutual security pact, on the model of the American-Japanese treaty. That pact will have stronger validity than many another to which the United States is presently a party because of America's longstanding special relationship with Israel.

Postscript: Marching to Peace by Leaps and Stumbles, 1977–1980

When President Carter and Prime Minister Begin finally met in Washington for the first time in July 1977, the two newly installed leaders decided to avoid confrontation after all. They tacitly agreed instead to tackle the differences between them as they went along, on the principle of "sufficient unto the day the troubles thereof."

Trouble there was aplenty in the days and months that followed, as the Carter administration pushed relentlessly for the convening of the Geneva Peace Conference with Palestinian participation. Nevertheless, the United States and Israel were able to accommodate each other, and, in the end, it was in the inadequately understood sands of inter-Arab differences that the Carter administration's drive to Geneva got bogged down.

At that moment, Egypt's President Sadat, whose imagination and courage were equal to his judgment and interest in a settlement, burst onto the scene with a peace initiative that revolutionized the entire diplomatic and psychological configuration. Although the momentum generated by his November 1977 trip to Jerusalem was soon largely dissipated in the friction of entrenched patterns of behavior, the vested interests that Sadat's initiative had created in its ultimate success impelled Carter, Sadat, and Begin to engage at Camp David in yet another extraordinary diplomatic exercise that resulted in another giant leap forward to peace.

The attempts of the parties to deal with the respective risks and costs incurred in the process of reaching agreement slowed down and then stalled their collective march forward mapped out in the Camp David Accords. However, their advance up to that point almost ruled out the possibility of retreat and once more impelled them to make an extraordinary effort, which led to the historic breakthrough of the signing of the Egyptian-Israeli Peace Treaty and an accompanying agreement on the West Bank and Gaza.

The execution of the Egyptian-Israeli Peace Treaty proceeded to the satisfaction of the parties, but the negotiations on the application of the agreement on the West Bank and Gaza stumbled over serious difficulties and failed to meet the May 1980 target date set for their conclusion. In contrast to similar situations in the past, efforts that were made to rescue the talks failed, because of uneven changes in the bargaining situation brought about by the Egyptian-Israeli treaty, false American moves, and the diplomatic semiparalysis induced by the American elections season. By the end of 1980 the situation was becoming fluid again, offering new possibilities of movement. What the new Reagan administration will make of these possibilities remains to be seen.

The Stalled Drive to Geneva

Contrary to the general expectation in the United States, Israel, and Arab countries, when President Carter and Prime Minister Begin finally met at the White House on July 19 and 20, 1977, they did not come to an open confrontation. The two leaders did express widely divergent views on several key issues, but they agreed to set the differences aside once Begin indicated that he was willing to go to the Geneva Peace Conference and that from his point of view "everything is negotiable." Begin, who was thoroughly skeptical about the Arabs' willingness to make peace with Israel, especially the "full" peace that Carter had said was necessary, sought in effect to toss the ball to the Arabs' court, instead of fighting out his differences with the United States. In the process, he was willing to absolve the United States of the obligation it had assumed in connection with the Sinai II Agreement to coordinate its position and strategy with Israel prior to any conference. Carter, for his part, was so eager to get the conference going that he did not bother to question Begin's premise or even to try to find out what Begin meant by everything being negotiable. Nor did the President attempt to dwell on the particulars of procedure—who would go to Geneva and how the conference would function—beyond mentioning that the Palestinians would have to be represented somehow and getting a vague nod from Begin on that point.

But a confrontation between the Carter administration and the Begin government was not to be so easily averted. On the first of August, 1977, Secretary of State Vance went on an eleven-day tour of Middle Eastern capitals to explore the position of the parties on some issues of substance and to try to achieve an agreement on procedure for the conference. He quickly discovered important differences among the Arab parties, as well as between them and Israel, on the crucial question of the nature and quality of the peace they envisaged, but these were overshadowed by more immediate divergent views on procedure. The Syrians wanted a unified Arab delegation and a specific PLO representation; Sadat favored linking the Palestinian delegation to the Jordanian in order to get the formal conference going and then, to carry on the real negotiations secretly in its shadow; the Saudis sought to bring about an American-PLO dialogue and told Vance that were the United States to agree to such a dialogue, the PLO would announce its readiness to accept Resolution 242, if it were modified to include recognition of Palestinian national rights; Jordan formally adhered to the position that the PLO should be specifically represented but hoped that the difficulties that this position would raise would compel the Arab parties to turn to Jordan and ask it to represent the Palestinians and the West Bank. Israel stuck firmly to the position of having no truck with the PLO and reminded the United States of its obligation to do the same as long as the PLO did not recognize Israel's right to exist and failed to accept Resolutions 242 and 338.

In view of these disparities, the most that Vance could achieve on his various stops was to get Israel and its neighbors to agree to send their foreign ministers to the United States for further discussions. In the meantime, Vance thought that the ideas presented to him by the Saudis were most promising, and he decided to cable to the President a recommendation to act on them even before he returned home. The President agreed, and, on August 8, 1977, announced that acceptance by the PLO of "the applicability of 242" would satisfy the conditions that the United States had set for dealing with it and would permit the opening of an American-PLO dialogue. Israel immediately protested this interpretation of the United States' obligation, but the administration persisted in it and in other attempts to lure the PLO, even after the PLO's Central Council at a meeting in Damascus on August 28, 1977, rejected the idea of even a qualified acceptance of 242.

The administration's attempt to accommodate the PLO shifted the argument back to the United States and Israel. On September 19, 1977, President Carter joined Secretary Vance in discussions with Foreign Minister Dayan on the question of Palestinian representation. Three days later, a formula was reached, but the Arabs rejected it, and the administration asserted that Israel had given the formula an unacceptable interpretation.

On October 1, 1977, Secretary of State Vance and Soviet Foreign Minister Gromyko concluded discussions they held at the margins of the United Nations General Assembly meeting by issuing a paper on guidelines for settling the Arab-Israeli conflict. The paper reiterated the language of Resolution 242 but did not mention it by name, and modified its content to include the necessity for "ensuring the legitimate rights of the Palestinian people." The paper also stated that the settlement of the conflict should be achieved by reconvening the Geneva Conference not later than December 1977, with the participation of representatives of all parties involved in the conflict, including those of the Palestinian people. The omission of any reference to Resolution 242, hitherto the only agreed-upon basis for a settlement, and the unilateral amendment of its language on the Palestinians by the two powers, coupled with the sudden reintroduction by the administration of the Soviet Union into the heart of the peace diplomacy, after former Secretary of State Kissinger had done his utmost to relegate it to a marginal role, immediately triggered a storm of protest. The protest was spearheaded by Israel and its friends, but the dissenters included partisans of a hard line toward the Soviets and members of the administration itself who favored Kissinger's approach. In the Arab camp, too, there was on one side dissatisfaction because the paper did not go far enough, and on the other indignation at the role gratuitously conceded by the United States to the Soviets.

Alarmed by the reaction, President Carter himself engaged Foreign Minister Dayan in a bitter marathon discussion, which was continued uninterruptedly by Secretary Vance and resulted in another American-Israeli compromise, known as "the October 5 working paper." In it the two sides agreed that the Arab parties would be represented at Geneva by a unified delegation that would include Palestinian Arabs; that after the opening sessions the conference would split into working groups comprising Israel, Jordan, Egypt, and the Palestinian Arabs; and that the agreed basis for the negotiations would be Resolutions 242 and 338. In a joint communiqué, the United States and Israel stated that all agreements and understandings between them on the subject remained valid, and that acceptance of the Soviet-American paper was not a prerequisite for anything. The paper was approved by the Israeli Cabinet a week later, though not before Foreign Minister Dayan threatened to resign if it was not. The storm and stress between the United States and Israel proved to have been in vain, for the Arab side, spearheaded by the PLO and the Syrians, rejected the working paper.

Sadat Opens a Way through Jerusalem

On November 9, 1977, President Sadat declared in a speech to the Egyptian National Assembly that, for the sake of sparing the blood of a single Egyptian soldier, he was "prepared to go to the ends of the earth, even to the Knesset in Jerusalem." The statement was picked up by the American media and made the basis of hectic exchanges, which culminated in a formal invitation from Prime Minister Begin that Sadat had promised to accept in advance. On November 19, 1977, Sadat landed at Ben Gurion airport.

At the time of the event and long after, the prevailing view among most observers was that Sadat's trip was an impulsive leap into the dark, triggered by the media's taking him up on his hyperbolic statement to the National Assembly. Subsequent information, however, confirmed the intimations, which very few had at the time, that Sadat's initiative was part of an imaginative design that had its roots in a sober recognition of the relevant politico-strategic realities, a clear-sighted assessment of the prospects of the diplomatic processes that preceded his initiative, and a cautious scouting of the grounds on which he proposed to advance.

Sadat's move rested on a clear grasp of the basic politico-strategic configuration underscored by the Yom Kippur War (see above, pp. 499 ff.). A key premise in that configuration was that the Arabs could not seek the destruction of Israel by force, because of Israel's last-resort nuclear option, the American commitment to Israel's survival, and the limitation of Soviet support to the Arab side. Consequently, the Arab objective vis-à-vis Israel must be scaled down to the recovery of the territories lost in 1967, and the Arabs' military and diplomatic choices must be assessed in relation to that limited objective. In principle, the constraints that ruled out a war for the destruction of Israel did not apply to the option of war to achieve the more limited objective; however, as the first stages of the Yom Kippur War had shown, Arab success in a war with a declared limited objective could be perceived by Israel as presenting a threat to its existence and would trigger either a nuclear response or American intervention on Israel's side to obviate such a response.

Israel's real military capabilities, as demonstrated in the final stages of the Yom Kippur War, were such that if the Arabs were to have better chances of success in another round, they needed first to build up an overwhelming margin of military superiority. Such an effort required the formation of an *enduring* Arab coalition comprising the oil-rich countries and the confrontation states, with the former bankrolling massive acquisitions of arms from the Soviet Union. Even if Egypt were willing to place itself back in a position of dependence on the Soviet Union, it was unlikely that the oil-rich countries would want to do so, or to bind themselves to radical Arab countries. And after all that, the United States could frustrate the Arabs' objective by increasing its military assistance to Israel. Should the Arabs, despite everything, begin to acquire a threatening superiority margin, Israel could pre-empt before the balance tilted decisively against it.

While a strategy aimed at recovering the territories by confrontation and war thus appeared to be extremely unattractive, the prospects of achieving the same objective by diplomatic means seemed to be much more promising. The key to such prospects was the premise that the United States had come to view its national interest as being bound with the achievement of an Arab-Israeli settlement, which Sadat accepted on the evidence of exertions of the previous two administrations in step-by-step diplomacy and the endeavors of the Carter administration to bring about a comprehensive settlement. The problem, as Sadat saw it, was that some of his Arab partners doubted that premise and that the Carter administration, rather than circumventing that difficulty, sought to attack it directly and got inextricably tangled in the web of inter-Arab differences.

Already in February 1977 President Sadat had intimated to President Carter in their first meeting that the Geneva Conference, which Carter was eager to convene, should be viewed as serving the essentially symbolic purposes of bringing all interested parties together in a peace conference and providing a forum for legitimizing agreements. The negotiations themselves should be pursued secretly and separately, with American mediation, between Israel and individual Arab parties, in Geneva itself or elsewhere. This was an adaptation of the model that Kissinger had followed, and it had the same object of allowing Egypt and Israel to advance toward agreement and then using that advance as a lever to prompt agreement between Israel and other Arab parties. Sadat thought that Carter understood this strategy and agreed to it, and he was therefore taken aback when the administration, instead of trying to finesse the problem of Palestinian participation as he had proposed, went instead for the Saudi proposal. Sadat feared that the administration would get bogged down in the problem of procedure, and that, in its effort to overcome the problem, it was apt to jeopardize the chances of success if the conference ever convened. The signing of the Soviet-American paper of October 1, 1977, confirmed these anxieties: while trying to open a way for the PLO, the administration lent its hand in that paper to undermining the status of Resolution 242, hitherto the only agreed legal basis for a settlement. Moreover, the paper gave the Soviets an effective role in the envisaged conference and thus placed them in a position wherein they could attempt to rally the Arab camp behind an all-or-nothing stance in order to isolate the United States. No agreement could result from such confrontation. In the process, Sadat would be placed before the impossible choice of joining the Soviet-Arab side and destroying a promising relationship he had developed with the United States, or joining the United States and Israel in open opposition to the Arab-Soviet camp.

Even before the American endeavors had reached a complete dead end, Sadat had begun to explore the prospects of his own strategy by sending his Deputy Prime Minister, Hassan Tuhami, on September 16, 1977, to meet secretly with Foreign Minister Moshe Dayan in Rabat, under the auspices of the King of Morocco. Dayan told Tuhami that Israel was prepared to return all of Sinai to Egypt in exchange for a separate, full-fledged peace, and the two discussed the desirability of additional meetings between themselves and also between their chiefs. The Rabat discussions thus confirmed Sadat in his sense that his basic strategy was workable: that Egypt and Israel could easily reach a peace agreement that could then be used to advance other agreements through the leverage of linkage and through American pressures and inducements. As the American efforts to take the parties to Geneva finally collapsed, Sadat thought the time ripe, and he needed only a suitable stage on which to play his scenario. The idea of a secret summit with Begin did not appeal to him because of the need to involve the Americans and to avoid the impression that he was only seeking a separate peace. This is when he thought of going to Jerusalem.

Begin's motivation in receiving President Sadat was somewhat less complex. From the moment he became Prime Minister, the feeling in Israel and abroad was that his government was going to be short lived. Not only did it have the slimmest of majorities in the Knesset, but all opinion polls showed that it had come to office in the first place much more because the voters wanted to punish the Labor Party for its mismanagement of the country's internal affairs than because they supported the Likkud's foreign policy platform. Consequently, the prevailing view was that, when Begin's government inevitably clashed with the American administration over the issue of the future of Judea and Samaria, it would lose some of its parliamentary support in the ensuing crisis and would fall. Begin himself expected such a clash, but he wanted to postpone it as long as possible, the better to prepare to deal with it when it occurred. This is why he proposed in his first meeting with President Carter in July 1977, to forgo any effort to coordinate positions between the two governments on substantive issues, and offered instead to go to Geneva and negotiate "everything." The success of this move made it possible for him to draw the Democratic Movement for Change, which had been sitting on the fence, into his coalition and thus to strengthen considerably his parliamentary base of support. He next engineered a near consensus in the Knesset on a set of resolutions opposing return to the 1967 boundaries, establishment of a Palestinian state, and negotiations with the PLO. These resolutions, in turn, became the basis for rallying the support of American Jewry and other friends of Israel.

Although Begin thus built up formidable defenses against a direct assault by the Carter administration on some of the basic positions he held, he remained vulnerable to the kind of indirect approach adopted by the administration, which spoke of a Palestinian "homeland" rather than a state, tried to make the PLO acceptable as a dialogue partner through qualified acceptance on its part of Resolution 242, and endeavored to give it an unofficial voice at Geneva under various banners. Begin's vulnerability to such tactics was driven home to him when his own foreign minister threatened to resign if he did not accept and press on his Cabinet the October 5, 1977 "working paper." The rejection of the paper by the Arabs afforded temporary relief, but the obsession of the American administration with going to Geneva portended additional politically unsettling pressures. Moreover, the problem of the almost certain confrontation over substantive issues if and when the conference convened remained entire.

In this context, when Sadat offered to come to Jerusalem, Begin had every reason to respond favorably. In the first place, Sadat's initiative bid fair to switch the peacemaking process off the Geneva track which, as far as Begin was concerned, could lead only to trouble with the United States. Second, Sadat's visit was bound to split the Arab world and switch the label of "intransigence" from him onto the Arab parties who would oppose Sadat's move. Thirdly, Begin reasoned that Sadat knew from the Dayan-Tuhami talks where Israel stood on issues relating to other Arab parties as well as on the Egyptian-Israeli question. If Sadat nevertheless chose to come to Jerusalem, he must have made up his mind to conclude a separate peace if necessary, rhetoric to the contrary notwithstanding. Given all this, Begin could hardly resist the chance to be the first Israeli leader to host an Arab leader in Israel's capital, to don the mantle of the de Gaulle type of statesman who alone can make the big decisions, and to bask in the limelight of the world media that would converge on Jerusalem to cover the historic event.

The visit unfolded in a euphoric atmosphere, despite the wide gap in the positions taken by Sadat and Begin in their respective speeches before the Knesset and the world media. It ended with a solemn pledge by the two leaders to shun war and to work for a comprehensive peace and a specific agreement to meet again soon to advance the process of negotiations. Beyond this, however, and beyond the intentions and calculations of the principals themselves, the visit altered fundamentally the entire configuration of the Arab-Israeli problem. Perhaps the most important change was the least tangible. The visit broke through the psychological barrier of fundamental mutual mistrust and alienation and planted the seeds of belief in the possibility of genuine Arab-Israeli mutual acceptance. Although Israel and its neighbors had accepted Resolutions 242 and 338 for some time, and although Israel and Egypt and Israel and Syria had concluded disengagement agreements that acknowledged peace to be their final goals, the idea of peace had remained an abstract utopian goal until Sadat's visit.

On a more concrete level, Sadat's initiative forced the United States to abandon the hopeless Geneva approach and committed it to Sadat's basic strategy. This entailed for it the risk of antagonizing Arab countries like Saudi Arabia and Jordan, whose good will it valued highly, and the certainty of antagonizing the Soviet Union, whose hostility it had sought to avoid. Since the risk and cost could be justified only by a happy consummation of Sadat's initiative, the United States' support for it entailed a strong commitment to see it through to at least some measure of success. The visit also generated enormous pressures on Begin to match the chances taken by Sadat in undertaking his unorthodox initiative and the risks taken by the United States in supporting it with equally daring moves to advance the peace process it opened up. The pressures were all the more weighty because they sprang from within Israel as well as from the outside, and from within Begin's own government as well as among the public at large. Finally, Sadat's initiative was severely criticized by many fellow Arabs as naive and ill-conceived, and two of his own foreign ministers successively resigned rather than associate themselves with it. However, the criticism of his judgment impelled Sadat to become doubly committed to vindicate it by seeing his initiative through to some concrete achievement. Thus, Sadat's initiative in a sense "trapped" him, as well as Begin and Carter, in situations in which the most plausible movement was forward.

Slip Back and New Leap Forward: From Ismailia to Camp David

The dynamics of the situation created by Sadat's visit to Jerusalem was demonstrated in more than one way in the subsequent course of events. The negotiations begun after the visit quickly ran into turbulent waters and, after nine months of ups and downs, ended up farther back than they had started. However, when definite failure appeared to be imminent, yet another highly unorthodox diplomatic method to save the situation was employed. In September 1978 the President of the United States, the President of Egypt, the Prime Minister of Israel, and their respective aides cloistered themselves for nearly two weeks at Camp David, where they devoted themselves exclusively, day and night, to intense negotiations. They emerged from that encounter with a historic agreement that seemed to set Egypt and Israel firmly within reach of peace.

Two weeks after Sadat's visit, a preparatory peace conference of Israeli, Egyptian, and American representatives had opened in Cairo, to which representatives of other interested Arab parties were invited but which none attended. The conference was attended by relatively lower-level officials and was primarily meant to give continuity to Sadat's initiative until Prime Minister Begin could respond to it more properly. That response came ten days later and took the form of a twenty-two point peace proposal, which Begin took to Washington on December 16, 1977, before presenting it to Sadat. Now that matters came to real negotiations, Begin, unlike in July, was anxious to secure in advance a measure of policy coordination with the United States.

Begin's plan had two parts. The first indicated Israel's willingness to acknowledge Egyptian sovereignty over the entire Sinai in exchange for peace and normalization of relations. While exercising its sovereignty, however, Egypt was to agree to certain security arrangements, such as demilitarized zones, and to the continued existence of eighteen Israeli settlements that would be subject to Israeli law and be under Israeli protection. The second and longer part of the plan consisted of a scheme for self-rule for the inhabitants of Judea, Samaria (the West Bank) and Gaza; it spelled out in great detail the structure and powers of the self-rule administration but retained ultimate authority for Israel in all crucial matters. The Carter administration found the first part highly encouraging, the second worrisome, though not without certain positive features.

Begin took his proposal to a summit meeting with Sadat at Ismailia on December 25–26, 1977. Like the American officials, Sadat was impressed by Begin's proposal regarding Sinai, despite the problem of the settlements. As for the West Bank and Gaza, Sadat argued in favor of an agreement on a few principles, worded in a manner to encourage other Arab parties to join the peace process, instead of the particulars of Begin's plan. Sadat was thus being faithful to his strategy, but some of Begin's colleagues believed that he was merely looking for a "fig leaf" to cover his readiness to go ahead with a separate Egyptian-Israeli peace, and they urged Begin to go along. Begin refused. His thinking at that point was that if he was going to give away all of Sinai, he wanted to have in exchange Sadat's explicit and specific agreement to his own scheme for Judea and Samaria. The result was that the summit came to no conclusion but decided to set up two committees, one military and one political, to pursue matters further.

Although Begin and Sadat, each eyeing his own critics, put the best face on the results of their summit, it became apparent before long that both had been bitterly disappointed. Begin felt that he made a most generous formal offer on Sinai but got nothing in return, and Sadat felt insulted that Begin wanted him to support explicitly indefinite Israeli control over the West Bank and Gaza in exchange for returning what was, after all, Egyptian territory. Sadat's indignation found echoes in hostile comments in the Egyptian press, much of them aimed at Begin personally and some even anti-Semitic in flavor (Mustafa Amin of *Al Akhbar* compared Begin to Shylock). Begin's frustration took the form of hints that his Sinai offer was subject to recall and of demonstrative action to reinforce some of the Sinai settlements.

The next act unfolded in this highly inauspicious atmosphere. In January, 1978, the political committee created after the Ismailia meeting gathered in Jerusalem, with the participation of a high-level American delegation headed by Secretary of State Cyrus Vance. Upon arriving at Ben Gurion airport, the Egyptian foreign minister deviated from the protocol for such occasions and read out a tough policy statement in which he said that Israel must withdraw from all occupied Arab territories, including Jerusalem, if it wanted to have peace. At a banquet speech the following evening, Begin retaliated by upbraiding the Egyptian representative for his remarks in terms the Egyptians considered insultingly patronizing. The next day Sadat exploded the conference by calling his delegation home in protest.

The breakdown of the Jerusalem conference shifted the burden of the negotiations from the Egyptian-Israeli base of the triangle to its American apex and caused the parties to harden their positions. Between February 4 and February 6, 1978, the Carter administration received Sadat in Washington and pressed him to come up with a peace plan of his own in response to Begin's. Such pressure succeeded only in eliciting a tough plan that would have Israel transfer authority in the West Bank and Gaza to Jordan and Egypt, respectively, who would make arrangements for securing Palestinian self-determination within five years. From March 17 to March 24, 1978, it was Begin's turn to come to Washington, and he matched Sadat's toughness by advancing the position that Resolution 242 did not apply at all to Judea and Samaria, the "withdrawal from territories" it called for being met by Israel's willingness to withdraw from Sinai. The administration reacted bitterly and threateningly to this position, and Begin returned home to face dissent within his own Cabinet, criticism from the ranks of the opposition, and demonstrations by a new citizens' movement calling itself Peace Now. Begin eventually came down from that limb, but in the meantime another development kept the peace process in abeyance.

Ever since Sadat's visit, the PLO had done its utmost to try to torpedo the peace process. In March 1978, a team of saboteurs finally succeeded in landing on a beach south of Haifa; they seized a bus full of passengers, whom they held hostage, forced it to be driven along the Haifa–Tel Aviv highway, and opened fire on any vehicle that came within range. Eventually they ran into a roadblock and shot it out with the police and the military who manned it while firing and exploding grenades among the passengers. Scores of people were killed and wounded—the worst carnage by terrorists in Israel's history. The Israeli reaction took the form of air attacks on Palestinian encampments in Lebanon, followed by a full-fledged invasion of the southern part of that country up to the Litani River aimed at searching for and destroying PLO personnel and positions. The Syrian troops deployed in central and northern Lebanon since Lebanon's 1975 civil war did not march south to meet the Israelis, so the PLO failed to provoke a large-scale Middle East war. Nor did it succeed in forcing Sadat to renounce his peace initiative because of the Israeli invasion of southern Lebanon. On the contrary, while denouncing both the terrorists' action and the Israeli reaction, Sadat pointed to these events as evidence for the need to end the situation that gave rise to them and as added justification for his peace initiative. Nevertheless, the actual peace negotiations could not be resumed in earnest until the Israeli forces were withdrawn from Lebanon (in June 1978), after yet another UN peace force was created and put into place in some of the evacuated positions.

In July 1978, the United States took the initiative of reassembling the political committee at Leeds, England. The conference made little headway in dealing with specific issues, but it accomplished two things that paved the way for the progress that followed. It eased the doubts that had built up over the previous months among Egyptian and Israeli leaders about the earnestness of the other side's intent to pursue a peace agreement, and it convinced the foreign ministers who participated in it about the need to get the top leaders together if a breakthrough was to be achieved. Early in the next month, President Carter sent Secretary Vance to Jerusalem and Alexandria to invite Prime Minister Begin and President Sadat to meet with him at Camp David the following month in an attempt to achieve that breakthrough.

The story of the negotiations that took place at Camp David between September 5 and September 17, 1978, must await the accounts of the participants, several of which are being written at the moment (January 1981). However, the basic dynamics that accounted for the success of the negotiations and shaped their outcome were apparent even before the final consummation: by dint of their own previous actions, all three leaders had placed themselves in positions in which the costs of failure exceeded by far the costs of the extra effort and the marginal concession needed to reach a meeting ground. They were the same dynamics that developed in the wake of Sadat's visit to Jerusalem.

From Sadat's point of view, failure at Camp David would have shown his entire peace initiative to be quixotic and would have gravely exposed his political position at home and in the Arab world. Even if he were able to survive such a blow, he would have to revert to a position in which his only options would be, at best, putting up with an indefinite and insecure stalemate of the Arab-Israeli conflict and, at worst, having to resume a hopeless, active confrontation with Israel alongside erratic and unreliable Arab partners. These consequences might be mitigated somewhat if the United States were to side with him in putting the onus for failure on Israel, for at least in that case he could assure himself of continuing American assistance and could bank on an American confrontation with Israel to open new possibilities in the future. However, to get the United States to take such a stance he would have to be deemed by it to have made very far reaching concessions while Begin remained unyielding.

For Prime Minister Begin, failure would have meant forfeiture of prospects that had excited the imagination of members of his own government, as well as the Israeli public at large, of taking the most powerful Arab country out of the war and concluding with it the first Arab-Israeli peace. Failure would also have meant a confrontation with the United States on which an isolated Israel had come to depend more heavily than ever, diplomatically, militarily, and economically. Disappointment at home and American pressure were bound to put a heavy strain on Begin's government and sooner rather than later cause its downfall. For Begin, too, failure might be tolerable if the United States were to side with him in putting the onus for it on Egypt. However, given the effort that American diplomacy had invested in Egypt, it was apt to do that only if it deemed Begin to have made very far reaching concessions while Sadat remained obdurate.

While either Sadat or Begin could at least contemplate the possibility of failure if he could get the United States to blame the other for it, for President Carter failure would have meant an unmitigated disaster. It would have meant the collapse of a peace endeavor in which he and his aides had invested nearly twenty months of unrelenting effort, first in the futile attempt to take the parties to Geneva and then in pursuing the path opened up by Sadat's initiative. Coming at a time when opinion polls indicated a very low estimation of his performance as President, a fiasco at Camp David could have destroyed him politically. If, in the process, he were to blame Begin, he would have to risk a confrontation with Israel that would add to his political travails while perhaps destabilizing the Middle East. If he were to blame Sadat, he could cause the United States to lose Egypt after having striven so hard to lure it since the Yom Kippur War. Were he to blame neither, he would be compounding the impression of his own ineptitude while acknowledging that the prospects of peace in the Middle East were hopeless. In that case he would still have to face the consequences of the collapse of the peace hopes in the area itself. The United States would find it extremely difficult to continue pursuing a policy oriented to Israel as well as to Arab countries and would be hard put to prevent the deterioration of the situation to confrontation and probable war.

The overall Camp David configuration gave the United States crucial bargaining levers, but their effective use required great tactical skill. Carter and his aides had to be flexible in their own mind as to what would be a desirable agreement, and they needed to refrain from committing themselves prematurely to positions on key issues that might draw the support of only one of the other parties. Instead, they needed to use the leverage of each party's need to have the United States on its side in order to nudge now one and now the other toward the middle. Finally, when the gap between the parties had been narrowed to the minimum, they had to come up with a comprehensive proposal to bridge it and put both parties on the spot. Whatever evidence has come out so far about the negotiations shows that that was basically what Carter and his aides did.

The Camp David summit produced two separate documents, one providing a framework for an Egyptian-Israeli peace treaty to be concluded within three months, the other providing a "framework for peace in the Middle East" and, particularly, for an agreement on the West Bank and Gaza. The two were not specifically tied, but clearly agreement on one depended on agreement on the other. The Egyptian-Israeli document was quite precise and inclusive, comprising virtually all the elements for a peace treaty. It provided, among other things, for complete Egyptian sovereignty over Sinai; Israeli evacuation of most of the area within three to nine months and of all of it within two to three years; normalization of relations, including full recognition, and diplomatic, economic, and cultural relations to begin after the Israeli interim withdrawal; measures limiting armed forces in Sinai and on the Israeli side of the border; recognition of the Strait of Tiran and the Gulf of Aqaba as international waters, free navigation for Israel in the Gulf of Suez and the Suez Canal, UN forces removable only by unanimous decision of the Security Council; and so on. The question of the Israeli settlements in Sinai was to be submitted to the Knesset for resolution, with Egypt making clear that their removal was a condition for validating both agreements.

The framework for the West Bank and Gaza, in contrast, was a compendium of ambiguous principles, specific points, and deliberate omissions that mixed, but did not blend, elements of the original positions of the parties. Its main feature was an agreement on setting up a self-governing authority for the inhabitants of the West Bank and Gaza for a transition period of five years, at the end of which the "final status" would be agreed upon. The framework comprised some of the principles and formulas sought by Sadat, such as the applicability of Resolution 242 to the West Bank and Gaza, recognition of the legitimate rights of the Palestinians, an end to the Israeli occupation administration and partial withdrawal of Israeli forces, self-government for the inhabitants during a limited transition period, participation by the Palestinians in determining the final status of the territories, and so on. The framework also included some of the key points sought by Begin, such as tacit acknowledgment of a special position for Israel in the West Bank and Gaza; a veto on such questions as the setting up of a Palestinian state and PLO participation in the peace process and the processing of returning refugees from the 1967 war; continuing Israeli military presence in the territories even beyond the transition period; a role in internal security; a key say in the determination of the specific powers and responsibilities of the self-governing authority; an evasive allusion to the refugee problem; and silence on the question of Jerusalem. Begin and Sadat merely recorded their position on that last issue in letters addressed to President Carter.

The fact that some elements of the framework were not mutually compatible and others were susceptible to divergent interpretations was not the result of merely careless formulation but was rather a reflection of the negotiators' intent. Given the feasibility of a complete agreement on an Egyptian-Israeli treaty, the unfeasibility of such an agreement on the West Bank and Gaza, and the avowed premise of avoiding a separate Egyptian-Israeli peace, and, on the other hand, given the necessity for the negotiators to move forward, the only way in which such movement could be achieved was by circumventing the West Bank obstacle through a framework that would permit each side to read into it much of its original intent. That this portended future disagreements was recognized by the parties, but each hoped that the political realities that would develop as a result of the two agreements would help to make its particular views prevail.

Another Slip Back and Another Peak: From Camp David to the Signing of a Peace Treaty

The Camp David Accords were easily ratified by the relevant constitutional bodies, and the Knesset approved removal of the Sinai settlements. Within less than a month after the Accords were signed, three delegations, headed by Secretary of State Cyrus Vance, Israeli Foreign Minister Moshe Dayan, and Egyptian Defense Minister Kamal Hassan Ali met in Washington, D. C. to negotiate an Egyptian-Israeli peace treaty. On October 13, 1978, the day after the opening of the conference, Secretary Vance presented a draft treaty, and within nine days the negotiators agreed to a final text subject to the approval of their governments. However, such approval was withheld by the Israeli Cabinet as well as by President Sadat; both proposed revisions which the negotiators could not readily reconcile. One month later, on November 21, 1978, the Israeli Cabinet approved a new American draft that the Egyptians rejected, and another month later the Egyptians agreed to an American proposal that the Israelis rejected. By then, the three-month target date for concluding a treaty which the parties had set for themselves at Camp David had been missed. After still another month of shuttle diplomacy by American Special Ambassador Alfred Atherton produced no breakthrough, President Carter called for another summit meeting in Washington for the end of February 1979. That proposal ran into difficulties and evolved into a separate Carter-Begin meeting in Washington. After that meeting produced an understanding, Carter himself went to Cairo and Jerusalem in March 1979 and successfully mediated the last difficulties.

On the face of it, the negotiations had stumbled over a number of specific issues such as "linkage" between the two Camp David Accords, a proposed provision for the application of self-rule to the Gaza Strip if the Palestinians of the West Bank refused to cooperate, the timing of the exchange of ambassadors, the modalities for reviewing the security arrangements, the supply of oil to Israel from wells it had developed in Sinai, and the question of the relative priority of the envisaged Egyptian-Israeli treaty and treaties obligating Egypt to come to the defense of other Arab countries. However, while all these issues were of some importance, none, except perhaps the one about priorities, was really crucial in comparison with the issues already resolved, and all of them could have been settled much sooner. If the negotiations extended to twice the three months originally set for them, reached several moments of crisis, and strained the relationships among all three parties, it was because considerations extrinsic to the issues in dispute intruded and caused both Sadat and Begin, at one time or another, to hold back. When a new set of external events developed that influenced all three parties in the opposite direction, a way was quickly found to overcome the remaining problems.

When Sadat had signed the Camp David Accords, he had done so on the assumption that Saudi Arabia, whose oil wealth had made it a pivotal Arab country, would at least tacitly endorse them, and on the related expectation that Jordan would explicitly adhere to them. The United States, which had its own reasons for seeking Saudi and Jordanian cooperation, had underwritten these assumptions and led him to believe that it would be able to "deliver" Saudi and Jordanian support. In fact, however, after the signing of the Accords, Saudi Arabia and Jordan responded to American efforts to obtain their endorsement with inquiries, delays, and ambiguous replies that gradually slid into unequivocal opposition. By November 1978, the two participated in an Arab summit in Baghdad which condemned the Accords, called on Sadat to repudiate them and rejoin the Arab ranks to pursue an all-Arab strategy, and threatened him with drastic sanctions if he went ahead to conclude a peace treaty with Israel. Sadat knew that he had gone too far forward to be able to retreat. He knew that the alternative strategy propounded by the Baghdad summit was no more viable now than when he had shunned it in favor of his own initiative. And he was convinced that either the Baghdad front itself would disintegrate before long and release the Saudis, or its radical core would make such extreme demands on the Saudis (and the Jordanians) as to force them to switch back toward him. But he needed time to allow these processes to take place, and so he had his negotiators fight for every nuance, raise new issues, and resist proposed compromises.

Begin, for his part, had signed the Camp David agreements in the conviction that, in exchange for returning Sinai and subscribing to some ambiguous formulations, he had secured a separate Egyptian peace and preserved, indeed, gained legitimacy for, ultimate Israeli control over the West Bank and Gaza. He was aware, of course, that Sadat might broadly interpret some of the general formulas in the framework for the West Bank and Gaza to make it approximate his original demand for Palestinian self-determination, including the possibility of a Palestinian state, but that did not bother Begin too much. It was another matter to discover, when he returned home, that the Labor Party opposition and members of his own government and his own party, while welcoming the framework for an Egyptian-Israeli treaty, expressed criticisms and apprehensions that the framework for the West Bank and Gaza indeed laid the foundations for a Palestinian state and certainly undermined Israel's ability to retain control over these territories. The points made by the critics were particularly disturbing to Begin because they found support in the position taken by a representative of the American government. In response to a series of questions that Jordan's King Hussein had raised when invited to assume the role assigned to him in the agreements, Assistant Secretary of State Harold Saunders gave replies that added up to putting as broad a construction as any that Sadat might have put on the agreement. Although Begin was able to assuage the criticism at home sufficiently to secure approval of the agreements, and although the Saunders interpretations were subsequently qualified by higher representatives of the American government, Begin was prompted to raise his guard. More than ever before he rejected any hint of a link between the two Camp David agreements, and he tightened his interpretation even of the Egyptian-Israeli agreement in order to bargain for the narrowest possible construction of the framework for the West Bank and Gaza.

The refusal of the Jordanians and the Palestinians to join the Camp David peace process and the clash between Egypt and nearly all the other Arab countries relaxed the Israeli position somewhat, leading to the Cabinet's acceptance of an American treaty draft in November. But these same events tightened Sadat's position, and when the United States sought to accommodate him, it was Begin's turn to refuse. Agreement was thus delayed, and the negotiations stagnated until the collapse of the shah's regime in Iran and the outbreak of war between South Yemen and North Yemen in January-February 1979 provided new incentives for all three parties to close the deal broached at Camp David.

The collapse of one of the pillars of American strategy in the Persian Gulf and the added threat to Saudi Arabia of the war between the two Yemens made it necessary for the United States to try to shore up the Arab-Israeli part of the Middle East arena, and for President Carter to compensate with a success there for the setback in the Persian Gulf. Sadat, for his part, expected that the Saudis' increased vulnerability and their enhanced dependence for security on the United States would cause them to swing around and assent to a peace agreement, if not openly support it. Moreover, he believed that the events of Iran and Yemen created new strategic responsibilities and opportunities for Egypt, in connection with the United States, that could best be met by putting the conflict with Israel formally out of the way. As for Begin, he, too, was attracted by the prospects that strategic realignments in the area might open for Israel once peace with Egypt was concluded, and he was therefore disposed not to pull too hard as he sensed a "give" in the American and Egyptian positions. The result was that after three days of tough bargaining with President Carter in Washington, enough of an agreement was reached between the two to encourage the President to go to Cairo and Jerusalem from March 8 to March 13, 1979, and wrap up the treaty. The Knesset endorsed it by a vote of 95 to 18 five days before its formal signing in Washington, D. C. on March 26, 1979.

In form, the treaty consisted of a preamble and nine articles, plus three annexes dealing with Israeli withdrawal from Sinai and security arrangements, and a protocol on the normalization of relations. A document called Agreed Minutes, comprising interpretations of certain articles of the treaty, and the annexes and maps were attached to the treaty. In addition, there was an agreement on the implementation of the Camp David framework for the West Bank of Gaza in the form of a letter addressed to President Carter and signed by President Sadat and Prime Minister Begin; an exchange of letters between Sadat and Carter and Carter and Begin regarding the timing of the exchange of ambassadors; a letter from Carter to Sadat and Begin embodying certain American obligations in connection with the treaty; and, finally, a note from Carter acknowledging that the expression "West Bank" was understood by Israel to mean "Judea and Samaria." In terms of substance, the following points are noteworthy:

1. While all these agreements were signed at the same time, only the annexes, protocols, and maps were an integral part of the treaty. The other agreements, although in principle equally binding, were given a different

and separate standing so as to accommodate various concerns of the parties, such as Begin's insistence on minimum linkage between the treaty and the framework for the West Bank and Gaza, Sadat's insistence on excluding the exchange of ambassadors from the treaty provisions, and Carter's concern to avoid giving the American commitments the standing of treaty obligations requiring the advice and consent of the Senate.

2. The treaty and the annexes fleshed out the Camp David framework for an Egyptian-Israeli peace but otherwise contained no innovation. The date for Israeli withdrawal from most of Sinai (El Arish–Ras Muhammad line) was set for nine months after the exchange of ratifications, and for the final withdrawal for three years after such exchange. Normalization of relations and (by separate agreement) the exchange of ambassadors were to take place after completion of the interim withdrawal. The much debated issue of priority was "settled" by a statement in the Agreed Minutes which essentially left it unsettled.

3. The connection between the two parts of the Camp David Accords was expressed only in the preamble of the treaty, but without any specific reference to the West Bank or the Palestinian question. Furthermore, a provision in the treaty (Article VI [2]) explicitly obligated the parties to fulfill in good faith their obligations under the treaty "without regard to the action or inaction of any other party and independently of any instrument external to this Treaty."

The instrument that did address the issue (the letter to Carter signed by Sadat and Begin) provided for negotiations to implement the Camp David framework for the West Bank and Gaza to begin one month after ratification and to go on continuously, with the object of providing "full autonomy" for the inhabitants. In the event that Jordan and Palestinians decided not to participate, the negotiations would be held by Egypt and Israel, who set for themselves "the goal" of completing them within one year. The self-governing authority would be elected "as expeditiously as possible" after agreement had been reached and would be inaugurated one month after the elections; the five-year transition period would begin at that point. Thus, both legally and in terms of timetable and procedure, Begin had his way almost entirely in keeping the application of the peace with Egypt separate from the issue of the West Bank and Gaza.

4. The United States' obligations in connection with the treaty took the form of identical letters from Carter to Sadat and Begin committing it, "subject to United States Constitutional processes," in the event of actual or threatened violation of the peace treaty, on request of one or both of the parties, "to consult with the Parties" and to "take such other action as it may deem appropriate and helpful" to achieve compliance with the treaty. This very loose obligation was supplemented by a specific commitment to conduct aerial monitoring of the security provisions as requested by the par-

ties, and to take the necessary steps to ensure the establishment and maintenance of a multinational force, if the UN Security Council should fail to provide for the permanent stationing of UN personnel in the limited force zone, as called for by the treaty. Apart from the treaty and related instruments, the United States obligated itself to provide Egypt and Israel with large-scale economic and military assistance, including specifically a promise to underwrite the cost of building two large air bases in the Negev to replace bases in Sinai that Israel had to give up under the treaty.

Moving Forward and Marking Time: From the Signing of Peace to December 1980

After the instruments of ratification were duly exchanged, the process of application of the agreements began in May 1979. As far as the Egyptian-Israeli treaty proper is concerned, the process went forward according to schedule remarkably well. When the UN Security Council refused to authorize its Emergency Force, stationed in Sinai since the end of the Yom Kippur War, to take up buffer positions between the Israeli and Egyptian forces as called for by the treaty, Sadat and Begin readily agreed to substitute for them joint Egyptian-Israeli patrols. By the time of the first anniversary of the signing of the peace treaty, March 1980, Israeli forces had pulled out of two-thirds of Sinai, Begin and Sadat had exchanged visits, delegations were regularly flying back and forth between the two countries, borders were open to civilians, trade in symbolic proportions had begun, Israeli ships were routinely sailing through the Suez Canal, and ambassadors had been exchanged. The leaders of the two countries had declared themselves repeatedly to be satisfied that the other side was scrupulously executing the terms of the Egyptian-Israeli treaty proper.

As for the framework for the West Bank and Gaza, the autonomy negotiations it called for ran from the outset into difficulties which got worse as time went on. Twelve months after the start of the talks, when the parties were supposed to have brought them to a conclusion, the prospects of agreement were perhaps even more remote than they had been when the talks started. The intervening negotiations and time had merely served to underscore the divergent intents of the parties and to define the differences in their positions more precisely. Although the negotiations were kept going, it was apparent that no progress was to be expected until at least the end of the American presidential elections. Remarkably, the stalemate in the autonomy talks did not affect the Egyptian-Israeli treaty beyond slowing down the pace of normalization and cultivation of potential joint interests.

The difficulties began when Jordan and the Palestinians of the West Bank refused to take part in the autonomy talks. On the contrary, Jordan joined Saudi Arabia and the great majority of the Arab states in breaking off diplomatic and economic relations with Egypt and applying other sanctions against it for signing the peace treaty, while the West Bank Palestinians dared not move on their own. Disappointed but unperturbed, Sadat took it upon himself to negotiate on Palestinian autonomy, as was provided for in such a situation. The Carter administration, on the other hand, went along with this arrangement but did not have its heart in it. It sought to develop an alternative approach to extending the peace process, and this proved to be the source of one of the main problems that paralyzed the autonomy talks.

Even before the actual signing of the peace treaty, President Carter had sent National Security Adviser Zbigniew Brzezinski to Riyad and Amman to try to persuade the Saudis and the Jordanians at least not to penalize Egypt for signing the treaty. Brzezinski thought he obtained the commitment he sought, but when the Arab states convened in Baghdad in March 1979, immediately after the actual signing, Saudi Arabia and Jordan joined the others in imposing severe sanctions on Egypt. Furthermore, Jordan complained publicly about American arm-twisting, and Saudi Arabia criticized the United States for promoting the peace treaty and went on to manipulate its supply of oil, in a market already made taut by the disruption of Iranian production, in a manner that sent oil prices rocketing. These developments, coupled with Saudi disenchantment with American policy in Iran and American resentment of Saudi ingratitude for the help given to them during the conflict between the two Yemens, brought American-Saudi relations to a nadir. On May 8, 1979, Secretary of State Vance made an unusual declaration that American-Saudi relations had deteriorated because of clear and sharp differences over the Egyptian-Israeli Peace Treaty.

Too much was at stake, however, in American-Saudi relations for them to remain that strained for long. In June 1979, Saudi Crown Prince Fahd initiated a reconciliation with a declaration that disagreement over the approach to peace should not affect these relations. He went on to urge the United States to open a dialogue with the PLO, expressed his belief that this could lead to PLO acceptance of Resolution 242, and indicated the willingness of Saudi Arabia to make peace with Israel if it withdrew to the 1967 borders. The next month Saudi Arabia decided to increase its oil production by one million barrels a day to compensate for the shortfall in Iranian production. The United States responded immediately. On July 31, 1979, President Carter compared the Palestinian cause to the civil rights movement in the United States and linked the United States peace efforts to the security of oil supplies. He indicated that the United States was seeking a formula for a UN resolution that could serve as a basis for bringing the PLO into the Middle East peace talks. On August 11, 1979, he tried to soften the impact of his statement by reaffirming his opposition to the creation of a Palestinian state, but a few days later it became known that United States Chief Delegate to the United Nations Andrew Young had actually met secretly with a representative of the PLO to discuss the kind of resolution to which the President had alluded. After initial denials, Young admitted that he had exceeded his authority, and he resigned. But the administration, while reiterating the obligation that the United States assumed in 1975 not to *negotiate* with the PLO before the latter met certain conditions, indicated that it regarded *contacts* with that organization to be important for the Middle East peace process and intended to have them under controlled circumstances.

Twice before the Carter administration had attempted to draw the PLO into the peace process (once by calling on the PLO to signify the "acceptability" of Resolution 242, and once by trying to circumvent 242 altogether, in the October 1977 Soviet-American paper), and twice its efforts were rebuffed by the PLO. The third American attempt fared no better, as the PLO Central Council rejected in August 1979 any UN resolution that did not recognize the right of the Palestinians to an independent state; but this time the attempt led to Sadat's joining Begin in resisting the Carter administration's seeming obsession with the "PLO option," and this alignment had far-reaching consequences on the fate of the autonomy talks.

Sadat, like the United States, was surprised that Saudi Arabia joined the other Arab states in imposing sanctions on him for signing the peace treaty. Unlike the United States, however, he believed that the Saudis' position was a temporary aberration induced by fear of the united front presented at Baghdad by Iraq, Syria, the PLO, South Yemen, and Libya, and anxiety about the Iranian revolution next door. He was convinced that the Saudis' anxieties would eventually compel them to seek closer relations with the United States, the ultimate guarantor of their security, and that at that time they would be forced to fall in line with the American-promoted Egyptian-Israeli peace and the Camp David approach. Crown Prince Fahd's June 1979 statement appeared to Sadat to signal the arrival of that time, but he was dismayed to see that the United States, instead of insisting that the Saudis should fall in line with its Camp David policy, itself went over to the course proposed by the Saudis. Although that course was foiled, the fact that the United States tried it caused it to miss an opportunity to rally the Saudis and, on the contrary, encouraged them to persist in the attempt to isolate Egypt. Sadat's policy following that episode was to insist more than ever before that the Camp David approach was the only valid way to peace and to wait for developments that would create another chance to rally the Saudis and Jordanians.

While the United States was pursuing its abortive initiative, Begin and Sadat went through the most harmonious period in their relationship. In July 1979, Begin was Sadat's guest in Alexandria. In August, the two of them separately conveyed to Special Ambassador Robert Strauss, Carter's representative in the autonomy talks, their strong opposition to the administration's endeavor. In September, after the administration formally renounced its initiative, Sadat was Begin's guest in Haifa. During that period, Begin gained a strong sense of the extent to which Sadat had become a prisoner of his own initiative and of his own strategy of waiting for the Saudis to come around. This, coupled with the rapid erosion of the Begin government's position at home, due to rampant inflation and discord in his Cabinet, prompted him to pursue more boldly a course he had hitherto followed only tentatively. He decided deliberately to mark time in the autonomy talks and to use it to consolidate Israel's hold on the West Bank by expanding settlements and in other ways, against the day when final decisions would have to be made or a Labor government should succeed him. This policy led to the resignation of Foreign Minister Moshe Dayan in October 1979, in addition to stirring up the opposition Labor Party and large segments of the public. It eventually brought about the resignation of Defense Minister Ezer Weizman seven months later, and Minister of Justice Shmuel Tamir thereafter, by which time half of the original Israeli team negotiating the autonomy agreements had quit. But the more politically beleaguered Begin felt, the more determined he seemed to be in pursuing his course. In the meantime, people in Sadat's entourage urged him to retaliate by taking actions to signal that the Egyptian-Israeli treaty itself was being endangered; however, except for occasionally going slowly on the cultivation of normal relations, Sadat resisted that kind of advice. Instead, he maintained a minimum level of relations with Begin and proceeded to cultivate Israeli parties and personalities of the opposition while awaiting a change of government.

The United States' role after the abortive UN-PLO episode continued to be beset by the lack of a coherent strategy, inconstancy of effort, and inconsistency of action. The administration spoke of progress in the autonomy negotiations as being very important for bringing the Saudis and other parties into the Camp David process, when analysis and experience suggested the reverse: using leverage to bring the Saudis to support, or at least not oppose, the process was the way to advance the autonomy talks. At the outset of the autonomy talks, President Carter had sought to underscore the importance he attached to them by appointing his close political associate Robert Strauss to head the American delegation as his special representative; Strauss had barely had the chance to get into the subject in earnest before he was undercut by the UN-PLO initiative and then resigned his position to become manager of the Carter reelection campaign. His successor, Sol Linowitz, approached his task with the same patience, dedication, and attention to detail he had displayed in the successful negotiation of the Panama Canal treaties; however, before he could get very far, his efforts were undermined by fuddled American reactions to one of Begin's actions in the West Bank. Following a decision of the Israeli Cabinet that asserted that Jews had a right to settle in Hebron, the United States voted on March 1, 1980, with the other fourteen members of the United Nations Security Council for a resolution which condemned Israel for increasing its settlements in Arab territories and included Jerusalem in the territories so defined. This was a departure from previous United States practice of abstaining on similar votes; but two days later, President Carter publicly disavowed the vote, stating that it was a mistake that had resulted from failure of communication within the administration. Secretary of State Vance gamely accepted responsibility for the failure, but when, several days later, President Carter told a New York Jewish audience that he had disavowed the vote because it violated United States policy and the Camp David agreements, the secretary of state denied before a congressional committee that it did so. This episode, coming not long after the Andrew Young fiasco, portrayed an administration whose left hand did not know what its right hand was doing, whose policy was made reversible by electoral politics, and which was not to be taken seriously whatever it did.

The final demonstration of the administration's loss of credibility occurred not long thereafter. On March 19, 1980, President Carter invited President Sadat and Prime Minister Begin to separate bilateral summits in Washington to advance the autonomy negotiations. With the election campaign in full swing, it was clear that Carter was in no position to provide the inputs which could alter the frozen situation. Sadat and Begin accepted the invitation for the sake of "old times" and future possibilities, but they were not prepared to do much more than that. Before the meeting, Sadat had suspended the autonomy talks in frustration with Begin while awaiting the American elections or a change of government in Israel. After the meeting, he promised to resume his participation in the talks but then pulled out of them again; he returned once more at Carter's behest. Before coming to Washington, Begin presided over a meeting of his Cabinet which adopted a specific plan to reestablish Jewish presence in Hebron (the subject of the American flip-flop vote) and announced that "only" ten more settlements would be created before the end of the year. After the meeting, he agreed to the resumption and even acceleration of the talks but did not budge on his settlement plans. Indeed, a few months later he capped his policy by allowing a private member bill to go through the Knesset formally annexing the Arab part of Jerusalem and proclaiming the whole city to be the indivisible, eternal capital of Israel. By then the May 1980 target date for the conclusion of the autonomy talks had long passed, and the delegates were meeting occasionally merely to keep the forum alive until the renewal or replacement of the American administration.

Prospects for a New Leap?

As the year 1980 drew to a close, the phase of stagnation appeared destined to come to an end and give way to a new one pregnant with possibilities. In the United States, President-elect Ronald Reagan had nearly finished assembling his administration after winning a sweeping mandate for a more determined and consistent leadership. In the Middle East, a war between Iran and Iraq had been sputtering for several months with no sign of ending and had already had major repercussions. An American armada was deployed within easy reach of the Strait of Hormuz to protect oil traffic lanes, and American AWACS planes were based on Saudi soil to help protect Saudi and neighboring oil wells and facilities as these worked near full capacity to make up for the collapse of Iraqi and Iranian exports. The Arab camp was divided several ways over the conflict, with Syria supporting Iran, Jordan backing Iraq, and the others spread between the two. In Egypt, President Sadat was eyeing the closer American-Saudi security relationship and looking to the Reagan administration to capitalize on it to impel Saudi cooperation in the peace process and to get it moving again. In Israel, Prime Minister Begin's government had just survived a no-confidence vote by the slimmest of margins and was approaching the end of its constitutional term in November 1981. Opinion polls had been consistently predicting a decisive victory for the Labor Party under the leadership of Shimon Peres. Former Secretary of State Kissinger was spending the last days of the year on a "private tour" of the Middle East to "educate himself" about the situation and the possibilities it offered, perhaps in preparation for taking on a new peace mission.

What the Reagan administration would make of the situation was not predictable. The President elect and his foreign policy team, comprising Secretary of State designate Alexander Haig and National Security Adviser Richard Allen, had given no indication of the direction of their policy beyond expressing the need for firmness and voicing the complimentary remarks and good intentions toward Israel customary in election seasons. Were one to venture a word about what the new administration *ought* to do, on the basis of the analysis of the tortuous diplomacy of the last three and a half years, then that word would be: stick to the Camp David approach; it is probably the only workable one.

BIBLIOGRAPHY

INDEX

BIBLIOGRAPHY

This bibliography is meant to provide suggestions to the reader who may wish to pursue subjects treated in this book further. Where there is abundant material, only key and representative works are cited. Where material is relatively scarce, as with military affairs and the diplomacy of recent years, the items mentioned come close to exhausting the English-language sources on the subjects, excluding periodical literature. Works in Hebrew and Arabic are cited only if they contain important material not available elsewhere. For additional material, the reader should consult as well the bibliographies appended to many of the works cited.

Bibliographical and Reference Works

American Jewish Committee. *The American Jewish Yearbook*. New York, 1899–. (Includes bibliographical section.)

American Universities Field Staff. *A Select Bibliography: Asia, Africa, Eastern Europe, Latin America*. New York, 1960.

Bank of Israel. *Annual Report*. Tel Aviv, 1950–.

Dotan, Uri. *A Bibliography of Articles on the Middle East, 1959–1967*. Tel Aviv, 1970.

Encyclopaedia Judaica. 16 vols. Jerusalem, 1971–1972.

Gilbert, Martin. *The Arab-Israeli Conflict: Its History in Maps*. London, 1974.

Howard, Harry N. *The Middle East: A Selected Bibliography of Recent Works, 1970–1972*. Washington, D.C., 1973.

Israel, Central Bureau of Statistics. *Statistical Abstract of Israel*. Jerusalem, 1950–.

Israel, Ministry of Labor. *Atlas of Israel*. Jerusalem and Amsterdam, 1970.

Israel, Prime Minister's Office. *Government Yearbook*. Jerusalem, 1950–.

Keesing's Contemporary Archives: Weekly Diary of World Events. London, 1931–.

Khalidi, Walid, and Jill Khadduri, eds. *Palestine and the Arab-Israeli Conflict: An Annotated Bibliography*. Beirut, 1974.

Middle East Journal. Washington, D.C., 1946– (quarterly). (Contains extensive bibliography of books and articles.)

Patai, Raphael, ed. *Encyclopedia of Zionism and Israel*. 2 vols. New York, 1971.

Shelach, Donna, Channah Harlap, and Shifra Weiss. *The Social Structure of Israel: A Bibliography*. Jerusalem, 1971.

History: From Ancient Times to the Rise of Zionism

Albright, William F. *Archeology and the Religion of Israel.* Baltimore, 1946.
Baron, Salo W. *A Social and Religious History of the Jews.* 2nd ed. 14 vols. New York, 1952–1969.
Ben-Sasson, H. H., ed. *History of the Jewish People.* Cambridge, Mass., 1976.
Katz, Jacob. *Exclusiveness and Tolerance: Jewish-Gentile Relations in Medieval and Modern Times.* London, 1961.
Parkes, James William. *A History of Palestine from 135 A.D. to Modern Times.* London, 1948.
Roth, Cecil. *A History of the Jews.* 2nd ed. New York, 1970.
deVaux, Roland. *Ancient Israel.* Vol. 1 *Social Institutions;* vol. 2, *Religious Institutions.* New York, 1965.

History: Zionism and the Emergence of Israel

Achad HaAm. *Selected Essays.* Philadelphia, 1972.
Balfour, Arthur James. *Speeches on Zionism.* London, 1928.
Baron, Salo W. *Modern Nationalism and Religion.* New York, 1947.
Bauer, Yehuda. *From Diplomacy to Resistance: A History of Jewish Palestine, 1939–1945.* Philadelphia, 1970.
———. *Flight and Rescue: Bricha.* New York, 1970.
Ben Gurion, David. *Rebirth and Destiny of Israel.* New York, 1954.
Berlin, Isaiah. *The Life and Opinions of Moses Hess.* Cambridge, Mass., 1959.
Borochov, Ber. *Nationalism and the Class Struggle.* New York, 1937.
Buber, Martin. *Israel and Palestine: The History of an Idea.* London, 1952.
———. *Israel and the World: Essays in a Time of Crisis.* New York, 1963.
Cohen, Israel. *A Short History of Zionism.* London, 1951.
Crossman, R. H. S. *Palestine Mission.* London, 1946.
Crum, Bartley. *Behind the Silken Curtain.* New York, 1947.
Dayan, Moshe. *Story of My Life.* London, 1976.
Dugdale, Blanche. *Arthur James Balfour.* 2 vols. London, 1936.
Einstein, Albert. *About Zionism: Speeches and Letters.* Ed. and trans. Levi Simon. London, 1930.
Esco Foundation for Palestine. *Palestine: A Study of Jewish, Arab, and British Policies.* 2 vols. New Haven, 1947.
Fitzsimmons, M. A. *The Foreign Policy of the British Labor Government, 1945–1951.* South Bend, Ind., 1953.
Friedman, Isaiah. *The Question of Palestine: British-Jewish-Arab Relations.* New York, 1973.
Goldmann, Nahum. *The Autobiography of Nahum Goldmann: Sixty Years of Jewish Life.* New York, 1969.
Graves, R. M. *Experiment in Anarchy.* London, 1949.
Great Britain. *Palestine: Royal Commission Report* [Peel Report] Cmd. 5854. London, 1938.
———. *Palestine: Statement of Policy* [White Paper]. Cmd. 6019. London, 1939.
———. *Report of the Anglo-American Committee of Inquiry Regarding the Problems of European Jewry and Palestine.* Cmd. 6808. London, 1946.

————. *Proposals for the Future of Palestine, July 1946–February 1947*. Cmd. 7044. London, 1947.

de Haas, Jacob. *Theodor Herzl: A Biographical Study*. 2 vols. Chicago, 1927.

————. *Louis D. Brandeis*. New York, 1929.

Halpern, Ben. *The American Jew: A Zionist Analysis*. New York, 1956.

————. *The Idea of the Jewish State*. Cambridge, Mass., 1961.

Haltis, Susan Lee. *The Bi-National Idea in Palestine During Mandatory Times*. Jerusalem, 1970.

Hertzberg, Arthur, ed. *The Zionist Idea*. New York, 1959.

Herzl, Theodor. *The Jewish State: A Modern Solution to the Jewish Question*. New York, 1970.

Hurewitz, J. C. *The Struggle for Palestine*. New York, 1950.

Katz, Jacob. *Exclusiveness and Tolerance: Jewish-Gentile Relations in Medieval and Modern Times*. London, 1961.

Katznelson, Berl. *Kitvei Berl Katznelson* [The writings of Berl Katznelson]. 12 vols. Tel Aviv, 1946–1949.

Kedourie, Elie. *Britain in the Middle East, 1914–1921*. London, 1956.

Kirk, George. *The Middle East, 1945–1950*. London, 1954.

Klieman, Aaron S. *Foundations of British Policy in the Arab World: The Cairo Conference of 1921*. Baltimore, 1970.

Laqueur, Walter. *A History of Zionism*. New York, 1972.

Litvinoff, Barnet, ed. *The Letters and Papers of Chaim Weizmann*. Vols. II, III. London, 1971, 1972.

Lowenthal, Marvin, ed. *The Diaries of Theodor Herzl*. New York, 1962.

Manuel, Frank E. *The Realities of American-Palestine Relations*. Washington, D.C., 1949.

Marlowe, John [pseud.] *The Seat of Pilate: An Account of the Palestine Mandate*. London, 1959.

Palestine, Chief Secretary. *A Survey of Palestine*. 2 vols. Jerusalem, 1946. (Report for benefit of the Anglo-American Committee of Inquiry.)

Patai, Raphael, ed. *The Complete Diaries of Theodor Herzl*. 5 vols. New York, 1960.

Pinsker, Leo. *Auto-Emancipation*. New York, 1956.

Rabinowitz, Ezekiel. *Justice Louis D. Brandeis: The Zionist Chapter of his Life*. New York, 1968.

Roth, Cecil. *A History of the Jews*. 2nd ed. New York, 1970.

Sachar, Howard M. *The Emergence of the Middle East*. New York, 1969.

————. *Europe Leaves the Middle East*. New York, 1972.

————. *A History of Israel: From the Rise of Zionism to Our Time*. New York, 1976.

Sacher, Harry. *Israel: The Establishment of a State*. London, 1952.

Samuel, Viscount Herbert L. *Memoirs*. London, 1945.

Schechtman, Joseph B. *Zionism and Zionists in Soviet Russia*. New York, 1966.

Silberner, Edmund, ed. *The Works of Moses Hess*. Leiden, 1958.

Stein, Leonard. *The Balfour Declaration*. London, 1961.

————, ed. *The Letters and Papers of Chaim Weizmann*. Vol. I. London, 1968.

Storrs, Sir Ronald. *Orientations*. London, 1937.

Sykes, Christopher. *Crossroads to Israel, 1917–1948*. New York, 1965.

Syrkin, Nachman. *Essays in Socialist Zionism.* New York, 1935.
al Tal, Abdallah. *Karithat Filastin* [The tragedy of Palestine]. Cairo, 1959.
Talmon, J. L. *Israel Among the Nations.* London, 1970.
United Nations Special Committee on Palestine. *Working Documentation Prepared by the Secretariat.* 5 vols. New York, 1947.
Urofsky, Melvin I. *American Zionism from Herzl to the Holocaust.* Garden City, N.Y., 1975.
Vital, David. *The Origins of Zionism.* London, 1975.
Vlavianos, B., and F. Gross, eds. *Struggle for Tomorrow: Modern Political Ideologies of the Jewish People.* New York, 1954.
Weizmann, Chaim. *Trial and Error.* New York, 1949.
Wilson, R. D. *Cordon and Search: With the Sixth Airborne Division in Palestine.* Aldershot, 1949.
Wise, Stephen S. *The Challenging Years.* New York, 1949.
Woodward, Sir E. Llewellyn. *British Foreign Policy in the Second World War.* London, 1962.

Geography, Society, Economics, Politics

Antonovsky, Aaron, and Alan Arian. *Hopes and Fears of Israelis: Consensus in a New Society.* Jerusalem, 1972.
Arian, Alan. *Ideological Change in Israel.* Cleveland, 1968.
———. *The Choosing People: Voting Behavior in Israel.* Cleveland, 1973.
Badi, Joseph. *The Government of the State of Israel.* New York, 1963.
———. *Religion in Israel Today: The Relationship between State and Religion.* New York, 1969.
Baker, Henry S. *The Legal System of Israel.* Tel Aviv, 1955.
Barkai, Chaim. *The Public, Histadrut, and Private Sectors in the Israeli Economy.* Jerusalem, 1964.
Begin, Menachem. *The Revolt: Story of the Irgun.* New York, 1951.
Bein, Alex. *The Return to the Soil.* Jerusalem, 1952.
Ben Gurion, David. *Israel: Years of Challenge.* New York, 1963.
Bernstein, Marver. *The Politics of Israel.* Princeton, 1967.
Bettelheim, Bruno. *The Children of the Dream.* New York, 1969.
Birnbaum, Ervin. *The Politics of Compromise: State and Religion in Israel.* Rutherford, N.J., 1970.
Bruno, Michael. *Economic Development: Problems of Israel, 1970–1980,* RAND Study. Santa Monica, Calif., 1970.
Caiden, Gerald E. *Israel's Administrative Culture.* Berkeley, 1970.
Cohen, Abner. *Arab Border Villages in Israel.* Manchester, 1965.
Dayan, Moshe. *Story of My Life.* London, 1976.
Deshen, Shlomo, and Moshe Shokeid. *The Predicament of Homecoming: Cultural and Social Life of North African Immigrants in Isarel.* Ithaca, N.Y., 1974.
Dror, Yehezkiel, and Emmanuel Guttman, eds. *The Government of Israel.* Jerusalem, 1964.
Eisenstadt, S. N. *The Absorption of Immigrants.* London, 1954.
———. *Israeli Society.* London, 1967.

Eliav, Arieh. *Land of the Hart.* Tel Aviv, 1972.

Elon, Amos. *The Israelis: Founders and Sons.* New York, 1971.

Fellman, Jack. *The Revival of a Classical Tongue: Eliezer Ben Yehuda and the Modern Hebrew Language.* The Hague, 1973.

Fein, Leonard. *Politics in Israel.* Boston, 1968.

Fisher, W. B. *The Middle East: A Physical, Social and Regional Geography.* New York, 1950.

Gal, Allon. *Socialist-Zionism: Theory and Issues in Contemporary Jewish Nationalism.* Cambridge, Mass., 1973.

Gordon, A. D. *Selected Essays.* New York, 1938.

Granott, Avraham. *Agrarian Refrom and the Record of Israel.* London, 1956.

Halevi, Nadav, and Ruth Klinov Malul. *The Economic Development of Israel.* New York, 1968.

Hammond, Paul, and Sidney S. Alexander, eds. *Political Dynamics in the Middle East.* New York, 1971.

Horowitz, David. *The Enigma of Economic Growth: A Case Study of Israel.* New York, 1972.

Isaac, Rael Jean. *Israel Divided: Ideological Politics in the Jewish State.* Baltimore, 1975.

Jiryis, Sabri. *The Arabs in Israel.* Beirut, 1968.

Katznelson, Berl. *Revolutionary Constructionism.* New York, 1937.

Klausner, Joseph. *A History of Modern Hebrew Literature.* London, 1932.

Kleinberger, Aharon F. *Society, Schools and Papers in Israel.* Oxford, 1968.

Landau, Jacob. *The Arabs in Israel.* London, 1969.

Leslie, S. Clement. *The Rift in Israel: Religious Authority and Secular Democracy.* New York, 1971.

Lissak, Moshe, *Social Mobility in Israeli Society.* Jerusalem, 1969.

Matras, Judah. *Social Change in Israel.* Chicago, 1965.

Medding Peter Y. *Mapai in Israel: Political Organization and Government in a New Society.* London, 1972.

Meir, Golda. *My Life.* New York, 1975.

Morris, Yaacov. *Pioneers from the West: A History of Colonization in Israel by Settlers from the English-Speaking Countries.* Westport, Conn., 1972.

Pack, Howard. *Structural Change and Economic Policy in Israel.* New Haven, 1971.

Patai, Raphael. *Cultures in Conflict.* New York, 1961.

Patinkin, Don. *The Israeli Economy: The First Decade.* Jerusalem, 1963.

Peretz, Don. *Israel and the Palestine Arabs.* Washington, D.C., 1958.

Popkin, Roy. *Technology of Necessity: Scientific and Engineering Development in Israel.* New York, 1971.

Preuss, Walter. *The Labor Movement in Israel: Past and Present.* Jerusalem, 1965.

Rackman, Emmanuel. *Israel's Emerging Constitution.* New York, 1955.

Rose, Herbert H. *The Life and Thought of A. D. Gordon.* New York, 1954.

Sachar, Howard M. *Aliyah: The Peoples of Israel.* Cleveland, 1961.

————. *A History of Israel: From the Rise of Zionism to Our Time.* New York, 1976.

Safran, Nadav. *The United States and Israel.* Cambridge, Mass., 1963.

Schwartz, Walter. *The Arabs in Israel.* London, 1959.

Segre, V. D. *Israel: A Society in Transition*. London, 1971.

Seligman, Lester G. *Leadership in a New Nation: Political Development in Israel*. New York, 1964.

Spiro, Medford E. *The Kibbutz: Venture in Utopia*. Cambridge, Mass., 1956.

————. *Children of the Kibbutz*. Cambridge, Mass., 1958.

St. John, Robert. *Tongue of the Prophets: The Story of Eliezer Ben-Yehuda*. New York, 1952.

Teller, Judd L. *Government and the Democratic Process*. New York, 1969.

Uri, Pierre, ed. *Israel and the Common Market*. Jerusalem, 1971.

Viteles, Harry. *A History of the Cooperative Movement in Israel*. Vols. I, II. London, 1966, 1968.

Weingrod, Alex. *Israel: Group Relations in a New Society*. New York, 1965.

Weintraub, D., M. Lissak, and Y. Azmon. *Moshava, Kibbutz, and Moshav*. Ithaca, N.Y., 1969.

Weitz, Ra'anan and Abshalom Rokach. *Agricultural Development, Planning and Implementation: An Israeli Case Study*. New York, 1968.

Wilner, Dorothy. *Nation-Building and Community in Israel*. Princeton, 1969.

Wars and Military Affairs

'Abd al Mun'im, Muhammad. *Asrar 1948* [Secrets of 1948]. Cairo, 1968.

Abu Nuwwar, Ma'an. *Fi sabil al quds* [For Jerusalem's sake]. Amman, [1968?].

————. *al Liwa al mudarra' 40* [The 40th Armored Brigade]. Amman, n.d.

Allon, Yigal. *The Making of Israel's Army*. London, 1970.

An Nahar Arab Report. *The October War*. Beirut, 1974.

Arad, Yitzhak, ed. *1000 hayamim* [The 1000 days: June 12, 1967– August 8, 1970]. Tzahal, General Staff. Tel Aviv, 1973.

Avnery, Ariel. *Pshitot ha-tagmul* [The retaliatory raids]. 3 vols. Tel Aviv, [1971?].

Barker, A. J. *Suez: The Seven Day War*. London, 1964.

————. *The Yom Kippur War*. New York, 1974.

Beaufre, General André. *The Suez Expedition*. New York, 1969.

Bell, J. Bowyer. *The Myth of the Guerrilla: Revolutionary Theory and Malpractice*. New York, 1971.

Ben Gurion, David. *Ma'arekhet sinay* [The Sinai Campaign]. Tel Aviv, 1959.

Blechman, B. M., and S. S. Kaplan. *The Use of Armed Forces as a Political Instrument*. Brookings study. Washington, D.C., 1977.

Burns, E. L. M. *Between Arab and Israeli*. New York, 1963.

Churchill, Winston, and Randolph Churchill. *The Six Day War*. Boston, 1967.

Dan, Ben. *The Secret War*. New York, 1970.

Dayan, Moshe. *Diary of the Sinai Campaign*. New York, 1965.

————. *Story of My Life*. London, 1976.

Dayan, Yael. *Israel Journal: June, 1967*. New York, 1967.

Glubb, Lt. General Sir John B. *A Soldier with the Arabs*. London, 1957.

Hashavya, Arye. *A History of the Six Day War*. Tel Aviv, 1969.

Heikal, Mohamed H. *The Road to Ramadan*. New York, 1975.

Henriques, Robert. *100 Hours to Suez*. New York, 1957.

Herzog, Chaim. *The War of Atonement*. London, 1975.

The International Institute for Strategic Studies. *The Military Balance.* London, 1958– (annual).

————. *Strategic Survey.* London, 1966– (annual).

Israel, Ministry of Defense. *Historiya shef milhemet hakomemiyut* [History of the War of Independence]. Tel Aviv, 1959.

Jackson, Robert. *The Israeli Air Force Story.* London, 1970.

Jane's All the World's Aircraft. New York (annual).

Jane's Fighting Ships. London (annual).

Joseph, Dov (Bernard). *The Faithful City: The Siege of Jerusalem, 1948.* New York, 1960.

Kimche, Jon, and David Kimche. *Both Sides of the Hill: Britain and the Palestine War.* London, 1960.

Lapierre, Dominique, and Larry Collins. *O Jerusalem.* London, 1972.

Lorch, Netanel. *The Edge of the Sword: Israel's War of Independence.* New York, 1961.

————. *One Long War: Arab versus Jew since 1920.* Jerusalem, 1976.

Luttwak, Edward, and Dan Horowitz. *The Israeli Army.* London, 1975.

Marshall, S. L. A. *Sinai Victory.* New York, 1958.

————. *Swift Sword.* New York, 1967.

Meir, Golda. *My Life.* New York, 1975.

Monroe, Elizabeth, and A. H. Farrar-Hockley. *The Arab-Isarel War, October 1973: Background and Events.* Adelphi Papers no. 111. London, 1975.

al Nafuri, Amin. *Istratijiyyat al harb didd isra'il* [Strategy of the war against Israel]. Damascus, 1970.

O'Ballance, Edgar. *The Arab-Israeli War, 1948.* London, 1956.

————. *The Sinai Campaign, 1956.* New York, 1960.

————. *The Third Arab-Israeli War.* Hamden, Conn., 1972.

————. *The Electronic War in the Middle East, 1968–1970.* Hamden, Conn., 1974.

O'Neill, Brad. *Revolutionary Warfare in the Middle East: The Israelis versus the Fedayeen.* Boulder, Colo., 1974.

Peres, Shimon. *David's Sling.* New York, 1970.

Perlmutter, Amos. *Military and Politics in Israel.* London, 1969.

Rabinovich, Abraham. *The Battle for Jerusalem, June 5–7, 1967.* Philadelphia, 1972.

Rolbant, Samuel. *The Israeli Soldier: Profile of an Army.* New York, 1970.

Roth, Stanley. *Middle East Balance of Power after the Yom Kippur War.* Cambridge, Mass., 1974.

Safran, Nadav. *From War to War: The Arab-Israeli Confrontation, 1948–1967.* New York, 1969.

Schiff, Zeev, and Raphael Rothstein. *Fedayeen.* London, 1972.

Schiff, Zeev. *October Earthquake: Yom Kippur, 1973.* Tel Aviv, 1974.

Slater, Leonard. *The Pledge.* New York, 1970.

Tahtinen, Dale R. *The Arab-Israeli Military Balance Today.* Washington, D.C., 1973.

————. *The Arab-Israeli Military Balance since October 1973.* Washington, D.C., 1974.

Talmi, Efrayim. *Milhamot yisrael, 1949–1969* [Israel's Wars, 1949–1969]. Tel Aviv, 1969.

Teveth, Shabtai. *The Tanks of Tammuz.* London, 1969.

Tlass, Mustafa. *Harb al 'isabat* [Guerrilla war]. Damascus, 1968.

United Arab Republic, Ministry of War, General Command of the Armed Forces. *al 'Amaliyyat al harbiyya bi filastin 'am 1948* [Military operations in Palestine, 1948]. 2 vols. Cairo, 1961.

Williams, Louis, ed. *Military Aspects of the Israeli-Arab Conflict*. International Symposium, Jerusalem, Oct. 12–17, 1973. Tel Aviv, 1975.

Young, Peter. *The Israeli Campaign, 1967*. London, 1967.

International Politics and American-Israeli Relations

Abdullah, King of Jordan. *Memoirs*. New York, 1950.

————. *My Memoirs Completed*. Washington, D.C., 1954.

Adams, Sherman. *Firsthand Report: The Inside Story of the Eisenhower Administration*. London, 1962.

al Ahram, Center for Political and Strategic Studies. *Harb oktobar* [The October War]. Cairo, 1974.

Alter, Robert. *America and Israel: Literary and Intellectual Trends*. New York, 1970.

American Jewish Committee. *American Jewish Yearbook*. New York, 1898– (annual).

Aron, Raymond. *DeGaulle, Israel, and the Jews*. New York, 1968.

al 'Azm, Khaled. *Mudhakkirat khaled al 'azm* [Memoirs of Khaled al 'Azm]. 3 vols. Beirut, 1972.

Balabkins, Nicholas. *West German Reparations to Israel*. New Brunswick, N.J., 1971.

Bavly, Dan, and David Farhi. *Israel and the Palestinians*. London, 1970.

Be'eri, Eliezer. *Army Officers in Arab Politics and Society*. New York, 1970.

Ben Gurion, David. *Israel: Years of Challenge*. New York, 1963.

————. *Pgishot 'im manhigim 'araviim* [Meetings with Arab leaders]. Tel Aviv, 1969.

Bernadotte, Folke. *To Jerusalem*. London, 1951.

Bovis, Eugene H. *The Jerusalem Question, 1917–1968*. Stanford, Calif., 1971.

Brandeis, Louis. *Brandeis on Zionism*. Washington, D.C., 1942.

Brecher, Michael. *The Foreign Policy System of Israel*. London, 1972.

————. *Decisions in Israel's Foreign Policy*. New Haven, 1974.

Bullock, J. *The Making of a War: The Middle East, 1967–1973*. London, 1974.

Campbell, John C. *Defense of the Middle East: Problems of American Policy*. New York, 1961.

Cohen, Aharon. *Israel and the Arab World*. New York, 1970.

Cohen, Saul B. *Geography and Politics in a World Divided*. New York, 1973.

Crosbie, Sylvia F. *A Tacit Alliance: France and Israel from Suez to the Six Day War*. Princeton, 1974.

Dagan, Avigdor. *Moscow and Jerusalem: Twenty Years of Relations between Israel and the Soviet Union*. London, 1970.

Dayan, Moshe. *Story of My Life*. London, 1976.

Deutschkron, Inge. *Bonn and Jerusalem: The Strange Coalition*. Philadelphia, 1970.

Draper, Theodor. *Israel and World Politics: Roots of the Third Arab-Israeli War*. London, 1968.

Eckman, Lester. *Soviet Policy toward Jews and Israel, 1917–1974.* New York, 1974.

Eden, Anthony. *Full Circle.* London, 1960.

Eisenhower, Dwight D. *The White House Years: Waging Peace, 1956–1961.* New York, 1965.

Eliav, Arieh. *Land of the Hart.* Tel Aviv, 1972.

Evron, Yair. *The Middle East: Nations, Superpowers and Wars.* New York, 1973.

Eytan, Walter. *The First Ten Years: A Diplomatic History of Israel.* New York, 1958.

Feingold, Henry L. *The Politics of Rescue: The Roosevelt Administration and the Holocaust, 1938–1945.* New Brunswick, N.J., 1970

Feis, Herbert. *The Birth of Israel: The Tousled Diplomatic Bed.* New York, 1969.

Finer, Herman. *Dulles over Suez: The Theory and Practice of His Diplomacy.* Chicago, 1964.

Freedman, R. O. *Soviet Policy towards the Middle East since 1970.* New York, 1975.

Fuchs, Laurence H. *The Political Behavior of American Jews.* Glencoe, Ill., 1956.

Gabbay, Rony E. *A Political Study of the Arab-Jewish Conflict.* Geneva, 1959.

Glubb, Lt. General Sir John B. *Britain and the Arabs: A Study of Fifty Years, 1908–1958.* London, 1959.

Golan, Matti. *The Secret Conversations of Henry Kissinger: Step-by-Step Diplomacy in the Middle East.* New York, 1976.

Goldmann, Nahum. *The Autobiography of Nahum Goldmann: Sixty Years of Jewish Life.* New York, 1969.

Hadawi, Sami. *Bitter Harvest: Palestine between 1914–1967.* New York, 1967.

al Hadidi, Lt. General Salah al Din. *Shahid 'ala harb '67* [Witness to the 1967 war]. Cairo, 1974.

Halperin, Samuel. *The Political World of American Zionism.* Detroit, 1961.

Hammond, Paul, and Sidney S. Alexander, eds. *Political Dynamics in the Middle East.* New York, 1971.

Heikal, Mohamed H. *The Cairo Documents.* New York, 1972.

————. *The Road to Ramadan.* New York, 1975.

Hoopes, Townsend. *The Devil and John Foster Dulles.* Boston, 1973.

Howard, Michael, and Robert Hunter. *Israel and the Arab World: The Crisis of 1967.* Adelphi Papers no. 41. London, 1967.

Hurewitz, Jacob C. *Diplomacy in the Near and Middle East: A Documentary Record.* 2nd ed. New York, 1972.

Hussein, King of Jordan. *Uneasy Lies the Head.* New York, 1962.

————. *My War with Israel.* New York, 1969.

Institute for Strategic Studies. *Sources of Conflict in the Middle East.* Adelphi Papers no. 26. London, 1964.

Johnson, Lyndon B. *The Vantage Point.* New York, 1971.

Kalb, Marvin, and Bernard Kalb. *Kissinger.* New York, 1974.

Kerr, Malcolm H. *The Arab Cold War.* 3rd ed. New York, 1971.

Khouri, Fred J. *The Arab-Israeli Dilemma.* Syracuse, N.Y., 1968.

Kimche, David, and Dan Bawley. *The Six Day War.* New York, 1968.

Kohler, Foy D. *The Soviet Union and the October 1973 Middle East War.* Coral Gables, Fla., 1974.

Krammer, Arnold. *The Forgotten Friendship: Israel and the Soviet Bloc, 1947–1953.* Urbana, Ill., 1974.

Kreinin, Mordecai. *Israel in Africa.* New York, 1964.

Laqueur, Walter *The Struggle for the Middle East: The Soviet Union in the Mediterranean, 1959–1968.* New York, 1969.

———. *Confrontation: The Middle East War and World Politics.* London, 1974.

Laufer, Leopold. *Israel and the Developing Countries.* New York, 1967.

Lucas, Noah. *The Modern History of Israel.* London, 1975.

Macmillan, Harold. *Tides of Fortune: 1945–1955.* London, 1969.

McDonald, James. *My Mission in Israel.* New York, 1951.

McLanvin, Ronald D. *The Middle East in Soviet Policy.* Lexington, Mass., 1975.

Meir, Golda. *My Life.* New York, 1975.

Moore, John Norton, ed. *The Arab-Israeli Conflict: Readings and Documents.* Princeton, 1977.

Nixon, Richard M. *U.S. Policy for the 1970's: The Emerging Structure of Peace.* A Report to the Congress. *Department of State Bulletin,* vol. LXVI, no. 1707, March 13, 1972.

Quandt, William B. *United States Policy in the Middle East: Constraints and Choices.* RAND Study. Santa Monica, Calif., 1970.

———. *Palestinian Nationalism: Its Political and Military Dimensions.* RAND Study. Santa Monica, Calif., 1971.

Reich, Bernard. *Israel and the Occupied Territories.* Washington, D.C., 1973.

Reisman, Michael. *The Art of the Possible: Diplomatic Alternatives in the Middle East.* Princeton, 1970.

Royal Institute of International Affairs. *British Interests in the Mediterranean and the Middle East.* London, 1958.

Rubin, Jacob A. *Partners in State-Building: American Jewry and Israel.* New York, 1969.

Sabri, Musa. *Watha'iq harb oktobar* [Documents of the October War]. Cairo, 1974.

Sachar, Howard M. *A History of Israel: From the Rise of Zionism to Our Time.* New York, 1976.

Safran, Nadav. *The United States and Israel.* Cambridge, Mass., 1963.

———. *From War to War: The Arab-Israeli Confrontation, 1948–1967.* New York, 1969.

Schechtman, Joseph. *The United States and the Jewish State Movement: The Crucial Decade, 1939–1949.* New York, 1966.

Silver, Abba Hillel. *Vision and Victory.* New York, 1949.

Snetsinger, John. *Truman, the Jewish Vote, and the Creation of Israel.* Stanford, Calif., 1974.

Stember, Charles H., et al. *Jews in the Mind of America.* New York, 1966.

Stevens, Richard P. *American Zionism and U.S. Foreign Policy.* New York, 1962.

Stock, Ernest. *Israel on the Road to Sinai, 1949–1956.* Ithaca, N.Y., 1967.

Talbott, Strobe, ed. and trans. *Khrushchev Remembers.* Boston, 1970.

Teveth, Shabtai, *The Cursed Blessing.* London, 1969.

Thomas, Hugh. *The Suez Affair.* London, 1970.

Truman, Harry S. *Years of Trial and Hope: The Memoirs of Harry S. Truman.* Vol. II. New York, 1956.

Tuchman, Barbara. *Bible and Sword.* New York, 1956.

U.S. Arms Control and Disarmament Agency. *Military Expenditures and Arms Transfers, 1966–1975.* Washington, D.C., 1976.

U.S. Department of State. *United States Foreign Policy, 1969–1970: A Report of the Secretary of State,* Washington, D.C., 1971.

U.S. Department of State. *United States Foreign Policy, 1971: A Report of the Secretary of State.* Washington, D.C., 1972.

U.S. Congress, House of Representatives, Committee on Foreign Affairs, Subcommittee on the Near East and Asia. *Jerusalem: The Future of the Holy City for Three Monotheisms.* Hearing, July 28, 1971. 92nd Congress, 1st Session. Washington, D.C., 1971.

U.S. Congress, House of Representatives, Committee on Foreign Affairs. *Soviet Involvement in the Middle East and the Western Response.* Joint hearings, Subcommittee on Europe and Subcommittee on the Near East and Asia, October 19, 21; November 2 and 3, 1971. 92nd Congress, 1st Session. Washington, D.C., 1971.

————. *The United States Oil Shortage and the Arab-Israeli Conflict.* Report of a Study Mission to the Middle East from October 22 to November 3, 1973. 93rd Congress, 1st Session, December 20, 1973. Washington, D.C., 1973.

————, Subcommittee on the Near East and South Asia. *United Nations Peacekeeping in the Middle East.* Hearings, December 5 and 6, 1973. 93rd Congress, 1st Session. Washington, D.C., 1973.

————. *After the War: European Security and the Middle East.* Report of a Study Mission to Geneva, Tel Aviv, and Vienna from November 15 to 24, 1973. 93rd Congress, 1st Session. Washington, D.C., 1973.

————. Subcommittee on the Near East and South Asia. *The United States Role in Opening the Suez Canal.* Hearing, May 8, 1974. 93rd Congress, 2nd Session. Washington, D.C., 1974.

————. *U.S. Foreign Policy and the Export of Nuclear Technology to the Middle East.* Hearings, June 25, July 9, 18, and September 16, 1974. 93rd Congress, 2nd Session. Washington, D.C., 1974.

————. *United States–Europe Relations and the 1973 Middle East War.* Hearings, November 1, 1973, and February 19, 1974. 93rd Congress, 1st and 2nd Sessions. Washington, D.C., 1974.

————. *Proposed Expansion of U.S. Military Facilities in the Indian Ocean.* Hearings, February 21, March 6, 12, 14, and 20, 1974. 93rd Congress, 2nd Session. Washington, D.C., 1974.

————. *The Middle East, 1974: New Hopes, New Challenges.* Hearings, April 9, May 7, 14, 23, and June 27, 1974. 93rd Congress, 2nd Session. Washington, D.C., 1974.

U.S. Congress, House of Representatives, Committee on International Relations [previously Foreign Affairs], Special Subcommittee on Investigations. *Economic Aid Allocations for Syria and Compliance with Section 901 of the Foreign Assistance Act.* Hearing, June 25, 1975. 94th Congress, 1st Session. Washington, D.C., 1975.

————. *Oil Fields as Military Objectives: A Feasibility Study.* Prepared by the Congressional Research Service, Library of Congress, August 21, 1975. 94th Congress, 1st Session. Washington, D.C., 1975.

————. *The Palestinian Issue in Middle East Peace Efforts.* Hearings, September 30, October 1 and 8, and November 12, 1975. 94th Congress, 1st Session. Washington, D.C., 1976.

U.S. Congress, Senate, Committee on Foreign Relations. *A Select Chronology and Background Documents Relating to the Middle East.* 1st rev. ed., May 1965. 91st Congress, 1st session. Washington, D.C., 1970.

———. *Emergency Military Assistance for Israel and Cambodia.* Hearing on S.2691 and H.R. 11088, December 13, 1973. 93rd Congress, 1st session. Washington, D.C., 1973.

———. Subcommittee on Multinational Corporations. *The International Petroleum Cartel, the Iranian Consortium and U.S. National Security.* Committee Print, February 21, 1974. 93rd Congress, 2nd Session. Washington, D.C., 1974.

———. Subcommittee on Near Eastern Affairs. *The Middle East Between War and Peace, November-December 1973.* Staff Report, March 5, 1974. 93rd Congress, 2nd Session. Washington, D.C., 1974.

———. *Foreign Assistance Authorization.* Hearings on S.3394, June 7, 21 and 26, July 24 and 25, 1974. 93rd Congress, 2nd Session. Washington, D.C., 1974.

———. Subcommittee on Multinational Corporations. *U.S. Oil Companies and the Arab Oil Embargo: The International Allocation of Constricted Supplies.* Report by the Federal Energy Administration, Office of International Energy Affairs, January 25, 1975. 94th Congress, 1st Session. Washington, D.C., 1975.

———. *Early Warning System in Sinai.* Hearings on Memoranda of Agreements between the Governments of Israel and the United States, October 6 and 7, 1975. 94th Congress, 1st Session. Washington, D.C., 1975.

———. *U.S. Missile Sale to Jordan.* Hearings on S. Con. Res. 50, July 15 and 21, 1975. 94th Congress, 1st Session. Washington, D.C., 1975.

———. *Early Warning System in Sinai.* Committee Report to Accompany S.J. Res. 138, October 7, 1975. 94th Congress, 1st Session. Washington, D.C., 1975.

———. *International Security Assistance.* Hearings on FY 1977 International Security Assistance Programs, March 26, April 5 and 8, 1976. 94th Congress, 2nd Session. Washington, D.C., 1976.

———. *Proposed Sale of C-130's to Egypt.* Hearings on Proposed Cash Sale to Egypt of Six C-130 Aircraft and Training of Egyptian Personnel, March 31 and April 2, 1976. 94th Congress, 2nd Session. Washington, D.C., 1976.

———. Subcommittee on Near Eastern and South Asian Affairs. *Priorities for Peace in the Middle East.* Hearings on The Arab Israeli Dispute: Priorities for Peace, July 23 and 24, 1975. 94th Congress, 1st Session. Washington, D.C., 1975.

Vali, Ferenc A. *A Bridge across the Bosphorus: The Foreign Policy of Turkey.* Baltimore, 1971.

Vatikiotis, P. J. *Egypt since the Revolution.* New York, 1968.

Whetten, Lawrence L. *The Canal War: Four Power Conflict in the Middle East.* Cambridge, Mass., 1974.

Zeine, Zeine N. *The Struggle for Arab Independence.* Beirut, 1960.

Biographies and Memoirs

Acheson, Dean. *Present at the Creation.* New York, 1969.

Adams, Sherman. *Firsthand Report: The Inside Story of the Eisenhower Administration.* London, 1962.

Bar-Zohar, Michael. *Ben Gurion: The Armed Prophet.* Englewood Cliffs, N.J. 1967.

Bein, Alex. *Theodor Herzl: A Biography*. Philadelphia, 1956.

Ben Gurion, David. *Recollections*. London, 1970.

———. *Israel: A Personal History*. New York, 1971.

Bullock, Alan. *The Life and Times of Ernest Bevin*. Vol. I. London, 1960.

Cohen, Israel. *Theodor Herzl: Founder of Political Zionism*. New York, 1959.

Dayan, Moshe. *Story of My Life*. London, 1976.

Edelman, Maurice. *Ben-Gurion: A Political Biography*. London, 1964.

Eisenhower, Dwight D. *The White House Years: Waging Peace, 1956–1961*. New York, 1965.

Elon, Amos. *Herzl*. New York, 1975.

Goldmann, Nahum. *The Autobiography of Nahum Goldmann: Sixty Years of Jewish Life*. New York, 1969.

de Haas, Jacob. *Brandeis: A Biographical Sketch*. New York, 1929.

Johnson, Lyndon B. *The Vantage Point*. New York, 1971.

Lie, Trygve. *In the Cause of Peace*. New York, 1954.

Lipovetzky, Pesah. *Joseph Trumpeldor: Life and Works*. Jerusalem, 1953.

Lipsky, Louis. *A Gallery of Zionist Profiles*. New York, 1956.

Litvinoff, Barnet. *Ben Gurion of Israel*. London, 1954.

Macmillan, Harold. *Tides of Fortune: 1945–1955*. London, 1969.

Meinertzhagen, R. *Middle East Diary, 1917–1956*. London, 1959.

Meir, Golda. *My Life*. New York, 1975.

Nutting, Anthony. *Nasser*. New York, 1972.

Perlman, Moshe. *Ben Gurion Looks Back*. London, 1965.

Prittie, Terence. *Eshkol: The Man and the Nation*. New York, 1969.

Rabinowicz, Ezekiel. *Justice Louis D. Brandeis: The Zionist Chapter of His Life*. New York, 1968.

Rabinowicz, Oscar K. *Vladimir Jabotinsky's Conception of a New Nation*. New York, 1946.

Samuel, Viscount Herbert L. *Memoirs*. London, 1955.

Schectman, Joseph B. *Vladimir Jabotinsky*. 2 vols. New York, 1956, 1961.

Simon, Sir Leon. *Achad HaAm—Asher Ginsberg: A Biography*. Philadelphia, 1960.

St. John, Robert. *Ben-Gurion: The Biography of an Extraordinary Man*. Rev. ed. New York, 1971.

———. *Eban*. New York, 1972.

Steinberg, Alfred. *The Man from Missouri: The Life and Times of Harry S. Truman*. New York, 1962.

Stephen, Robert. *Nasser: A Political Biography*. New York, 1971.

Syrkin, Marie. *Golda Meir: Israel's Leader*. New York, 1969.

Talbott, Strobe, ed. and trans. *Khrushchev Remembers*. Boston, 1970.

Teveth, Shabati. *Moshe Dayan*. London, 1972.

Truman, Harry S. *Memoirs*. 2 vols. New York, 1953, 1955.

Weisgal, M. W., and J. Carmichael, eds. *Chaim Weizmann: A Biography by Several Hands*. New York, 1963.

Weizmann, Chaim. *Trial and Error*. New York, 1949.

Wilson, Harold. *The Labour Government, 1964–1970: A Personal Record*. London, 1971.

Winer, Gershon. *The Founding Fathers of Israel*. New York, 1971.

Wise, Stephen S. *Challenging Years*. New York, 1949.

INDEX

Abdallah, King, 336
Abraham: covenant with God, 6, 7
Abu Egeila, 243, 245, 246
Abu Rodeis, 76, 297; oil fields in, 541–545, 551, 554, 556, 558, 591, 593, 598
Achdut Haavoda, 141, 143, 157, 159, 167–170, 175, 176, 412
Acre, 48, 71
Acre-Haifa Bay, 71, 72, 242
Adabiya, 310
Adan, Avraham, 292, 298, 306–310
Aden, 375
Adenauer, Konrad, 376
Africa: East Africa as alternative site for Jewish state, 20; and location of Israel, 69; Jewish immigration from North Africa, 89–90
African nations in Middle East politics: from 1957 to 1967, 377, 378, 379, 380; in 1973 and after, 495–496
Agranat Inquiry Commission, 185, 186, 282, 287, 314, 327, 513, 529–530
Agranat, Shimon, 181, 185
Agricultural settlements: built by political parties, 152; role in defense, 229
Agriculture in Israel, 70–74, 79–80, 87, 104, 105, 110; and imports, 120; government investment in, 112, 116; production efficiency of, 116–117; exports of, 119
Agudah, 184, 191, 196, 205, 212
Agudat Yisrael, 141, 142, 153, 158, 161, 183, 192, 202, 205
Al Ahram, 279
Aircraft industry, 230, 234
Air force of Israel, 233, 234, 239, 256; in Six

Day War, 240–241, 245, 246; in war of attrition, 264–265; in fedayeen warfare, 271; after war of attrition, 272–275; in Yom Kippur War, 279–282, 286–287, 289, 292, 294, 296, 297, 299, 302, 303, 305, 309, 313
Airline, international: hijacking attempts against, 451
Alcalay, Rabbi Judah, 15
Alexander II, 17
Alexandretta district, 379
Alexandria port, 256
Algeria in Middle East politics: in 1973, 315, 499; from 1967 to 1970, 428; in 1967, 390, 402, 403; from 1957 to 1967, 380; from 1949 to 1956, 354, 355, 369, 370
Aliyot: prestatehood, 84–89, 105, 187; poststatehood, 83, 84, 89–106
Allenby bridge, 54
Alliance Israélite universelle, 85
Allon Plan, 101, 537
Allon, Yigal: rivalry with Dayan, 175, 177, 188, 474; as military hero, 175, 412; in security and foreign affairs, 190, 284, 490, 537–538, 541–542, 544–546, 553; from military to politics, 322
Almogi, Yosef, 162
Almohade, 11
Aloni, Shulamit, 183, 184, 185
Altalena, 143, 151
Amer, Abdel Hakim, 404
American Council for Judaism, 201
American Israel Public Affairs Committee, 574
"Americanization" of Israel, 573–574

Amin, Idi, 495
Amman, 258, 453–454
Anglo-American Commission, 31, 32
Anglo-American Treaty of 1924, 35, 36
Anglo-Egyptian agreement, 227, 350–351
Anglo-French Suez War, 238. *See also*
  Sinai-Suez War
Anti-Lebanon range, 252
Appointment Committee (for judges in
  Israel), 132
Aqaba, 258. *See also* Gulf of Aqaba
Arab Common Defense Council, 402
Arab countries: early view of Zionism, 5–6;
  opposition to Jewish National Home,
  28–30, 32; opposition to partitioning of
  Palestine, 38, 40–41, 43–48; and Jewish
  War of Independence, 43, 48–60;
  bordering Israel, 69; as threat to Israel's
  security, 69, 107, 109, 143–144, 166–168,
  181, 222–227, 267, 315; economic
  boycott of Israel, 109, 114; view of
  political parties in Israel, 143–144, 166;
  population of, 225; resources of, 226;
  strategy after Six Day War, 257–258; in
  Yom Kippur War, 278–281; relations with
  Israel (1949–1956), 334–358; relations
  with U.S. (1949–1956), 348–353; military
  of, 596. *See also specific Arab countries*
Arab Higher Committee, 43
Arab League, 49, 564; military committee of,
  45, 46; Joint Defense Council of, 466
Arab Legion of Transjordan, 53–55, 58, 59,
  60, 73. *See also* Transjordan
Arab Liberation Army, 45–46, 47, 50, 53, 59
Arab Socialist Union, 459
Arab Union, 363, 373
Arabian Sea, 375
Arabs in Israel: population of, 70, 71, 73, 74,
  83, 94–95, 99–104, 106; land owned by,
  80, 81; labor on Jewish farms, 85, 87;
  impact of, 99–104, 108, 116; political
  representation of, 143, 144; and military
  service, 232; civil liberties of, 318
Arad, 74
Arbitration Courts, 132
Argentina: Jewish agricultural settlement in,
  27
Arif, Colonel (Abdel Salam), 365, 366
El Arish, 56, 60, 76, 77, 243, 245, 246, 248
El Arish–Ras Muhammad line, 513, 518
Armistice agreement (1949), 415
Army, *see* Military

Ashdod, 72, 78
Ashkenazi Jews, 12–13, 144, 204, 212, 217,
  325
Asian countries: Jewish migration from,
  89–93; in Middle East politics
  (1957–1967), 377–379, 380
Asluj, 59
Assad, President Hafez, 476, 479, 516–517,
  528
"Assurances from USG to Israel", 557–558
Assyria, 8, 69
Aswan Dam, 352, 354, 355
Atoms for Peace program, 576
Attlee, Clement, 36
Auja, 56, 60
Australia, 482
Austria: persecution of Jews in, 27
Automobiles: in Israel, 77, 108, 230
Avigdor, Colonel, 300

Bab el Mandeb Strait, 312, 511, 515, 527,
  559, 594
Babylon, 8, 10, 69
Badran, Shams, 389, 391, 404
Baghdad, 366
Baghdad Pact, 579; as threat to Israel's
  security, 167, 349, 353; Egypt's
  self-exclusion from, 351–352, 354, 379;
  demise of, 360, 364, 375, 380; Jordan in,
  361; and Cold War in Middle East, 367;
  French view of, 370
Balfour, Arthur, 24
Balfour Declaration and Mandate: as root of
  Israel, 6; and Britain's rule in Palestine, 5,
  46, 53; and recognition of Zionist
  movement, 21, 63, 345; Britain's motives
  in issuing of, 24–26, 28; and internal
  development of the Yishuv, 26–28;
  external political aspects of, 28–31; ending
  with U.N. resolution to partition Palestine,
  32, 39, 48; supported by Brandeis, 34; U.S.
  support of, 35; territory involved in, 67, 71
Banias, 252, 253, 255
Banias River, 386
Bank of Israel, 195. *See also* Commerce and
  banking
Bar Association of Israel, 132
Bar Kochba, Shim'on, 9, 10
Barbour, Walworth, 442
Bardawil, Lagoon of, 76
Barlev, Chaim, 187, 284, 287, 298, 305,
  307–308, 324, 443

Barlev Line, 264, 272–273, 287, 289–292
Basel Program, 63
Bashan, 75
Basic Laws, 129, 130, 132
Bat Gallim, 351
Ba'thists, 362, 365, 383, 385, 387
Bedouin nomads, 76, 229
Beerot Yitshak, 56
Beersheba, 56, 74, 77
Begin, Menachem, 173, 197, 199, 561, 563, 569–570, 595
Beirut, 67
Beit Shaan, 53
Ben Gurion, David: in War of Independence, 46, 49, 55, 62, 64, 167, 320; in Sinai-Suez War, 352; on eve of Six Day War, 173; in Provisional government, 142; as Prime Minister and Defense Minister, 189, 321–338; political reforms of, 155–156, 320–321, 323; and Lavon affair, 151, 405; replaced by Sharett, 168; in Rafi, 170, 171; and religion-state problem, 207; meeting with Adenauer, 376; as effective leader, 417
Ben Yehuda, Eliezer, 84, 85
Bernadotte, Count Folke, 58, 59
Bernadotte Plan, 39, 342
Bethlehem, 73
Bethlehem-Hebron area, 247, 250
Bevin, Ernest, 31, 341–342, 345
Bibas, Rabbi Judah, 15
Bible: and origins of Israel, 6–9, 13, 80, 85; Israeli locations mentioned in, 70, 71, 73, 75; national cultural importance of, 142
Biluim, 85
Bir'am, 318
Bir Gafgafa, 243, 287, 297
Bir Lahfan, 243, 245, 246
Bir Thamada, 243
Bitter Lakes, 298, 306
Al Bizri, Brigadier Afif, 362
Black Panthers of Israel, 96
Bnei Yisrael, 210
Bnot Yaacov bridge, 53, 293, 295 (map), 297, 299
Borokowsky, 214, 217
Brandeis, Louis D., 27, 34, 35
Brezhnev, Leonid, 310, 478, 479, 485–487, 490–494, 541, 550, 587
Britain: Zionism in, 5, 22, 25; support of Jewish National Home, 24–26, 28–29; administration of Jewish National Home, 26, 29–31; Palestine policy affected by Arabs, 28–31, 32, 38, 46; and U.N. plan to partition Palestine, 32, 38; interests in Greece and Turkey (1947), 37; in War of Independence, 38, 45–48, 53, 54, 60, 237; command of Arab Legion of Transjordan, 53, 54; administration of Palestine, 67, 87; interest in Middle East area, 69; and railway system in Israel, 77; influence on Israeli government, 128–133, 144, 148, 154, 155, 160; in Middle East politics (1949–1956), 166, 167, 227, 334–335, 338, 340–343, 345, 346, 349–358, 401, 425, 576, 579; in Six Day War, 267, 389, 409; in Middle East politics (1957–1967), 359, 361, 362, 364, 367, 373, 375, 380, 453, 581; attitudes from 1970 to 1973, 453; in Yom Kippur War, 482, 489, 497, 499
Bromine: as natural resource, 78, 112
Brookings Institution: Middle East report, 565–566, 598
Brzezinski, Zbigniew, 565
Bundists, 21, 22
Burma, 377-378, 379
Byroade, Henry, 354

Cabinet of Israel, 128, 129, 130–131
Cairo, 304, 306, 308, 351; after Six Day War, 259; in war of attrition, 264; in Yom Kippur War, 286, 309, 310
Cairo-Suez Road; and kilometer 101 meeting, 512, 513, 515, 518, 521, 525–527, 532
Cambodia, 378, 439, 586
Carmel, Moshe, 322
Carter, Jimmy, 194, 561, 564–569, 594–595
Censorship: on defense matters, 319
Central America: relations with Israel, 378, 380
Central Intelligence Agency, U.S., 386
Central Treaty Organization, 349
Chamberlain, Neville, 30
Chamoun, Camille, 364
Chinese Farm, 306, 307, 308
Chovevei Tzion, 18, 19, 85
Churchill, Winston, 23; White Paper of, 29, 30, 31, 36
Citizens Rights Movement, 158
Citriculture in Israel, 72, 119
Civil liberties: defense effort affecting, 318–319
Civil War (1947–1948), 44–48, 222

Clements, William P., 564
Climate of Israel, 78
Cold War, 324, 340, 343, 367, 534, 579
Commerce and banking, 105, 114; and
  political parties, 153
Communal problem in Israel, 89–97, 98,
  105, 144. See also Oriental Jews
Communications, 112, 114, 115; and
  political parties, 152, 153
Communist party, 141, 142, 143, 159, 164,
  169, 173, 183
Comptroller, State, 129
Conciliation Commission, 335–336
Congo, 383
Constitution of Israel, 126, 128, 129,
  133–135, 138
Constitution, Law and Judicial Committee,
  134
Construction industry, 115–116, 120;
  government investment in, 112; imports
  for, 120; and political parties, 152, 162
Copper mining, 74, 78, 112
Crusades, 12
Culture: impact of defense on, 325–330;
  impact of U.S. on, 573–574
Cyrus the Great, 8–9
Czechoslovakia, 27, 47, 57

Damascus, 258; in Six Day War, 252,
  255–256; in Yom Kippur War, 302–304,
  311
Damia bridge, 54, 247, 250
David, King, 8
Dayan, Moshe: in War of Independence, 52;
  and Israel Workers' list, 170; as Minister
  of Defense, 173–175, 178–179, 215, 218,
  321–323, 390, 405–406, 412–413; rivalry
  with Allon, 175, 177, 188, 474; resignation
  from and return to government, 185–190;
  in 1977 elections, 197; reform of military,
  231; in Six Day War, 257, 320, 411; and
  Open Bridges policy, 268, 318–319; in
  1973 war, 283–286, 294, 296–298, 308,
  488, 490; activities (1970–1973), 450,
  458, 459, 473–475; activities (1973–1974),
  515–517, 519, 521, 523, 524, 529
Dayanim Law, 212
Dead Sea, 71, 74, 78–79, 247
Declaration of Independence of Israel, 113
Defense Army of Israel, 320, 327. See also
  Military; National security; Tzahal
Defense Ministry, 160

Defense (Emergency) Regulations of 1945,
  134
Degania Alef, 52
Degania Bet, 52
De Gaulle, Charles, 389, 401, 409, 432
De Hirsch, Maurice, 19, 27
Democracy in Israel, 126–135; American
  support of, 571, 572
Democratic Front, 192
Democratic Movement for Change, 191, 192,
  196, 197, 198, 199
Deversoir, 306
Diamonds: as exports, 118, 119
Diaspora, 92
Dimona, 74, 77; nuclear reactor in, 321, 370
Dinitz, Simcha, 481, 483, 489, 490
Disengagement agreements: with Egypt and
  Syria, 184, 185, 521–534, 590–594;
  discussion of possibility of, with Jordan,
  189, 191, 536–539, 591
Dobrinin, Anatoly, 433, 492–493
Douhet, Giulio, 275
Dreyfus affair, 19
Druzes, 75, 232
Dühring, Karl Eugen, 19
Dulles, John Foster, 348–350, 352, 355, 359,
  371, 577, 579

Eastern Front: in Egyptian strategy, 262
Eban, Abba: in Six Day War negotiations,
  389, 400–402, 409–411; in 1973 peace
  negotiations, 474, 490, 514, 520;
  departure from government, 187; views
  from outside government, 193; mentioned,
  439, 462
Ecclesiastical Courts, 132
Economy of Israel, 107–125, 127, 381; and
  growth of Jewish Palestine, 27–28, 29;
  geographic factors in, 70–82; expansion
  of, 107–111; role of government in,
  111–114; and patterns of production,
  114–118; foreign trade in, 118–120;
  problems and prospects of, 120–124; and
  impact of Yom Kippur War, 124–125;
  immigration affecting, 162–163, 169;
  affecting internal politics, 177; reform
  attempted by Rabin, 193, 194–195;
  military influence on, 228–231, 236, 280,
  316, 324–325, 329, 522; after Six Day
  War, 260; affected by Open Bridges policy,
  269
Eden, Anthony, 348
Education: and school system, 87, 90–91;

levels attained by population, 111; and political parties, 152, 153, 162; religious influence on, 204–205, 211, 212; financial support by American Jews, 573

Egypt: Jews in, under Roman rule, 10–11, 69; in war against Israel (1948–1949), 43, 44, 46, 49, 50, 55–60; geography of, 69, 76; and 1955 arms deal with Russia, 167, 168, 227, 228, 238, 577, 579; in 1956 Suez-Sinai War, 238–239, 335, 353–358; in Six Day War, 173, 240–246, 248, 320, 386–404, 406–409, 411–413, 582; position after war of 1967, 67, 258–261, 414; and 1969 war of attrition, 177, 261–266, 271–273; in prelude to Yom Kippur War, 278–288; in course of Yom Kippur War, 288–311, 315, 476–502; in Yom Kippur War at sea, 311–312; policies (1949–1956), 335, 337–338, 341–344, 349–358, 401; policies (1957–1967), 359–380, 382–384, 386, 387, 580–582; policies (1967–1970), 415, 416, 419–447, 584–585; policies (1970–1973), 272–274, 276, 448–475, 586–587; policies (October 1973 to May 1974), 506–534, 588–591; policies (1974–1977), 535, 537–548, 550–558, 560–567, 591–593, 597–598

Egyptian Intelligence, 266

Egyptian Third Army, 507–511, 513, 589–590

Ehrenburg, Ilya, 345, 346

Eilat, 74, 76, 77, 78, 226, 263, 312

Eilat-Ashdod oil pipeline, 69, 74, 119, 380

Eilat-Haifa oil pipeline, 69, 74, 380

Ein Gev, 50

Eisenhower Doctrine, 360–363, 371, 372, 374, 581

Eisenhower, Dwight, 324, 348, 576

Eitan, General Raful, 296, 297, 300, 302

El Al airline, 78, 118, 119

Elazar, General David, 186, 253, 284–287, 297–298, 307–308

Elections: in 1949, 140–141; from 1949 to 1973, 158–159; in 1973, 180–183, 514, 518, 522; in 1977, 191–192, 196–199

Elections Ordinance (1948), 128

Electoral process: and development of proportional representation, 145–148; affected by strong party affiliations, 153–160; immigration affecting, 162–165; and reform movements, 198

Electricity: generation of, 79; government investment in, 112

Electronic warning system: for defense, 545, 546, 554, 557, 593

Elon, Amos, 92

Emek Yizreel, 72, 78

Emigration from Israel, 107, 108

England, *see* Britain

Entebbe rescue, 194, 564

Equal Rights for Women Law, 211, 212

Eretz Yisrael, 101

Eshkol, Levi: in 1967 war, 173–174, 189, 320, 388–390, 396, 405–409, 411–412, 417; replaced as Defense Minister by Dayan, 173, 320, 321, 322; struggle with Ben Gurion, 151, 170, 405; attempt to unify party, 177

Ethiopia, 379, 496

Etzion bloc, 53–54

Euphrates, 69

Eurasia, 69

Europe: and life of Jews under Christian rulers, 11–13; Jewish migration from, 12, 88, 89, 162; emancipation of Jews after French Revolution, 16; Zionism in, 21–22; persecution of Jews in, 27; policies in (1973), 497–498, 503–504; 588; policies in (1973–1974), 509, 519, 534, 590; policies in (1974–1977), 540; policies in (1957–1967), 580. *See also individual nations*

European Common Market, 120

European Jews in Israel, 89–93, 95–97, 99; political representation of, 144

Fahd ibn Abdel Aziz, *see* Ibn Abdel Aziz

Fahmi, Ismail, 508–509, 520, 524

Fanon, Franz, 267

Al Fatah, 266, 267, 386

Fawzi, Muhammad, 388, 391, 394, 395

Fayid air base, 308

Fedayeen warfare, 258, 266–271, 337, 352–353, 356, 357, 466

Feisal, Prince, 363, 385; King, 428, 468, 500, 550

Finance Committee, 133

Firan oasis, 75, 76

Firdan, 298

First Temple: period of, 8

First Zionist Congress, 20

"Five principles": of U.S. policy, 584

Five-Star Shipping Line, 378

Ford, Gerald, 538, 541, 545, 548, 551–554, 563, 564, 568, 591

Foreign Affairs Ministry, 160. *See also* International politics

Foreign aid to Israel, 110, 114; dependence on, 121, 123, 124, 163

Foreign policy: affected by potential Arab aggression, 166, 167. *See also* International politics

Foreign trade of Israel, 118–120; imports, 116, 118, 120, 121, 123–125; exports, 117–125

France: support of Zionism, 22, 85; claims to Palestine, 26; Tripartite Declaration (1950), 166; policies (1949–1956), 167, 335, 338, 343, 350, 353–358, 401, 425, 576, 579; in War of Independence, 237; in 1956 war, 321; policies (1957–1967), 360, 362, 364, 369–370, 375, 380, 581; and 1967 war, 389, 401–402, 409; policies (1967–1970), 423, 434; and 1973 war, 497, 499

Frankfurter, Felix, 35

Free Center Party, 158

Gabriel sea-to-sea missile, 275, 276

Gachal, 169, 175, 177, 178, 180, 442, 447, 448, 458

Gadna, 234–235

Galilee, 47, 50, 53, 58, 59, 226; geography of, 70, 78

Galilee, Sea of, 71, 75, 80, 297, 385

Galili Document, 179, 181, 183, 474

Galili, Yisrael, 458

Galuth and Geullah, 13, 16, 92

Gamassi, Abdel Ghani, 310, 513, 518

Gas fields in Israel, 79

Gaza and Gaza Strip: in War of Independence, 56, 59, 60; Palestinians in, 62, 266; after Six Day War, 67, 94, 99–101, 328, 434; geography of, 71, 72, 75, 78; during Six Day War, 242, 243, 388, 394, 395; and fedayeen warfare, 270; after Sinai-Suez War, 319, 368, 372, 579; in 1954 raid, 351, 352; in Sinai invasion (1956), 356, 357; Brookings report on, 566; Begin's view of, 595

General Federation of Jewish Workers, 21, 87, 152. *See also* Histadrut

General Zionist party, 141, 142, 143, 153, 158, 163, 168, 169. *See also* Liberal party

Geneva Peace Conference, 181, 510, 527, 528, 532, 590; groundwork for, 514–520; proceedings of, 520–521; and reconvening

considerations, 543–544, 546, 549–550, 552–554, 559, 565–567, 592, 596

Geography of Israel: affected by Six Day War, 67–70, 73, 258–259, 415–417; physical and economic, 70–82; occupied territories in, 75–77; political and physical, 226, 236; affecting Israel in war, 267, 280

Germany: Zionism in, 22; persecution of Jews in, 27, 29, 31, 35; Jewish migration from, 88; reparations payments to Israel, 110, 122, 163. *See also* Nazis; West Germany

Gesher, 53

Geullah, 13, 16, 92, 201

Ghana, 378

Gibraltar, Strait of, 559, 594

Gida pass, 305–306, 515, 518, 525

Givati brigade, 57

Glassboro summit meeting, 428, 429

Glubb, General, 361

Golan area: from 1970 to 1973, 454, 473; from 1973 to 1974, 523, 529; from 1974 to 1977, 550, 561–563

Golan Heights: in Six Day War, 67, 175, 252, 253, 255, 256; geography of, 75; Syrian batteries in, 226; in Yom Kippur War, 232, 281, 284, 287–288, 293, 296, 297, 300, 301, 303, 311, 313, 479; geostrategic importance of, 258, 259

Gonen, Shmuel, 287, 291–292, 296, 298, 305

Goren, Shlomo, 214–219

Government of Israel, 126–135, 138–139; role in economy, 111–114; democracy in, 126–128, 134; judiciary and legal system in, 126, 128–129, 132–133, 134; Knesset in, 126, 129–134; Provisional, 128–129; Britain as model for, 128–133; President of, 129–130, 131–132, 133; Cabinet of, 128, 129, 130–131; affecting party system, 143, 148, 153, 161–162; coalitions in, 156–160, 169, 170–171; military influence on, 319–325, 329–330, 406; decision-making problems, 404–406, 416. *See also* Mandatory government

Government of National Unity, 173, 175, 176, 177, 185, 447

Grechko, Andrei, 467

Greece: and ancient Palestine, 9, 69; and U.S. interests in Middle East, 37; policies (1973), 497

Gromyko, Andrei, 345, 346, 427, 429, 433;

during 1973 war, 485; activities
(1973–1974), 517, 532; at Geneva
Conference, 520
Gross national product, 108–117, 121, 122,
152
Guerilla action: and terrorism, 222 223, 227,
237. *See also* Fedayeen warfare
Gulf of Aqaba; 69, 74–77; blockade by
Egypt, 173; and 1956 Sinai invasion, 357,
368, 372, 377–379; in Six Day War,
388–390, 395–398, 400, 401, 403, 410
Gush Emunim, 212

Hadassah Medical Center, 573
Haganah, 31, 44–46, 64, 320; during World
War II, 64
Haifa, 88, 91, 226, 337; in War of
Independence, 46, 47; geography of, 71,
72; and transportation network, 77, 78;
population changes in, 106
Halakha, 184, 212
Hapoel Hammizrachi, 141, 142, 153, 159,
169
Harel, Issar, 405
Hashomer Hatzair, 141, 142, 143, 150, 161,
168
Hasmonean family, 9
Hauran, 75
Hausner, Gideon, 216, 218
Heath, Edward, 489
Hebrew: as national language, 26, 93, 94;
revival of, 84, 85, 87
Hebrew University, 54, 73
Hebron, 56, 72, 73, 84
Heikal, Muhammad, 279
Heine, Heinrich, 18
Hellenism: influence on Jews, 9, 10
Henderson, Loy, 362
Hermon, Mount, 75; in Yom Kippur War,
283, 288, 293, 300, 302, 303, 311
Herod, 9
Herut, 141–144, 152, 158, 163, 169, 173,
175
Herut-Liberal Bloc, *see* Gachal
Herzl, Theodor, 14, 18–20, 146, 149
Hidjaz railway, 75, 77
High Court of Justice, 132, 133, 134
Highway system in Israel, 77, 112
Histadrut, 87, 105, 112, 113, 152–153, 164,
165, 195, 573; influence on education,
205. *See also* General Federation of Jewish
Workers

Histadrut Sick Fund, 195
Historical origins of Israel, 4–6; and Jewish
connection with Palestine, 7–13; and
Zionist movement, 14–23; and Balfour
Declaration and Mandate, 24–31; and role
of U.N. and U.S., 32–42; and War of
Independence, 43–64
Hitler, 22, 27, 29, 30, 35
Hofi, Yitzhak, 283–284, 288, 303
Holland, 497
Huleh, Lake, 71
Huleh Valley, 75, 226
Humphrey, Hubert, 390, 403
Hungarian Jews, 85
Hushniya, 296, 299
Hussein, King: in 1967 war, 174, 247–248,
389, 398–399; and 1970 cease-fire
agreement, 270; break from Egypt's
domination, 361–362, 369; and Iraqi
revolution, 364, 373; position after Six
Day War, 422–423; and 1970 Syrian
invasion of Jordan, 450–454, 586; policy
on armed conflict, 466; attempt at
Israeli-Jordanian disengagement
agreement, 536–539, 591
Husseini clan, 46

Ibn Abdel Aziz, Fahd, 569
Ibn Saud, King Abdel Aziz, 36, 361, 363, 365
Ickes, Harold, 36
Ikrit, 310
Immigration in Israel, 82, 107–109, 334,
338, 340, 341, 381; and prestatehood,
27–31, 35, 36, 39, 40, 64, 83–94, 153; and
poststatehood, 83, 84, 89–106; affecting
economic development, 109, 111,
113–115, 121, 122; impact of, 127;
policies of, 128, 133; affecting party
system, 161, 162–165, 169; and
religion-state problem, 208, 213; military
affected by, 230, 232
Imports, *see* Foreign trade
Income: distribution of, 90, 105
Independent Liberal party, 169, 192,
195–196, 216, 218, 553; from 1967 to
1977, 183, 184, 199
India: discrimination against Jews from, 210;
and Middle East politics, 467
Indian Ocean, 69
Industry in Israel, 70, 71, 72, 74, 105, 110,
117–120; and government investment in
manufacturing, 112; exports of, 119;

imports of, 120; and political parties, 152; affected by military needs, 230; military, 274, 323, 324, 330
Institute for Arid Zone Research, 74
Intelligence Branch of Israel, 281–285, 351
Internal politics of Israel, 138–219; and religion-state problem, 132, 133, 139, 142, 143, 160, 162, 164, 169, 200–219; prestatehood, 140–160; party system from 1948 to 1967, 161–171; party system from 1967 to 1977, 172–199
International Court of Justice, 372
International politics: affecting internal politics, 177; from 1948 to 1957, 334–358, 578–579; from 1957 to 1967, 359–380, 579–582; in 1967, 381–413, 582–583; from 1967 to 1970, 414–447, 583–585; from 1970 to 1973, 448–475, 585–587; in October 1973, 476–505, 587–588; from October 1973 to May 1974, 506–534, 588–591; from June 1974 to May 1977, 535–570, 588–591; and overview of American-Israeli relations, 571–598
Iran, 378, 379, 380; during Yom Kippur War, 480
Iraq: in war against Israel (1948–1949), 43, 46, 49, 50, 53, 59; air force of, 241, 242, 275; in Six Day War, 241, 242, 247, 389, 390, 394, 399, 402, 403, 413; military posture after Six Day War, 258; in war of attrition, 262; in Yom Kippur War, 301, 303, 304, 310, 315, 480, 482, 489; policies (1949–1956), 341, 342, 349–350, 354, 355, 357, 579; policies (1957–1967), 359–367, 373, 375, 379, 380, 382–384, 426, 581; policies (1970–1973), 452, 453; policies (1974–1977), 563
Irbid, 453
Irbid Mafraq, 258
Irgun, 44, 45, 47, 48, 63, 142–143, 151, 320, 325
Irrigation, 70, 71, 72, 74, 79–80, 112, 116
Isdud, 56, 57
Islam, 11
Ismail, Ahmad, 279, 283, 304, 309, 310
Ismail, Hafez, 470–471
Ismailia, 286, 289, 306, 308, 310
Israel Workers' list, 170
Istiqlalists, 365
Italy, 497

Jabotinsky, Vladimir, 63
Jacob (Israel), 7
Jaffa, 46–48, 72, 77
Japan, 378, 519
Jarring, Gunnar: 1967 negotiations of, 430–431; 1969 negotiations of, 434; 1970 negotiations of, 265, 441, 585; 1971 negotiations of, 457–460, 462, 466; 1973 negotiations of, 472, 587
Jebel Libni, 243, 245
Jebel Musa, 75
Jenin, 53, 59, 247, 248, 250
Jericho, 71, 247, 250
Jerusalem, 77, 78, 83, 84, 88, 174, 226, 416, 434; as ancient religious center, 8; destroyed by Romans, 9; during War of Independence, 46–48, 50, 54–60, 566; division of, 59, 60, 69, 73; after World War I, 67; geography of, 73–74; population changes in, 106; in Six Day War, 246–247, 248, 250
Jewish Agency, 26, 27, 30, 112, 128, 162
Jewish culture: in ancient civilization, 8, 9, 10; in Babylon, 10; in Alexandria, 10–11; in Spain, 11; in Europe, 11–13; in Age of Enlightenment, 16
Jewish history: in ancient Palestine, 7–10; and Diaspora and idea of return, 10–13
Jewish National Fund, 80
Jewish National Home, *see* National Home
"Jewish problem", 16–19, 113; in France, 16, 19; in Rumania, 17; in Russia, 17–18, 149–150, 167; in central and western Europe, 18; in Europe, 91; in Asian countries, 91–92; in Poland, 149
Jewish Territorial Organization, 20
Jews: and Arab conquests, 9, 10–11, 69; assimilation in other cultures, 11, 17, 18, 19, 21; national unity of, 93, 94, 95–97; and world Jewry aid to Israel, 123, 125
Jews in Israel: population of, 83; school system of, 87; and defining who is Jewish, 208, 212, 213
Jews in U.S., 571–577; influence in Israel, 573–574; influence on U.S. policies, 574–577
Jezreel Valley: during War of Independence, 46, 47, 53; railway through, 77; in Six Day War, 248; geography of, 72
Johnson, Lyndon: aid to Israel (1965), 374; during 1967 war, 388–391, 398–401,

409–411, 425–426; aid to Israel after 1967 war, 418, 431; at Glassboro summit meeting, 428–429; 1969 peace negotiations, 432; "Five Principles" of Middle East policy, 584

Johnson Plan, 385, 582

Jordan: after War of Independence, 60; Palestinian Arab refugees in, 62; territory changes in, 67; and international division of Jerusalem, 69, 73; bordering Israel, 69, 226, 239; in Six Day War, 174, 240–242, 246–252, 389, 390, 398–399, 402, 403, 413; 1975 peace negotiations, 189, 191, 197, 536–539; position after Six Day War, 258, 260, 261, 415, 416, 422–423; in war of attrition, 262; guerrilla movement in, 270, 271, 438, 442, 446; policies (1970–1973), 275, 450–456, 462, 466, 586, 587; in Yom Kippur War, 280, 302–304, 310, 315, 489, 499; policies (1949–1956), 336, 337, 355, 356; policies (1957–1967), 359, 361–367, 373, 375, 380, 382, 385, 453, 581; approval of Resolution 242, 430; in 1969 peace negotiations, 434–435; in 1970 peace negotiations, 441; policies (1973–1974), 520–521, 530. *See also* Hussein, King; Transjordan

Jordan River: dividing Mandate territory, 67; irrigation with, and dispute with Arabs, 70–71, 79–80, 385, 392; bridges over, 77; in Six Day War, 247, 248, 252, 258, 259; and Open Bridges policy, 268; and fedayeen warfare, 271; in Yom Kippur War, 293, 296, 297, 536; hydroelectric project on, 348–349

Jordan Valley, 454; agriculture in, 71; climate of, 78

Joshua, 7

Judaism, *see* Jews

Judea, 595; climate of, 78; after Yom Kippur War, 181, 182, 184, 198, 212, 536; after Six Day War, 416. *See also* West Bank

Judiciary and legal system, 128, 132–133

Jumblat, Kamal, 563

Kafr Kassem incident, 329

Kalisher, Rabbi Zvi Hirsch, 15

Kantara, 56, 245, 286, 289, 298

Kashrut, 204

Kassem, General Abdel Karim, 365–367, 382–384

Kennedy, John F., 374, 581

Kenya, 496

Kenyatta, Jomo, 496

Kfar Darom, 56

Kfar Etzion, 53

Kfar Sirkin, 242

Kfir fighter-bomber, 274

Khartoum summit meeting, 428

Khrushchev, Nikita, 167, 366, 384

Kibbutzim, 87; and agrindustrial collective village, 117; affected by strong party affiliations, 150, 166; hired labor in, 163–164

Kiddush hashshem, 218

Kilometer 101 agreement: on Cairo-Suez Road, 512, 513, 515, 518, 521, 525–527, 532

Kiryat Arbaa, 73. *See also* Hebron

Kiryat Shmona, 531–532

Kishon River, 71

Kissinger, Henry: policies (1970), 438–441, 444, 445, 586–587; during 1970 Syrian invasion of Jordan, 453–456, 586–587; 1971 China trip, 461; 1973 secret negotiations with Hafez Ismail, 470–471; and 1973 Washington summit, 472; policy in Yom Kippur War, 301, 310, 473–483, 486–495, 503–504; negotiations from October 1973 to September 1975, 506–560, 588–594; policies (1974–1977), 535, 557, 561, 563, 565, 591, 595

Knesset, 126, 129–134, 140, 144, 148, 154–155, 157–159, 211

Knesset Committee, 132

Kohens: marriage laws affecting, 211, 215

Korean War, 339, 343, 346

Kosygin, Aleksei: during 1973 war, 309, 484–485; and 1966 Egyptian-Syrian joint defense treaty, 387; during 1967 war, 389, 399, 411; 425–428; at Glassboro summit meeting, 426; 1970 note to Nixon, 440

Kulturkampf, 206, 217

Kuneitra, 75, 252, 253, 255, 293–294, 300, 302, 529, 532

Kuntila, 243, 245

Kusseima, 245

Kuwait: policies (1957–1967), 375, 382, 383; policies (1967), 390, 402, 403; policies (1973), 499

Kuwatly, Shukri, 362

Labor Alignment, 512–513, 518, 521, 522, 529, 530. *See also* Maarakh
Labor Party: domination of government, 113, 180; formation of, 159, 176; factional strife in, 177, 322; and Galili document, 179, 474; in Yom Kippur War, 180; and Rabin, 184–185, 188, 530, 537; and Dayan, 186, 322, 474; in 1977 elections, 191, 194–199, 595; and religious problems, 212, 217, 218
Lachish region, 72
Land: reclamation of, 72, 74, 79, 112, 127; tenure system, 80–82, 116; purchase laws, 128, 133
Langer, Chanoch and Miriam, 214–218
Lanner, General Dan, 296, 299–300, 302–303
Laos, 378
Latakia, 311, 368
Latrun, 55–56, 58, 247, 248, 250
Lausanne Protocol, 336
Lavon affair, 151, 170, 171, 189, 212, 351, 405
Lavon, Pinchas, 321
League of Nations, 67, 520; approval of Balfour Declaration, 26
Lebanon: in War of Independence, 43, 50, 53, 59, 60; Palestinian refugees in, 62; geographical features of, 69, 70, 252; 1976 civil war, 193–194, 560, 562–565; fedayeen in, 270, 271, 442, 517, 531–532; in Yom Kippur War, 315; policies (1949–1956), 337; 1958 civil war, 359, 361, 363, 364, 382, 385, 426, 453, 581
Lechi, 44, 45, 320
Legal system, 128, 132–133
Legislative process, 129–132, 134
Lenin, 21
Liberal party, 169. *See also* General Zionist party
Libya, 275, 305, 315, 326, 361, 366, 367, 390, 403, 435, 436, 459–460, 474, 497, 499, 500, 563
Likkud: in 1973 elections, 180–185, 189; in 1977 elections, 191–192, 197–199, 561, 595; in 1973 war, 513; in 1974, 537. *See also* Gachal; Herut
Lod, 58, 77, 78, 230
Lodge, Henry Cabot, 35

Maalot, 531–532
Maarakh: formation of, 169; in National Unity government, 176–178; in 1973 elections, 180–185, 189, 190, 473–474; in 1977 elections, 192, 199; and Hausner bill, 217; and Eshkol, 412. *See also* Achdut Haavoda; Labor Alignment; Mapai; Mapam
Mack, Julian, 35
Magen, General Kalman, 298, 308, 310
Maghreb, 499, 500
Mahmud, Sidki, 404
Majdal, 56
Malaria, 71, 72, 79, 82, 85
Malkieh, 53
Mamzerim, 211, 213–219
Mandate of Palestine, 24–31, 67, 77, 78, 573. *See also* Balfour Declaration
Mandatory government: affecting laws of Israel, 128, 133, 134; political parties in, 140–160; religion and state in, 202–204, 206
Manganese, 76, 78
Manufacturing, *see* Industry
Mapai party: in 1949 election, 141, 143, 144; during 1946, 150; and Lavon affair, 151, 405; control of Histadrut, 152; dominance in government, 155, 157–160; and reforms of Ben Gurion, 156; activities (1948–1967), 162, 163, 166–170, 206–207, 211, 212, 315, 377; activities (1967–1977), 173–176, 179, 187, 191; and Eshkol, 412; activities (1948–1967), 141–144, 150–151, 159, 163, 164, 166–168
Mapam, 175, 176, 180, 183, 184, 216–218, 553
Marriage: intermarriage between members of different communities, 93; religious vs. civil law, 210–211, 213–219
Marxism, 141, 142, 168
Mas'ada, 252, 255
Massada (kibbutz), 50, 52
Matt, Colonel Dan, 306–309
Mediterranean Sea, 69, 259
Megiddo, 242
Meir, Golda: 184–190, 455, 547; as Third Aliyah member, 87; in 1969 election, 177, 417; and party unity, 178, 417; and Galili document, 179, 474; and religious question, 215–216; during 1973 war,

284–286, 297, 477, 481, 482, 484,
487–491; in Six Day War, 320;
ambassador in Moscow, 347; 1963
meeting with Kennedy, 374; in 1970
negotiations, 442–443, 446, 450, 452,
453, 456; in 1971 negotiations, 458, 460,
463, 466; in 1973 negotiations, 471, 473;
in negotiations from October 1973 to May
1974, 508–513, 517, 525, 527, 529–530,
537
Memorandum of Agreement: with U.S.,
557–559, 593–594
Mendler, Albert, 287, 291, 292, 298
Merchant fleet of Israel, 77, 118–119
Middle East Defense Command, 339, 340,
343
Midrash, 10
Mikve Yisrael, 85
Military: establishment, 231–235; the reserve
system, 228–231; 232, 272, 276, 278,
281–283, 285–286, 292, 296, 300–301,
313, 322–323, 326, 522; relation to
economy, 107, 109, 111–115, 117–118,
120–122, 124, 194, 195, 274, 275, 596;
and politics and the polity, 134, 152, 165,
194, 317–330, 406; action in War of
Independence, 43–60; action in 1956 war,
232, 356, 368; action in 1967 war,
240–256; action in war of attrition,
261–271; action in Yom Kippur War,
281–282, 288–312; strategy (1949–1967),
235–239; after Six Day War, 257–258,
262–264, 268–271; in 1970–1973,
271–277; in Yom Kippur War, 281–286,
297, 301–303, 305–307; flaws in defense,
312–313; strategy after Yom Kippur War,
314–316; service for women, 211; imports
of equipment, 274, 316. *See also* Air force;
National security; Navy
Military-agricultural settlements, 179. *See
also* Nachal
Millet system, 203, 204, 209
Mineral resources in Israel, 71, 74, 76,
78–79, 80, 112
Mining, 71, 74, 76, 78–79, 112, 117;
government investment in, 112
Mishmar Haemek, 47
Mishmar Hayarden, 59
Mishna, 9
Mitla pass, 515, 518, 525
Mitzpeh Ramon, 74

Mizrachi party, 141, 142, 153, 159, 169;
influence on schools, 205
Moked, 159, 183, 192
Mongols, 69
Morocco, 302, 304, 382, 499
Morrison-Grady plan, 40
Moscow Doctors Plot, 166, 344
Moses, 7, 75
Moshav, 87
Mossul province, 365, 366
Movement for Citizen's Rights, 183, 184,
185, 192
Movement for the Integral Land of Israel,
328
Muhieddine, Zakariya, 390, 403
Munich: murder of Israeli athletes in, 473
Muslims, 11, 12, 75, 162, 209
Muslim Brethren, 46

Nablus, 73, 248, 250
Nachal, 229, 234, 271
Nafekh, 296
Nag'Hamadi, 263
Nahariya, 71
Nasser, Gamal Abdel: 235, 359–369,
435–437, 457, 580; in Six Day War, 173,
222, 406–409, 411, 582; in war of
attrition, 177, 261, 264, 431, 433,
444–447; after Six Day War, 246, 258,
279, 418–425, 427, 428; death of, 273,
456, 459, 496; arms deal with Soviet
Union, 351–354, 579; in Sinai-Suez War,
353–357; and Arab nationalism, 359–369,
581; peace negotiations with Israel (1955),
338; and Rogers proposal, 437, 442–447,
451, 456; in 1970 negotiations, 438, 440;
and oil embargo, 499–500
Natanya, 242
National Home of the Jewish People, 15, 17,
20–23, 86, 149; and attitudes of Britain,
24–26, 28–31; internal development of,
27–28; Arab opposition to, 28–30; and
secular vs. religious movement, 202
National Insurance System, 231
National land, 129
National Land Authority, 80
National Museum, 73
National Religious Front, 169
National Religious Party, 169, 190, 196, 199;
in elections (1949–1973), 158; and Dayan
in 1967, 173; in 1973 elections, 183–185,

189, 192; in 1977 elections, 191–192, 569; views on Judea and Samaria, 212; and case of mamzerim, 216

National security: threats to, affecting internal politics, 139, 165–171; and reliance on military strength, 168; as priority in national policy, 189; policies (1949–1967), 222–239; and test of Six Day War, 240–256; policies (1967–1973), 257–277; in Yom Kippur War, 278–316; defense effort and Israeli polity, 317–330. *See also* Military *and individual wars*

National Unity Government, 173, 175, 176, 177, 185

National Water Carrier, 80, 385

Nationalism, Jewish: and Zionist movement, 4–6, 63, 208; American support of, 572

Natonek, Rabbi Joseph, 15

Natserat Illit, 70

Natural resources of Israel, 78–79, 107, 109, 113, 114

Navy of Israel, 230, 233, 234, 259; in Six Day War, 245, 256; growth after Six Day War, 276; in Yom Kippur War, 311–312

Nazareth, 59, 70

Nazis: persecution of Jews, 5, 27, 31, 36, 40, 41, 63, 151; and Jewish migration from Germany, 88

Nebi Yusha, 53

Nebuchadnezzar, 8

Negba, 57, 59

Negev, 226; in War of Independence, 47, 48, 57–59; geography of, 70, 73, 74, 80; phosphate mining in, 78; in Six Day War, 247; after Six Day War, 258; population changes in, 106; development plans of Ben Gurion, 376

Nepal, 378

Nes Tzionah, 85

Neturei Karta, 201

Nile, 69

Nirim, 56

Nitzanim, 56

Nixon, Richard: policies compared to Johnson, 432, 584–585; policies (1970), 438–441, 452, 458, 584–585; and policies of Rogers, 441, 444–448, 586; policies (1971), 461–462, 466–468; and Jordan crisis, 452, 454, 455, 586; policies (1972), 463, 587; policies (1973), 470–475, 587; during Yom Kippur War, 479, 482, 483, 486, 489–491, 493–494; policies

(1973–1974), 508–511, 527, 589; policies (1974), 535–538, 541; policies compared to Carter, 568

North Atlantic Treaty Organization (NATO), 167, 343, 497, 504, 506, 534, 578, 590, 597

Notre Dame convent, 55

Nu, U, 377, 379

Nuclear weapons, 483, 489, 596–597

Occupations: distribution in Israel, 105, 114–118

Occupied areas: geography of, 67, 75–77, 83; affecting Jewish character of Israel, 99–104, 116; and legal basis for military rule of Arabs, 134; plan for political use of, 174, 175, 178, 179, 180; and views of religious parties; 212–213; guerrilla warfare in, 267–271; and Arab employment in Israel, 269; civil liberties in, 318–319; policies on (1967–1970), 433, 434, 447, 583; policies on (1970–1973), 459, 464, 472, 473, 474; during Yom Kippur War, 481, 484, 485; policies on (1973–1974), 516, 518, 523, 529, 530, 532, 589, 590; policies on (1974–1977), 536–537, 541, 551, 559, 565–566, 598

Ofer, Avraham, 196

Oil: and Middle East politics (before 1948), 34, 35, 36, 37, 39, 40, 41; passage through Israel, 69, 74, 380; in Sinai peninsula, 76; in Israel, 78, 112; and politics (1967), 260–261, 390, 402, 403, 582; and politics (1973), 313–314, 476, 481, 486, 496–504, 588; and politics (1948–1957), 341, 343, 354, 357–358, 578–579; and politics (1957–1967), 382, 580; and politics (1967–1970), 435; and politics (1970–1973), 452, 471, 472, 474, 586, 587; and politics (from October 1973 to May 1974), 506, 508–510, 512, 514–516, 519, 529, 534, 589, 590; and politics (1974–1977), 540, 541, 558, 564, 575, 596, 597; at Abu Rodeis, 541–545, 551, 554, 556, 558, 591, 593, 598

Olives, 70

Open Bridges policy, 103, 268–269, 271, 318

Open Door policy, 35

Ore deposits in Israel, 78

Organization of African Unity, 496

Oriental Jews, 13, 89–93, 95–97, 99, 104, 111, 127, 198, 325; affecting party system,

164–165; and religion-state problem, 209–210. *See also* Communal problem
Oron, 78
Orthodox Judaism, 201, 207–208, 213, 218
Ottoman Empire, 67, 76–77, 85, 133, 134, 203

Palais des Nations, 520
Pakistan, 349, 467
Palestine, 67; ancient history of Jews in, 7–10; Jewish dispersion from, 10–13; as National Home for Jewish People, 15, 17, 20–24, 26, 63, 86; U.N. plan for partitioning of, 29–30, 32, 38–44, 46, 48, 60, 62, 67, 142; possible political entity in, 101
Palestine (Defence) Order-in-Council, 134
Palestine Liberation Army, 385
Palestine Liberation Organization (PLO), 102, 104, 532; in Lebanon, 194; supported by Arab leaders, 385, 549, 591; in Jordan, 389, 536, 537–539, 586; strategy of, 423; attempts at airline hijacking, 451; and Geneva Conference, 517, 534, 549–550, 559; in clash with Syria over Lebanon, 562–567; recognition of, 594. *See also* Palestinians
Palestinians: as refugees, 63, 224, 225; in Six Day War, 242, 243; guerrilla movement of, 262, 266–271; representation of, 514, 517, 518, 549–551, 566, 568, 591–592, 595; nationalism of, 572. *See also* Palestine Liberation Organization
Palmach, 57, 320
Paris-Cairo railway system, 77
Peace Conference of 1919, 27, 34
Peled, Binyamin, 292, 296
Peled, Musa, 299–300, 302
Pentateuch, 9
People of Israel, 83–106; formation and transformation until 1967, 84–94; wars of 1967 and 1973 affecting, 94–104. *See also* Population
Peres, Shimon: in Rafi, 170, 186–187; association and rivalry with Rabin, 187–190, 194; and Yadlin, 195; as head of Labor list in 1977 election, 197, 199; in 1958 negotiations with West Germany, 376; and Eshkol, 405; in 1975 negotiations, 544, 546
Persia, 8–9, 69
Persian Gulf, 375, 379, 380

Petach Tikva, 85
Philharmonic Orchestra of Israel, 573
Philistines, 8
Philippines, 378
Phosphate mining, 78, 112
Pineau, Christian, 353
Pinsker, Leo, 14, 17–18
Poalei Agudat Yisrael, 141, 142, 158, 161, 183, 192
Poalei Tzion Smol, 141
Podgorny, Nikolai, 419, 427, 460
Pogroms in Russia, 85, 86, 150
Poland: opposition to Zionism, 21; Jewish migration from, 87–88; Jews in, during Enlightenment, 149
Political party system, 138–199; in prestatehood, 140–160; from 1948–1967, 161–171; from 1967–1977, 172–199. *See also* Internal politics *and specific parties*
Politics: internal, 138–219, *see also* Internal politics; international, 332–598, *see also* International politics
Pompey, 9
Popular Front for the Liberation of Palestine, 451
Population of Israel, 70–74, 83–106, 225; and growth of Jewish Palestine, 24, 27–28, 29, 30; changes after War of Independence, 62; stratification of, 104–106; rural-urban distribution of, 106; affecting government, 127; affecting guerrilla warfare, 267
Port Said, 76, 259, 310, 312, 356
Portugal, 497, 546, 548, 591
Potash, as natural resource, 78, 112
Prague Trials of 1952, 166
President: role of, 129–133
Prime Minister: role of, 129, 131, 133, 160
Prisoners of war: Israelis in Syria, 506, 507, 510, 511, 513, 514, 517, 518, 528, 529, 530, 532
Progressive party, 141, 158, 169
Provisional Council, 128
Provisional Government, 128–129, 133, 142–143, 148

Qaddafi, Colonel Muammar, 500

Rabat Arab summit meeting, 436–437, 539, 540, 549, 591, 592
Rabin, General Yitzhak: and Six Day War, 175, 406; formation of new government,

184–190, 530; in 1977 elections,
192–197; and relations with Jordan,
453–456, 537; *Haaretz* interview in 1974,
541–542, 561; in 1975 negotiations,
544–545, 547, 548, 551–554; in 1977
negotiations, 561–562, 567
Rabbinate, 203–204, 210
Rabbinical Council, 203–204, 205
Rabbinical Court, 214
Rabinowitz, Yehoshua, 195, 196
Radio Damascus, 255
Rafah, 56, 77, 179, 243, 245
Rafi party, 159, 170, 171, 173, 176, 187, 188
Rafid, 299
Railway system in Israel, 77, 112
Rakah, 159, 183, 192, 199
Ramalla, 73, 248, 250
Ramat David air base, 248
Ramat Rahel, 55, 56
Ramleh, 58
Red Sea, 69, 259, 312, 375, 559
Reform Judaism, 213
Religion and state, 132, 133, 139, 142, 143,
160, 162, 164, 169; and religious political
parties, 183–185, 206–207, 210–212;
origins of problem, 200–202; pattern of
relations in, 202–206; and religious
councils, 202, 205–206; and religious
courts, 203, 210; laws and regulations
relating to, 204, 210–215; dynamics of
problem with, 206–213; and case of the
mamzerim, 213–219
Religions, Ministry of, 202, 205
Repression of Jews, 11–12, 16–19, 21–23,
162, 344; affecting support for Israel, 572
Reshef missile boat, 274, 276
Resolution 242 of U.N., 414, 430–432; as
basis for negotiations, 441, 482, 485–491,
498, 569, 585; acceptance by Israel, 442,
447; Sadat's view of, 471; and views of
Palestine Liberation Organization, 559,
567, 594; U.S. view of, 584
Resolution 338 of U.N.: formulation of, 487;
as basis for negotiations, 498, 506, 514,
527, 532, 556, 569; and views of
Palestine Liberation Organization, 559,
594
Resolution 339 of U.N., 493, 507
Revisionist party, 142, 152
Rhodes format, 434
Richards, James P., 361
Rifai, Zeid, 536

Rikhye, Indar Jit, 388, 394
Rishon le-Tzion, 85
Riyad, Mahmud, 388, 395, 434
Rockefeller, Nelson, 510
Rogers, William P.: initiative of, 177,
441–444, 446, 448, 585, 586; plan for
Arab-Israeli settlement, 435, 437,
439–444, 446, 471, 567, 585; erosion of
policies; 449–464, 465, 505; in 1969
negotiations, 264, 435; in 1970
negotiations, 438–439; 441, 453, 585;
relations with Kissinger, 456, 586; in 1971
negotiations, 457–459, 461, 463, 470, 473
Roman rule of Judea: revolts against, 9, 69
Roosevelt, Franklin, 36
Rosh Pinna, 85
Rothschild, Baron Edmond, 20, 24, 85
Rumania, 17
Rusk, Dean, 389, 427, 429
Russia, *see* Soviet Union

Sa'ar, 276
Sabha, 338
Sabri, Ali, 459, 460
Sadat, Anwar: and 1971 as year of decision,
273–274, 459–62, 466; in 1972
negotiations, 279, 464–470; and Yom
Kippur War, 304, 309, 310, 476, 508; in
1973 negotiations, 470, 479–481,
484–485, 487, 489, 493–494; in
negotiations after Yom Kippur War, 510,
512, 514–527, 535; in 1974 negotiations,
539–542; in 1975 negotiations, 542–545,
550–553, 561; in 1976 negotiations, 562;
in 1977 negotiations, 567, 598
Sadeq, Muhammad, 279
Safed, 46, 84; geography of, 70
Safwat, Ismail Pasha, 46
Said, *see* Port Said
St. Catherine Monastery, 75, 76
Samakh, 50, 52, 252, 253
Samaria: in War of Independence, 53, 54;
after Yom Kippur War, 181, 183, 184,
198, 212; as territorial problem, 416, 536,
595. *See also* West Bank
Samuel, Herbert, 25
Sapir, Pinchas, 178, 179, 186–188, 190, 474
Saudi Arabia: policies (1957–1967), 361,
362, 366, 367, 373, 382, 385, 582; in Six
Day War, 403; policies (1967–1970), 258,
428, 436; during Yom Kippur War, 315,

476, 486, 499–500, 502; policies (1970–1973), 452, 468; policies (1973–1974), 516, 530; policies (1974–1977), 542, 550, 564, 566, 567, 569, 592, 597
Saul, King, 8
Scali, John, 471–472
Scopus, Mount, 54, 248
Scranton, William, 432
Secularists, 209
Security Law, 134. *See also* National security
Sefaradi Jews, 13, 144, 204, 217, 325
Selassie, Haile, 496
Senegal, 496
Senghor, Leopold Sedar, 496
Settlements, 179, 229, 236, 473, 474
Shaar Hagolan, 50, 52
Shafrir air-to-air missiles, 274
Shapira, Moshe, 412
Sharett, Moshe, 168–169, 189, 338, 339, 377
Sharm el Sheikh, 76, 245, 312, 395
Sharon, Ariel, 180, 181, 187, 192, 257, 292, 298–299, 306–310, 513
Sharon Division, 243, 245–246
Sharon, Plain of, 71–72
Sharon, Samuel Flatto, 192
Shawwaf, Colonel, 365
Shazli, General Sa'd al Din: in Six Day War, 242, 243, 245; in Yom Kippur War, 279, 309, 310; at Arab League's Joint Defense Council, 466
Sheehan, Edward, 545
Sheikh Jarrah, 54
Shekhem, 73
Shelli, 192
Shlomtzion, 192
Shomron, 73
Shukairy, Ahmad, 389
Siddur, 10
Sidki, Aziz, 469–470
Sinai Agreement I, 184, 185, 521–527, 554, 556, 590
Sinai Agreement II, 76, 191–193, 535, 539, 554–556, 559–562, 570, 593–594, 598
Sinai Desert, 72, 74, 259
Sinai, Mount, 75
Sinai Peninsula: after Six Day War, 67, 69; geography of, 75–76, 258–259; railway system in, 77; after Yom Kippur War, 181, 182, 509, 513, 518, 523; Egyptian batteries in, 226; in Six Day War, 242, 320,

388, 390, 394–397, 399, 409; as territorial problem (1970–1973), 261, 457, 459, 461, 466, 473; in Yom Kippur War, 288–292, 311; withdrawal from, 319, 372, 579; and negotiations of 1974–1977; 540–546, 550, 551, 554, 591, 593, 598
Sinai-Suez War; reserve forces in, 232; casualties in, 234; strategy in, 236–239; causes of, 266, 335, 354–356; and Kafr Kassem incident, 329; events during, 356–357, 579; Egypt's position after, 357–358, 387; and positions of Britain and France, 357–358, 581; Israel's position after, 358, 368–380, 415; U.S. in, 425, 579; Soviets in, 426
Sisco, Joseph, 433, 438, 441, 453, 460, 461, 463, 473, 511–512, 515
Six Day War: casualties in, 47, 234, 246, 248, 250, 256; and territorial changes, 67, 69–70, 73, 94, 99; immediate causes of, 76, 387–413, 476; affecting people of Israel, 83–84, 89, 94–104; and communal problem, 94–97; affecting economy, 112, 119, 122, 123, 236; impact of issues raised by, 127; impact on political party system, 138–139, 171–179, 199, 323; mobilization of reserves in, 232, 236; strategy in, 236–237, 243–245, 247–248, 253; events during, 240–256, 388–413; Egypt in, 240–246, 247, 257, 258; Syria in, 240, 241, 242, 247, 248, 250–256, 258, 266; Jordan in, 240, 241, 242, 246–252, 257, 258; air force in, 240–241, 245, 246, 248, 250, 253, 255, 256; land forces in, 243; and Israel's strategic-diplomatic position, 257–261, 318, 414–447; and position of Iraq, 258; fedayeen in, 266; and military influence on government decisions, 320; remote background of, 381–387, 476; and U.S. diplomatic position, 417–419, 423–424; and position of Soviet Union, 419–420, 421, 422, 423, 447; compared to Yom Kippur War, 477; as turning point in U.S.-Israel relations, 578, 582–583
Six-Point Agreement of 1973, 511–514, 516, 527, 590
Slansky, Rudolph, 344
Sodom, 74
Solomon, King, 8, 74
South America: relations with Israel, 378, 380

652 / *Index*

Soviet Union: "Jewish problem" in, 17; Jewish repression in, 17, 21, 86, 166, 208; Zionism in, 21, 25, 97; and role of Jews in Revolution, 25; Jewish migration from, 27, 83, 84, 86, 87, 89, 94, 97–99, 101, 108, 111, 213; affecting U.S. interests in Middle East, 37; support of partitioning of Palestine, 38, 142; naval power in Middle East, 69; pogroms in, 85, 86, 150; and views of political parties in Israel, 143, 151, 166–168; Jews in, during Enlightenment, 149–150; and 1955 Egyptian arms deal, 167, 227, 228, 238, 347, 352, 353; and Jewish War of Independence, 38; in Six Day War, 95, 253, 389–392, 399–401, 403, 407, 411–412, 414, 582; after 1967 War, 258, 260, 276; in war of attrition, 177, 261, 264–266, 271–272; in Yom Kippur War, 279, 284, 301–304, 309, 311, 313, 477–495, 497, 588; policies (1949–1956), 334–335, 338–340, 343–347, 356, 357, 577, 578–579; policies (1957–1967), 359–369, 371, 374, 379, 380, 382–387, 418, 579–582; policies (1967–1970), 416, 419–423, 447, 584–585; policies (1970–1973), 271–274, 448–449, 452–473, 585–587; policies (1973–1974), 499, 502–504, 506, 508–510, 514, 517, 519–524, 530, 532, 534, 588–590; policies (1974–1977), 535, 539–541, 543, 546, 549–552, 559, 565, 570, 592, 596, 597

Spain: Jews under Arab rule in, 11; Jewish migration from, 12; aid to Arabs, 497

Stalin, Joseph, 166, 347

Standard Oil, 34

Stein, Leonard, 25

Stern Gang, 44

Strauss, Franz Joseph, 376

Sudan, 379, 390

Suez Canal: from 1948 to 1956, 53, 56, 350–351, 353–358, 369, 401; in Six Day War, 76, 175, 242, 245; after Six Day War, 69, 258–260, 380, 437, 441, 443; in war of attrition, 262, 263; and fedayeen warfare, 270; from 1970 to 1973, 272, 274, 459, 461, 462, 465, 470; in Yom Kippur War, 279–282, 287–294, 296, 298–299, 304–310, 479, 481, 484–485, 489–490; from October 1973 to May

1974, 507, 509, 515, 516, 518–519, 522–527, 530; from 1974 to 1977, 539–540, 544, 550, 556, 593; and Israeli trade, 577

Suez City, 286, 310, 493, 511, 523

Suez, Gulf of, 306, 310, 312, 541

Sulzberger, C. L., 466

Supreme Court of Israel, 128, 132, 133

Sweden, 105

Sykes, Mark, 26

Syria: and ancient Palestine, 9, 69; Palestinian refugees in, 62; after World War I, 67; bordering Israel, 69; and Jordan River, 70–71; and guerrilla warfare against Israel, 266; air force of, 275; in war against Israel (1948–1949), 43, 45, 50–53, 59, 60; arms deal in 1955 with Russia, 227–228, 238; in Six Day War, 67, 71, 75, 240–242, 247–256, 266, 320, 386–399, 402, 406–408; after Six Day War, 256, 258, 260, 261, 276; in war of attrition, 262; in prelude to Yom Kippur War, 278–288; in Yom Kippur War, 278, 293–297, 299–304, 311–312, 315, 476–480, 487–489, 492, 499, 501–502; relations with Israel (1949–1956), 337, 356; policies (1957–1967), 359–367, 369, 379, 380, 383–387, 426, 581; policies (1967–1970), 415, 416, 419, 422–423, 425, 427, 431, 442, 584; policies (1970–1973), 451–455, 459–460, 475, 586; policies (October 1973 to May 1974), 514–518, 522, 528–535, 590–591; policies (1974–1977), 195, 535, 536, 540, 544, 548, 550, 557, 560–566, 597

Tal Division, 243, 245

Al Tal, Wasfi, 466

Talmud, 10

Tassa, 298, 306

Tel Aviv, 46, 50, 56, 57, 58, 72, 88, 91, 106, 195, 226, 248

Tel Fakhir, 255

Thailand, 378

Thant, U, 388, 394–395

Third World, 519, 580

Thousand-day war, *see* War of attrition

Tiberias, 46, 84, 242

Tiberias, Lake, 71, 78, 226

Tih Plateau, 76

Timna copper mines, 74, 78

Tiran Island, 76
Tiran, Strait of, 242, 320, 337, 357, 389, 390, 395, 400, 402, 408, 425
Titus, 9
Tobacco, 70
Torah, 9, 10
Torah Front, 141, 183
Tourism, 119
Trade, *see* Foreign trade
Transarabian pipeline, 252
Transition Law of 1949, 131
Transjordan: and Churchill White Paper, 29; in war against Jews (1948–1949), 43, 48–50, 53–55, 58–60; and Mandate of Palestine, 67; in War of Independence, 73; policies of (1947–1949), 341, 342. *See also* Jordan
Transportation network in Israel, 77–78, 105, 112, 114, 115, 118–119, 124; government investment in, 112, 116
Treasury Ministry, 160
Tripartite Declaration of 1950, 166, 338–340, 343–348, 353, 361, 576, 579
Truman Doctrine, 37, 340, 341
Truman, Harry S., 6, 31, 33, 36–40, 44, 349, 576
Tulkarm, 247
Tunisia, 382
El Tur, 76
Turkey, 25, 34, 37, 335, 343, 349, 354, 362, 363, 377, 379, 497, 546, 548, 591
Tzahal, 165, 173, 174, 175, 194, 276, 278, 312, 321, 328. *See also* Air force; Military; National security; Navy; *individual wars*

Uganda, 495
United Arab party, 192
United Arab Republic, 363, 365, 366, 367, 369, 373, 384
United Jewish Appeal, 542
United Nations: partition plan and birth of Israel, 5–6, 31–44, 46, 48, 56–60, 62, 344, 345, 573, 576; discussion of trusteeship proposal, 38–39, 47; involvements, debates, and resolutions through 1956 war, 237, 335–336, 339, 342, 345, 348–349, 356–357, 577, 579; in 1957–1967, 364, 368, 372, 378; in 1967–1970, 414, 425–430, 432, 496, 585; in Six Day War, 246, 247, 253, 388–391, 394–400, 407, 409, 412; in war of

attrition, 265–266; during 1973 war, 315, 478, 480, 481, 484, 493–495; in 1970–1973, 457–466, 471–472; from October 1973 to May 1974, 507, 508, 510, 511, 514, 520, 523, 525, 532; in 1974–1977, 536, 544–545, 548, 550, 554–556, 565, 569, 593–594; and Palestinian Liberation Organization, 539, 559, 562
United States: and Zionism, 5, 6, 21, 22; and Balfour Declaration and Mandate, 25, 26, 35; role in birth of Israel, 31–42, 47; Jewish migration to, 86, 88; Jewish migration from, 89, 94, 97–99, 101, 111; financial support of Israel, 110, 123, 125, 166–167; compared to government of Israel, 126, 130, 138, 144–145, 148, 152–156, 160; and views of political parties in Israel, 143, 166, 168; policies (June 1974 to May 1977), 191–196, 535–570, 591–598; policies (1967–1970), 258, 260, 261, 267, 414–447, 584–585; in war of attrition, 177, 263, 264, 265; and Yom Kippur War, 283, 301, 303, 306, 312, 313, 315, 316, 476–505; relations with Israel, 330–598; policies (1949–1956), 334–358, 401, 578–579; policies (1957–1967), 359–380, 382–387, 579–582; and Six Day War, 381–413, 587–588; policies (1970–1973), 178, 181, 273, 448–475, 585–587; policies (October 1973 to May 1974), 506–534, 588–591; special connection with Israel, 571–577; overview of Middle East policies, 571–598; next stage in relations with Israel, 594–598

Vance, Cyrus, 566–567
Vietnam: and Middle East politics, 378, 469, 546, 548, 552, 582, 584–587, 591

Wafd, 342, 343
Wailing Wall, 29, 174, 213
Waldheim, Kurt, 520
War(s), *see specific wars*
War of attrition: causes of, 222, 279; and peace negotiations, 265–266, 435, 441–442, 463, 585; threat of resumption, 271–277; and General Sharon, 257; events during, 261–266; results of, 279, 414, 447;

Soviet Union in, 426, 433, 435–436, 463, 585
War Cabinet, 298, 305, 488
War of Independence, 5–6, 38–39; and course of civil war, 44–48; and course of regular war, 48–60, 237–238; and boundaries of Israel, 69, 73; consequences of, 60–64, 143, 222, 334, 415, 421; and division of Jerusalem, 73; agricultural settlements in, 229; and women in armed forces, 235; and military influence on politics, 323; and Rhodes format, 434
Water resources of Israel, 79–80; irrigation with, 70, 71, 72, 74, 79–80, 112, 116; and National Water Carrier, 80, 385
Watergate affair, 478, 536, 538
Weizmann, Chaim, 25, 27, 30
Weizmann, Ezer, 187
West Bank: after Six Day War, 67, 73, 94, 99–101, 328, 416; geography of, 70, 72–73, 75, 258; in 1973–1974 period, 184, 189, 198, 521, 532; in Six Day War, 246–248, 403; and fedayeen warfare, 270; in Yom Kippur War, 298; after Sinai-Suez War, 373, in 1970–1973 period, 473; in 1974–1977 period, 536–537, 566, 570. See also Judea; Samaria
West Germany, 321, 375–376, 380, 497
White Paper of 1939, 341, 342
Wilson, Harold, 389, 390, 402, 409
Wilson, Woodrow, 33, 34, 35
Wise, Stephen, 35
Women's International Zionist Organization, 211
World Jewish Congress, 376
World War I, 25: and U.S. involvement in Middle East, 33–34; affecting Palestine, 67; affecting immigration, 87
World War II: affecting growth of Jewish Palestine, 28, 30; and U.S. interests in Middle East, 36–37
World Zionist Congress, 80, 147
World Zionist Organization: Herzl in, 18, 20; growth of, 21; Jabotinsky in, 63; and prestatehood Aliyot, 85, 86; Jewish Agency and, 112; affecting political parties of Israel, 140, 144–148, 170

Yad Mordecai, 56
Yadin, Yigal, 196, 231
Yadlin, Asher, 195, 196
Yammit, 179, 473

Yariv, Aharon, 187, 513, 518
Yarkon River, 72, 80
Yemen, 361, 363, 374, 375, 380, 382–383, 385, 393, 394, 407, 428, 581–582
Yemenite Jews, 144
Yeshivot, 153
Yevsektzia, 21
Yishuv: history of, 27–28; in 1940–1949 period, 31, 32, 88, 345; in War of Independence, 32, 43–45, 49, 64; agricultural settlements of, 82; in 1934–1939 period, 88; egalitarianism in, 92, 105–106, 137, 164; economic policy of, 102, 114; in Provisional Government, 128, 142, 151; origins of political parties in, 140, 144, 145, 148, 170, 187; and Mapai party, 175, 191; and religion and state problem, 210; military of, 326
Yoffe Division, 243, 245, 246
Yom Kippur War: affecting people of Israel, 94–104, 328, 330; impact on economy, 122, 124–125, 194; and position of Israel, 127, 234, 311–316, 318, 495–505, 507–534; affecting political parties, 139, 153, 178, 179–191; course of, 223, 288–311, 319; initial forces in, 286–288, 293, 232; diplomacy during, 236, 426, 477–495; prelude to, 257, 272, 277, 279–288, 476–477; at sea, 311–312; affecting military establishment, 322, 327; and Israeli-Egyptian disengagement agreement, 521–527, 532, 590; and Six-Point Agreement, 527, 590; and Israeli-Syrian disengagement agreement, 528–534, 556, 590–591; and U.S. in Middle East politics, 575, 587–588; and Jordanian-Israeli disengagement, 591
Yosef, Ovadia, 217
Yost, Charles, 403
Youth Guard, 45

Zacharov, Matvei, 427
Zangwill, Israel, 20
Zarmi, Meir, 195
Zeira, Eliyahu, 284
Zhdanov Doctrine, 346, 347
Zichron Yaacov, 85
Zionist Movement: and origins of religion–state problem, 4–5, 14, 22, 201–202, 328, 330; Britain affecting, 5; United Nations affecting, 5, 6; United States affecting, 5, 6, 573; and early Arab

view, 5–6, 102–103, 500; Germany affecting, 5, 27; and yearning for return, 14–20; early leaders of, 15; and building of National Home, 20–23; opposition to Churchill's White Paper, 30; development of ideology in, 30, 32, 149–150; military vs. peaceful means of achieving goals in, 63–64, 328–329; and land tenure system, 80–81; and Second Aliyah, 86–87, 187; and Third Aliyah, 87–88, 187; and Oriental Jews, 92; and structure of society, 92, 106; in Soviet Union, 97, 166, 344–347; affecting economy of Israel, 113, 115, 116, 121; in Provisional Government, 128; affecting political parties, 140, 142–152; influence on education, 205; and agricultural settlements, 229; and assimilation of immigrants, 325–326

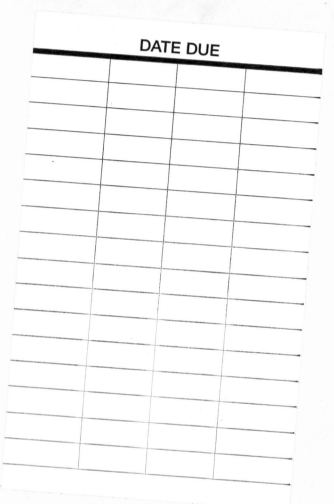

DATE DUE